THE VOYAGE
OF
FRANCOIS PYRARD

VIEW OF LAVAL.

Before the construction of the modern Embankment.

THE VOYAGE
OF
FRANCOIS PYRARD
OF LAVAL

TO THE EAST INDIES, THE MALDIVES, THE MOLUCCAS AND BRAZIL

TRANSLATED INTO ENGLISH FROM THE THIRD FRENCH EDITION OF 1619 AND EDITED WITH NOTES,

BY ALBERT GRAY

FORMERLY OF THE CEYLON CIVIL SERVICE

ASSISTED

BY H. C. P. BELL

OF THE CYLON CIVIL SERVICE

IN TWO VOLUMES—VOL. 1

GYAN

Published by

GYAN

Gyan Publishing House
5, Ansari Road
Daryaganj, New Delhi-110002
Phone: 011-47034999, 9811692060
E-mail: books@gyanbooks.com

Distribution Network
gyanbooks.com
India, USA, Canada, UK, Australia, France

ISBN : 978-81-212-4200-4 (Set)
ISBN : 978-81-212-4769-6 (HB)
First Published, 1887

2nd Impression 2020

Printed at: Gyan Press, Delhi.

The Voyage of Francois Pyrard
Author: Albert Gray

THE VOYAGE

OF

FRANÇOIS PYRARD

OF LAVAL

TO THE EAST INDIES, THE MALDIVES, THE MOLUCCAS AND BRAZIL.

TRANSLATED INTO ENGLISH FROM THE THIRD FRENCH EDITION OF 1619
AND EDITED, WITH NOTES,

By ALBERT GRAY,

FORMERLY OF THE CEYLON CIVIL SERVICE.

ASSISTED

By H. C. P. BELL,

OF THE CEYLON CIVIL SERVICE.

IN TWO VOLUMES.—VOL. I.

LONDON:
PRINTED FOR THE HAKLUYT SOCIETY,
4, LINCOLN'S INN FIELDS, W.C.

M.DCCC.LXXXVII.

COUNCIL

OF

THE HAKLUYT SOCIETY.

CONTENTS OF THE FIRST VOLUME.

	PAGE
INTRODUCTION - - - - -	ix
CHRONOLOGY OF PYRARD'S VOYAGE - - -	xlix
ADDENDA ET CORRIGENDA - - - -	l
TITLE PAGE OF THE THIRD FRENCH EDITION - -	li
DEDICATORY EPISTLE - - - - -	liii
HEADINGS OF CHAPTERS - - - -	lv
VOYAGE: PART THE FIRST - - -	1-452

LIST OF ILLUSTRATIONS.

1. View of Laval (from a photograph) *to face title-page.*
2. Mâlé Harbour - - - - - 120
3. Ground-plan of the exterior arrangement of the Chief Mosque (Hukuru Miskítu) at Mâlé - - *opposite page* 126
4. Minaret and portion of Mosque at Mâlé - - - 132
5. Arena for the Sports at Mâlé - - - - 142
6. Young Girl and Old Man - - - - 162
7. Maldive Woman - - - - - 166
8. Principal Entrance to the Palace - - - 219
9. Maldive Larin - - - - - 232
10. Ceylon Larin and modern Maldive Copper Lári - - 234
11. Old Fort Wall at Mâlé - - - - 246
12. Map of the Maldives - - *end of volume.*

Nos. 2, 4, 5, 6, 7, 8, and 11 are from photographs by Mr. BELL.

"Ὦ ξεῖνοι, τίνες ἐστέ; πόθεν πλεῖθ' ὑγρὰ κέλευθα;
Ἤ τι κατὰ πρῆξιν ἢ μαψιδίως ἀλάλησθε
Οἷά τε ληϊστῆρες ὑπεὶρ ἅλα; τοί τ' ἀλόωνται
Ψυχὰς παρθέμενοι, κακὸν ἀλλοδαποῖσι φέροντες."

Od. ix. 252-5.

"In istâ Indiâ sunt insulæ multæ, et ut audivi, plus quam decem millia habitatæ: ubi sunt multa mirabilia mundi."

FRIAR JORDANUS.

INTRODUCTION.

At the end of the fifteenth century, while the Pope was still regarded as standing arbitrator in the disputes of Christendom, Alexander VI had decreed to Portugal the discoveries of the East. The discovery of the Cape route to India was the first-fruits of that dispensation, and, for the greater part of the succeeding century, Portugal was admitted to hold in lawful possession, not only the territories of her conquest in India, but also the ocean ways which led thither. From the first landing of Da Gama at Calicut in 1498, the policy of the Portuguese was to maintain an absolute supremacy in Eastern waters. Their aim was not territorial dominion, but only command of the seas and of trade routes, in pursuance of which they sought positions of advantage, whether ports or islands, some of which they won by force, others by diplomacy. It was a curious feature of the age that the other nations of Europe in some sense acknowledged their right to the possession of the Cape route,[1] without acknow-

[1] The doctrine that the ocean is the common property of the human race was asserted first by Elizabeth and her bold seamen, and afterwards defended on legal principles by Grotius in his

ledging their exclusive right to Eastern trade. So it was that the Dutch and English navigators, believing they had an equal right to Indian trade, if they could only get at it by some other route, spent long and toilsome years of maritime apprenticeship in their search after the North-west Passage.

The French were the first to set at nought the restrictions of the Papal Bull. Paulmier de Gonville[1] is believed to have rounded the Cape in 1503, and to have reached Madagascar. The brothers Parmentier[2] of Dieppe, following the same route, reached

Mare Liberum. Owing to the disputes with the Dutch as to the North Sea fisheries, the doctrines of Elizabeth were abandoned by James, whose legal champion, Selden, replied to Grotius by his treatise, *Mare Clausum.* It is hardly necessary to add that time has been on the side of Grotius.

[1] He is said to have sailed from Honfleur in June 1503. The evidence upon which his existence and his voyage rest is the statement of the Abbé Binot Paulmier de Gonville, the great-grandson of a female relative of this captain, by her union with a Malagasy named Essomericque, whom de Gonville brought back with him (see Guerin, *Nav. Franç.*, pp. 50-55). M. Estancelin would make out that de Gonville was the discoverer of Australia (*Nav. Normands*, p. 165); but when patriotism comes in at the door, facts fly out of the window.

[2] The voyage of the brothers Jean and Raoul Parmentier is well authenticated. They left Dieppe 28th March 1529, with two ships, the *Pensée*, of 200 tons, and the *Sacre*, of 120. They touched at the Maldives [see App. A], and reached Ticou, in Sumatra, where Jean died of fever, 3rd December 1529. The journal of the voyage remained in MS. until 1832, when it was lent by M. Tarbé to Estancelin, and published by the latter in his *Navigateurs Normands* (pp. 241-312). Jean Parmentier, the gallant leader of this expedition, was born in 1480, or, as some say, in 1494. He was a poet and classicist. Before he started on this voyage, he had translated the *Catiline* of Sallust, and spent

Sumatra in 1526. These, however, were isolated enterprises, and led to nothing. The same national listlessness, which afterwards proved fatal to the schemes of Dupleix, characterised the French at this period. None of their countrymen followed these early pioneers, and the conquest of the East was left to be wrested from the Portuguese by the Netherlanders and the English.

During the last twenty years of the sixteenth century history was made apace. The United Provinces had achieved their independence; Philip II had ascended the throne of Portugal, and the whole conquests of the Eastern and of the Western world were brought under a single sceptre. At this time the distribution of Indian goods throughout Europe was managed by the Dutch merchants, chiefly of Amsterdam, who received them from the Portuguese car-

his leisure on this voyage in working on the *Jugurtha*. He took with him his friend Pierre Crignon, also a poet, who, in the preface to his own works, speaks thus warmly of the discoverer:—"Car quant au regard dudit Jan Parmentier, cestoit ung homme digne d'être estimé de toutes gens savants, et lequel sy les sœurs et déesses fatales luy eussent prolongé le fil de sa vie estoit pour faire honneur au pays pour ses haultes entreprises et belles navigations. C'est le premier François qui a entrepris à estre pilotte pour mener navires à la terre Amérique qu'on dit Brésil, et semblablement le premier François qui a descouvert les Indes jusques à l'isle de Taprobane, et si mort ne l'eust pas prévenu je crois qu'il eust été jusques au Moluques" (see *Le Discours de la Navigation de Jean et Raoul Parmentier de Dieppe*, par Ch. Schefer, Paris, Leroux, 1883, 8vo.). Estancelin identifies Jean Parmentier with the "gran capitano del mare francese del luogo di Dieppa" of Ramusio; and the allusion of Crignon to previous voyages to America goes far to corroborate the suggestion.

racks at Lisbon. One of Philip's first measures, at once revengeful and impolitic, was to prohibit the Dutch from frequenting Lisbon. This was a vital question to a newly emancipated nation of seafaring traders. The Lisbon traffic had given them a knowledge of the products of the East: many Dutchmen were in business houses in Lisbon and Seville. They had ample information at their command, but they hesitated to run the hazards of the navigation of the Cape.

Meantime the English were not idle. The circumnavigation of the globe successively by Drake and Cavendish, and their harrying of the Spanish Main, precipitated a crisis, and the destruction of the Invincible Armada in 1588 was a death-blow to the Spanish and Portuguese theories of property in ocean routes. No longer content with mere fighting and the capture of rich freights, the English were determined to open up a direct trade with the East. The first expedition of three vessels in 1591, under Raymond and Lancaster, was unfortunate.[1] In the year following, however, a fresh spur was given to English enterprise by the capture of the great Portuguese carrack, the *Madre de Dios;* and her "Notable Register and Matricola of the whole Government and Trade of the Portuguese in the East Indies", became in fact the prospectus of our first East India Company.[2]

[1] Two accounts of this voyage are contained in the *Lancaster Voyages* (Hak. Soc.), taken from Hakluyt.

[2] The English voyages incidently referred to in these volumes are as follows:—

Nearly seven years were allowed to elapse after the defeat of the Armada, ere the Dutch began to take its lessons to heart. They pressed on doggedly in their search for the North-west Passage, but it was not till February 1595 that Cornelius Houtman left the Texel with four vessels to reach India by the Cape route. He was at Sumatra in July 1596, and returned to Amsterdam in August 1597.

During the next few years fleets were despatched from the several Netherland ports as fast as they could be built and equipped. By the summer of 1601, when the story of these volumes begins, they had, in a space of six years and a half, despatched no less than forty-nine ships to India by the Cape route.[1]

The *first* voyage (1600-3) under Lancaster; the *Red Dragon*, *Hector*, *Ascension*, *Susan*, and *Guest*.

The *second* voyage (1604-6) under Middleton; the *Dragon*, *Hector*, *Ascension*, and *Susan*.

The *third* voyage (1606-9) under Keeling; the *Dragon*, *Hector*, and *Consent*. Capt. William Hawkins, who commanded the *Hector*, left his ship at Surat and proceeded to Agra.

The *fourth* voyage (1608) under Sharpeigh; the *Ascension* and *Union*.

[1] These include the fleets of C. Houtman in 1595, of C. Houtman, J. van Neck, W. van Warwyk, S. de Weert, and O. van Noort in 1598; of S. van der Hagen and P. van Caerden in 1599; of J. van Neck in 1600. The expeditions which left Holland in 1601 and following years are incidentally alluded to in the text of these volumes. They left as follows:—April 1601, W. Harmansen, 5 ships; J. van Heemskerk, 9 ships; May 1601, J. van Spilbergen, 3 ships; June 1602, W. van Warwyk, 14 ships; December 1603, S. van der Hagen, 13 ships; May 1605, C. Matalief, 11 ships; April 1606, P. Van Caerden, 8 ships;

Instigated at length by the successes of the Dutch and English, some citizens of St. Malo, Laval, and Vitré formed a company, and equipped two vessels for the purpose of "sounding the ford", and showing the French the way to the East Indies. How the merchants of towns so far inland as Laval and Vitré came to take part in the enterprise does not appear. St. Malo was at that time of a commercial importance second only to Dieppe, though its townsmen had for ages enjoyed a wider reputation for piracy than for legitimate trade. The vessels fitted out were the *Croissant* and the *Corbin*. The general of the expedition, and captain of the *Croissant*, was Michel Frotet de la Bardelière; the *Corbin* was under the command of François Grout. Both were men of position at St. Malo. The majority of the crews doubtless hailed from the same town; but the narrative shows that there was a substantial complement from Laval and Vitré; and of the two chroniclers of the expedition, the one, François Pyrard, who sailed in the *Corbin*, was of Laval; the other, François Martin,[1] who went in the *Croissant*, was a native of Vitré. Nor were the crews entirely French; for we find frequent mention of Flemings and Hollanders as having been on board the *Corbin*. Some

December 1607, P. W. Verhoeven, 13 ships. The journals of most of these voyages were published separately soon after their respective terminations, and all, with the exception of the Houtman voyage of 1598 (*v. i.*, p. 30, note 3), are contained in the Dutch collections.

[1] As to his book, see below, p. 2, note 2.

of these received higher pay, in consideration of their skill as gunners or carpenters, or by reason of their having already been to the Indies ; and one at least of the crew—viz., the pilot of the *Corbin*—was an Englishman. The ships were of dimensions similar to those employed by the Dutch, the *Croissant* being of 400, and the *Corbin* of 200 tons, the former being less than half the size of a large Portuguese carrack. The plan generally adopted by the Dutch and English, of sending, with the principal ships, a victualler or store-ship, which should supply gaps in the ranks of the ships' companies, and after being emptied of its stores, could be abandoned at the Cape or beyond, was disregarded by the French. This neglect is, at the conclusion of the voyage, remarked by the author as a grievous error.

The ships were officered as follows: each commander had a lieutenant, and each ship carried a pilot and second pilot, a mate and a second mate, a merchant and a second merchant, a clerk, two surgeons, two pursers, two cooks, and two chief stewards. In addition to these were a master-gunner and five or six gunners. A notable omission among the "personnes de commandement" was that of a priest, who by his influence, and by the regular performance of divine service, might have done much to moderate the swearing and blasphemies of the sailors, and to assuage the jealousies and quarrels of the officers and men, to which the author chiefly attributes the ill-success of the voyage.

Let us now turn our attention for a moment to François Pyrard himself, and in the first place to his birthplace.

The chief town of the *Département de la Mayenne*, situate upon the river of that name, and what is more important, on the direct railway line between Paris and Brest, Laval is at the present day a flourishing commercial town of 27,000 inhabitants. The broad spaces of low-lying ground have given the modern town free room for expansion, and have thus left the old town to itself. The principal feature of the latter is the fine old château, whose machicolated round tower dominates the river, and to whose sides cling a mass of quaint, irregularly built houses, the homes and shops of many generations who lived and died under the shadow and protection of the feudal lord. The streets, with their antique appearance, preserve their antique names, and we find here the Rue *du Four*, *du Pin Doré*, *des Serruriers*, *du Jeu du Paume*, *des Orfèvres*, *des Chevaux aux Mesles*, *du Roquet*, etc. The château and old town, viewed from the other side of the river, still present a very picturesque appearance; but within the last few years all the old houses on the river have been swept away to give place to a new and elegant embankment. The woodcut which is given opposite the title-page of this volume shows the town as it was before this modern improvement, and probably very much as it was at the close of the sixteenth century. Laval was a very ancient fief of France[1]; it is said to take its name from *vallum*, —*vallum Guidonis*, as it is called in the old charters, for every Count of Laval was a Guy. These lords, like the Princes of Reuss, are all chronologically numbered. During the youth of Pyrard, Guy XX reigned; and the last of his race, Guy XXV, died in due time before the Revolution, in 1741.[2]

In this old town was born François Pyrard, the author of these volumes. The date of his birth and the quality of his parentage are alike unknown. From his remark at the commencement of the work, that he went the voyage for the purpose of seeing the world, we may assume that he was then, in 1601, a young man between twenty and thirty. His only relative—and, indeed, the only other person of his name—known to fame, is one who was probably his brother, viz., Pierre Pyrard of Laval, who joined the Society of Jesus in the year 1602, being then twenty-one years of age. If François and

[1] The following works may be consulted:—*Annalles et chroniques du pais de Laval*, 1480-1537, by Guillaume Le Doyen, with notes by L. la Beauluère, 1859, 8vo.; *Documents rel. à l'hist. de Laval*, 1860, 8vo.; *Etudes archéologiques sur la Cathedrale de Laval*, by L. T. Hamard, 1885, 8vo.; *Histoire de Laval*, 818-1855, by St. Couanier de Launay, 1st edit., 1856, 2nd edit., 1866, 8vo.; *Mém. ecclés. conc. la ville de Laval*, 789-1802, 1846; *Notices hist. sur les hôpitaux de Laval*, by Léon Maître, 1868, 12mo.

[2] Laval has given birth to one greater man than any of these five-and-twenty Guys, and has done herself the honour of placing in the principal square of the town a statue of Ambroise Paré, the father of French surgery. The pedestal bears for its legend his own words—"Je le pansay, Dieu le guarist."

Pierre were brothers, the fact that Pierre was a literary and philosophical Jesuit[1] would seem to indicate that François had received, at least, a fair education. Of his youth or life, however, previous to his departure for India, he himself discloses nothing; nor has the diligence of local antiquaries succeeded in gleaning any facts relating either to him or to any descendants of his family.[2]

[1] Pierre Pyrard attained considerable eminence in the Society of Jesus as a professor of theology and philosophy. He was a director at various times of the colleges of Pau and Limoges, and on one occasion represented his province at a General Assembly at Rome. He is the author of a single controversial work, *Responsum ad Jarnacensem ministrum Calvinianum*, Burdigalæ, 1616, 8vo. He died at Pau, 3rd April 1667, aged 87 (*Bibliotheca Sotwelliana;* Haureau, *Hist. Lit. du Maine*, i, p. 193).

[2] Notices of Pyrard, which add nothing to our information, appear in Haureau, *Hist. Lit. du Maine*, tom. i, p. 193; Steph. Couanier de Launay, *Histoire de Laval*, 1856, 8vo.; *Bulletin de la Societé de l'Industrie de la Mayenne*, tom. iii, 1867 (article by Jules Lefizelier); *Annuaire de la Mayenne*, 1841, p. 36 (article by M. Levèque Bérangerie); *Bibliographie du Maine*, 1845, by N. Desportes. MM. Lefizelier and Bérangerie have made every search for traces of the family in the neighbourhood of Laval, but without success. The former adverts to a strange mistake, to which currency had been given by M. Ferdinand Denis, a writer generally well versed in voyages. It seems that one Baron de Saint-Genois, in his *Navigateurs Belges* (1846, 2 vols., 12mo.), claimed Pyrard as a Belgian, born at Stembert, near Verviers, and that his family still existed at the villages near that place. The statement was based upon a supposed claim of descent from Pyrard, made by the Abbé Duval Pyrau, before the Revolutionary Tribunal at Liége. M. Denis fell into the trap, and in the *Magasin Pittoresque* of March 1866, in an article on "Cauris", endorsed the Belgian myth. M. Lefizelier, while preparing his paper on Pyrard, wrote to M. Denis, and appealed from Saint-Genois to

He does not tell us whether he invested any money in the voyage, or merely sailed as one of the crew; nor does he even say in what capacity he shipped. One of his biographers rates him as surgeon,[1] another as supercargo[2]; and though I am aware of no explicit authority for either assertion, I am inclined to think that a probable conclusion may be arrived at by a negative line of reasoning. Besides the captain, Grout, and the lieutenant, Pepin, and one who succeeded the latter, he makes mention of the mate, the second mate, the pilot (an Englishman), and the second pilot. That he was not an officer connected with the navigation, would also seem probable from the fact that he had not been to sea before, and never seems quite at home with nautical terms. Nor was he ship's clerk, for the man who held this office was his bosom friend. On only one occasion does he mention the performance of any duty or task by himself personally, and this was merely to carry a message, on the evening preceding the wreck, from the captain on his sick-bed to the officers on deck. It is not of itself sufficient to lead to the conclusion that he was one of the surgeons; and his allusions to surgery and medicine throughout the book do not exceed the knowledge of a layman of the time. He

Pyrard himself. M. Denis then re-read our traveller, and seeing his mistake, suggested, what is no doubt the fact, that the person with whom the Abbé claimed relationship was not François Pyrard, but Claude Pyraux, another traveller, who died at Bussorah in 1773!

[1] *Sorberiana*, p. 195.

[2] M. Alfred de Lacaze, in *Nouv. Biog. Univ.*, art. "Pyrard".

mentions the merchant and the second merchant, deploring a lasting quarrel between the former and the captain. That he was not a gunner may be inferred from his mention of certain of his comrades as gunners, at times and places when his own skill in that line would most likely have been remarked. The pursers, of whom there were two on board, are the only officers he does not mention personally; and as I think he was an officer, I am disposed to argue, from the remarkable interest which he takes at all times and in all places in matters of trade, and specially in bazaar commodities and their prices, that he was one of the ship's pursers.

The ships set sail from St. Malo on the 18th May 1601. The first omen of misfortune was the breaking of the *Corbin's* foremast at a distance of only nine or ten leagues out. La Bardelière, owing to the rising insubordination of the crews, refused to return to port, and the mast was repaired by the carpenters as best they could. On the 21st they fell in with nine Dutch ships, which may be identified with the fleet of Heemskerk, who left the Texel on the 23rd April. The Canaries were sighted on the 3rd June, and the Cape Verd Islands on the 12th and 13th. On the 14th July they were off the coast of Sierra Leone, and there they saw for the first time the two ships of Joris van Spilbergen. The line was passed on the 24th August, and on the 30th they made land at Annobon. Here the Frenchmen met with a treacherous reception at the hands of the Portuguese and their negro slaves. Thomas

Pepin, the lieutenant of the *Corbin*, was killed, and several others were wounded during the endeavours to obtain fresh provisions and water. Spilberg had been there only a few days before, and had considerable and similar difficulty in obtaining the necessary supplies.

After six weeks spent at this island in fruitless attempts to gain water and fresh food, the French admiral determined to weigh anchor and make sail for Saint Helena, which was reached on the 17th November. The nine days' sojourn here was of great service to the sick, especially to those stricken with the scurvy.

The voyage was continued on the 26th November; the Abrolhos were passed three days later, and on the 28th December the ships had rounded the Cape. There they again fell in with Spilberg's ships, and divers courtesies were exchanged. A short acquaintance, however, gave the Dutch captain an insight into the laxity of discipline on board the French vessels, and determined him not to sail in their company.

Small progress was made during the month of January 1602. In the early part of February a violent storm off the Natal coast scattered and shattered the two small fleets, and on the 19th the *Corbin* found refuge in St. Augustine's Bay, Madagascar. Here she was joined by the *Croissant*, and later by the *Ram*, the Dutch vice-admiral, under Guyon le Fort. This captain, though born in Holland, was the son of a citizen of Vitré, and the three crews foregathered on shore and on board in all friendliness. The author remarks, as an indication of better fortune, or better equipment and discipline, that while the French ships had then a large number of scurvy patients, the *Ram* had not a single man on the sick-list. All three ships required considerable repairs. The Frenchmen remained at St. Augustine's Bay from the 19th February until the 15th May. During this period six of the sailors, lotus-eating truants, deserted the French encampment, and made their way inland to seek refuge among the natives. Their courage had been broken alike by the storm from which they had lately escaped, and by the alarming increase of sickness. "Utterly consumed with sharp distress," they no doubt thought:

> "Surely, surely, slumber is more sweet than toil, the shore
> Than labour in the deep mid-ocean, wind and wave and oar."

A few days of jungle wandering, however, disappointed their expectations. The natives showed no inclination to receive them, and at length, exhausted from want of food and water, they returned in penitence to their comrades. Meantime sickness and mortality made dreadful havoc among the crews, and, in order to supply the needful complement of hands, resort was had to a plan of kidnapping natives. This proved abortive, and, further intercourse being now impossible, the ships were forced to pursue their course.

The state of the crews, owing to sickness and mortality, was now such that it was necessary to seek some other harbour of refuge before attempting to cross the Indian Ocean. Leaving St. Augustine's Bay on the 15th May, the ships arrived at Malailli, one of the Comoros, on the 23rd. A stay of fifteen days here vastly improved the health of the men, and the scurvy almost disappeared.

A course was now laid across the ocean: the line was crossed on the 21st June: on the 1st July some islands and reefs were sighted. The Dutch pilot of the *Croissant* believed them to be those of *Diego de Roys*, a supposed group of islands placed in the charts of the period near the equator, in about long. 70 E.; but the Englishman of the *Corbin* more correctly recognised them as the Maldives. During the following night, which by order was to have been passed in beating about, the *Corbin* was practically left to herself. The captain was ill and below, the mate and second mate were drunk, the lights of the binnacle were allowed to go out, and the watch were asleep. In these circumstances disaster was almost inevitable: and in the early morning of the 2nd July the *Corbin* struck heavily on the reef of what is now known as *Goidú*, or Horsburgh Atoll. The scene of hopeless panic which ensued is painted in vivid language by the author. All the ensuing day was spent in arduous efforts to get out the galion, and on the morning of the 3rd the crew were landed at the island of Fuladú.

The survivors numbered about forty men. Many, including the captain, were still sick of the Madagascar fever; others, by drunkenness, had fallen a prey to tropical disorders; all were exhausted with fatigue. They were in pressing want of good food and careful treatment. Some, whether from greed or precaution, had, however, supplied themselves liberally with silver money from the ship's chests, which they secreted about their persons or in the sand. The natives raised their prices for the bare necessaries of life, and thus gradually reduced them to the greatest straits. News was carried to Málé of the wreck and of the money landed by the men, and commissioners were despatched to Fuladú to secure the king's rights, the ship with all its contents being, by Maldive law, a casualty of the crown. The Maldivians, on this occasion, as must be admitted, belied their general character for humanity, though their conduct may partially be excused on the ground of the silver question. We may compare the sufferings of the Frenchmen here with the far greater afflictions of the Spaniards wrecked from the Armada on the coast of Ireland.[1] One little band of twelve men, under the mate, stole a boat, and succeeded in making the mainland at Quilon, where they were consigned to the Portuguese galleys. Whether any of them got back to France is uncertain: Pyrard seems to have heard nothing of them in India. The captain died at Málé six weeks or so after the wreck, being treated

[1] See Froude, *Hist. of Eng.;* and also an interesting article by the Earl of Ducie, in the *Nineteenth Century* for September 1885, entitled "An Episode of the Spanish Armada". This story is closely parallel to that of the French at the Maldives.

to the last with the utmost barbarity by his own men. The little band rapidly diminished by deaths and desertions, and out of the shipwrecked crew of forty who were landed at the Maldives only four survived the captivity.

Almost from the first Pyrard obtained exceptional treatment. This was due to his prudence in setting himself forthwith to the study of the native language, whereby he brought himself under the notice of one of the king's commissioners. On removal to Málé he thus was able to interest the Sultan and to obtain favour for himself and his comrades. He was lodged with a lord who was the Sultan's most trusted adviser, and for four years was allowed to go from island to island in company with the islanders, and for his own purposes of trade. With the exception that he was a captive, and deprived of the public exercise of the Christian religion, his term of exile was in most respects tolerable. In February 1607 an expedition arrived at Málé from Chittagong, incited, as Pyrard afterwards heard, by the prospect of obtaining the excellent cannon saved from the *Corbin.* The Sultan endeavoured to escape to the southern atolls, but was pursued and slain, and Pyrard and his three remaining companions, on being discovered not to be Portuguese, were taken to India by the invaders.

The account of the Maldives occupies the greater part of the present volume (ch. v-xxiii). First, we have the circumstances attending the wreck, the escape of the mate and his party, other attempted escapes, and the arrival of the author at Málé (ch. v-ix). Next, a general description of the Maldive islands, details of the religion, manners, and customs of the people, the government and the court, trade and commerce (ch. x-xvii). Thirdly, traditional and current history of the islands, and memoranda of occurrences during the author's captivity, closing with the Bengal invasion, which gave him his liberty (ch. xviii-xxiii). As we shall see hereafter, the greater portion of the Maldive section of the book was not put in writing till long after his return, and four years of varied adventure intervened between his departure from the Maldives and his arrival in France. So vivid, however, was his recollection, so accurate had been his observation, that Mr. Christopher and Mr. Bell, our two modern authorities, writing their accounts of the islands with Pyrard before them, find but little to add and less to amend.

The Bengal ships, laden with booty and carrying Pyrard and his friends, touched first at Minikoy (Maliku) and the Laccadives, and then sailed for Chittagong. Here the Raja endeavoured to induce the Frenchmen to remain with him, but put no obstacles in the way of their departure. After a month's sojourn, they were offered a passage in a ship bound for Calicut, where they expected to be able to put themselves into the hands of the Dutch.

After a three weeks' voyage, they were landed, not at Calicut, but at Muṭṭungal, a port of the Malabar pirates between Cananor and Calicut.

At this and the neighbouring towns, the Frenchmen, as being enemies of the Portuguese, were received with great distinction, and even enthusiasm. His sojourn at the pirate ports enables our author to throw much light upon the relations of the Malabars with the Samorin, and of both with the Portuguese. Although much pressed to remain, Pyrard and his friends proceeded to Calicut by land, arriving there about the end of June 1607.

Their reception at Calicut was no less warm and hearty. An eight months' residence at this famous city gave our author time to observe and admire the conditions of prosperity of a great commercial town under native rule. Unfortunately, they were not the only Europeans at Calicut. Two Jesuits, whom the Samorin found it useful to have at his court for the purposes of his diplomatic intercourse with Goa, induced the Frenchmen to accept their letters of safe conduct to Cochin. One of the party, a Flemish Protestant,[1] who had before found himself in the clutches of the Portuguese, scented treachery, and refused to leave Calicut. Pyrard and his two other friends were kidnapped by a party of Portuguese outside Calicut, and conveyed to Cochin as prisoners.

The description of the Tronco of Cochin, into which our travellers were now thrown, reads as horrible as that of any prison in those dark days of legal cruelty. It may be read, but cannot be para-

[1] Described by Pyrard as a tailor and a trumpeter, and also as a clever carver in wood.

phrased here. The captives, after an imprisonment of nine or ten days, were well-advised in making an application for intercession to the Jesuits' College. Finding them to be Frenchmen and Catholics, the fathers interested themselves in their behalf, and obtained their enlargement. They remained six weeks longer at Cochin, and were then shipped for Goa by the armada of the South, which, after a twenty days' passage, reached the metropolis of Portuguese India in June 1608.

The first volume closes with the author's arrival at Goa. The remainder of his adventures may be allowed to stand over for the present. Suffice it to say that he was pressed into the Portuguese service on shipboard, and visited Ceylon and the Eastern Islands. On his return from the far East he was again at Goa for the latter part of 1609, and got a passage in a carrack, which set sail in January 1610. After a sojourn in Brazil, where the carrack was abandoned, he made his way to Europe. The ship made land at the Bayonne Islands, on the coast of Galicia. Here Pyrard bade farewell to his two companions, who had thus far shared his fortunes, and, after paying his promised vows at Compostella, took ship for Rochelle, and, after an absence of nearly ten years, arrived at Laval on the 16th February 1611.

After a short stay in his native town, Pyrard seems to have proceeded to Paris, where, in the same year, he brought out the first edition of his book. It is in one volume, 12mo., containing twelve chapters,—a Treatise of Animals, Trees, etc., and an

Advice for Navigation in the Indies,—in all, pp. 372. The title-page is as follows :—

"*Discours* | *du voyage des* | *François aux Indes* | *Orientales,* | Ensemble des divers accidens, | adventures & dangers de l'auteur en plusieurs | Royaumes des Indes, & du | sejour qu'il y a fait par dix ans, depuis | l'an 1601 jusques en ceste année 1611 | CONTENANT | la description des pais, les mœurs, loix, facon de viure, Religion | de la plus part des habitans de l'Inde, l'accroissement de | la Chrestienté, le trafic & diverses autres singularitez, | non encore écrittes ou plus exactement remarquees. | TRAITE ET DESCRIPTION DES | animaux, arbres & fruicts des Indes | orientales, obseruees par l'Auteur. | Plus un brief Advertissement & Advis pour | ceux qui entreprennent le voyage des Indes. | Dedié a la Reyne Regente | en France | Par *FRANÇOIS PYRARD* de Laval | A PARIS, | Chez David le Clerc, ruë Frementel, au | petit Corbeil, près le puits Certain | M. DC. XI. | Avec privilege du Roy. | "

The privilege is not inserted.

The book itself is dedicated to the Queen-Regent, Marie de Medici ; the Treatise to the President Jeannin. From the former dedication it would not appear that he had obtained any actual assistance from her Majesty. The commencement of the latter, however, intimates that the patronage of Jeannin was of a substantial character. It begins thus : "Ayant esté apres un accueil si favorable induit par vous à mettre par escrit ce qui estoit de mon voyage," etc. Both dedicatory epistles are in other respects worded in the adulatory style of the times.

The second edition was published in 1615. The book was, in great measure, re-written, and now appears in two volumes, 8vo. It was published at Paris, "par Remy Dallin, au mont S. Hilaire, rue de Sept Voyes à l'image S. Hilaire." The first volume, like the first edition, is dedicated to the Queen mother, now no longer Regent; the second to "Monseigneur Messire Leonard Destrappes, Archevesque d'Aux, conseiller du Roy en ses conseils d'Estat et Privé"; and the author acknowledges the great favours he had received from the Archbishop in his house.

The third edition[1] was published in 1619, 8vo. It was the last issued in the lifetime of the author, and contains the Maldive vocabulary, and is thus the most valuable. Its title-page will be found below.

The first volume contains a Dedicatory Epistle to G. du Vair, Bishop and Count of Lisieux, a Table of Contents, pp. 486, and an Index. The second volume has a shortened title-page; a Dedicatory Epistle to Charles Duret, Sieur de Chevry; a Table of Contents; the remainder of the Voyage, pp. 1-361; a Treatise of Animals, Trees, and Fruits, pp. 363-412; an Advice for the Navigation of the East Indies, pp. 413-434; a Vocabulary of Maldive words (unpaged); and an Index.

Pyrard is said to have died in 1621, but it does

[1] An edition of 1616 is mentioned by Ternaux-Compans as having been published at Paris by S. Thiboust; but I believe this to be a mistake, founded upon the error of Boucher de la Richarderie, who, omitting the edition of 1611, and giving the first (wrongly) as of 1615, and the third (rightly) of 1619, says there was a second, of which he does not know the date.

not appear upon what authority the statement is based. For bibliographical purposes the exact date is unimportant, as, in the course of nature, he must have died long before the next edition appeared.

The fourth and last French edition appeared in 1679. This was in one vol. 4to. It is edited by P. Du Val, Geographer in Ordinary to the King, and published at Paris by Louis Billaine, who apparently writes the preface. The book is divided into three parts, with separate pagination :—the first contains the Voyage as far as Goa, pp. 327 ; the second, the remainder of the Voyage, pp. 218 ; the third, the Treatise of Animals, etc., and the Advice, pp. 1-48, followed by a discourse on voyages in general—a description of the Coast of Africa, by "M. N. N.", pp. 49-72 ; Geographical Observations on Pyrard's Voyage, by Du Val, pp. 73-144 ; and an Index. The added appendices are valueless so far as Pyrard is concerned. That of "M. N. N." has no reference to the book at all ; while Du Val merely airs his geographical knowledge, without elucidating the text in any particular. The Maldive vocabulary is ruthlessly discarded, to give place to this trash. The text is a fair reprint, but in some places unneeded polish is given to the style; in others, words and names are corrected according to the superior notions of Du Val ; in others, passages excised. Far from being "la plus recherchée", as B. de la Richarderie extols it, this edition is, to the book-lover, a comparatively worthless possession.

Since 1679 the book has never been reprinted as

a whole. Nor, with a single exception, has it been translated. A professedly complete Portuguese version was published at Goa, the first volume in 1858, the second in 1862, by Señor Joaquim Heliodoro da Cunha Rivara. Unfortunately, the text used was that of 1679, and the translation accordingly reflects the demerits of the original. The notes, especially those to the second or Goa volume, convey some historical and local information of considerable value. These have been used in the preparation of the present edition; though, in many instances, where the original authorities are cited, Mr. Rivara's guidance will not be acknowledged. One feature of this and other work from the hand of that eminent Goanese antiquary must not pass unnoticed, viz., the eminent candour with which the evils of the Portuguese system, and the misdeeds of the Portuguese officers, are admitted without exculpation. It is highly to the credit of Portuguese India that the sole translation of a work, which unveils a scene of so much national disgrace and misfortune, should have proceeded from the press of Goa.

While the book has been but once translated as a whole, it has been abridged a score of times. The following may be instanced :—In French : Prevost, *Hist. des Voy.*, 1753, tom. 10 ; Charton, *Voyageurs Anciens et Modernes*, Paris, 1856, tom. 4 ; Guerin, *Navigateurs Français*, Paris, 1846. In German: Schwabe, *Allgemeine Historie der Reisen*, Leipzig, 1747-74, vol. 8 ; *Berliner Sammlung der besten und neuesten Reise beschreibungen*, vols. 13, 14 ;

Sammlung mehrer Geschichte, etc., Brandenburg, 1783. In English: Purchas's *Pilgrimes*; Harris's *Collection of Voyages*, vol. 1; *The World Displayed*, London, 1774-8, vol. 10; Duncan's *Mariner's Chronicle*, 1805, vol. 4.

A few words are necessary upon the authorship of these volumes. Prone as bibliographers are to the discovery of mare's-nests, it will certainly surprise all readers, who are even tolerably acquainted with the geographical and ethnographical knowledge of the period, to learn that Pyrard figures in the black-list of M. Querard's *Supercheries Littéraires Dévoilées*. On investigation of this charge, it is found to rest upon several authorities of the seventeenth century, though none of them can be assigned to an earlier period than 1650. They would seem to be independent, and are certainly conflicting. None of these *dicta* are dated; approximately, however, they come in the following order:

(1.) Samuel Sorbière [b. 1615, d. 1670] has this note on Pyrard in his *Sorberiana*[1]:

"Les voiages de Pirard, en deux volumes, où l'auteur s'amuse à nous raconter beaucoup de petites avantures particuliéres, que le lecteur lit avec autant de dégoût qu'il les écrivoit sans doute avecque plaisir. Tout ce que j'y apris fut l'histoire du Cocos, dont il parle fort long. On m'assure que le livre avoit été composé par Mr. B. . . . . . sur les mémoires de Pirard Chirurgien, assez idiot, et qui n'eût pas été capable de former un discours de longue halaine" (p. 195).

The two vol. edition referred to, of which Sorbière

[1] *Sorberiana, sive Excerpta ex ore Samuelis Sorbiere.* Toulouse, 1694.

was so unworthy a student, was either of 1615 or 1619. The Mr. B. to whom the authorship is attributed, is either Jerome Bignon or Pierre Bergeron. The number of dots after the initial is one too many for the former, and one too few for the latter. Bergeron was a well-known literary ecclesiastic, and, if he had been intended, he would probably have been designated by a clerical title. I am therefore inclined to think that Sorbière meant to refer to Jerome Bignon.

(2.) The copy of the 1619 edition, formerly owned by Bishop Huet of Avranches [b. 1624, d. 1721], and now possessed by the Bibliothèque Nationale of Paris, contains in the fly-leaf the following MS. note :

"*Le veritable auteur de ce liure est Pierre Bergeron, qui ayant oui parler des diuerses avantures de Pyrard, lorsqu'il fut de retour à Paris, il le prist chez soy, et se les fist raconter auec toute l'exactitude que l'on peut remarquer dans cet ouurage. Comme Pyrard estoit toujours yure, Bergeron pr̄ discerner la verité de ses paroles luy faisoit dire plusieurs fois et à divers tems une mesme chose, et qd̄ il la rapportoit constamm̄ d'une mesme façon et sans varier, il la prenoit pr̄ veritable : sinon, il la rejettoit coē suspecte. Je tiens cela de Mr. Conrart.*"[1]

This note, which I have examined, is not signed, but I have no reason to question its authenticity. The information it contains must be dated prior to 1675, the year of Conrart's death.

(3.) The publisher's preface to the 1679 edition of

[1] Founder of and secretary to the society from which sprung the French Academy.

Pyrard, already referred to, contains the following passage :

"Il y a des avantures si extraordinaires qu'elles passeroient pour les incidents de Roman, si l'on n'estoit pas persuadé de la sincerité de l'auteur, qui n'estant pas homme sçavant, avoit pris la précaution de communiquer ses cayers, et de prendre les avis des plus sçavants hommes de son temps, et entr'autres de feu Monsieur HIEROSME BIGNON, Advocat General ; qui a esté un des premiers hommes de son siecle, et qui a eu la bonté de redresser notre voyageur dans les choses qui surpassoient ses connoissances."

(4.) The last authority is that of Tallemant des Réaux [b. 1619, d. *circa* 1700], in his *Historiettes*, not published till the present century.[1] In *Hist*. No. CCCV, on M. et Madame de Blérancourt, he states that this lady was much given to study, and proceeds :

"Bergeron, chanoine de je ne sais où (M. Despesses dont il avoit été précepteur lui avoit fait donner cette prébende), fui celui dont elle se servit pour s'instruire. Elle a fait, dit-on, un *Discours de l'amour conjugal ;* mais on ne l'a point vu. Bergeron demeura avec elle tout le reste de sa vie. Ce bonhomme aimoit fort les voyages ; il tint Pyrard deux ans à Blérancourt[2]; de temps en temps il le faisoit parler des mêmes choses, et marquoit ce qu'il lui disoit, pour voir s'il ne vacilloit point : car Pyrard n'étoit qu'un brutal et un ivrogne. C'est ainsi que le bonhomme Bergeron a fait le livre de *Voyages de Pyrard ;* il prit tout ce soin-là parce que c'est la seule relation que nous

---

[1] Edited by M. Monmerqué. 1st edition. 6 vols., 1834 ; the 3rd edition is published by Garnier Frères. 10 vols. in 5.

[2] This fine château is situate near Noyon, and has been engraved by Israel Silvestre.

ayons des Maldives. Ce bon vieillard n'y mit point son nom, non plus qu'à la première partie de Vincent le Blanc, qu'il ecrivit aussi tout le même, car les autres parties ne valent rien; et quelqu'un, après le mort de M. de Peyresc, chez qui étoit le manuscrit, y a ajouté le reste pour grossir le volume. Il y a encore un traité des navigations de la façon de M. Bergeron, au bout de la *Conquête des Canaries*, par Bethencourt."[1]

These are the nearest to contemporary records we possess. In the eighteenth century, while the notes of Huet and Tallemant des Réaux were still hidden in manuscript, the Abbé Pérau, in his *Life of Bignon*,[2] was able to assign the book, without fear of contradiction, to his hero. Under the year 1615 we have this passage (p. 88):

"M. Bignon ne donna rien à l'impression depuis ses notes sur Marculfe: on lui est cependant redevable de la relation d'un *Voyage aux Indes Orientales, Maldives, Moluques, et au Brésil*, qui fut imprimé à Paris in 8° en 1615. Mais comme il n'avoit été que le rédacteur de ce qu'il avoit appris du voyageur, il n'eut garde de se l'approprier et il le fit paroître sous le nom de celui qui étoit censé en être le premier auteur. Ce voyageur s'appelloit François Pyrard, originaire de Laval: c'étoit un homme d'assez bon sens, mais peu capable de s'énoncer par écrit. M. Bignon ayant eu occasion de faire connoissance avec lui, l'entendit avec plaisir et trouvant que les découvertes qu'il avoit faites pourroient être avantageuses au public, il lui proposa de les mettre au jour. Cette entre-

---

[1] Published by the Hakluyt Society in 1872, under the editorship of Mr. Major, who refers in his Introduction to this edition of Bergeron.

[2] *La Vie de Jerome Bignon, Avocat Général et Conseiller d'Etat.* Par M. l'Abbé Pérau, Licentié, de la maison et Société de Sorbonne. Paris, 1757, 8vo.

pris paroissant au dessus des forces de Pyrard, M. Bignon l'attira chez lui, et sur les conférences qu'il eut habituellement avec ce voyageur il en forma une relation qui parut comme j'ai dit en 1615 en deux volumes in 8°. Il y en eut une nouvelle édition en 1679 augmentée de divers traités."

The notices of the bibliographers are not of much value. Before the publication of the Bergeron theory, most of them subscribed to the Bignon authorship; afterwards, *more suo*, they merely stated or tried to reconcile the conflicting accounts. The eighteenth century editions of Moreri attribute the work to Bignon. Niceron follows suit; but Chauffepié, who read the book, doubts whether the book could have come from other than Pyrard's hand:—"Cela paroit un peu difficile à comprendre, quand on lit le voyage même, ou l'auteur parle toujours en première personne. La manière dont la chose est exposée dans l'Avertissement qui est à la tête du livre est bien plus naturelle." He then quotes the passage from the preface of 1679.

Bechman and Zeidler follow the Bignon theory. Brunet and Ebert, Barbier and Querard, merely quote the conflicting notices of Huet and Pérau. M. Cyriès, in his article on Pyrard in Michaud's *Biog. Univ.*, attributes the fulness of detail for which the book is remarkable to the notes taken by Bignon in conversations with Pyrard, and adds:—"Ces matériaux soigneusement transcrits furent confiés à Bergeron, qui les mit en ordre et les publia sous ce titre" (citing the edition of 1615). This reconciliation of the two stories is, I believe, a mere conjecture: there is no authority for the statement that the manuscript notes passed from Bignon to Bergeron; and the notices of Huet and Tallemant des Réaux are express to the effect that the book was made up by Bergeron from Pyrard's lips.

We are, unfortunately, without any data for testing the Bignon theory. As regards Bergeron, we are in a better position to judge. He undoubtedly made a special study of voyages, and in 1629 published an edition of Bethencourt's *Conquête des Canaries*, together with a treatise of ancient and modern voyages. In this latter work reference is twice made to Pyrard. Writing of the caution and provision necessary to be taken in regard to the Indian voyage, he proceeds :—

"De cela on en peut prendre de très-bon aduis du sieur Pirard sur la fin de son liure des Indes Orientales où il donne une bien particulière instruction pour tous ceux qui voudront entreprendre tels voyages; et entr'autres il remarque les defauts tres-grands de nos François, tant pour leur desobeyssance aux chefs, & pour leur querelles entr'eux, que pour beaucoup d'autres fautes & desordres, à quoy toutes les autres nations sçauent mieux pourvoir" (p. 187).

Coming to the mention of particular voyages, he writes :—

"Pour le regard des grands voyages de quelques particuliers és Indes depuis que le pas en a esté ouvert par les Portugais et Castillans, les autres nations, entr'autres nos François, en ont esté assez soigneux, soit pour le trafic, soit par simple curiosité de voir & d'apprendre, comme sont ceux de Pirard, Mocquet, Martin & autres mis en lumière. Quant à Pirard, outre la description assez exacte des costes de l'Inde Orientale, d'Afrique & du Bresil, il en fait une bien particulière des Isles *Maldiues*, qui n'estoient quasi cognuës que de nom auparavant" (p. 195).

This is followed by a note on Mocquet, the well-known voyager whom Pyrard met in India.

In neither of these passages does Bergeron drop the slightest hint that he was personally responsible for Pyrard's book. This omission is by Tallemant des Réaux attributed to modesty, and the voyages of Vincent le Blanc are instanced as an example of like magnanimity. Now the first edition of Le Blanc was published in 1648. The title-page informs us, "Le tout recueilly de ses mémoires par le sieur Coulon." The so-called second edition was issued in 1649, but this is the same as the former in all respects except the title-page, where, in place of the above, we have "Redigez fidellement sur ses mémoires et registres tirez de la Bibliothèque de Monsieur de Peiresc, conseiller au Parlement de Provence et enrichis de trés-curieuses observations par PIERRE BERGERON Parisien." Peiresc died in 1637; and thus the sting of Tallemant's gibe, that Bergeron wrote the real Le Blanc, and that "some one" after Peiresc's death added the worthless matter, is removed. Either Bergeron edited the edition of 1648 under the name of Coulon, or his name was used in 1649 to sell the "remainder" of a book which had not gone off well.

Even assuming that Bergeron did write or edit the Le Blanc voyages, a superficial comparison of that book with Pyrard's will prove, independently of the matter, that the two works did not come from the same hand. The authority of Conrart, conveyed to us by Bishop Huet, is indeed high, and when confirmed by the circumstantial account of Tallemant des Réaux, is entitled to due recognition. But when, in 1679, the publisher of Pyrard makes no mention of Bergeron, and merely alludes to the friendly assistance of Bignon, and, above all, when we read Pyrard's book itself, we must inevitably come to the opinion of Chauffepié, that the matter of these volumes is Pyrard's, and his alone. There can be little doubt, upon the authorities, that, between 1611 and 1619, Pyrard spent much of his time in and about the houses of great and learned men. Some of these, such as Jeannin, Bignon, and Bergeron, must have seen clearly that the book of 1611 contained but a small part of the author's experience and knowledge; and it is probable that by repeated conversation they revived his memories, and induced him to make in the next edition a more ample record. Taking as a test the description of the Maldives, we find that, in the edition of 1611 (the authorship of which has never been in question) this is comprised in 74 pages. The same section of the voyage in the edition of 1619 extends over 223 pages, each of which contains about twice as much matter as one of the earlier volume. And there was not a man then alive (except, perhaps, Pyrard's own fellow-captives, whose names even are unknown) who could have written a single page of this account.[1]

[1] The fulness of the description of Portuguese India in the

If, then, the charge against Pyrard be confined to this, that the proof-sheets were corrected by these learned men, or that by their advice he enlarged his treatment of various portions of his voyage, or amended his arrangement of details, or even that parts of the book were written by others to his dictation,—in any such case, the fact is of no discredit to him as an author, and affords no grounds for a charge of literary fraud.

We may pass lightly, though not with silence, the sad picture of Pyrard's later years, drawn by Huet and des Réaux. Both state that he was a drunkard. Readers of these volumes will not require to be told that, down to the time of his return to France, far from being a drunkard, he had passed unscathed through his great misfortunes and long captivity, chiefly by the virtue of sobriety, wherein many of his comrades were so deficient. With the sole exception of an episode in his Brazilian sojourn, there is not a trace in these volumes of even levity of conduct. He presents himself to us truthfully, so far as we can judge, as a pious Catholic, little used to the world, to whom the drunkenness and blasphemy of his sailor comrades were alike abhorrent, and in whose eyes the one redeeming feature of the Portuguese character was

second volume is perhaps to be attributed to the prior publication of Linschoten's *Itinerary*, which had appeared in Dutch in 1596, in German and English in 1598, and in French in 1610, and had in all probability been read by Bergeron, and used in his conversations with Pyrard.

the sobriety of that race. It would seem that, on his return to France, he failed in striking into the tide of the ordinary civil life of his class. His book of 1611 made him a marked man, and his time was probably spent in shiftless lounging in the ante-rooms and at the serving-tables of the great. Unable to deny the charge as laid, we may at least contend that he probably maintained his former good character till 1615, when his first full narrative had been written. It is in the preface to the edition of 1619 that, for the first time, we find an indication that things had gone wrong with him. If, indeed, he was by this time given over to habits of intoxication, and was without the distraction of trade or business, his health, perhaps still suffering from the effects of Maldive fever and spleen-disease, would soon be broken, and his death in 1621, if not authentically proved, was only a probable consequence.

Whatever may have been the failings of the man, he has given us a book in which each volume possesses a peculiar interest. The first contains his description of the Maldives, on which it is the standard and almost unique authority: the second, with which for this purpose we may include the last five chapters of the first, gives us a picture of Western India at the commencement of the seventeenth century, during those critical years when the Dutch, aided by the Malabars, and at times by the English, fairly grappled with the Portuguese—years which witnessed the sieges of Mozambique and Malacca, the first interference of the Dutch in

Ceylon, and the periodical blockade of Goa itself. The Portuguese were stunned, but they little realised the situation: their great capital was still abandoned to the luxurious habits and official corruption which had characterised the period of undisputed monopoly; and in Pyrard's second volume we have the delineation, by an intelligent and disinterested foreigner, of a scene, which with our present knowledge of the magnitude of the issues then at stake, is not lacking in tragic interest. Nor is the demeanour of the Portuguese without its lesson for us, who are now treading the same stage.

The interest attaching to the first volume is of a different character. The Maldives, even in those days, came little into the current of Indian politics. They are remote in the broad Indian Ocean: of the innumerable little islands of which the group consists, the largest is no bigger than an ordinary English common. Each inhabited island is a little village, separated from its neighbours by sea or lagoon; yet the whole forms and, as far back as we can trace the islands in history, has formed a compact kingdom, with a well-designed constitution, a cabinet of ministers, a body of executive and judicial, religious and revenue officers, all in due subordination. Were not the whole aspect of Maldive civilisation coloured and penetrated by Mahomedanism, that ever-present factor in the East, we might regard Pyrard's description of this little kingdom, so strange and yet so particular, as one which might have come from the hand of Swift or Defoe.

Since Pyrard left the Maldives in 1607, very few Europeans have visited them, and most of these have been shipwrecked mariners. The last detailed account of them is given by my coadjutor, Mr. Bell, in his valuable report to the Ceylon Government of a visit made by him in 1880. The visit was, unhappily, but a short one, but, from his position at Galle and Colombo, he has had frequent intercourse with Maldive merchants and sailors, and he has made a special study of the language. But for the aid he has afforded me, both by his report and by his notes, this volume could not have been edited: and I gladly take this opportunity of stating that most of the notes to the Maldive portion are merely pieced together by me from the very full information on all points which he has placed at my command.

One other modern authority, however, whose name is frequently quoted in the notes, must not pass unnoticed here, especially as he is one of the many noble Anglo-Indians whom untimely death has deprived of what are called the substantial rewards of this world, and whose names should therefore be rescued from oblivion.

Lieut. Willmott Christopher, of the Indian Navy, was a lieutenant on the *Benares*, under Captain Moresby, when the survey of the Maldives was carried out in 1834-5. The crews of the two ships suffered much from illness at the islands, and in June 1835 the survey had to be temporarily abandoned. Lieutenants Christopher and Young, desirous of learning further the language and customs of the islanders, bravely volunteered to remain at Malé. The permission of the Bombay Government was obtained, and the *Benares* left them with a few men in June 1835. Three weeks afterwards, Young fell seriously ill of the fever, and two months later Christopher himself was seized. In the meantime he had been of the greatest service to the crew of an English ship wrecked on one of the atolls. On his return to Malé in August, his friend and the men left, and Christopher, after struggling on for another month, was forced to follow them to Ceylon. The description of the Maldives compiled by the two lieutenants was published in vol. i of the *Transactions of the Bombay Geographical Society* (pp. 54-108), and a Maldive vocabulary, collected by Christopher, appears in vol. vi of the *Journal R. A. S.* The two papers, the result of but a few months' work, in combination with arduous public duties and under the most depressing influences of sickness, form a record of painstaking investigation. They had read either Pyrard or an abridgment, and their papers form a valuable supplement to our author.

After this service Christopher was engaged in the survey of the East Coast of Africa, and there met M. Antoine d'Abbadie, who has in letters to me expressed admiration of his character and abilities. In 1848, *per mare et terram*, the Indian Navy took part in the siege of Mooltan. "During the first siege", writes Mr. Low,[1] "Lieutenant

[1] *History of the Indian Navy*, ii, 218-220.

Willmott Christopher, who, as Assistant Superintendent of the Indus flotilla, had been engaged in transporting men, guns, and stores to Mooltan, took advantage of this opportunity to indulge his love of adventure and unbounded energy, and joined the hastily raised levies of the late Sir Herbert Edwardes, when his intimate knowledge of Mooltan and its neighbourhood was of essential service to that officer." Sir H. Edwardes' own opinion of him may be gathered from the following[1]: "Another volunteer went with me into the field and assisted me greatly in carrying orders—poor Christopher, of the Indian Navy, whose zeal proved fatal to him so shortly after. On this occasion he rode about with a long sea-telescope under his arm, just as composedly as if he had been on the deck of his own vessel."

In the terrible night attack of the 9th September 1848, Christopher received his death-wound. "Captain Christopher", continues Sir H. Edwardes, "had from his first arrival with the steamers at Mooltan shown the usual willingness of his profession to co-operate with his brother officers on shore. On the night in question he had once already conducted some reinforcements to Colonel Pattoun's assistance; but the fighting at the outposts still raged with unabated fury. Another reinforcement came up, but had no guide. 'Will no one show us the way?' asked the officer of the party, looking round on the tired occupants of the trenches. 'I

[1] See Sir H. Edwardes's *A Year on the Punjaub Frontier.*

will,' replied Christopher, and putting himself at their head, steered them with the steadiness of a pilot through ditches and gardens, under a roaring fire of musketry. A ball hit him in the ankle, and shattered the joint to pieces. A few weeks later (9th October 1848), he was borne by the grateful British officers to a rude grave beside a well near the village of Sooraj Khoond, and I myself read the service over him. A better or braver man fell not beneath the walls of Mooltan."

I am far from intending to confine the expression of my obligations to Mr. Bell to the commentary on the Maldive chapters of this book. He has assisted me in all parts of it, more or less, as well by suggestion and original information, as by criticism and answers to queries. I regret that his residence in Ceylon prevented me from profiting by his perusal of the translation and notes in their final form, and that to this cause are due many slight errors in the transliteration of Maldive words, and a few graver mistakes.

I owe a heavy debt of gratitude to our respected President, Colonel Yule, who, regardless of his many other duties and avocations, while not, I am sure, neglectful of them, has rendered me assistance at every turn from his abundant store. While this volume was in preparation, his invaluable *Glossary* was in the press, and he at all times gave me free access to the proofs. In many cases, even where I have appended a reference to his work, my notes were drawn before I saw Colonel Yule's proofs: had it been otherwise, I should frequently have profited by his better choice of quotations. Over and above the aid given by his published work, Colonel Yule has too often spared neither time nor trouble, in my behalf and the Society's, in making searches in reference to obscure or interesting matters occurring in the text. He has put me under further obligation by carefully revising the proof-sheets, to their great benefit.

Lastly, I have pleasure in thanking M. Louis Brière, the well-known antiquary of Le Mans, for placing at my disposal all the information available with reference to the author, and for his kind welcome to me during a short visit to Le Mans. His kindness did not end here, for, being unable at the time to lay his hand on the above-mentioned article of M. Berangerie, M. Brière, after my departure, took the pains to make for me with his own hands a full and careful copy of the whole article of twenty-seven pages. My hope is that the great interest which M. Brière took in the project of this English edition of his countryman's voyages, may not be disappointed by the execution.

A. G.

CHRONOLOGY OF PYRARD'S VOYAGE.

(VOL. I.)

---

18 May 1601, the *Croissant* and the *Corbin* leave St. Malo; 21 May, fall in with 9 Dutch ships; 3 June, sight the Canaries; 12 June, sight the Cape Verd Islands; 14 July, sight Spilberg's ships off coast of Guinea; 29 Aug.—16 Oct., at Annobon; 17—26 Nov., at St. Helena; 27—28 Dec., double the Cape of Good Hope; 6 Jan. 1602, severe storm; 4 Feb., sight Madagascar; 7—11, another storm; 18 Feb., again sight Madagascar; 29 Feb.—15 May, at St. Augustine's Bay; 23 May—7 June, at the Comorros; 21 June, cross the line northwards; 2 July, wreck of the *Corbin* at the Maldives.

July 1602—Feb. 1607, captivity of Pyrard at the Maldives. Aug. 1602, death of Captain Grout; Sept. 1602, escape of the mate and 11 others; Jan. 1604, escape and death of 4 Flemings; 12 Oct. 1605, eclipse of the sun; —, 1606, arrival at the Maldives of Martin Domburgh and another Hollander; also of Adrian de Gouveia, an ambassador from Goa.

Feb. 1607, arrival of hostile fleet from Chittagong, death of the king, and departure of Pyrard and three surviving companions with the fleet; March 1607, Pyrard, after touching at Minicoy and the Laccadives, arrives at Chittagong; *circa* 23 April, leaves Chittagong; May, arrives at Muṭṭungal, on the Malabar coast; May—June, visits Chombaye, Vadakkara, and Kôṭṭakal, and arrives at Calicut. June 1607—Feb. 1608, residence at Calicut. March 1608, taken prisoner to Cochin; May, leaves Cochin for Goa, touches at Cananore; June 1608, arrives at Goa. [End of Volume I.]

ADDENDA ET CORRIGENDA.

Page 23, line 5 from bottom, for "*Formosa*", read "*Tormosa*".

Page 32, line 5 from top, for "some", read "two".

Page 51, line 16 from top, for "he", read "they".

Page 59, line 5, after "Pouladou", add "where we had first landed".

Page 64, line 6 from top, for "hours", read "days".

Page 72, line 17 from top, after "women", read "and had them beaten".

Page 73, line 10 from bottom, for "more highly in his esteem", read "better treated out of consideration for him".

Page 79, note 3, for "*gananawa*", read "*geniyanavā*".

Page 83, note 3, for "*du*", read "*dú*", and for "*duwa*", read "*dúwa*".

Page 90, note 3, for "*miru*", read "*mīru*", and strike out "and is one of the three ministers of the Sultan".

Page 94, note, for "*etula*", read "*atula*".

Page 95, note 2, for "*dolos*", read "*doḷos*".

Page 96, note 1, for "Mr. Bell", read "Mr. Christopher".

Page 97, note 1, for "Sin. *hækiri*," read "*Eḷu hækiriya*".

Page 97, note 2. The following are the numbers of inhabited islands in ten of the atolls in the year 1882, according to information gleaned by Mr. Bell from well-informed islanders: Malosmaḍulu 32, Málé 13, Ari 18, Felidu 5, Mulaku 10, Nilandu 14, Koḷumaḍulu 13, Haddumati 13, Suvádiva 21, Aḍḍú 7.

Page 127, note 3, for "*namadawā*", read "*namanara*".

Page 160, *dele* last half of note. The corresponding year of the Christian era to A.H. 994 is 1616, not 1677. The tombs so dated are therefore of men who were contemporary with Pyrard, during whose time there was no Portuguese invasion.

Page 184, line 4 from top, for "do otherwise", read "deformed".

Page 202, 10 lines from bottom, for "call", read "called".

Page 248, note, for "Viyadou", read "Viyadoru".

Page 255, note 1, add "or as Mr. Bell suggests, a misprint for *Mauvaye*, the modern *Mává Kilage*, a title, as Kambadi Kilage, confined to ladies.

Page 325, line 12 from top, for "padoes", read "padocs".

Page 339, line 5 from top, for "*Moussey*", read "*Moussez*".

Page 343, note 2, for "*Chastiganes*", read "*Chastaignes*".

Page 355, line 15 from top, for "Moussey", read "Moussez".

Page 375, line 12 from top, for "Goa", read "Cochin".

Page 392, line 8 from bottom, for "parents", read "priests".

Page 393, line 12 from top, for "silver", read "silk".

Page 404. *Auiards* is probably the Morathi *Awar*, a fence enclosing a yard round a house (Wilson).

VOYAGE

DE

FRANÇOIS PYRARD

de Laual.

CONTENANT SA NAVIGATION aux Indes Orientales, Maldiues, Moluques, Bresil: les diuers accidens, aduentures & dangers qui luy sont arriuez en ce voyage, tant en allant & retournant, que pendant son sejour de dix ans en ce païs là.

AVEC LA DESCRIPTION DES PAYS, mœurs, loix, façons de faire, police & gouuernement; du trafic & commerce qui s'y fait; des animaux, arbres, fruicts, & autres singularitez.

DIVISÉ EN DEVX PARTIES.

TROISIESME ET DERNIERE EDITION, REVEVÉ

Corrigée & augmentée de beaucoup outre les precedentes.

Avec vn petit dictionaire de la langue des Maldiues.

A PARIS

Chez SAMVEL THIBOVST, au Palais en la galerie des Prisonniers.

ET

Chez la veufue REMY DALLIN, au mont S. Hilaire, ruë de sept Voyes, à l'Image S. Hilaire.

M. DC. XIX.

DEDICATORY EPISTLE

TO

MESSIRE

GUILLAUME

DU VAIR, BISHOP

AND COUNT OF LIZIEUX

And Keeper of the Seals of France.

MONSEIGNEUR,

At a time when all France hath so much reason to render thanks to God for that in this calamitous age it hath pleased him to call you to the said illustrious office, which you administer so worthily to the well-being and satisfaction of all,—I desire not to be the last, albeit the least of all, to come forward in recognition of that sovereign virtue, which amid the greatest and most important affairs of the estate which it supports, disdains not to admit all the wretched to its protection. Receive then, MONSEIGNEUR, *if it please you of your wonted kindness and humanity, the relics of this living wreck, who, having survived so many strange and luckless adventures, in so many quarters of sea and land, even now in the very port fails not every day to experience all the rigours and violence of his habitual misfortune. And in truth it would be utterly heart-breaking to find myself thus furiously pursued and persecuted of fortune, even on the soil of France herself, my beloved country, were not my last hopes (after God) in your singular goodness, which hath so sensibly affected all that in their necessities have recourse thereto. This it is which hath made me resolve the more willingly to dedicate to you this last edition of the history of my voyages, whose story I have edited in better form than heretofore, with the addition moreover of many facts supplied from my memory. Should it please you,* MONSEIGNEUR, *betimes to cast a glance on this little work, you will see herein the unvarnished and truthful image of all that is most wondrous in nature, as also the most remarkable diversity of events and occurrences in the life of man. For my part, I venture to promise myself with assurance that this my book, with the approbation and favour of your great name, will be better received by all persons of curiosity and virtue, who, already holding in admiration your worthy and laudable deeds in other affairs, will deem it to their credit to esteem that which you have deigned to approve. Thus am I under such obligations to you that in the future I shall have no greater care or desire than to render myself worthy to receive the honour of your commands, and to remain for ever,* MONSEIGNEUR,

Your very humble and obedient servant,

FRANÇOIS PYRARD.

⁂ Guillaume Du Vair, to whom the first volume of the edition of 1619 is dedicated, was born at Paris, 7th March 1556. At the age of 21 he was Counsellor in the Parliament of Paris. He ranged himself on the side of the Moderates. Henri IV appointed him to important posts in Provence. In 1603 he became an ecclesiastic, and in 1616 was nominated Keeper of the Seals, but was soon afterwards forced to resign owing to his disfavour with the Queen-Regent. In 1617 he became Bishop of Lisieux, and was soon after recalled to official life. He died at Tonneins, 3rd August 1621.

TABLE OF MATTERS CONTAINED IN THE FIRST VOLUME.

CHAPTER I.

PAGE

Narrative of the voyage from the embarking at St. Malo to the Cape of Good Hope - - - - 5

CHAPTER II.

Of the Cape of Good Hope and the Cape of the Needles.—Violent storm off the coast of Natal - - - - 20

CHAPTER III.

We anchor in St. Augustine's Bay, at the island of St. Lawrence.—Of our landing and long sojourn there.—A description of the island, and of the manners and customs of the inhabitants - 29

CHAPTER IV.

We touch at the Comorro Islands.—Our sojourn at the road there, and our agreeable refreshment - - - 42

CHAPTER V.

Pitiable wreck of the ship *Corbin*, wherein the author was, on the reefs of the Maldives.—How the men were saved at an island with much trouble, and the miseries endured by them - 48

CHAPTER VI.

What happened to the men who were saved from the *Corbin*, and the miseries they endured - - - - - 60

CHAPTER VII.

Arrival of a lord bearing the king's commission at the is'and of Paindoüé, who at length takes the author back with him - 69

CHAPTER VIII.

Arrival of the author at the island of Málé, where he salutes the king.—The putting to death of four Frenchmen for attempting to escape.—Arrival of his other companions, and the reasons which prevented the king from sending them to Sumatra - - - - - - - 76

CHAPTER IX.

Grievous sickness of the author, which left him in evil plight.—Escape of four Flemings, and the ill-favour of the king towards those who remained - - - - - 82

CHAPTER X.

Description of the Maldive Islands, of their situation, and the people who inhabit them - - - - - 93

CHAPTER XI.

Of the religion of the inhabitants of the Maldives, and the ceremonies which they observe - - - - - 123

CHAPTER XII.

More of their ceremonies at betrothals and weddings, at obsequies and funerals - - - - - - 150

CHAPTER XIII.

Of the form of their apparel, of their manner of living, ordinary exercises, and other peculiar customs which they observe in their conduct - - - - - - 161

CHAPTER XIV.

Form of the government of the State.—Of the magistrates, of justice and the laws - - - - - - 197

CHAPTER XV.

Orders of the people and of the nobility; the great offices and dignities, and their rank - - - - - 208

CHAPTER XVI.

Of the king's palace; a description of it.—Of his manner of life, and of the queens, his wives - - - - - 218

CHAPTER XVII.

Of the revenues of the king, of the money, traffic, and commerce of the Maldives, and of the merchandise imported and exported - - - - - - - 227

CHAPTER XVIII.

Curiosity of the Maldive king.—His genealogy.—Political changes at the islands.—The king's wives, and other matters - 242

CHAPTER XIX.

The Maldives, when peopled.—Of many other memorable events which occurred at these islands, and in the neighbourhood, during the sojourn of the author there.—Of a vessel of Tananor, and the story of a Malabar captain's dealing with the Maldive king, and his hapless fate.—The adventures of the king's nephew and brother-in-law - - - 265

CHAPTER XX.

Accidents and casualties to ships at the Maldives.—Arrival of Hollanders.—A wandering Jew.—A captain of Mogor and his adventures, and of some ships wrecked there - - 277

CHAPTER XXI.

Of a captured Portuguese vessel that was wrecked.—An ambassador from the king of the Maldive Islands.—A vessel of Achen.—A Malay native.—A Maldive confession.—The discovery of a strange island, and other events - - - 292

CHAPTER XXII.

Divers judgments passed for adultery, lewdness, and other crimes.—Amorous humour of the Indian women.—Of the Grand Pandiare, and the strange resolution of a Mulatto - - 302

CHAPTER XXIII.

Of the expedition of the king of Bengal to the Maldives.—The taking of Málé Island.—Death of the Maldive king.—Voyage of the author to Bengal, with a description of the islands of Malicut and Divandurou - - - 309

CHAPTER XXIV.

The kingdom of Bengal, and some observations thereon - 326

CHAPTER XXV.

Voyage to Calecut by way of Montingué, Badara, and Marquaire; also concerning the famous Captain Cogni-aly - - 336

CHAPTER XXVI.

Arrival of the author at Calecut, and a description of that kingdom.—The king and people, their manners, religion, and ways of life - - - - - - - - 361

CHAPTER XXVII.

More of Calecut.—Classes of the people: Bramenis, Nairs, Moucois, and others, and characteristics of the country - 371

CHAPTER XXVIII.

Of the kingdoms of Chaly, Tananor, and Cochin.—Imprisonment of the author, and other occurrences - - - 420

CHAPTER XXIX.

Voyage from Cochin to Goa.—Of the kingdom of Cananor, and the estate of the Malabars.—An accident which happened to the author - - - - - - 439

THE
VOYAGE OF FRANÇOIS PYRARD.

VOYAGE OF FRANÇOIS PYRARD.

FIRST PART.

THE abundance of all kinds of wealth which France produces, and the favours which the bounty of Heaven hath so liberally poured upon her soil, may have been the cause why the French have so long neglected the sea. And this is so not only in their case, but with most of the nations who have enjoyed that felicity even in a less degree. They have enough to do with the land, which supplies them with a sufficiency of wealth, and take no thought to seek more amid the perils of the treacherous sea. On the other hand, we see that nations whose territory is poor and sterile, or too confined, have sought a recompense in navigation, whereby they have not only supplied their deficiencies, but have also made their cities in all respects rich and opulent. These are the peoples who have excelled in naval science. Yet in truth France, in neglecting trade, deprives herself of riches, which nature offers in addition to her other wealth; for she is washed by two productive seas and furnished with many good harbours, by means of which she might communicate and negotiate with many nations far from her two coasts, as though they were her neighbours, on the east and west, and even with the most distant countries. It must be confessed, too, that the trade of the sea is of the most noble and excellent kind, bringing, amid great risks, the riches and peculiar products of other lands to profit one's own country, and carrying of her abundance to those that are in need. It

is like depriving oneself of the use of a limb, for example, cutting off an arm. We are now seeing our mistake, for the French, after neglecting countless fair opportunities (which the Portuguese and Spaniards have not only taken but eagerly sought), are constrained to receive from those nations, in retail, the gold, spices, and the curious things of the East, in place of having fetched them themselves, and distributing them to others. So at present the Portuguese and Spaniards are trying to keep to themselves those elements which are common to all, and by all manner of wrong-doing to chase from the seas the French and other nations who would voyage and traffic therein. This it was which principally induced a merchant company of St. Malo, Laval, and Vitré, in the year 1601, to sound the ford (*sonder le guay*), and seeking a path to the Indies, to show the French the way; in short, to draw from the fountain-head.[1] With this intent, they equipped two ships, the one of 400 tons, named the *Croissant*,[2] the other of 200, named the *Corbin*, which were de-

[1] Pyrard seems to believe this voyage to have been the first undertaken by any Frenchman to the East Indies; and Martin, in his journal of the voyage of the *Croissant*, also so describes it. (See next note.) Both seem to have been ignorant of the voyage of Jean Parmentier of Dieppe, who reached Sumatra in 1529, and, like Pyrard, visited the Maldives. The reason of this ignorance is that no account of Parmentier's voyage was published until 1832, when M. Estancelin obtained a MS. journal, in possession of M. Théodore Tarbé, and included it in his *Discours de voyages et descouvertes des navigateurs Normands* (pp. 241-312); for the Maldive portion, see App. to this volume. There is an excellent new edition of the Parmentier voyages by M. Ch. Schefer; Paris, Leroux, 1883, 8vo.

[2] The fortunes of the *Croissant*, so far as they concern the narrative of Pyrard, will be noted in the course of this work from other authorities, and chiefly from the journal of François Martin, published under the title of *Description du premier voyage faict aux Indes Orientales par les François*. Of this rare book there are two editions; the first published early in 1604 (the privilege bearing date 3rd Feb.), a very few months after the arrival of the author at Plymouth. The second edition, of which is the copy possessed by the Brit. Mus., was pub-

spatched under the command of the Sieur de la Bardeliere,[1] a burgess of St. Malo, with François Grout,[2] Sieur du Closneuf, Constable of St. Malo, as his vice-admiral and captain

lished in 1609. In the title-page of the latter the words "par les François" are an addition—that is, if the title of the first edition be correctly given by Ternaux Compans.

[1] The admiral's full name and title, as given by Martin, was Michel Frotet, sieur de la Bardeliere (*Martin*, p. 13). He was born at St. Malo, 31 Dec. 1549, and was descended of an ancient family of that town, and, like his cousin, Frotet de la Landelle, was one of the most determined supporters of the League. On the 29th March 1589 he was nominated one of the four captains-general of the militia, and throughout the wars of 1589-91 had several important commands and performed many signal services, on account of which his townsmen gave him the name of the St. Malo Ajax (Cunat, *St. Malo illustré par ses marins*, Rennes, 1857, 8vo., p. 77; see also article by Cunat in Lovet, *Biographie Bretonne*).

[2] Grout was of an old St. Malo family, which claimed kinship with the Dutch family of Groot, soon after this time to be made illustrious by the name of Hugo Grotius. Grout's father, also François, was born at St. Malo in 1518, and had his Christian name from Francis I, who happened to be at the town on the day of his baptism. The event is recorded thus: "Le 5e jour d'Octobre 1518 fut baptizé ungn filz à Jehan Grout et Jehanne Brulle sa femme: et fut grand compère noble homme Franczoys Galleaze, grand écuyer de France, et fut nommé Franczoys au nom du roy, lequel est alors présent en Saint-Malo: et petit compère Michel Brulle, et commère Perrine Chenu, baptizé par le vicaire-curé, Maistre Lancelot Ruffier" (Cunat, *St. Malo illustré par ses marins*, p. 369). The date of the birth of the younger Grout is uncertain; he was captain of a ship in 1597, and was appointed Constable of St. Malo in 1600, "en recognoissance des agréables et fidelles services qu'il avoit faicts à Henri IV tant à la réduction de ladicte ville, que ès priuses de l'isle de la Roche-au-vay, Dinan et aultres lieux." (Manet, *Biographie des Malouins célèbres*, St. Malo, 1824, 8vo., pp. 85-6). Whether Grout was married and left issue when he set out on this ill-fated expedition is not known, but it may be mentioned that the family appears again in later days in the person of Grout de St. Georges, who was captain of the French ship *l'Invincible* in the action with the English under Lord Anson on the 14th June 1747. His valour on this occasion won the admiration of Anson as well as of his own countrymen, and when he died at Mozambique, in 1763, in command of the *Fortuné*, Louis XV granted a pension to his brother, M. Grout de la Grassinais. His portrait is now hung in the Hôtel de Ville at St. Malo (Cunat, *ibid.*).

of the *Corbin*.[1] I was of the number, being not less desirous of seeing the world than of getting rich, and embarked in the *Corbin*. This ship had a worse fate than the other, and was lost,[2] and I have at last escaped, after many troubles. Since it has pleased God, contrary to all expectation, to bring me safe and sound to my native land after suffering so many hardships and running endless risks, not only having been borne about to most of the maritime regions and to the Indian islands, making almost a circuit of the world and visiting all four continents, but also having lived for the space of ten years among various races, and in my long sojourn learnt their manners, laws, and customs, perhaps better (as I may say without vanity) than any other Frenchman—nay than even any Portuguese or Hollander,—I have been constrained to put in writing whatever strange things I saw in my long travel, that so my countrymen may share them. My tale may also serve to give warning to those who would make the same voyage, to avoid the troubles into which I fell, or rather which I saw happen to others, so that by learning those mistakes in our navigation which caused our disaster, they may make the enterprise with more circumspection.

[1] Martin adds the name of the chief merchant, Christofle Moreau, sieur du Poisçant (*Martin*, p. 12). This man seems to have taken a prominent part in the League, for he appears at the head of the list of proscribed persons in a decree and ordonnance of the Seneschal of Rennes, 30 April 1590 (Dubois, L. F., *Essai sur l'histoire de la Ville de Vitré*, Paris, 1839, 8vo., p. 141).

[2] He would seem to imply here that the *Croissant* got safely home, but, as we shall see hereafter, she was abandoned almost within French waters, and sank in the sight of her remaining crew, who were rescued by the Hollanders.

CHAPTER I.

Narrative of the Voyage from the embarking at S. Malo to the Cape of Good Hope.

WE left St. Malo with a north-east wind to begin our voyage on the 18th of May 1601. When we were but nine or ten leagues to sea the foremast of our ship split and broke in half, and this was a beginning of misfortune. We fired a cannon-shot to give notice to our commander on board the *Croissant*, and to know from him if we should put back to get another mast; but he being resolved to continue his course without delay, sent us the carpenters of his ship, who with ours mended the mast as best they could. The truth was, he was afraid of losing the voyage, for most of the mariners had taken this mishap, trifling though it was, for an evil omen, and said aloud that if we put into any port of France they would be off and give up the business. As for me, I never had a good opinion of our voyage since the embarking, not on account of this chance breaking of the mast, but of the bad order and discipline in the ships; for there was no piety or devotion, but plenty of oaths and blasphemy, disobedience to officers, mutiny and carelessness, and every day quarrelling, assaults, thefts, and the like vices.

On the 21st of the said month we sighted nine large Hollander vessels called "hulks" (*hourques*),[1] which put about to

[1] *Hourque*, "a hulk or huge flyboat" (Cotgrave); "a hulk or double flieboat of the burden of 250 tons" (*Cumberland's Voy.*, in Hak., iii, 774). The name was applied to the old canal-boat, or flyboat, of Holland and Flanders, which was flat-bottomed, with broad buttocks, and with stem and stern much alike. It had originally but one mast and a bowsprit The Dutch sea-going vessels were made on the same model, but squared off at the stern, and when built of considerable tonnage, had three masts and carried seven sails, viz., six square sails and one lateen. The latter ships, preserving the above features of hull, took the same name. They were very similar to the *Marsiliana* of the Venetians. *Hourques* ranged

salute the ships of France. In fact, they passed to leeward of us, which is the greatest mark of submission at sea; and they each fired a cannon, but the gunner of their vice-admiral fired with ball, which struck our ship in the sail and tore it to pieces. When we saw that, we feared that they wanted to fight, and hoisted our ensign or flag on the foremast to inform our commander. This caused him to bring to at once, while we began to barricade the ship all round (these barricades were of red scarlet, with the arms of France worked on cloth of gold),[1] putting our cannon in order, and loading all with shot. We armed ourselves and took up our positions, the captain on the poop and the lieutenant at the bows, and the four gunners with their assistants at the four quarters of the ship. This done, we fired two shots at the sails of the vessel which had attacked us, to know what they would say before we gave them a broadside. But they did not put themselves in an attitude of defence. Our commander, who handled his sails and helm exceeding well, bore down the

from fifty and sixty tons up to 200 and 300, "et il y en a qui font le voiage des Indes orientales, montées seulement de cinq ou six matelots" (Aubin). The words *hourque* and *hulk* are usually derived from the Greek ὁλκάς; but this is contested by Jal (see Aubin, *Dict. de Marine*, s. v. *hourque* and *heu*: Jal, *Archéologie Navale*, i, 141; ii, 216: also *Glossaire Nautique:* Pantera, *Armata Navale*, Rome, 1614: Skeat, *Etym. Dict.*, s. v. "hulk": and Smyth's *Sailor's Word-Book*). From the clumsy build of the Dutch vessels, and its supposed connection with "hull" (erroneous), the word "hulk" has come to be applied to any superannuated ship which is kept moored in rivers or harbours for coaling or other purposes.

[1] These barricades or screens (*bastingues* or *pavois*) were of cloth, stretched all round the upper decks, and also at the tops, of ships of war, to screen the crew from the enemy's sight during combat. At this time they were of a red material, as the author states; in 1670, the king, by an ordonnance, required that in future they should be blue, worked with yellow *fleurs de lis*, and bordered with broad white bands. Sometimes they were strengthened on the inner side so as to resist musket-shot, and this was generally done in galleys to protect the oarsmen (Aubin, *Dict. de Marine*; and Jal, *Gloss. Naut.*, s. v. *pavois*; Cotgrave, s. v. *pavoisade*).

wind, all sail set, towards the Hollander Admiral, and firing a shot, commanded him to strike amain; which he did promptly though much astonished, as he knew nothing that had happened. On being informed, he summoned his vice-admiral, who told him that one of his gunners, being drunk, had made the mistake. The Admiral sent for the gunner and presented him to our commander, begging him to forgive the injury, and offered to give over the offender to be punished as he might wish, or to do it himself on the spot and hang him at the yard-arm. But our General, being satisfied, said that he required nothing more, and prayed the Admiral to pardon the poor gunner. I doubt not he was incontinently punished, for the Flemings and Hollanders never let offences go unpunished on board their ships, keeping better discipline than we do on ours, which is the cause their voyages succeed better. At length we parted, with many mutual excuses.[1] They told us they were bound for the Cape Verd Islands, for cargoes of salt from the Isle de Mayo.[2]

On the 3rd of June following we sighted the Canary Islands, which are in 28°, 29°, and 30° northern latitude, and passed through them.

On the 12th and 13th of June we sighted the Cape Verd Islands. They are ten in number; the first from this side is

[1] This affair has recently been not a little magnified by the patriotism of the St. Malo biographer:—"Apres un combat contre six hourques hollandoises, combat qui eut lieu par la faute de ceux qui les montaient, puisque la guerre n'était pas declarée, le commandant hollandois rendit toute satisfaction à La Bardelière, et les équipages se séparerent bons amis" (*Cunat*, p. 77).

[2] It is probable that the fleet here spoken of was that of Heemskerk, who left the Texel with nine ships on the 23rd April, in company with five others under Wolphant Harmansen. These fleets parted on the 8th May. It is likely enough that the Dutch commander gave out that he was bound only for the C. Verd Islands, as he would not wish it to come to the ears of the Portuguese that he was sailing to the Indies (*Rec. des Voy.*, 1702, ii, 359, *et seq.*). The *rencontre* with the French is not mentioned in the Dutch journals. Martin mentions eight Dutch ships only (p. 13).

Saint Antoine, the second *S. Vincent*, the third *S. Lucar*, the fourth *S. Nicolas*, the fifth *del Sal*, the sixth *De buena vista*, the seventh *de Mayo*, the eighth *Santiago*, the ninth *del Fuego*, the tenth *Bravo*.[1] They begin at lat. 10° N., and reach down to lat. 14°. The Portuguese inhabit and cultivate some of them; the others are only inhabited by animals, such as goats, which are very numerous. They have fruits and provisions in abundance. The principal island, on which the others are dependent, is *S. Nicolas*; it is the seat of the Bishop and of justice.[2] The proximity of Cape Verd on the mainland, only fifty or sixty leagues off, where the Portuguese carry on a continual traffic in negro slaves, causes these islands to be much frequented because of this merchandise, which is carried to the West Indies and to Brazil, as well as to Portugal. In one of the islands, *de Mayo*, there is found such a quantity of rock-salt that one can load as much as one wishes without cost, for the island is uninhabited, and loading and transport are quite easy. You see in another island a mountain which throws out from its summit flames by night and smoke by day. On that account it is called "Isla del Fuego".[3]

On the 29th of the same month we were in lat. 5° N., and

[1] The Portuguese names are more properly as follows:—S. Antão, S. Vicente, Sta. Luzia, S. Nicolao, do Sal, da Boa Vista, Mayo, Santiago, Fogo, and Brava. The C. Verd Islands were discovered in 1456 by the Venetian Cadamosto, under the auspices of Prince Henry of Portugal. The first sighted was Boa Vista, and thence so called (Major's *Prince Henry*, p. 163).

[2] Sir R. Hawkins, who visited the Cape Verd Islands in 1593, says that Santiago was then the chief island, the seat of the Audiencia and the Bishop. This island was sacked by the English under Sir Anthony Sherley in 1596, and the government was then perhaps temporarily transferred to S. Nicolas (*Hawkins's Voyages*, Hak. Soc., pp. 129-30). The established seat of government has always been, as now, Santiago.

[3] "The second island is Fuego, so called, for that day and night there burneth in it a vulcan, whose flames in the night are seene twentie leagues off in the sea" (Sir R. Hawkins, in *Hawkins's Voyages*, Hak. Soc., 130).

saw the North Star very low, and at the same time sighted the Southern Constellation, or Antarctic Pole, otherwise called the *Croisade*, from being composed of four stars in the form of a cross, though it is distant 27° from the Pole. Yet it is the nearest by which the pilots can be guided as to their latitude. Here you see a strange quantity of fish, about as big as those called mullet, which have wings like bats, by means of which, when pursued by the larger fish, they dart out of the water and fly a long way until their wings are dry. So, on the other hand, when they are in the air, the sea birds, of which there is a vast multitude, give them chase and catch them, unless they first regain the sea. Many of them fell on our ships, and when once they fall on something hard where there is no water, they cannot raise themselves again. Thus we got some fresh food (and much pleasure too in watching the chase), for this fish is delicate and good eating. But it was a marvellous sight to see in so deep sea and in this quarter so vast a number of fish, that we might say we saw the whole sea covered with them, and all in a turmoil, though it was calm.[1] There were also big ones, such as bonitos and albachores,[2] and many other kinds, of which we caught with lines enough to supply the ship; and porpoises too, with harpoons attached to pieces of wood, then lifting them by strength of arm. I have seen these flying fish everywhere near the line, both on this and on

[1] For another description of the flying fish see *Hawkins's Voyages*, Hak. Soc., pp. 60, 152. Sir Richard Hawkins likens the pursuit to the chase as conducted by men: "The dolphins and bonitoes are the houndes, and the alcatraces (cormorants) the hawkes, and the flying fishes the game."

[2] Both kinds of tunny, and mentioned by nearly all voyagers. The word *albacora*, as it is written in Sp. and Port., is evidently Arabic. Dozy and Engelmann, however, express themselves unable to trace it in the Arabic dictionaries. It is probably *el-bakra*, "the cow-(fish)", according to the common practice of naming marine animals after those of the land.

the other side of the Cape of Good Hope, and both N. and S. of the line.

On the 14th of July we perceived the coast of Guinea, that is, the land of *Sierra Liona.* We thought we were more than 100 leagues off, but, owing to the calms and the currents, we had been drawn in against our will. We sighted two ships, one of which came near enough to look at us.[1] This coast is very unhealthy and inclement.

On the 24th August we passed the equinoctial line; for on this day, when we took the sun at the usual hour, viz., at midday (which sailors call the observation), there was found to be no elevation, so that we understood that we were under the line. The latitude is taken with the astrolabe from the sun, or from the stars by Jacob's-staff, called by sailors the *arbaleste.*[2] From lat. 7 or 8 N. to the same on the south

[1] These ships were afterwards met at the Cape, and proved to be two Dutch ships, the *Ram* and the *Sheep*, and a yacht, the *Lamb*, under G. Spilberg as admiral, with Guion Le Fort as vice-admiral. Their voyage is described at length in the *Recueil des Voyages*, ii, 421-552. This little fleet was destined to play a great part in the history of India, for Spilberg and his comrades were the first Dutchmen who gained a footing in Ceylon; and it was in that island more than elsewhere that the struggle of the Dutch and Portuguese for Eastern empire was fought and determined (see Tennant, *Ceylon*, ii, 34, *et seq.*). The Dutch chronicler does not mention having sighted the French ships here on the Guinea coast, but Martin, who was on board the *Croissant*, records the meeting thus: "Nous apperceusmes deux navires et une patache que nous jugions estre Flamens : la patache se mist en devoir de nous approcher et voyant que nous ne l'attendions, s'en retourna vers ses navires." (*Martin*, p. 17.)

[2] The astrolabe is an instrument of great antiquity, the treatise on it by Chaucer, written in 1391, being the first on a scientific subject published in England (Craik, *Eng. Lit.*, i, 367). The Jacob's-staff was one of many forms of the cross-staff. In England it was distinguished from the cross-staff proper (see *The use of the two mathematicall Instruments, the Crosse-staffe ... and the Jacob's staffe, set forth Dialogue wise in two briefe and plaine Treatises, etc.*, by Thomas Hood, London, 1596). All the chief authorities as to these instruments are collected by Capt. Markham in a valuable Appendix to his *Voyages and Works of John Davis*, Hak. Soc., 1880. The Portuguese also used several forms of

we were much harassed by the inconstancy of the weather and the bad climate. The heat is violent and stifling in the extreme; it destroys most of the provisions; the water becomes putrid and full of big worms; all kinds of meat and fish go bad, even the most carefully salted; all the butter we had brought was melted to oil, and so were the tallow candles. The ships began to split in those parts which were not under water; the pitch and tar likewise melted; and it was as impossible to remain below as in an oven. Nothing is so inconstant as the weather, but there it is inconstancy itself; in a moment it becomes calm as by a miracle; in half an hour there is on all sides thunder and lightning, the most terrible that can be imagined: this is chiefly when the sun is near the equinox. Suddenly the calm returns, then the storm begins again, and so on. All at once the wind rises with such impetuosity that it is all you can do to lower all sail in time, and you would suppose that the masts and yards would give way and the ship be lost. Often you see coming from afar great whirlwinds, which the sailors call *dragons*[1]; if they pass over ships they break them up and send them to the bottom. When they are seen coming the sailors take naked swords and strike them one against the other, in the form of a cross, on the bows of the ship, or in the direction where they see the storm coming, and they consider that that prevents it coming upon the ship and turns it aside. More-

cross-staff, *e.g.*, *radiometro*, *raio astronomico*, *bordão de Jacob*, *vara de ouro*, and others (Rivara, *Pyrard*, i, 9).

[1] This passage would seem to be the *locus classicus* for the term *dragon*. Jal (*Gloss. Naut.*, s. v. "Superstitions") quotes it from Père René François, *Essay des Merveilles de Nature*, second edition, 1622, ch. xii, who took it and other passages in the same chapter direct from Pyrard: this father, however, does not acknowledge his authorities. The word is used here for a waterspout, and in much the same sense by John de' Marignolli, in his description of a storm: "And such wondrous things we beheld! The sea as if in flames, and fire-splitting dragons flying by, etc." (Yule's *Cathay*, p. 356). Compare the Greek *typhon* and the Chinese *lung*.

over, in this region the rains are very dangerous, for if one is soaked and does not change one's dress promptly, the skin is shortly after covered with tumours and pimples, and worms are engendered in the clothes, so that there is much trouble to those who have a change of clothing, and bad results to those who have none. We were obliged to cover our ships with wax-cloth, and to make awnings to ward off the rain and the sun, and still we had much to bear. It would be impossible for me to relate in detail all the extremities, the labour, the discomforts, and fatigue which we endured for three months owing to these calms and *trauades*[1] (so they call these squalls), which do more mischief than heavy wind or a storm, and ships are soon worn out by them. Ours shook and reeled from side to side from the violence of the great *loüesme*[2] in those seas; but with the wind aft the sails

[1] *Travados*, "gusts of wind which the Portuguese call *Turbades* or *Travades*. These hurricanes, attended with excessive rains, fall on a sudden upon the ships, and toss them so violently that one would think they would perish immediately. But they don't last above an hour and half; and when they are over the air is so calm, that the surface of the sea is as smooth as glass" (*Collection of Voyages undertaken by the Dutch East India Company*, London, 1703, p. 97). The following is from Bluteau:—"Segundo João Jacobo Hofman no seu *Lexicon Universal*, tom. 4, fol. 491, col. 1, derão os Portuguezes este nome a huns ventos do mar Atlantico, que mais frequentemente regnão entre o Brasil e a Africa debayxo do Equador na altura de Guinè, do Cabo de Boa Esperança para o Cabo de Guardafu. Repentinamente sahem de hũa navem e são tão impetuosas que revolvem tudo de cima para bayxo."

[2] This word, which, as will be seen, Pyrard uses frequently in the sense of rollers or swell, as distinguished from a stormy state of the sea caused immediately by wind, is not found in any of the French dictionaries, nor even in Jal's *Glossary*. M. Charton has this note:—"Ce mot ne se trouve dans aucun glossaire. M. Jal, que nous avons consulté, pense qu'il doit avoir le sens de *houle*, ou celui de *grande lame* de fond, ou peut-être enfin de *ras de marée*. M. le docteur Roulin croit que c'est une imitation incorrecte du mot anglais *whelm*, qui signifie 'couvrir d'eau une surface', et que nos marins des bords de la Manche avaient adopté dans le sens de 'spoon-drift', 'embrun', écume des lames chassées par le gros vent, et pendant sa durée" (Charton, *Voy.*, iv,

keep the ship steady, and if she is close to the wind she lies on one side only. These calms try vessels much, chiefly those heavily laden, and too often make their timbers start, so that after one such storm they cannot stand the sea long.

On the 29th August, our pilot, who was an Englishman,[1] being aloft, descried land ten leagues distant. This delighted us exceedingly, for we were in need of fresh water, and yet did not know where to find land, believing that we could not have been driven so near to Guinea, which we intended to pass a hundred leagues off; but the calms and currents had brought us in once more. At the good news our captain quickly hoisted the ensign on the foremast (for only a chief or commander can fly it on the mainmast), and firing a shot to call our General's attention, learned from him that it was the island of *Anabon*.[2] As he was now behind we did not go forward, but put our ship about and waited till the morning, ere we cast anchor at the island: this the mariners call "beating"; it is practised when they want to keep in view of land and to remain in the same part of the sea or coast, first they go one way, and then, tacking about, the other.

Next day, the 30th, after anchoring, we treated amicably with the Portuguese, who are masters of the island. As they had accepted some presents from us, and had also sent us some fruit, we trusted to their good faith, and our General got

243, *n*.). It seems more likely to be a nautical corruption of "lame" than of "whelm", the use of which word does not seem to be correctly appreciated by the Docteur Roulin.

[1] The name of this pilot is not given. English pilots, as Mr. Bell reminds me, were in request in those days, especially when they had been the Indian voyage before. Thus John Davis was pilot to the Dutch voyage of the *Moucherons* in 1598; William Adams to Mahn's fleet of the same year; Mellish, who had sailed with Cavendish, was pilot in Van Noort's fleet.

[2] The island of Annobon, in lat. 1° 30′ S., long. 5° 40′ E., so called from its discovery by Martin Fernandez on the 1st January 1471. It was ceded to Spain in 1778, and is said now to contain about 1,000 inhabitants.

ready his gallion and put in it a number of vessels for the water, fruit, and other provisions, sending for this purpose some sailors and soldiers. With them also six officers of the two ships desired to go for refreshment, and though it was against the General's intention, he did not care to stop them. When they were landed, the six officers were well received by the Portuguese, so that they trusted them entirely, and let themselves be conducted whither they would. They then sent the boat with the sailors round to the other side of the island for the water, as had been arranged. They were led by a party of negroes, who, however, would not enter the boat—a circumstance which was of itself enough to show their want of good faith—but made round the island, they by land, and we by sea. Soon after, the six were surrounded and attacked by a large number of Portuguese and negro slaves in arms, who had been in an ambuscade. One of the six, the lieutenant of the *Corbin*, named Thomas Pepin of St. Malo, began to defend himself, and in fact wounded several of them, but being overpowered by numbers, he was mortally wounded and carried ashore, while the other five were made prisoners. The Portuguese then sent the wounded man on a raft to the ships, accompanied by our General's negro servant, who had gone with the six; but as soon as he was laid on the ship the lieutenant breathed his last. The General at once fired two shots to warn the sailors on the other side to return if they could with the boat, and not to engage in any fighting, which they did promptly. The next day the Portuguese sent on another raft (for they have there no other vessels) one of the five prisoners, to say that they were very badly treated, being kept in chains in the mountains and separate from one another. These mountains are high, and all covered with wood. Moreover, they said that a ransom was put on their heads, which was at length agreed to, viz., 1,500 cruzados, some wine, biscuit, powder, muskets, and other implements, the prisoners being severally delivered up at each part payment. The Portuguese then sent a pig, some rice, fruit, and other provisions, and told us that we might go freely and safely about the island; but we would not trust them any more, though we were in need of fresh water. Therefore we went by night in our boats, well armed, to fetch the water, but got only a little, for the stream is at the bottom of a valley near the sea, and the islanders would not let us have it, but took up a position on the hills above, and attacked us with muskets, wounding in the shoulder one of our ship's boys. They also wounded us with stones thrown or rolled down the hill, so that the work was very dangerous. This continued for six or seven weeks, while we were at the coast.[1] In place of the dead lieutenant, another was constituted, not elected on the spot, but one that had been nominated to succeed by the Company at St. Malo, who had made appointments to all the offices in case of death, so as not to leave that in the discretion of the ship's company, which might give rise to some disorder. And here is to be remarked that one who is promoted to a higher grade, or changes his office, gets no more wages than he had before, because the wages of a deceased officer always run on to the return home of the ship, and are paid to his widow, children, or heirs, just as though he were alive.

This island belongs to a Portuguese lord, to whom the King of Spain has given it[2]: the other Portuguese who reside there are his factors and agents. All the people of the island are his slaves, and with them he drives a great trade as

[1] An interesting cut, representing the attack of the islanders upon the French, will be found in the Dutch journal of Spilberg's voyage, drawn, no doubt, from the description given by the Frenchmen of the *Croissant* and *Corbin*, when they met Spilberg's ships at the Cape and Madagascar.

[2] The Portuguese lord lived at the little dependent island named St. Omer (Martin, *Voyage*, p. 95). Pyrard here, as elsewhere, properly speaks of the King of Spain, Portugal having been subject to Spain since 1580. The island now, in fact, belongs to Spain, by virtue of Art. 13 of the Treaty of 11th March 1778 (Rivara's *Pyrard*, i, 13, *note*).

well in Spain as in the West Indies, exporting every year a certain number, according to their increase. They are all negroes, and go naked, men and women, save that they cover with cotton their privy parts; the women carry their babes on their backs, and give them suck over the shoulder, their breasts being so long that the children grasp and suck them from behind. This island is situate under the altitude of a degree and a half south latitude, and has a circuit of about five or six leagues. It is high, mountainous, and covered with wood, and always green. All the time we were there, not a day passed but it rained more or less. The roadstead on the north-west is very dangerous by reason of the shoals and rocks. Fruits grow there in abundance, such as oranges, bananas (which serve for bread); cocos,[1] which supply the people with wine; sugar-canes, pine-apples, other fruits which they call *Panana*,[2] and also rice and millet. A quantity of cotton is collected, and this forms the sole revenue of the island. The fishery is abundant, and the fish being good, we were greatly refreshed thereby. At a league and a half from Anabon is a little island all burnt up and without any verdure, yet is it so covered with birds that one can hardly walk a step in any direction without treading upon them or their eggs. They are called *Pingui;* they are a little bigger than our pigeons, of about the same plumage, of excellent flavour and good eating, albeit the flesh is very black.[3] We ate many

[1] The word "coco" being applied exclusively to the nut, Rivara is right in pointing out that Pyrard makes a slip here, inasmuch as the wine is drawn from the tree itself.

[2] It is not clear what fruit is here intended; he has already mentioned bananas and pineapples (*ananas*), for which the word might be supposed to be a misprint. In the first edition (1611) it appears as *panaua*; and Martin (p. 22), also writing of Annobon, says: "Et autres fruicts qu'ils nomment *Panama*"; but neither of these various readings help us. The sweet-potato may be meant, or the word may be connected with *pão*, bread, and indicate *cassava*, which grows at Annobon.

[3] As pointed out by Guèrin, in his abridgment of Pyrard, the birds here called penguins were really *manchots* (*Les Navigateurs Français*, p. 218, *note*).

of them, going every day to that little island to take our walks and catch them. One of our fellows, who had been recognised as lieutenant of the *Corbin* in place of him deceased, in pursuing these birds, fell between some rocks and broke his leg, and much trouble we had to get him out at all. We were beset by all manner of misfortunes during our sojourn at this road, for besides this we had many others, and most of them happened to our ship, where arose a great quarrel between our Captain and the chief factor or merchant. They almost came to blows, and were like to have caused a general revolt and mutiny, so that our General had need to come with a competent guard to restore order; nevertheless, this dispute lasted the whole voyage, neither speaking to the other. I leave you to consider how all could go well when the chiefs, who ought to show a good example to the others, themselves created disorder. There was also another mischance, viz.: when the men were getting into the boats to fight for a supply of water, fire reached some powder in one of ours wherein our Captain was, and many were burned and injured. But the last accident was this: on weighing anchor, we were all the morning endeavouring to raise one of ours; and although those on board the *Croissant* came to our aid, we could not get it up, and the cable gave way, though it was as thick as a man's thigh and quite new. The anchor itself was lost—a matter of no small moment at such times.

Having thus sojourned at the anchorage at this island for the space of six weeks, on the 16th October our General gave order to weigh and to hoist sail, and steer a course for St. Helena, because we had not been able to get fitting refreshment here, and we were beginning to have some sick of the scurvy. Those on their way to the Indies do not ordinarily fetch that island (St. Helena), the winds not being favourable, and great risk attending the attempt to make it; indeed, our pilot said that he did not expect we should of certainty reach it. However, on the 17th November, we did at daybreak happily sight the island of St. Helena,[1] situate under the 16th degree toward the Antarctic Pole, and distant 600 leagues from the Cape of Good Hope. We found on the altar of the chapel many letters, which gave notice that the Hollanders had passed there. We looked to find there some timber to refit our foremast, but there was none fit for the purpose. Our sojourn at this island was nine days, and this was of great service to our sick, inasmuch as the water, the flesh, and the fruits there are very wholesome, and the air very pure and healthy: so we were replenished with all the water we stood in need of. I will not tarry here to describe the beauty, fertility, plenteousness, and commodities of this excellent island, postponing a more particular description against my return, because the long stay we then made gave me a better knowledge of it.

On the 26th November 1601, our sick being now recovered, we weighed anchor and set sail, and pursued our route towards the Cape of Good Hope.

Three days afterwards we doubled the *Abroilles*. These are banks and shoals off the coast of Brazil, under the 18th degree beyond the equinoctial line. They stretch a distance of some 70 leagues; the Portuguese call them *Abrolhos*,[2] that is to

[1] St. Helena, in lat. 16° S., long. 5° 50′ W., discovered by João de Nova on St. Helena's day (18th Aug.), 1502, was held under the nominal authority of the Portuguese till 1651, when it was taken by the English. The Portuguese, for reasons stated by Pyrard in his subsequent description of the island, never garrisoned it, nor indeed allowed it to be colonised. It was accordingly used freely for refreshment and as a post-office by Portuguese, Dutch, and English. As Pyrard postpones his fuller description, we may also postpone our fuller notes.

[2] *Abre-olhos!* "Keep your eyes open!" This fanciful derivation was at one time generally accepted. Pyrard was not the first to give currency to it; thus, Sir R. Hawkins writes the word *abreoios* (*Hawkins's Voyages*, p. 171). It is, however, undoubtedly taken from *abrolho*, the water calthrop, which has a secondary meaning, in military use, of a *cheval de frise*, and in nautical use, of pointed rocks or breakers. (See Rivara's *Pyrard*, i, 16, *note*; *Linschoten*, Hak. Soc., i, 16, *note*.)

say, "Open your eyes", because these shoals are exceeding dangerous, and it is very necessary to keep a good look-out and to give them a wide berth; for if you were to fail to double them, and were to get caught in them, it would be very difficult to get out; and even if you did get out, the voyage would be lost, and you would have to return whence you set out. This is the reason why ships going to the Indies, out of care to keep them at a distance, fall away too much on the other side towards Guinea, where the air is exceeding unwholesome, and where they meet with such calms and currents, that very frequently vessels are lost, or else many men languish and die of grievous ailments; wherefore the dexterity of good pilots lies in not approaching too near the coast of Guinea, and also in not striking these banks of the *Abroilles* on the Brazil side, but in taking their measure, and in so doing they will have plenty of room, for the distance between the coast of Africa and that of Brazil is put down at about a thousand leagues. Having thus doubled these banks, we had a merry-making, and appointed by lot a king to rule during the feast, which lasts a whole day; and there was served out to each a pint of wine more than ordinary. This was in imitation of the Portuguese, who do this, men being always accustomed to imitate rather bad customs, than such as are good and laudable. For my part I nowise approve those feasts and banquets at sea, which result only in consuming the ship's wine and victuals, and in making the mariners drunk and incapable of doing their duties, besides giving rise to quarrels and assaults.[1]

[1] To pass the Abrolhos was with the Portuguese the first crisis of the voyage; the Cape was the second. The same festivities were observed on board the *Croissant*:—"A ceste consideration les Portuguais ayant doublé ces bancs ont accoustumé en signe de regiouissance faire un Roy, eslisant celuy à qui eschet un certain billet, et à leur imitation nous en fismes un, et Dieu voullut que le sort tomba sur moy, et celuy qui est Roy a tout pouvoir durāt ceste solennité, laquelle dure ordinairement quatre

CHAPTER II.

Of the Cape of Good Hope and the Cape of the Needles.— Violent storm on the coast of Natal.

Meanwhile our vessels were daily making their way towards the Cape of Good Hope, and after some days we perceived the signs whereby proximity to the Cape is known. Fifty or sixty leagues out are seen floating in vast numbers the stalks of reeds, with about nine or ten reeds (more or less) attached to each stalk: these are called *trombas*[1];

ou cinq jours, qui ont accoustumé de se passer en festins et joye; le jour de ma promotion je fists deliurer quelques prisonniers qui estoient à la chaine" (*Martin*, p. 32). So Davis, in his Dutch voyage of 1598: "The 10th we passed the Abrolhos, which was the greatest of our feare . . . whereupon our Baase (for so a Dutch Captaine is called) chose a Master of Mis-rule by the name Kesar (*i.e.*, *Keizer*, 'Emperor'). Now the authoritie of riot lay in this disordered officer, who after dinner could neither salute his friends, nor understand the lawes of Reason. And those that ought to have been most respective, were both lawlesse and witlesse. In this dissolute manner we wasted three days, which being ended, and having againe recovered our former discretion, we shaped our course for Cape Bona Esperanza" (*Davis*, Hak. Soc., p. 134). Compare the Whit-Sunday festivities mentioned by Linschoten (Hak. Soc., i, 17), at which some idle words led to a dangerous brawl.

[1] Port. *tromba*. These reeds, together with the various birds, are alluded to by most navigators as signs of the Cape. "The signs and tokens whereby they know themselves certainly to have passed the Cape [homeward bound], are great heapes and peeces of thicke reedes, that alwaies thereabouts drive uppon the water, at least 15 or 20 miles from the land" (*Linsch.*, Hakl. Soc., ii, 250). "Le 31 ils commencèrent à voir floter des *trumbas*, ou poignées de joncs avec leurs racines, ce qui est une marque qu'on n'est pas loin du Cap de Bonne Espérance" (Houtman's voy., *Rec. des Voy.*, i, 211). "There are also other signs of land being near, as those they call *caravels of Brittany*, being weeds, or rather reeds, like the Indian canes, or rather like grass, but as thick as one's finger" (Merolla, 1682, in *Churchill*, i, 665). "These *trombas* are a kind of great canes, about the bignesse of a man's arm, and three or four foot long, which flote upon the water with their roots" (*Mandelslo*, Eng. trans., 248).

also, a multitude of white birds speckled with black spots, which the Portuguese call *mangue de velade.*[1]

On the 27th December 1601, towards midnight, while it was blowing a strong gale with rain, the night being very dark, we suddenly found ourselves close upon land, and but for a mariner, who by accident perceived it, we had been lost, for the seas at that part are passing heavy and stormy, and there are some great rocks projecting out into the sea. As soon, therefore, as this was descried by the mariner, we tacked sails and ship and put about to sea, and fired off a gun to give our General warning. At daybreak it was observed that we had passed the Cape of Good Hope, and that the cape we saw was that of the Needles.[2] This cape

[1] Properly *mangas de vèlludo*, "velvet sleeves". Thomas Stevens, the Jesuit, whom Pyrard afterwards met at Goa, thus writes, in 1579: "Fowles of sundry kindes followed our ship...... The Portingals have named them all according to some proprietie which they have: some they call *Rush-tailes*, because their tails be not proportionable to their bodies, but long and smal like a rush; some *Forked-tailes*, because they be broad and forked; some *Velvet-sleeves*, because they have wings of the coulor of velvet, and boweth them as a man boweth his elbow. This bird is alwaies welcome, for he appeareth neerest the Cape" (*Hakluyt*, i, 161). Linschoten says: "We saw there also divers of the birds called *Mangas de Velludo*, that is to say, Velvet-sleeves, for they have upon the ends of their wings blacke points like velvet, all the rest being white and somewhat grey, which they hold for a certain sign of the land that lyeth within the Cape de Bona Esperanza (Hakl. Soc. edition, ii, 243; so *Mocquet*, edition 1645, p. 227). Rivara points out that Pyrard has misdescribed the "mangas de velludo", which is white with black wings, and has given the description of another and commoner Cape bird, known by the Portuguese as the "Feijão frade" (see *Linsch.*, ii, 250), which is white, freckled with black spots. Dr. Fryer mentions "*Pintado* birds, *Mango faleudos*, *Albetrosses*, the first remarkable for their pointed spots of black and white" (p. 12), without describing the "velvet-sleeve". Mandelslo gives a correct description: "*Mangas de valeudo*, a kind of sea-mews, being white all over the bodies and having black wings" (Eng. trans., p. 248).

[2] *I.e.*, *Cabo das Agulhas*, the name by which it is still known. It is the southernmost point of the African continent. Pyrard places it in 35° S.; Linschoten (Hakl. Soc., ii, 249) in 34½°; it is really in 36° 5′ S.

advances out into the sea further than that of Good Hope by fifteen leagues, and is situate under the altitude of 35 degrees of Southern latitude. It is named the Cape of the Needles, because at this place the compasses or needles remained fixed, pointing directly to the north, without any declination to the east or the west; when it is doubled, they begin to decline to the north-east. On this day we sighted two Hollander ships and a pinnace coming out of a bay that is by the Cape *des Aguilles*, called *Baya Sardeigna*,[1] where they had gone for refreshment. It was, however, impossible for us to approach one another all the day long, because of the wind and of the sea, which was running high and tempestuous; nevertheless, their smaller ship, with great difficulty, ran down the wind toward us and told us who they were. On the morrow we came together, and for two days visited each other and gave mutual entertainment with all friendliness. They were very small ships from Camfer,[2] in Zeeland, their General by name *Spilbert*.[3] They told us it was them we had sighted on the Guinea coast, and that had our General waited until they had sent their pinnace after us, the misfortune that befell us at the island of *Anabon*

As to the non-variation of the compass, see Davis (*Voyages*, Hakl. Soc., p. 136): "We doubled Cape das Agulios, which is the most southerly promontorie of Africa, where the compasse hath no variation."

[1] *Saldanha* bay, called after Antonio de Saldanha, who went to India in 1503. *Baya Sardeigna* is a misnomer, which Rivara accepts by his translation, *Bahia das Sardinhas* (*Viagem de Pyrard*, i, p. 18). As pointed out by Mr. Corney (*Middleton's Voy.*, Hakl. Soc., p. 6) and Mr. Clements Markham (*Lancaster's Voy.*, Hakl. Soc., p. 62), the Saldanha Bay of the Portuguese, Dutch, and English voyagers of this period is our Table Bay. Pyrard's statement that the Dutch were met coming out of a bay near the Needles Cape is incorrect; Spilberg had put into Table Bay and nowhere else, and the two fleets met off the Cape of Good Hope (Spilberg, *Rec. des Voy.*, ii, 438-44).

[2] Veer, Terveer, or Campveer, a small town and fort commanding the Veergat, on the north side of the island of Walcheren. It was taken by the British during the ill-fated expedition of 1809.

[3] Joris van Spilbergen, generally called Spilberg.

had not come to pass. For they related to us how they had landed, and put no confidence in the people of the island as we did; yet they obtained a sufficiency of water, losing, however, two of their men, and having six wounded. They told us, moreover, that if we had been all together in company we should have been strong enough in men to have made ourselves masters of the island: that no great resistance was possible, and so we should have been enabled to refresh ourselves and make provision of water. Thus was our General partly to blame for all that misfortune, because he did not await the Hollanders as he ought. We gave them a mainsail, of which they stood in need, and in exchange they gave us two perriers,[1] or small iron cannon. They were also bound for the Indies, and we should have been glad enough to make the voyage in their company. But this could not be, because they had to go by the passage between the mainland and the island of St. Laurence, in order to meet their countrymen who were awaiting them there, a rendezvous having been appointed at the *Baya Formosa*,[2] on the Melinde coast. Our intention, on the contrary, was to pass outside the island, wherefore we parted and took leave of each other with much cannonading.[3] This done, we took our course outside the island of St. Laurence.

[1] *Perrier*, "the ship's artillery called a fowler" (Cotgrave); "(petit canon de fer), a *pederero* or *petterero*, a fowler, a sort of gun" (Boyer). The word is a corruption of Fr. *pierrier*, Port. *pederero*, and is taken from an engine used for casting stones, which was in use before the discovery of gunpowder. In the sixteenth century there were *pierriers* and *demi-pierriers*, ranging from 35 to 20 quintals. It was a gun proper for use on the main-tops, and in boats (Jal, *Gloss. Naut.*, s. v.).

[2] Near Melinde, in latitude 3° S., longitude 40° 20′ E. In the text it is misprinted *Tormosa*.

[3] The following account of the meeting with the Dutch ships, given in Spilberg's voyage (*Rec. des Voy.*, ii, 444), shows how the laxity of discipline on board the French ships struck the foreigner, and indicates, even in these petty details, the vital difference between the seamanship of the French and Portuguese on the one hand, and that of the Dutch and English on the other:—"Le 27 [Dec. 1604] nous découvrîmes

The 6th January 1602, being Twelfth Night, while all were making merry and crying "le Roy boit",[1] arose a violent

le Cap, et deux vaisseaux François de S. Malo, dont Mr. de Bardelière étoit Amiral, et Mr. le Connétable de Vitré Vice-amiral. Un des Pilotes étoit Flamand, et se nommoit Mayor Wouter Willekens. Après qu'on lui eut parlé, nous fîmes route de compagnie. Le même jour, notre Général aïant beaucoup d'envie de s'entretenir plus particulièrement avec eux, dans l'espérance d'aprendre quelques nouvelles, se rendit à leur bord, accompagné de Corneille Specx : et le lendemain les François passèrent au sien. Ils lui dirent qu'ils avoient aussi relâché à Annobon, où on leur avoient montré des tombeaux de quelques uns de leurs gens, qu'on disoit avoir été tuez en combattant contre trois vaisseaux Flamands. Ces Messieurs les François de S. Malo s'imaginoient être là en grande seureté, parce-qu'ils étoient Catoliques Romains : surtout en descendant à terre, pour aller ouïr la Messe. Mais la Messe leur coûta bien plus cher que qu'ils en eussent paié la façon au Prêtre : car les Portugais en massacrèrent quelques-uns et en retinrent d'autres prisonniers, pour qui il fallut paier de grosses rançons, jusqu'à mille écus en argent, avec diverses marchandises.

"Le 1 de Janvier 1602 les François aïant déclaré qu'ils vouloient aller par l'est de Madagascar, et par conséquent prendre un autre cours que nous n'avions résolu, on se sépara bon amis. Au reste il n'étoit pas à propos que nous fussions plus longtems avec eux. Nos gens n'avoient par semaine que chacun trois livres de biscuit, et tous les dix jours deux pintes de vin ; au lieu que les tonneaux de vin étoient toujours percez dans les navires François, chacun en pouvant aller tirer quand il lui plaisoit. On y avoit le biscuit à commandement : on y jettoit à la mer le stocfiche tout cuit. Chaque ration de vin étoit de six pintes par semaine pour chaque homme, et encore ne s'en tenoient-ils pas à cette règle ; souvent ils alloient plus loin, et s'en faisoient donner davantage. Cet example étoit dangereux, et il ne devoit pas être longtems devant nos yeux, puis-qu'il nous étoit impossible de le suivre, et qu'il auroit pu servir à faire murmurer nos gens, de ce qu'ils n'étoient pas ainsi traitez." The Dutch, perhaps intentionally, misinformed the French as to their route, in order to get rid of them. The course they had resolved to make was first to a point near Cape Sta. Lucia, then across to Cape St. Mary, at the south end of Madagascâr, thence to the Comorro Islands (*Rec. des Voy.*, ii, pp. 432, 433).

[1] In France, the chairman at the Twelfth Night festival was called "Le roi de la fève" (King of the bean). His first act, on taking the chair, was to drink to the company, who responded with a loud shout of "Le roi boit!" The celebration, which in the early Middle Ages consisted of a procession in which the three Kings or Magi took the principal

squall, which required us to lower sail, and one of our mariners, a man of St. Malo, fell into the sea. It was impossible to save him: his messmate,[1] however, would have flung himself after him had he not been restrained; but I think this was more because he had taken too much wine than out of affection, for these sailors have not much friendship. All along this coast we saw all night many fires on the tops of the mountains. Thus continuing our voyage, we passed without any storm the land of Natal, which is on the Ethiopian coast,—an unwonted occurrence, because violent storms are usually met with between the 33rd and 28th degrees.

On the 30th January, in the altitude of 26 degrees, our General asked his pilot[2] on which side of the island of St. Laurence we were; he replied, on the outside; nevertheless, this was not so, for we were between the coast of Africa and the island, contrary to our intention. This was due to the ignorance of the pilot, as well as to our amusing ourselves too long with the Hollanders' ships. Having the weather calm, we let our ships go at their will, carrying generally only lower sails; while the Hollanders' vessels, being better sailers than ours, duly kept their course along the coast of Africa, and we followed them unconsciously. Our General, doubting the fact, demanded to sight the island for his assurance; but after sailing for two days and two nights without sighting it, he gave orders to put about on the opposite

part, had by this time degenerated into a mere jollification; nowadays, in England at least, the sole remaining relic is a cake. The whole history of Twelfth Night will be found well described in Chambers's *Book of Days* (January 6th), where also may be seen a copy of an old French print, exhibiting a party of revellers crying "Le roi boit!" as described by Pyrard.

[1] As the author explains in his Advice at the end of vol. ii, each of the sailors had his messmate: an arrangement made with a view to friendship and mutual assistance.

[2] Probably the Fleming named Mayor Wouter Willekens mentioned by Spilberg (v. s., p. 23, note 3).

course. This done, we sailed on till the 4th of February, when we began to sight the island of St. Laurence on its inner side, whereupon our General was highly incensed against the pilot. Forthwith he gave order to work back out of the strait and to return to the outer course, because he was afraid of not being able to make the passage by reason of the contrary winds which are ordinarily to be met with in the season we were then in.

On the 7th February 1602, while coasting back along Natal to get without the island of St. Laurence, a course we had already made happily without mishap, there arose suddenly a violent squall from the south-west. We had no thought of it; the Portuguese, on the other hand, when they make the passage in this latitude, prepare for these storms, and take precautions in time. Our galleon had been lowered to send a man on board the *Croissant* to confer between the General and our captain on some business concerning the voyage; and just a moment before, I had myself returned from visiting some of my friends that were very ill, amongst others, a young man of our town, Laval, whom I loved dearly. Some of our men who were on board the *Croissant*, seeing the sea wax high, got into the galleon or boat and returned to us. But they made so little haste that they could hardly have been got on board, had we not flung them a cable, which gripping, it was as much as they could do to get on board in safety. It was, however, impossible to hoist the galleon so promptly; it was only lashed, as best we could, with a heavy cable, and this broke, so the galleon filled with water and went to the bottom before we could do anything to save it; this loss was of the utmost trouble to us. I believe it impossible for those who have not experienced it to conceive the horror and fury of this storm, for all we had experienced heretofore was mere child's-play in comparison. It became so dark at high noon that we could not see the sky nor recognise one another. Our two ships got far parted, and in an instant our sails were torn to shreds: the rain and wind were so furious in our faces that we were wounded and bruised as by strokes of rods: the collars of our shirts were torn, and smote us on the face so that we had to wrench them off. The waves also ran so terribly high that you would have said that the ship was at one time tossed up to heaven, at another plunged into an abyss, and all the while rolling from side to side in such wise that it was no easy matter to keep within the ship, and very perilous to remain on deck: for we were continually struck by the heaviest seas, and sometimes by one (roller) *louesme;* more than twenty hogsheads of water were shipped, which passed over the vessel and only partly escaped on the other side. With their violence these would carry away all they met, and so it behoved a man to hold well to the deck. Fortunate was it for us that our ship was so tight and staunch that not a single leak was sprung in her nether timbers by the fury of this storm, and she made no more water than ordinary. All the water she made came in from above when she was struck by these seas and topping waves, which passed over her and drenched not only the men on the deck and those under cover, but also the ship's provisions and furniture. We had hardly hands enough to empty the ship with the pumps, and our captain was foremost at the job. There was nothing that was not soaked and spoiled; and this entailed the greatest hardships; for during the four days and four nights the storm lasted, we were perpetually drenched with salt water, and afterwards had nothing dry for change. We ate nothing but a little biscuit and a little wine, being unable to cook anything; to sleep or get the slightest repose was out of the question. At such a time, all who were wise turned to their own thoughts; as for the mariners, it is then they swear and blaspheme more than usual. At the height of the storm at midnight the question arose of cutting the main topmast. The method of so doing is to cut the standing and running rigging on the leeward side, next to cut the mast half across, then to cut the ropes on the windward side, whereupon it falls of itself without injuring anyone. This was a perilous job, owing to the difficulty a man had in keeping his hold during the violent tossings of the ship. In this task they employed our chief carpenter, a Hollander, and one of the best ship's carpenters living; he received double wages and double portions of wine, but in truth he did as much work as any three men. With great difficulty he managed to cut the mast, and then, unable to keep his hold, fell with it to leeward and beyond the ship's side. By a miracle, however, he encountered the great yard, which being lowered and lashed crosswise, stretched out beyond the ship some nine or ten feet. There were here some ropes, which the poor fellow caught and gripped so firmly that he managed to save himself, though with the utmost difficulty. We thought, too, that another grave accident was to befall us. There were four or five heavy iron cannon, which were dismounted and lashed and belayed below on the first deck. By force of the storm these got loose, but God permitted that some men below should observe it; and these men ran forthwith with mattresses, sacks, and other soft baggage, and cast them on either side to stay the guns, and so to get them re-lashed; otherwise the slightest blow they would have given in their rolling to the ship's side would have driven a hole in her. During this storm our rudder-trunk broke, and this was a great trouble to us, for it deprived us of the necessary use of the helm. Our pilots and the oldest seamen said they had never endured a more violent storm, nor one that had so driven them from their wits and daunted their resolution. But the truth is that they had never before experienced the violence of the sea in those parts, where ordinarily it is much more heavy and stormy than elsewhere. For my part, on my return I came through seas quite as furious, under the same altitude, but not on the same coast.

CHAPTER III.

We anchor in St. Augustine's bay, at the island of St. Laurence. —Of our landing and long sojourn there.—A description of the island, and of the manners and customs of the inhabitants.

The storm lasted until the 11th of the said month of February. When it subsided we were in great trouble by reason we had lost sight of the *Croissant*, our General. What gave us the more anxiety was that we observed a great mast floating on the sea, and believed that the *Croissant* had gone down, and that the mast was hers. By this time the most of our wearied crew were sick and half-dead; wherefore the Captain took counsel whether we ought to make land, and the opinion was to make the nearest we could, which was the island of St. Laurence.[1] Forthwith our course was directed thither, albeit we were somewhat afraid, because we had no pilot nor mariner who had been to the Indies before, saving one Flemish gunner, who was an ignorant fellow.

Approaching the island, at thirty or forty leagues off, we observed the sea to become changed: it was yellowish and exceeding frothy, covered with sea-urchins, canes, reeds, and other floating herbs, and these continued till we reached the island. At length, on the 18th February, we sighted land.

On the morning of the 19th February we cast anchor in a

[1] *I.e.*, Madagascar, first discovered by Soares on the 1st Feb. 1506: it was called St. Laurence, owing to a later discovery by d'Abreu on that saint's day (August 10th in the same year), and was so known all through the Portuguese period.

> "De São Lourenço-vê a ilha affamada,
> Que Madagascar he d'alguns chamada."
>
> (Camões, *Lus.*, x, 137.)

In course of time the native name Madagascar, supposed to be derived from Makdishu (Magadoxo), on the Zanzibar coast, asserted itself (*Linschoten*, Hakl. Soc., i, p. 19, *note*).

bay, surnamed of St. Augustine,[1] situate under the altitude of 23½ degrees south, under the tropic of Capricorn. It is a large and commodious bay, with a good bottom of slime and sand. At midday we perceived a large vessel in the offing. Thinking at the first it was a Portuguese ship, we put on our arms and prepared ourselves, and began to stretch our quarter-nettings for our defence; but when it came nigher we found it was the *Croissant*, from which we had been separated about the space of twelve hours; she brought up close alongside. This was a matter of much joy and comfort, saving that we found her to be in worse plight than ourselves, her furniture in sorry condition, her timbers open, and her crew almost all sick. Towards evening we perceived another ship, without masts or sails, except a single spar fixed amidships, with a little sail for her assistance. She anchored four or five leagues from us, not daring to come closer, and then despatched a boat with three or four hands to reconnoitre us. When they perceived who we were, they approached and came aboard our ship, where they were welcomed and told us who they were. The vessel was one of the two Hollanders we had seen at the Cape of the Needles, and had been grievously dealt with by the gale.[2] Presently the barque returned to inform their captain, who forthwith came and cast anchor alongside of us. He was named Le Fort, the son of a Frenchman of Vitré, but born in Holland.[3] He had

[1] St. Augustine's Bay, in latitude 23° 30′ S.; longitude 43° 35′ E.

[2] It was the *Ram*, one of Spilberg's ships, which got separated from her consort soon after leaving the Cape. The violence of this gale is described in Spilberg's voyage in much the same terms as by Pyrard (*Rec. des Voy.*, ii, pp. 449-53). The *Ram* did not meet the *Sheep* again till the 3rd July, when she joined her at Batticaloa, in Ceylon. Her crew recounted their adventures to their friends, and it is added, "Ils avoient vu dans cette baie [St. Augustine's] deux vaisseaux François de S. Malo, aussi tout-désemparez" (*ib.*, p. 479).

[3] Guyon Lefort, the captain of the *Ram*, the vessel here met with by the Frenchman, had already been to the East in the expedition sent out in 1598 from Middelburg by the Company of the *Moucherons*. The

already been to the Indies, and died on this voyage at Achen. It was said the King of Achen liked him and made much of him. The three ships being now together, our General and our Captain and the Hollander, with the chief men of the three vessels, took counsel what they should do for the common advantage, and, according to the general agreement, a place on shore was chosen, the best we could find, to land such as were sick of the scurvy—a great number on board our vessels, but among the Hollanders not a man. A place was chosen and marked out at the foot of a high mountain, on the banks of a river that falls into this bay; it was enclosed with a palisade of thick stakes, planted and driven in close to one another, and interlaced with big branches and with bastions of the same work, all covered with sails; while for the defence of this fortress we brought ashore some small cannon. Nor could we do otherwise, because there is no stone there fit for the purpose, and no means of making trenches and ramparts, the ground being all shifting sand. We landed there our scurvy-stricken men, and for their

vessels were the *Leeuw* (Lion) and the *Leeuwin* (Lioness), commanded respectively by the brothers Cornelis and Frederik de Houtman. Lefort was on board the *Lion*, in the capacity of Treasurer. In a treacherous attack made on the ships at Achin, Cornelis de Houtman lost his life, and Frederik was taken prisoner. The Dutch lost in all sixty-eight men. Lefort was one of the prisoners, but was subsequently sent back with a message from the Achin Raja; and on the opening of the sealed letters containing the appointment in case of death, he was found to be nominated to the command of the expedition. He brought the ships safely home in July 1600. No Dutch account of this voyage exists; but the story is told in a graphic narrative by our great navigator, John Davis, who was pilot to the expedition. According to Davis, Lefort was the son of "a French merchant, dwelling in Seething Lane" (*Davis's Voyages and Works*, Hakl. Soc., Introduction, pp. lxiv, lxv, and pp. 145, 153; also *De opkomst van het Nederlandsch Gezag in Oost Indie*, door Jhr. Mr. J. K. J. de Jonge, 'sGravenhage, 1864). Lefort died at Achin on the 7th March 1603. Spilberg charged him and his crew with conspiracy, and before his death he was removed from his command (Spilberg's voyage, *Rec. des Voy.*, ii, p. 532).

defence sent some that were able-bodied with arquebuses, muskets, and other arms to keep guard night and day. The Hollanders, not having a single sick man, did not wish to take up their quarters on shore, so they only pitched a tent a hundred paces from our fort, with two small cannon mounted for their protection; thither they sent some of their men for the refitting and re-apparelling of their ship, which they set about with all diligence, and in the morning landed and joined our company. After we had settled everything at the fort for the safety of the sick and sound alike, we sent some arquebusiers into the country to reconnoitre. Having advanced a little way within the island, they perceived some natives, who fled for fear of them. In order not to frighten them they did not follow them further, but returned, according to the orders of our General. The inhabitants, thus apprized that there were ships at anchor and strangers on their shores, came down to the number of fifteen or twenty, armed and accoutred in their fashion, bringing only a cow and a ram. Their design was to reconnoitre us and to try us whether we would treat with them freely and frankly, before they would make up their minds to traffic with us. Wherefore, approaching us, they for some time made signs to us, for neither we understood their language, nor they ours; they then turned away with their two beasts, as though they would not barter, although we had shown them many things whereof they seemed to make much account. Incontinently thereafter (having concluded, as may be believed, that we were men of good faith, forasmuch as we had not done them any violence or outrage, and had not even followed them) they came back in a little while, and frankly gave us the cow and the ram, while we gave them some little knives, scissors, and such like implements as they do greatly prize. Thus did we make friends with them, in such wise that, during the remainder of our sojourn there, they came without fail every four days with good store of animals, fowls, milk, honey, and some fruits, amongst others, *pateques*,[1] as large as pumpkins, excellent eating and highly refreshing. They bartered all these for ironware, and little Flemish and French bagatelles of the most trifling value, insomuch that for two counters (*jettons*), or one copper or tin spoon, we got a cow or bull, or three ewes or rams, for they have neither wethers nor oxen, being ignorant of castration. One day it happened that the pilot of the Hollander ship, who had about his neck the silver whistle which he used, advanced among the islanders while trafficking with them. This whistle took their fancy so much, and they became so enamoured of it, that they thought no more of our little trinkets and merchandises, and would not give us their beasts till we gave them this whistle, so were we constrained to sell it piece by piece, for it was hung upon several little chains: and in like manner we had to sell all the other whistles we had on board our ships. Provisions thus became dear, and a cow or bull that had cost us but one or two sols began to go up to eight or nine. Soon after there came toward us one of their people who had not been seen before, and showed us the buckle of one of these chains and a little piece of wood cut round; we understood thereby that he was asking for reals of forty sols, the piece of wood being of that size, roundness, and thickness, but we would not show him any. He knew quite well the value of silver, wherefore we concluded that further inland were peoples more civilised and better educated than the rest.[2] It was strictly forbidden

[1] *Pastèques*, "water-melons". The word, which Pyrard uses again hereafter for the melons of Malabar, is a corruption of the Arabic *al-baṭṭîkh*. See *Littré*, s. v. *Pastèque*. The word had already been introduced by the Moors into the Peninsula, where it survives in the Port. *albudieca* and Catalonian *albudeca*. After the Portuguese conquests it was re-introduced as *pateca*; but both forms have given way to the modern *melancia*. Fryer speaks of *putacho* "melon" at Bombay (*Fryer*, p. 76); see also *Garcia de Orta*, 141*b*.

[2] The real cause was that St. Augustine's Bay had been frequented

among us for any to buy or traffic on his own account, as well Hollanders as French, so that all provisions and refreshments should be held in common. The Hollander ship received a fourth part and paid a fourth; as between our two ships the proportion had been fixed at St. Malo: that is to say, of all purchases the *Corbin* paid two-fifths and the *Croissant* three-fifths, because the latter had the larger crew. We thought we were arrived at this island most seasonably for our own refreshment, for the benefit of the scurvy stricken, and also for the refitting of our ships, that were sorely in need thereof. But the result was quite otherwise, for they almost all died, and none recovered his health; even those that were whole fell sick of a burning fever, with frenzy, whereof they died at the end of two or three days. The disease was contagious, insomuch that a considerable number of the chiefest among us, and those of gentle birth, to the number of forty-one out of the two ships, died there as well of the scurvy as of the fever; and many that were stricken died full soon thereafter on sea. Our captain also fell sick of that disease, whereof he afterwards died at the Maldives, as we shall relate anon. As it was believed that those sick of the fever had contracted it on shore, they were carried aboard, the air there being fresher than on land, while those sick of the scurvy, which is an ailment proceeding from the sea and its fatigues, were carried ashore. We laid our dead to earth, or rather to sand (there being no earth there), in a spot which we named "The Cemetery of the French".[1] We

previously by Portuguese and Dutch ships, *e.g.*, by Houtman's in 1595, on which occasion tin spoons were in greatest request (*Rec. des Voy.*, i, pp. 231, 233).

[1] Orig.: "Nous enterrasmes, ou pour mieux dire nous ensablasmes (n'y ayant point de terre là) nos morts en un lieu que nous nommasmes le cemetiere des François." At and near this bay Houtman lost a number of his men, who were buried at a little island, which was in consequence called the cemetery of the Hollanders (*Rec. des Voy.*, i, pp. 224, 232).

had much difficulty in digging the graves and laying them therein, for all was moving sand, which filled up again at once; we had to use long pieces of wood, which men bore by the two ends, the body being suspended therefrom with ropes, and thus were they laid in the sand. For my part, during the fourteen months of our outward voyage and the twelve months of our homeward voyage, I was, thanks to God, never at all sick, though I was very ill in the Indies.[1] Certainly the place was very unhealthy, situate directly under the tropic of Capricorn, where the sun was close overhead, and beat upon us perpendicularly, at the foot of a high mountain covered with an infinite number of great lizards, though these were nowise hurtful and gave us no trouble. We had been much more harassed by the heat but for our proximity to a great wood which clothed the river banks, where, by day, those that were well enough went to walk and take the air, besides which we had the benefit of bathing in the river and the sea. Moreover, this wood was so full of apes and little monkeys that nowhere could more be seen. It is vastly pleasing to see these little animals playing together and leaping from tree to tree, as do our squirrels here. There was also a marvellous number of birds of all sorts, principally parrots, some having plumage of five or six different hues; and we had great amusement in listening to the varied music of their cries. Many strange fruits were also to be found there, whereof some were good eating, others not so. At that place and all around was nothing but shifting sand; the river water was unwholesome and salt by reason of the tide, but in default of other we were constrained to use it. The heat was so vehement that many of our men got their

[1] This is inconsistent with the author's statement in his Advice (see vol. ii), where he says that he was twice attacked by fever, the first time being on his arrival at St. Laurence on the outward voyage; though it agrees with his remark in ch. vi. The reference to his illness in the Indies is to a bad fever he had at the Maldives (see ch. ix).

feet burned, for all they had shoes and stockings; thence were generated ulcers, very troublesome to heal, which prevented them from walking. Another thing was that the majority of them, unable to govern their appetites after their long fast at sea, glutted themselves beyond measure with fresh meat, which the excessive and violent heat rendered more difficult of digestion. Furthermore, we suffered vast inconvenience by day from the flies, which persecuted us with the utmost fury, and by night from the mosquitos or gnats, which probe the flesh to the blood and cause the place to swell as by the sting of our honey-bees. In broad daylight they are powerless, and retire within the shady coverts of the woods and dwellings; but at night they swarm abroad. They are in such multitudes, and bite so keenly, that it is impossible to exist without covering the hands and face; while to get any sleep, we were constrained to make a fire well charged with smoke and to lie all around. Many of our sick put themselves in closed sacks, leaving but a small hole for breathing. At the Maldives (whereof I shall treat below), where these creatures are a vast nuisance, they use curtains, made on purpose, of a fine web, which these little flies cannot penetrate. This is a common annoyance throughout all the torrid zone.

The island of St. Laurence is of immense size, being more than 700 leagues in circuit—a fact of which I can speak with assurance, having coasted round both sides, as well on my outward as on my homeward voyage. The one end toward the south is under the 26th degree of latitude; that toward the north under the 14th.[1] It is very abundant in animals; the ewes bear three or four lambs at a time, as I learnt by experience, for we killed some that were big with young, and they had that number in their wombs. The tails of rams and ewes are wondrous big and heavy; one we

[1] Cape St. Mary, the southern point, is in latitude 26° S., and Cape Ambar, the northern, in latitude 12° S.

weighed turned twenty-eight pounds. Bulls, cows, rams, and ewes are so numerous all over the island that they are common property, belonging to any that can catch them. The reason is that the natives eat them but little, being, like the rest of the Indians, not flesh-eaters; they lay more account by fish, fruit, and milk diet. You will see there herds of 300 and 400 of these animals together. And while we were there we witnessed a wonderful habit of these bulls and cows: when they would cross from one side to the other of the said river, which is as broad and deep as our Seine, the larger bulls advanced in front, the cows following and placing their heads on the buttocks of the bulls, and the calves placing theirs on the buttocks of their dams; and when there were more cows than bulls, one cow would lean on the buttocks of another, and so they passed over. These oxen have on their necks a big hump of fat, good and delicate eating, and of the same flavour as the sheep's tails. Nevertheless, the flesh of these animals is neither so good eating nor so nourishing as that of ours here. There are vast numbers of monkeys and parrots, whereof we ate so many that betimes we would have as many as fifty or sixty in the pot together: they are as good eating as large pigeons. There is likewise an abundance of poultry, partridges, pheasants, and other kinds of birds. You see there also many chameleons, large lizards (whereof some are as big as a man's thigh), and bats that are bigger than crows. In the river, hard by which we were lodged, were good store of fish, whereof we took an abundant supply; there were also plenty crocodiles, several of which we killed. Herein we observed a remarkable fact, viz., that on killing one or more crocodiles, and cutting them open and gutting them, the entrails cast abroad a most excellent savour and perfumed most sweetly all the air around.[1] By night we set ourselves on

[1] Vincent le Blanc mentions, with reference to a crocodile killed in his presence at Pegu: "It was flead (flayed), and the flesh distributed

the watch to catch them, having by day cast on the sandy bank of the river a quantity of cows' and sheep's entrails; when night was closed in they failed not to come to the carrion, and then we shot them. Sometimes they were only wounded, and escaped; but even then this same odour as of musk hung about the place all the night long.

The people are of an olive and tawny complexion, approaching red; they are tall, straight, and shapely; clever and intelligent. All go naked, saving that they wear a little bit of cotton cloth about the privy parts; they wear their hair long, arranged in tresses and plaits. For arms they use only darts and javelins, called by them *Azagayes*,[1] which they fling with great dexterity; beyond all things they do fear arquebuses, at noise whereof they flee away. The women have a cloth covering them from above the breasts to the waist, and another from the waist to the knees; they keep the head uncovered and shaven of all hair; their bravery and ornaments consist of bracelets of copper, tin, or iron, of which they are very proud. It is said this island was formerly peopled by the Chinese by the means of one of their ships which was wrecked at this place, the crew taking up their abode there. And in truth the people resemble the Chinese much in face, but not in colour, for the Chinese are white and they olive; that, however, comes from their living under the torrid zone and going always naked. The island at the present is thickly peopled, and contains many kings who wage war one with another. Among the inhabitants are some that hold the Mahometan religion and are circumcised; the rest are pagans and Gentiles.

amongst the courtiers, and is as sweet as musk, which occasioned one of our gang to say he thought ambergris proceeded from these creatures" (Eng. trans., p. 115).

[1] As Dozy has pointed out, the word is the Berber *zaghaya*, with the Arabic article prefixed (see Yule and Burnell, *Disc. Gloss.*, s. v.). It is frequently used by the Portuguese writers, but cannot have been a Madagascar word.

While we were at this island, six of our mariners that were carpenters, gunners, and other craftsmen necessary to the ship's service, were debauched by one of their fellows, a Fleming, who bore a grudge against the mate of the *Corbin*. He persuaded them that it was better to quit the ships, where was nought but trouble, labour, and misery for them, and to escape ashore, where, without doubt, they would be welcomed and received by the kings of the country; and they hearkened to him the more readily because he had already been to the Indies. So it was that one night they went forth of our vessels without the knowledge of the rest, taking with them some biscuit, and each his own baggage and an arquebuse furnished with ammunition, with design to return no more.[1] This being discovered the next morning caused us the utmost vexation, seeing how short-handed we were. We also feared lest they should frighten the inhabitants and hinder them from bringing us provisions—as indeed was the case, for they ceased to come for a time. But at length, constrained by necessity, our men returned. Our General received them back and pardoned them by reason of the great need wherein we were; otherwise they had been punished. They told us they were seven days without finding water, enduring much from the pangs of thirst and the excessive heat, whereby they were compelled to drink their own urine; as for eating, they were in no stress, having taken some biscuit, and meeting with game frequently and fruit sometimes. They often saw numbers of the inhabitants with herds of cattle, but these fled away, so that they could not come nigh them. They also said that they had found a number of little huts constructed of canes and reeds, at which they saw nothing but some cotton nets for catching fish, with some common wood in place of cork, and some big shells and

[1] This is but one of many instances that might be given from actual history of "Lotos-eaters" in the tropics; in fiction see, besides Tennyson's poem, a well-known passage in Kingsley's *Westward Ho!*

periwinkles in place of lead; also heaps of fishbones. Sometimes they found trunks of large trees cut and hollowed, wherein was a little rain-water.

Now to return to the story of my voyage. We endured much hardship at this island during the three months we spent there. Our vessels were in grievous plight, the *Croissant* all open, and ours not better at her forepart. We made a new stem for our foremast from a tree of this island. The Hollanders made some masts of several pieces, and after a six weeks' stay took their departure, without losing a single man. For our part we made the greatest haste, but our men were perpetually falling sick, one dying after another; this caused us to prolong our sojourn. Having thus at length refitted our ships we had to take measures for our departure. To this end we made provision of flesh for the two ships, which was not very good, nor well adapted for preserving; but we were obliged to use it. We cut it in very thin and clean slices while yet quite fresh, then salted it forthwith, and put it in the sun to dry, suspended on ropes; the thicker slices would not dry rightly, and worms were engendered therein. All the viands of that country take the salt less readily than those of our country, and for all we could do, they became spoiled; let alone that they are not such good eating. Our vessels being thus ready, refitted and refurnished, we took in wood and water, re-embarked the remainder of our sick and all our goods that were on shore, and prepared to set sail. But forasmuch as we had lost a third part of our company,[1] and the voyage was still but little advanced, we resolved to take some of the inhabitants of the island for our assistance, for we were too feeble and short-handed in comparison of the size of the *Croissant*. For this

[1] He has said above that they lost 41 men at St. Augustine's Bay, so that the combined crews, including those lost at Annobon, must have numbered about 125 men when the ships left St. Malo. The *Croissant*, having three-fifths of the whole complement, thus had a crew of 75 hands; the *Corbin*, about 50.

purpose our General gave order to go at early morning and hide some carbines, pistols, and swords at a certain spot between the place where the poor natives came to meet us, and the place where they were wont to tarry with us trafficking for their cattle and other goods. At the same time he placed some of our men in two several ambuscades hard by, in order that, when they should come at nine or ten o'clock, as was their custom, and according to their promise expressed on the last occasion by signs, seeing us to be without arms, and not mistrusting us at all (for they were then on very friendly terms with us), they should be easily caught by our men, who were to run speedily for the hidden arms, and by those in ambush. This scheme was thus artfully devised, because out of their great fear of firearms they would never approach us when we were armed; and because, notwithstanding all this familiarity with us, they were yet exceeding cunning and suspicious, regarding all our actions and deportment with the utmost care. Thus did we design to give them a sorry farewell and an ill-requital for their service. But God permitted not this perfidy to succeed. They came not on that day at all; whereupon our General changed his plans, and gave order to make ready to sail on the morrow. It was a great mercy for us on board the *Corbin* that we did not take any of these islanders, for had they been with us when we reached the Maldives, as you shall hear anon, they would have had us all put to death for pirates.

On the 15th May 1602 we weighed anchor. But inasmuch as there were amongst us still many sick, including our captain of the *Corbin*, and three persons having already died since we began to set our sails, we therefore resolved to bear away towards the Comorro Islands.

CHAPTER IV.

We touch at the Comorro Islands.—Our sojourn at the road there, and our agreeable refreshment.

On the 23rd of the same month we sighted the Comorro Islands, which are in 12½ degrees of southern latitude, between the island of St. Laurence and the continent of Africa, distant about seventy leagues from Mozembic. They are five in number,[1] each possessing its own king; the one in the midst of the four others is called *Malailli,* at the roadstead of which we cast anchor. On our arrival, our General incontinently sent a boat ashore to reconnoitre, and to see if we could get some refreshment for our sick, who could not recover their health at the island of St. Laurence; on the contrary, after many had died, the soundest of us fell ill. The boat having taken land on this island of Malailli near a village—one of many we saw there lying close to one another, and of considerable size, the houses being of wood covered with palm leaves—our people were well received. Many of the inhabitants came to meet them with all appearance of friendship, bringing them good store of fruits, in exchange for which our men gave them some cheap ironware, and then

[1] There are four principal islands, Comoro, Mohilla (the *Malailli* of the text), Mayotta, and Johanna (or Anzuan). They were well known to the Portuguese in their intercourse with Mozambique. Davis, who visited Mayotta, mentions five, viz., Mayotta, Ansuame, Magliaglie, Saint Christofero, and Spirito Sancto (*Davis's Voyages*, Hakl. Soc., p. 137). Martin speaks of three only, Malailli, Jonani, and Gonarsige. Dr. Fryer gives views of Mayotta, Mohilla, and Johanna, as seen above the horizon. He visited Johanna, and gives a full description (pp. 15-22). Sir Thomas Herbert also counts five, with two lists of the names, viz.: (*a*) Cumro, Meottis, Joanna, Mohelia, and Gazidia; (*b*) John di Castro, Spirito Sancto, Sancto Christofero, Anguzezia, and Mayotto. He gives a full description, especially of Mohilla (*Travels*, pp. 25-30). For an amusing modern description of Joanna, see W. F. W. Owen's *Narrative of Voyages, etc.*, 1833, i, pp. 177-186.

returned to the ships. The next day we sent again to truck with the islanders, but with great diffidence and circumspection, for we feared to be deceived as we were at Anabon. We had two boats, in one of which was the merchandise for trafficking, with the men to conduct it, and some sailors, two of whom went ashore at the place where the islanders brought their goods: the other boat tarried behind, well equipped with arquebusiers and musketeers, to prevent any harm befalling our men on shore. The islanders also bore their arms, viz., alfanges[1] or scimitars, javelins, bows and arrows. In trucking with them we were not obliged to use signs, as at the island of St. Laurence, for there were some that spoke Portuguese. First they asked us who we were, and we replying that we were French, they asked us if we were friends and allies of the Portuguese. When one of our people said yes, they retorted that we should have gone and anchored at Mozembic. We continued to traffic with them every day in like manner. Three or four days after, they told us we had not quitted us of our duty: that it was customary when a foreign ship arrived at the road of these islands to go and salute the king of the island, who dwelt two leagues inland, with a fair present. Our General, who was in the boat with the soldiers, made answer that he should be held excused, because he knew not the customs of the country, nor that the king dwelt in that island, and that he would give satisfaction in this matter on the following day. Soon after, the General came on board the *Corbin* to visit our captain, who was very sick, and caused to be got ready the present for the king, viz., a pretty piece of gilded glass of Venetian work, and some other little things. So, on the morrow, our General went ashore with his boat to the place where the islanders were assembled; there, after mutual salutations, they were greatly pleased with the present, and offered to conduct those that should land to bear

[1] "Cutlasses", from Arab. *al-khandjar* (Dozy).

the present to the king. But our General, saying that he would send two of our men, demanded two of theirs for hostages. They then began to consult together, and afterwards made answer, that their people were unwilling to enter our boats, being men ignorant of the world; and that he should not fear to land with all assurance, for that they would pledge their word and honour we should incur no damage or incivility. We, who had been once deceived at Anabon out of too much confidence, were careful not to be taken in a second time, so we replied that we would not send our men unless they gave us the hostages. But they added that if none of our men would go and salute the king, at least we might deliver them the present, and that they would salute the king on the General's behalf. To which he replied, that unless he or one of his men should go, he was not minded to send the present, which perchance might be lost and never delivered to the king. This matter did not, however, interrupt our traffic, which was continued as before, each party keeping their guard. I know not why they acted thus, whether their intentions were good or evil, but I know full well that among all the peoples of India there is but little confidence, whether their religion or the humour of the country be the cause, and it is all the same whether they be Mahometans or Gentiles. None of them have any faith, nor respect for aught but profit, taking from those who will give them most; friends now with one party, now with another: even the Chinese are much the same. I know, too, that the Portuguese throughout all the East Indies give counsel to the peoples with whom they are in alliance or friendship, and even earnestly solicit them to do and practise all manner of treachery and surprises upon the ships of the French, English, and Hollanders, and go as far as to promise them recompense for such conduct: so that I would not trust myself in the hands of any of these nations, whether they were allies of the Portuguese or not, unless I had first made an alliance and treaty with the latter; and even then it were better not to have too much confidence, and ever to keep on one's guard with discretion. Now to return to the islands of Comorro. The inhabitants hold the Mahometan religion, for during our traffic with them they told us on a Thursday that the morrow was their feast-day, and that they could not give their minds to merchandise on that day, but would return on the Saturday: this I afterwards found to be the same in the Indies. They are a mixture of several races, as well from the coast of Ethiopia, Caffres, and even Mulattos, as Arabs and Persians; they are also great friends of the Portuguese. I leave you to imagine whether they be wanting in intelligence, counsel, and cunning. I heard afterwards, in the Indies, that they made a design to surprise an English ship that was at anchor in their road. They had become so familiar with the English that they went freely to and fro one with another, and very often budged not from the ship-board for their meals, and sometimes slept there. One night, seeing that they were not suspected, they designed to make themselves masters of the ship, and after waiting till the English were all asleep, they slew twelve or fifteen of them, and would have quite attained their end, had not the rest awakened in time and defended themselves valiantly, and slain a number of these islanders; the remainder escaped by swimming.[1] See how little trust can be placed in these

[1] The ship referred to is probably the *Union*, Captain Rowles, which sailed with the *Ascension*, Captain Sharpeigh, in 1608. The two ships parted in a storm after rounding the Cape early in 1609. The *Union* called at St. Augustine's Bay in Madagascar, and at Comorro, in hopes of finding her consort. Samuel Bradshaw, whose account of the *Union's* voyage is the only one we possess, mentions this attempt made upon her by the natives, but not in the same detail as Pyrard. The incidents mentioned in the text were probably given to Pyrard by Richard Wickham, the merchant of the *Union*, who was afterwards kidnapped near Zanzibar and carried to Goa, where Pyrard met him; he returned to Europe in the same fleet (see vol. ii). See Bradshaw's letter in *Purchas*,

peoples. While we were at this road, and the traffic in fruits continued in the customary manner, our mariners desired to go and make provision of water at the other side of the island, near another village apart from that with which we had been trafficking, because the place seemed convenient for drawing a large quantity. But the inhabitants of that village, who had not been made aware of our arrival, and had drawn no profit therefrom, when our men landed there, assembled all together in arms, and hindered them from taking the water, saying that they would not allow them unless they should give them money: so that our men were constrained to return back empty-handed. Our General hearing this, and not willing to use any violence (the better course, seeing how short-handed we were), gave some money to the mariners to go back withal, and pay the natives. They did so, and on payment of about five or six crowns we were permitted to take as much water as we wanted. These islands are very fertile in fruits; very big bitter oranges and small sweet oranges, citrons of two sorts, cocos, bananas, honey, betel, and rice, which when cooked is of a violet colour. Every day we were at anchor there we bought three or four boat-loads for the most trifling price—to wit, some little ironware and other Flemish bagatelles. Flesh is not so plentiful, for they sell it as dear as in this country, or more so; they have, however, good store of cattle, such as oxen, cows, goats, and sheep. These latter do not resemble those of the island of St. Laurence, because they have the tail large and broad, but not round, and are liker the Barbary

ii, 232-4; *Cal. State Papers, E. I.*, vol. i, p. 639; references to the *Union* in *Lancaster's Voyages*, Hakl. Soc. The *Union* pursued her voyage from Zanzibar to Socotra, thence to Achin and Priaman. On her return she met Middleton at St. Augustine's Bay in 1610. According to the journal of that voyage (*Lanc. Voy.*, p. 147), the *Union* had lost her captain and chief merchants "at *Conggomare*, in the north-east part of the Island of St. Laurence". She was ultimately abandoned near Morlaix in Brittany (*Purchas*, ii, pp. 234-5).

sheep. There is also good store of poultry, partridges, turtle-doves, pigeons, and other birds. I did not learn that these islands had other wealth than that of fruits, wherewith they lade their barques, all made of the coco tree, in the fashion of those of the Maldives, which I shall describe hereafter, and convey the same to Mozembic, a distance of only seventy leagues, getting in exchange what they require, such as cotton, cotton cloth, gold, ivory, and such like things. The Portuguese of Mozembic likewise come and traffic there. These islands are of the utmost convenience to Mozembic and to the Portuguese who dwell there, for the supply of provisions, because the country all around there is exceeding poor and sterile. I also learnt in India from all who had been or resided there that living was very dear.

All the refreshments bought by our people were in the name of the General and at the expense of the ships: the fruits were then divided equally among all; nor was any permitted to traffic on his own account, save that towards the end our General gave permission to everyone to buy for himself what each would, for the space of two days only. But I must not omit to notice a rare sight observed by us. Being in a boat a league from shore, and returning to our vessels that were in the road, we saw appear on the surface of the water a fish of monstrous shape. We only saw the head, which resembled a man's in shape and size, at the chin a kind of beard like a fish's fins, and the head somewhat long and pointed, and covered with scales. But when we would approach it nearer, it plunged its head into the depths of the sea, giving us only a glimpse of its back, which was scaly, and appeared no more.[1]

[1] Probably a dugong or a manatee, one of which animals was also seen here by Sir Thomas Herbert, and described by him (*Travels*, p. 26). Mocquet (1645, p. 231) gives a very fanciful description, representing the animal with its back erect as a pillar, having a shield before its head and a saddle on its back, and making a horrible noise as it passed the ship.

We remained at the road of these islands for the space of fifteen days, and the utility and comfort to us of this sojourn is past belief. All our scurvy patients recovered their health, and the others got an alleviation of their ailments, as well by aid of the good air as of the good water and fruit. I have remarked that for this malady of scurvy, which is so frequent at sea, there is no better or more certain cure than citrons and oranges and their juice: and after using it once successfully everyone makes provision of it to serve him when in need. At length we set sail, the 7th of June 1602.

The 21st of the same month we repassed the equinoctial line toward the North or Arctic Pole; but I remarked nothing more than I have already described of my first crossing, except, however, that we did not fall in with so many calms or *travades,* nor experienced such hardships as we had encountered on the coast of Guinea.

CHAPTER V.

Pitiable wreck of the ship "Corbin", wherein the author was, on the reefs of the Maldives.—How the men were saved at an island with much trouble, and the miseries endured by them.

What I have said of the discomforts and troubles of our voyage up to this point is as nothing compared with what happened after. I shall now describe misery, the greatest that can be imagined, and I am assured there are none in reading it but will deplore an event so sad and lamentable, which ruined and completely overpowered us. This is how it happened.

The first day of July 1602, being 5° N. of the line, with fine weather, neither too calm nor too much wind, we perceived at break of day that the *Croissant* had lost her big boat, which she had towed from St. Laurence, where it had been made use of as a pinnace.[1] It had been arranged at St. Malo, between our commander and the Merchant Company, that we should build a pinnace at the first land we touched on the other side of the Cape of Good Hope, and for this purpose we had brought all suitable timber, a mast and ropes, ready prepared, and requiring only to be put together. It is very necessary on long voyages to have a pinnace to reconnoitre with in unknown places, to land with on occasion, and to enter rivers where a big ship cannot or dare not venture. I mention particularly the loss of the boat used as a pinnace, and our want of the latter, for with it the *Croissant* might have saved our men. Soon after, we sighted at a distance great reefs, which surrounded a number of small islands, amid which we perceived a little sail. We approached our General, and let him know that we no longer saw the boat. But we were told that in the past night it had been filled by a heavy sea, and had broken the tow-rope and had gone to the bottom. After this our mate, who alone spoke on these occasions (the captain and lieutenant being both ill, and our English pilot speaking no French), asked what islands they were we saw. The General and his pilot replied that they were called the islands *de Diego de Roys*.[2] In truth,

[1] "Le 1 jour de Juillet 1602 ayăt cinq degrez d'eleuation, la nuict il fit un orage lequel emplit d'eau nostre gallion qui estoit attaché au derriere de nostre vaisseau ce qui nous retarda fort longtemps ; desirant le sauuer nous abbaissasmes les voiles. Au point du jour nous eusmes la veuë de plusieurs bancs et Isles qui s'appellent les Maldives, ceste perte neătmoins, fut cause de nous sauuer la vie : laquelle sans miracle nous eussions perduë : si de nuict nous fussions arriuez en lieu si dangereux, duquel nous pensions estre esloignez de quatre vingts lieuës" (*Martin*, p. 45).

[2] There is much confusion as to these *de Roys* islands. In Gastaldi's map of 1561 will be found a group of islands to the south-west of the Maldives, and near them: they are marked "Ye desabitate". There can be little doubt that these are intended for the Chagos. Subsequent maps pushed the group further north, and fixed them on the equator,

we had left the *de Roys* Islands four and twenty leagues behind us in the west. There was great dispute between those of the *Croissant* and ourselves as to these islands and reefs; for our captain, pilot, mate, and second mate held that they were the Maldives, and that we must take care: the General and his pilot thought otherwise. We saw little boats, which seemed willing to approach and pilot us—as, indeed, I afterwards learnt from the natives was the case; but our General would not wait, and imprudently took no notice of them. All day passed in this discussion; we continued our course, keeping near each other till the evening, when our ship went down the wind to bid the General good-night, and to get his orders for the night. Then our mate asked if the passage was open, and the General said it was, and that he was certain they were the de Roys Islands, and no other; nevertheless, as these were unknown parts, and for fear lest there should be other rocks or reefs before us, the best thing was to put about after dark in the opposite course, and sail towards the west until midnight, and after midnight to tack about and get the ship to her previous position, running east to arrive by daybreak where we then

in long. 70° E., and gave them the names of Diego de Roys, de Royz, de Ruiz, or de Rais. The Chagos, being found to be further south, were entered independently. These mythical islands, no doubt, were duly entered in the charts of the *Croissant*. The island of Diego Rodriguez is in lat. 19° 40′ S., long. 60° 45′ E., a long way off; and its name was certainly corrupted into *de Roys*, as Davis (*Voy.*, p. 165) and Mandelslo (p. 246) so use it. How this name got to be used for islands supposed to be near the Maldives is difficult to imagine: there may have been some confusion with *Diego Garcia*, the southernmost of the Chagos, or possibly with *Garayos*, the name of some shoals to the east of Madagascar. However these supposed islands got their names, they maintained their position upon the equator in long. 70′ E. in the maps of Speed (1626), of Hondius (1636), Visscher (1657), Seller (1678), De l'Isle (1723), Vaugondy (1751), and lastly, in Wyld's atlas of 1828. The survey of the Maldives and Chagos by Moresby, soon after this put an end to their existence. The pilot of the *Croissant* was not so far out, if only the islands had been there.

were, or a little further on, so that we should not make any more way in the night, and get lost before we knew where we were. At nightfall we obeyed the orders of the General. The captain, who was very ill, charged me to warn the mate and second mate to keep a good look-out (*bon cart*, as the watch is called which is kept by the mariners every night, each in his turn, as by sentinels), for in his opinion we were in a dangerous part of the Maldives, notwithstanding the opinion of the pilot of the *Croissant*.

Our General intended to pass by the north of these islands, between the head of them and the coast of India; but, on the contrary, we were running right into the midst of them, to our peril. The pilots said they would be careful; for all who have the duty of navigation in those parts must cautiously avoid the dangerous banks and reefs from a hundred leagues off, if he can, otherwise there is great risk in passing through these islands without losing your ship. But misfortune was pressing close upon us, and notwithstanding the foresight of our captain, who could not set right the others' ignorance, that which had not happened once during the voyage now came to pass, viz., everyone was fast asleep that night, even those on watch. The mate and second mate had been carousing, and were drunk. The light usually kept on the poop for reading the compass was out, because the man at the wheel, who had charge of the light and the hour-glass, had fallen asleep, as had also the ship's boy that attended him; for it is customary for the man at the helm always to have a ship's boy by him. What was worse, the ship was steered to the east half-an-hour, or three-quarters at most, too soon. So, while we were thus all asleep, the ship struck heavily twice, and as we started with the shock, she suddenly struck a third time, and heeled over. I leave you to imagine the condition of all on board,—what a pitiful spectacle we presented,—the cries and lamentations of men who find themselves wrecked at night on a rock in mid-ocean, and await a certain death. Some wept and cried with all their might; others took to prayers; others confessed to each other; and far from having a captain to command and encourage us, we had one that aggravated our sorrows. For it was a month and more since he had left his bed; but the fear of death caused him incontinently to rise in his shirt, and, feeble as he was, fall a-crying among us. The ship having half-heeled over, we cut the masts to prevent her going quite over, and then fired a cannon-shot to warn the *Croissant* to keep back. But she was in no danger, as she was well behind us, and was keeping a good look-out. We all thought that the ship must go to the bottom, as we could see nothing but heavy waves going over us; and that, in fact, must have happened if we had struck upon a rock. About three-quarters of an hour after, dawn appeared, and we sighted some islands at not more than five or six leagues distance beyond the reefs, and the *Croissant* quite close to us, but unable to succour us.[1] Our ship remained firm on her side, and being on a reef, could still hold together for a while; for had it been on sand, she must have heeled over altogether, and we should have been drowned to a man. This gave us some consolation, and the courage to endeavour to save our lives and to get to land, although in our present plight there was but little hope of that, seeing what a dis-

[1] "Le 2 jour de Juillet 1602 à l'aube du jour nous vismes le Corbin esloigné d'un quart de lieuë de nous qui auoit perdu son grand mast, incontinent apres au point du jour nous vismes qu'il estoit eschoué sur le banc, la Mer passant par dessus le corps du Navire, il avoit encore son mast de mizene, et sa voile haute, lequel tomba peu de tẽps apres; ce nous fut un fort piteux spectacle voir nos compagnons perir sans leur pouuoir ayder, et ne sçauions que esperer de nous, estant encores si proches d'une infinité d'Isles et de bancs, que nous craignions ne pouuions doubler, le vent nous estant plus contraire que fauorable, de façon que nous estions en grand angoisse; sur les deux heures nous apperçeusmes un batteau à la voile entre les Isles et les bancs qui alloit vers les lieux ou s'estoit perdu le Corbin. Nous auions de hauteur 5 degrez trois quarts" (*Martin*, pp. 45, 46).

tance the land was off: and even then we ran the risk of being denied a landing, or of being killed by the natives. We then bethought us to prepare some craft to carry us, as we could no longer expect to get out the galion[1] or the boat. We took spars, rods, and those stout beams called *antennes*, which are at each side of ships, and are useful for spars and rods when occasion demands. And because they are only for use in case of need, they have this name *antennes;* but being in the shape of spars and rods, they are called *materaux, ou verges de beille,*—that is, extra.[2] These we bound together in the manner of a large hurdle, and on to that we nailed a number of planks and boards brought up from below. This kind of raft is called a *panguaye.*[3] This

[1] The use of the word *galion* for a boat carried by a ship is unusual. A *galion* was a mixture of the "round" and the "long" form of vessel. The former was for sails, the latter for oars; the *galion* was for oars and sails; and whereas the proportion of breadth to length in a round ship was 1 to 3, in a *galion* it was 1 to 4 or 5. The name got applied to larger ships of this build, which never used oars. When small, they generally carried three lateen sails (Jal). The *Corbin's* jolly-boat was probably of this build and rig.

[2] *Antenna*, the classical Latin for "yard", has passed into all the Romance languages, but in these, confined to yards of the latin, or, as we say, lateen rig. Such a yard is swung not at its middle, but considerably towards one end. According to M. Rivara, the word *antenna* is used among the Portuguese in the same sense as here; but formerly only for the yards in actual use (Rivara's *Pyr.*, i, 45). There is of course no connection between the word and the sense of spare or extra spars.

[3] As Rivara points out, Pyrard mistakes the use of the word *panguaye*, or, as the Portuguese write it, *pangaio*, which was a small sailing canoe: "hũa pequena embarcação composta de taboas unidas e atadas com cordas, sem prego algum" (Bluteau). Rivara says the word is still used in Portuguese India and Africa for a two-masted barque with lateen sails. It is mentioned in *Lancaster's Voyages* (Hakl. Soc., pp. 5, 6, and 26), where it is described as being like a barge with one mat sail of coco-nut leaves. "The barge is sowed together with the rindes of trees and pinned with wooden pinnes." See also *Alb. Comm.*, Hakl. Soc., iii, p. 60, *note;* and Dr. Burnell's note to *Linschoten*, Hakl. Soc., i, p. 32, where it appears that the word is used so early as 1505, in Dom

was sufficient to carry us all easily, and to save a large quantity of baggage and merchandise to boot. We were working at this raft or *panguaye* all hands, and with all our power, from daybreak until two or three hours after noon; but our labour was all in vain, as it was impossible to get it over the reef and afloat. This made us lose all courage and hope; besides, as I have said, there seemed no chance of getting the galion, which was well forward in the ship below the second deck, and all the masts were cut, and there was no means of fixing a pulley to raise it withal; moreover, the sea was so heavy and stormy that the waves and swell (*louesme*) were going right over the ship to the depth of a pike and more, and we were every moment in danger of having them over us. In addition to this, the sea was so tempestuous (for we saw the waves break for more than two miles distance, with a horrible noise, over the reefs and rocks) that the galion could not have resisted its violence.

Such being our condition, we perceived a boat approaching us from the island, as if to reconnoitre, but it did not come within half a league of us. When we saw it, the best swimmer among us threw himself into the water and made for her, begging the men in her by all manner of signs and cries to come to our aid; but they would do nothing for all his efforts, so that he was constrained at his peril to return. We could not imagine the reason for this inhumanity and barbarism. But I afterwards found that all persons were strictly prohibited from boarding or approaching a wrecked ship,[1] except by command of the king or by leave of the nearest king's officers, who in such case are allowed to save the men, giving information at once to the king. For the rest, I could not sufficiently wonder that, in the midst of our misery, many

Manoel's letter. What Pyrard probably means is *jangada*, the word for raft, which the Portuguese borrowed from the Malayālam *sangāḍa* (see *Linsch.*, Hakl. Soc., ii, p. 181).

[1] *E.g.*, the case of the Ceylon ship, in ch. xxi.

of the sailors and mariners ceased not to drink and eat, and to consume the ship's victuals even beyond the necessities of nature, saying to the others of us who remonstrated, that we were all as good as lost, and that they preferred to die in that fashion. Then they swore and fought, and some broke open the chests of others whom they saw at their prayers (having ceased to think more of the things of this world), and no longer acknowledged their captain, making no more account of him than of their comrades, and saying that, as the voyage was at an end, they were no longer bound to obey him. I was horrified at this; and I make bold to say that seamen of this temper, of whom I have seen but too many, leave their souls and conscience on land, so irreligious, demoralised, and insolent have I seen them to be.

To return to my story. Though we despaired of our lives, we made an attempt to get out the galion, at which we worked our best, as we had done at the raft in the morning. Having got it out with vast trouble, we all did our best to equip it and put it to rights, all broken as it was by the waves; but darkness came on before it was quite ready, and we remained the following night on board in our evil plight, and amid great distress and danger, the ship being very full of water, while the waves frequently passed over our heads and drenched us again and again.

Next day, the 3rd July 1602, in the morning, we got the galion over the reefs with great trouble and risk, ourselves swimming the while. This done, we all got on board, taking with us swords, arquebuses, and small pikes, and pulled towards the islands. Our galion, being heavily laden, made much water, and almost capsized several times by the violence of the winds and waves. At last, after much fatigue, we got ashore at one of the islands called *Pouladou.*[1]

[1] *Fuladu* (in the Admiralty Chart wrongly spelt *Furudu*), in Goidu or Horsburgh atoll, lat. 4° 54′ N. This atoll is a small one immediately

As soon as we reached the shore, the natives who were waiting for us would not permit us to land till we were first disarmed by them. So we having surrendered at discretion to the islanders, they permitted us to land and then pulled up our galion, and took out of it the rudder, masts, and other things necessary for its equipment, and sent them all to the neighbouring islands, whither also they pulled all the boats of their own island, leaving not a single one behind. I perceived from this first view that they were a spirited and quick-witted race. As their island was small (not a league in circumference), and its inhabitants numbered only twenty or twenty-five, they had to fear the arrival with arms of a greater number than themselves, lest we should make ourselves masters of their island and escape by aid of their boats, which would have been easy enough had we known their weakness; but, as I have said, they took the right measures.

On our disembarking we were all led to a building in the middle of the island, where they gave us some fruit, coconuts, and limes. Thither, too, came the lord of the island, called *Ybrahim* and *Pouladouquilague*,[1] who appeared to be of great age. He knew some words of Portuguese, by means of which he put many questions to us; after which his people

to the south of Malosmadolu atoll, and in the division of the atolls for administrative purposes deemed part of it. This explains Pyrard's remark below (ch. x), that he was wrecked on Malosmadolu atoll.

[1] "Lord of Pouladou." The word *quilague* must not be confounded with *calogue*. Quilague, or, more properly, *Kilagé*, has the sense of suzerainty, and is used (i) by itself, meaning the regent of the kingdom (see ch. xv and xviii); (ii) in *renequilague*, "queen", and appended to the name of a queen, as *Manaye quilague* (ch. xviii); (iii) to lords of islands, as here. The word, as will be seen, is common to both genders. *Calogue*, on the other hand, merely implies that the person is of gentle birth, and is used after proper names; in the Vocabulary (vol. ii), Pyrard gives the feminine *camulogue*. The distinction may perhaps be observed even in Ibn Batuta, who calls the grand vizier *Calaky*, and the cadi *Fandayarkâloû* (*Ibn Bat.*, iv, p. 133).

searched us and took away everything we carried, saying that all that appertained to the king, after a ship was wrecked. This lord of the island was a great lord, and, as I afterwards learnt, nearly related to the Christian king of the Maldives, who is at Goa.[1] Seeing that we had a piece of scarlet, he asked us what that was. We replied that we had brought it to present to the king; and although all that was in the ship was his, yet was that brought to be presented to him whole and nnspoiled by the sea water. As soon as they heard that it was for the king, not a man of them dared to take it or touch it, or even to look at it.[2] We were, nevertheless, minded to cut off a piece, about two or three ells, for a present to the lord of the island, in hopes that we should be the better treated. He took it, and thanked us with effusive gratitude, but made us promise not to tell anyone, otherwise he would rather have died than taken it. Soon after, hearing that some officers of the king were coming, he changed his mind, and brought it back, begging us not to tell that he had so much as handled it. For all that, the king heard of it at least six months later, and was wroth against him, and would have sent for him, had he not been then in the last stage of a disease, whereof he died at the age of seventy-five years.

When we had been in this building for the space of a day they took our mate and two sailors away to the king, forty leagues off, in another island, called *Malé*, which is the capital island (all the others being dependencies of it); and there the king resides. Our mate took with him the piece of scarlet and presented it to the king, and was well received, being lodged within the palace. However, this was done

[1] As to the Christian kings of the Maldives, see the text *passim*, and Appendix B.

[2] Mr. Bell, in 1879, took as a present to the Sultan forty yards of red silk, which was highly appreciated, and could not be touched by any inferior person with impunity. In South Sea phrase, it was "tabu".

not so much by way of favour or honour, as to secure his person; for afterwards I came to understand the general distrust.

The king soon sent his brother-in-law with a goodly number of soldiers in barques to go to our wreck and get from it all he could. This was the brother of the chief queen, and was entitled *Ranabandery Tacourou*,[1] his own name being Mouhamede. When he came to the island *Pouladou*, where we were, we were treated better on the occasion of his arrival, and were taken often to the ship to help in getting out the merchandise, baggage, and all the wearing apparel. But they laughed at the advice we gave them, for they knew better than we. As it was impossible for the boats to go over the reef, they fastened a cable to the ship, while the other end was lashed to a big rock of the reef; and so, by holding on to this rope with one hand, we could go and come over the reef to the ship in safety; while so doing, the waves only passed over our heads, and could not overthrow us nor carry us off. For the rest, they had a very pretty contrivance for getting off the cannon and other heavy things, although these were all in the hold, as I shall tell in the proper place.[2]

[1] *Ranabandery*, probably the same as *Ransbandery*, in ch. xv, where it is explained as "Treasurer". *Rana* or *rans* = Sin. *ran*, gold; *bandery* = *bender* or *bandhāra*, treasury; *cf.* Skt. *bhāṇḍārin*, a steward or treasurer; Jav. *Bendárá* and Malay *Bandahāra*, the title of one of the higher ministers in the Malay states. *Takourou* must be Skt. *ṭhakkura*, "an idol, a deity", Hindi. *ṭhākur*, "lord, master". In Pyrard's time it was used only for the greatest lords; in later days it was conferred upon persons of inferior rank, provided they were of good birth. Thus we find it borne by a pilot in 1682 (see *J. Geog. Soc.*, ii, 76). Mr. Bell states that "many persons of respectable birth receive from the Sultan the titular rank of *Takuru-fánu*". He compares with it the common Kandyan name *Tikiri*. He adds that Takuru-fánu is nowadays not so respected a title as *Maniku-fánu* (*Report*, p. 63). As we shall see hereafter, this Ranabaḍéri Takuru-fánu (his correct title) succeeded to the throne after the death of Sultan Ibrahim.

[2] See below, ch. x.

So for several days they got out our merchandise and took it away to the king; but before that, the king's brother-in-law, by virtue of his commission, separated us one from another, and distributed some of us among the surrounding islands (the greater number remaining at *Pouladou*), and on his return took with him our captain, ill as he was, and five or six others. He was presented to the king, and was well received. The king promised to get a ship ready to carry him to Achen, in the island of Sumatra, whither our General had gone; and I know not but he might have kept his word. Our captain, however, died at Malé, the residence of the king, about six or seven weeks after.[1] In all expeditions to the ship they took some one of us in the same way. As for me, the king's brother-in-law, in separating us, took me away from those at *Pouladou*, and put me with two others on a little island called *Paindoüé*[2] (distant from *Pouladou* a league only), where there were no more people than in the other. Here my two companions and I were well received from the very first, and, thanks to the lord who brought us, we had a sufficiency of food.

[1] That is, in the middle of August 1602. M. Manet is, therefore, in error in giving the 10th June 1603 as the date of Grout's death (Manet, *Biographie des Malouins célèbres*, p. 86).

[2] *Fendu*, or *Fehendú*, a small island next to *Fuladu*, in Horsburgh atoll.

CHAPTER VI.

What happened to the men who were saved from the "Corbin", and the miseries they endured.

I have related in detail, as far as I have been able, the circumstances of our shipwreck and our misfortunes down to our reaching land, when it appeared that we had escaped the dangers of the sea; but those I have now to tell of were no less. Bad luck, when long continued, ends in bad health: so those who were rescued from the midst of waves and floods found no alleviation of their ills on land. We numbered about forty persons. Hear now what followed.

While we were still on board, we bethought us to get out all the silver we had, and all our most precious merchandise, and to take on shore most of it, to the end that we might be recognised as good merchants, and not pirates and robbers, and so might get a more favourable reception. This was our captain's advice; but we could not get at any of it, as it was in the *soutes* (which are close-fastened bunkers where the merchandise and victuals are stowed), and right at the ship's bottom, where the sea was so deep that it was all we could do to hold on to the ship's sides. So it remained in the ship with the rest of the merchandise, and in default we took what remained of the silver belonging to the ship's crew, which amounted to about 500 crowns, and what individuals had brought in their chests, which amounted to another 500 crowns. All this was secreted in the men's waistbands. Most of us had these waistbands, but others not, for there were not enough for all. This was not for a present to the king, which it might have been, had we been able to bring away all the silver, but to meet the necessities of us all. Nevertheless, the event showed that it became the occasion of the greatest trouble, and those who took the money turned out the greatest sufferers. The first night we spent at *Pouladou* we buried this silver, for fear lest we should be searched and it be found upon us, and we resolved not to unearth it except for the needs of the whole body. But at length, when our comrades who were left at *Pouladou* found that they got nothing to eat and were dying of hunger, they were constrained to unearth it and offer money for food, and the people indeed gave them food for the silver. The mischief was that the smallest piece of money they had was the twenty sols piece of Spanish money, and the islanders, seeing our men's ignorance, never gave them any change: so that for a thing of the value of two *liars*[1] they had to give one of these pieces, so that at this rate for five or six pieces a man sometimes hardly got a meal. Had our men had the cunning to do as they use at the islands and all over India (where money of every kind and mint is accepted so long as it is of good metal)—that is, to clip it in small pieces, and then to weigh it out when required—their silver would have lasted them much longer. But, as I said, for the smallest commodity they gave a whole piece. So by this waste the silver lasted but a little while to most of those who had it; and to them the natives would give nothing except for money, so they endured all manner of discomforts. Others who had more (for it was not given in equal shares, but handed to individuals for the common use) hid it from their comrades and did not in any way assist them. From this cause many died of hunger, getting no help either from the islanders or even from their fellows, and this was deplorable indeed. On the other hand, those who had money, and who by this means could obtain food, filled their bellies without discretion; and being in a country where the air is very unhealthy for all strangers, even for those of a similar climate,

[1] *Liard*, "petite monnaie de cuivre qui valait trois deniers, le quart d'un sou, et un peu plus qu'un centime" (*Littré*). Its etymology is uncertain. Tavernier says that the Indian *pecha* ("pice") was worth "about two of our liards" (Eng. trans., pt. ii, p. 22).

they fell ill, and died one after another; nay more, in place of receiving aid and consolation from their fellows, those who were without money and in great need came and stripped them, and took their money before they were dead; and for that which was found upon the dead, the healthy who survived fought one with another who should have it, and banded themselves two against two, and finally messmate against messmate,[1] with so little charity, that they would see their comrades and fellow countrymen die before their eyes without giving them any assistance or succour. I have never seen a sight so pitiable and deplorable.

As for me, I was taken by the king's brother-in-law, as I have said above, to the island *Paindoüé*, with two others. We had not taken belts of money, and had nothing in the world. This caused us some trouble at first, but by-and-bye we found we were better off for having nothing. The others who had money were better supplied for a short time, but afterwards experienced the greatest hardships. At first the natives of *Paindoüé* gave us some food, little by little; but when they saw that our companions in the other islands had so much money, and spent it so profusely, they resolved to give us no more subsistence, being concerned that our arrival had brought no profit to their island, as to the others. So, in order to try us whether by extremity of hunger we should not be constrained to give them some of that which they believed we had concealed, they betook them with their boats to the island of *Pouladou*, to sell to our companions their fowls, fish, fruit, and other provisions. This, however, was in secret, for they are strictly prohibited from selling anything to strangers saved from shipwreck, and from taking money or merchandise of them, as all that belongs to the king when once the ship is wrecked (they may, however, give them provisions, and treat them with such humanity as seems good to them): and, in fact, some time after, a strict inquiry was made of those

[1] See p. 25, *note*.

who had taken anything—as I shall tell hereafter. By this conspiracy of the islanders against us, which was to give us nothing more, my two companions and I were reduced to the most terrible straits imaginable. All we could do was to seek for the sea-slugs[1] on the sand, and to eat them; and sometimes perchance we found a dead fish cast up by the sea, which we boiled with divers sorts of herbs unknown to us, salting our food with a little sea water; and if by chance we got hold of a lime we put it in, and days passed sometimes ere we got any such thing. We were in this extremity a good while, until the natives, concluding that we had no money, and having, as may be believed, some pity in them, began to be less shy and barbarous; for before, most of them, and all the women and children, hid themselves from us, fleeing us as though we were monsters, and did not allow us to enter their villages or their houses. They even used us to terrify and frighten their little children withal. At length, discovering that they were becoming less distant towards us day by day, we began to accost them and to offer our services for any job in which they would employ us, which services they accepted. They often took me in their boats to sea and to the neighbouring islands to help them in getting coco-nuts and in fishing, in return for which they gave me a share of fish at the fishing, and coco-nuts, rice, millet, and honey for other work. My companions did their best to win something in the same way, for they took me only to the fishing—for what reason I know not—and then we brought all we got into a common stock and lived on it. Thus were we brought so low, that for fish and coco-nuts we were fain to do the most vile handiwork and the most painful labour—in a word, work which slaves would not or could not do. All this was without force or compulsion: we went ourselves and begged them to employ us; otherwise we should have died of hunger, for they would give us nothing unless we worked for

[1] *I.e., bêche de mer* (M. *ihi*).

it, and then so little, that we were but ill-sustained by what we got; for they fish only in calm weather, their sails being composed of coco-fibre, which they wish not to spoil[1]; and their bodies being naked while at this exercise, they fear the rain, and when they are having a day's fishing they do not return sometimes for eight hours or more. Such was our condition as regards food. As for lodging, during rain by day and for sleep by night we retired to a wooden hut on the sea-shore, which had been put up a while ago for building a boat. We had thus sufficient cover overhead; but at the sides all was open. As it was then winter there—that is, during the months of July and August, when the rains are continuous and heavy—I leave you to imagine the distress we suffered from the wind, the rain, and sometimes the big waves, which were only ten paces off our hut. Owing to these great and grievous discomforts my two companions fell ill. As for me, thanks to God, not having been ill during all our voyage, I held out for a good while.

While I was thus working for my living I was obliged to learn the language of the country as well as I could, though my companions despised it, saying there was no need to learn the language peculiar to these islands, for that they hoped to be sent at length to Sumatra to the General, as the king had promised our captain, and as the islanders told us. I did not despair; but the fear I had that this would not come to pass made me resort to every expedient. I saw, too, the misery in which we were, and I essayed to learn the language to serve my purposes, and got great assistance from it. With this purpose in my mind, an occasion presented itself of learning the language quickly and easily: for the lord of the island *Paindoüé*, where we three were, called *Aly Pandio Atacourou*,[2] who was a great chief and a relative

[1] Mr. Bell says this is literally true of their fishing-boats (*mas-odi*) at the present day.

[2] *I.e.*, Ali, lord of Pandio, or Paindoüé (now *Fehendú*). *Atacourou* is a misprint for *Tacourou*. It would now be written *Ali Takuru-fánu*.

of the king through his wife, seeing that I was trying to learn their language, thought more highly of me, and took a liking to me: and in truth I did my best to make myself agreeable to him and his wife, and to all the people of the island, by obeying them in all things. He was a man of great honour and courtesy, knowing and inquisitive. He was also a good navigator, and had possessed himself of the compasses and marine charts of our ship, the use of which he often inquired of me, theirs being made of another fashion. In short, he was at all times well pleased that I should be of his company to entertain him, and to answer all the questions he put to me about our manners and customs. This casual conversation, with the trouble I took, soon made me understand much of the language; and on that account the lord became more and more well disposed towards me, and I began to be not quite so wretched as before, and often received additional provisions through his kindness.

To return to our people who were at *Pouladou*. When their money was spent they were worse treated, and more afflicted with famine than we, inasmuch as their number was greater than ours. The lord of our island, *Paindoüé*, went often to *Pouladou* to visit the lord of that island, who was his relative. One day, after I made his acquaintance, he took me with him to give me the satisfaction of seeing my companions. By this means I became aware of the miserable condition to which they were reduced and the afflictions they had to suffer. When I was with them we all together searched the sea-shore to see if we could chance to find something to eat; for they were dying of hunger, and had to do as we had done at first at *Paindoüé*. We found a very large turtle (for in the Indian Sea they grow to a prodigious size) turned upon its back; it had 500 or 600 eggs, each as big as the yolk of a hen's egg. We were well pleased at our discovery; we cut it in pieces, and boiled it with fresh

F

water in a boiler which they lent to us, and then ate it. The flesh was extremely fat and tasty, like veal, and the eggs were very good; but afterwards we had all such a stomach disorder that we thought we should die, and I was the first seized. I suspect it was because we were famished, and having nothing else, ate that to excess.[1] We had forgotten, too, to cook it in sea water, and so to season it; for, as I afterwards learnt at the Maldives, fish cooked in sea water is more wholesome, and does not go bad so soon, and will keep a long time after being dried. The natives always cook it in sea water. I then learnt the fearful misery to which my comrades, and especially the sick, were reduced by famine, and that they gave no assistance to one another. I slept at this island; next day, the lord of *Paindoüé* took me back with him, and when he returned on another occasion, took me again with him.

Meanwhile, the king's people came day after day to take what they could from the ship, chiefly the lead with which it was bottomed: this they prize highly in that country. They took even the nails, and as much of the timber as they could. And as they came and went they took from time to time some of our men, who were glad enough to go; and those who had silver gave it, to be taken. We were told that the king was to give a ship to our captain, and when it was got ready we should all be taken. Our people died one after another, clinging to this hope. Our captain, chief clerk, second mate, and many others were already dead. The mate had been the first to pay his respects to the king; but he asked leave to return to the ship to get some clothes, which was readily granted to all of us, as the natives had no use for such things. So, when the mate saw that they did not come and look after us, and that the captain was dead, he formed

[1] The turtle was of a non-edible species, probably the "loggerhead"; M. *musimbi (Couanea olivacea)*. He relates this incident again in his Treatise (see vol. ii).

a design to escape, which he long revolved in secret and unknown to some of us, to whom he would not discover his mind. The second time I saw him he communicated his design to me, and regretted that he could not include me, as he had not sufficient means. I told him I did not believe that he would succeed, for that the natives were very suspicious of us, and on that account had left [at the island] neither boats nor barques; nay more, the king's people had sent some soldiers, as well to keep watch over us, as to discover what people of the island had received silver from our men, and to make them give it up; nevertheless, the mate conducted his enterprise so dexterously that at length he seized the ship of the lord of *Paindoüé* while he was at *Pouladou* seeing his relative, as on the two occasions when he took me with him. He had well chosen his opportunity, which was just after midday, when the people of the island least suspected anything. So, having stored the ship with fresh water and coco-nuts, of which he had previously hidden a good supply in the wood, he embarked with eleven others, leaving eight of our men (four sick and four sound), without whose knowledge he set sail. The inhabitants soon perceived it, but they had no boats to pursue him. They came to give the news to the men of our island on a raft called *Candouepatis*[1] (of which I shall speak in its place), so that our people had plenty of time to get beyond the reefs before the people had found their boats, and they were already a long way off, out of view and of danger, when the islanders were embarking to pursue. This enterprise was a success so far as they were concerned,[2] but it was the cause of a sea of troubles to the eight who remained; for the soldiers, out of revenge, exercised upon them all imaginable severities. They bound those who were in health, and beat them savagely, and then took from them all the money and victuals they had;

[1] M. *Kadufati*, a raft made of the *Kadu* tree. (See below, ch. x.)

[2] As to the subsequent fortunes of these twelve, see below, p. 80.

then they came to the sick, compelling the healthy to carry them to the shore, and so close to the sea, that when the tide came their legs were soaked, while at the same time they were exposed to the inclemencies of the sky, the sun, and the rain, which was incessant at that season. Moreover, they held them so rigorously that the healthy were not even permitted to carry them fresh water to drink, the only thing which the healthy themselves obtained. So the poor sick fellows died of hunger, and were then thrown into the sea, as the islanders did to all our men who died, not giving us even permission to bury our dead friends. This, however, was done without the knowledge of the king, for he caused some to be buried at the sea-shore, chiefly those who died at the island where he resided. But to return to *Pouladou*,—those who were left told me that the poor sick crawled about in great agony, and lay on their faces, so as to eat the grass beneath them, and so were frequently found with grass in their mouths. The lieutenant of our ship, a man of good family at S. Malo, died in this condition. Of the others who kept their health, there was one who, constrained by hunger to climb a coco-tree by night to try to get some fruit, fell from the high tree-top and was killed, though he had several times before climbed it without accident. His remaining comrades suffered severely; they even ate rats when they could catch them.

As for us three who were at *Paindoüé*, the escape of our friends brought us no other harm than our own fears. The natives of the island assembled together with sticks in their hands (for arms they are not allowed to wear except they be of the gendarmerie, and while they are in the king's service),[1] and came to us in our hut by the sea-shore. There they insulted and threatened us; they even gave us some blows; but as they had never seen us with money, they did not go beyond that, and treated us better than our friends

[1] This rule is strictly enforced still.

at *Pouladou.* The lord of the island, too, a very humane man, prevented them from maltreating us, and gave me proof of his kindness, as did his wife and the elders of the island.

CHAPTER VII.

Arrival of a lord bearing the king's commission to the island of Paindoüé, who at length takes the author back with him.

I have above related our condition during the three months and a half following our shipwreck. Then arrived from the king's island a great lord named *Assant Caounas Calogue.*[1] The first who had been sent was the king's brother-in-law, and, as I subsequently heard, the king had learnt that he had not obeyed his orders, and had retained something from the ship for his own use, and was so enraged that he even boxed his ears, and never sent him again. In his stead he sent one of the highest nobles of his court, whom he consulted on the most important affairs, having more confidence in him than in any other. His orders were to get out of the ship and to convey to the king all he could, chiefly some cannon, and the rest of the lead and iron, and also to make search for the silver which the islanders had received from us. He was assisted by another lord named *Oussaint Rannamandy Calogue,*[2] who had authority over all ships, barques,

[1] *Assant*, no doubt, is *Hassan: caounas*, I cannot explain. It may be the name of his island, as Mr. Bell suggests, and as in the case of *Ali Pandio Tacourou*, and *Misdoue Quilague.* As to *calogue*, v. s., p. 56, *note.* This lord and his family, with whom the author had the warmest friendship, are mentioned several times hereafter.

[2] This would now be written *Husain Ranahamádi Kalógc-fánu.* The title *Ranahamádi* survives, and the holder is still chief of the *Kalási* or "sailors", but distinct from the *Velándá* (Bell).

boats, captains, and mariners, but not over soldiers; in short, he was chief of the marine, or, as we might call him, superintendent of the galleys and ships of the king, but not admiral. On his arrival he was received as it is the custom to receive the king's officers of high rank who come in his service. I have witnessed a reception of this kind. From a distance the barque or the boat (called *ody*[1]) in which the lord is makes a signal with a red flag, furls its sails, and casts anchor at a gun-shot from the island. Then the lord or chief man of the place sends to inquire who it is, and being informed, gives order for his reception, and goes out to meet him, accompanied by as many men and boats as are available, leaving only the *Catibe,*[2] or curé, with four or five of the *Mouscoulits,*[3] or elders of the island. The boats are laden some with coco-nuts, others with bananas, betel, and other fruits with which the island abounds, everything being arranged in baskets and white boxes made of coco-leaves. These are made for the occasion, and are not used again; for these leaves are so common, and the people so clever in making the baskets, that they never require to use them twice; they also make them so that one cannot get out the fruit or other things from within, without cutting them and breaking them up, and they are then cast aside. On presenting these, the lord of the island enters first and salutes the other, saying *Sallam Alecon,*[4] which is their common salutation; then stooping down, touches his feet with his right hand, which he then raises and puts on his own head, as if to mean that he would put his head under the other's feet. All the others in attendance do the same, and bring all the presents, two at a time, with a rod on their shoulders, at the middle of which the present is suspended. This salutation

[1] M. *oḍi;* Tam. *oḍam.*

[2] M. *Katibu*, from the Ar. *Katib*, "scribe".

[3] *Muskuli;* see ch. xiv.

[4] Ar. *Salaam aleikum.*

and present is called *Vedon à Rouespou.*[1] After this the lord of the island makes his speech, and begs the visitor to land, and to do him the honour to take his lodging at the place prepared. Thither he proceeds, accompanied by his host and his followers. As the great lord nears the island, the *Catibe* and the others who have remained behind are waiting on the strand, and come forward before the guest, wading in the sea up to their waists, and carrying each his cloth or turban on his left arm. This cloth is half silk and half cotton, very well woven, and coloured red, an ell and a half in length, and three-quarters of an ell in width. Then the *Catibe* and his followers salute him in the customary way, and make a speech, offering him cloths and other presents, which are courteously received, and taken in charge by his attendants. That done, as soon as the lord desires to land, one of the chief *Catibes* or *Mouscoulits* comes forward to offer his shoulder—a function much esteemed—and the other gets on his shoulders; and so, with a leg on each side, he rides him horse fashion to land, and is there set down. Great care is taken that his feet do not get wet, for that they hold a great disgrace. He is then conducted in great honour, accompanied by all the residents, to the lodging prepared for him and his suite. There the people salute him again, and he talks with them for half-an-hour or so, and then all take their leave. Then they bring him a bath of lukewarm water, nicely prepared, and after that odorous oils to rub his body withal, after the custom of the Indies. Next they gave him wine of coco to drink, the finest and most tasty to be got, along with many portions of betel, very neatly served, and supplied with all the requisite ingredients, which I shall describe in the proper place.[2] Thus refreshed and rested, he

[1] Chr. gives *wedung*, "present", and *wedung oḍi*, "offering boat". The latter part of Pyrard's phrase is, according to Mr. Bell, a courtly suffix, properly written *aruvaifi*, or *aruvaifu*.

[2] See vol. ii, Treatise, ch. viii.

proceeds to the principal temple, which they call *Oucourou misquitte.*[1] There he says his prayers for upwards of an hour, and then returns to his lodging, where meanwhile his table has been prepared with all the delicacies of the country. While he is upon the island, all people of quality and means send him presents, such as savoury dishes, fruits, and betel, neatly served and borne by the hands of women, with the greatest ceremony and honour possible,—not that he has not always his own kitchen and daily meals: sometimes, indeed, he neither eats nor tastes any of all these things [that are brought]; but such is the custom of all these islands.

This lord having arrived in this fashion, and all these ceremonies being ended, he straightway executed his commission at the ship, and when that was done he went to the island of *Pouladou,* where he made inquiry for those who had had money from our vessel; and to get hold of it he arrested all the inhabitants of the island, even the women, to see if they would confess. Then he had their thumbs put into cleft sticks, squeezed and bound with iron clasps, to the end that by this pain they might be constrained to admit the truth,—as, in fact, they did, and gave up the money; but not all, for the king's people could not discover the full quantity. They also made accusation against those of other islands, to which the king's people were at once sent. In fine, the greater part of those who had touched our money were obliged to give it up, and for a year or two some one was always being discovered in possession of some that had been concealed till then. Even the soldiers who were left there on guard were convicted of it. The people of *Paindoüé* were in no trouble, for we exculpated them; and on that account they always liked me, and sent me presents while I was there; and it was proved that they had taken nothing of us.

All these things happened in fifteen days during which the king's commissioner sojourned at *Paindoüé, Pouladou,*

[1] *Hukuru miskitu,* "Friday mosque" (*Bell,* p. 58).

and the neighbouring islands, sometimes at one and sometimes at another, executing the king's commission. The lord of *Paindoüé* and the *Catibe*, as well as the people who took a liking to me, presented me to him, and strongly recommended me, all thinking that I was some great lord from this part of the world [*i.e.*, Europe]; and I did not correct their opinion, seeing that it served me. Owing to this recommendation, the lord sent from the king took me into his friendship, as well as because he saw that I already knew enough of their language to express myself and to make myself understood a little, and that I was taking pains to learn it every day. I have remarked that nothing served me so much, or so conciliated the goodwill of the people, the lords, and even of the king, as to have a knowledge of their language, and that was the reason why I was always preferred to my companions, and more esteemed than they. And so, while he was in those parts, he always desired that I should accompany him and be near him, whether in his boat at the place of the wreck, or at the other islands. Among others, he took me to a little island called *Touladou*,[1] distant ten leagues, whither he had gone to see one of his wives, and he had the greatest pleasure in my conversation. Also, it was on account of this affection that my companions and I were in no want, being more highly in his esteem. The day before he returned, he asked me if I would like to go with him to *Malé*, where the king lives. I told him that I had long desired it. I had, nevertheless, some fear lest he should change his mind, and on the morrow I never went out of his sight; so, when he was ready to start, one of the soldiers of his suite took him on his shoulders, as the custom is, and bore him through the sea to his barque: from there he called me, and got me on board. I was vastly pleased to go; but I was also sad at thus leaving my two companions at *Paindoué*

[1] Tuládu (in the Admiralty Charts spelt *Turahdou*), in lat. 5° 1′ N., at south end of Málosmaduḷu atoll.

and those at *Pouladou,* of whom only four now remained surviving their great calamities. They all, on seeing me depart without them, wept piteously. The lord, perceiving this, asked me, as their interpreter, what caused them to weep; and having the reason of their affliction explained to him, he bade me console them, and tell them from him not to be troubled; that the king would send and fetch them soon; that he himself was desirous of satisfying them, but that he dared not do so without the express command of the king. That did not console them much, seeing that I was going and they were remaining; so that they continued, or rather increased, their tears and lamentations. This distressed me, though I dared not show it, for I had already learnt the humour of the natives on this point, which is that they cannot tolerate in their presence sad and melancholy persons or dreamers, saying that such persons are plotting some treason or mischief in their minds.[1] So one who wishes to be well received among them must be happy and joyous, must laugh and sing if he can, although without occasion or desire, nay, though the contrary be the case. I restrained myself as much as I could, but he, being a man of intelligence, saw well through my disguise the sorrow I bore at my heart. Then he pressed me to tell him what troubled me; this I did, and confessed frankly that besides my sorrow

[1] The Maldivians were of much the same opinion as Julius Cæsar:—

"Yond Cassius has a lean and hungry look;
He thinks too much: such men are dangerous.
. . . .
. . . . . he loves no plays,
As thou dost, Antony: he hears no music;
Seldom he smiles, and smiles in such a sort
As if he mock'd himself and scorn'd his spirit
That could be moved to smile at any thing.
Such men as he be never at heart's ease
Whiles they behold a greater than themselves,
And therefore are they very dangerous."

(*Julius Cæsar*, Act i, sc. 2.)

at leaving my companions and seeing them weep, mourning their condition and the misery they would have to endure, even as they had already suffered, I had, said I, a more particular cause of grief, viz., that one of my two companions at *Paindoüé* and I had, from the day of our coming on board in France, made mutual profession of the warmest friendship; that I had always helped him and he me, in a greater degree than the others, and I could not but confess the great grief I had at parting with him; that, acknowledging the kindness for which I was under daily increasing obligation to him (the lord), that emboldened me to beg him on this occasion to have regard to my affliction, and to give me the satisfaction of taking this man along with us, and to be merciful to those who remained. This speech, and my countenance bedewed with tears, which my extreme sorrow drew forth against my will, affected the lord, whom I ever found in the highest degree kindly and merciful, as well as generous and magnanimous; so much so, that I venture to assert that in disposition and good manners he would yield to no gentlemen of Europe. He at once spoke privily with the other lord, the superintendent of the king's galleys and ships of whom I have spoken, and to the other chief men who were about him, and after consulting with them he told me that to please me he would gratify him, and forthwith caused the man to embark whom I indicated. As for the five who remained, he gave orders that they should be separated, and that they should be placed one in each of the neighbouring islands, enjoining the chiefs and more important inhabitants there present at his departure to treat them humanely, and to take care that they should be in no distress, and to feed them at the public expense until they should receive the king's command to send them. Then I bade adieu to my companions, more easy in mind than before, even as they too were, praying me to keep them in remembrance, that so they might not remain long in these little islands separated one from another. That done, we set sail and made way for the rest of the day.

CHAPTER VIII.

Arrival of the author at the island of Malé, where he salutes the king.—The putting to death of four Frenchmen for attempting to escape.—Arrival of his other companions, and the reasons which prevented the king from sending them to Sumatra.

At nightfall we reached a little island called *Maconnodou*,[1] belonging to the general of the galleys, where we slept: for it is their custom never to sail by night. On the following morning, when it was time to go on board, the lord told me we were within fifteen or sixteen leagues of Malé, where the king was, and that he would not dare to take my companion, not knowing whether it would be agreeable to the king, and that he proposed to leave him there for some days, until he should have spoken with the king about fetching him; that he was sure it would be well with him, and that he had given orders to that end. We arrived at length at Malé, where, on landing, he went at once to salute the king and render an account of his journey, bidding one of his people conduct me to his house. He did not omit, among other matters, to speak about me, the immediate consequence of which was that I was sent for by command of the king. At the palace I remained about three hours in waiting. In the evening I was introduced into a court where the king had come out to see all that had been brought in the last voyage from our

[1] A small island on the north-west side of Málé atoll, in lat. 4° 31′ N., now called *Makunudu*. Mr. Bell visited it in 1879, putting in there for the night, just as Pyrard did. He describes it as being about a quarter to half a mile in circuit.

vessel—*i.e.*, the cannon, balls, arms, and other implements of war and navigation, which had been brought to his magazine there. I was bidden to approach, and then I saluted the king in the language and in the mode of the country—which I had carefully studied the moment I was admitted, and had been particularly instructed in beforehand.[1] This pleased him, and induced him to inquire of me the uses of some of the things brought from the ship, which he did not know; these I explained to him, expressing myself as best I could. It being now night, he bade the lord who had brought me to give me lodging and entertainment, and me to come every day to see him along with the other courtiers. This done, we retired.

On the following days I was entirely occupied in attendance upon the king, in answering all his questions concerning the manners and customs of the people of Europe and of our France, the dress, arms, and estate of the kings, of whom he made particular inquiry. While I discoursed upon the greatness of the kingdom of France, of the generosity of its noblesse, and their dexterity in arms, he said he was surprised that they had not conquered the Indies, and had left it to the Portuguese, who had given him to understand that their king was the greatest and most powerful of all the Christian kings. The king also let me see the queens, his wives, who in like manner kept me many days replying to their inquiries, being especially curious to hear of the figures, dress, manners, marriages, and customs of the ladies of France; and often they sent for me without the king's knowledge, a thing not allowed in the case of others.

As I have already said, fifteen or sixteen of our people had already been brought to the island of Malé, where the king dwells. When I arrived there I found no more than three—

[1] This would imply some customary mode of obeisance. Christopher, however, states that, at the Durbar, no salutation is expected (*Trans. Bomb. Geog. Soc.*, i, 67).

two Flemings, and a Frenchman who was in the last stage of sickness, and died eight days after. At first, when our people came there, a Portuguese ship[1] of 400 tons was at anchor in the roads, having come from Cochin with a full cargo of rice, to take away *bolys*,[2] or shells, to Bengal, where they are in great demand. The captain and merchant were Mestifs, the others Indian Christians, and all habited in Portuguese fashion. They showed much enmity towards our men, and spoke evilly of us to the king, who believed them; and this was in part the cause why we were not so well treated as we had been. They asked the king to let them take us all to Cochin, whereto he consented—in fact, asking our captain and chief clerk if they wished to go, and telling them that they might. They made reply, with all the others who were present, that they would rather die than go. In truth, they had good reason to fear them, as it was not to do us any good, nor for our advantage, that they wished to take us; so our men trusted always that the king would send them in a barque to Achen in Sumatra, as he had promised. Soon after, the captain and chief clerk died; the others followed one by one, worn out by the fatigue they had already endured, and by the bad climate and water of that island, which make it impossible for most foreigners to live there. Moreover, when the news came to the king of the escape of the mate and the other men from Pouladou, he was so enraged, that he swore a solemn oath that he would not let one of us go. I was assured by several of the lords that otherwise he would have provided us with a barque, as we desired. The pilot, hearing this resolution, which confined him for life to these islands, designed to get a barque and escape, like his friends of Pouladou. To this end he conspired with three of our sailors, and hid in a wood all that

[1] This ship is again referred to in ch. xvii.

[2] *Boli*, "cowries"; Sin. *bella*. The traffic in these shells is more fully described below.

was required. Their design was discovered by the islanders, who had remarked their goings to and fro the wood by the shore, and played spies over them. They then gave information to the six elders, called *Mouscoulis*, who rule the highest affairs of state, and they in turn informed the king. Careful observation was made of the carriage of these four, and on the night on which they were to embark they were taken in the act by the soldiers, who put their feet in irons. Two days afterwards the soldiers took them in boats, feigning to take them to some other island; and when they were upon the sea they cut off their heads with blows of the *caty*,[1] which is made like a large bill-hook of this country, and of excellent steel, well-polished and highly worked: it comes from the Malabar coast, and cuts exceedingly well. They felled them by many blows; and one who dealt only one blow was esteemed no good soldier [of the king]. Thus do they always when they execute their king's orders, and so would they to their near relative, even their own brothers, to testify their zeal in the king's service. So, when the king likes anyone, all the world likes him; and if the king wishes one ill, all the world hates him, and no one associates with him, nor even looks at him. The four corpses were flung into the sea.[2] After all, it is no wonder that the king was enraged at these attempts to escape on the part of our men, for it is high treason to steal a barque or boat and to depart beyond the realm: that may not be done without passport, and a special and precise permit of the king, even though the boat were one's own. Without that, it is death and unpardonable, and no one need hope for the king's mercy if convicted. This crime is called *odican anpou.*[3] I heard this sad news, and

[1] M. *Katu*, a bill-hook = Sin. *Kætta*.

[2] This unfortunate pilot, as above observed, was an Englishman. His name is not given.

[3] This would have been nearly right if he had written *odi-ganan-pou*. The modern M. is *odi gengosfu*, "having taken away a boat". As to *ganan*, *cf.* Sin. *gananawa*, "to take away".

that of the natural death of our other comrades, as soon as I arrived at Malé, where the Cochin ship still was; it took away the greater part of the equipment of our vessel, which the king sold to it, consisting chiefly of things he could not use. At the same time one of the king's pilots told me that the twelve of *Pouladou* who escaped with the mate of our ship had arrived at Coilan, on the coast, and had been put in irons on a Portuguese galley, where he had seen them, and would be taken to Goa.[1]

I was then one of three at the island of Malé, along with the two Flemings. I petitioned the king to send for my comrade who had been left on the way at the island of *Maconnodou*, which he did at once, and we were only parted from one another for ten days; thus we mustered four, he, I, and the two Flemings. Two months afterwards, I managed to get the five brought who were left scattered among the little islands near the scene of the wreck; this done, we numbered nine, four Frenchmen and five Flemings, all kindly treated by the king and his lords. But we had no good understanding betwixt us, and this was due to the Flemings, who all five held themselves apart from us, and ever through interpreters spoke evil of us to the lords and to the people. The cause of this discord was that they were jealous of seeing me more courteously received than they were, and well liked and esteemed by the king, always at his side, and in consequence graciously entreated by the nobles. Thus they persuaded

[1] Referred to again in ch. xviii: these men succeeded in reaching Quilon, but received an unfriendly welcome at the hands of the Portuguese. They were the only party, according to Pyrard, who did escape from the Maldives, besides himself and three companions. Martin, however, writing of the 22nd Oct. 1602, says that some Portuguese arrived at Achin from Pedir, and assured the crew of the *Croissant* that they had seen twenty-five men saved from the *Corbin* in two boats, one containing fourteen and the other eleven men, and that they had made land between Cape Comorin and Ceylon, at the pearl fishery (*Martin*, p. 59). Pyrard is more likely to be right.

themselves that my three French companions were more welcome than they, and that I favoured these more than themselves, who were strangers to me. Nay more, because I spoke the Maldive language with some facility, while they understood it not at all, they imagined that I spoke evil of them, and that I was the cause of their being less at their ease: yet verily the truth was far otherwise.

The king's oath in his anger was the cause why his promise to give us a barque was not carried out; and, moreover, all our people were dead, saving nine; so there was no glimpse of hope that we should ever leave the place. This was a grievous affliction for us to think of, and we sought consolation of God and of each other. I have mentioned the reason given by the king for not treating us with courtesy; for, in truth, in the case of all the other ships which were in like manner wrecked during my sojourn there, he gave the men the means of departing, retaining only the money and merchandise. But, besides the reasons mentioned, I have thought that he had yet another, viz., the money which had disappeared, which one may say was the chiefest cause of misfortune, and of the death of the greater part of our crew; inasmuch as the king, being informed that some money was taken from the ship, and imagining that what our folk had concealed was a large sum, perhaps as large as that he found in the ship, he would not that this money should go out of his country; and while he searched for more than he had, most of our men died. I believe that, coming after that, the escape of the mate and the attempt of the pilot nettled him still more. It had been proposed not to take any of the silver at all, or to convey it all to the king, like the piece of scarlet. On one occasion he told me plainly that my companions had concealed the silver, and had made him a present of the piece of scarlet only because they could not hide it like money, and that they had all acted wrongfully in that matter, and were unworthy of his favour.

CHAPTER IX.

Grievous sickness of the author, which left him in evil plight.—Escape of four Flemings, and the ill-favour of the king towards those who remained.

I was for about four or five months in fairly good health, and, except for the want of the free exercise of my religion and liberty, was comfortable, well housed, fed, and treated by the lord who had brought me, my lodging being in a little apartment within the enclosure of his house. One of his servants waited upon me at all hours, and brought me my food with separate utensils, for they never eat with one who is not of their religion. He loved me as one of his own sons, of whom he had three, of nearly the same age as myself, and they loved me as their brother. This lord was in favour with the king, who placed all confidence in him; they had been attached to each other from the time they were four or five years old, and each was now fifty. Such being my condition, I fell ill of a severe burning fever, very common there and very dangerous, especially to strangers, so much so that few get over it; still less the Christians, for whom there is no sort of cure, for they are not disposed to obey the sorcerers, and get cured by charms and enchantments, as the islanders use. I was ill and in great danger for more than two months, and it was ten months before I was quite well. Not a day passed but the king and the queens sent to get news of me and my condition; he sent at all hours the choicest dishes and the most delicious morsels from his own table; and in order that I might be treated more at my ease, and might the better ask for what I wanted, he sent one of my own comrades, whom he charged with the care of me, in addition to the house servants. The sickness was severe and very troublesome; it is known through all the Indies under the name of Maldive fever: they call it *Malé ons.*[1] It is the sickness of which most of my companions died, as all strangers fail not to be soon attacked; and when one gets over it one may be sure he will recover from the other maladies to which the climate will subject him; for a man changes by habit with the climate and manner of living, and this malady, as it were, makes him a new body, and he feels quite inured. And, indeed, if a stranger, whom in their language they call *Pour-addé,*[2] recovers from it, they say that he is *diues,*[3] as who should say naturalised, and no longer a stranger. For this kingdom in their language is called *Malé-ragué,*[4] the kingdom of Malé; but by the other Indians it is called *Malé-diuar,* and the people *diues.*[5] To return to my illness. I was eight days without swallowing anything but water, and that too is a bad thing. The country people refrain from drinking

[1] M. *Málé hung* (Bell); Sin. *una*, "fever". The Maldivians also use the word *homan* (Ar. *hummā*); see ch. xiii, and Vocabulary (vol. ii). All travellers bear witness to the baneful effects of this intermittent fever and ague. Ibn Batuta says, "In the midst of all this a fever seized me, and I was very ill. Every one who goes to that island must inevitably catch the fever" (App. A). The Indian Navy Surveyors of 1834-6 suffered severely (Taylor's *Sailing Dir.*, pt. i, p. 569; *Journ. Geo. Soc. Bom.*, i, 55, 67; *Bell*, 7, 8). I have also had an account of the difficulties which constantly recurred during the survey, in supplying fresh crews owing to this cause, from the lips of Capt. Chas. Campbell, one of the few survivors of that meritorious service.

[2] *Furadi míha*, "voyage man" (Chr.).

[3] *Dives*, or more properly *divehi*, is the adjectival form of *diva*, or *du*, "island"; Sans. *dwípa;* Sin. *duwa*. In modern times "islanders" is expressed by *divehi míhun* (*Bell*, p. 3), and the "island letters" by *divehi akuru; cf.* the *divi* of Ammianus Marcellinus, as to which see App. A.

[4] More commonly *Divehi rájjé;* see Sultan's letter of 1795 (*Bell*, 78).

[5] There seems some little confusion here. He has already said that *dives* was the Maldivians' name for themselves, and I believe he means *Malé divar* as the continental name for the Maldivian people, not kingdom; the form *divar* would seem to be Dravidian. The Sinhalese usually call the Maldivians *gundara-kárayo*, "the *gundara* (boat) men", and the islands *Mála diva*, or *Máladiv dúpat* (*Bell*, 3).

anything but lukewarm water, with a little powdered pepper in it; this prevents the inflammation, which would otherwise ensue when the fever passes off. I could not, however, take this beverage, which does nothing to quench the thirst. After the fever left me my legs and thighs swelled greatly, as if I had the dropsy. All foreigners suffer in the same way. Besides, I could not see for more than ten or a dozen paces before me, and I was afraid I should become blind. The fever also left me an obstruction and inflammation of the spleen, which caused me great difficulty of breathing. This spleen disease is very common among them, and they all have it rather large; they call the disease *ont cory*[1]; and, in fact, it so remained with me all the time I was at the Maldives. About the same time the king fell sick, and on this account I could not see him when I was on my feet again—until, on his recovery, as he was going to the mosque, I saluted him. He was much surprised to see the state to which I was reduced by this inflammation, and said that his illness had prevented him doing more for me. He at once bade his attendants see to it, and sent to find men who were skilled in curing this ailment, and told them to take the unguents from his own stock; for the king always keeps a quantity of drugs, medicines, and recipes of all sorts for the sick, even charms. The people would go and ask for them, and he was well enough pleased to do this kindness to all comers; and by this means also to know who were ill, who recovering, and who dying, and so to provide for the burial of those who died. It was his wont to do this for the poor and for such as were without means, in manner suitable to the degree of each. Thus did many busy themselves with my illness; but I did not get well until my legs burst and the water which caused the swelling escaped; my eyes then recovered their former power. But the mischief was that the ulcers in my legs became very large and deep, and so painful that I got no rest

[1] Below, ch. xiii, spelt *on cory*, properly *huṇ-korhi*.

by day or night, and the humours taking their course by this channel, it was difficult to close the wounds up. In this condition I remained for four months; the king causing me to be attended to and cared for to the best of his power. There was a little island within sight of Malé called *Bandos*,[1] where dwelt a man esteemed expert in that line. The king sent for him, and bade him cure me if he knew how, and he would reward him handsomely. The man promised to do so; but he added that if it should please the king to permit him to take me with him he could cure me much sooner, for the air was much better and more bracing, and the water better at that island than at Malé. The king permitted him, and gave word to his officers to serve out to him everything he asked for my support; so I was indeed well treated and cared for by this man. But meanwhile happened an accident to my comrades, which grieved me much and entailed much discomfort to me. This was, that of the five Flemings that were at Malé, four made resolve to escape from the islands by stealing a boat, seeing the desperate position to which we were reduced by being unable to depart with the king's permission. Two of the Flemings had arrived at Malé with our captain and the others brought with him; and having been with these men when they died, they succeeded to the money which they had kept concealed; thus they had every means of procuring the requisites for embarking. See now how they pursued their enterprise. The factor of the Christian king of the Maldives kept a banquecalle,[2] or storehouse, on the sea-shore at Malé. He was an Indian of Cochin, of the race of Canarins, and a Christian, though a bad one, as I afterwards came to understand. These Flemings

[1] *Bados.* There are two islands of this name in lat. 4° 15′ N. *Bodu-* and *Kuḍa-Bados* (big and little); the former only is inhabited, and is, therefore, probably the one intended here. The Adm. charts give the names *Burrah Bunduse* and *Coorah Bunduse.*

[2] As to the history of this word, see Yule and Burnell, *Disc. Gloss.* and *New Eng. Dict.*, s. v. "Bankshall".

made friends with him, and so plied him with money that he let them put and keep in his store the provisions and baggage which they required. It remained only to await an opportunity for seizing a boat, which was a long time in coming. At length it happened that one of the followers of the lord who brought me to Malé left his boat near the place on account of the rain; and as he was hour by hour expecting the fine weather, he did not take out the rudder as usual. The boat was all equipped for the fishing, but very small, being no more than eight times the length of an arm, which is the most common measure used (it is called *Riens;* another smaller measure is used for cloth, viz., from the elbow to the tips of the fingers, this is called *Moul*;[1] all this by the way). The boat was called *Donny*,[2] *i.e.*, "bird", because it was a quick sailer, and it was equipped with provisions and water for several days. Our people having made this discovery, embarked at nightfall with their goods, and made off; but bad luck had it that this night and the day following there raged the most violent storm imaginable, not a whit less than that we came through off the coast of Natal. Even the islanders said they had never seen so many coco-trees blown down in four-and-twenty hours. I leave you to imagine whether it be possible that our poor fellows could have saved themselves in such a storm, in a little frail bark, not knowing the channels and passages which they ought to take in the midst of so many rocks and reefs. So it was that afterwards there were found upon the beach some pieces

[1] More correctly *riya* and *murhe.* The Sin. *riyana* is a cubit; the Maldivian *boḍu riya* (big riya) = length of the arm; *kuru riya* (little riya) or *murhé* = cubit; and *baya murhé* (half murhé) = span (*Bell*, 119).

[2] Rivara identifies this word with the Tam. *tóṇi*, "boat"; but the author distinctly says it was called *donny*, *i.e.*, "bird", because it was a good sailer: the word is repeated in the Vocabulary as the equivalent of "birds". Correctly written, as by Christopher and Bell, it is *dúni*. Pyrard may have confused *doṇi*, "boat", with *dúni* "bird", but there is not enough to forbid us taking the passage to mean that "Bird" was the name of the boat.

of the boat's equipment, which led to the belief that they had perished—as, in fact, they had; for nothing was ever heard of them again, neither at the islands nor on the mainland. The king was greatly incensed at this third escape, as well on the account already stated, that it is high treason to steal a boat and depart without leave, as because one of the four Flemings was a good gunner, and he liked him for that. This gunner was engaged at S. Malo for the voyage. Having received some money as an advance, he married, and was no longer willing to come, and offered to return what he had received. This our captain would not agree to; on the contrary, he had him seized and carried on board, neck and heels, by four men, on account whereof he was never afterwards well disposed, and even on several occasions when some of the ship's crew were offended at the captain for some punishment, conspired with them to make a wrong course, and to wreck the ship, and so get ashore. This he confessed to us at the Maldives. He also behaved with barbarous inhumanity towards our captain while he lay at the point of death at Malé, for he took off him by force a night-shirt which he was wearing; nor was he dissuaded from the act by all the prayers of the poor sick captain, only saying that he wanted it, and that he no longer recognised the captain after the loss of the ship. This disaster happened to these poor Flemings about eighteen months after our shipwreck. I reflected that by God's assistance, amid so many tribulations, I had never engaged in these attempts at escape, which all turned out ill, as I have related.[1] Two days afterwards, my comrade with whom I had vowed so warm a friendship died after a long illness. This was to me an intolerable affliction. He was from Vitré, and in our vessel had the office of clerk. I believe that he was at length brought down with vexation and melancholy, having

[1] The mate and his eleven friends did indeed reach the coast of India, but were there consigned to the Portuguese galleys.

left a wife and children to make this voyage, and now saw no hope of return. To come back to the Flemings who had gone off. When it was discovered, and the king was informed, messengers were sent to our people's lodgings to see for a fact who were left. They found two Frenchmen, one Fleming, and the man who was dying, as I have said. The six elders assembled at the king's palace, the accustomed place, and summoned our three men, whom they kept there by the space of four or five hours, telling them that they were accomplices in the others' treason, and threatening them with death. At length, seeing that they were not guilty, they let them go; but the king gave orders not to give them any more rice as provision from his store,—not however, preventing those who would from giving them victuals: for his part, he would never again believe a Frenchman. And, in fact, they did not by reason of that order fail to get a livelihood.

All these things grieved me excessively: my long and tedious illness, the loss of our men, the death of my friend, and the anger of the king, which waxed against those of us who were left. On my recovery, which was at the end of two months after I was taken to the little island of *Bandos*, I desired to tarry there, thinking thus to avoid the wrath of the king, which by this delay might be appeased; but at length I was advised not to add by contumacy to my transgression (for so they referred to our friends' mishap), and to return at once to the king. I took the advice, and on arrival, as the custom is, I put myself in the way of the king before going to my lodging. He happened to be going out at one of the lower courts, next to his sleeping apartments. I saluted him in the usual way, without any difference. Then he spoke to me, and asked if I had been well treated, and was quite well, and even wished to see the place of my sore. This gave me good hope that I was again in his favour as before; but I was greatly deceived, for he forbade them to give me anything from his house, any more than to my comrades. I was vexed—not, however, for the victuals, for the lords let me not want for aught; but for this cause, that, there, a man to whom the king does not give food is of no account, and has no position. And even the great lords accept rice of the king, and it is a high honour, too; so, on the contrary, is it a kind of infamy to be deprived of it. My especial friends did not, however, cease to favour me and help me, as they saw that the king did not speak ill of me, and that he acted thus to inspire me with fear for the future; otherwise, when the king is in good earnest incensed against anyone, that man would not find a single friend, and those who had been his friends would abandon him.

Two months passed in this disgrace, but for all that I did not cease to go regularly to the palace to present myself to the king. I was warned that by the custom of the country one should not absent oneself when the king is angry, nor cease to go to the palace regularly, until by long patience the king speaks and again receives you into his favour.[1] I again fell ill of a fever. The lord with whom I lodged apprised the king of it, and he bade him treat me well and spare nothing. Nor did he; and to give me better hope, he assured me that the king was not at all angry with me, but on the contrary was solicitous for my health: and, indeed, the king bade them give me the ordinary provision of rice, and to my three companions, too. The illness was short, and I was soon well again. Six weeks afterwards I was fairly astonished to be summoned to the palace by the six elders, and to be told that they were informed that we had a design to escape. They gave me orders, on the part of the king, not to have any dealings with my companions, nor to speak French to them; and that I was to give them the same order. It was very diffi-

[1] This custom is quoted from Pyrard, with approval, by Montesquieu, as "disarming the prince's indignation" (*Esp. des Lois*, liv. xii, ch. 30).

cult, lodged so near each other, to obey this order and not to speak or communicate with one another,—which, indeed, we did in secret. For all that, fifteen days after, it was reported to the king, who was much offended, and commanded that my three companions were to be taken to an atollon named *Souadou*,[1] which is eighty leagues to the south of Malé. You have to pass the line to get there. That is the place where the king exiles those who displease him; it is an island far removed from his court, where foreign vessels never touch, whose inhabitants are very unmannerly, rude, and boorish. This order was given to the master or Intendant of the royal ships, who is called *Maé dau da elle*[2]; this person had conceived an ill-will towards me, out of jealousy of the lord who had brought me from *Paindoüé*, with whom he was there, for he had made me promise on the journey that I should lodge with him, and I could not do it, for the king made me lodge with the lord who had brought me. By way of revenge, he sent word to me by one of the royal sergeants, who are called *Mirvaires*,[3] that I was to come to him to be embarked for Souadou with the others. I could not refuse

[1] The atoll *Suadiva*, or *Huadiva*, is here probably intended to include the smaller atoll Addú, and the island Fua Mulaku. This remote portion of the Maldive kingdom was treated as a sub-kingdom, the exiled King Dom Manoel describing himself as "rei das ilhas de Maldiva e de tres Patanas de Cuaydu" (Letters Patent in *Arch. Port. Or.*, Fasc. 3). As appears here and elsewhere in the narrative, Suadiva atoll was the place of exile for political offenders and a place of refuge for unsuccessful conspirators; and, as Mr. Bell informs me, contains at this day the descendants of several occupants of the throne.

[2] This office was that of captain or superintendent of the king's private ships, and must not be confounded with that of *velannas*, or admiral. The duties are described above at pp. 69-70, where the name of the officer is given. The title *Mádadahelu* is still in use.

[3] M. *miru baharu* (Bell); Ar. *Emir-el-Bahr*. In Pyrard's time (see below, ch. xv) there were two of these officers, having the duties of harbour masters, in subordination to the *velannas*, or admiral. Nowadays there is one *Miru Baharu*, who is port surgeon at Málé, and is one of the three ministers of the Sultan.

nor resist this order, and in great sorrow went to embark, when one of the sons of the lord with whom I was, well knowing that the king had given no such order with regard to me, promptly informed him of it; the king at once ordered that I should be disembarked, saying that he did not intend that I should be elsewhere than near himself. By this means I was freed. Some of the lords begged of the king to let one of the three others also remain, or that he should go at another time. This was because they liked the man for being a good tailor and a trumpeter: and this gave him much custom and acquaintances in all ranks. The king consented, so that only two were embarked, a Frenchman and a Fleming, and we two remained; for after the departure of the others there was no word of sending him, as they thought that we could not effect our escape. The king sent for me and reprimanded me for our disobedience; adding that he was annoyed that I had entertained a design to escape, and that he did not wish me to go and drown myself as the gunner had done. I humbly excused myself, and assured him that I had not participated in any such enterprises. It was then that I began to be in the greatest favour with the king. Two years afterwards, my two comrades who had been banished to Souadou were recalled on this wise. One of them, the Fleming, was a very clever cutter of soft wood with the point of a knife; and having more leisure than he cared for, took it into his head to make a little vessel in the Flemish fashion, no longer than an arm's length, but so neatly done that it had all its proper sails, ropes, utensils, and equipment, no less than a big ship of 500 tons. He sent it to the king, who admired the little work so highly that he sent orders that the workman should be sent back at once, and out of esteem for him, his companion too. So we were again all four together for the space of fifteen months.[1]

[1] As will be seen hereafter, Pyrard left the Maldives in February 1607; the date of the return of his two comrades from Suadu would,

The king gave me a lodging close to him, and every day I had rice and other provisions brought from his house. He also supplied me with a servant to wait upon me, besides some money and other presents; by means of which I became somewhat rich, according to the notions of the country, to which I conformed in every possible way, as well as to their habits and customs, so as to be the better received among them. I trafficked with the foreign ships which arrived there, and with so much address, that they put entire confidence in me, and left large quantities of merchandise of all kinds for me to sell in their absence, or to keep against their return, and gave me a certain share. I remained also in the king's favour, whom I went to salute every day, and

therefore, be about Nov. 1605. No more deaths occurred, and these four, besides the twelve who escaped from Pouladou, were all who reached India out of the *Corbin's* crew. This will be a convenient place to summarise the misfortunes of the whole party. About forty survived the wreck (p. 60). The mate and two sailors were the first taken to Malé (p. 57); then the captain and five or six others (p. 59). Pyrard and two others were taken to Paindoüé (*ib.*). Many at Pouladou died (p. 61), and his own two companions fell sick (p. 64). The king's officers take others to Malé, where the captain and second mate die (p. 66). The mate and eleven others escape from Pouladou, leaving eight, of whom four were sick (p. 67). Of these latter, four die, one falling from a coco-tree (p. 68). Pyrard goes to Malé, with one of the two at Paindoüé, leaving four at Pouladou (p. 76). Fifteen or sixteen had already been brought to Malé, of whom P. found only three surviving, two Flemings and one Frenchman, the latter dying eight days after P.'s arrival (pp. 77-78). The pilot (an Englishman) and three sailors had been put to death for an attempted escape (p. 80). P.'s companion, who had been left at Maconnodou, is now brought to Malé, making four, two French and two Flemings. Two months later he gets the five brought from Pouladou, *i.e.*, nine at Malé—five Flemings and four French (*ib.*). Four Flemings escape and are drowned (p. 86), leaving four French and one Fleming. His great friend, a Frenchman, dies (p. 87), leaving two French (besides Pyrard himself, who was then at Bandos) and one Fleming. These four were taken to India in 1607 by the Bengal invaders. It is not known whether the mate or any of his eleven friends got back to Europe.

was consequently well received by the grandees, and treated with the warm friendship of many.

I had a number of coco-trees of my own, which are there a source of riches. I had them tended by labourers, who give their services for hire. In a word, I wanted nothing but the exercise of the Christian religion, and I was much grieved to be deprived of that, and to lose all hope of returning to France. So it is that my long sojourn in these islands gave me a great knowledge of them, of the people who inhabit them, and their manners and customs, and I am now disposed to leave on record, with some particularity, the information I thus acquired.

CHAPTER X.

Description of the Maldive islands, of their situation, and the people who inhabit them.

The Maldive isles[1] begin at 8 degrees from the equinoctial line to the northward, and terminate at 4 degrees to the southward. Their length is thus great—about 200 leagues; their breadth is only 30 or 35 leagues. They are distant from the continent—that is, from Cape Comorin, Coilan, and Cochin—about 150 leagues. The Portuguese account it 4,500 leagues by sea to reach them from Spain.

They are divided in thirteen provinces, called by them *atollons*,[2] which is a natural division, according to the situa-

[1] The Maldives extend from latitude 7° 6′ N. to latitude 0° 42′ S., and from longitude 72° 33′ to longitude 73° 44′ E., a space 470 miles in length north and south, and seventy miles east and west. Ihavandiffulu, the northernmost atoll, is distant about 350 miles from Cape Comorin, and Málé atoll about 400 miles from the nearest port of Ceylon (Bell, *Rep.*, 1; Taylor, *Sailing Dir.*, 1874, pt. I, pp. 567-9).

[2] The Maldive is *atolu*, and is perhaps the only word which that language has given to European vocabularies. The word used by Ibn

tion of the places. For each atollon is separated from the rest, and contains in itself a great number of little isles. It is a marvel to see each of these atollons, surrbunded on all sides by a great bank of stone, and no human device could so well wall in a space of land as it does. These atollons are either round or oval, each thirty leagues, more or less, in circumference, and all in a line, end to end from the north to the south, without touching each other. Between every two there are channels, some broad and some narrow. Standing in the middle of one of these atollons, you see around you this great reef of rock, as I have said, which surrounds and defends the islands from the impetuosity of the sea. But it is a fearful thing, even to the most hardy, to approach this reef, and to see the billows from afar come on and break with fury all around; for I assure you, as a thing which I have seen an infinity of times, that the crests and foam of the breakers rise higher than a house, of the whiteness of cotton, so that you see around you, as it were, a wall of exceeding whiteness, chiefly when the sea is high.

Batuta is *aklīm*, *κλίμα*; while the exiled Maldive king at Cochin, in his letters patent of the year 1561, describes himself as "King of the Maldive islands and of the three *patanas* of Suadu, and of the seven islands of Pullobay" (*Arch. Port. Or.*, Fasc. 5, No. 350; see also Barros, *Dec. III*, liv. iii, c. 7. Rivara's *Pyrard*). The word *patana* is a Sinhalese word, meaning in Ceylon a patch or stretch of mountain land on which jungle does not grow. As there were three atolls, Suadu, Addu, and Fua Mulaku, which, being distant from the rest and near each other, ordinarily went under the name of Suadu, the word *patana* would seem to be synonymous with *atolu*. Colonel Yule (*Enc. Brit.*, article "Maldives") finds the word *atollon* in Zeidler's *Univ. Lex.*, published in 1732, and I am not aware of an earlier use of it as a borrowed word. Mr. Bell considers the word to be connected with the Sin. *étula*, "within"; and Mr. Burnell, who had suggested the Malayâlam *aḍal*, "closing, uniting" (see *New Eng. Dict.* s. v.), was satisfied with this derivation (Yule and Burnell, *Disc. Gloss.*). Mr. Bell is of opinion that Pyrard's *atollon* is a misprint for *atollou*; but the word appears so frequently in the former form, and never in the latter, that it is more likely Pyrard intended by the soft French final *n* to give his notion of transliteration.

Within each of these enclosures are the islands, great and small, in number almost infinite. The natives informed me that there were as many as 12,000[1]; but my notion is that there is not the appearance of so great a number, and that they say 12,000 to indicate an incredible number, which cannot be counted. Yet, true it is that there is an endless number of little ones which are mere sandbanks, altogether uninhabited. Moreover, the king of the Maldives puts this number among his titles, for he called himself *Sultan Ibrahim dolos assa ral tera atholon:* that is to say, "Ibrahim Sultan, King of 13 provinces and 12,000 isles."[2] However that may

[1] The number of the islands has been variously stated. According to Ptolemy, there were 1,368 islands in the vicinity of Ceylon. Moses Chorenensis increased the number by four:—"Taprobane insularum omnium maxima......atque insulas minores circumjectas habet, ad mille trecentas septuaginta duas" (Whiston's edition, 1736). The following also have reference to the Indian islands generally:—John of Montecorvino puts the number at over 12,000 (*Cathay*, p. 215); Friar Jordanus had heard of 10,000 or 12,000 inhabited (Hak. Soc. ed., pp. 28, 53); and Marco Polo asserts as a fact that there were 12,700 inhabited and uninhabited. To come now to those who speak more definitely of the Maldives. Suleyman, in the ninth century, gives the number 1,900 (Reinaud, *Relation*, etc.). Masudi says "there are counted of them 2,000, or more exactly 1,900" (Sprenger's edition, i, 335). Hieronymo di Santo Stefano says seven to eight thousand (*India in the Fifteenth Century*, Hakl. Soc., p. 8). De Barros derives the name "Maldiva" from *Mal*, the Malabar (?) for 1,000, and *diva*, "islands" (*Dec. III*, liv. iii, c. 7); while Garcia de Orta, by way of correcting him, says they are not called Maldiva, but *Naledica*, "because *nale* in Malabar signifies '*four*', and *diva*, 'island'; so in the Malabar tongue they are said to be 'the Four Islands'" (*De Orta*, 11; see also *Mandelslo*, pp. 62, 116). Padre Lucena says "11,000 inhabited" (*Vida de S. Franç. Xav.*, liv. ix, c. 20), and he is followed by Bartoli (*Asia*, lib. iii, p. 201), by Philippus a Sant. Trin. (French edition, p. 226), and by other clerical writers. Mandelslo (Eng. trans., p. 116) says "near upon a thousand". Valentyn heard that they numbered 13,000. Captain Owen believed the total number was three or four times 12,000 (*J. R. G. S.*, ii, p. 84).

[2] *Dolos*, "twelve", Sin. the same; *assa*, "one thousand, or ten times 96", according to Pyrard (see Vocabulary, vol. ii), Sin. *dāsa*; *ral*, "country" (see Vocab.); Chr. has *ray* (*g* mute), "island"; *cf.* Sin. *rata*; *téra*, "thirteen"; the old Sin. is *tera* or *teles*, the mod. is *dahatuna*.

be, the currents and heavy seas are continually diminishing the number, as I was told by the natives, who also said that the inhabitants were decreasing in proportion, and are not so numerous as in ancient times.[1] One would say, in looking at the interior of one of these atollons, that all the little islands and the sea between them form but one continuous shoal, or that it was of old but one island, afterwards broken and divided into many. And in fact those who sail near the Maldives perceive the interior to be all white, by reason of the sand of that colour which covers all the shoals and reefs. The sea is calm and of little depth, at the deepest place not being twenty fathoms, and there are but few such places, for nearly everywhere you see almost to the bottom. This bottom is everywhere stone reef, rocks, and sand, so that when the sea is low it would not come up to the waist, and in most places only to the knee; so it would then be easy to go without a boat to all the islands of the same atollon, were it not for two things which prevent that: first, the great fish called *Paimones*,[2] which devour men, and break their arms and legs when they meet them; in the second place, the rocks at the bottom of the sea, for the most part, are sharp and pointed, and these give countless wounds to such as walk thereon. Moreover, one meets also a mass of branches of a thing whereof I cannot say whether it be tree or stone, only it is like white coral, and is also branched and pointed, but not polished at all; on the contrary, it is very rough, and all hollow and pierced with little holes, and

[1] Mr. Bell notes the prevalence of this notion, that the islands are wasting away (p. 2), and mentions in confirmation that the black soil of the islands is in some places to be seen below low-water mark; but adds that it is admitted that additions are made to the inhabited islands. Valentyn states that, according to Sinhalese tradition, Ceylon and the Maldives were formerly one island.

[2] M. *Femunu* (Chr. and Bell). In his Treatise (see vol. ii), Pyrard mentions a smaller kind, called *tuberons* (tuberão) by the Portuguese, which may be identified with the M. *miyaru* (Chr.).

quite porous; nevertheless, it is hard, and in weight like stone. In their language the natives call it *aquiry*,[1] and use it for making honey and sugar of cocos, bruising these with little stones and boiling with coco-water: thus are their honey and sugar prepared. That substance (*madrepore*) greatly incommodes those who bathe or wade in the sea; and it was therefore difficult for me to go from isle to isle without a boat; those, however, who are accustomed to it often do so.

Of the islands, an infinite number—that is, as I believe, a large majority—are entirely uninhabited,[2] and have only trees and herbs; others have no vegetation, and are merely shifting sand, some being for the most part submerged at high tides, and laid bare when the sea is low, the remaining part being covered with large crabs, called *cacouué*,[3] and crayfish, or else with numbers of birds called *pinguy*,[4] which lay there their eggs and young, and in quantities so prodigious that one could not (and I have often tried it) plant one's foot without

[1] Madrepore, M. *hiri* (Chr.). Mr. Bell compares the Sin. *hækiri*, also the Sin. *hirigal*, "coral stone". Chr. gives *hiri*, "white coral", and *mudu*, "madrepore".

[2] It would be a difficult, if not an impossible task, to attempt to count the uninhabited islands, even with our very excellent Admiralty charts. The number of inhabited islands is as follows:—

Atoll.	Inhab. Islands.	Atoll.	Inhab. Islands.
1. Tiladummati . .	17	9. Mulaku . . .	8
2. Miladummadulu .	32	10. Kolumadulu . .	11
3. Fádiffolu . .	2	11. Haddummati . .	12
4. Málosmadulu . .	30	12. Huvadú . . .	17
5. Ari	13	13. { Addu / Fua' Mulaku } .	7
6. Málé	8		
7. Felidu . . .	5		
8. Nilandú . . .	13	Total .	175

Colonel Yule has numbered 602 islands with names on the Admiralty Chart.

[3] M. *Kakuni* (Chr.); Sin. *Kakuluwa*.

[4] There are no penguins at the Maldives; he means probably *manchots*.

touching their eggs or young, even the birds themselves, for they fly not away at the sight of men. For all that, the islanders eat them not, good eating though they be; they are as large as pigeons, and of a black and white plumage. These islands, which I have said are uninhabited, appear from a distance as white as if they were covered with snow; this is from the exceeding whiteness of the sand, which is as loose and fine as that of an hour-glass, and so warm that these birds' eggs are easily hatched in it. These islands but rarely have fresh water; the others which are covered, whether inhabited or not, have it, excepting some, whose inhabitants have to go to the neighbouring islands to fetch it; they have also contrivances for catching that which falls from heaven[1]; and though they have water on these islands, it is not all alike, being better in some places than in others. All their well water is not good and wholesome. They make their wells in this fashion: by digging for three or four feet, more or less, they find fresh water in abundance, and what is a very strange thing, at four paces from the beach, even in places that are often washed by the sea. I have observed that the water was quite cold by day, especially at noon, and at night was quite warm.

But to return to the thirteen atollons. Hear their names,[2] commencing from the most northern, which is at the head of the rest, and on that account called by the Portuguese *Cabexa de las ilhas*, and in the Maldive language *Tilla dou matis*, with the same meaning, that is, "the highest point"; it

[1] Mr. Bell informs me that the natives use two simple contrivances for catching the rain: (1) a cloth is stretched horizontally, with a stone in the centre of it, under which vessels are placed to catch the water as it filters through; (2) coco-nut leaves are tied tightly round coco-tree trunks near the ground, and the rain as it runs down is conducted into vessels.

[2] The names of the atolls, according to the more correct modern system of transliteration, will be found above, p. 97, *note*. Compare the names given by Ibn Batuta, see App. A. The termination *dou*, *dous*, or *doue*, also written *diva*, is the Sansk. *dwípa*, Sin. *duwa*, "island".

is under the eighth degree from the line to the northward, at the same altitude as Cochin,[1] and no more. So the first atollon is called *Tilla dou matis;* the second, *Milla doue madoue;* the third, *Padypolo;* the fourth, *Malos madou;* the fifth, *Ariatollon;* the sixth, *Malé atollon*, which is the principal one, having in it Malé island, the capital of all the others; the seventh, *Poulisdous;* the eighth, *Molucque;* the ninth, *Nillandous;* the tenth, *Collo madous;* the eleventh, *Adoumatis;* the twelfth, *Souadou;* the thirteenth, *Addou* and *Poua Molucque*, which are two little ones, distinct and separate like the others, but so small that they are only counted as one. Generally *Addou*, being the chief, gives its name to the other. During my sojourn I was in all the atollons, and sailed about them with the natives.[2] Each of these atollons is separated from its neighbour by a sea channel, and these vary, some being narrow and some wide; but whichever they be, you cannot pass them in large ships without disaster. Albeit, there are four much wider than the others, which the largest ships can pass; but even these are very dangerous, and it is hazardous to go by them, especially by night; for then you are infallibly lost, as we were, for you must meet with some shallows and reefs, which ought to be avoided. I have seen at the Maldives many marine charts, in which all this was very precisely laid down.[3] The people

[1] The northernmost island of the Maldives is in 7° 6′ N.; Cochin is in 9° 55′.

[2] This statement may be taken generally. He does not describe any trips made round the atolls.

[3] These charts (M. *muruba*, Chr.; *mouraban*, Pyr., Voc.) have been seen in Ceylon (Tennent, *Ceylon*, i, 612, *note*). Sir A. Johnston, a former Chief Justice of Ceylon, obtained two of them, which he presented to the Royal Asiatic Society (Christopher's paper in *J. R. A. S.*, vol. vi); but these appear to have been lost. Mr. Bell has in his possession several charts of the coasts of India and Ceylon; but he never saw among them any of the Maldives themselves. From the photographs of these charts most of them seem fairly good copies of European originals: the one of Ceylon and the Coromandel coast given here is the worst of the lot, *i.e.*, the most purely native production.

also were wondrous clever at avoiding them and in getting out of the most dangerous passages without harm. I have often seen them pass through the midst of reefs, shoals, and rocks, by channels so narrow that there was room only for the boat, and sometimes so tight was the fit that she would scrape both her sides on the rocks, and for all that the natives would go with confidence through these hazards, and with all sails set, while I, travelling under their conduct, suffered the gravest apprehensions: this often happened to me. But I was never so afraid as on one occasion when I was with some of them in a little boat of not more than four arm-lengths, in a sea towering above me two pikes high, more stormy and swollen than ever was. Every moment it seemed that a wave would carry me off the boat, wherein I had much trouble to hold myself, while they recked nothing of it, and only laughed; for they fear the sea not a whit, and are exceedingly adroit in managing their barques and boats, being brought up to it from their youth, as well the great lords as the poorest of the people: not to understand these matters would be esteemed a disgrace. So it would be impossible to tell the number of barques and boats upon all the islands, for the poorest will have a boat of his own, and a rich man will have many. They never navigate by night, wherefore they fetch land every evening; they steer only by eyesight and without compass, except when they go beyond their own islands on a long voyage. For the same reason they take not much provisions, buying from day to day whatever they require at the several islands. A great number of the islands within an atollon are also surrounded by a shoal, with only one or two openings, very narrow and difficult to notice, and therefore much need for them to know how to manage their barques dexterously; otherwise, if they made the least mistake in the world, their barque would be upset and their merchandise lost. As for the men, they can swim so well that in these sea passages they always save themselves; and, in truth, they are half fish, so accustomed are they to the sea, in which they pass their days, either swimming or wading or in boats. I have seen them many a time within the reefs where the sea is calm—I have seen them, I say, swim after fish, which they have suddenly caught sight of while bathing, and catch them in their course. That is quite a common thing. And yet they often lose their barques, with all their dexterity. They are most troubled by the currents *oyuarou*,[1] which run now to the east, now to the west, through the island channels, and in other parts of the sea, six months one way and six months the other; and not six months for certain either way, but sometimes more and sometimes less, and this is what deceives them, and usually causes the loss of their vessels. The winds are often steady, like the currents from the east or the west; but they vary even more, and are not so regular, sometimes veering to the north or south; while the current always keeps its accustomed course until the season changes. This, as I have said, is variable, and is the cause of disasters to the shipping. I shall note some instances hereafter.

In connection with this there is also a feature well worthy of note. It is that the atollons, which, as I have said, are all in a line and end to end, separated by the sea channels, have openings or entrances opposite each other, two on one side and two on the other, by means of which you can go and come from atollon to atollon and have communication at all times: in which thing is to be observed an effect of God's providence, which leaves nothing imperfect. For if there were only two openings in each atollon—that is, one at each end—it would not be possible to pass from atollon to atollon, from opening to opening, owing to the strength of the currents, which run six months to the east and six months

[1] M. *oyivaru* (Bell); Sin. *oya*, "river". As to the plural form, *varu*, see Professor Childers, in *J. R. A. S.*, New Series, vii, 35. According to Mr. Bell, however, this form is used for singular as well as plural.

to the west, and suffer you not to cross, but carry you down. And in cases where the two openings were not opposite each other, but one on towards the east and the other towards the west, you could easily get across and enter, but you could not return until after the six months were past and the current changed.

As the entrances are disposed, you can go from one atollon to another, notwithstanding the current, at all seasons, and traffic and communicate freely, as in fact they do. For each atollon has an opening at four places, corresponding to its two neighbours; for example, there is an opening toward the east, which is almost directly opposite the entrance to the other atollon; and on the western side there is another, which is likewise over against that of the neighbour on that side; so that if the current is running from east to west, you cannot cross direct from opening to opening; but in this case you set out from the eastern opening, which is the higher up the current, and over-thwarting it, enter the other atollon by the western opening. And so you can speedily return at all times without awaiting the change of season; but then you must set out from the eastern opening, which is opposite the one you started from, and, over-thwarting the current, make the western opening of the other atollon. When the current changes, and runs from west to east, you must do the opposite to what I have said: that is, set out from up the current, and enter by the opening of the other atollon, which is down the stream, that will be towards the east. The utility and necessity of these openings further appear in this, that notwithstanding them, barques and boats are very often lost, being carried out of their course by the currents, and chiefly when they are caught by calms or contrary winds on their passage; but if these openings were not where I have described them, it would be much worse, and you could not navigate from atollon to atollon.

For the rest, these entrances to the atollons vary in size,

some are broad, some narrow; the broadest is not more than two hundred paces or thereabouts; while some are hardly thirty, and even less. At each side of these entrances to each atollon are two islands, and you might say that they were for the very purpose of guarding the entrance; for, in fact, it would be easy with cannon to prevent ships from entering in, seeing that the broadest is no more than two hundred paces.

As for the channels, called by them *Candou*,[1] which separate the atollons, four of them are navigable for large ships passing the Maldives; all sorts of foreign craft use them, but not without danger, and many are lost every year. It is not that men choose to pass through: on the contrary, they avoid them as much as possible; but these islands are so situated in the midst of the sea, and are of such extent, that it is difficult to avoid them; the currents, more than anything else, carry the ships out of their course during calms and contrary winds, when sails are of no avail to escape the currents. The first (channel) to take from the north is that at the entering in whereof we were wrecked on the reef of Malosmadou atollon. The second, nearer to Malé, is called *Caridou*,[2] in the midst of which is the largest of all the islands, surrounded by reefs, as I have described. The third is beyond Malé, to the south, and is called *Addou*. The fourth is called *Souadou*, which is directly under the equinoctial line, and is the widest of all, being more than twenty leagues broad.[3] The islanders, while going among the islands

[1] M. *Kaḍu* (Chr. and Bell). The same word is used for "channel" and for "sea" (Chr. and Pyr., Voc.). In the former signification, *cf.* Tam. *kaḍi*, "to cut"; in the latter, Tam. *kadal*, "sea".

[2] So named from the island *Kaharidú*, or *Karhidú*. If the latter be correct, it would seem to mean the "Coco-nut Island", from *karhi*, "coco-nut".

[3] Mr. Bell understands the first of these to be the Moresby Channel (M. *Dekuna Kaḍu*); the second, the *Kaharidú*, or channel of Cardiva island; the third, the *Ariyadú*. The *Souadou* is generally known in

and atollons, do not use the compass; but only on long voyages beyond, and on crossing this wide channel, they use it. All the other channels between the atollons are quite narrow, and full of shoals and flats, and can only be crossed in small barques; and even then a good knowledge of the ground is required to escape danger. I have been surprised, while sailing with the islanders on the channel which separates Malé and Poulisdou (it bears the name of Poulisdou,[1] and is seven leagues broad or thereabouts), to find the sea as dark as the anchor; and for all that, if you put it in a pot, it was just like other water: I saw it ever bubbling in dark eddies, like water over a fire. The sea does not flow at this place as elsewhere, and this was fearful to behold: it seemed I was in a whirlpool, as I did not see the water flow one way or the other. Nor can I assign a cause for this; but I know well that the natives are afraid of it: they often meet with storms there.

As I have said that these islands are so near the equinoctial line on each side, you may imagine what is the quality of the air (viz.), that it is very intemperate, and the heat excessive. The night and the day are of equal duration at all seasons; the nights are quite cool, and bring an abundance of dew. It is on account of this coolness that this country may be lived in without inconvenience, and herbs and trees abound, notwithstanding the heat of the sun. Winter begins in April, and lasts six months; summer, in October, and likewise lasts six months. There is no frost in winter, but continual rain. The winds then are stronger from the west; on the other hand, the summer is extremely hot, and there is no rain; the winds are then from the east.

English charts as the One-and-a-half Degree Channel. But Pyrard omits two others, the Véimandú, or Kolumadulu, and the Equatorial Channel, south of Suadiva atoll, both of which are regularly used by large ships (*Bell*, i, 4; Taylor's *Sailing Directory*, i, 567–9).

[1] M. *Fuḷidú Kaḍu.*

It is believed that the Maldives were formerly peopled by the Cingala (for so they call the people of Ceylan); but I find that the Maldivians do not in any way resemble the Cingala, who are black and ill-shapen, while the former are of good form and proportion, and differ but little from ourselves, saving in their colour, which is olive.[1] Yet it may be believed that the climate and lapse of time have rendered them more fair than were those who first peopled the islands. Add to this, that a large number of foreigners from all parts meet there and make it their home; besides many Indians who from time to time are wrecked there, as we were, and remain at the islands. This is why the people living at Malé and the neighbouring parts toward the north are more polished, genteel, and civilised, while those toward the south are ruder in language and habits, and also are less well-formed in body, and darker; and you see many women, chiefly the poor, go about naked, without any shame, with nothing on but a little cloth to cover their private parts.[2] The northern parts, therefore, are more frequented by foreigners, who usually marry there. There, too, pass all the ships, which enrich the country and tend to civilise it, and so people of quality and means go there more willingly than to the south, whither, as I have said, the king sends those whom he would punish with banishment; albeit the people of the south are no less well-informed and clever than the rest, perhaps more so in some ways; but as for the

[1] See further below, ch. xix. The Maldivians may, as a rule, be fairer than the low country Sinhalese, but are, I believe, no fairer than the Kandyans. As will be seen in his chapter on Ceylon (vol. ii, chap. x), Pyrard knew little of that island, and probably nothing of the interior. Mr. Bell is distinctly of opinion that our author is wrong in his contrast, and that the Maldivians compare badly with either the Kandyans or the low country Sinhalese, whether in face or figure.

[2] In all parts of the Maldives, nowadays, the women are decently attired.

nobles, they are all in the north, where, too, the soldiers are obtained.[1]

In short, the people are exceeding adroit, much given to the manufacture of all kinds of things, and excelling therein, even in letters and science, according to their notions; but more especially in astrology, of which they make great business. They are a prudent and circumspect people, very cunning in trade and in social life. And while they are valiant, and courageous, and skilled in arms, they live under a complete system of law and police.[2] As for the women, they are pretty, for all they are of an olive complexion; and yet you find some as fair as in Europe, albeit their hair is always black; but that they esteem a beauty, and many make it come so by keeping the girls' heads shaven up to the age of eight or nine, only leaving them a little hair all along the forehead,[3] to distinguish them from the boys, who have none at all, except the eye-brows; and from the time the children are born they shave their heads every week, and this makes the hair very black, though it would in some cases have been otherwise, for I have seen some children with it almost fair.

[1] Our knowledge of the southern atolls is, unfortunately, very limited. One authority, however, the captain of the s.s. *Consett*, wrecked on Suadiva atoll in 1880, gives a pleasant picture of the islands there. He describes the people as "very obliging, kind, and friendly", not ignorant, having books in their own language, and carrying on manufactures of coir yarn and rope, fine rush mats, fans, and tatties. The children are taught to read; the women are prettily dressed, and morality is good (*Bell*, 19).

[2] The following character of the Maldivians, given by Barros, shows the unjust notions current among the Portuguese: "A gente destas ilhas, com quem os nossos tem communicação, é baça fraca e maliciosa, cousas que sempre andam juntas, não somente com a natureza dos homens, mas ainda nos brutos animaes, donde se pode verificar uma paradoxa, que todo fraco de animo é malicioso em cautellas" (*Dec. III*, liv. iii, c. 7).

[3] Or, as the practice now is, leaving a rim of hair all round the head.

Their hair, then, is in general black, and the blackest is the most admired, as well in men as in women. This blackness, as I have said, comes from their being shaved every week from their birth. It is a beauty among women to have the hair very long, thick, and black; they dress and bathe it often, and clean it with water and washes made on purpose; and after bathing and cleaning their heads and hair, they let it all float in the wind (that is, within their own house-yards) until it be perfectly dry, then they apply oils, very odoriferous, in such wise that their heads are always soaked and oily.[1] For they never wet their bodies, men or women, but after they have oiled,—*i.e.*, two or three times a week for the hair, and for the body sometimes oftener than once a day. They are not obliged to wash their hair except when they have company, and especially every Friday, which is their Sabbath, and on all the other great feasts; the men on the Fridays, and the women on the great feasts only, and besides then as often as they like or require.

The women also perfume their heads, however small their means, and so, after washing, oiling, and perfuming the hair, they dress it, and that is by taking all the hair from the front behind, and drawing it as tight as possible, so that not a hair strays hither or thither; then they tie it up behind and make a large knotted bunch; and in order to enlarge that they use a perruque of man's hair (but as long as a woman's), in form like a horse's tail; to hold this, they fix it in the thick end of a kind of thimble, to which all the rest of the hair is fastened. This thimble, of gold or silver, is set with pearls or precious stones, according to their means; and some of them wear two of these false tresses, which serve to form the knot of hair behind, and to enlarge the bunch. Some-

[1] They use, as Mr. Bell informs me, at least four descriptions of hair oil: (1) plain coco-nut oil; (2) the same, scented with jasmine; (3) the same, with champak; and (4) a fish oil.

times, but not always, they insert the sweet-smelling flowers of the country, which are never wanting.[1] And all this is so well managed that not a single hair stands out beyond another.

As for the men, it is only allowed, as I have said, to the soldiers, officers of the king, and nobles to wear their hair long, as these do for the most part, and as long as the women. They take just as much trouble, too, as do the women, in washing, cleaning, oiling, and perfuming it with flowers; and there is no other difference except that the men tie theirs on one side or on the top of the head, and not behind, as the women use; moreover, they never wear a false perruque. Nevertheless, they are not obliged to wear their hair so, but short or long, as they think fit, as moustaches or whiskers are worn with us.[2] I have seen there the king and the princes and most of the lords and soldiers wear their hair short, and some of those who generally wore it long, when they got tired of it, or when it ceased to grow, cut it off and sell or give it to the women; for the false perruques are only those of men; the women never have their hair cut, alive or dead. Most of these false tresses come from the mainland, from Cochin, Calicut, and the Malabar coast, where all the men grow their hair long, and then cut it and sell it to the women of their own country and to foreigners. Their hair grows much faster than ours, because, as I fancy, they wash and oil it so often; also by reason of the excessive heat, which makes the hair grow more thick and strong: never, however, curly,

[1] No false perruques are now used; but where the hair is insufficient for an ample *koṇḍé*, or chignon, a pad of a certain root is inserted, and the hair dressed over that. No gold or silver hairpins are used, nor other ornaments, except flowers; and these, in the atolls as far south as Málé, must be concealed by the head-kerchief, of which, by the way, Pyrard says nothing.

[2] Whether in obedience to the custom of Indian Mussulmans, or to convenience, as the author's subsequent remarks seem to indicate, the universal practice of Maldivians at the present day, from the Sultan downwards, is to shave the entire head.

as among us. The men are very hairy in their bodies: one could not imagine a covering more thick; they pride themselves in it, as in that in which the strength of a man is. This is not, however, true of them all; and if a man be not thus hairy, they say he is more like a woman than a man, and despise him accordingly. The women are not so, and have hair only on the ordinary places. There are in that country no regular barbers, and every man knows how to shave himself, as well men as women. They use a razor only for that, and they have no combs; but they have scissors of copper and of iron, and mirrors also of copper, which they use for guiding the razor, which is of steel, but not made like ours, which they do not value.[1] They shave themselves in the same way (as we do); but the king and the great lords have men who are proud to do this for them,—not for gain, but from affection, being men of quality; albeit the king makes them some presents at the end of the year.

So, throughout all the islands there is no person, man or woman, rich or poor, gentle or simple, who after the age of fifteen has not a private set of implements for treating the hair, which they are very careful to brush aside when it teases them but a little. As for the girls, they are shaven in youth every week; but to distinguish them from the boys, they have a small fringe left. They wear no clothing up to the age of eight or nine, save only a cloth reaching from the waist to above the knees, and this is first worn when they begin to walk; the boys, however, do not wear it till the age of seven, and until they have been circumcised. They say, with regard to their daughters, that there is no need for them to wear clothing before the time mentioned, for it is then that the breasts begin to swell and rise, and it behoves them to cover them, as parts which they take as much shame in

[1] It need hardly be said that copper scissors and mirrors and Maldivian razors have long since given place to the wares of Sheffield. Glass mirrors, combs, and brushes are in common use.

exposing as we here other parts. Then, too, they let their hair grow, and cut it no more. They are dressed and decked out, as being then eligible for marriage. Before that they are considered children, and no one, man or boy, may talk to them of love, inasmuch as, up to that time, they are not recognised nor attired as girls.

The men, when they grow old, are covered with hair, as I have said; not being clothed from the waist upwards, they shave only as far as the chest and stomach, but in such fashion betimes, cutting it in one place and leaving it in another, that it looks like a slashed doublet. They wear their beards in two styles; the one, which is allowed only to the Pandiares, Naibes, Catibes, and other clerks, and to all who have made the journey to Mecca and Medinatalnaby[1] in Arabia (where is the sepulchre of Mahomet), is to wear the beard as long as possible, and only to shave it under the throat, and above and below the lips: for they would not for the world have anything that they eat or drink touch their hair, that being one of the most disgusting pollutions: therefore they have no hair around the mouth; nay, I have sometimes observed that when they found a single hair upon a dish of meat, they would not touch it, and would rather remain fasting, and give the food to the birds and other animals, no one else caring to touch it. The other kind of beard for all other people and the commonalty is to wear it small, in the Spanish style, shaved round the mouth and under the throat, but without moustaches; on the cheeks they cut little spaces with the scissors, quite close to the skin, but so, however, that some hair is seen. At the chin it is pointed, as with us at present.[2] Moreover, they keep with care the cuttings of their hair and nails, without letting any drop; these they are careful to bury in their cemeteries with a little water; for they would not for the world tread upon them nor cast them in the fire,

[1] Medïnat-en-Nabi, "the city of the Prophet".
[2] These two styles are still observed.

for they say that they are part of the body, and demand burial as it does; and, indeed, they fold them neatly in cotton; and most of them like to be shaved at the gates of temples and mosques. They are very handy in this matter, and use no warm water for shaving; their razors cut exceeding ill. They only pass a little cold water over the surface, and however bad a business they make of it, they make no complaint, and aver it gives them no pain. I used to take greater precaution, and had the water warmed, and soaked my hair a long while; but sometimes I thought they would rasp all my skin off and tear up my hair by the roots. It is a matter of habit with them, for otherwise they would be as sensitive as we. But it is time to come to a particular description of these islands.

The Maldives are very fertile in fruit and other commodities necessary for human life. There is millet in abundance, which they call *Oura*, as well as another small grain called *Bimby*,[1] which is like millet, except that it is black like turnip-seed. These grains are sown and reaped twice a year. They make of them a kind of flour, whereof they concoct a gruel with milk and coco-milk, and also cakes and fritters, and many other comfits. There grow there also roots of divers kinds, on which they live; among others, one called *Itelpoul*,[2] which is plentiful without being sown; it

[1] M. *urá*; Sin. *tana hál* (Setaria Italica); M. *bimbi*; Sin. *kurakkan* (Cynosurus corocanus). Mr. Bell mentions the former as grown in the southern, the latter in the northern atolls. He also mentions a second kind of millet—M. *kudibai*; Sin. *menéri* (Panicum miliaceum)—as found in the south (*Report*, 84). "All the Maldive islands are destitute of grain, except that in the province of *Souweid* (Suádiva) there is a cereal like the *anly*, which is brought thence to Mahal (Málé)" (*Ibn Bat.*, iv, 112).

[2] M. *hittala-fu* (*fu* = "flour"); Sin. *hiritala* (Dioscorea oppositifolia). From it, as Ibn Batuta says, "the natives prepare a flour, with which they make a kind of vermicelli, and this they cook in coco-nut water; it is one of the most agreeable dishes in the world. I had a great taste for it, and ate it often."

is round, and as large as the two fists, or thereabouts. They crush it upon a very rough stone, then they put it on a cloth in the sun to dry; it then becomes very white, like starch or flour, and keeps as long as is desired. They make it into thick soup, cakes, and biscuits, which are very good eating, except that they are too filling for the stomach, and must be eaten fresh, to be wholesome. There are also other kinds of roots called *Alas*,[1] good to eat and plentiful, which are sown and cultivated; one kind red, like beetroot, others white, like turnips; they are in general larger than a man's thigh. They are cooked and served in several ways; and to preserve them the year round (for they are ripe only at the end of winter, in the month of September), they mix them with honey and coco-sugar, and that compound forms a great part of the food of the people. Wheat, which is called *Godam*,[2] and rice, called *Andoue*,[3] do not grow at all; but plenty of rice is brought from the mainland by the merchants, and therefore they use it much, and it is cheap. It is served and eaten in divers ways: it is cooked by itself in water, and eaten with other viands in place of bread, or else mixed with spiceries; sometimes with milk and coco-sugar; sometimes cooked with chickens or fish, which dishes they serve with great neatness and propriety. They also cook it, and then dry and pound it; and with this flour, along with eggs, honey, milk, and coco-butter, they make tartlets and other very excellent cates. Herbs and trees abound everywhere in the islands; a large number bear fruit, others not at all; yet of these latter the leaves are eaten, being sweet

[1] M. *alu*, Sin. *ala*, "root". He particularises the two common kinds of yams, the red and the white. *Ālu* is now in Hind. the common name for the potato; originally that of an esculent *arum*. Yams in Hind. are called *rakt-ālū*, *i.e.*, "red ālū".

[2] M. *godan*; Sans. *godhama*; Tam. *kothumei*.

[3] In the edition of 1619 printed *Indoue*, but corrected as above in edition of 1679. The M. is *hadu* or *hanḍu*.

and delicate[1]; others are applied to every sort of use. I shall describe them in detail in another place: it will suffice to have made this mention of them here. As for fruits, there are limes, pomegranates, and oranges, in the greatest possible abundance; bananas, which the Portuguese call Indian figs,[2] but the Maldivians *Quella*.[3] It is a large fruit, which multiplies fast, tasty and very nourishing, so much so, that they feed their babes upon it in place of pap. There are ever so many more which I cannot name, some of which resemble our plums, pears, figs, cucumbers, and melons, though they grow on trees. None, however, is more useful than the coco or Indian nut, which they call *Roul*,[4] and the fruit *Caré*,[5] which is more plentiful at the Maldives than elsewhere. The islands supply many neighbouring countries, and the natives there know better than others how to extract its substance and the commodities it yields. It is, indeed, the most wondrous manna imaginable; for this single tree can supply everything necessary to man, furnishing him in plenty with wine, honey, sugar, milk, and butter. Besides, the kernel or almond is good to eat with all kinds of viands instead of bread: there, they neither make bread nor ever see it; indeed, I was five years or more without tasting it, or even seeing it, and I got so accustomed to that style of living that it seemed not strange to me. Moreover, the wood, bark, leaves, and nuts provide the greater part of their furniture and utensils. But I had rather not tarry in its description here: that were too long a tale, and would take

[1] Mr. Bell states that they eat the leaves of the *manga* and the *kullofilá* trees.

[2] *Figos da India*; see *Garcia de Orta*, fol. 95.

[3] In orig. (and here only) misprinted *qualla*; M. *keyo*; Sin. *kehel*; Hind. *kelā*; Skt. *kadalī*. There are many sorts.

[4] M. *rú*; *cf.* Sin. *ruka*, "tree".

[5] In orig. *cate*, an evident misprint for *caré*, as the M. *karhi* is printed in the Vocabulary, in vol. ii.

me from the course of my story. In another place[1] I will more conveniently give a particular description of this marvellous tree, which will perhaps be more ample than any previous accounts; for I knew it thoroughly; I lived upon it, and had a large number in my possession for a long time. As for firewood, there is so much that it is not bought and sold, the country being quite covered with all kinds of trees, which give capital shade, and a pleasant freshness to the air. People are free to go and cut such trees as are only fit for firewood, at their pleasure. Some of the islands, too, are entirely covered with such timber, which people send their servants and slaves to fetch for their use. With all this abundance of fruits, as I have said, it is a remarkable thing that each of the thirteen atollons yields different produce: for though all are under the same sky, yet each hath not everything needful, and the growth of products cannot be spread from one to the others. You would say that God had willed that these people should visit each other, such diversity is there; what is plentiful in one island is rare in another. I have often wished that some plant which grew abundantly in one place should grow elsewhere; but it will hardly do so, and is not so good or so natural as is grown in those atollons and islands proper to it; in other places it is a forced production. The people, too, in their domiciles have followed a similar rule, for the craftsmen are collected in different isles—for instance, the weavers in one, the goldsmiths, the locksmiths, the blacksmiths, the mat-weavers, the potters, the turners, and the carpenters in others; in short, their craftsmen do not mingle together; each craft has its separate island.[2] But they communicate

[1] See vol. ii.

[2] This is, to some extent, the case still; thus, two islands of Nilandu atoll, Ribadu and Huludeli, are exclusively occupied by men of the jeweller caste and craft. Three islands of Tiladummati atoll, Uligan, Berimadu, and Tiffardu, are occupied by toddy-drawers, and Takandu,

with the other islands in this way. They have boats covered with a little deck, whereby they go from isle to isle, working and dealing in their goods, and it is sometimes more than a year ere they return to the island of their home. They take with them all their male children from the age of four or five upwards, to teach them the business. At their halting-places they always sleep, eat, and drink in their boats, and generally work there too. I remember seeing the tinkers' boat thus going from village to village. I might here specify the atollons and islands which produce peculiar fruits and commodities, but that would be superfluous.

Among their animals are poultry in great plenty, which cost only the catching, for they are wild; and in the market they are sold at a sol apiece, and about thirty-six eggs for the same price. It is the flesh they use the most, next to fish. There are also quantities of pigeons, ducks, rails, and certain birds[1] most resembling sparrow-hawks, spotted with black and grey, which do not, however, live on prey, but on fruits; there are other different species, all wild and undomesticated. The crows annoy the natives much, for they are so bold that they will enter houses to take anything, though people are there, and are not a whit afraid; this seemed very strange to me, and at first I thought they were tame. They are so numerous as to be beyond counting, and the people do not kill them. The bats there are as large

in the same atoll, by tinkers. Mat-weaving is confined to the islands of Huvadú, and the manufacture of cotton-cloth is carried on chiefly in Málosmadulu, Addú, and Huvadú atolls. In the remoter parts of Ceylon, villages are exclusively peopled by distinct castes; all are now cultivators of the soil, though they to some extent also pursue their hereditary calling. There, a potter or a blacksmith village would be but a few miles off. At the Maldives, where the island of a particular craft was probably leagues away beyond the channels of ocean, the segregation of trades is remarkable evidence of the endurance of caste after four, and now nearly seven, centuries of Muhammadanism.

[1] The spotted *koil* of India; M. *dindi-koveli.*

as ravens. Much annoyance, too, is suffered from the mosquitos or gnats, which bite keenly. They are as much or more of a nuisance there than at the island of S. Laurens, or anywhere in the Indies. But what trouble the people most are the rats, mice, and ants, which are everywhere, with other kinds of animals and vermin, which come into their houses, and eat and spoil their grain, provisions, fruit, and soft goods; so that they are constrained, in order to obviate this, to build houses and granaries on piles in the sea, at 200 to 300 paces from shore, and thither for safety they convey in boats their grain and fruit. Most of the king's magazines are built in this wise.

There are no venomous animals, except some snakes. There is one kind of snake in the sea which is very dangerous.[1] One sees numbers of cats, polecats, and ferrets.[2] That is all I have to say of the animals native to the islands. I have seen others of all kinds, but they came from abroad. There are no beasts of burden, nor other large animals, either wild or tame. It is true there are about four or five hundred cows and bulls, but they belong to the king, who keeps them at his island of Malé. They had been brought from the continent as a curiosity, and had multiplied to this number, as they are never eaten, except four or five times a year at the great feasts, when the king has one killed, and sometimes to give to foreign ships which the king desires to gratify. I have also seen some sheep, which also belong to the king.[3] He has no dogs: the people have a horror of them. While I was there, the Portuguese of Cochin sent him two, as a

[1] Two kinds of water-snakes are much dreaded by the natives, the *veṇ-harufá* (Hydrophis spiralis), and the *máridá* (Pelamis bicolor) (Bell, *Report*, 85).

[2] By "polecats and ferrets" he evidently means the mongoose (M. *mugari*).

[3] The few sheep and cattle at Málé all belong to the Sultan or great men, and are still kept for the purposes stated. Mr. Bell was presented with a kid on the occasion of his visit.

curiosity, which he incontinently drowned. If a native had been touched by one of them, he would go and bathe at once to purify himself.

The sea yields fish in wondrous wise, of all kinds, great and small: chiefly on account that it is shallow and calm within the atollons, and for other reasons peculiar to those shores. The fishery is of great yield, and it is the chief employment of the islanders; so their principal food is fish, either fresh, with rice or other viands, or fried with coco-oil, or cooked in sea-water and dried as a preserve; and they are daily despatching ships with cargoes of this to Achen, in Sumatra, and elsewhere. Among the fish are some large ones which trouble them, seeing that they devour men when they come to bathe or fish. I myself was within an ace of being devoured by them. One sees many people who have lost arms and legs, or are otherwise maimed.

This great abundance makes living easy, and everything is cheap. You get 400 coco-nuts for a larin,[1] which is of the value of eight sous; 500 bananas also for a larin; for about the same price, 100 large fish, a dozen fowls, or 300 pounds of roots, and so on; so that there is not a country in India where foreigners enrich themselves so fast, for the trade is good, and living costs but little. So they have a proverb, that they themselves will never get rich, but only the foreigners. In my opinion, it is the easy means of living which renders them indolent and negligent, and this prevents them getting rich; for most of them care only for the wherewithal to live, without ambition, desire, or trouble for aught beside.

The principal island, as I have said, is called Malé, which gives its name to all the others; for the word *Dives*[2] means a number of little islands collected together. It is about the

[1] In recent years the price has been 90 coco-nuts for 1 rupee.

[2] M. *divehi*, applied to the whole Maldivian group. They call themselves *divehi-mihun*, "the island men".

middle of the other islands, and is about a league and a half in circumference. It is the most fertile of all, and the emporium both for them and for foreigners. It is the residence of the king and of the court: for this reason it is the most thickly peopled; but it is also the most unhealthy, for which they assign this cause, viz., that, time out of memory, the kings have resided here, and there have died a vast number of people, who have been separately buried, so that the whole island is full of corpses, and the sun, beating down upon the soil, has caused noxious vapours to arise. The water, too, is very bad,[1] wherefore the king is compelled to send, for the use of himself and his house, to a neighbouring island,[2] where it is better, and no one is buried. The nobles and people of means at Malé do the same.

Throughout the islands there are no walled towns—not even in the island of Malé; but over the whole island are scattered here and there houses and buildings, both of the lords and of the commonalty; and so at the other islands. Sometimes the houses are separated by streets and into quarters, with neat arrangement; and everyone knows his own parish.[3]

The houses and buildings of the common folk are of coco-wood, cut from the trunks of the trees; they are thatched with the leaves of the same tree, plaited together double. The nobles and the rich build houses of stone, raised from the

[1] Mr. Christopher states, with reference to this passage, that there are wells all over the island of Málé; but he never heard that the natives entertained this bad opinion of the water (*T. B. G. S.*, i, 58). Mr. Bell, on the other hand, informs me that the water is not good. He does not know of any neighbouring island from which a pure supply could be obtained; but the Sultan and great men do occasionally have it brought from Kurendú, in Fadiffolu atoll, where it is of excellent purity.

[2] Probably *Bados;* above, at p. 85, he says that the water was better there.

[3] M. *avaru*, of which Málé now has four; other islands are similarly divided.

shallows of the sea, where they get as much as they want, both as to length and thickness.[1] It is polished, and of good grain, very white, but a little hard in some cases for cutting and working; in time it loses its natural hardness and whiteness, and at length becomes quite black, after being beaten with rain or soaked in fresh water. The manner of drawing up this stone from the sea is remarkable. There grows, in these countries, a kind of tree called *Candou*,[2]

[1] The general use of stone has not been maintained. Mr. Bell, in 1879, found only one house built of it at Málé, besides the Sultan's. The dwellings of the well-to-do natives are now of wood; those of the poor of coco-thatch, or wattle and daub, with thatched roofs, resembling the "lines" of Tamil coolies (*Report*, 56). Pyrard may be going too far in saying that the houses of the nobles were built of stone; if this were so, some of them would probably be standing still. Ibn Batuta states that stone was used in his time for the foundations, and the Indian surveyors of 1835 found only the ruins of a few houses built of madrepore. The following account is still true: "Their houses are ill-built and dark, having at most only one small window, and frequently none at all; in fact, they are but large-sized huts with a peaked roof, in general about 28 feet long by 12 broad, and 15 feet high to the top of the roof. They are made of a substantial frame-work of wood, thatched all over with coco-nut leaves; the floor is plastered, and the sides are sometimes boarded; a partition near the middle divides the house into two rooms, one of which is private and the other open to visitors. In this public room there are two ranges of seats; the one on the right side on entering is considered the most honourable, and the other on the left (carried across the house) is appropriated for the common people" (Chr., in *T. B. G. S.*, i, 59). Mr. Bell supplies the Maldive names for this description. The inner or private room is the *eteri-gé* or *maval-gě;* the outer, or public room, is *béru-gé;* the range of seats on the right is *kuḍa-arhi;* the other is *boḍu-arhi* (*Report*, 56).

[2] M. *kadu*, pronounced *kandu*. It is now used precisely as Pyrard describes. There are two kinds, *mas kadu* and *varu kadu*. Only the former is sawn into planks; it has a larger leaf, and is the heavier. *Varu kadu* (which Pyrard evidently intends to describe) has leaves like the *suriya*. The fruit is small; the nut is not eaten, but is useful for furnishing an oil with which the native boats are caulked. The timber, light as cork, is used for rafts, etc. The species is certainly identical with the Sinhalese *kenda*, of which Moon, in his Catalogue (pp. 10, 160), gives the following five varieties: *Aṇ-* (horn), *alu-* (ashy), *lunu-* (salt), *savu-* (sago), and *ul-* (pointed) *kenda* (Bell).

which is as large as the walnut here, with leaves like the aspen, and as white, but extremely soft. It bears no fruit, and is not even good for burning; when dry, it is cut into planks, which are used as deal is with us. It is the lightest wood possible, more so than cork. On espying, in the sea, a stone which they would have, they make fast a cable to it. That is a common thing for them; for, as I have said, they are half-fish, and very adroit swimmers; their women even swim as well as, or better than, the men of these parts: so that any will, at the slightest need, dive to the bottom of the sea, be it fifteen

Málé Harbour, showing the Breakwater.

or twenty fathoms of water, and will remain there a long time surveying the bottom, very often to see if it is a good place for an anchor; and sometimes, in place of throwing an anchor, they choose some big rock at the bottom of the sea and belay a cable to it. So, when they have chosen the stone they want, and made fast their cable to it, they take a piece of this Candou wood, and fasten it to the cable close to the stone, or if the wood is pierced, run the cable through it, and above that they add as many more like pieces of wood as may be necessary. That wood being marvellously light and buoyant, floats up the stone or other heavy substance, even though it may be of the weight of 100,000 pounds. I have seen this done nearly every day. The cannons of our ship, which were at the bottom of the sea, also the anchors and other heavy things, were got up in this way, in the presence of all of us, who thought to give the people some advice, but they knew how to do it much better than we. By the same means, which is common and ordinary with them, I have seen the harbour of Malé, which was formerly so full of big rocks that ships could not sail nor anchor there in safety, to be cleared and improved and rendered navigable, with a good anchorage, in less than fifteen days.[1] With this floating wood they drew the stones ashore and took them out to a deeper place, and then, cutting the cables, which are made of a certain fine bark,[2] let them fall to the bottom. Stones for their building are got in the same way; but when the wood is soaked with water it must be dried in the sun, otherwise it would not float. I will add two other uses which this Candou wood serves, since I have said so much about it. This is one: they take five or six large pieces of wood, and lash them together in a row, and then place upon them sawn planks of the same timber, so that it makes a level and well-fitted raft; all around the surface they put little benches in front, behind, and at the sides and in the middle, to sit upon. This serves them to go upon the sea, and to pass from island to island. I have been one of ten on board, and it is chiefly with this craft that they do their

[1] Mr. Bell thus writes of Málé: "An unbroken reef, just awash, renders its south side inaccessible; but the rest of its circumference has a lagoon or harbour, formed by an artificial bank of coral, 3 to 4 feet above water, and 6 to 8 feet in width, roughly renewed from time to time, which serves as an effective breakwater against the monsoon storms. As the depth of the water inside is from 6 to 14 feet, this harbour gives excellent shelter to both the trading and fishing boats of the natives (*Report*, p. 12).

[2] M. *digga-vakka*: *i.e.*, the bark of the *digga* tree (Bell).

big fishings. Each man has his own, for it is very handy, and requires only one to manage it, whatever the weather may be,—I mean within the atollons and channels, and not upon the high seas. No need to fear that it will capsize, for that wood always floats ; and, moreover, in making the raft, they know the proper measurements of wood, and the ordering and balancing of the pieces, so that it never is upset ; all they have to fear is lest the pieces should become detached. This (raft) is in their language called *Candoupatis*,[1] from the tree of which it is composed. The Candou tree has another property, viz., that by rubbing small pieces of it one against another, fire is generated, and so they light their fires, using it as we do steel.[2] Thus is their stone for building obtained from the sea in the manner described ; as for lime, it is made from the shells found on the sea-shore, and binds exceeding well.

But, since I have spoken of the people, it is meet, before going further, to add a word about their language and what it is.

There are two languages in use. The first is peculiar to the Maldives, and is a very full one. In the five years and more which I spent there, I had mastered it as though it were my mother tongue, and was quite familiar with it. The second is the Arabic, which is highly esteemed, and learnt by them as Latin is with us. It is also used daily in their prayers. There are, besides, extraordinary languages, such as those of Cambay, Guzerat, and Malaca, and even Portuguese, which some learn for the sake of commerce and of the intercourse they have with that nation. In the Sou-

[1] M. *Kadu-fati* (Bell), still made and used as above stated. It is provided with benches, and worked with an oar at the stern, but without sails, and will carry ten persons. As to *fati*, *cf.* the Sin. *pata*. It is used in compounds, as *gilćfati*, "necklace".

[2] Only the *mas kadu* is used for this purpose, the *varu kadu* being too soft (Bell).

adou atollon, and towards the south of the Maldives, a language is spoken difficult to understand, rough and barbarous, but still it is the common tongue.[1]

CHAPTER XI.

Of the religion of the inhabitants of the Maldives, and the ceremonies which they observe.

The religion which they profess is that of Mahomet, and there is no other throughout the islands,[2] save among the

[1] The language of the Suvadiva group still preserves more of the Sinhalese character than that of the northern atolls (Bell, *Report*, 69), and the natives of the north have considerable difficulty in understanding those of the southern atolls; but Mr. Bell considers the difference to be no more than exists between our own provincial dialects.

[2] Pyrard does not class as a religion the worship of Nature and of the elements, which undoubtedly existed in his day, and indeed still survives: all such observances he ranks as superstitions. Apart from all these remains of a primitive faith, there lies the question whether Buddhism ever ruled at the atolls. In his time, Buddhism was but little understood, and he himself seems to know nothing of it, so that we need not be surprised to get little or no information from him. We may bear in mind, too, that in India, except where Jainism prevails, traces of Buddhism are to be found in ruins and sculpture, but hardly at all in the religious observances of the people. Further than this, Mahommedanism has in all cases made a cleaner sweep of all pre-existing forms of worship than any other missionary religion. Yet it seems likely that further investigation will justify the conjecture already made by me (*J. R. A. S.*, vol. x, new series), that there was an intervening Buddhism at the Maldives. The Sinhalese chronicles and sacred books are found to contain no reference either to the Maldivians or to their religion. Christopher, however, notes that at the Maldives the body is buried in the posture of the recumbent Buddha—*i.e.*, on the right side, with the right hand under the right ear, and the left placed along the thigh. But this was the mode used with Muhammad himself, and adopted throughout all Islam (Burton, *Pilgrimage*, *etc.*, vol. ii, ch. 2). Christopher was also informed by a learned Buddhist priest that there were formerly on

foreigners who land there; albeit of these the most frequent are Arabs, Malabars, and Indians of Sumatra, who hold the same faith. Their temples are called Mesquites,[1] which are

the Maldives two noted temples of Buddha. He gave the names of the islands, but Christopher "could not recognise them as perpetuated to the present day". The name of the priest is not given, and no Sinhalese priest now knows anything of the matter. Mr. Bell, however, has it on the assertion of trustworthy natives, that there are on the island Fua Mulaku "jungle-covered ruins of a tope or dagaba, and amid them the stone image of a Buddha in the *sthánamudrá*, or standing position." The tope is described as resembling the solid bell-shaped dagabas, rising from platforms, usual in Ceylon. Such ruins the islanders of the southern atolls term *astabu* (Aḍḍu atoll), *havitta* (Fua Mulaku), and *vére* (atolls further north), in which it is easy to recognise the Sanskrit *stúpa*, *chaitya*, and *vihára*. One of the islands in Ari atoll is called *Vihama-furhi*, and one in Málé atoll *Vihamaná-furhi*, meaning "the island of delightful Viharas". Mr. Bell notes an island called *Muñña-furhi*, perhaps = *Munipura*, "Buddha's city"; and another, *Huludeli*, Sin. *saladaḷa*, "Bo-tree island". He also mentions that the term applied by the Maldivians to their first sovereign converted to Muhammadanism is *Darumavanta*, *i. e.*, *Dharmmavanta*, "religious", "just". Christopher further states that the Bo tree (*Ficus religiosa* or *Pipal*) is said to be "still suffered to stand alone in the vicinity of mosques, when all other shrubbery is cleared away for the burial-ground." As to this, Mr. Bell remarks that only two Bo trees (M. *bói gas*) are known to be growing at the present day on the Maldives: one in Suvadiva atoll, the other at Málé, near the palace, but not within the walled enclosure or burial-ground of any mosque. So little is known of the islands individually, that it is rather premature to conclude that there are not more Bo trees, or that it is not held in some veneration. The evidence of names is not of great value, unless coupled with other testimony; but the existence of actual dagabas, witnessed by any European who knows a Buddhist building, will settle the question (see Christopher, *Trans. Bom. Geo. Soc.*, i, pp. 313-14; Bell, *Report*, pp. 59, 74, 75). Since the above went to press, a pamphlet on the island of Minicoy has appeared, from the hand of Mr. O. Bartholomeusz, the medical officer who served there during the erection of the lighthouse. He states that "the general belief of the islanders is that their ancestors were Buddhists"; and that there still exist, in close proximity, the ruins of a Buddhist temple and of an artificial tank. But whether the temple be a *dagaba* or a *vihara*, and upon what evidence its Buddhist character is determined, he does not indicate.

[1] M. *miskítu*.

well built of fair worked stone, and well bonded; they have thick walls, and stand in the middle of a large walled square, which is their cemetery, where they bury their dead,—or rather, some of them: for they choose burial-places where they will, and everyone likes to have a place for his own. The temple is square, facing the west, for that, they say, is the direction of the sepulchre of Mahomet. It has three doors, and at the entrance to each, on the outside, there is a large well, descended by steps, the bottom and sides of which are paved and fitted with flat stones, well polished and neat, to accommodate them at their ablutions; and thence to the door is a paved way of the same stone (for all the rest of the close or cemetery is only sand), so that they may not be soiled after bathing, and then they must mount eight or nine steps to the elevation of the temple. The paved floor of the temple is covered with pretty mats and carpets; and they are careful to keep it neat and clean; none durst even spit or blow his nose there; and if they have no handkerchief, and have a mind to spit, they must go to the door-step and spit outside. The superstructure is of wood, the carpentry of which I admired much, for it could not be better polished or worked. The walls are wainscoted with wood, worked and fitted in the same way; and the whole of the woodwork, outside and in, is put together without nail or bolt of any kind, and yet holds so fast that one could not take it to pieces unless one knew the artifice. You see large slabs, either of stone or wood, fixed to the walls in divers places, on which are engraved letters and inscriptions in the Arabic language. At the end of the temple, towards the west, there is a little enclosure, like a chapel in the choir of a church (that is, in the temple of Malé), where the king sits along with his nearest relative, who carries his sword and shield, the Pandiare, one of the Catibes, and the four Moudins.[1] Next to this enclosure are two large galleries, where the

[1] M. *Fadiyaru*, *katíbu*, *mudímu*.

soldiers and their captain sit with their arms. And generally throughout the temple, which is spacious and of large extent, there are partitioned spaces for certain persons—not, however, for a single person, but for those of a certain order, estate, age, or quality.[1] And this order is so well observed, that no one would dare to set himself in a place ordained for one of another condition, otherwise he would be fined in a penalty prescribed in this behalf; so there is no jealousy or dispute about places, and a commoner could as easily get a great lord fined on the spot for taking his place, as the lord the commoner. In this temple are lamps kept burning continually; there are coco-trees set apart as an endowment for this purpose by every man and woman householder, who help to keep it up. These temples, or mesquites, are very numerous in all the inhabited islands, and in some islands one sees as many as nine or ten; but their festival is celebrated in one only, which is ordained for the purpose, and is in consequence greater than the others, the latter being like chapels or oratories for praying in, founded by the devotion of individuals. The principal one, in which the festival is held, is built and maintained at the common expense, and is called *Oucourou mesquite.*[2] It is also to be remarked that the festival is not celebrated in any island unless it has forty persons above the age of fifteen years, not counting the Catibe; consequently, in such an island there cannot be a Catibe, who is the principal officiating minister in the ceremony. In such case the inhabitants go to a neighbouring island; albeit, they have one or more mesquites in their own

[1] I am indebted to Mr. Bell for the accompanying plan of the chief mosque at Málé, and the interior arrangements at present. He has obtained this from his Maldive pandit, who, on hearing Pyrard's account interpreted to him, bore witness to its substantial accuracy. The walls of the partitions are said to run to the roof, or at least above a man's height. They are loopholed or trellised, so as to allow of hearing, and, to some extent, of seeing through.

[2] M. *Hukuru miskítu*, *i.e.*, Friday mosque: *Jamu' Masjid* of India.

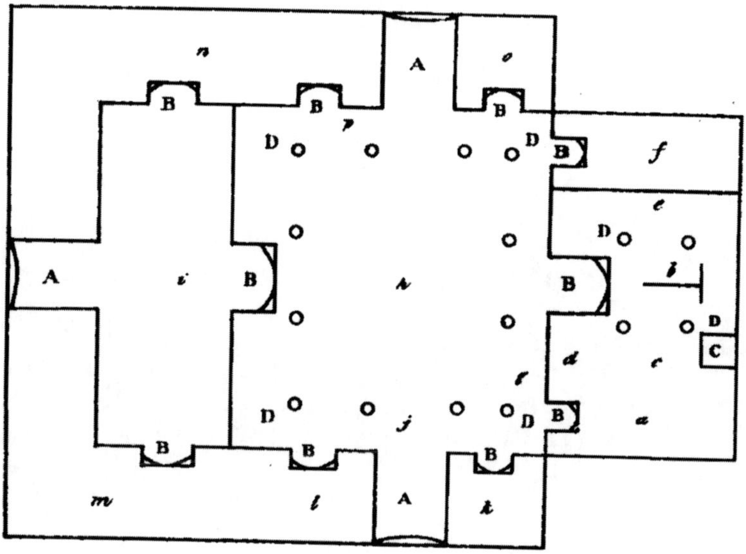

GROUND PLAN OF THE INTERIOR ARRANGEMENT OF THE CHIEF MOSQUE (*HUKURU MISKĪTU*) AT MÁLÉ.

A. Principal doors.
B. Entrances to partitions.
C. Pulpit.
D. Pillars (16).
a. The Sultan.
b. Katību (officiating).
c. Mudimun (priests).
d. Vazīrun (ministers of state).
e. Dari-kalun (Sultan's children).
f. Kilagé-fanu (lords).
g. Sáhibun (nobles).
h. Laskarun (soldiers).
i. Rayyetun (commonalty).
j. Askaru-muskulin (?).
k. Kudi-bé-kalun (palace guard).
l. Dorhun, special attendants of Mosque.
m. Miskitu mīhun, attendants of Mosque.
n. Abudálun (fakirs).
o. Majalis-bé-kalun (?).
p. Askarun (?).

island for their daily prayers. Each mesquite has its own priest, called a *Moudin*,[1] who receives the revenues and takes charge of it as a chaplain does of his chapel. The islands which have a sufficient number of people have also a Catibe, or rector, who is a superior priest of their religion, and says the public prayers, and delivers sermons and homilies, having under him the moudins of the several mesquites. All work together in teaching the people the law of Mahomet, and especially the moudins, who teach the children to read and write the language of the country, and that of Arabia, in return for which the parents give them some fitting reward.

Every day of the week they go at daybreak to the temple, and for this they give a reason according to their belief, viz., that the world is flat, and not round, and that there is a wall of copper all around which prevents the world from being submerged by the waters which encompass it[2]; and that the devil, the enemy of the human race, is at hand all night trying to pierce and undermine this work, and when the day breaks he must nearly have worked a hole. By reason whereof all the men from fifteen years of age upwards go at break of day to the mesquites to make their orisons, for without prayers the world would perish. Four other times during the day they enter it,—at noon, at three in the afternoon, at sunset, and at ten at night, remaining in the mesquite each time for about half-an-hour. The women never enter the temples, but remain at home and say their prayers there. Nevertheless the men need not go to the temples on week days if not so disposed, but may say their prayers and perform the ceremonies called *Namandé*[3] at their own

[1] M. *mudímu;* Ar. *muaddhin.*

[2] The Arabs believe the earth to be flat and surrounded by the ocean (el-Bahr el-Moheet), which is surrounded by a chain of mountains called Kaf. The latter are described by El-Kazwini as composed of green chrysolite, like the green tint of the sky. These mountains are the abode of the Jinn (Lane, *Ar. Soc. in the M. Ages*, pp. 100, 104).

[3] M. *namādu*, Sin. *namadawā*, Pers. *namāz.*

houses or elsewhere; and what is more, no one is compelled to say prayers. If, however, it were known that a man did not say them at all, no one would eat or hold intercourse with him: that is all the punishment that would befall him; and such a one, they would say, was not a good Mussulman; and for this reason they nearly all do it; yet it is a heavy tax upon their time, whether they are busy or not. They also use beads, as we do, but without crosses.

Before entering the temple they wash their feet, hands, ears, mouth, and eyes, using the while certain ceremonies and prayers, which vary according to the hour, festival, or other occasion; for example, when they have performed the offices of nature, or touched their privy parts, they have to wash and to say prescribed prayers; so also, after sexual intercourse they must bathe the whole body,[1] and say other prayers; if it has been with his own wife, they must be of another kind, for they hold themselves polluted by it, and they would not omit this ceremony for anything, believing that by this means they are purified of their sins and defilements. What I considered indecent, besides the superstition of their damnable and abominable errors, was their washing and bathing all in the public gaze, and many together, and saying their prayers quite loud, whereby from their various prayers one became aware of their most secret doings,—when they had slept with their wives, and when not, and when with other women.

All are circumcised (they call circumcision *Seunat*[2])—that is to say, the male children—when they reach the age of seven; then they hold a feast for all comers, which lasts for ten

[1] The references here are to the greater and less ablutions, *ghusl* and *wuḍû*, the former being used after such pollutions as he mentions, the latter on every occasion before prayer (see Sale, *Koran*, Prel. Disc.).

[2] Ar. *sunnah*, "the duty". Christopher gives the M. verb *gebaindang*, "to circumcise". The age varies between six and sixteen among Mahommedans, but the rite is not performed until the boy can distinctly pronounce the profession of faith (Sale, *Koran*, Prel. Disc.).

days, according to their means, and there is dancing to the music of flutes and tambourines, and other rejoicings. For circumcision there are operators who only circumcise, and do nothing else. This is the manner of the proceeding. Six or seven hours before the circumcision, the child is bathed in the sea, and kept there till the hour arrives, for they say that this causes the member to shrink, and renders the skin more soft. A shed is constructed on purpose in the yard of each man's house, covered all round with cloths, or silk stuffs; the floor of it is covered with fine white sand. The child is then brought into the shed, where, to prevent him struggling, two or three moudins are stationed, who meanwhile chant the proper verses and prayers. The operator, taking a little white lime, marks all round the member the line where he has to cut, then draws the prepuce as far as he can and ties it with a little cord, and then performs the operation with a razor used only for that, and very keen and sharp. The boy is tended and doctored by the operator himself, until he is recovered. Meanwhile, the relatives and friends of the parents come to visit him, bringing presents for the operator, who also receives payment from the father. Recovery takes about fifteen days, and then the operator takes the circumcised boy to the sea and bathes him, saying prayers and performing ceremonies the while; then he puts into his hand a little palm or coco-branch, fixing at the end of it a little piece of white taffetas, cut to a point like a little pennant, and called *dida*.[1] This they offer, with all their vows and offerings, as we do wax candles; but they offer divers other things, as I shall describe. Before a child is circumcised they say that he is innocent, and cannot sin; and, indeed, most of them before this time wear no cloth to cover their private parts, for they say that one who cannot sin has no shame; but after circumcision they fail not to cover them. For their daughters, there are no feasts or ceremonies, except

[1] M. *dida*, Sin. *dada*, "a flag".

that for their circumcision they draw two or three drops of blood when they reach the age of two years. When the children grow up they hold in great respect the man who circumcised them, and call him their master.

Throughout the year they celebrate many festivals. In the first place, the Friday of every week is kept solemn. They call this festival *Oucourou*,[1] and in Arabic *diu matil*,[2] and all the people join in it—*i.e.*, the men and youths, but not the women, nor the boys until they have attained the age of fifteen, or are at least proficient in the faith, and have been through the whole of the Alcoran, which they call *Couroan*.[3] On Thursday evening, the eve of the festival, some have vespers said at home: this they call *Saluat*[4]; others have prayers made for the dead, and with this view prepare some food and drink, sending the same to their priests or Moudins of the mosques near which the deceased are buried; or else they bid them to come and say the prayers at their houses (this prayer is called *Pastia*[5]), and entertain them; so that often the Moudins cannot partake of the repast, and put off saying prayers for some, for fear lest they should be obliged to eat when they cannot. All this evening they use quantities of perfumes, as well in their temples as in their own houses.

This Friday festival is celebrated with great ceremony and in great style, as I have seen it done at Malé. In the morning, the man whose duty it is to make public proclamations on behalf of the king, goes round the island, bearing in his hand a kind of metal bell called *coly*,[6] which resembles the cover of an alembic, with a wooden mallet, with which he strikes the bell; and at every cross-road he stops and admo-

[1] *I.e.*, "Friday". M. *hukuru*, Sin. *sikura-dā*.

[2] Ar. *juma*.

[3] *Kurán:* in Maldive, *guruán* or *guruván*.

[4] M. *salátu;* Ar. *salah*.

[5] Ar. *fátihah*.

[6] M. *Koli*.

nishes the people that it is their *Oucourou* festival. He is assisted by three persons carrying straight trumpets, in their language called *Tarapilly*,[1] which are blown at the same moment. The people, on receiving notice of the festival, cease from their labours, which they may not resume for the rest of the day. They go to bathe and wash, saying certain prayers, which vary according to the occasion or feast at which the ablutions are made; everyone puts on his best clothes, and dons the finest he can, according to his means and quality, and all from the age of fifteen upwards are obliged to be present. Meantime, over the gateway of the king's palace, the players of instruments, different kinds of drums, flutes, hautbois, fifes, etc. (for they have no stringed instruments[2]), play continuously from morning to mid-day. The trumpets, too, are blown; all these have certain single notes, which harmonise very well. The four royal Moudins also are there; they are men of quality, of birth and education, their office being one of honour and dignity; and no one can become Catibe of the king's island unless he has previously been one of these four. They are not like the Moudins of the mosques who minister to the people on all occasions; for they perform service only on the feast day and at other solemnities. These four Moudins all together ascend a stone building of great height, which adjoins the mosque, and putting their hands to their ears, cry out three times in unison, with all their might and in fearful tones, these words in Arabic, "*Alas, alas aquebar*,"[3] that is, "Great God," and add something about Mahomet. Afterwards they go to the king's palace and do the same; and then the king, if he wishes to attend (as, indeed, he seldom fails), sends a carpet of silk

[1] M. *tála fili*.

[2] *Beru*, "tomtoms" or "drums"; *dummárhi*, "flageolets" or "hautbois"; *tára*, "tambourines", are instruments mentioned by Mr. Bell (*Rep.*, 62).

[3] *Allahu Akbar!* "God is great!"

to be put at his place: if he does not so, it is a sure sign that he is not coming. Thence the Moudins proceed to the house of the Catibe, and do the like. On receiving the notice, he attires himself in a long vestment of white cloth, putting over it a cassock, or gown made in the Arab style, with slippers of gilded leather. The Moudins attend him, as he attends the king. If the king is going, all the lords, gentlemen, captains, and soldiers proceed to fetch him at his palace, and accompany him in line, all with their arms, and to the sound of trumpets and drums, in great magnificence.

Minaret and portion of Mosque at Málé.

If he does not go, he comes out at his usual hour at mid-day. The Catibe also has his head veiled with a white veil, and over that a large white Turkish turban, which covers him completely, so that he cannot see, and one of the Moudins leads him by the hand, and conducts him to the mosque, where he is the last to arrive. By this time all the people have assembled, and the king is there, and has said his prayers; but as soon as the Catibe enters he must begin at once. So the Catibe (who is a kind of parson), taking his place at the end of the temple, ascends a pulpit of wood, constructed for the purpose, six or seven steps from the ground. There, holding a naked sword in his hand, pointed downwards, he brandishes it to and fro, and recites his usual prayers. During this, all the people are at their prayers, and do their Namandé unceasingly, putting themselves in divers postures, sitting, standing, kneeling, with foreheads to the ground, hands raised and lowered, and then crossed, heads and eyes turned hither and thither. It would be hard to describe all their gestures and antics during this interval. At that time they lay down their arms, and even their knives, and they would not dare have anything upon them but their clothes, which, however, must be of the cleanest. The Catibe changes the prayers every Friday until the end of the year, and then begins afresh. He repeats them all by heart; yet for all that, one of the Moudins holds the book (before him), and if the Catibe haply were to miss a single word, nay, even a syllable or a letter, the Moudin would correct him loudly and distinctly; for they hold that if there should be the slightest fault the festival would be null and void. I have seen them in anxious discussion, one with another, upon this point. In the island of Malé there are two Catibes,[1] who relieve one another, and celebrate the festival in turn, week by week: the other islands have only one. The service lasts about two hours. Sometimes the grand Pandiare, who is the religious superior of all the islands, gives a sermon or homily, according to the occasion, and adds a prayer for the health of some one, or for the downfall and destruction of their enemies, as the case may be. This done, everyone salutes his neighbour, taking hands, and saying, *Salan à lescon*,[2] which is the ordinary salutation of all Mahometans.

When the king returns from the temple he has a finer

[1] So at present.

[2] *Salaam aleikum!* "Peace be with you!"

retinue than on his going thither, for the Pandiare, the Naibes, Catibes, Moudins, and gentlemen of quality, besides those who conducted him thither, like to accompany him to the palace in the same ceremony wherewith he came. Then he thanks them, and sends them so fine a repast, that they spend the rest of the day enjoying themselves with good cheer at the king's expense. This is never omitted when he goes to the mosque; but the order of their eating is that those of the same rank and quality are together, apart from the others, as I have said above.

On new moon days throughout the year a like festival is held, and a general rejoicing as soon as the new moon is observed. They put in order their houses, courtyards, and all the streets; while at the entrances of the mosques, and at all house doors, as well without as within, they place on each side coco-nut shells cut in half, like wooden bowls, full of white sand, upon which they lay embers, and throughout the night they burn thereon aromatic gums, scented woods, and perfumes, and inside their houses in like manner, at the corners of their beds and elsewhere. On all feast days they daub and decorate their doors and furniture with sandal and other aromatic woods and paste of perfumery; but above all they solemnise four new moons in the year more than the others.

In the month of December, about the new moon, they observe a fast, called in Arabic *Ramedan*, and in their language *Rodet.*[1] I say about the month of December, for I cannot with certainty designate the time, seeing that their month and year are lunar, and are not fixed as ours are. This solemn fast begins at the new moon, and ends at the new moon of the following month. It does not, however, commence exactly at the time of the new moon, but when they first observe it; so that in some atollons and islands it begins a day sooner or later, according as they descry the

[1] *Ródá*, the Maldive form of the Pers. *Rózu*, "fast".

crescent. The months are reckoned in the same way; it is not counted a new month till the moon is seen, which is very uncertain when the sky is thick and cloudy. Sometimes the months are different in different places. In order to observe the moon, everybody betakes him to the highest eminence in the island, and each one is very keen to be the first to discover the moon, and show it to the others. Forthwith the king has volleys of cannon and musketry fired; and trumpets, drums, and other instruments are played. This takes place at all the new moons; but at the four above mentioned, more of it, and at that one (Ramedan) most of all. Forthwith they say their prayers, and take each other's hands, giving their ordinary salutation; then put their hands over their eyes, and cover their faces for a long space, and so continue their devotions throughout the following day. This happens at the beginning of every month; but at the month of Ramedan the ceremony is much more grand. On that night, men and women go separately to pay visits, regale themselves in company at banquets, dances, and amusements, and retire not till it be nearly dawn. Before it be day, all go to bathe and perform ceremonies peculiar to this night alone, whereby they hold themselves to be purified of all their past sins, and prepared for the fast ensuing. They dress themselves and wash their teeth well, and put aside their betel, though so used to it that they can but ill afford to want it; then they go to bed. Thenceforward they fast all day long until the night, and with so much scruple, that not only do they taste nothing, but they would not even wash their mouths, nor put their fingers in them, nor swallow their spittle; so they are obliged to spit frequently: and this is very inconvenient, especially when they go to the temple, where, it not being lawful to spit within, they have on every occasion to go to the door. The men may bathe, provided they do not immerse the head, for fear lest a drop of water should enter by the mouth or the ears; but the women may not, for they might admit water elsewhere, so great is their superstition. Half an hour before sunset all the men and boys above fifteen years betake themselves to the temple, so as to be there exactly when the sun disappears. During the half-hour they wash and clean their teeth and their mouths very thoroughly, and for this purpose the Moudins of the mosques throughout the fast supply large packets of toothpicks,[1] scrapers, and little coco-wood implements expressly made for cleaning the mouth and teeth. This done, the Moudins cry out three times, and enter the temple. One of the Moudins then advances as far as possible in front, no one being at either side of him, but all behind. So it is they make their prayers at the temple, while the women make theirs at home; and afterwards they make good cheer with their friends, entertaining each other in turn. Nobody does otherwise; all are fond of entertaining their friends. And for a long time before, they make the necessary provision by laying up a store of meats and luxuries. You would be surprised to see how curious and exact they are in all this; how careful they are to scour and clean all their kitchen and table utensils, their furniture, and their houses, too, in such wise that I think I have hardly ever seen such cleanliness and neatness. Even the poorest do the like, and save all they can to make good cheer during Ramedan with their relatives, friends, neighbours, and those of their own class; and they spend more in that one month than in the six preceding. On some days the king entertains large numbers of persons,—on one day the lords, on another, the soldiers, on another, the Pandiare, Catibe, Moudins, and other clergy, and so on through all the people of the island, never inviting but one class on the same occasion. This he does with great magnificence and at great expense, in the style of the country, and with perfect order and propriety; the lords, too, do the same with their friends

[1] M. *dai-konna-karhi.*

and equals: for it is a rule which they scrupulously observe, not to eat with persons of a different order. The captains entertain the soldiers, and so everyone in his own rank of life, from the lowest to the highest. This supper is called *Rodet pillauay*,[1] as who should say "breaking the fast". Only the men and boys feast in this wise: the women are never present; yet true it is, that by night they send each other presents and eatables, and they bathe every evening, when the men are not allowed to do so. They say that throughout Ramedan men abstain from their wives during the fasting days, but not during the night; and when they do indulge, both are bound to go and bathe, and say certain prayers the same night and before daylight. Every day during this month, until the new moon following, they fast in the manner described, and abstain all the time as far as they can from committing any sin, more so than at other times, and are very zealous in good works. If haply they have broken their fast any one day or more by some slight act, they add at the end as many days as they have missed. This happens often, for they are very superstitious, as I have said, and even believe that the fast is null if they have lost blood at any part of the body; moreover, they will none of them do any work during the month of the fast, how poor soever they may be; and they make up their minds neither to go out of their island, nor to send any thence. Nevertheless, they are not forbidden to work: they prefer not to do so. The Pandiare gives a sermon every day at three in the afternoon, lasting two hours, either at the king's palace, or at the temple, or at his own house, which all the inhabitants of Malé are careful to attend; it is given in the native language, sometimes in Arabic, and thence interpreted. They employ the rest of their time in the exercise of arms and in divers games, such as the game of ball, of which they have three kinds; it is kicked with the feet, and they

[1] M. *róda villán*, "to keep the fast".

assemble in bands and companies to play it.[1] On their part the women and girls pay visits at each other's houses, and play little games suitable to their sex and to their bringing up; and of these they have many kinds and varieties.

In this month you see boys and girls caressing and making love of their own accord, more than at other seasons.[2] Then they send songs, sonnets, and verselets, written on coco-leaves, which are as white as paper, the letters being graven with bodkins. The boys cull the fairest and sweetest flowers, and arrange them in garlands very prettily, and send them to the girls, who in return send some betel, nicely ordered and prepared. This is their way of making love. They are not allowed to marry by day in this month, but must await the night. In short, during this month they seek out every means of passing the time gaily. So the fast of Ramedan lasts from one new moon to the next. The women and girls are obliged to fast eight days longer than the men at the close of the month, on account, as they say, of their courses.

Three days before the close of Ramedan, the bell, or *coly*, and the trumpets go round the town in the usual way, as when a festival or a royal command is announced, and warn the people on behalf of the Pandiare (whom the Arabs call *Cady*), that all the Maldive islanders should bring or send in writing the names of all, both great and small, men and boys, women and girls, to be registered; those of Malé to the Pandiare, and those of the other islands to the Naibe of their atoll. When they do this, they have to give in for each person an offering of half a larin, equal to four sols of our

[1] The game of football, not practised by the Sinhalese, was probably introduced from the Malay countries, where it is a favourite amusement.

[2] Though, according to the above description, the Maldivians observed Ramadan in strictness, the youths would appear to be somewhat lax, it being unlawful even to touch a woman during the fast (Sale, *Prel. Disc.*, sec. iv).

money, or its equivalent in goods; this is done quite voluntarily and faithfully, for they believe that without it their fast would be of no effect. It is called *Pitourou*,[1] as being the tribute which they pay to God and Mahomet; and those who have not wherewithal to pay this offering, beg it of the rich, who willingly give for that purpose. Those who wish not to be obliged to others, nor to have the shame of being paid for (as indeed it is a badge of shame and of poverty; the king pays for everyone who asks him, as do the lords and the rich), and those who have not at the time a half-larin or its equivalent, make a written declaration that they cannot pay till after the festival, and thus make a debt of it. Fathers and mothers pay not only for themselves but also for their children, as soon as born, until they marry or cease to live with them, and also for their servants and slaves. The money collected is divided into three parts, which amount to a great deal according to the country notions. For receiving and guarding this *Pitourou* there is a very good system, for there are four receivers chosen for this office alone from among the men of means and the officers of the Pandiare. One of these officers represents the king, another the clergy, the third, those who are only recently of their religion, and the fourth, the poor. There are also eight persons who make entries in writing of everything presented, refusing nothing that is brought, be its value or price what it may. All the money and goods are put aside until after the festival, when all is received, for a fair and proper division. The first part belongs to the priests—*i.e.*, the Pandiare, Naibes, Catibes, Moudins, Deuanits[2] (who are the sergeants), and other like functionaries;

[1] M. *fituru*, Ar. *al-fiṭr*, "the breaking of the fast", used elliptically for *ṣadaḳatu'-l-fiṭr*, "the alms of the breaking of the fast". According to *Qanoon e Islam*, p. 57, the alms portion is said to be two-and-a-half seers of some grain or fruit, payable by all but wives and grown-up sons.

[2] M. *dévâni*.

the second is given to those who have recently become of their religion; and the third is for the poor; and if anything remains over to be paid, that is the priests' concern, for they are responsible for it, as being church money; but they never lose any.

The fast ended, they celebrate a grand festival, and one of the greatest solemnity with them, called *Ydu.*[1] The day is no more certain than the commencement of Ramedan, for it is the day of the new moon following,—*i.e.*, when it is seen; and this renders it somewhat uncertain year by year. They hold the same festival and solemnities at the sight of this moon as of its predecessor; the bell and trumpets make a round of the island to announce the festival, as also next morning early, in like manner. All rise very early, wash and bathe the whole body, with ceremonies peculiar to this occasion. It must be noted that their fast is not over until the service and prayers are performed, and they go forth of the temple; then they come out with scents and perfumes, and put on the finest clothes they have, which are made expressly for this day and the festival following, and after that are preserved with great care, in order to be placed after their death upon their coffins when they are borne to the grave. They are early at the temple—that is, about seven or eight o'clock, and not at mid-day, as on Fridays. The service lasts an hour and a half, being shorter than usual; and afterwards, when the king goes forth, he returns to his palace with a braver retinue of grandees than on other days; cannon are fired, and the air resounds with the noise of drums, flutes, and musketry. When the king enters the second court of the palace, a bullock and a ram are brought forth

[1] Ar. *'íd.* The festival which celebrates the close of Ramadan is known as the *'Ídu-l-fiṭr*, or the *'Ídu-s-saghír*, i.e., "the minor festival"; in India, the *choti*, or little, *'Íd.* As it is in some parts celebrated with more rejoicing than the "great festival", it has sometimes been so called by travellers and even eminent Orientalists; never, however, by the Arabs (Lane, *Ar. Soc.*, p. 22).

and slain in the presence of him and his retinue, as a kind of sacrifice; they are cut up into pieces and distributed among the grandees of the island, or others to whom the king is pleased to send, for he gives his directions there in person. The recipients esteem it as high an honour as among us it is to receive the consecrated bread. Those who get a good share call together their neighbours to participate, if they are so minded, for it is a mark of friendship so to do; and those who can get a morsel to eat think themselves in luck. This done, the king retires to his apartments, whence he goes not forth until, after dinner, he comes to see the games and amusements. Meanwhile, he provides a banquet of all the luxuries of the country, for all classes of people in his island, according to their rank and quality, in separate rooms and sheds, which are hung with pretty cloths. The festival lasts two days longer. The nobles and captains entertain their friends, soldiers, and servants; after dinner there is nothing but games, dancing, and rejoicings, which take place in front of the king's palace only. On the third day these are held in front of the houses of the nobles and persons of quality, who are greatly honoured thereby. The chief sports[1] are with arms, the buckler and naked sword. They fence with

[1] Mr. Bell gives the following picture of these sports, which are still observed:—"On fête days at Málé, sports (M. *kuli jahan*) are exhibited, under rules and restrictions, to prevent injury to the performers. The arena is simply a portion of one of the main streets, with thatched buildings on either side, from which the Sultan and ladies of the harem may view the sports. All the male spectators stand round in a ring. The sports consist entirely of mimic hand-to-hand combats between successive sets of performers, two at a time, armed with sword (M. *kaḍi*) and targe (M. *addana*), lance (M. *daḍi-haliya*), or quarter-staff (M. *kuli jaha daḍi*). The players do little more than posture at each other *ad nauseam*, and show but little skill in managing their weapons. The Sultan and by-standers alike appear to evince no real interest in the proceedings, which are conducted from first to last in gravity and silence, and repeated for days together with wearisome monotony. It is not considered beneath the dignity of the principal men to take part in these games (*Rep.*, p. 62).

dexterity, but suffer no harm, all the blows being received on the buckler. They use also pikes, hung with bells, in which case they receive the thrusts in like manner upon the buckler. All join in this mimic warfare with good temper, dancing and leaping to the music of drums, trumpets, flutes, etc., which play incessantly. The king comes to view the scene, but he remains not long. The queens, too, and their ladies

Arena for the Sports at Mâlé.

look on; but they are concealed by jalousies and curtains, so that they cannot be seen. There is no other kind of dancing, nor at any other time, neither on the part of the men nor the women, save it be of some good-for-nothing creatures, who play the buffoon by night to make their neighbours laugh. Some folks disguise themselves in foreign dress, and construct large and roomy ships, which they run along the streets and highways with armed parties on board, and when the ships approach one another they have a fight; and this affords great amusement. The king gives betel and areca to his whole court, both small and great (this is much thought of), as also do the chiefs and captains to their followers, soldiers, and subordinates.

At the last quarter of the moon following this festival they have another, called *Mas Ydu*, *i.e.*, "grand festival", lasting three days, when they observe the same ceremonies. It is the holy day upon which the Mahometan pilgrims assemble at Mecca to visit the sepulchre of Mahomet.[1] More ceremonies are then performed than during all the rest of the year: on that day they come from all parts of the world, and sometimes when they have arrived too late, and it is over, they have to await the return of the festival for ten or eleven months.

About the month of April, or May, at the full moon—a day before and a day after—they have a festival, called *Poycacan*,[2] that is to say, "full moon". It is more of a rejoic-

[1] The festival referred to is the *'Idu-l-kurbán*, or *'Idu-l-azhá*, the "feast of the sacrifice", commonly called the greater Beiram. It is generally regarded as in commemoration of the sacrifice of Ishmael, whom the Moslems substitute for Isaac. The great day is the 10th of the month Zu'l Hijjah, when the pilgrims, halting in the valley of Mina, on their return from Mount Arafat to Mecca, perform their sacrifice. This festival continues three or four days (Lane, *Ar. Soc.*, p. 21; Burton, *Pilg.*, vol. ii, ch. 5; Sale, *Prel. Disc.*, sect. vii).

[2] M. *foi-kakkaṇ*; *cf.* Sin. *poya*, a change of the moon, and *kanavá*, to eat. This festival is evidently not Mahomedan, and is probably the Buddhistic celebration of the full moon (Sin. *depoya*) of the month *Wesak* (May), when the Sinhalese commemorate the attainment by Gautama of Nirvána. Whether its introduction to the Maldives had anything to do with that of rice, we are likely never to know. The description of the observance is, however, a true picture of the Kandyan festival at this day. Many a time have I been present at these nocturnal festivities, made weird and fantastic by hideous disguises and pantomimic gestures, displayed to crowds of gaily-dressed Kandyans. The whole scene is lighted by flaring torches, amid the sombre shadows of the temple trees, while here and there groups stand or sit round little fires at which coffee and *appas* are being prepared for the

ing than a (religious) festival. When it is evening, the neighbours assemble, gentle and simple (I bethought me it was like St. John's with us[1]), each bringing his portion of rice; they make a big fire at the nearest cross-roads, and there cook their rice. While they are all around the fire, instruments of music are played; and betimes some merry-andrews, disguised as birds, wild beasts, or such like, come and dance, indulging in lascivious and indecent gesture, even in the presence of women and girls, who are there along with the men. This goes on throughout all the islands, but at the palace the king gives rice to the soldiers for doing it. They say it was at this moon that rice was brought to the islands for the first time, and on that account they have from time immemorial kept this holiday, which lasts three days.

In the month of June, or thereabouts (for, as I said, their months do not accord with ours), they keep a festival of the dead, with many superstitious observances. On the day, the king, with all his wives (who have not permission to go without their houses but on this day only), pays a visit to the sepulchres of his predecessors, and to those of persons held to be saints in their religion; there he makes offerings, burns perfumes, and presents some *dida*,[2] as we should candles.

sustaining of exhausted nature. No indecent gestures or behaviour are now to be observed, though these were characteristic of some of the Ceylon festivities too, until they were suppressed in Knox's time. That traveller, however, expressly says that the orgies he describes were never performed in presence of women (*Knox*, p. 97).

[1] The Nativity of St. John the Baptist, June 24th. The reference is, however, to the Eve or Vigil, to the celebration of which all the popular ceremonial was confined. This consisted in bonfires, torchlight processions, dancing, etc., the celebrants adorned with garlands, ribbons, and other gewgaws. It was a superstition of the Middle Ages, probably transmitted from pagan times, that it was advisable to keep watch through this night, to prevent a temporary wandering of the soul from the body. An account of the festival will be found in Chambers's *Book of Days*.

[2] *I.e.*, flags; see p. 129.

Everybody, too, goes to visit the graves of his kindred and friends, and presents as many portions of food as he has dead relatives and friends. The food is laid aside by the Moudins of the neighbouring temples, who offer as many separate prayers as there are portions. All the graves of those who have kinsmen and friends living are visited, and replenished with white sand on that day, and perfumes are burned while the prayers are said.

Next day there is a general almsgiving at the king's palace, the king giving to all the poor with his own hand; and they, well aware of the day, come up from the most distant islands for it. He makes inquiry first what people they are, and if they be indeed in want: for to those who are not he gives only a little silver ring worth half a larin, of which he has a large number made against this day to give to folks of the lowest estate, who bring there all their children to receive of the king each his ring. On this same day all householders likewise give alms, according to their means, being bound to give to the poor the fifth part of their goods, provided they are worth at least 100 larins; and those who are not worth 100 larins are not obliged to give anything in alms.

About the month of August or September, for two days the king has a large quantity of rice cooked very thin, or half mixed with honey and coco-milk; this is carried about the island in tubs containing about a hogshead apiece. The bearers of it have cups and ladles to serve out to all they meet, and no one declines, be he beggar or lord. Everyone does the same on his own account, and even the poorest must cook some rice and send it to his neighbours. They told me that they keep this festival in remembrance of a miracle which Mahomet did as on this day, while he was at the wars, and they call it *Candis cacan.*[1]

[1] M. *Kandi-kakkan*, "kanji-eating"; Sin. *kenda*, "kanji" (rice gruel), and *kanavá*, "to eat", past tense, *kakā*.

There is yet another very solemn festival about the month of October, which takes place at night, and is called *Maulude*[1]; they say it is the night whereon their prophet Mahomet died. This is the ceremony: they begin a month before the festival, by meeting to elect officers to make arrangements and to supervise; these number at least fifty, all men of quality, and act as our "valets de feste". Their duty is to go from house to house collecting from every man the sum at which he is rated, according to his means; they go also to ask people to take part, and to arrange everything; though, indeed, the people of the parish fail not all to assist at this festival, which is diligently observed in all the islands. At Malé I have seen it performed at six places. The king bears the expense of one celebration, which takes place at his palace. At the four corners of the island it is celebrated by the people in their several parishes, and one general celebration for all the people is held in the middle of the island, in front of the principal temple. At each of the six places is erected for the occasion a wooden house, sixty feet long by forty broad, or thereabouts; the roof is of coco-branches; the wood of which it is constructed must not have been, nor may in the future be, used for any other purpose, not even for the festival of the following year. The ground is covered with fine white sand to the depth of half a foot. This house within is hung with cotton or silk cloths of all colours, and of the finest and richest description available. Above, to serve for a ceiling, they stretch pieces of cotton cloth, very white and very fine, and to support them they run cotton cords, dyed black, from side to side at right angles and aslant, so cleverly that the white above seems to

[1] M. *maulúdu*. Moolids, or, more properly, Mólids, are great periodical or annual festivals held on the anniversaries of saints (Lane, *Ar. Soc.*, 71). Mahomed died at noon on the 12th day of Rabia el Awwal of the 11th year of the Hejira. The 1st, 4th, 8th, and 12th of this month are observed as maulúdu at the Maldives.

be cut into squares and lozenges of exactly the same size: it is very neat.[1] On the sand wherewith the ground is covered they spread pretty new mats, on which each one sits, and there are no other seats. On all sides are hung copper lamps to the number of about thirty; each is large and has two wicks, so that it is almost as bright as daylight. By contrivances with air-holes, odorous perfumes are introduced within, though burnt without, for the heat of the place of itself is well-nigh insupportable: only the fumes and the odour come within. There are other conduits, too, for the introduction of water, which is very necessary, for they often wash their mouths by way of refreshment after chewing betel, which they do the whole night long.

In the middle of this hall there is a table of the height of the knees, whereon are arranged little wicker baskets, and polished lacquer vessels containing divers kinds of cates made of rice flour with coco-sugar, like little macaroons, of the thickness of the thumb: these are excellently well served with all kinds of native fruits. The table is covered with sweet-smelling flowers, while all around are jars containing drinks of different mixtures, chiefly [flavoured with] amber[gris] and musk. The whole is covered over with a large cotton cloth worked with a coloured pattern. The people rig themselves out in their bravest style; but only the men and boys are present, and no women. The men of quality of the parish do not go, for it would be beneath their dignity; it is a feast of the common folk. They assemble at eight o'clock in the evening, and sit in places assigned to them, according to their rank, by the stewards of the festival. All night long the Pandiare, Catibes, Naybes, and Moudins, with all the rest of the clergy, and other good singers, cease not to chant with all their might in alternation like a choir; nor is their chanting without rule, for some of them who know not how

[1] This description will be well understood by all who have enjoyed the hospitality of the native Sinhalese.

to sing have to take lessons from a master: so the harmony is good, and the singing far from disagreeable. They call this chanting *Zicourou,*[1] and say that they are the Psalms of David.[2] On the stroke of midnight everybody with one accord lies down at full length with his face to the ground, and so remains for a space of time. Then of a sudden the Pandiare or the Catibes stand up, and all the rest after them, and set a-leaping upon each other as they were madmen or lunatics, crying, at the top of their voices, "*Aly alas Mahomedin*", again and again; this lasts for some time. I have inquired of them why they did this, and they asking "What?" and I replying, "These mad leapings and dancing," they told me they knew nothing of having danced or done any such thing, but only remembered that for a space of time they had been rapt with ecstasy and had been partakers of heaven and the joys of their paradise. Sometimes the Pandiare remains for an hour or more like dead; they say then that he is transported to heaven, and that it is a mark that he is a righteous man. The king does not take part in this festival the whole time; he comes to see what is going on for an hour or two, and then returns. In this manner I have many a time seen it in his

[1] Ar. *zikr.* These performances consist of chorus chanting at night, the name of God being perpetually repeated, accompanied by motions of the head, hands, and whole body. The munshids at intervals sing religious odes or love-songs to the accompaniment of a kind of flute. (Lane, *Ar. Soc.*, p. 72.)

[2] The Psalms of David are well known even among remote Mahomedan communities (Mungo Park, *Travels*, c. xi). Compare the quaint account of Lancaster taking his leave of the Sultan of Achin:—"And when the general tooke his leaue, the king said vnto him: Have you the Psalmes of David extant among you? The generall answered: Yea, and we sing them daily. Then said the king: I and the rest of these nobles about me will sing a Psalme to God for your prosperitie, and so they did very solemnly. And after it was ended the king said: I would heare you sing another Psalme, although in your owne language. So there being in the company some twelue of us, we sung another Psalme: and after the Psalme was ended the generall tooke his leaue of the king" (*Lanc. Voy.*, Hak. Soc., p. 97).

company. Fifty persons are elected to minister to the rest; this is a great honour, and there is no one but is glad enough to accept the office, for none but distinguished men and scions of good families get the offer. These officers distribute during the night to all ranks of the people, seated in their proper order, a portion of betel and areca, arranged and prepared in a different style from their ordinary (I mean of the common folk, for the king and the great lords always use it prepared in the same way). They give as many as a dozen portions to each person, whoever he may be; in like wise they present to all who have a mind to drink, beverages of the country brew, in large copper bowls, exceedingly well fashioned and worked, and with a cover on the top. Now and then are brought like bowls full of water, with basins, for washing the mouth and hands; they would not for the world let a drop of water or any refuse fall to the ground. The people are arranged in lines, and at intervals are vacant spaces for passing between them.

Towards the close of the night the chanting ceases and the Pandiare and Catibes say prayers, after which they proceed to the midst of the hall, where the aforesaid table is spread; this they uncover, and all crowd around, and each one receives a portion; this they take great care of, and carry it home to show that they have been to the festival. At the same time the officers, taking some aromatic waters in vases placed there, sprinkle it upon the bodies of all present, touching them with their hands; and this is received by them as a benediction of great efficacy. This done, they must lay to the eating, for they have no celebration of solemnities without that. So the officers bring basins of water for washing their hands and mouths, they having done nothing but chew betel the night long; then they make a circle of nine or ten together, but always of the same class, and grouped according to the prescribed order. Viands are brought upon large heavy dishes, each of which contains other small ones, in which are divers meats, well served, and these are placed in the midst; it takes three to carry them. And when they have done eating, they go home to bed.

CHAPTER XII.

More of their ceremonies,—at betrothals and weddings, at obsequies and funerals.

At their weddings, which are called *Caueny*,[1] they also use formalities and ceremonies not a few: it is the Pandiare or the Naybes to whom alone they address themselves on this occasion; these send their *deuanits*,[2] or sergeants, to make the inquiries I shall speak of. If everything is settled, the girl or woman sends her father, or in default, her next of kin on the father's side, and gives him the power to represent her. This person and the future husband present themselves before the Pandiare or Naybe, who being certified on all points, takes the bridegroom's hand, and asks him if he wills to take the woman on the conditions proposed, and then of the father or kinsman he demands the same; and if they answer yea, he goes through the prescribed formalities, taking the attestation of the witnesses present—namely, the kinsfolk, sergeants, and others—to the promise of marriage, and to all the proceedings. Thereupon they go to the woman, who is waiting at her house, and assure her of all that has passed. That done, they all sit down to a banquet at the expense of the bridegroom, according to his means, music being played all the day long. Many people come to visit and salute them, the visitors receiving betel, which is their token of respect, as we should give refreshment here. To the Pandiare or Naybe are sent two larins, a dish of food, and a box

[1] M. *káveni*. [2] M. *dévani*.

of betel. Likewise, those who marry are wont to give presents to the king and the queens, to the great lords and ladies,—that is, the bridegroom to the king and lords, and the bride to the queens and other ladies, as well as to their own kindred and friends. On the other hand, when the king marries, he receives presents from all his subjects, as well lords as commoners, men as women, who present themselves in good order, each with those of his own quality, class, parish, and sex, with their offerings of cloths, robes, turbans, meats, flowers, etc., according to the means of the giver. The people of Malé appear in person, those of the other atollons and chief islands generally by deputies; the great lords tarrying awhile to have the pleasure of saluting him in person. For all that, the king goeth not forth nor showeth himself on these days, but hour by hour his attendants come and tell him what persons have arrived at the hall, of what quality, how arrayed, and with what presents, and at the last these are laid before him. They amount to a great deal, and all appertain to the newly married queen.

A man may have three wives at once,[1] but no more, and these only if he is able to support and maintain them. If all three wives live in the same island, the husband is obliged by their law to sleep as many nights with one as with another; but they do not observe this. It is but an ill-considered law for these countries, where three husbands would not suffice for one wife, so lewd are the women.

The women have no marriage portion; it is for the husbands to provide them with everything necessary, and to bear the expense of the wedding in manner suited to their rank. So they settle for them a jointure, called *Rans*,[2] according, not to the means and quality of the husband, but to the

[1] Mahomed allowed four (*Koran*, Sura iv), but Maldive usage may have limited husbands to three, which seems to have been the number kept by the Sultan.

[2] M. *ran*, "gold", and the same in Sin.

quality of the wife, and to what her mother and grandmothers had: for she must have no less. For this cause the Pandiare or Naybe full often sends them away without marrying them, when he finds that the bridegroom's means suffice not for such a jointure; even though both parties ask to be married without thought for the jointure. Most of the women take this *Rans* for the traditional honour of their house, and most of them of their own accord give up a part or all of it a few days after marriage. If the husband dies, she is allowed to take her jointure with her own goods; but the husband's heirs will make a composition with her; whereas, if she has parted with it during the life of the deceased, she can ask none of it back.

The impediments to marriage, of which the Pandiare or Naybe informs himself before he marries anyone, are the being brother and sister, or cousins-german, or foster-brother and sister, or having formerly called each other in token of friendship by the name of son or daughter, father or mother, brother or sister: in such cases they may not marry together.[1]

Youths may marry when they list, but girls may not till they have attained the age of fifteen years,—I mean, when they are orphans, or rather, bereft of their father,—for a mother would have no authority, neither any of the kindred on the mother's side. In default of a father, their brother gives them in marriage; if no brother, the nearest male relative on the father's side. Fathers, however, give their daughters in marriage as soon as possible after the age of ten years, thinking it a great sin to let a girl want a husband; wherefore they hand them over at the age of ten or eleven to the

[1] See *Koran*, Sura iv, where the actual relationship of brother and sister, or foster-brother and sister, is a bar; but no mention is made of the fictitious brother- and sister-hood of friends. This latter is, however, a well-established Sinhalese relationship. It is common to hear a man say, "M. is not my brother, but I call him brother."

first that asks them, without making any bother, be he old or young, man or boy: provided only there is little difference in their quality, that is all they think of.

A man can leave his wife when he will, provided that she agree (they call divorce *Varicor*[1]); otherwise, if she do not consent, the man may still leave her, but would be obliged to pay her jointure. But this does not happen, for what displeasure soever the wife may feel, she will not ask for her jointure, for that would be to her a reproach among women. They would despise one of their sex who was so mean-spirited and unworthy as to fear she could not get other husbands; and, indeed, no one would court such a one: so that public opinion prevents them enjoying what the law ordains. The wife, too, can separate from her husband, provided he consents; otherwise not. This divorce, which is very common among them, must be made in the presence of witnesses, all or some of whom must be present when either of the parties expresses a desire to marry another, otherwise the Naybe would not perform the marriage. This is the source of many quarrels, for full often, in a sudden choler, they divorce each other by consent, and soon after one of the parties rues it, and the other does not. Thus do they frequently come before the judge, bringing their witnesses to prove their divorces and marriages.

When the divorce is effected, the parties may marry again when they like; and they can marry each other again as before; but only three times, and no more, save when the woman after three marriages has married another man, and he has left her.[2] As they are flighty in their notions about

[1] M. *vari-kuraṇ*. As to the Mohamedan law, see *Qanoon e Islam*, pp. 145-7; *Hughes*, p. 182.

[2] "Ye may divorce your wives twice. . . . . But if the husband divorce her a third time, she shall not be lawful for him again, until she marry another husband. But if he also divorce her, it shall be no crime in them if they return to each other, if they think they can observe the ordinances of God" (*Koran*, Sura ii).

marriage, it often happens that, after three marriages and three divorces between the same parties, they wish to come together again, and are prevented by the law. But hear now the means they contrive. Vile and abject beings are found who, for a money consideration, contract a marriage with the woman, and sleep a night with her, but without touching her (for she would not suffer him, and it is so understood); next day he swears that he has had her company, and then two or three days after he quits her in the presence of witnesses. By this means the letter of the law is obeyed, and, three months after, the former pair are married afresh. The highest ladies in the land are constrained to go through the same business in like case. These middlemen are called *Medu piry*,[1] as who should say "middle husband"; they are held in great contempt even of the common people, as infamous creatures without honour or conscience. It is a grievous slander even to be called *Medu piry*. Even if it happens by chance that a man marries a woman already divorced three times, and after awhile he leaves her, and her old husband takes her to wife again, he would be greatly offended, as having been got to take the part of a *medu piry*, and his honour would be gone, did he not avenge himself. For the rest, they cannot make use of a *medu piry* more than twice[2]: after that they cannot marry together again; and it is to be noted that there is no expense in the wedding or in presents when the same parties are remarried. So it is, by these frequent

[1] If such a custom were known in Ceylon, the "middle husband" would be called by an almost identical name, viz., *mada pirimi*. That he was designated by a Maldive, and not an Arabic, term, shows, as the fact would seem, that the feigned marriage was a legal fiction invented at the Maldives.

[2] As the *medu piry* marriage was the fourth, after three marriages with the first husband, a second *medu piry* marriage would imply that the lady had gone through the marriage ceremony at least eight times; she could then be married three times more to her first husband, and only then would the law step in and put an end.

divorces they marry many a time, and change marvellously often. A man may in his life have had eighty wives and more; among others, the Pandiare, who died shortly after I resided at the islands, had as many as a hundred. In like manner the wives have a vast number of husbands; but, far from that being imputed to them for any kind of blame, they are prouder the oftener they have changed husbands; and when they are courted they tell the number, names, and quality of their former husbands as a high recommendation. Nor are they less esteemed by their gallants, but rather more; and less is thought of one who is still a virgin than of one who is no longer so, except it be by the king and the great lords. Yet, notwithstanding this common changing, you will find men and women who remain for a long time together, by reason that they love and cherish each other more than all the world.

After the dissolution of the marriage by divorce or death, the women cannot marry again quite so soon. When a husband dies, four months and ten days are ordained for the widow to mourn him; and then, to marry again, it suffices not for the woman to say off-hand that her husband is dead, for she must prove his death by three witnesses, who speak to the time, manner, and cause thereof. If, however, the husband were absent from the kingdom, and the wife had nothing of his, she could remarry a year after. So in divorce is there a time prescribed: for the woman must certify that since the separation she has had her courses three times, and she must wait till then ere she marries again. This is done to avoid the uncertain status of the issue, if she should be with child. Wherefore the Pandiare or Naybe informs himself particularly of this, and has the woman who desires to marry examined by three other women of the same parish and of good repute; and in addition he makes her swear that she has had her courses three times.

Burial is with them called *Calbalolan*,[1] and is a matter of much consideration, as to which they are highly superstitious. First of all, the dead body is washed by six men; if it is a woman, by six women. They use more than a hogshead of water in the washing, and say certain prayers the while; this done, they cover it with cotton, and shroud it with two cloths of white cotton, the one over the other, placing the right hand upon the ear and the left along the side. They place it in a coffin of Candou wood, laid upon the right side, until the time for burial comes.[2] The women of the family and of the neighbourhood assemble and bewail the corpse, telling all the praises of the deceased. The six men and six women are public officers, and they must be good people and without reproach; for if they were proved to be otherwise, they would lose their offices. These they buy for money of the king, and they have besides to give a sum of money to their comrades, which is divided among them. Their earnings are for the common stock, and are equally divided among the six men and six women, whether it be a man or woman (who is dead), and whether the men or the women have had most work. When the body is taken away these women set up the most fearful crying and yelling, and continue their wailing throughout the obsequies. The body is borne to the grave by six of the kindred or best friends, the place having been chosen and arranged by the deceased in his lifetime; for these people take such thought for their burial, that from

[1] M. *valuḷān*, Sin. *valalanavā*, "to bury".

[2] As will be seen, he says of the actual burial only that the body is laid with the face toward Mecca: the posture of the body here described would, of course, be unchanged. "The Prophet's body, it should be remembered, lies, or is supposed to lie, stretched at full length on the right side, with the right palm supporting the right cheek, the face fronting Mecca, as Moslems are always buried, and, consequently, the body lies with the head almost due west and the feet due east" (Burton, *Pilgr.*, vol. ii, ch. 2). At the Maldives the body would thus be laid with the head to the north, the feet to the south.

the time they marry and have the means, they make ready with great care all the requisites for their burial—the place, the coffin, stones for the tomb, folding sheets, and so on. They even put aside and collect little by little the money required for that occasion, and would sooner die of hunger than touch it. This fund they call *Capon*.[1] Each of them, too, has two suits, of the richest he can afford, according to his quality, which are worn at the festival *Ydu*, and then preserved in their boxes, as I have said, against the day of their burial, to be then placed upon their coffin. These suits are afterwards divided among the priests of the temple. The relatives and friends accompany the corpse, together with a large number of people not invited, who walk on all sides of the body confusedly, and without order. From the house to the place of burial they scatter over the road *bolys*[2] (which are little shells, of which I shall speak in their place), to the end that the poor may collect them and make a profit. They bring also a quantity of packages of rice and millet, which they distribute on the way to the poor. They cut also a large number of small bits of gold and silver, according to the wealth of the deceased and his heirs, who put their several shares in little pieces of cloth and give to the chief officiating minister, whether Pandiare, Naybe, or Catibe, to distribute among all the others who have assisted in praying for the deceased; but all do not share in this, for it belongs, say they, to the clergy only. Sometimes others take it if they like; this depends upon the wealth of the deceased and his heirs. Before the body walks a man with a bottle full of water, scented with aromatic flowers; this he sprinkles over all he meets along the road, which is neatly swept and brushed from the house to the mosque at which the burial is to be. For this duty this person receives a piece of silk or new cotton, according to the means of the deceased; as also

[1] M. *kafun*.

[2] M. *boli*, "cowries".

do the six who bear the body.[1] The burial of the nobles and the rich is usually in the cemeteries around the mosques, where ground is bought dearly enough: except when they have themselves built the mosque, in which case they are wont to reserve a site for themselves and their family adjoining the mosque; and this is the most honourable place. This money is distributed, with other like profits, among the priests of the mosque; for besides the Moudins, every mosque has a certain number of other priests called *Quiauany*,[2] who are maintained for the service of the temple and cemetery out of the funds settled by the builders of the temple. These incumbencies are very honourable, and are even bought. Only those of that temple can perform the funeral service at a burial there, not those of another. Yet some people desire to have a large number of priests at their funeral, and then those of the temple call in as many as are wanted from the neighbouring mosques. These priests chant continually during the three hours the ceremony lasts. Over the hole of the grave a large coverlet of silk or cotton is stretched, until it is filled up and the interment completed; it then goes to

[1] Christopher witnessed the funeral of the grandmother of Sultan Muhammad 'Imád-ud-dín, who ascended the throne in 1835, and thus describes it:—"The body was conveyed to the mosque, where prayers were read over it. The men who carried her coffin walked on cowries, which (to the value of 100 rupees) were strewed on the road from the house. As the procession moved on, handfuls of the small copper coin (50 of which go to a rupee) were scattered, for which the lower orders of the people kept up a scramble, very much out of character with the occasion, and ill-according with the rest of the scene. All the men were attired in full costume, consisting of a red waist-cloth with black and white borders, and a head-piece corresponding to it, both of native manufacture. At the burial, a gaudy canopy of various colours, supported on four poles, was elevated over the body, and the Fatha was read. After a temporary hut had been erected over the grave for the readers of the Koran, the company adjourned to the Sultan's palace, to partake of a dinner prepared for them" (*T. Bo. Geo. Soc.*, i, 63).

[2] M. *kiyaveni* (*bé-kalun*), *i.e.*, "readers"; *kiyavāṇ*, "to read".

the Moudin. Upon and around the grave they strew a quantity of fine white sand. When they lay the body within, they turn the face in the direction of the sepulchre of Mahomet, and then cover it with white sand, and sprinkle it with water from a bottle, by way of refreshing it, and over the grave they lay a large cotton sheet. After that, the relatives, who have brought a quantity of food, give to all the assistants to eat thereof.

When it is a great lord, there is no more ceremony, save that the chanting continues longer, even for the space of a year; and day by day dishes of meats are sent to the place, along with some betel: these are taken by the Moudin. If it be a king or queen, this continues during the life of the heir. For the rest, prayers are said for the deceased night and day until the third Friday after the burial; and most frequently the priests chant and eat their meals at the tomb itself, where there is a hut erected for the purpose: this is taken away at the conclusion of the service, on the third Friday after the funeral. At the close they have a great feast, to which they invite all the kindred and friends, along with the priests and Moudins, saying that they are then despatching the soul of the defunct to Paradise. On that day they place at the two ends of the grave, two stones of the same size, and fixed upright, high or low, according to the quality of the dead person. Upon these they engrave the name of the deceased and his praises. Every year, on the same day, they have a similar feast, with the same ceremonies, in the courtyard of the dead person's house, or in that of his principal heir, in a hut just like the former one.[1] In short, the expense in all this is often so great that their means are exhausted. Every year, at the festival of the dead, they

[1] "They are careful, in erecting tombstones over their lost relatives, to preserve the date of their death, the anniversary of which is observed by almsgiving and prayer on the part of the surviving members of the family" (*T. Bo. Geo. Soc.*, i, 63).

place some fresh white sand on the grave, and burn a quantity of perfumes and incense. Such as have the means, leave funds in the hands of certain persons in trust to keep their graves covered with white sand, to tend them every morning, and to keep them enclosed with little wooden posts and rails, so that none may tread thereon; for they have a horror of treading on ground wherein anyone is buried, and take care not to do so, deeming that the dead would feel insulted, and that it is a great sin. Some sepulchres they hold sacred, and at them keep many lamps burning continually.[1] Moreover, they hold in great reverence the bones of the dead, and when they are digging a grave, or on other occasion discover any, no one, not even the Pandiare or the Catibes, would dare to touch them but with a cloth; wherefore they never bury two bodies in the same place.

I have never observed that they used any mourning garments, or other than their ordinary; only this, that the kinsmen, on the way to a funeral, take off their turbans and walk bareheaded, and so continue for that day and some

[1] "A remarkable object on the island is a tomb erected over the remains of a person who is regarded by the natives as the most eminent of their saints. The building, which is surmounted by a cupola and a short spire, is thirty feet high; the gate, over which a lantern is placed, is of copper network" (*T. Bo. Geo. Soc.*, i, 63). Christopher also mentions tombs at the S.E. point of Málé island as being specially sacred. They are said to be of certain Persians who came in search of a countryman (Tabriz, or from Tabriz), who is believed to have reintroduced Mahomedanism after the expulsion of the Portuguese. Only two out of about sixty tombs were legible, and these were dated A.H. 994 (A.D. 1677), more than a century after the Portuguese conquest, and more than forty years after the last abortive Portuguese attack, viz., under Ferreira Belliago in 1632. They might possibly be the tombs of some heroes who took part in the repulsion of the Portuguese on this last occasion. That anyone buried in the seventeenth century had anything to do with the re-establishment of Islam is, of course, palpably absurd; for although one at least of the Portuguese armadas contained a *posse* of padres with missionary intention, the faith of Mahomed was never in peril. Possibly Pyrard refers to some of the older tombs in the same locality.

days thereafter, if so minded; for there is no fixed time; and, moreover, they abstain from chewing betel.

Such as are slain in battle against men of a contrary faith are buried without ceremony, in their own clothes, on the spot where they have been slain. No prayers are said for them, for they are deemed sanctified and blessed, and are called *Chaydes*,[1] and in fact are invoked in time of affliction.

They never transport a corpse from one island to another; even were it the king, he is buried where he dies.[2]

If, haply, one of them dies at sea, the body is washed and prepared for burial, with all the ceremonies aforesaid; it is placed in a coffin fixed upon three or four pieces of Candou wood, so that it may continue afloat, and then is cast into the sea. In the coffin they put some money, according to their means, with a writing mentioning the religion of the dead man, and entreating those who may meet with it to take the money and to bury the body honourably: this have I seen done many a time.

CHAPTER XIII.

Of the form of their apparel, of their manner of living, ordinary exercises, and other peculiar customs which they observe in their conduct.

As for their garments, see how they apparel themselves. First, the men bind all round their private parts a broad band of cloth, lest in coming or going, or in doing some work, these should be discovered. Over this they wear a small cotton cloth, dyed blue or red or some other colour, reaching only as far as the knees. Above this they wear a large cloth of cotton, or silk, if they be at all rich and well off; this reaches to the ankles, and is belted with a fine square ker-

[1] Ar. *Shahíd* (*i.e.*, "martyrs"); M. *Sahídu*. [2] See *infra*, ch. xxiii.

chief, embroidered with gold and silk; this is folded in three, drawn round the loins, and tied in front. Then, for braver adornment, they add a little piece of silk of divers colours, fine as crape or gauze, and short, not reaching further than the mid thigh; and after all this they gird themselves with

Young Girl and old Man.

a large silken sash, like their turbans, with pretty fringes, the ends whereof they let hang down in front.[1] In this

[1] Compare Mr. Bell's description of the Maldivian male attire at the present day:—"The ordinary dress of the men consists of short drawers (M. *haruválu*), a cloth wrapped round the waist, after the Sinhalese fashion (M. *mundu*), and a plain handkerchief twisted over the head (M. *rumá*). On board their vessels, and in foreign parts, some don a

girdle, which serves them for a purse, they keep their money and their betel on the left side, while on the right they carry their knife, by which they lay great store; every one carries it, not excepting even the king himself. These knives are exceedingly well made, all of excellent steel,—for they have not the invention of blending iron with steel. Men of means have the haft and sheath all of carved and worked silver. At the upper end of the sheath is a silver buckle, from which hangs a little chain, also of silver, to which is attached a tooth-pick and an ear-pick, and other little implements. Other folks, who cannot afford to have them so costly, use a sheath of carved wood and a haft of fish-bone, either of whale or other marine animal: for they like not to wear the bone of any land animal. They are careful of these knives, and would not consider themselves to be properly dressed without their knife at the waist; and there is none, how vile or mean soever, but wears it: it is their means of defence.[1] Other arms none is allowed to bear. It is only the soldiers and

thin shirt, generally white (M. *kuru libás*), and Turkish waistcoat (M. *saduriya*), which, with the peculiar coarse blue waistcloth edged with red, and the red handkerchief, mark a Maldivian at once among other races. The upper orders, and those who have been the Haj, wear, besides the waistcloth (particularly on Fridays, when attending mosque), a kind of long dressing gown (M. *digu libás*), reaching to the ankles, somewhat similar to those worn by Mahomedan priests in Ceylon. The dress of the men, as minutely described by Pyrard, must formerly have been richer and more elaborate, including the use of turbans, silk scarfs, silver chains, and fancy knives. No Maldivian not of the priesthood now ventures to wear a turban (M. *fagudi*) in the royal presence or island, this head-dress being retained by the Sultan exclusively" (*Report*, 55). See also Christopher (*T. Bom. Geo. Soc.*, i, 58). For Ibn Batuta's description, see App. A.

[1] "Ordinary Maldive waist knives (*vali*), chastely inlaid with silver and mother-of-pearl, leave nothing to be desired in portability and serviceableness, whilst for shape and handsome finish the larger silver-mounted knife-dagger with ivory handle (*fiyohi*), worn exclusively by grandees and soldiers, is unique. Knife handles are carved from *kuradi* wood, black coral (*endiri*), and whale's teeth (*bodu-mas dai*)" (Bell, *Report*, 88).

king's officers who may; nor they, indeed, save when they are in the service of the king at Malé, or elsewhere on his commissions. These have usually at their side a waved dagger called a *Cris*, which comes from Achen in Sumatra, from Java, and China. When they walk in the street they also bear a drawn sword in one hand, in the other a buckler or else a javelin. The soldiers have another peculiar mark, and that is, they wear their hair long, done up all together and tied in a large bunch.[1] Their chief bravery is to wear all around their waist many silver chains; and every person of any substance, be he man or woman, boy or girl, likes to have them, but always in number according to their means and quality. In these they lay out all their treasure, and usually destine them to pay the expense of their obsequies. But it is only the great nobles or foreigners who may wear them above their clothes and let them be seen: all others wear them concealed beneath; yet they must needs have them to talk about and to display in private. The rest of the body from the waist upwards is left naked,—I mean by the common folk; for the gentlemen of quality do not so; and yet on festival days they put on their doublets and gowns of cotton or silk, fastened with buttons of gilded copper; for they durst not have them of gold, that being for the king only.[2] These gowns are of divers colours, but all have borders of white and blue. The sleeves reach only to the elbow; for they say that if they were to come to the wrist, as with us, they would not have the free use of their arms. Along with these are worn coloured drawers, close-fitting and covering the body from the waist to the ankles, where they are fastened also

[1] Mr. Bell states that the men now, without exception, shave the head (*Report*, p. 55). The long hair of the soldiers described by Pyrard would seem to be a relic of Sinhalese custom. Every Sinhalese man, even at the present day, wears his hair long, and tied in a bunch at the back of the head.

[2] The wearing of gold ornaments is still confined to the Sultan and those of royal blood.

with gilt buttons. The nobles don these doublets and gowns every day. There are others, a great number, who on festival days wear no doublets, but use another sort of bravery, which is this: they pound some sandal and camphor, or other odorous wood, on very smooth stones brought from the mainland; that they mix with distilled essence of flowers, and then with the paste so made cover all the body from the waist upwards, describing with their finger all sorts of patterns, according to their fancy. They appeared to me like slashed and patterned doublets; and the scent was very pleasing. Sometimes they paste on themselves flowers, the fairest and sweetest to be found. It is their wives and lady friends who deck them in this sort, figuring upon their backs such designs and flourishes as they fancy. This kind of bravery is exceedingly common; but they dare not present themselves in this guise before the king nor in his palace.[1]

Those who have been to Arabia, and have visited the sepulchre of Mahomet at Mecca, are held in high respect by all the world, whatever be their rank, and whether they be poor or rich; and, indeed, a great number of the poor have been there. These have peculiar privileges: they are called *Agy*[2]; and in order to be recognised and remarked among the others, they all wear very white cotton frocks, and on their heads little round bonnets, also white, and carry beads in their hands without crosses; and when they have not the means to maintain themselves in this attire, the king or the nobles supply them, and fail not to do so.

All wear on their heads turbans of red, or chequered of divers colours. Most people have these of silk; but such as cannot afford silk, of the finest cotton. The soldiers and officers of the king wear them arranged in a style not per-

[1] This practice seems to have died out. See below, ch. xxvii, where it seems this mode of adornment was practised by the Samorin of Calicut.

[2] According to Professor Robertson Smith (Yule's *Glossary*, s. v. "Hadgee"), the correct Ar. for one who has made the pilgrimage is *ḥājj*; but the incorrect form *ḥājjī* is used by the Turks and Persians, and, as appears here, by the Maldivians.

mitted to others, most frequently tying round their heads the broidered kerchiefs of which I have spoken, and other things which the rest may not wear. Their hair, which is long like the women's here, is not concealed by the turban.

All go barefooted, and most often barelegged. Nevertheless, at their homes they use a kind of slippers or sandals[1] of wood; and when a person of greater quality comes to visit them, they put off these sandals and remain barefooted.

Maldive Woman.

As for the women, first of all they have a large coloured cloth of cotton or silk, which covers them from the waist to the ankles, and serves as a petticoat. Above this they wear a robe of taffetas, or of very fine cotton, but very long, reaching to the feet, and with blue and white borders. To give a notion of its shape, I cannot better describe this robe than

[1] Called *mara vali*.

by comparing it to the chemises which the women here wear. It is a little open round the neck, and fastened with two little gilt buttons, and likewise open at the throat in front, but no further at the breast; so that when they want to give suck to their babes, they have to lift these robes, without, however, making any exposure below, which is saved by the petticoat cloth of which I have spoken. Their arms are charged with heavy bracelets of silver, sometimes from the wrist up to the elbow; some of them have them mixed with tin, chiefly the poor, while the rest have them of fine and massive silver, in such sort that some of them carry as much as three or four pounds of silver on their arms. In addition, they have the silver chains round the waist, which are not seen, save sometimes when the robe is very transparent. Around the neck all women of means and quality have a number of gold chains, to which are threaded some pieces of gold money from Arabia or the mainland.[1]

Their hair is plaited, and sometimes they add a false peruke to make the bunch seem larger: this is of men's hair, for the women never cut theirs; it is covered with a gold netting, which the great ladies stud with precious stones. At their ears they wear as rich pendants as they can afford, but of a different sort from those worn in these parts; for mothers bore their daughters' ears at a tender age, not only at one place in the lobe, but at several places all along the cartilage, and insert cotton thread to keep the holes open, in

[1] "Like the Sinhalese, the women wear a waistcloth, generally of native manufacture, coarse in texture, the ground of a chocolate colour, relieved by black and white stripes (M. *féliya*). The upper part of the body is covered by a loose-fitting, red-coloured jersey reaching to the knees, short sleeved, and edged at the neck with silver tinsel lace (M. *libás*), whilst round the high-worn *kondé* is twisted a handkerchief matching the *libás* in colour, the *tout ensemble* forming a very becoming and picturesque costume. A profusion of bangles, with necklace, ear-rings, and other ornaments, deck the person. The use of gold trinkets is no longer rigidly restricted to women of quality" (Bell, *Report*, 55).

order, when they grow up, to fix therein golden clasps, to the number of twenty-four in the two ears. The front of the clasp is commonly adorned with a precious stone or a pearl. Besides these, there is in the lobe of the ear another pendant of a peculiar shape. When the women walk in the street by night or day, though it is but rarely they go forth by day, they wear a veil over the head. This, however, they take off in the presence of the queens and princesses, or even of ladies of higher quality than themselves,—not, however, before men, nor even before the king: on the contrary, that is the time to conceal themselves, when they think they are observed of men.[1]

I have said that they wear gold chains at the neck and precious stones in their ear-pendants; but it is to be remarked that no one, be it man or woman, saving a prince or a great noble, would dare to wear either rings or precious stones, bracelets or necklets, ear-rings or gold chains, without the permission of the king in the case of men, or of the queens in the case of women, and granted by letter. This permission is bought for ready money, unless given gratuitously, as is often the case to women. Only the queens and princesses may wear bracelets and rings of gold on the arms or legs; but other ornaments they may use of gold: and although the toe-rings and anklets may be of silver, such may not be worn but on payment of a certain sum, saving by those of high quality and birth; nor may any but the queens wear rings except on the thumb. The princesses and great ladies may wear them on the middle finger and the other two, with permission, but the men only on the thumb. So each knows his own rank and quality, and what he may use in

1 "The liberty enjoyed by the women is remarkable. Though their apartments are considered strictly private, they are not kept from the view of strangers, nor now debarred from openly walking abroad unveiled in the daytime. Even now (however) Maldivian ladies of the upper classes do not walk, but pay their visits in closed palanquins" (Bell, *Report*, 62).

the way of ornament, himself and his wife, and there is no confusion in these matters. For instance, if any man's wife who was not aforetime accustomed to much finery began to adorn herself more, or a man were to wear finger-rings,—albeit in this they were not exceeding their rights,—they would be taxed more heavily for that, excepting the officers of the king and of the queens, who pay no tax, and excepting also the inhabitants of Malé.[1] These, however, are subject to other charges and to many extraordinary expenses. Strangers and their wives have the privilege of dressing as they please, and of wearing any ornaments or bravery without permission, in like manner as the great princes and the king himself; and in many other things I have remarked that strangers have many rights and privileges denied to the natives of the country. So, too, the Pandiare, the Naybes, and Catibes, as well of Malé as of the other islands, many dress and adorn themselves as they will, and are not constrained by laws as others are in this respect. But to return to our discourse: the women are careful in dressing and adorning themselves with propriety, in bathing every day, in anointing their hair with scented oil, and in perfuming themselves. They have also a custom of colouring their feet and finger-nails red. It is the country notion of beauty. It is done with the sap of a certain tree,[2] and endures till the nail grows again, and then they do it afresh. And in truth they seemed to be pretty and engaging enough, as much by reason that they are neatly dressed as that they are well formed, of good figures, and winsome ways; albeit they are of an olive skin, for the most part, although you will find many brunettes, and many quite fair, just as in these parts.[3]

[1] The people of Málé are still free of taxation (Bell, *Report*, 67; Christopher, *T. Bom. Geo. Soc.*, i, 60).

[2] The juice of the Eastern privet, *Lawsonia* (M. *híná*), taken from the leaf; Pyrard mentions it later as *innafa* (*híná-fai*); *fai* = "leaf".

[3] "The women are short, usually of a more olive colour than the men, much resembling, in this respect, the fair-skinned Kandyans, with

The people at large, as well men as women, have many peculiar customs in their ways of life and deportment. First, they never eat together unless they are of the same quality and condition: it is dishonourable even to be at the same table with an inferior: so they never meet to feast together except at the religious festivals already described. If, however, they wish to entertain their friends, they cause to be prepared at their houses a large dish containing many courses, which is served up on a large round table with a cover of taffetas, and sent to the house of the person to be entertained: this is esteemed a great honour. When they are at home, they like not that others should see them eat, wherefore they retire to the back of the house, and let down all their screens and curtains towards the front, so as not to be seen. They say prayers before meals, and likewise before going forth. They have no other table but the floor of the house, covered with a neat little mat, on which they sit cross-legged. Linen they use not at all; but, to avoid soiling their mats, they use large banana leaves, whereon they place their food, and others in front of these to serve as ashets.[1] They take their food so nicely that they spill nothing, not even a drop of water, though they wash the mouth before and after dinner in basins served on purpose. The vessel used is of earthenware like that of Fayance,[2] fashioned in the native style, and imported from Cambaye; or else it is of China porcelain, which is very common, and used by almost all. But they use not any plate of earthenware or of porcelain, saving one kind of round box, polished and lacquered, with a cover of the same; it is manufactured in the island. When closed, this box is covered with a square piece of silk of

oval-shaped faces, regular features, and shapely figures. Clean and healthy in appearance, they are generally good-looking, some decidedly pretty" (Bell, *Report*, 55).

[1] I may be permitted to use the common Scotch form of the French *assiette*.

[2] *I.e.*, the coloured ware called after Faenza, 18 m. S.W. of Ravenna.

about the same size, which is worked in various styles of needlework and of all colours.[1] Even the poorest use these covered dishes, for the boxes cost but little. Their use is by reason of the ants, which exist in such wondrous multitude that they swarm everywhere, and it is difficult to keep anything from being incontinently covered with them. The people are so careful in their feeding, that they would not taste any food upon which has dropped a fly or an ant, or any other little creature, or the least dirt; in such case they would give it to the birds. They would not think of giving it to the poor, for they give to them nothing but what they would care to eat themselves, and prepared as for themselves. On this subject I have remarked that when the poor come to their doors, they make them enter the house and enjoy the same cheer as themselves, holding them to be as much the servants of God as they are. But to return to their ways of life, and to the utensils used at table. The greatest nobles have no other vessels, nor more costly than the rest, and use only the one already described. Although they could well afford vessels of gold and silver if they liked, yet their law forbids it, and for that reason they use them not. If haply their vessel should be a little cracked, they eat no longer thereout, putting it aside as polluted. No spoons are used either for eating rice or honey, nor even for liquids such as broth or gruels, neither there nor in the rest of India, but everything is taken with the fingers, which they are accustomed to do so neatly and dexterously that nothing is soiled. It is with them the greatest possible incivility, and very blameworthy, to let drop anything while

[1] These lacquered wooden dishes (*kurandi*) are mentioned by Mr. Bell (*Report*, 88). He has had a set of cups, saucers, and plates of this work presented to him, and reports them pretty. Although Pyrard (*v. s.*, p. 114) mentions a potter caste, the Maldivians seem to have done little in this line, earthenware being among the imports from Portuguese India (Correa, *Lendas*, i, 341; Bell, *Report*, 97). See also Ibn Bat., App. A.

eating. During the meal none present would dare to spit or cough: he must rise and go out to do that. Nothing they abhor, or consider so indecent and undignified, as spitting. In eating they never use the left hand, by reason that it is used for another purpose. They like to eat a half-ripe coconut when they begin their meal, and to drink its water, deeming it very healthy, and a laxative for the bowels. For the rest, all eat with much greediness and in great haste, holding it the best manners not to tarry at their food. Moreover, if they are (eating) in company they utter not a word one to another. To drink during a meal is bad manners: they never do so, and mock us for the habit; but after eating their bellyful, they drink once. Their commonest beverage is coco-milk, or coco-wine drawn the same day. They have also two other sorts of a more choice nature; the one is a warm drink composed of water and coco-honey with some pepper (much used in their other food, and called *Pasme*[1]) and another grain called *Cahoa*[2]; the other is cold and more delicate, being made of coco-sugar dissolved in water. But these drinks are for the king and the great lords, or for the solemn banquets at their festivals. They drink out of copper cups, exceeding handsome and craftily worked, which also have covers. After meat, when they have washed, a portion of betel is served in place of dessert, for fruits are served along with the meat. Most part of them have no fixed hour for their meals; they eat at all hours of the day when the fancy takes them, even the great lords and ladies.[3] The

[1] The M. is *asé-mirus;* the Sin. for pepper, generally, is *miris*, the variety being shown by an affix. Mr. Bell thinks Pyrard's initial "p" is an error; he cannot otherwise account for it.

[2] *I.e.*, coffee; Ar. *kahwa*. For the varied history of the word, see Yule's *Glossary*. Coffee does not grow at the Maldives; this would therefore be the real berry of Mocha or Yemen, where alone it was grown in quantity in those days, and not Ceylon coffee reshipped from Aden, as the most genuine of our Mocha is said now to be.

[3] Mr. Bell confirms this, and adds: "The usual meal of the natives consists of rice, often only half boiled, mixed with a few chopped

women and girls prepare the meals and look to the cooking, and not the men. The greatest insult that can be passed upon a man is to call him *cisdy*,[1]—that is to say, "cook"; and if any are found to be addicted to it (and there are some, chiefly among the grandees, who find that they can cook better than the women), they are mocked and despised of all men, in such sort that they are looked upon as women, rather than men: they even durst not associate but with women, nor engage in other exercises; so no difficulty is made in leaving them with the females.[2]

When they require to slay any animal for food there is much mystery in the matter. They cut the throat, turning themselves towards the sepulchre of Mahomet, and say their prayers, and after quitting their hold of the animal, or throwing it down, they touch it not again till it be quite dead; and should any touch it sooner, they would cast away the flesh and would not eat of it. Nor is this all: the throat must be cut at a certain place only, otherwise none would eat of it; nor does everyone know of that place, but chiefly it is known to the priests and Moudins. They who take in hand to slay an animal should be elders, and not boys: they should be fathers of children themselves. I have been amused to observe, at the common business of killing a

chillies, a little fish, 'fish sugar', and scraped coco-nut. This they consume in silence, even when eating in company, and with a haste that savours of greediness. A draught of water closes the repast" (*Report*, 56).

[1] "The contemptuous term *sídí*, applied to men who descend to this menial service, retains its old force" (Bell, *Report*, 56). The word is not to be derived from a Sinhalese source; Mr. Bell is inclined to think that it means merely "negro slave", the term "Sídí" being applied generally in Western India to East African negroes. The Zanzibar negroes on our men-of-war are still known as "Sidi-boys". See Yule and Burnell, *Glossary*, s. v. "Seedy".

[2] The suggestion here, which is obvious, seems to confirm Mr. Bell's derivation; the negro slaves at the Maldives would be generally, or at least frequently, eunuchs.

fowl, how they run about a whole island to find a man who knows how to do it,—ay, and who will be willing, for they refrain from the job as much as they can.[1] When they skin a fowl they throw away the skin, neck, back, and entrails, and eat the rest.

In all their actions they are scrupulous and superstitious, even in the smallest matters. After sleeping, whether by day or night, they fail not, as soon as they awake, to bathe their eyes and face, and rub them with oil, putting some black stuff[2] upon the eyelashes and eyebrows; nor would they dare to speak or to say good-day to anyone ere they had done all that. They are very particular in cleaning their teeth, and are further of opinion that the red colour of the betel and areca, which they are continually chewing, is good for them; so that they all have red teeth by reason of the betel-chewing, and they deem it a beauty. They carry betel always on them in the folds of their waist, and it would be a dishonour to a man to be found wanting it; it is the custom, when they meet one another on the road, each to give of his own. They bathe many times a day, not only when they list, but as their religion requires; and when they enter a temple they bathe the extremities, as I have said: this, in their language, is called *voulos*.[3] So, too, after making water, or otherwise obeying nature, they wash their parts with the left hand, or else bathe the whole body (this is called *Innan*[4]), with divers forms and ceremonies proper to the several festivals. So, when they bathe in public, as is their wont, it is well seen why they are bathing,—as, for example, when they have had the society of their wives, whether by day or night, you see them plunge the head three times under water: this is exceed-

[1] A probable, though very slight, trait of former Buddhism.

[2] See also Ibn Bat. They call it *galadun*.

[3] Ar. *wuḍu* or *wuzu*. "This consists in washing the hands, mouth, nostrils, face, arms, as high as the elbow, the right first, each three times; and then the upper part of the head, the beard, ears, neck, and feet each once" (Lane, *Ar. Soc.*, 11).

[4] M. *hinán*, to bathe; Sin. *nánda*.

ing indecent. When they are seated in any place, others must take care to pass behind them, for to do otherwise would be held a great indignity, and would bring about some untoward result; but if it is necessary to go in front of another, the one who does so crouches full low, and holds his hands down to the ground, saying *Assa*,[1] as who should say, "Be not displeased." It is a grave indiscretion for one seated in the presence of others to swing the legs; they are much offended at it, and hold it to be a sign of bad luck and a piece of bad manners. So, when they set out on any voyage, they like not to meet or touch any person; and if aught untoward or unfortunate should happen, they will lay it at the door of him who touched them. Above all, when they go a-fishing, one must not salute them nor give them good-day.[2] From sunset on Thursday until three or four o'clock on the following day, they suffer none to take anything from their houses; should it be their greatest friend or their father who would borrow anything, they would not lend it then, nor would they give up anything which another had sent to demand, even if it did not belong to them; nevertheless, they make no business about receiving anything or admitting anything to their houses at that time. I have noted as worthy of praise that when they have disputes and quarrels, or are at enmity, they refrain above all things from abusing the food and drink which they may have received from one another; if any should do so, all would vent their anger upon him.

When at sea, if they are caught by contrary winds, by calms, or by storms, they make vows to him who rules the winds, who is called not God, but King; and there is no island

[1] Probably a contraction of the Sin. *avasara*, "leave" or "permission", which word is used on precisely similar occasions in Ceylon. Mr. Bell says the expression seems to have died out, at least in the northern atolls, the modern phrase being *amuru-devvá*, "grant leave".

[2] See the interesting collection of Sinhalese omens on commencing a work or a journey, given by S. Jayatilaka Mudaliyar in *Ceylon As. Soc. Jour.*, vii, 147-161; and Mr. Bell's paper on Sin. customs connected with Paddy cultivation, in the same journal for 1883.

but has a *siare*,[1] as they call it, which is a place dedicated to the King of the winds, in a corner of the island remote from the world, where those who have escaped from danger

[1] The title of "king", in place of "god" of the winds, is, no doubt, a concession to the monotheistic principles of Islam; and the passage gives a curious insight into the primitive worship of the islanders. It may first be observed that the powers of wind and sea are separately worshipped, the Maldivian sailors having to contend not only with monsoons but with currents; next, that the stage of culture when the sea and wind are themselves the objects of worship has been passed, and personal, if not anthropomorphic, deities have been conceived. As to the character of the worship of the two kings, the author is not so precise as might be wished. The proceedings at the *siare* (M. *Ziyára*, Ar. *Ziyarat*, "visitation", in orthodox Mah. usage meaning, the visiting of sacred places, as opposed to the Haj, and vulgarly the place so visited) are by way of thanksgiving for safety, offered, it would seem, exclusively to the king of the winds; the worship of the king of the sea is deprecatory, and it does not appear whether it is paid at the *siare* or elsewhere.

The worship of wind and sea is ancient and extensive. Cicero writes: "Ergo imbres, nimbi, procellæ, turbines Dii putandi. Nostri quidem duces, mare ingredientes, immolare hostiam fluctibus consueverunt" (*De Nat. Deor.*, iii, 20). Thus would a successful voyage be secured while the elements were still uncertain. Both this method, and the propitiatory ceremonies as employed by Mahomedans during a storm, are well exemplified by Père Dan in his description of the Barbary pirates of the sixteenth century. The pirates' wives would light a little fire, in which they burned incense and myrrh; then they cut the throat of a cock, sprinkling the blood in the fire. They scattered the feathers to the wind and tore the body to pieces, casting most of it into the sea (Dan, *Hist. de Barbarie*, 1637, liv. III, c. iii). The pirates themselves appeased a storm as follows: first they sacrificed a sheep, disembowelling it alive, casting one-half the body into the sea on the starboard side, the other on the port. If this were unsuccessful, they would next pour two barrels of oil on the water, one on each side of the ship. This, as recent experiments have proved, would be efficacious for a time; but when the storm again prevailed, they placed lighted candles on all their cannon, allowing them to burn out. This failing, one resource only remained, never resorted to but in the last extremity; they constrained the wretched Christians, chained to the galley-benches, to make vows to the Virgin, St. Nicholas, or some other saint, they cared not which! (*ib.*, liv. III, c. vi). In no part of the world has this sea-worship been so strongly marked as on the Guinea coast of Africa. Bosman says: "When it rages, and hinders us bringing our goods on

come to make offering daily of little boats and ships fashioned on purpose, and filled with perfumes, gums, flowers, and odoriferous woods. The perfumes are set on fire, the little boats are cast upon the sea, and float till they are

shore, when no ships have been there for a long time, and they impatiently wait for them,—on these occasions they make great offerings to it, by throwing into it all sorts of goods. But the priests do not much encourage this sort of sacrificing, by reason there happens no remainder to be left for them" (*Pinkerton*, vol. xvi, p. 500). Snelgrave describes the sacrifice of an old woman, who was fortunately picked up by the English boats before the sharks got her (*New Account of Guinea*, pp. 101-105). The same practices survived to our own day: "In Dahome the Ocean has a special priest, who, at stated times, repairs to the beach, and there begs the Ocean god not to be boisterous, throwing in rice and corn, oil and beans, cloth, cowries, and other valuables. Occasionally the king of Dahome offers a human victim, who is carried in a hammock to a canoe, and thence delivered to the sharks" (Burton, *Dahome*, i, 141). The races of India proper are so little addicted to navigation, that they contribute few instances of this worship; we find, however, that at Carwar, on sight of the new moon in August, the effigy of Ganesa "was carried in procession to the river's side and thrown into the river, upon which all rivers which have bars are opened for navigation" (Alex. Hamilton, *New Acct.*, i, 274-5). Further east, among the Lampongs of Sumatra, we find the most ancient and simple adoration of the sea itself. When the inland natives behold it for the first time, they make it an offering of cakes and sweetmeats, deprecating its power of doing them mischief (Marsden, *Sumatra*, 256).

The sacrifice of a model boat, filled with perfumes, gums, etc., and set on fire, described by Pyrard as a thank-offering, is, with the Malays of Larut, resorted to, in almost identical form, as a means of enticing away the evil spirits from a sick person (see *Medical Hist. of the Laroot Field Force*, by Surgeon-Major Davie, in App. to *Army Med. Dep. Rep.*, 1876, quoted in *J. R. A. S.*, new series, vol. x, p. 202, note 2.

The sacrifice at the launch of a new ship still survives at the Maldives, as described by Pyrard. "On such occasions a small vessel, three or four feet long, being decked out with flags, and having samples of the various fruits of the island, is set adrift; should it be a boat newly built, other ceremonies are observed, accompanied with feasting, music, etc. The miniature vessel is decorated with flowers, and her gunwales are hung with fruits, for which, as soon as she enters the water, there is a general scramble" (Christopher, in *T. Bom. Geo. Soc.*, i, 75). Exactly the same offering of a miniature canoe is made to Ganga Bandera, a

burned, for they too catch the fire, and this, say they, that the king of the winds may accept them. So, when they have any difficulty in launching their ships or galleys, they kill some cocks and hens, and cast them into the sea in face of the ship or boat which they desire to launch. Likewise they believe in a king of the sea, to whom in like sort they make prayers and ceremonies while on voyages; or when they go a-fishing, they dread above all things to offend the kings of the winds and of the sea. So, too, when they are at sea, they durst not spit nor throw anything to windward for fear lest he should be offended, and with like intent they never look abaft. When I was in their boats, they were concerned to see that I observed not these superstitions. All boats, barques, and vessels are dedicated to these powers of the winds and of the sea; and, indeed, they treat their boats with as much respect as their temples, keeping them exceeding clean, and abstaining from all filthy or indecent actions on board. Likewise they hold in honour the kings of the other elements (as they call them), as him of war, and pay them all great ceremony.

They lay great store by certain charms, called *Tauide*,[1]

malignant river-demon in Ceylon (*Pridham*, p. 165; *cf.* translation of the poem "Gangárobaniya", in *Ceylon Friend*, 1879-80, p. 282). And generally, see *Qanoon e Islam*, pp. 31, 99-101; Barbot, in *Churchill*, vol. v, pp. 143, 344, 375).

Since writing the above, Mr. Bell informs me that some of this demon worship exists in the southern atolls, though the natives are loth to give him information on the subject. He has, however, obtained the names of the following ten devils:—1, Gharaguginni Rannamári (the "king of the winds"); 2, Nabajaháge; 3, Aku-isanja' javija; 4, Lajjígavisa-navi; 5, Gálígóti; 6, Jajjálu; 7, Habbóráza; 8, Dihabórajañí; 9, Kosmoyázabadu; 10, Laggitúḍí. One of the last nine is probably the king of the sea.

[1] M. *tavídu*, Ar. *ta' wíz*. Sorcery is, with the Maldivians, *faḍita* (Sin. *paṇḍita*), "the learned (science)". Mr. Bell (*J. Ceyl. Br. R. A. S.*, vii, 119) gives two examples of these *mantras* from the southern atolls, remarking that they come under the Sanskrit category of *Stambhana*, or of *Vibhíshana*, *i.e.*, intended to procure illicit intercourse and effect discord. The

which they carry under their dress, enclosed in little boxes, which the rich have made of gold or silver. They wear these either on their arms, neck, or waist, or even at the feet,

first runs as follows: "Gada istiri vari tura' kurákan haivakaru abaku de míhunge rúfa kurahai *hadduru harruḷi nuvá gihí badili elagoḍí* abu gahani." Translation: "To completely estrange a desirable woman (from her husband), make a teak nail (and) an image of both persons, (mutter) 'hadduru harruḷi nuvá gihí badili elagoḍí' [unintelligible], and drive in the nail." The second is as follows: "Gada istiriye' liame karhi male' fari nuvanís kaḍágen au vaḷie' hanulaigen mi malu effurhu *Al Kadr Sura* lie ane' furhumati *Vajahatu* lie mi malu rúfa kurahá váhaka vará oḷun lie *Al Rahmán Sura* huswáden lie' vá' rónu' fas tan bede rakas boḍe' Katiláeige lein kaḷiko' dumarhí bávvai hikkai tin duvas véinái nagaigen gos múdu aḷani kakú fenu eḷi nama balai fonavani fúḷu fenu eḷi nama audei." Translation: "Write (the name of) a desirable woman; pluck an unopened bud of the screw-pine flower; sharpen a new knife; on one side of this flower write *Al Kadr Sura;* on the other side write *Vajahatu;* make an image out of this flower; write particulars of the horoscope; write *Al Rahmán Sura* from beginning to end; tie (the image) in five places with left-hand (twisted) coir; cut the throat of a bloodsucker (lizard); smear its blood (on the image); place it on a loft; dry it for three days; (then) take it and enter the sea—if you go in knee-deep (she) will send a message; if you go in to the waist (she) will come."

The *tavídu* of the Maldives correspond in all respects to the *huniyam* of Ceylon. In the *Jour. Cey. Br. R. A. S.*, vol. vii, p. 116, Mr. Louis Nell gives a photograph (actual size, about two inches) of a *huniyam* image, which was discovered in a little tin box in a hollow tree. A most valuable account of them is given in the same journal for 1865, by Dandris de Silva Mudaliyar, under the title "Sinhalese Demonology". The Mudaliyar there writes:—"*Koḍivina*, or *Huniyam*, is the name given to evils of whatever kind inflicted by the agency of charms . . . . There are said to be 84,000 (charms) of every degree of malignity, most of which, more or less, contribute to bring to an untimely death the person affected by this influence, though that event may be deferred for many years."

Of the Maldivians' skill in charms, Barbosa writes:—"As gentes dellas nao tem armas, e sao homens fracos, mas muito engenhosos, e sobre tudo grandes encantadores" (*Noticias das Naçoes Ultramarinas*, tom. ii, p. 352, Lisbon, 1812). This passage, unfortunately, appears in Lord Stanley's *Barbosa*, Hakl. Soc., p. 164, in this disguise: "The inhabitants are ill-formed and weak, but are very ingenious and charming."

according to the subject of distress; for they serve all purposes, as well offensive as defensive, as well for loving as for gaining love, for raising hatred, for making well or making sick. The magicians and sorcerers sell them for money, and say that they bring good luck, and will heal or preserve one from many a sickness; and in their sicknesses they have but few remedies, and then by recourse to these magicians and sorcerers, who are their only doctors; they have none other. Likewise they all believe that evil is brought by the devil to harass them withal, and that he is the sole cause of death and sickness. They invoke him, accordingly, and offer him flowers, and prepare a banquet of all sorts of meats and drinks, which they place in a secret spot and leave to be wasted, unless peradventure some poor folk take them away. With the same design, they kill some cocks and hens, turning themselves towards the sepulchre of Mahomet, and then leave them, praying the devil to accept them, and to take himself off and leave the sick person at ease: they call this sorcery *Cauuery*.[1]

But since I have spoken of their cures by sorcery, it seems needful to tell what are their sicknesses, and then I shall add something of the natural remedies which they practise. Fever is very common there, and is called by them *homan*[2]; but it is most dangerous to strangers sojourning there, whom it does for in but a few days. I have already spoken of it from my own experience, having seen many of my comrades die of it, and having had it myself. It is

[1] In ch. xix, more correctly *Quenuery* (M. *Kanvcri*). "This is the savage theory of demoniacal possession, which has been for ages, and still remains, the dominant theory of disease and inspiration among the lower races. Disease being accounted for by the attack of spirits, it naturally follows that to get rid of these spirits is the proper means of cure" (Tylor, *Prim. Cult.*, second edition, ii, 124, 125; see, too, p. 127, and the authorities there given; also Knox, *Ceylon*, p. 78).

[2] Ar. *hummá*; yet at p. 83 he calls Málé fever *Malé ons* (M. *hung*, Sin. *una*).

known throughout all the Indies under the name of "Maldive fever". Every ten years there comes a sickness called *cariuadiri*,[1] in the presence of which they abandon one another as if it were the plague. It is like the chicken-pox which our children have, and of this malady many die. The eye-sickness[2] is common enough, and you see great numbers of people blind by it, and most of them have short sight. Often, too, when they have been for long in the sun during the heat of the day, when the sun sets they cannot see at all, though they are near a fire or a light, even were it a hundred torches: it does not otherwise harm them. This evil or ailment is called *rosnans*.[3] To cure it they cook the liver of a cock, writing over it certain words and charms, and swallow it at sunset. My comrades and I were much troubled by it at times, till at length, being apprised of this recipe, we took a cock's liver, rejecting the charms, to see if it would serve us, and found that it cured us as it cured them, without the use of their sorceries. They suffer much from the itch, which they call *caz*[4]; but they cure it with coco-nut oil. They are also greatly troubled with ringworm, and have no cure for it, for there are some whose bodies are nearly covered with it. These diseases come from the quantity of salt fish they eat, and by reason that nearly all their food is salted only by being steeped in sea-water. In winter, when the rains are continuous, they still go barefooted, and then there attaches to their feet and between the toes a kind of worm, generated in the mud, causing pustules and tumours; and these, when they burst, raise ulcers, which impede their walking. These worms are called in their

[1] *I.e.*, small-pox; M. *karhivaduri*. Mr. Bell relates that on small-pox breaking out among the crew engaged at the wreck of s.s. *Seagull*, on the island Gaufaru, in 1879, the natives fled *en masse* to another island (*Report*, 8).

[2] Ophthalmia.

[3] M. *róná* (Bell). This is night-blindness, a well-known tropical ailment. The *roshuwandu* of Chr. is the appropriate medicine.

[4] M. *kas*, Hind. *khaj*, Sin. *kushta*.

language *Quilla panis*,[1] that is to say, "dirt worms". In the other parts of the body, too, they are much troubled with worms. All alike have the spleen enlarged, and besides that, they are subject to having it obstructed, with the abdomen distended and tight, whereby they are much troubled. They are of opinion that this comes from the water of the islands, which is not good; and from the same cause they get the fever. This malady they call *Oncory*.[2] The cure they use for this, as for all other kinds of inflammation or local pain, is to apply large button-cauters to the swollen or painful part. This makes an issue and wound passing large, to which they apply cotton steeped in oil of cocos, whereby they get much relief. I have seen men thus burnt and cauterised in five or six places. As for me, when I was sick, I declined to let them practise this remedy upon me. As to ulcers, to which they are greatly subject, and chiefly on the legs, they cure them by putting over them copper plates, which entirely heal them, as I found by experience. Besides these remedies I have described, they have some recipes and compounds of their herbs and drugs for divers ailments, most of all for wounds, which they cure with great dexterity. Yet are they ignorant of the art of using bandages and linen for wounds, for they apply ointments only, as we do here to horses. Catarrhs and rheums annoy them betimes, as also gout in the bones. Venereal disease is not so common, albeit it is found, and is cured with China-wood,[3] without sweating or anything else. This disease they call *farangui baescour*,[4] from its coming to them from Europe, whose

[1] M. *kila fani* (kilá, "earth", *fani*, "worms"); *cf.* Sin. *panuwa*, "worm".

[2] See *supra*, p. 84.

[3] *Bois de la Chine;* elsewhere he writes *bois d'Eschine*. It was formerly called *China radix*, but latterly *Smilax China* (Linn.); also vulgarly *chine* and *squine*. "A red and spungious Indian root, good against the gout" (Cotgrave); Linschoten has a long chapter upon it, and asserts its virtues for both these diseases (*Hakl. Soc.*, i, 239; ii, 107-12).

[4] *Cf.* Ar. *bāsūr*, "piles".

inhabitants they call by a common name, *farangui*, or *frangui*, from the French, the most renowned people of the West.[1] I have remarked that they know not what it is to suffer from toothache: and this seems to be caused by their habit of chewing betel, which strengthens the gums; and, indeed, by adopting their practice, I never had toothache there, though I have always suffered much from it elsewhere.

In nursing their babes, they have some peculiar customs and habits, which I have not observed elsewhere. As soon as their children are born, they bathe them in cold water six times in the day,[2] and then rub them with oil, which they continue a long while; moreover, as often as they obey the calls of nature they bathe their parts with water, just as if they were grown persons. Mothers nurse their children themselves, and would not think of letting them be suckled by others, not even the queens, for they are wont to say that all animals suckle their own young; yet they keep servants to tend, carry, and manage them. Besides the breast, they give

[1] Rivara (*Viagem de F. Pyrard*) is sarcastic:—"O auctor devia saber que tambem na Europa o nome desta molestia traz a sua derivação da mesma origem, privilegio que as outras nações não invejam por certo aos Francezes." Dr. Burnell (*Linsch.*, Hakl. Soc., i, 239, *note*) cites the evidence which goes to show that syphilis was not introduced into Europe by Columbus's crew *circa* 1493, that it was an old disease known both in Europe and Asia, and that only a fresh and notable outbreak occurred towards the end of the fifteenth century. He quotes the statement of Varthema, that he found the Samorin of Calicut suffering from it in 1505, and argues that he could not have got it from the Portuguese,—*sed quære*. Whether it existed in India before the Portuguese period I will not examine here; the name given to it at the Maldives shows that the natives there attributed it to the Portuguese; and this opinion is universally entertained in Ceylon and elsewhere in the East.

[2] *Cf.* Virg., *Æneid*, ix, 603:—

> "Durum ab stirpe genus, natos ad flumina primum
> Deferimus, sævoque gelu duramus et undis;"

and Claudian (*in Ruf.*, ii, 112), of the Germans—

> "Et quos nascentes explorat gurgite Rhenus."

them gruel of rice or millet, pounded and soaked, and then cooked with coco-milk and sugar[1]; most of them—that is, the poorer folk—give them bananas. They never swaddle them, but let them go free; nor have I ever seen them do otherwise. They put them to bed suspended in the air, in little cord beds, or little cradles, in which they are swung and rocked. About the age of nine months they begin to walk; at nine years they begin to be taught the studies and exercises of the country.

Their studies are to read and write, and to learn their Alcoran, and so to know how they have to live. Their letters are of three sorts[2]: the Arabic, with some letters and points

[1] This particular kind of kanji they call *furahani*.

[2] In other passages (*supra*, pp. 138, 142, and vol. ii, Introduction to Vocabulary) he speaks of the languages at the Maldives; this is the only reference to the characters used. The letters thirdly mentioned are perhaps the Tamil, those only being common to Ceylon and India. But there is little or no evidence of intercourse between the Maldives and the Tamil country; along the Malabar coast, with which the Maldives had so much to do, the language and alphabet used are almost universally Malayâlam; this latter, however, is not used at all in Ceylon. The matter must be left in doubt. The second character referred to is, doubtless, the *Divehi akuru*, or *dives ákuru*, "island letters", the more ancient alphabet of the Maldives. Christopher (*J. R. A. S.*, vol. vi) gave a plate showing the principal consonants and vowel-signs, which I reproduced in my paper on the Maldives (*J. R. A. S.*, new series, vol. x); but Mr. Bell says the alphabet has never been published in full, and M. d'Abbadie, who met Christopher on the Nubian coast, and had from him his own copy of the letters, tells me that this is so. "It consists of twenty-five letters", says Mr. Bell, "not counting duplicates, capable of some hundreds of vowel-mutations." "One peculiarity", says Christopher, "in the alphabet is, that some of the consonants change their form according to the various vowel-sounds with which they are united, the construction of the letter being altogether different." This character is clearly a modification of the old Vaṭṭeḷuttu of S. India, the parent also of the Sinhalese (see Dr. Burnell, in *Ind. Ant.*, i, 229; and *Elements of S. Indian Palæography*). It is largely used in the old Maldive tombstones and walls, and, from the appearance of these inscriptions, must have been in use long before the Arabic. It is not known now in the northern atolls except by the Faḍiyáru, and a few of the

which they have added to express their language; another, whose characters are peculiar to the Maldive language; and a third, which is common to Ceylon and to the greater part of India. They write their lessons on little tablets of wood, which are whitened, and when they have learned their lesson

learned at Málé, though said to be still prevalent in the south. In Christopher's time all orders for the southern atolls had to be transcribed into it, but, according to Mr. Bell, this practice is now discontinued. Like the Sinhalese and other Indian writing, it was written from left to right.

What form of writing Pyrard exactly means by the Arabic, "with some letters and points which they have added", is somewhat difficult to say. That the Arabic character in its entirety was, and is, used, is proved both by Mr. Christopher and Mr. Bell, and the former states that it is written in two different ways, the old and the new. Somewhere about Pyrard's time, however, a change was introduced, and an alphabet called the *Gabuli tána* came into vogue. It consists properly of eighteen letters, nine of which are the first nine Arabic numerals, the other nine being adopted from the *Divehi akuru.* It has also some auxiliary letters borrowed from the Arabic and Persian. Vowels are not inherent, but are supplied by diacritical strokes common to the Arabic. Unlike the *Divehi akuru*, these letters do not admit of being joined in writing. This alphabet will be found in *J. R. A. S.*, vol. vi; *J. A. S. Beng.*, v, p. 784; and *J. R. A. S.*, new series, vol. x. The mode of writing this character is from right to left, following the Arabic, as appears by the facsimiles of Maldive letters given by Christopher (*J. R. A. S.*, vol. vi), and by Mr. Bell (*Rep.*, plate, App., 78). Mr. Prinsep, however (*J. A. S. Beng.*, v, p. 784), gives a few words written by a Maldivian nakodah in this character, which are written from left to right, so it may be that in or for the southern atolls the modern character was then used in the old direction. A similar change was made by the Tagals of the Philippines, who formerly wrote from top to bottom, and after the Spanish conquest adopted the left-to-right method (see *De Morga*, Hakl. Soc., p. 295, *note*). It may be added that there are several kinds of *Tána* writing; Mr. Bell mentions the *Harha tána* and the *Defo' tána*, "but these are awkward and rarely employed." As, according to Christopher, the modern Arabic form and the *Gabuli tána* were introduced about the same time, after the expulsion of the Portuguese,—a date which is, I believe, fixed only by tradition,—and as it does not appear whether Pyrard knew Arabic writing, it must for the present remain doubtful whether the Arabic which he refers to was really Arabic or the mixed *Tána* alphabet.

they efface what they have written, and whiten them afresh, unless the writing is required to be preserved[1]; in that case, they write upon parchment made of the leaves of the tree *Macare queau*,[2] whose leaf is a fathom and a half long and a foot broad. They make books of it, which last as long or longer than ours, without decaying. In teaching their children to write, they use wooden boards made on purpose, well polished and joined, and spread thereon some fine, powdered sand; then they make the letters with a bodkin and bid them imitate them, effacing betimes what they have written, and using no paper for this purpose.[3] They all treat their masters with the same respect and honour as their own fathers, by reason whereof they may not contract marriage together, as though related in affinity. Among them are men who make a pursuit of study, and are esteemed vastly learned in their knowledge of the Alcoran, and in the ceremonies of their law: these are chiefly the Moudins, Catibes, or Naybes. These two offices are compatible; the Catibe may be a Naybe, and the Naybe a Catibe.

Mathematics are taught and much cultivated, especially astrology, which is studied by many, seeing that the astrologers are consulted at every turn. None would care to engage in any enterprise without previously taking their advice. And not only do they like to know their nativities and have their horoscopes taken, but also when they have to do any building, whether in wood or stone, they must go

[1] They whiten boards with a kind of clay (*marhi*), and write on this surface with ink of native manufacture; the whole washes off.

[2] M. *mâ-karhikeyo*, the "pandanus". Paper has now almost entirely superseded these leaves as writing material (Bell, *Report*, 70, 84). Pyrard gives a further description of this tree in his Treatise, in vol. ii.

[3] The Maldive children are still taught in the same manner; it is called *vorhufilâ liyaṇ*. The Sinhalese use the same, calling it *vëllé-liyanavâ*.

and inquire of the astrologer at what hour it were better to commence it, that so it may be done under a good constellation; and the same if it be the building of a ship, but with differences proper to the different uses which the vessel may be building for; thus, they choose a different day or hour for a ship of war, for a merchantman, and for a fishing-boat. Moreover, when they undertake a voyage or any other enterprise, in like wise it is not without first inquiring of the astrologer what will be the issue of it, and whether the day be good or bad, and the planet favourable or unfavourable; and so, if anything untoward befalls them, they attribute it to the day, and accept it with patience, saying that the will of God has been done. The king at all times keeps a number of these astrologers about him, as well as other mathematicians, and ofttimes employs their services. They also study magic and sorcery.

These islanders practise themselves greatly in arms,—how to use the sword with the buckler, how to draw the bow with ease, how to fire the arquebuse and handle the pike; they also have schools of arms, whose masters are highly honoured and respected, they who take this office being in general great lords.[1] They have no other games but ball (large and small), which they catch and throw with much address, though they use the feet only.[2]

[1] *Vide* ch. xix.

[2] They have two ball games, as Mr. Bell informs me, in which the feet are used, but not entirely, viz., *suvá* and *lubómandl.* These games would seem to have been introduced from the Eastern Archipelago, whose natives are very expert at them. "They have a diversion similar to that described by Homer amongst the Phæacians, which consists in tossing an elastic wicker ball from one to the other in a large party. They arrive to a great degree of dexterity in the sport, receiving it with equal facility on the foot or hand, the heel or the toe, from whence it is thrown either perpendicularly into the air and caught again, or obliquely to some other person of the company, who stand in an extended circle" (Marsden, *Sumatra*, p. 239; see also Crawfurd, *Ind. Arch.*, i, 117).

They employ themselves also in manufactures, and are exceeding apt and adroit therein, in such sort that there are among them a great number of different crafts for the making of furniture, utensils, and other commodities.

Their chiefest and most common employment is fishing, wherein all the people indifferently in all parts of the Maldives take part; nor are there only certain persons of this employment, as elsewhere, nor certain places for it, reserved from the public. Natural freedom prevails, and every man may fish where he likes and as much as he likes.[1] It is deemed an honourable employment, even the greatest lords joining, and taking great pleasure in it, as they do here in the chase; but they care not otherwise to profit in the takes. On the contrary, all men of honour and quality, when they go a-fishing and catch any, send them to their friends or give them to any who come and ask of them, or else they have a quantity cooked with green bananas, called at the Maldives *quella*,[2] and call all their neighbours to come and eat; this they do without other ceremony, by way of merry-making. The kings themselves have officers to wait upon them when they would enjoy this sport. Being islanders, with but a small extent of land, with them fishing is what the chase is to other nations. Twelve persons are appointed to work and man the king's boat, and to do the needful when he goes a-fishing. They are all great lords who are appointed to these offices; they think themselves highly honoured, and purchase them dearly. Over them is a captain, one of the highest grandees, who must work the rudder of

[1] Owing to the abundance of the fishery, no restrictive rules or limits were necessary. Very different is the case in Ceylon, where the utmost jealousy exists between the coast hamlets as to their respective fishing grounds, and local feuds have as long a duration as those between the British and French fishermen of the Newfoundland banks, which have for so many years exercised the highest diplomatic talent of London and Paris, and are still unsettled (1885).

[2] M. *kéu*, and in the southern atolls, *kéli*; Sin. *kehel*; Hind. *kelá*.

the vessel. The king gives each of the twelve a heavy silver ring or bracelet,[1] to put on his right arm, of the weight of a quarter of a pound (which is called a *gaux*,[2] and is like our weights), and to the captain one of gold: these they wear when the king goes to fish. Nevertheless, the king who reigned when I was there went a-fishing but rarely.

Fishing is done at the Maldives in several ways. The chief fishery, that of the fish in which is the greatest trade, is pursued beyond the reefs and atolls in the deep sea, six or seven leagues out, where that kind of fish always lies. A marvellous quantity of large fish are caught there, of seven or eight sorts, which are all of the same race and kind, though not of the same appearance or size; for example, *bonites, albachores, daurades*,[3] and others, which are very like each other, and of the same taste, and have no scales, no more than mackerel; they are all found together in the same grounds, and are caught in the same manner,—that is, by a line of a fathom and a half of thick cotton cord, fixed in a big cane, which is a wood of great strength. The hook at the end is of a different sort from ours. It is not bent, but is longer, and pointed at the end like a needle, without barb or tongue, resembling in all respects the letter "h" written

[1] A badge adopted, perhaps, from the Malabar coast. "The principallest or chiefest of those Nayros, which are leaders or captaines of certaine numbers of Nayros, weare a gold or silver bracelet or ring about their armes, above their elbowes; as also their Governours, Ambassadours and Kings, whereby they are knowne from other men" (*Linsch.*, Hakl. Soc., i, 282). Compare the use of the *annulus aureus* among the Romans (Smith, *Dict. Gr. and R. Ant.*). See also below, ch. xix.

[2] M. *gau*, or *galé*; *cf.* Sin. *gala*, "stone"; now also = ¼ lb. A *Cypræa mauritiana* shell, bearing the Sultan's seal in wax, is the regular "Imperial *gau*" in the southern atolls (Bell, *Report*, 118).

[3] *I.e.*, *bonito*, the *Thynnus pelamys* (Day); *albacore*, a kind of large mackerel, *Thynnus albucora* (Lowe), perhaps the same as *T. macropterus* (Day); and *dorado*, or "gilt head", the sea-bream (often called "dolphin"; see *Hawk. Voy.*, Hakl. Soc., p. 148); the *Coryphæna hippurus* (Day).

in the French running hand. No bait is attached, but the day before, they provide a lot of little fish of the size of little roach or whitebait, which are found in great abundance on the reefs and shallows; these they keep alive in net-bags of coco-nut cord of small meshes, and let them drag in the sea at the stern of their barques. When they get out to the deep sea to the fishing ground they cast abroad these little fish, and at the same time put in their line. The big fish, seeing the little fish—a rare sight in the deep sea,—rush up in numbers, and are caught at the hook, which is whitened and tinned on purpose,—for this kind of fish is exceeding greedy and foolish, so to be taken by a white hook, which it mistakes for a small white fish.[1] They have then only to draw the line into the boat, where the fish drops at once, being hardly hooked; the line is speedily put back into the sea, and thus a marvellous quantity are taken, in such wise that in less than three or four hours their boats are nearly full: and this, be it remarked, while they are going full sail. The fish which is taken there is commonly called in their language *Cobolly masse*,[2] that is to say, "black fish", for they

[1] This is equally true at the present day both of the Maldivian and Ceylon fish: they have learned neither wisdom nor self-restraint.

[2] M. *kaḷu-bili-mas*, *i.e.*, *kalu*, "black"; *bili*, "bonito", Sin. *balayá*; *mas*, "fish". It is vulgarly pronounced *komboli*, or *kommala mas*, and is known in Ceylon as *umbala kada*. Ibn Batuta calls it *koulb al más* (see below, App. A). Pridham (*Ceylon*, 605) writes *komblĕmas*; the Hindustani form is *kumbala*.

With the *komboli mas* of the Ceylon and Indian bazaars, though chiefly bonito, pass several other kinds of fish, such as the *godá*, *kanneli*, and *rágoḍi*. There are several methods of cutting up the fish for curing, all of which are fully described, with diagrams, by Mr. Bell (*Report*, pp. 93-5). The preparation is then as follows:—"The pieces are washed with salt water, then thrown into a cauldron of boiling salt water and allowed to remain a few minutes only, to prevent the flesh becoming too soft. It is said to be important that the water should be boiling from the first. On being taken out they are placed on the wattle, loft, or shelf (M. *mehi*, Sin. *messa*) above the fire. There they are left three or four days till well blackened and dried, after which, if necessary, they

are all black. They are cooked in sea-water, and then dried in the sun upon trays, and so when dry they keep a long while; wherefore there is great traffic in them, not only in the country, but throughout the rest of India, where they are in great request. For the rest, the largest and finest fish caught must go to the king, and as soon as the boat lands, one of the chief men takes the fish and reeves a cord or osier through his gills, and then carry him with a rod over the shoulder to the king's kitchen. Next, they give some to the clergy, to the poor, and to their friends, and the remainder are divided amongst themselves; but however small the catch, this division must always be made.

There is another kind of fishing, which is done at night on the reefs around the atolls, and only twice a month, when the moon is in conjunction and again when it is full, three days each time.[1] It is done from these rafts, called *candoue patis*, of which I have spoken above.[2] Long lines of fifty or sixty fathoms are used, of thick and strong cotton, blackened with the bark of a tree, which serves them in place of charcoal or pitch: this is to preserve the line for a long time from rotting. At the end are hooks to which baits are attached, in like manner as with us. With these lines they catch a quantity of fish, of a kind I have not seen elsewhere; it is three or four feet long, and broad in proportion, and all red; but within quite white and firm when cooked. It is most excellent and delicious eating, by reason whereof these people—who, in the names they give to things, full nearly express their nature—call this fish "the

are exposed to the sun to be finished. Thus dried, they are, as is well known, of the appearance and consistency of blocks of wood" (Bell, *loc. cit.*; also his paper in *Ind. Ant.*, xi, 196).

[1] This is called *fő'-mas*, or *fői-mas*, Sin. *poya-mas*, the fishing of the *poya* or festival days.

[2] At p. 122.

king of the sea".[1] They eat it fresh, and salt it not at all. Likewise they catch many other kinds of fish in marvellous quantity; it would be impossible for me to distinguish them, so great is their variety: fishes unknown to us in these parts, and by me not seen in any other region of the world. It will suffice here to mention them thus generally, to give a notion of the principal source of the wealth of the country; and if there be aught else to remark in particular, I will reserve it to speak of elsewhere. Also they have all kinds of nets, lines of cotton thread, weels, and implements of fishery, as we have, for catching fish in various ways in the shallows of the sea; but these are only for eating fresh, and there is no traffic therein. On the seashore, where it is but shallow, they for a pastime take pleasure in fishing for little fish resembling sardines, and exceeding delicate eating, with a net of cotton twine of large extent, having all over it little pieces of tin to keep it taut; this they cast with great art when they perceive a shoal of these little fish, which are caught in the width of the net by means of the tin, which draws the net over the bottom and encloses them all.[2] But see one other manner of fishing, which I have noted, a manner most strange and laborious.

For twice a year, at the time of the equinoxes and the high tides, they have a general fishing, and a great number of people assemble at certain places on the sea. To understand the manner of this fishing, you must know that then the tide not only flows and rises higher than during the rest of the year, but also ebbs proportionally, and on so going back discovers shoals and rocks which are seen at no other time. In such like places, when the sea is gone back, they note some convenient nook, and plant all around large stones

1 *Rat-veri-mas*, *i.e.*, "the red chief of fish"; Mr. Bell identifies it with the Rangoo (*Lutianus*).

2 This net is called *ellá-dá*, "cast-net", corresponding to the *baru-dæla*, "weighted net", of the Sinhalese.

one upon another, in such wise that it seems like a round wall or a ravelin. This enclosure is forty paces round or thereabouts, and an entry is left of two or three paces wide. They assemble thirty or forty men, each of whom carries fifty or sixty fathoms of thick coco-cord, at every fathom of which is attached a piece of dried coco-husk to keep the cord always floating, just as cork is used with us. The cords brought by each are tied together, and the whole stretched round the shoal. I leave you to imagine the extent of the circle. The marvel is that the fish within this cord are all caught, though there are neither nets, nor gins, nor line depending, but the cord only. Yet the fish fear the cord and the shadow of the cord, in such sort that, instead of escaping away under it, and not letting themselves be thus encircled, they flee before it, thinking there is a line beneath it which would arrest them. The men all come round towards this stone enclosure of which I have spoken, drawing the cord little by little, some in boats, others in the water; for in these shallows the sea is of little depth, and reaches no more than to the neck, or mostly short of that. Thus, as they draw the cord, the fish flee and crowd towards the enclosure, so at length the cord being nearly all drawn in, the fish enter within; then at once the men fill up the entrance with bundles of coco-branches and leaves, tied end to end, twenty or thirty fathoms, and of the thickness of a man, so that when the sea goes down the fish are left on dry land.[1] Then it is great sport to see the fish struggling and leaping, and in such quantity that sometimes there are ten or twelve thousand or more caught. They fill sacks and net-pockets of small meshes with them, placing these at the opening and chasing the fish from within, in such wise that they lose not one. And some of them I have seen so huge that it

[1] This mode of fishing seems a combination of the *má*, or *boḍu dá*, Sin. *má dæla*, and the *mas-hifá-korhi*, Sin. *mas korotuva*. It is a fish-kraal, and may be seen on the rivers and sea-shore of Ceylon.

was all a man could do to carry one. I have been often at this fishing, and have had for my share more than a hundred large fish, although I was a stranger, and of the least account among so many, where all had their full share; yet in truth I had to endure more than they, for they were accustomed to go barefooted on the reefs and rocks, and I was not, and on some occasions I had to go nearly half a league in this fashion, and always in the sun. All this fish is used for their food in banquets and treats, there being no traffic in this kind; yet they cook and dry it on trays, else they could not keep so great a quantity for a length of time without rotting. This fishing is practised only once in six months in each shoal, and each time for fifteen days; they change the place every day, and do not often return to the same place for the same mode of fishing, except it be at the other equinox.

The fish found on these shoals or within the reefs of the atolls is called in the Maldive language *phare masse*, as who should say "shoal" or "reef fish"—from *phare*, that is to say, a reef or bank, and *masse*, "fish".[1] The other sort taken in deep sea, as I have said, is called *combolly masse*, that is, "black fish", in which they have their great traffic, supplying therewith all the coasts of the main. The fish of which I speak is cooked in sea-water and dried, for other mode of salting they have none; and when betimes they salt some of it, it is left in the brine till wanted. But it is not this kind that they send abroad. No salt is made at the Maldives: what they use comes from the coast of Malabar, and would not suffice for the quantity of fish they catch every day, both for the food of the people and for trade; for in truth there is no place in all the Indies, nor elsewhere (in my belief), so rich in fish and abundantly supplied therewith.

I omitted, before closing my discourse of the manners and exercises of the islanders, to say a word of their behaviour, which, though it might easily be gathered from their conduct

[1] M. *faru mas*; *cf.* Sin. *para*, in *galpara*, "reef".

as I have represented it, yet may conveniently here be somewhat touched upon. This people is quick and apprehensive, subtle and crafty in most part of their actions. Courage also they lack not, and love arms and exercises. They are industrious in arts and manufactures, and polite of manners: a people superstitious beyond measure, and much devoted to their religion, yet, in their indulgence of women, lascivious and intemperate. Adultery, incest, and sodomy are common, notwithstanding the severity of the law and penalties. As for simple lewdness, nothing is more common; they think it no sin, neither wives nor unmarried girls, and make no work about submitting themselves to their male friends and afterwards (a most execrable practice) voiding their fruit, or bringing about abortion, or making away with their bastard babes. The women are strangely wanton, and the men are no better; but they have less of force and spirit. Their chief desire is to find, if they can, some recipe wherewithal to satisfy their wives, and to get themselves greater strength to practise their lechery; and I believe they would give all their substance for such a thing. They have often asked me if I knew of any such means, even the highest nobles, and so often, in fact, that I was quite sick of the subject. They talk thereof continually, even in the presence of their wives, of whom they have as many as three, as I have said, so that they are unable to satisfy each. Then the air is exceeding sultry, and causes some part of the natural force to evaporate; moreover, their manner of life is against them in this matter, their nerves becoming slack by being continually in the water; add that the most of them eat opium, or, as they call it, *aphion*,[1] which intoxicates and stupefies them.

Notwithstanding this, they are all given to this vice without moderation, as well men as women, not to say more of their abominations.

The women conceal their nipples and breasts as carefully

[1] M. *afihun*, Ar. *afyún*.

as the private parts, and there is the same modesty and shame in showing or uncovering them. Even to speak of a breast is with them most lewd and shameful. Kissing is made as much of as sleeping together, and is as improper to speak of. For the rest, though they be exceeding lewd in their conversation, they restrain themselves before their kindred and respect their presence. If a word such as I have spoken of should escape a man in talk with a woman before one or more of his kindred, they would retire and be highly offended at him; he would have to make his excuses, and say that he was not aware he was among his kindred, otherwise, if they should think he said it of design, they would complain to the judge, to have from him that uttered these shameful words in their presence an acknowledgment that he held them for men of virtue and honour.

A man durst not enter a place where a woman is bathing, or even where she has cast off her robe, though she might still have the cloth which serves them for a petticoat: for, as I said, they deem their breasts and bosom to be private parts. When a man and a woman are seen together and are met by other people, you must not ask of the man if the woman is his wife, his daughter, or his sister; for if she was his daughter, and you asked if she were his wife, he would be insulted as much as if you had accused him of incest. You must only ask if she is related to him, and he will tell the degree of relationship. While the women have their courses they bathe not at all, neither wash, save their hands and mouth, nor change their robes while these last: also they sleep not with their husbands, nor eat or hold converse with anyone. I have said above that the women go forth but rarely by day: all their visits are made by night; but I have omitted to mention something peculiar in their customs which I may without inconvenience add here. In their visits by night they must have a man to bear them company, to walk before them, and when he hears anyone coming, he says three times, *Gas*,[1] that is to say, "Beware"; men warned by this signal leave that side of the road on which the women are coming, without seeming to see them or wishing to be accosted by them, so great is their respect. And if other women should meet them, each takes her own side, and gives no salutation unless they be intimate acquaintance. You do not knock at a door, for there is no knocker; and you do not call to anyone to open the door, for the chief gate of the courtyard is always open to a certain hour, that is, till eleven at night, when all have retired; wherefore, you enter the courtyard, which is close to the house, and that is also open, saving only that it has a curtain of cotton, or other stuff, hung in front. As you approach this door you only cough, at the sound whereof those within come forth to see if they are wanted for anything. In like manner, when men walk in the streets by night, they frequently cough on purpose to put others on their guard, for fear of running against, or wounding one another, for all (I mean the soldiers and king's officers at Malé) carry drawn arms. Whatsoever remains to be said of their manners will be better understood by what I shall describe hereafter, and by the history of what passed at the Maldives during my sojourn there.

CHAPTER XIV.

Form of the government of the state, of the magistrates, of justice and the laws.

The government of the Maldive state is royal, very ancient and absolute; the king is feared and dreaded, and everything depends upon him. I have said that the islands are divided into thirteen atollons,—a natural division, which

[1] Probably a misprint for *gos*, "having gone", *i.e.*, "begone!"

has been followed in government; for of these are constituted thirteen provinces, over each of which is a chief called a *Naybe.*[1] These Naybes, or chiefs of provinces, are priests or doctors of the law, who have an eye as well to all matters of religion and education, as to the administration of justice in the province, giving their orders to the priests under them. For the atollons are again divided into many islands, and in each one containing more than forty-one men, as I said, there is a doctor called a *Catibe*, the religious superior of that island, who has under him the priests incumbent of the mosques. All these see to the instruction of the people in the law: they are supported in part by fruits, which everyone is bound to yield, and in part from certain endowments assigned to them by the king, according to their degree. But the Naybes, besides their duties and authority in religion, are also appointed to administer justice, each in his own government. They are the sole judges in the land, as well in matters civil as criminal; and if one wants to go to law, he must go find the Naybe or attend his coming to the place. For the Naybes four times a year go the circuit of the islands in their several governments, and hold visitations as well ecclesiastical as judicial.[2] This brings them in great revenues, for it is then the people pay their dues, besides which they receive many presents from a multitude of people, and of such they are very greedy. Be it remarked that throughout the Maldive islands there are no judges but these thirteen Naybes, for the Catibes and the priests of the mosques are overseers only. Over these Naybes is a superior, who resides at Malé, and is always near the person of the king; he

[1] Ar. *naib*. The Naibs are only the ecclesiastical and judicial chiefs of the atolls. No doubt, in Pyrard's time, they were superior to the collectors of revenue, *atoḷu-veri*, but the latter are much the bigger men now.

[2] It is said that the Naibs "travel the circuit" only twice a year now.

is called the *Pandiare*,[1] and not only ecclesiastical superior of the whole kingdom, but also sovereign judge. Wherefore, if any, after pleading before the Naybe, is loth to obey his judgment, be it in a matter civil or criminal, he appeals to the Pandiare, who decides all matters brought before him, taking the advice of some Naybes who are about him, of the Catibes, and of certain personages called *Moucouris*,[2] that is to say, doctors or learned men, who for all that are not officers: and he gives no judgment but by the assistance of four or five of such persons at the least. These Moucouris know the whole of their Alcoran by heart (all others read it only), besides having a knowledge of other sciences. They are invited in state to all feasts, preachings, and ceremonies, and are greatly respected and honoured of all men. There are but few of them, not fifteen in all the islands. The Pandiare is called *Cady* in the Arabic tongue. And yet after the judgment of the Pandiare some will plead to the king himself, who gives order for justice to be done and executed, and this by six lords, his chief officers, who manage the most important affairs of the realm. They are called *Mouscoulis*,[3] as who should say "elders".

The Pandiare, assisted by the two Catibes of Malé island, and by the Naybe of the atollon, along with some of these doctors, also makes his visitation throughout the island of Malé, just as each Naybe in his atollon. He is also assisted by his officers, who carry a long whip, of which I shall speak hereafter, for correcting the delinquents: he makes what inquiries he thinks fit, with especial regard to all matters of religion and justice. All he meets without exception he causeth to say their creed, and some prayers in Arabic, and

[1] M. *Faḍiyaru*, or *Fanḍiyáru;* derivation uncertain, but perhaps connected with the Tam. *panḍaram*, "religious mendicant, monk, or friar" (Winslow).

[2] *Mugari-bé-kalun ; bé-kalun* is the ordinary ending of all class-terms.

[3] M. *Muskuḷi*, "elders". They are now called *vazíru*.

then asks them the interpretation of the same in the Maldive language. If they know it not, he hath them whipped and scourged on the spot by his officers. The women durst not show themselves while he passes along the street, and if he should meet one without her veil, he would have her head shaved. So it is ordained by their law, and the Naybes do the like.

Besides the Naybes, there is in each province or atollon a man appointed and employed by the king to collect and levy his dues and revenues, and those of the Christian king at Goa, to carry out his orders, and, in short, to manage his affairs. These are called *Varuery*,[1] and they are highly honoured and respected. Such as come with any commission from the king address themselves to them, and they furnish whatsoever is needful in the way of attendants and guides for the islands of their atollon.

All the islands have each its separate wards and parishes, in like manner as Malé, where there are five wards, each with its headman, called *Mouscouly auare*,[2] the alderman of the ward, and nothing is done there but he knows of it; and if anything in the ward is required, whether for the use of the king or the people, he must be applied to, and no other, as having charge of everything there; and if anything

[1] M. *atolu-veri*, or *Váru-veri;* i.e., *váru*, "tax", and *veri*, "man". Mr. Bell thinks that *váru* may be connected with the Sin. *varuva*, a paddy-heap, and may be traced to a time anterior to the separation of the races, when taxes were paid in kind. These collectors are appointed to an atoll, or part of an atoll, by the Sultan on the recommendation of the *Hadégiri*. They do not necessarily reside in their districts. The majority reside at Málé, and employ sub-agents (*rarhu-veri*). The emoluments of the office are considerable, and it is frequently held by relations of the king, and by the ministers themselves. It is held for life or during the sultan's pleasure, and at the decease of an *atoḷu-veri* his estate is held liable for any balance due to the treasury (Bell, *Report*, 67).

[2] M. *Muskuḷi ava'*; *cf.* Sin. *avadhi*, "limit", "division". There are only four of these wards now.

is missing, it must be sought of him. The people of the ward treat him with great honour and respect,—not that he can do nothing without the counsel and advice of the other elders and counsellors of the ward, but when he has any project in view, he summons them to his house or other place as it pleaseth him, to consider together of what is to be done; the same goes on at the other islands, for each one has a superior unto whom the folk of the ward give ear.

Law in their language is called *Sacouest*,[1] and is administered at the house of the Naybes, or at Malé at the house of the Pandiare, with the assistants above mentioned, and betimes also at the king's palace when the case is of grave importance.

When one willeth to commence a suit, he applies to the judge or Naybe, and he sendeth one of his sergeants, of whom each hath a certain number, called *Deuanits*,[2] to cause the party appealed to appear; and if he be not in the same island, he is entitled to a writ of the Naybe, whereby he is directed to come to where the Naybe is, provided it be a place within his jurisdiction. For if it be in that of another, the Naybe has no power therein, and in such case he is served with a writ of the Pandiare, who may summon a man from any part of the realm to the king's island where he resides. The writ is delivered to the Catibe, the headman of the island, who in presence of all delivers it to the person appealed, straitly warning him to go. In the which he dare not fail, for as many as disobey the behests of the law are not admitted to the company of the others, to go to mosque, or to eat or drink with them, and are treated as outside the pale of their law. If a man, for example, some grandee, will not obey, the king sendeth his soldiers to constrain him. And if one liketh not to plead before the Naybe, whether

[1] M. *Sakuvá*; probably connected with the Sin. *sákiya*, "evidence"; *cf.* Skt. *sākshin*, "a witness".

[2] M. *Dévāni.* Now six in number (Bell, *Report*, 65).

for cause that he is ill-disposed towards him, or that he favours him overmuch, then the plaintiff or the defendant who is appealed applies to the king, who makes order that justice be done by indifferent judges; the cause is then heard at the palace of the king, in the presence of all the grandees of the island.

The parties plead their own causes. If it is an issue of fact, each brings three witnesses; and if they have none, the defendant is believed upon his oath, which he takes by touching with his hand the book of their law, the judge presenting it; and the plaintiff, if he be at all a man of the world, scrupulously observes whether his opponent really touches the book, and at the proper place. If the issue be one of law, it is adjudged by the law. The judges receive nothing for their judgments, and nothing is due, save that the deuanits or sergeants get a twelfth part of the judgment debt or penalty.

Slaves may not be witnesses, and their word is of no avail as evidence; and in like manner that of three women is taken as of one man. The slaves are such as have become so, or have been brought from abroad and sold, for strangers wrecked there lose not their liberty if they had it before; if they were slaves, they remain so. In good truth, the slaves, who are call *Allo*,[1] are of much more sorry condition than the rest. They can have but one wife, while all [others] are permitted to have three, and they can put them away and take them back but once only. The penalty for beating a slave is only half that for beating or assaulting a free man.

Debtors are obliged, if they have no means of paying, to go into servitude, not as slaves, nor treated as such, but as natives of the country; they serve only their creditors or others who pay the money for their redemption. These

[1] M. *ala*; *cf.* Sin. *válá*.

bondsmen are called *Pemousseré*,[1] which is to say "bondsman on loan", and this lasts till they be acquitted, and their

[1] M. *femuséri*. The custom of debt slavery, evidently of great antiquity, is mentioned by Ibn Batuta (see App. A), and exists at the present day. Christopher states that the men of Málé become "dependents of any of the chiefs, most of whom retain as many followers as they may be able to support, a large retinue being considered a sign of rank and power" (*Trans. Bom. Geo. Soc.*, i, 60). Mr. Bell says, "A curious custom, still surviving, permits an insolvent debtor to work off his debt as his creditor's servant. These bondsmen are called *Femuséri*" (*Report*, p. 65).

In Ceylon the custom was in full force in Knox's time (*Knox*, 102), and lasted until some time after the British occupation. The following account is given in Sir J. d'Oyly's MS., *Laws and Constitutions of the Kandyan Kingdom*, a copy of which is in my possession:—"If the debtor have no property, the chief sometimes delivers him to his creditor, who is thereupon authorised to confine him in his house, and if he cannot obtain satisfaction, to employ him as a servant, or rather as his slave, treating him as such, and supplying him with victuals and clothing" (p. 180). The author proceeds to say that the creditor could also, by leave of the chief, enter upon and cultivate the debtor's field, and that he sometimes (illegally) seized his child. In times of great scarcity people voluntarily became bondslaves, and sold their children (p. 235). In some cases the king paid the debt by way of largess out of the royal treasury, in others it was raised by public subscription (p. 395).

It is in the Eastern Archipelago, however, that the practice obtains most widely and persistently. The best account is that given by Marsden:—"When a debtor is unable to pay what he owes, and has no relation or friends capable of doing it for him; or when the children of a deceased person do not find property enough to discharge the debts of their parent, they are forced to the state called *mengeering*, that is, they become a species of bondslaves to the creditor, who allows them subsistence and clothing, but does not appropriate the produce of their labour, to the diminution of the debt. Their condition is better than that of pure slavery, in this, that the creditor cannot strike them, and they can change their masters, by prevailing upon another person to pay their debt and accept of their labour on the same terms. Of course, they may procure their liberty if they can by any means provide a sum equal to their debt; whereas a slave, though possessing ever so large property, has not the right of purchasing his liberty" (*Sumatra*, 214; see also pp. 190-2, 335; also Crawfurd, *Ind. Arch.*, iii, 98; Raffles's *Java*, second edition, i, 394, *note*).

Debt slavery was found to be in full force, with its attendant abuses,

children continue to be so for ever if they do not pay. Sometimes, when they are badly treated, they can get released by binding themselves to another, who pays for them; all their hire is their food and maintenance, and when they die their master takes all they had; and if that is not enough for the debt, the children remain in bond till the whole be paid. A great number of the people seek to be the *Pemousseré* of grandees and men in office, and so to gain support and favour, for while they belong to nobody they are tormented by one another.

In the matter of crimes a man must plead for justice to be done, and he must be a person of capacity to sue, except it were a crime punishable by the law, otherwise there is no public process in case of crime or injury committed on the person of another—unless, as I say, it is a crime against their law. A wife cannot appeal in the court for the murder of her husband, but only the children or kindred; and if the children are of young age, time is given till they attain the age of sixteen years, to see if they desire to be avenged for the death of their father. In the meantime, the judge condemns him that is suspected of the murder to support the children of the deceased, and to teach them some art or craft; then, when they come of age, they may demand justice, or release and pardon the murderer; if not, he may be accused at any time thereafter. For there, in the matter of an injury done to any private person, the person injured must be the complainant, otherwise the crime is annulled; nevertheless, if the king wills, he has justice done, without any other party to the cause; but that happens rarely.[1]

in the Malay states of Perak and Selangor, on the assumption of the British protectorate a few years ago. It has now been abolished by a scheme of compensation from and after the 31st December 1883. See *Parliamentary Papers*, C. 2410 (1879), C. 3285 and C. 3429 (1882), and C. 4192 (1884). The custom was abolished at Sarawak by Sir James Brooke, but is still in use in the native states of Borneo.

[1] We have here, succinctly stated, the same double modes of prosecu-

The usual penalties are banishment to the desert islands of the south, as I have already said, mutilation of a member, or the scourge,[1] which is the most common, but infinitely cruel. It is of thick leather straps, as long as the arm and as broad as the four fingers, and as thick as two; of these, five or six are fixed together in a haft of wood. With this, malefactors are chastised, and so cruelly beaten that full often they die of it. It is the usual penalty for great crimes, such as sodomy, incest, and adultery. Women taken in adultery, besides the said penalty, have their hair cut off.[2]

False witness and perjury are punished in the same way, the guilty party being also amerced in a money fine, which is given to the poor.

If a wife or a daughter be ravished, the guilty party is punished as an adulterer, and in addition is obliged to settle a portion upon the wife or daughter.

A thief who has stolen any article of value has his hand cut off.[3]

tion which obtained in English law for many centuries, viz., the prosecution by the king, in which case the charge was called a "plea of the crown", and the prosecution by the injured party, called an "appeal". The intricate technicalities with which the latter procedure was incrusted may be studied in the pages of Bracton, Britton, and Hawkins. As lawyers are aware, this mode of prosecution, after being for long deemed obsolete, was revived by an "appeal of murder" in the year 1818, with due "wager of battle", and was only then abolished by statute. The main difference between the English and Maldive appeal was, that in the former the right was primarily confined to the widow, and only passed to the heir when there was no surviving widow.

[1] Below, in ch. xxii, he calls this scourge *gleau*. Christopher states that flogging is done with "two or three rattans held together in the hand". He confirms Pyrard as to the severity with which it is inflicted, adding that "sometimes death ensues" (*Trans. Bom. Geo. Soc.*, i, 78).

[2] According to Christopher, if the woman has not given encouragement, the man is severely flogged, the injured husband being the administrator (*Trans. Bom. Geo. Soc.*, i, 78).

[3] This is the punishment prescribed by the Koran: "If a man or woman steal, cut off their hands in retribution for that which they have committed: this is an exemplary punishment appointed by God, and

In the matter of injuries a prosecutor is not free to hush up the charge; the penalty is exacted when there is proof of heinous wrong.

If a man has committed some offence against the law, he must do penance in a public manner, as a public apology. For the rest, they hold it for certain that they could never enter Paradise did they not pay and perform whatsoever the court has ordered. For the execution and scourging of malefactors they have no executioner: that office is performed by the *deuanits* or sergeants.

As for the penalty of death, though their law ordains it for a homicide, the judges never pass the sentence.[1] All the time I was at the Maldives, I never saw one condemned to death by the ordinary judges. They would not dare to do so, but by the express command of the king, which is given but seldom. Moreover, it is a common saying with them, that they could not afford thus to lose their men; and that if all were put to death that merited it, in course of time the islands would be dispeopled, and so that the human race in other parts would not suffice to pay the penalty, and that the world would come to an end. Yet true it is that the king sends some of his chosen soldiers, and condemns, and puts

God is mighty and wise" (*Sura*, 5). Ibn Batuta (below, App. A) mentions that this penalty was unknown or unpractised before his arrival at the Maldives, and states that when he, as Cadi, had a thief's hand cut off, the bystanders all fainted! Christopher was shown a stone block on which offenders' hands were chopped off in former days (*T. Bom. Geo. Soc.*, i, 78). The real humanity of the islanders had reasserted itself, in defiance of the Koran. Mutilation is unknown and forgotten now (Bell, *Report*, 65). Note in the above passage, "any article of value", as indicating, perhaps, a similar distinction to that which obtained in English law, between "grand larceny", where the thing stolen was of the value of one shilling or over, and "petty larceny", where it was under; our law was the more cruel, the penalty of the former being death, of the latter, whipping.

[1] Murder is now punished by flogging and banishment to the southern atolls (Chr., in *Trans. Bom. Geo. Soc.*, i, 78; Bell, *Report*, 65).

to death such as merit it, or have offended him. For though the processes of justice are in the hands of the doctors of the law, and they are the judges, yet the king is the sole arbiter and dispenser of it; he alone has the power of life and death. Appeal is made to him, and he gives his orders for justice to be done as he wills it, as well to the judges and doctors, as to his lords and officers. And to speak generally, he is absolute throughout his whole realm, and disposes all things according to his pleasure, and that in most tyrannical sort at times, though chiefly in his dealings with the vulgar, a most abject and caitiff herd. Among other kinds of chastisement, he maketh use of one peculiar to the lot of such as have incurred his displeasure, for he causeth them to lie upon their bellies on the ground, their four limbs held by four persons; they then receive some stripes upon the back with a rod or kind of cane, which is called *Rotan*,[1] and comes from Bengal: this takes off the skin, and the weals and scars remain ever after to mark such as have displeased the king. I have also observed, as a matter pertaining to the forms of their judicature, that they put not the process or the pleadings in criminal causes into writing, nor the indictments, nor the depositions, nor the judgments: all is very prompt and summary. And it is the same in civil actions, except in suits for hereditaments, or coco-trees (which are immovable property), wherein judgments are delivered by the Pandiare or the Naybes. In such case they grant writs [of possession], sealed with their seal in ink,—for I have never seen them use wax for sealing,—and these serve for evidence to their posterity, to the end that thenceforth neither he that hath gained the cause, nor his heirs, may be disquieted in their possession.

[1] *Rattan.*

CHAPTER XV.

Orders of the people,—of the nobility, the great offices and dignities, and their rank.

As for the orders and distinctions of the whole people, according to their condition and quality, be it remarked there are four sorts of persons.[1] In the first are comprehended the king, called *Rasquan*,[2] the queen, called *Renequillague*,[3]

[1] It will be observed that the first, third, and fourth classes are distinctions settled by birth; the second so-called class includes all dignities and titles of honour granted by the king. 1. Persons of the blood royal are termed *Baṇḍâra*, or *Baḍâra*, the term applied also to the children of the Sinhalese kings. By including the "great lords" in this first class, Pyrard probably refers to the titles of *Manipul*, assumed only by the nearest relations of the sultan, and *Dídí*, applied to remoter scions of the royal house and descendants of former sultans. 2. The second class of dignities, viz., those conferred on individuals, include the officers of state and titles conferred out of court favour or bought. The highest is that of *Kilagé-fánu* (Pyrard, *quilague*), formerly confined to the regent acting in the absence of the sultan, but now given to several grandees. Among titles independent of office are *Kalege-fánu* and *Takuru-fánu*, the former of which can be purchased for a few rupees. Masters of vessels get the titles of *Nákhudá*, *Néví*, and *Málimi*, as implying skill and experience in seamanship. 3. The third class is that of the aristocracy generally, viz., the *Maniku*. The wife of a *maniku* man is termed *manike* (*cf.* the common Sin. name, *meṇika*). When a *maniku* man receives a title of honour, he is called *maniku-fánu*. Some of this class preserve the relics of Portuguese influence, and call themselves *Don Maniku*. Either Pyrard is wrong in stating that children's status comes from the mother, or the law is now changed. Mr. Bell is informed by the highest Maldive authorities that the status of the father governs; *e.g.*, a *maniku* woman marries a *Dídí*, the children are *Dídí*. It may be noted here that Pyrard also states (ch. xviii), that nobility comes "from the mother as well as from the father". 4. The common people are termed *Kalo* (fem. *Kamulo*). He does not here speak of the slaves, *alu* (see p. 202); nor does he refer to the handicraft castes.

[2] M. *raskan* or *rasge-fánu*; *cf.* Sin. *rajan*, *radu*, and *rada*.

[3] M. *rani-kilage-fánu*. This would seem to be the title of a reigning queen or princess regent, as of the queen Aminá (1754). The sultan's wives are called *Rasge-fánu Abi-Kabalun* (Bell, *Report*, p. 76).

and those who are of his race and of the lineage of former kings; princes, called *Calans*,[1] princesses, *Camenaz*,[2] and great lords. The second is the order of dignities, offices, and rank granted by the king, in the which precedence is likewise carefully observed; the third is the nobility; the fourth, the common people. I will begin with the third, that being the rank conferred by birth, and separating its possessors from the common people. Dignities and offices are casualties independent of this rank. There are a great number of nobles here and there throughout the islands. Such as are not nobles durst not sit with them, nor even in the presence of a nobleman so long as he is standing; and should they see one how far off soever coming behind them, they must needs wait and let him pass before them. So, if one has a cloth or anything else thrown over his shoulder, he takes it down.[3] Noble women, though married to men of inferior condition, lose not their rank: even the children the issue of such marriages are noble by virtue of the mother's estate, even were the father of the lowest order. So women of low quality married to nobles are not ennobled by their husbands, but retain their former rank; everyone keeps his own place, and there is no confusion on this subject. But besides the nobility by birth, the king ennobles whom he will. When that happens, the king, besides a grant of letters (patent), sends one of his officers, specially appointed for this duty, to make publication thereof throughout the island to the sound of a kind of bell, which is a plate of metal struck with a hammer. As for the dignities, hear which are the principal, and the rank of them. After the king come the princes of his blood, and such as are descended from other

[1] M. *kalâ-fânu*, Pers. *kalân*, "great". Mr. Bell informs me that the Sultan of Pyrard's time is still known by this title, specially applied.

[2] M. *kamana-fânu*; *cf.* Sin. *hâmini*, "lady".

[3] The Sinhalese hardly ever omit these marks of respect when they meet a chief or a European in the road.

kings, his predecessors; these, though of a different line, are all held in honour and respect. Next, the great officers of the realm,[1]—to wit, the *Quilague*, whom we might call the king's

[1] We are fortunate enough to possess tolerably full lists of the ministers composing the "Cabinet" of the Sultan, at periods covering the last five hundred years; and it will be seen that the offices and their respective status have been altered, probably from the like causes of the necessities of the times, as our own high offices of State. The authorities as to those offices are the same as for other events of Maldive history, viz., Ibn Batuta (A.D. 1344), Pyrard (1602-9), Christopher (1835), and Mr. Bell at the present day.

I. Ibn Batuta (see below, App. A) gives the following offices:—

1. *Calaky*	... ...	Grand Vizier or Sultan's Lieutenant.
2. *Fandayarkalou*	...	The Kádi.
3. *Hendidjéry* ...	...	Preacher.
4. *Fámeldáry* ...	...	Chief of the Treasury.
5. *Máfácalou* ...	...	Receiver General of Revenue.
6. *Fitnáyec*	... ...	Minister of Police.
7. *Mánáyec*	... ...	Admiral.
8. *Déherd*	... ...	General of the Army.

After describing the offices of the first seven, he says, "All these have the title of Vizier." The eighth is mentioned incidentally in his subsequent narrative as a Vizier.

II. Pyrard's list of dignities is as follows:—

1. *Quilague* (*Kilagé*). Same as Ibn Bat.

2. *Parenas* (*Fáruná*, and in southern atolls, more correctly, *Fárhiná*). Not traced in other lists; no distinctive duties assigned. The title is now given to the Regent or Lieut.-General.

3. *Endequery*. The same in title, but not in functions, as Ibn. Bat., 3.

4. *Velannas* (*Veláná*). Admiral: under him—
   (*a*) two deputies called *Mirvaires* (*Míru Baharu*).

5. *Dorimenaz* (*Dorhiméná*). General of the Militia.
   (*a*) *Acouraz* (*Hakurá*), his lieutenant.

6. *Manpas* (*Máfai*). Chancellor; *cf.* Ibn Bat., 5.

7. *Carans* (*Karaní*). Secretary.

8. *Mas bandery* (*Má badéry*). Intendant of Finance; probably corresponding to the Auditor-General of British colonies.

9. *Rans bandery* (*Raṇ baḍeri*). Treasurer.

III. Christopher, in 1834, found a Cabinet of six Viziers, whose titles are given here according to the more correct spelling of Mr. Bell:—

lieutenant-general, because, next to the king, and in his absence, he is the most powerful in the government of the state,

1. *Dorhiménâ.* Chief or General of the Army. See Pyrard, 5.
2. *Hakurá.* See Pyrard, 5 (*a*).
3. *Velánâ.* See Pyrard, 4.
4. *Fámudéri.* Pyrard mentions (ch. xviii) a *Pammedery calogue* as a great lord, but does not place him among the ministers,—but see Ibn Bat., 4.
5. *Máfai.* See Ibn Bat., 5, and Pyrard, 6.
6. *Dáhará.* See Ibn Bat., 8. Pyrard (ch. xix) mentions a *Darade Tacourou* as a "Count" or "Duke", but does not place him among the ministers.

IV. Lastly, Mr. Bell (1879) finds that the Sultan now employs only three chief ministers, viz.:

1. *Hadégiri*, or *Bodu Badéri*, "Chief Treasurer of the realm". See Ibn Bat., 3, and Pyrard, 3.
2. *Dáhará.* See Ibn Bat., 8, and Chr., 6.
3. *Míru Baharu* (Ar. *Emir-el-Bahr*). See Pyrard, 4 (*a*).

The *Hadégiri* (preacher in Ibn Batuta's time, a lord privy councillor in Pyrard's, and now chief treasurer), though not placed by Christopher among the six ministers, was a high officer in his day, as he says he "is vested with authority to enforce the payment of revenue when complaint is made to him by the *Atolwari*". Mr. Bell says, "He seems to rank above the other two ministers, and to possess greater influence in the community. A staff of accountants and clerks are employed to assist him in the revenue duties at Málé."

The *Dáhará*, Mr. Bell observes, "has no specific department of public business to supervise. But for a certain voice in the military and municipal affairs, his office would be a titular sinecure."

The *Míru Baharu*, according to the same authority, "is the Port Doctor and Master Attendant of Málé. He visits all vessels that arrive, and refuses permission to land until it has been ascertained to his satisfaction that there is no sickness on board. Generally speaking, the entire management and control of all public business not falling within the province of the *Hadégiri*, and distributed a few years back among the six Viziers, devolve now on the *Míru Baharu* and the *Dáhará*."

It will be observed that the *Pandiare*, or Kadi, is included in Ibn Batuta's, but in no subsequent list. Although in Pyrard's time, as at present, he was supreme in ecclesiastical and judicial affairs, he was not supposed to interfere in the executive government.

Mr. Bell considers that a good many of the offices mentioned above may be traced back to the offices in the ancient Sinhalese monarchy,

and without his authority nothing is done. So, if the king wills to do, observe, or execute anything, he is the first to be

which occur in the *Mahawanso:* thus, he traces the *Hadégiri* to the *Bhándágáriko amachcho*, the Lord High Treasurer of Ceylon (Turnour's *Mahawanso*, pp. 231-3); *Dorhiménâ* to the *Dvára-náyaka* (*ib.*, 260); *Fámudéri* to the *Amachcha Pámukha* (*ib.*, 69), Sin. *pámok, déta; Máfai* may be derived from *maha*, "great", and *pati*, as in *Senápati*, *Chamupati* (Mah. *passim*); the *Dáhára* would seem to be the *Dovárika* (*ib.*, 117); the *Mánáyec* of Ibn Bat. is clearly enough the Sin. *maha náyaka.* (See Ibn Batuta; Christopher, in *Trans. Bom. Geo. Soc.*, i, 70-72; Bell, *Report*, 66, 78.)

Departmental Government.—(i). *Ecclesiastical and Judicial.*—These formed one department under the Pandiare, who was and still is chief priest and chief justice. Under him were the Naibs, thirteen in number, one for each atoll. These, according to Pyrard, were the sole provincial judges. Under them were the Catibs, of whom there was one in each island containing upwards of forty inhabitants. They were the religious superiors of their respective islands, but in judicial affairs they were "overseers" only. There were at Málé a Naib and two Catibs, who assisted the Pandiare in both departments. Subordinate again to the Catibs were the *Moudins*, or incumbents of mosques: every mosque had its Moudin. At Málé there were four "king's Moudins" (p. 147), who were of much greater consequence than ordinary Moudins: they were, in fact, royal chaplains, and the Catib of Málé was chosen from among them.

Christopher states that the Naibs were also called Catibs, and intimates that residence in their atolls was not obligatory, six or seven being usually at Málé (*Trans. Bom. Geo. Soc.*, i, 70). He states, in corroboration of Pyrard, that the Naibs were supported by the islanders; but he seems to be wrong in asserting that the Naibs and Catibs were identical, for Mr. Bell confirms the distinction of Pyrard, and states that at Málé the Pandiare is now assisted by four Naibs and two Catibs (*Report*, p. 65).

The last officers to be mentioned in this department are the *devanits* (M. *dévâni*), who performed, as they still do, the functions of peons, process-servers, and executioners. They are assigned to the Naibs as well as to the Pandiare. Mr. Bell states that the Pandiare has six, "who for their general services receive a small monthly allowance of rice, and one-twelfth share of the awards and proceeds of sale" (*Report*, p. 65).

(ii). *Revenue.*—Pyrard does not state specifically what officer presided over this department; he may have been the *Pammedery calogue* mentioned by him as one of the great lords,—and Ibn Batuta's list would lead to this conclusion,—or he may have been the same officer as at the

deputed and to receive his commands. There is next to him another of great authority, called the *Parenas;* then an *Endequery,* whose office is to be ever by the king, and to counsel

present day, viz., the *Hadégiri* (Pyrard, *Endequery*), who embraces the functions of the Treasurer (Pyrard's *Rans bandery*), and probably also those of the *Mas bandery* (Bell, *Report*, p. 66). Each atoll had, and still has, its collector, called by Pyrard the *Varuery*, or, as correctly given by Mr. Bell, *Váru-veri*, or *Atolu-veri*. They are now appointed by the Sultan on the recommendation of the Hadégiri. "They do not necessarily live in the respective atolls assigned to them. The majority remain at Málé, and employ sub-agents, *varhu-veri*, who are frequently Catibs. Each atoll has a storehouse (*váru-gé*), where the Government revenue is temporarily warehoused until required to be transmitted to Málé. The emoluments of this office must be considerable, as it is held by the relations of the Sultan and chief ministers, and frequently by the ministers themselves. Its tenure lasts for life, or during the Sultan's pleasure; and at the decease of an atolu-veri his estate is held liable for any balance due, or alleged to be due, for his division. The revenue of the different atolls, usually paid in native produce and manufacture, is collected into the treasury (*bodu-badéri-gé*) at Málé, whence it is shipped in the Sultan's and private vessels, on Government account, to different parts of India and Ceylon" (Bell, *Report*, p. 67).

It would seem from Christopher's account that the revenue officers have acquired in some measure the judicial powers formerly exercised by the Naibs and Catibs.

(iii). *Admiralty.*—Pyrard calls the High Admiral, *Velannas;* and says that he had two subordinates, *Mirvaires* (*Emir-el-Bahr*). Christopher calls him *Wilono Shabander*, and mentions also one Emir-el-Bahr, whom he describes as Master Attendant of Málé. Mr. Bell, as stated above, finds the *Velánú* gone altogether, and the Emir-el-Bahr (M. *Miru-Baharu*) elevated to a seat in the Cabinet.

(iv). *Military.*—The Maldive militia was under a general, called by Ibn Batuta the *Deherd*, and by Pyrard, *Dorimesna* (*Dorhiménú*). His lieutenant, not mentioned by Ibn Batuta, is by Pyrard called *Acouraz.* In Christopher's time the second Vizier retained his title (*Hakurá*), with no distinct duties. The gendarmerie of Málé (there appears to have been no military force in the other islands) was divided into six companies, raised in the six wards of the town. The company of each ward (*auare*) was under one of the six *Mouscoulis* or Viziers. Mr. Bell finds the militia still divided into six companies, with a nominal strength of 100 men each. The Sultan's body-guard of forty men is under a separate officer (*Report*, p. 68). The officer entitled by Ibn Batuta *Fitndyec*, or "Minister of Police", cannot be traced in later times.

him on all occasions and in all matters. Next, he that hath charge of the marine, called the *Velannas*, as we should say the admiral: I have said something of him above. He it is who keeps watch over all ships which arrive, and what merchandise they carry, having the care of lodging strangers, and representing their wants; in general, he hath an eye to all that concerns the shipping, and what comes by the sea. He is wont to board ships as they arrive, even the smallest barques, to take their rudders and have them borne to the king's house, for fear they should depart without leave. Under him are two sergeants, called *Mirvaires*, who keep watch over ships arriving, and render him an account of them, and otherwise carry out his orders and those of the king among the country people. These sergeants are known by reason that they carry in their hand a thick bâton of Bengal cane, which others than they durst not bear. There is also a general over all the militia, called the *Dorimenaz*, who has a lieutenant, called the *Acouraz*.

Besides these, there is the Chancellor, called *Manpas*, who applies to all letters the king's seal, which is nothing but his name in Arabic, graven in silver, dipped in ink, and pressed upon the paper. The secretary is called *Carans*[1]; the director of finance, *Mas bandery;* the treasurer, *Rans bandery;* and besides these are divers other minor offices which it were superfluous to describe in detail. Be it noted that all these above-mentioned great officers are often summoned to give counsel to the king, when he desires it, along with six persons of age and experience, and of the highest rank and learning, called *Mouscoulis*, that is, elders, of whom I have already spoken. They are nominated by the king, chosen

[1] From the Skt. *karan*, "a doer"; *cf.* Sin. *karanavá*, "to do". The word may have reached the Maldives from any part of India, where it was in general use for "a clerk". Ibn Bat. twice, at least, uses *kiráni* for a ship's clerk, and *cranny* is modern Anglo-Indian for a clerk or copyist. (See Yule and Burnell, *Gloss.*, s. v. *Cranny.*)

and deputed by the other grandees to assist the king, and give advice on all occasions, to avoid the necessity of calling together the whole council on every matter; in short, they manage all kinds of business, and are ready at all times to carry out the king's pleasure. It is the six elders, too, who administer justice in the palace to such as have appealed to the king, not being satisfied with the judgments of the Naibes and the Pandiare. They have command of six companies of men-at-arms, each his own.

Many other dignities there are of divers degrees, which the king grants unto such of the nobles as he hath a favour to, assigning to them certain islands for pension and salary, as he doth to all the above named, more or less, according to the rank and quality of each; we might say they are like the dignities of Count, Marquis, Baron, etc., with us. But besides the revenues of certain islands apportioned to these officers, the king also gives them rice for their maintenance, as he doth to the soldiers for their pay, with the tolls and dues from the barques and vessels that come to traffic at the Maldives: these the king allows to them for their support, besides some little presents which he gives them on certain days. The highest honour in that land is to eat the king's rice, and to be of the number of his officers; wanting that, a man is but little thought of, noble though he be; insomuch that, after the office bearers, the soldiers get the most honour and privilege, and a gentleman is of but small account if he be not enrolled in the militia.

This militia[1] consists of soldiers of the king's guard to the

[1] The Maldivians have never been a warlike people. Ibn Batuta says of them, "In body they are weak, and have no aptitude for combat or for war, and their arms are prayers." As will be seen hereafter, the military organisation described by Pyrard was totally unfit to meet the Bengal invaders, who slew the king and gave the author his liberty. Here is Mr. Bell's description of the present state of things:—"The sole military force consists of a nondescript militia (*Hagu-bê-kalun*) at Mâlé, divided into six companies, numbering nominally 100 men each, but

number of six hundred, divided into six companies, and commanded by the six Mouscoulis or elders; ten other great companies are also kept up. These ten companies have each for its captain one of the greatest lords in the kingdom. These latter do not keep the guard, but serve the king when he requires them, not only as soldiers to march and fight, but also to do whatsoever he bids them, as to launch a ship, or to haul it ashore, or to do other heavy labour wherein many hands are needed, even to build the king's palace, if occasion required, or to construct any other work or building for the king. They are called out by the sound of the bell of which I have spoken. They are divided into two regiments, for there are five companies which are more honourable, the nobles only being admitted to them; they also get more pay than the rest. As for the other five, they are of all sorts of people, and are less esteemed. The revenue of many islands is set apart for the payment of these companies. They have many privileges; among others, none durst strike them; and it is permitted to them to habit themselves differently from the rest, to wear a thick gold ring on the finger to assist them in drawing the bow, which others may not wear; in a word, to be more brave and fine in their dress. So there are few men of means but choose to

with an actual strength at the present day of probably not less than 1,200 all told. These companies were formerly under the command of the six viziers as captains (*Bodu-bé-kalun*). The soldiers bear no arms, and are under no sort of discipline beyond that which results from the habit of assembling, without much order or arrangement, when called together. Their duties, according to Christopher, are so anomalous that they often serve as sailors on board the public boats. A body of forty men (*Kudi-bẽ-kalun*) is required to mount guard in rotation at the Sultan's palace, and is in charge of an officer called *Má Baḍéri Takurú-fánu*. These men have certain privileges, and are distinguished from the *Hagu-bé-kalun* by their head-herchief. A small body-guard (*Dagedetere-bẽ-kalun*), bearing muskets, escort the Sultan whenever he appears in public" (Bell, *Report*, 68; also Christopher, in *Trans. Bom. Geo. Soc.*, i, 72).

join; albeit, they must have the permission of the king; and it costs them sixty larins to enter, whereof twenty go to the king for permission, and forty to be divided among the company which one desires to join. Slaves cannot enter them, nor may those whose business it is to gather and draw the produce of the coco-tree, nor other sorts of mean labouring men, nor such as know not to read or write, nor those who serve others. For the rest, most of the offices are bought of the king, and are much sought after by the rich for the sake of the honour, power, and authority which they get thereby over their fellows; but they may not sell them again, or transfer them to others.

All the islanders have but a single name apiece, without any surname or family name, those in most common use being *Mahomet, Haly, Hussum, Assan, Ibrahim*, and the like; but for the sake of distinction the name of their rank is added to their name: for instance, the nobles in blood add to their names *Tacourou*,[1] which shows who they are, and their wives, *Bybis*[2]; and besides that they add the name of the island which belongs to them. Such as are noble only by office or rank are called *Callogues*,[3] and their wives and daughters, *Camullogues*.[4] This name is used not only by the officers whom I have named, and others in actual service and pay, but also by many others who obtain sinecure rank from the king, so as to be distinguished from the common herd, and so to have a certain position and be respected accordingly. This is bought of the king dearly enough, yet such names and qualities are limited in number, to the end that the honour, being granted to but a few, may be more prized nor soon degraded. The common folk are called by the name

1 As pointed out above, the title of *Takuru-fánu* is, in these latter days, sold. Takuru is probably the Skt. *Thākur*, which survives in Bengal as *Tagore* (see Yule's *Gloss.*, Supplt., s. v. *Thakoor*).

2 *Bibi* (see Yule's *Gloss.*, s. v. *Beebee*).

3 *Kaloge*.

4 *Kamulo*.

Callo,[1] along with their own names, besides which is added the craft or condition of which each is. Their wives and daughters are called *Camulo*.[2]

CHAPTER XVI.

Of the king's palace,—a description of it; of his manner of life, and of the queens, his wives.

To come now to a description of the king's palace.[3] It has been mentioned several times above, that the king resides ordinarily at Malé, which is in consequence the chief of all the other islands, his palace being there.

It is built of stone, and consists of several houses well constructed, yet without much ornamental architecture, and of a single story. All around are orchards and gardens, with fountains and ponds of water, enclosed within walls, and paved with large polished stone. These places are guarded perpetually by men appointed to that duty; for it is there the king and his queens bathe, and it is strictly forbidden to all others to bathe there.

In the close of the palace, called in their language *gan-*

[1] *Kalo.* [2] *Kamulo.*

[3] The Sultan's palace seems to have been rebuilt or enlarged since Pyrard's time. Chr. gives the following description of it:—"The Sultan's palace is a large, upper-roomed house, with a peaked roof, covered with thick sheet-copper, in a walled enclosure, which is surrounded by a shallow moat, comprising an area of about a square mile. Within this space there is also a well-built magazine, besides several other houses, and a neat building raised on stone arches, from which the ladies witness the games exhibited before the court on festivals. One of the above-mentioned buildings is said to contain a variety of arms and relics taken from wrecked vessels; and it is currently reported and believed that there is a tank near the palace filled with ambergris" (*T. B. G. S.*, i, 53). Christopher was not admitted to view the interior, nor was Mr. Bell.

doyre,[1] which is of great extent, there are many buildings, and also courtyards, in each of which is a well, set off with fine white stone. In one of these courtyards are the two royal magazines; in the one the king keeps his cannon, in the other all his other sorts of arms.

At the entering in of the palace there is a guard-house, where you see some pieces of cannon and other arms. The gateway is made like a square tower, on top of which

Principal Entrance to the Palace.

the musicians play and sing on feast days, as I have described.

[1] M. *gaḍuvaru*, or *ganḍuvaru*. The meaning of the word is not quite clear. *Gaḍu* is "piece", or "part", as in *mas-gaḍu*, the best cut of fish; *re-gaḍu*, "the night (part of the day)". It also has an honorific sense, as in *alu-gaḍu-men*, "I", when used as our royal "we"; *fen-gaḍu*, water for the Sultan's use; *veḍun-gaḍu*, said of the present annually made to the Governor of Ceylon. The *varu* is, perhaps, only a plural suffix, as in *oyivaru*, "currents"; cf. *váru-veri*, above.

Proceeding thence, you come to the first hall, where the soldiers attend; further on, another great hall for the lords, gentlemen, and qualified persons: for nobody, be he lord, gentleman, or commoner, man or boy, woman or girl, durst go further than this, saving only the domestic officers of the king and queens, and their slaves and servants. Hear now how these halls are built. The floor is raised three feet above ground, and is laid with wood nicely joined and highly polished. It is for a precaution against the ants that the floor is thus raised, and it is the same in all the houses of the country, except that, as you may suppose, if builders' work can be done better at one place than another, it will be at the king's palace. The floor is all covered with little mats made at the islands, interlaced of divers colours, with figures and other patterns prettily worked, and marvellously fair to see. The walls are hung with silk tapestry; while above, the ceiling is covered also with silk tapestry from which hang pretty fringes as those of a curtain. In the hall of the soldiers and strangers the king had spread upon the ceiling the great ensign and banner of our vessel, which was blue, with the arms of France in gold, beautifully worked. He was greatly proud of this, showing it off as a curiosity to strangers; and ofttimes he made me explain what was represented in the arms, as indeed I did, not without causing him to wonder at the greatness of our king. In these halls, over the place where the king sits, there is another kind of ceiling and curtain of a richer character, under which is a large space raised two feet, and covered with a large carpet, on which he seats himself cross-legged, for they use no other seats. On the mats throughout the hall, the lords, when they come to court, sit in the same fashion.

At this court[1] the order of ranks is strictly observed; for

[1] According to Christopher, "the customs and etiquette observed in the Durbar are remarkable for their simplicity. The courtiers and officers take stations according to their respective ranks" (*T. Bo. G. S.*,

those of lower condition remain standing, unless the king, or in his absence the grandees who may be there, bid them to be seated. The places next to where the king is wont to sit are the most honourable, and so on in proportion to the distance. For the gentry of Malé, and other regular courtiers, who are bound to come and salute the king every afternoon, tarry sitting in this second hall, and may not proceed further; there they amuse themselves conversing with one another until the king comes forth, or some domestic officer shows himself, whom they bid tell the king that they have come to pay their respects, or convey some special request to him. Such is the manner of holding court in that country. Sometimes, while they are sitting there, the king sends them dishes of fruit and betel, which they esteem a great honour and favour. Once a week, or fortnight, as he pleases, the king comes to sit in this hall to take part in their deliberations, and to take counsel with them on affairs of state or other. The nobles of the other islands, who are very numerous, often come to court, and observe the same procedure as do those of Malé and the ordinary courtiers; but they never come for a fresh visit without bringing a present: for no one, whether noble or merchant, is admitted to salute the king unless he brings an offering. Likewise, those lords who hold islands of the king, bring the tribute due to him. By this manner of offering presents a man is soon aware whether he is in his good graces or not, for if the king accepts his present, he is assured of his goodwill; but if not, or if the king says not a word to the messenger who announces his arrival and conveys his respects, it is a certain sign of disfavour and disgrace. When the king receives strangers, it is in the first or large hall, where the guards attend.

The king's private apartments and the corridors are also much adorned, and are hung with silk tapestry, worked richly

i, 67). A court regulation requires that all persons wear dress of native manufacture when they come into the Sultan's presence.

with flower and branch patterns in gold and divers colours; this dazzles the eye, as well with the richness of the gold and the colours, as with the wondrous work of it. These hangings come for the most part from China, Bengal, Masulipatan, and St. Thomas, and are also made at the Maldives. The (common) people use cotton hangings, composed of pieces of cotton cloth of all colours, arranged together in various ways, and upon them figures and patterns in needle-work, or other pieces applied and sewn on. From Bengal comes also another sort of hanging, of fine linen painted and ornamented with colours in a very agreeable fashion: these they call *Iader*.[1]

The beds are suspended in air by four cords from a bar supported by two posts; the pillows and sheets are of cotton and silk, the whole covered with precious curtains of silk and cloth of gold. The beds of the king, the grandees, and the wealthy are in this style, as they are thus more comfortably rocked to sleep.[2] They are also accustomed, when they go to bed, to have their bodies handled and chafed, and gently rubbed by their attendants, and to be patted with both hands; they say this is good for their spleen disease, and that it cures the pain; it also puts them to sleep sooner, and makes them forget the pain in the part patted and rubbed. The ordinary domestics of the king sleep on cotton pillows laid on boards fixed on four posts four feet high.

The ordinary habit of the king was a gown, of exceeding white and fine cotton, or rather a cassock, falling to the waist or rather lower, with a border of white and blue, and fastened in front with buttons of massive gold. With this he wore

1 Probably the Hind. *chadar*, "a sheet", the Anglo-Indian *chudder* (see Yule and Burnell, *Gloss.*, s. v.)

2 Marco Polo, bk. III, ch. xvii, states that the wealthier people of the Coromandel coast had bedsteads of light canework, in which they were drawn up by cords nearly to the ceiling, in order to escape vermin during the night.

a piece of red taffetas, edged, reaching from the waist to the heels. This taffetas was girt with a long and large waistband of red silk with gold fringes, and by a heavy gold chain, fastened in front by a fine buckle larger than the hand, set with the rarest gems known. He carried also a knife, after the manner of his country, but richly ornamented. On his head he wore a little bonnet of red scarlet, which is highly prized in that country and permitted to the king alone: this bonnet was trimmed all round with gold, while on the top was a big button of solid gold with some precious stone, signifying in a way his royalty, the whole bound round with a turban of red silk like the waistband. And although the greatest lords and the soldiers like to wear their hair long, as has been said, yet he was wont to shave every week. He went always barelegged, like the rest, and wore on his feet only gold-sewn leather slippers,[1] brought from Arabia, and made like sandals. These no person in the kingdom, of whatever rank, would dare to wear, saving the queens and the princesses of his house. As for the princes, though they might, or could easily get permission, yet they care not to use aught but certain wooden sandals,[2] and those at home only, leaving to the king this mark of distinction between them and him, though he has another by which he may easily be recognised: for when he goes forth, a white umbrella or parasol[3] is borne over him. This is the chief mark of royal majesty; neither is it, nor would it be allowed to any other person whatsoever, except to foreigners, who are permitted to dress as they please, and carry what they like. Walking by the king on all occasions are pages, one carrying a fan, another the king's sword drawn and a buckler, a third his box of betel and areca, of which he partakes every hour.

[1] *Fai-rán-koḷu; koḷu* is a royal suffix, like *gaḍu*.

[2] *Maravali-koḷu*.

[3] *Hudu-hai-koḷu; hudu* = Sin. *hudu* or *sudu*, "white"; *hai* = Sin. *sat*, "umbrella".

A doctor of the law also follows, never losing sight of him, reading a book in his presence and admonishing him of his religion.

At table, where he eats alone, he is served by the chief of his household in the same manner as I have related of his subjects, except that he is served with greater care, honour, and reverence. His plate is neither gold nor silver, for that is forbidden by their law; but of porcelain, or of other China fabric, or of copper, neatly fashioned and worked at the Maldives; he also uses the boxes of polished and lacquered wood.[1]

His exercise and ordinary pastime was not to go forth frequently, or to go a-fishing, as I learnt from the islanders was the habit of kings that preceded him, but to tarry most of his time shut up in his palace, entertaining his queens, seeing his courtiers, and superintending numbers of workmen and artisans, such as painters, goldsmiths, embroiderers, cutlers, bead-makers, turners, joiners, armourers, and divers others, whom he kept at his palace, supplying them with materials, and paying them for their work as it was finished; he then stored the articles with care in various places in the palace, and sometimes made presents of them. In this occupation he took much delight and spent much of his time; he also used himself to work, and would say it was a sin to be idle. He was of quick and ready wit, knowing something of most things; he worked at several crafts and trades, and was ever anxious to learn; he sought out such as excelled at anything; and if he met with any foreigner who knew something that neither he nor his islanders knew, he paid him great attention, to the end that he should teach him his art.

When he goes out he is accompanied by his soldiers, of whom a hundred are on guard daily. On Fridays, when he goes to the mosque, it is in fine array and in grand pomp, as

[1] See above, at p. 170-1.

I have to some extent described above, for the soldiers march in order, one company before and the other behind, his ordinary officers beside him, along with the greatest men of his court, while drums, flutes, trumpets, and other instruments are played with a harmony most pleasing to the ear.[1] The service done, he returns to his palace in the same order, the soldiers marching to the sound of the instruments, and dancing and capering in front of the king with their arms, and with their swords striking the shields of one another: in this they show their address, for to avoid confusion they strike not all together, but two at a time only, and one after another continuously. The residents of the island who have taken part in the festival escort him back, and it would be a shame for any not to go. Arrived at his palace, the king keeps the Pandiare, the Naybes, Catibes, and Moudins, as well as the chief lords, gentlemen, and soldiers, or such as he selects on each occasion to dine at the palace, and after dinner he sits to administer justice. When the king used to go out, he went always on foot (since on none of the islands are there any horses or other beasts for riding), except when he was carried in a chair on the shoulders of his slaves; but that happened rarely or never, for, being strong and healthy, he liked better to walk afoot; besides, the island is of but little extent. At Malé the streets and roads are not paved, and still less elsewhere, wherefore the inhabitants, to prevent weeds growing upon them, are obliged to sweep them; this they do principally at the festivals, for then they know that the king or the queens must come and walk about the island, and on that account they are careful.

When the king walks in the street, the people quit that side and leave it free, and go to the other, so that there be none where the king goeth; for the king never passeth between two persons, and great care is taken not to touch

[1] See Ibn Batuta's description of the Vizier's procession to the mosque, App. A.

him. The great lords are treated in the same way in their own islands by their inferiors.

It is also to be remarked that when one speaks to the king or the queens or their children, or to the princes of the blood, or when one speaks of them to others, it is in terms applied only to them, and such as one durst not apply to others; as, for example, when you say of a man that he sleeps, of the king you would say he slumbers, or takes rest; and these terms are never used but with respect to the king.[1]

The king's wives are habited in the same style as I have described the great ladies, save that they are more profuse with gold, pearls, and gems, in the richness of their ear-pendants, gold chains, and bracelets, and in their carkanets on the neck, arms, and legs.

The ladies that are wives or daughters of the grandees of the island are expected to go and visit them in the evening, to pass the time with them and to take them presents.

Sometimes the queens go abroad, but that is rarely, and then they have women and slaves who go far ahead to warn men to keep out of the way, and not show themselves on the road: only women are allowed. Indeed, the women assemble from their several wards, and come forward with little offerings, such as flowers and fruits. Four chief women bear over the heads of the queens a silk curtain reaching to the ground, in such wise that they cannot be seen.

When they are with child, they also go out to bathe in the sea, like all the other women, for it is a custom of the country, and esteemed healthy. For this purpose a little shed or enclosure of posts and sticks is erected in the sea, and covered all round with cloths. There the queens and grand ladies bathe at their ease, after which they come out into

[1] So in modern Maldivian and Sinhalese; of an ordinary person it is said, *nidáoti*, "he sleeps", Sin. *nidáganuavá;* of the Sultan or other great person it is said, *avahárafụla*, "he slumbers", Sin. *sætapenavá.*

another little house built on purpose, where they have another bath of fresh water nicely served.

In the apartments of the queens, princesses, and great ladies, no daylight is admitted, but only lamps are kept burning continually. They withdraw to a part of their chamber where they are shut off by four or five several curtain-hangings, which have to be raised one by one before a person gets to where they are; but no man or woman, domestic or stranger, whoever it might be, would dare lift the last, although they might not be asleep, taking their meals, or doing anything. One must first cough and say who it is, and then the ladies call to him, or send, according to their pleasure. By the way, I omitted to say that all women and girls when they go to bed take off only their robe, and wear their waist-cloths; but these are cloths solely for night use, and men have the like, and they would not think of doing otherwise.

CHAPTER XVII.

Of the revenues of the king, money, traffic, and commerce of the Maldives; and of the merchandise imported and exported.

The revenues of the king consist of his domains, many islands being held of him in seignory; next of the dues[1] paid by his subjects of the produce of the land, that is to say, the fifth part of all grain sown; a certain share of the cocos

[1] "Each atoll is bound to pay yearly a certain portion of its produce, said to be levied as a poll-tax upon every male or female over twelve years of age, at the following rates:—1 *kotta* of cowries, 12 *cadjans* (M. *fan*), and 1 *tula* (28 lb.) of coir for every woman and girl, and for each man and boy the same, with the addition of 50 dried fish, 100 coco-nuts, and 50 *adubá* of jaggery" (Bell, *Report*, 67). "Native money is now occasionally accepted in lieu of produce" (*ibid.*).

and lemons has also to be paid; but they compound with him by a fixed annual contribution of honey[1] or fruit. Besides these dues, the king imposes on his subjects an ordinary tax, according to their means, consisting of coco-cordage, of shells called *Boly*, of which I have spoken, and of dried fish in those islands where it more abounds and the fishing is best,—for they never pay him these dues and taxes in money, except when they buy rank or office, or the permission to don their braveries. Also he requires the inhabitants of the islands to make and furnish annually as much cotton-cloth as he delivers to them of raw cotton: this is for the use of the soldiers, to whom he gives these cloths three times a year, besides their pay.[2] The king's revenue consists also of merchandise; for all ships that put in there in the first instance report themselves to him and declare their cargo; then he compounds with them at a certain price for what he wants to take, and this is most often the greater portion: afterwards the people buy the rest at a price fixed at higher rates than the king has paid, and then the king distributes his merchandise abroad among the richer islands at such prices as he pleases, though they have no need of the goods, while he takes from them in exchange such merchandise as he wants at no more than half its value.[3] Ofttimes, too, he despatches ships to foreign parts, laden with the merchandise of his island, insomuch that his revenue cannot with any certainty be told, for it is variable, now more, now less; and sometimes he has a loss, chiefly when his ships are wrecked, or fail to make a good port.

[1] *I.e.*, jaggery or palm-sugar.

[2] "A payment of cloth and mats is also exacted from atolls where these are manufactured" (Bell, *Report*, 67). Christopher says that the Sultan makes an annual distribution of red cloth to the Viziers for the soldiers under their command, each man receiving a piece of cloth and 30 pice in money (*T. Bom. Geo. Soc.*, i, 72).

[3] The Sultan still asserts a right of pre-emption at low rates on all cargoes imported from foreign parts (Bell *Report*. 67).

Besides these revenues, the king has certain dues appurtenant to him—for instance, all that is found on the sea-shore belongs to him: a man dare not touch such a thing with a view to keeping it; he is bound to collect it, and bear it to him, whether it be wreckage, timber, chests, or other casualties; or ambergris, called by them *gomen*, and when prepared, *Meuuare*,[1] of which more is found there than in

[1] *Goma*, the Maldivian name for ambergris, is also the Sinhalese for cow-dung, which it somewhat resembles in appearance and consistency. No doubt they thought it was whales' dung, as did the Japanese, according to Kœmpfer. *Meuuare* is for *mávaharu* (= *maha*, *vaharu*), the "very sweet smelling" substance. Ambergris, the origin of which was so long obscure, is now known to be a secretion formed in the stomach or intestines of the *Physeter macrocephalus*, or spermaceti whale. It is found chiefly in those whales which appear torpid and lean, whence it appears to be the product of disease (McCulloch's *Dict. of Com.*). It is opaque and soft, and when heated gives out a peculiarly agreeable perfume. It is now used only for perfumery, but was formerly employed in medicine as a cordial and an aphrodisiac (*G. de Orta*, f. 14).

The first notion as to the origin of ambergris seems to have been that it was a kind of fungus, produced at the bottom of the sea (see Reinaud, *Relation des Voyages par les Arabes*, i, p. 4). The knowledge that it came from the whale is, however, found in *Mas'udi*, i, 335. Marco Polo (Yule's edit., ii, 341) states the same, and that in his time whales were killed with harpoons, for the possession of their ambergris. Friar Jordanus, in the fourteenth century, mentions it as *embar*, and says it is like wood (p. 43). Barbosa, who says that large quantities were found at the Maldives, relates (p. 165) that the Moors informed him that it was the droppings of birds, which, torn from the rocks by storms, floated on the sea, and was afterwards swallowed by whales. Kœmpfer (*Hist. of Japan*, Eng. trans., i, 111-12) says it is chiefly found in the intestines of whales, but retails the current stories of its nature, as birds' dung, a sea-sponge, and also a bituminous substance, or a kind of earth or clay. Garcia de Orta (f. 13) does not believe that it comes from the whale. Sir R. Hawkins states that some think it to be found in the bowels of the whale, or voided by him, "and maintaine for certaine that the same is ingendred by eating an hearbe which groweth in the sea. This hearbe is not in all seas, say they, and therefore, where it wanteth, the whales give not this fruit" (Hawkins, *Voyages*, 155). P. Vincenzo says that it is produced at the bottom of the sea, and afterwards refined in the whale's belly (ed. 1678, p. 242). Though so much

any of the East Indies; it, too, belongs to the king, and he that would dare appropriate it would have his hand cut off. It is the same with a certain nut, cast up by the sea from time to time, and as big as a man's head, which one might liken to a couple of large melons joined together: this they call *Tavarcarré*,[1] believing that it comes of certain trees

was known, Tavernier thinks its origin still an open question—"there is no person in the world that knows either what it is, or where or how it is produced" (pt. II, ch. xxi).

Ambergris is of several descriptions. Barbosa (*loc. cit.*) mentions the white (*ponabar*), the greyish (*puambar*), and the brown (*minabar*). The lightest in colour is the best, though Herbert (4th edit., p. 372) says the grey is better than the white. It was always rare, and fetched high prices, and being a product of the sea, was generally (but not in Japan, according to Kœmpfer) regarded as royal property. It may be superfluous to note here that the *'anbar* of the Arabs, and of all these travellers, was solely the whale-secretion. The application of the word to the yellow amber, as we now use it, is modern. Large pieces of ambergris were occasionally found. Kœmpfer speaks of a piece found in Japan, weighing 100 *cattis*, or 130 lb. Dutch, and of another weighing 185 lb., sold by the King of Tidore to the Dutch E. I. Company for 11,000 rix-dollars, or about £2,000. Tavernier mentions two pieces of 33 and 42 lb. respectively as being large. Capt. Hamilton saw a piece belonging to the Raja of Cananore "as big as a bushel, and valued at Rs. 10,000, or £1,250 sterling" (*New Acct.*, etc., i, 298). But these are small compared to that recorded by J. los Santos as having been found on the coast of Melinde, which was so big that a man could hide behind it! (Fr. trans., p. 105).

Tavernier states that the Governor of Mozambique was in the habit of getting 300,000 pardaos of ambergris during his three years' term of office, one pardao being equal to about 2*s*. 6*d*. Its value in the Portuguese time is difficult to determine, owing to its variety of quality; some information will be found in the *Livro dos Pesos*, etc. (p. 13), and the *Lembranças* (p. 46), contained in *Subsidios para a Hist. da Ind. Port.*

Ambergris is found throughout all the tropic seas, and, in former times at least, was occasionally washed ashore in Spain and England (Hawkins, *Voy.*; Tavernier, *loc. cit.*).

[1] This is the celebrated sea coco-nut (*coco de mer*), *Lodoicea Seychellarum*. From the mistake as to its habitat it was termed *Cocos maldivicus* by Rumphius, and, from its fancied medicinal properties, *Nux medica* by Clusius. The species *Lodoicea* grows only on the Seychelles; the trees being close upon the sea-shore, the fruit is floated across the

under the sea: the Portuguese call it "coco des Maldives"; it is an article of medicine, and fetches a high price. Often at the season for this *Tauarcarré*, or for grey and black amber (as this too is found there), the king's servants and officers harass the poor people when they suspect them of having found any; nay more, when they have a grudge against a man, they impute to him this charge, as they do here that of false money, to the end that he may be searched; and when

Indian Ocean, and being occasionally picked up at the Maldives, was supposed, at first, to be a product of these islands, and afterwards, when the tree was not forthcoming, of a species which grew under the sea. See, as to this tree, Sir W. J. Hooker, in *Bot. Mag. and Reg.*, vol. xii; Macleod (L.), *Eastern Africa*, i, 224-7; G. de Orta, 69-71; Sonnerat, *Voy.*, Eng. trans., pp. 2-6; Thunberg, *Travels*, 3rd edit., iv, 133, 159; Labillardière's *Voyage in Search of La Pérouse*; and Yule's *Glossary*, s. v. "Coco de mer".

Like many other products, the sea coco-nut was a remedy for all manner of ailments, such as the flux, epilepsy, and apoplexy (Thunberg), colic, paralysis, and nervous infirmities (G. de Orta). Above all, it was an antidote to poison; and Faria-y-Sousa says it is "a greater antidote against poison than bezoar stone"; while de Orta, with greater medical experience, believed the bezoar to be better. The shell was made into goblets for kings of the East and West, and set in gold and diamonds, and it was supposed that those who drank a poisoned draught out of those marvellous cups would escape unhurt. According to de Orta, the Queen of Portugal sent every year for these nuts. The Emperor Rudolf II is said to have offered 4,000 florins for a single specimen (*Malte Brun*, iv, 420). It is thus described in the *Lusiads* (x, 136):

> "Nas ilhas de Maldiva nasce a planta
> No profundo das aguas, soberana,
> Cujo pomo contra o veneno urgente
> Hé tido por antidoto excellente,"

The name *tavarcarré* is given in Piso's *Mantissa Aromatica*, and also by Sonnerat and Thunberg; and no doubt they borrowed it from Pyrard. Sonnerat says the meaning of the word is "treasure", but it is clear that he has mistaken the passage following, where Pyrard says that when a man becomes suddenly rich, he is said to have found *tavarcarré*, or amber, "as though it were treasure". The Maldivian word, as Mr. Bell informs me, is *tâva' karhi*, or *tava karhi*, *i.e.*, the "hard (shelled) nut"; M. *tava* = Sin. *tada*.

one becomes suddenly rich, it is commonly said that he has found *Tauarcarré*, or amber, as though it were treasure. There is also a plentiful fishery of black coral,[1] which belongs to the king, and he keeps numbers of men employed at it.

The coin of the realm is silver only, and of one sort. These are pieces of silver called *larins*,[2] of the value of eight sous

Maldive Larin.

or thereabouts of our money, as I have said, as long as the finger, but doubled down. The king has them struck in his island, and stamped with his name in Arabic characters. All other coins are foreign, and though they are current, they are only taken at their just value and weight, and they must be

[1] M. *endiri.*

[2] This coin takes its name from the city Lar, in Persia. The earliest mention of it by a European writer is, so far as I am aware, in the *Lembranças das Cousas da India* (*Subsidios*, iii, 53), that is, in 1525, and the following table is given :—2 *fules* =1 dinar; 12 dinars =1 tanga; 3 tangas 10 dinars =1 new larin; 3 tangas 9 dinars =1 old larin. At Cambaye, the same writer says (p. 38) that 1 *tanga larin* = 60 reis, and that 45 of these larins weighed 1 Portuguese marco, *i.e.*, 50 grammes each (*Subsidios*, i, 61). We get the following values from Antonio Nunes (1551), in his *Livro dos Pesos*, etc.: "At the port of Bengala, 80 cowries =1 *pone;* 48 *pones* =1 larin" (*Subsidios*, i, 61). The editor of the *Subsidios*, taking a *marco* of silver in the reign of João III as being equivalent to 2,500 reis, notes that the larin would then be worth 51.012 reis.

The early Portuguese writers do not mention the shape of the larin, but there is no reason to doubt that it was as Pyrard describes it, that is, in the form in which it was current all over Western India in the seventeenth and eighteenth centuries.

The earliest Dutch authority describes it as current at Goa and the Malabar coast :—"Ils usent aussi une monnoye venant de Perse nommée *Larrin*, du nom de la ville *Lar*, où on les forge ; elle est longue comme gros fil d'argent, doublé : ayant à l'un costé un signe ou caractère du Roy de Perse; elle est de pur argent sans aucune mixtion : valent la pièce 105 ou 108 Basarucos selon que le change va" (*Premier*

gold or silver; all others are rejected. For in India and the adjacent parts, where there are many kingdoms and lord-

Livre de la Nav., p. 53, f. *b*). In Pyrard's time the larin was worth a little more than the tanga; he says a larin was worth 8 sous, and a tanga 7½ sous. The author of the *Premier Livre, loc. cit.*, likewise gives a pardao as being 6 tangas or 5 larins.

Mendelslo, in 1637, in describing the money of Persia, indicates that the larin which was formerly coined by Shah Ismail was then no longer minted (Eng. trans., p. 299); but Tavernier, about the same time, states that the Arabian merchants coming to Persia take nothing but larins for their goods (Eng. trans., pt. ii. p. 1). Chardin, at the end of the seventeenth century, states that the larin was no longer minted, but was still current all along the Persian Gulf (*Voyage*, 1711, p. 92).

In Ceylon, the larin is traced almost into the present century. Valentyn says that the cinnamon and cardamoms of Ceylon were exported to Persia, and paid for in ready cash: this cash was in all probability larins. Tennent (*Ceylon*, i, 463) says that the Ceylon larins are stamped with Persian characters; but this cannot be true of them all, for Knox (1660-79) writes: "The shape is like a fish-hook; they stamp what mark or impression on it they please" (*Knox*, 98, mispaged 97).

Thunberg was informed that larins were struck by the king of Kandy; he describes them thus:—"It consists of a silver cylinder, hammered out, which in the middle is bent together, the ends being afterwards turned up like a hook, and the upper end distinguished either with certain letters or stars, or else with engravings. One of them which I procured by barter cost 12 Dutch stivers, and another, of a smaller size, 9; both of them were of fine silver" (Thunberg, *Travels*, iv, 210-2). Fra Bartolomeo thinks the larin was introduced by a modern king of Kandy, and describes it as "a piece of silver wire rolled up like a wax taper. When a person wishes to make a purchase, he cuts off as much of this silver as is equal in value to the price of the article." According to Davy, it had a definite value equal to 7*d*. English.

There are some interesting papers on the *larin* in the *Numismatic Chronicle*, viz., by Mr. W. B. Dickinson, in vol. xi, at p. 161; vol. xii, p. 82; vol. xiii, p. 61; and by Prof. H. H. Wilson, in vol. xvi, at p. 179. The first-named writer gives some excellent illustrations of various forms of the larin in vol. xi; and Prof. Wilson gives a plate of some specimens of a parcel of 397 larins found at Sangameswara, in the Ratnagiri collectorate, in 1846. These latter seem to have been all of the straight variety, *i.e.*, bent only once. The legends of most were illegible, owing to the silver being too narrow for the stamp; but, by collation of various specimens, Prof. Wilson read the legend of one

ships, there is a great variety of money, both as to form and stamp, not only of gold and silver, but also of another

side as "Sultan Ali Aadil Shah", and of the other, "Zarb Lari—Dangh Sikka", *i.e.*, "Struck at Lari" (or rather, "a Lari", as Mr. Thomas suggests)—"stamped tanga", and of date A.H. 1071, *i.e.*, A.D. 1659. Notwithstanding this legend, the probability is that the coins were struck at Bijapur. Mr. Vaux read, on some larins of the British Museum collection, the legend, "Mohammad the prophet of God", and the word "Melek" (king). There is no sufficient proof of the currency in India of the larin in the eighteenth century, as Prof. Wilson believes, in reliance upon a Sattara document of 1711, wherein is mention of "Dabul larins", as, long before this time, the word had become a mere expression in the territories where Portuguese influence prevailed.

Ceylon Larin (fish-hook).

The cut given on p. 232 of a Maldive larin obtained by Mr. Bell (it has long since gone out of use) shows that it was identical in shape with the Persian coin (see the cuts in Tavernier, and in the *Premier Livre*, etc.). The Ceylon coin, as will be observed from Thunberg's description, was first doubled flat, and then bent in the shape of a fish-hook, as stated by Knox. To the present day it is known in Ceylon as the "fish-hook" coin. Cuts of it will be found in Davy's *Ceylon*, p. 245, and in *Tennent*, i, 463, as well as in the *Num. Chron.*, *ubi supra*, and in Mr. Rhys Davids' article in *Numismata Orientalia* (part iv, p. 34). The British Museum possesses between twenty and thirty specimens, most of them presented by Mr. Marsden, but, unfortunately, it is not known where any of them were found, and the characters of but few are legible; I am therefore unable to say whether the Ceylon hook-form is common to the larins of other countries.

Although, as stated above, the silver larin is now obsolete at the Maldives, the name has passed to copper coins of the ordinary shape.

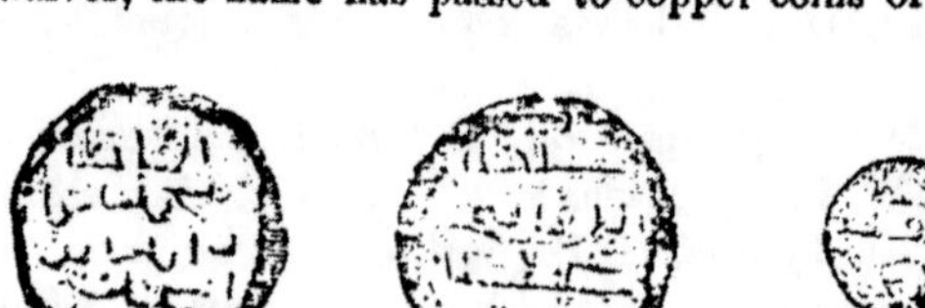

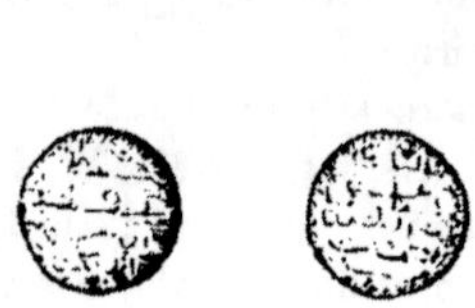

Kuda lári.

Bodu lári.

These are of two kinds, the *bodu lári* (big lari) and the *kuda lári* (little lari)—25 of the former and 100 of the latter going to a rupee. Mr.

metal called *Calin*,[1] which is white like tin, but harder, purer, and finer, and much used in the Indies: coin is also made of iron. But this kind of money is only current in the territory of the prince that coins it; so that in this matter there is great diversity, by reason of the multitude of duchies, in such wise that the Portuguese at Goa struck coin of calin or of iron, which would be of no use in Portugal, nor even at the town of Cochin, which also belongs to them, in India, and is not far from Goa; so that there they likewise employ a peculiar coinage. But gold and silver, of whatever form or stamp, is taken in all the kingdoms at its proper value, which nevertheless is very different from ours, seeing that silver is in greater demand, and is dearer than here, and gold cheaper. Spanish reals fetch a high price, the silver being very good. Now to return to the Maldives: the king coins larins only; other pieces of less value he coins not at all; insomuch that for the uses of trade they cut the silver and pay by weight for the value of the goods bought: but this is not done without some loss, for in cutting the larin they lose a twelfth part. They take no silver without weighing it and trying it in the fire to prove it; and everybody

Bell has specimens of these larins dating from 1716 down to 1877 (*Report*, 118, 121).

[1] This was, in fact, Malayan tin. The word is originally Malay (*kalang*); it appears in Arabic as *ḳala'i*, and in the Portuguese writers as *calaim* (*Livro das Monçoes*, ii, 181; *Subsidios*, i, 6; ii, 17, 256; iii, 54; Correa, *Lendas*, ii, 256). The form *calin* seems to have been adopted by French writers from Pyrard (see Marsden, *Sumatra*, 22). As to the history of the word, see, further, Yule's *Glossary*, s. v. *Calay*, where it will be seen that other writers of the period, like Pyrard, conceived it to be a distinct metal. Tin coin was in use at Malacca long before the Portuguese conquest (Correa, *Lendas*, ii, 256; Da Cunha, *Indo-Port. Num.*, p. 16). A *calaim* there was worth 100 caixes, or 11 Port. reis (*Dalb. Comm.*, Hak. Soc., iii, 78, *note*). The metal was introduced into the Portuguese coinage by Albuquerque, but chiefly as an alloy with lead, and the name *calaim* as a coin then disappeared.

has weights in his house for this purpose. Then, in place of copper and small change, they use the shells of which I have said somewhat above, and will presently say more; 12,000 of them are worth a larin. For the rest, all the gold and silver comes from abroad; there are no mines in the islands. In all the public markets and in their private traffic they most frequently barter one thing for another.

There is a great trade at the Maldives, and they are much frequented for their commodities. You see merchants from all quarters, as Malabar men from Barcelor, Onor, Bacalor, Cananor, Calecut, Tananor, Cochin, Coilam, Cael[1]; Guzeratis from Cambaye, Surat, and Chaul; Arabs, Persians, men of Bengal, St. Thomas, and Masulipatam, Ceylon, and Sumatra, who bring goods that are in demand there, and take away what the Maldives produce in abundance. First, of the coco tree, which grows naturally at the islands without any cultivation, they make many sorts of goods in demand with the foreigners: for instance, cordage, with which all the vessels of the Indies are equipped; the coco fruit, which is carried in such quantity to the coasts of Arabia and Malabar and throughout India, that more than a hundred ships are laden with it every year, as well as with the oil and honey of the same tree; and the leaves which serve for sails: but the greatest trade is in cordage.

There is another kind of wealth at the Maldives, viz., certain little shells containing a little animal, large as the tip of the little finger, and quite white, polished, and bright: they are fished twice a month, three days before and three days after the new moon, as well as at the full, and none would be got at any other season. The women gather them on the sands and in the shallows of the sea, standing in the water up to their waists. They call them *Boly*,[2] and export to all parts an infinite

[1] These Malabar ports are mentioned separately hereafter.

[2] The cowry, *Cypræa moneta*, M. *boli*; *cf.* Sin. *bella* (*animate*), and pl. *b.li*, "shells" (*inanimate*); well known as a very ancient and still the

quantity, in such wise that in one year I have seen thirty or forty whole ships loaded with them without other cargo. All

most widely used shell-money. Pyrard writes it here *boly*, and elsewhere *bolli*. The earlier geographers, the two Mahomedans of the ninth century, Masudi in the tenth, and Edrisi in the twelfth (*vide infra*, App. A), all describe the cowry as being taken by casting wood or branches into the sea, the creatures fastening themselves thereon in great numbers. The same method is stated by de Barros (*Dec. III*, liv. III, c. iv), and by Capt. Hamilton early in the eighteenth century. Ibn Batuta (see App. A) does not say how they are taken, but mentions that they are placed in pits in the sand in order to rot. According to Pyrard, corroborated by Mr. Bell, they are taken by men wading up to the waist.

In the Arab *Relation*, i, p. 5, they are said to be called on the islands *al-kabtaj;* Edrisi writes *el kendj;* and Albiruni refers to the M. as *Diwa kandha*, *i.e.*, Cowry Islands. Ibn Bat. calls them *wada'*, a frequent Arabic word for them. The Portuguese, Dutch, and English have all adopted the word cowry from the Hind. *kauri*, though the Portuguese commonly referred to them as *buzios*, "shells".

All these quoted writers state that a large trade was carried on from the Maldives in these shells, that they formed the king's treasure, and in fact were used as money. Ibn Batuta is the first to give measures and values. He describes them as sold by the *syah* (100), *fâl* (700), *cotta* (12,000), and *bostou* (100,000). At the Maldives the market value ranged from four to twelve *bostou* to a dinar of gold, probably = 10*s*. 6*d*. As to the value of the *dinar* in Ibn Batuta's time, see *Cathay*, 439. Even then it seems cowries were current all over Africa, distance adding greatly to their value; for Ibn Bat. adds that a dinar of gold, which would purchase four to twelve *bostou* at the Maldives, was given in the Soudan for only 1,150 shells. It is somewhat strange that, though these shells have been for so many centuries current coin in Bengal and all over Africa, they seem never to have been adopted for monetary purposes on the neighbouring coast of Malabar (see *Varthema*, p. 131, *note*), nor even in Ceylon. The Portuguese bought cowries at the Maldives by the *cotta* (spelt *cota*, *Subsidios*, i, 35), 4½ cottas being taken as weighing a quintal: the price in Portuguese currency is not stated. Nunes, the author here quoted, however, gives the value at the ports of Bengala, where of course the price has always been much higher. There, in 1554, cowries were current coin, 80 = 1 *pone* (= *paṇ*, which is still used in Bengal for 80 cowries), and 48 *pones* = 1 larin; and a quintal was worth 700 reis (*ib.*, 37). In Bengal, therefore, a larin purchased only 3,840 cowries, while at the Maldives it would purchase 12,000.

go to Bengal, for there only is there a demand for a large quantity at high prices. The people of Bengal use them for

Pyrard gives the current price as 12,000 = 1 larin = 8 sous, which would, at the then rate of exchange, equal about 7½*d*. English.

The period of Dutch supremacy in Ceylon, which included the suzerainty of the Maldives, was also the great period of the African slave trade, and large quantities of cowries were exported *viâ* Ceylon to the European markets, to be thence employed in purchasing human beings on the Guinea coast. In 1740 the Dutch Governor fixed the price at 2½ rix-dollars for a cotta of 24 lb. The annual home demand was then 400,000 lb., which, he says, would sell for fl. 1,100,000 (£8,300), but even then was not a profitable business (Lee's *Ribeyro*, App., p. 175). If the price so fixed was what the Dutch paid the Maldive Sultan, it results that the impetus given by the slave trade had sent up the market for cowries. But the most interesting account of these shells in connection with the slave trade occurs in the narrative of an anonymous Dutch gentleman, published in English in 1747 (*A Voyage to the Island of Ceylon*, etc., by a Dutch gentleman, London, 1754):—"The Dutch drive a considerable trade with the inhabitants of the Maldives for those little shells called *cowries*, where are prodigious quantities of them, and not only on the shore, but in the very ground, being probably deposited there at the time of the Flood, and left there when the ocean receded from the land. What we call money being arbitrary, and its nature and value depending on a tacit convention betwixt men, these shells, in several parts of Asia and Africa, are accounted current money, with a value assigned to them. This is established by a reciprocal consent, and those who are pleased to show a contempt of them don't reflect that shells are as fit for a common standard of pecuniary value as either gold or silver; they certainly forget that they themselves are obliged to do what they ridicule, and take them for ready money. In 1740, 2,400 *cowries* [probably 24,000, or 2 cottas] were equal to a *rupee*, or about a crown at three guilders of our money.

"But their great currency is on the coast of Africa, particularly *Guinea*, where the negroes value them as much as gold and silver, and call them *bougies* [Port. *buzios*]. An instance of the great consumption of these shells, that the French merchants of the kingdom of *Whydah* usually give forty pounds of these *cowries* for every piece of common linen manufactured by the natives, and proportionably for the products of the country, as wax, ivory, gold, etc. The company it is which supplies the European nation with the far greater part of this negro money, if I may be indulged the expression. The esteem in which these shells are on the coast of *Guinea* must appear surprising. They are not only, like gold and silver, the measure and instrument of commerce betwixt

ordinary money, although they have gold and silver and plenty of other metals; and, what is more strange, kings and great lords have houses built expressly to store these shells, and treat them as part of their treasure. All the merchants from other places in India take a large quantity to carry to Bengal, where they are always in demand; for they are produced nowhere but at the Maldives, on which account they serve as petty cash, as I have said. When I came to Malé for the first time, there was a vessel at anchor from Cochin, a

the negroes, but worn as ornaments in necklaces and bracelets, strung in one or more rows, which looks something odd, yet not amiss, by the contrast of the whiteness of the shells with the blackness of their skins.

"Formerly twelve thousand-weight of these *cowries* would purchase a cargo of five or six hundred negroes; but those lucrative times are now no more; and the negroes now set such a value on their countrymen, that there is no such thing as having a cargo under twelve or fourteen tons of cowries.

"As payments in this kind of specie are attended with some intricacy, the negroes, though so simple as to sell one another for shells, have contrived a kind of copper vessel, holding exactly a hundred and eight pounds, which is a great despatch to business. However, the *Maldives* must not be thought the only place which affords these shells; they are also found in the *Philippine* islands, but they don't come up to the *Maldivian*, either in colour or clearness. The chief European market for these shells is Amsterdam, where there are spacious warehouses of them, the French and English merchants buying them up to send to Africa."

The rate of exchange in Bengal at the end of last century, given by Fra Bartolomeo, was 60 to the pice, or 3,840 to the rupee (*Fra Bart.*, Eng. trans., 86). In 1820 the Bengal rate was 6,000 to the rupee, *i.e.*, Rs. 2 the cotta (*Prinsep. Ind. Ant.*); the same price obtained at Málé in 1835 (*T. Bom. Geo. Soc.*, i, 85). In 1843 the exchange in Bengal was at 64 cowries to the pice, which would now purchase about six times the number. At Málé the price in recent years has generally been R. 1.50 the *cotta* = 25 lb., or Rs. 5 the cwt. It is a far cry from Masudi to Mincing Lane, but I may conclude this note with the following extract made by Mr. Bell from a recent Produce Market Report:—"Cowries, Maldive small, 15*s.* to 18*s.* per ton; medium, 10*s.* to 12*s.*; large, 6*s.* Very dull. Bombay large common Maldive, 8*s.* to 10*s.* per cwt.; medium Calcutta, 20*s.*"

town of the Portuguese, of 400 tons burthen; the captain and merchants were Mestifs,[1] the others Christianised Indians, all habited in the Portuguese fashion, and they had come solely to load with these shells for the Bengal market.[2] They give 20 *coquetees*[3] [? kegs] of rice for a parcel of shells: for all these *Bolys* are put in parcels of 12,000, in little baskets of coco leaves of open work, lined inside with cloth of the same coco tree, to prevent the shells falling out. These parcels or baskets of 12,000 are negotiated there as bags of silver are here, which between merchants are taken as counted, but not by others: for they are so clever at counting, that in less than no time they will take tally of a whole parcel. Also in Cambaye and elsewhere in India they set the prettiest of these shells in articles of furniture, as if they were marbles or precious stones.

The Maldives have also an infinite abundance of fish of all kinds, as I have said before. And so rich is the fishery, that not only have they always enough to fill their own bellies withal, but they also sell a large quantity, both cooked and dried, to foreigners. This commodity is in great demand in all parts of India, notably in Sumatra, whither whole shiploads are carried.

Tortoise-shell, called *Cambe*,[4] is much valued in the Indies.

1 *Mestif*, or *métif*, is the Fr. corruption of the Port. *mestiço*, a half-caste; though Pyrard elsewhere, and also Mocquet, write *métice*. Cotgrave has *mestif*, a mongrel. The now obsolete Anglo-Indian form was *mustees* or *mustice* (see Yule, *Glossary*, s. v.)

2 See *supra*, p. 78.

3 From *coquet*, the syn. of which are "caque", "baril", and "tonnelet" (see earlier editions of Ducange, s. v. *Cochetus*).

4 M. *kahabu*; Sin. *kæsubu* or *kæsumbu*. The tortoise-shell of commerce is, according to Mr. Bell, supplied by the "hawksbill" variety (*Caretta imbricata*). Pyrard describes it more fully hereafter in his Treatise (vol. ii). The natives take it both on land and as it floats on the water (*T. Bom. Geo. Soc.*, i, 79). The price of this article, as we shall see later, was 1 larin the *gau* (=¼ lb.). Maldive tortoise-shell is of first-rate quality, and always finds a ready sale in Ceylon and

It is found at the Maldives, and is largely traded in. It is a tortoise of an uncommon kind, found only there and at the Philippines. It is pretty and highly polished, and quite black, with much natural marking. It is in greatest demand at Cambaye, where it is made into women's bracelets, and into pretty boxes and caskets set in silver.

The people of the Maldives likewise make a good traffic in rush mats[1] of perfect smoothness, which they make very prettily of divers colours, adorning them with patterns and figures so neatly that nothing can be nicer. The Portuguese and Indians alike prize them, so that there is much trade in them. So also with cloth of cotton and silk, which is brought to them raw, and by them worked up. They do not make white cloth, but only patterned and figured, and in small pieces of an arm's length and a half in width for their dress, and other kinds for the women, and for turbans, all exceedingly beautiful and fine.[2] So the Maldives are frequented

Bengal. What is purchased at Málé at Rs. 16 to Rs. 25 per cwt., is sold in Ceylon at Rs. 5 to Rs. 10 per lb. The average value of the annual imports into Ceylon since 1856 is £1,296; in one year, 1875, they amounted to £2,184 (Bell, *Rep.*, pp. 85, 105).

[1] "The well-known Maldive mats (M. *tuḍu kuna*) are made only in Suvádiva atoll, from a rush (M. *hâu*) which thrives best there. In delicacy of pattern, in happy combination of the only three colours adopted,—black, yellow-brown, and white,—and in permanency of dye, these fine mats surpass anything in the same line the world over, and have justly obtained unqualified commendation. The best quality are worked up on Gaddú island, the ordinary mats at Havara-Tinadú, and a small kind on Gemaná-furhi" (Bell, *Rep.*, 88). The large fine mats are valued at Rs. 5 to Rs. 6 even at Málé, and can rarely be procured in Ceylon under Rs. 8 to 10 (*ib.*, 106).

[2] "Two or three qualities of cotton cloth are woven, chiefly in Málosmadulu (Eda-furhi island), Aḍḍú, and Suvádiva atolls, though occasionally made elsewhere for private use. A peculiarity in this article consists in the uniform tasteful colouring of the waist and head-cloths, sometimes plain red, or blue edged with red an inch wide, but more commonly of a rich chocolate colour, relieved by a black stripe between two of white on either side, and finished at the ends by a narrow yellow silk border and a neat fringe. The dyes employed are excellent, particularly the

from all quarters for their commodities, inasmuch as they possess so many things that foreigners prize and require. In exchange, everything that the islanders are in need of is imported from elsewhere, such as rice, white cotton cloth, raw silk and cotton, oil of a certain odoriferous grain, used only to rub the body after bathing; areca for chewing with betel, iron, steel, spices, porcelain—in short, everything they have not; and all these at favourable prices, by reason of the number of ships touching there, and the easy access. Gold and silver are also imported, and, once entered, never allowed to leave the country. They would not give the least bit of it to any foreigner, but keep it as treasure, or make it into trinkets for the women.

CHAPTER XVIII.

Curiosity of the Maldive king.—His genealogy.—Political changes at the islands.—The king's wives, and other matters.

Having said enough of the island, I come now to tell more particularly of the king of the Maldives, his genealogy, wives, conduct, and divers events that happened in his time. This king often asked me about the king of France, his age, manner of life, wars, armaments, ships, cannon, and other matters, and if the two ships we came in belonged to him. I answered him in some detail on these points, and said that if

red and chocolate, which are extracted from a root, M. *ahi* (*Morinda citrifolia*). The black dye is obtained by boiling gall-nuts and rusty iron together in coco-nut water. The price of cloths of native manufacture is much higher than that of the various coloured ones imported from India, in consequence of the demand induced by all persons being expected on public occasions to wear the former. The natives also spin a large quantity of foreign cotton. The spinning-machine (*tatun*) is simply a large and small wheel of light framework" (Bell, *Rep.*, 88; and see *T. Bom. Geo. Soc.*, i, 81).

our king were to send ships to the Indies, it would not be two or three only, but two or three hundred, which surprised him much. He also inquired if the French were the *Franki* or *Franqui* who were spoken of in the Indies. This question I could not well resolve at the time, but since then I have learnt that this name Franki signifies all the Western peoples: to wit, the French, Italians, Spaniards, and other Europeans, but principally the French, who in former days, by their great conquest in the holy wars of the East, wherein they took the leading part, have left their name in the Indies, since then applied in common to the rest.

The king of the Maldives asked me many other questions, among others, of the court of our king, which I described to him at length as best I could. Then I enlarged upon the greatness of the king and his state, with all which he was highly pleased. On their part, the queens, princesses, and other ladies inquired much of the queens and princesses here, and how many wives the king had, and were greatly astonished to hear that, though so great and powerful, he had but one. But chiefly they desired to know how the ladies here conducted affairs of love—for they cared to talk and hear of nothing but love. They were vastly amazed when I told them that the ladies of these parts had no male intimates but their husbands. They also thought it a strange custom to salute wives with a kiss before all the world, and wondered at the great liberty I told them our wives had; yet they praised and commended it highly in contrast to themselves, who are always shut up. They put many more questions to me on the subject of love and women, and their conversation with men.

Thus was I ever a welcome guest at the palace, and went frequently to entertain them with various stories in answer to their questions. The king, among other things, liked to hear in detail all about the building and management of our ships. He was much astonished when I told him that the dye of red scarlet[1] was made with the urine of men who drank wine only, in so much that he flung away a scarlet bonnet he wore, and on that account would no longer use it. They had found in our vessel some brushes of pigs' bristles and scrapers of the same; but when he knew what they were, he had them burned outside his palace, and was much annoyed at having used or even touched them. He also wanted to burn some boxes and chests covered with sea-wolf[2] skin, thinking that it, too, was pig's skin. He wanted to know about everything, and to what uses each was put. He much admired the art of making parchment and paper, and above all was curious to learn our science of navigation, and often made me bring the charts and marine instruments, the knowledge of which I imparted to his pilots. He could hardly believe all I told him of our France and its king, whereof he had never heard tell before.

But to come to the genealogy of this king of the Maldives. I shall tell what I heard there, how he and his family came to the throne. His father had been Catibe of an island. About fifty years before this time the king of these islands, who was of noble and ancient lineage, seeing that he was but

[1] "Scarlet" was a woollen cloth, generally of that peculiar shade of red to which it has given the name. Here Pyrard speaks of "red scarlet"; in vol. ii he mentions "violet scarlet". Froissart, in the fifteenth century, speaks of white scarlet; and Marot, in the sixteenth, of green. The derivation of the word, which appears in French of the twelfth century as *escarlate*, must still be considered uncertain. Littré favours *Galaticus*, *i.e.*, of Galatia, but admits the want of any intermediate form. In English, Piers Plowman and Chaucer use the form *ciclatoun*, which seems identical with the Pers. *saqalát* or *saqlatún*, and which Mr. Skeat thinks may be the original of the word scarlet. The Pers. terms are now applied to European broadcloth, but there is evidence of their application in the middle ages to some kind of silk and gold brocade. See Yule's *Marco Polo*, Bk. i, ch. 58, *note*, and especially his *Discursive Glossary*, s. v. "Suclát", where will be found the best history of the word.

[2] *I.e.*, some kind of seal. In the *Hawkins' Voy.* (Hak. Soc., p. 196), we read of "sea-wolves or seals".

ill-obeyed, and was unable to withstand a formidable rival who wished to depose him, was inspired of God with a resolve to quit all. He departed secretly with his wife and some of his family, without saying a word of his destination to anyone. He went straight to Cochin, where he became a Christian, along with his wife and some of his followers, sending back such as would not be baptized. For this cause his rival, who was his near relative, was at once accepted as king. The name of the latter was *Haly*, of the former *Assan*. The ordinary title is *Rascan*, which signifies "King"; but when they sign, they always put "Sultan", as do all the Mahometan kings. They say there are but five kings of their religion who have a right to use the title Sultan, which means Sovereign—that is to say, the Turk, the Persian, the Mogor, he of the Maldives, and the king of Achen or Sumatra.

This former king, then, when he became a Christian at Cochin, wrote word to all his subjects that they should become Christians, and pay him their wonted tribute, otherwise he would come and see to it with a large army of Portuguese, who had promised him their aid. The new king and the Maldive people made answer that they would no longer acknowledge him; that if aught was due to him he might come and get it; and that if he preferred to be a Christian he should remain where he was; as for them, they would sooner die than change their faith. Hearing this, he asked the aid of the Viceroy of the Indies at Goa, who promised it, but on terms that he should not go in person, as it was feared that he would not agree with his people, or might bring the Portuguese into difficulties. The Portuguese army then set out, but were not able to effect anything, and lost a galley with three ships, and a goodly number of men, and so were constrained to retire. The following year they returned with a stronger force and better pilots, and the new king went out bravely to meet them, though he knew himself lost; he might perhaps have escaped, but he preferred to die in battle rather than to retreat with shame. He was vanquished and put to death, and the Portuguese made themselves masters of Malé, where they built a fortress,[1] and thence sallied forth to compel the submission of the other islands, and put many of the inhabitants to the sword. Then they assembled all the chiefs of the islands, and told them

Old Fort Wall at Malé

they desired to leave them at peace, and not to constrain them in any way, nor to change their religion, if only they

[1] "The fort, being at present (1835) filled up with earth, is a solid mass, in height about twenty feet, faced with stone, and on it are mounted ten guns, which, though very old and almost useless, are taken care of by being covered in. As no native inscription is to be found on this fort, similar to those on the bastion built at the angles of the wall that partly surrounds the island, and as it exhibits signs of more skill than has been evinced in the other defences which appear to have been constructed by the natives, having a round front and gentle slope upwards from the inner line of the base, it seems probable that it is an erection of the Portuguese" (Christopher, in *T. Bom. Geo. Soc.*, i, 57). Mr. Bell says that it has been partially excavated since Christopher's time: he also noticed some twenty or thirty iron guns lying about in the rank vegetation, and two brass guns with Arabic inscriptions.

would pay the king his dues. These terms being accepted, they left one of the island chiefs to govern, and to remain always at Malé with the Portuguese commandant, on terms that he should take no political measures but after consulting the Portuguese and the island chiefs, and that all the trade should be in the hands of the Portuguese alone.

I have heard it said by the islanders that the trade and prosperity of the islands were never so great as when the Portuguese governed there. The governor appointed by the Portuguese to rule under them as viceroy was a lord, a native of the island, and of their religion; but he did everything in the name of the Christian king who lived in the Portuguese territory. This lord was grandfather to the wife of him that was king in my time. The Portuguese in this way ruled the islands in peace for the space of ten years, during which time the father of this king and his brother were Catibes, each of his own island, but, with the pride of their race, would never submit to the Portuguese yoke, nor obey the governor whom they had left in power. On the contrary, they rebelled and levied a force of men and galleys for war, and retired to the atollon *Ouadou,* otherwise *Souadou,* at the southern extremity of the islands, while the Portuguese dared not follow them, nor cross the *Candou* or channel of the said atollon; so that this atollon, and the islands belonging thereto, were never subject to the Portuguese, nor any of the other islands and atollons to the south of that channel.

These two brothers then built a strong fort, and being distant about eighty leagues from Malé, where the Portuguese were, they became in time so strong in men, arms, and ammunition, that they, as it were, held Malé and the Portuguese in check, so that they durst not come out without daily experiencing a harassing war. This lasted for eight years, at the end of which arrived four galleys of Malabar corsairs for the purpose of war and pillage, as was their wont. The two brothers accosted them, and agreed with them to make war upon the Portuguese on terms of half the booty; so one day, getting word that the captain of the fortress and island of Malé was gone to Cochin with a goodly number of Portuguese soldiers, they could not miss the opportunity, and resolved to attack the fortress: which project they carried out so well, that one night they surprised it by escalade, and made themselves masters of the place, putting to death upwards of 300 men that were within, and taking prisoner the native governor who was set there by the Portuguese. The place being taken and sacked, the Malabars, having got their agreed share of the spoil, were going home, leaving the two brothers masters of the town; but they, jealous to see so much of the riches of the islands being carried off, resolved to attack the Malabars. This they did, and, after a long engagement, at length were left victorious, and got both the booty and the galleys, sending the men back to the Malabar coast, and thus repaid with treachery the good service they had of them.[1]

[1] Tradition still keeps alive in the Maldives the story of those stirring times, and of the national heroes who threw off the Portuguese yoke. The following is from the mouth of Mr. Bell's Maldive pandit, a native of Nolivaran-faru, in Tiladummati atoll:—"When Sultan Hassan, who was the son of Sultan Yusub, left the islands, Ali, his rival, reigned in his stead. Incited by Hassan, who had become a Christian, the Portuguese made an attempt to take Málé, but failed for want of ammunition. They returned two or three times, and after four years' war took Málé, and slew the Sultan Ali. His death was on this wise,—being faint and parched with thirst during the final attack, he was seen by a toddy drawer from the neighbouring island of Viligili, who, crossing on a coconut-shell raft (*sic*), offered the wearied Sultan some sweet toddy. As he drank, a shot put an end to his life. His body was washed ashore on an islet westward of Malé (only dry at low tide), called to this day *Ali Rasgefánu Ziare.*

"The Portuguese left as their governor at Málé a half-caste named Andiri Andiri (? Andrea), whose father was the sole survivor of a wreck at Huvadu atoll, and married a Maldive woman, leaving two sons, Andiri and another. During the Portuguese rule there was also a Viyadou (? Port. *Veador*) living at Bára, in Tiladummati atoll, as

In this manner the two brothers became kings of the islands, and equally shared the throne without any quarrel between them. They were both men of great valour, and were acknowledged as such by the people. All the lords and chiefs of the islands submitted to them, and such as would not, had permission to retire to their own private islands without taking part in any way in affairs of state. There were many who would not obey, esteeming themselves of better lineage than the two brothers, who nevertheless knew how to make themselves feared; and when one would not obey them, they sent a force at once to sack and pillage his island. They married wives of the best houses of the country, and were acknowledged throughout all the islands and atolls as absolute kings. As for the Portuguese, they were indignant at the rebuff they had received at the Maldives, and

Atoluveri [*cf.* the 'thief of Baura', referred to in the letters patent of the Christian king, Dom Manoel, *i.e.*, Hassan, dated October 2nd, 1561; see post, App. B]. At Utimu, in Tiladummati atoll, lived Husain Katibu Takuru-fánu, father of the noble brothers, Muhammad Bodu-Takuru-fánu and Hassan Kilage-fánu. On the death of their father, the brothers, with a lad named Ali Dadahelu, went to Málé to obtain for one of the brothers the title and office of *Katibu*, held by their late father. They asked, 'In which of our two names?' 'In that of the elder,' replied Andiri. Henceforth the elder was always styled *Bodu Takuru-fánu*.

"This elder brother induced the *Viyadou* at Bára to build a *gundara*, which he stole, and therewith yearly visited the Malabar coast, and at length surprised and killed the Viyadou. The brothers and the lad then removed their families to Minicoy, and carried on for years a desultory war throughout the atolls. They gradually regained them from the Portuguese, and finally captured Málé and slew Andiri, the governor. The elder brother then occupied the throne till his death. He was succeeded by his son, Kalá-fanu [Sultan Ibrahim of Pyrard's time], who came to his death by the hands of some strangers, and was buried at Kanimidu, in Kolumadulu atoll."

It will be seen that the tradition differs from Pyrard's narrative only in minor points, such as that the Portuguese governor was a half-caste. As to the Sultan Hassan, who became a Christian under the name of Dom Manoel, and the Portuguese accounts of their invasions of the Maldives, see App. B.

were resolved to avenge it; so the next year they sent an army to the islands, and carried on the war for a long time; but the two kings defeated all their forces. This war lasted three years. These kings were very powerful, and possessed two fortresses, that of Malé, and the other at the atoll of *Souadou*, or *Ouadou*, in an island called *Game.*[1] At length both parties considered that it would be for the good of the country and of trade to come to some sort of understanding, rather than to continue this war to a doubtful issue; accordingly, they made a treaty, with these conditions: that the Maldive kings and their people should be left in peace to possess the islands in like manner as their predecessors, save that they should give a certain pension to their Christian king, his successors and heirs, to be rendered at Cochin, but without acknowledging him in any other way; on the other hand, that the Mahometan kings at the islands should not be allowed to take the title and name of king, though they were to be absolute in all things, but only that of prince, duke, or the like. Also, that those two only should be entitled to this name, in their language *Quilague*, and that they should be responsible for the payment of the pension of the Christian king, who on his part was allowed to have a factor there. Furthermore, all natives of the Maldives desiring to traffic with other countries, were bound to take a passport from the Portuguese, as were all the other Indians that were at peace with them. Such were the terms of this peace, which has endured to the present day.

As for the Christian king, he gave a third part of his revenue to the king of Portugal: this revenue consists of these *bollis* and *cairo*,[2] which is rope made of the coco-tree.

[1] *Gan*, in Huvadu atoll, lat. 0° 17′ N., spelt *Ghang* in the Adm. Charts. It is doubtless the same word as the Sin. *gama*, "village". There are said to be traces of an old fort still visible.

[2] So called by the Portuguese, from Malayálam *kayár*, Tam. *kayiru*, hence our form "coir". See Yule, *Gloss.*, s. v. The M. is *rónu*.

They (the Maldive kings) send every year at their own expense four ships, of 150 tons burthen each, laden with it, and that is at the risk of the Maldivians until the ships get beyond the banks at the [northern] end of the islands: beyond that point, the risk is with the Christian king. Notwithstanding this peace,[1] the Maldivians bear a deadly hatred to the Portuguese.

The two brothers reigned together in peace for twenty-five years. The personal name of the elder was *Mahomet;* he was also called *Bode ta Courou*,[2] signifying "great lord"; he married the wife of the king who was slain at Malé by the Portuguese. The younger was called *Assan Quilague*, and married the daughter of the same king, so that the two brothers had for their wives a mother and daughter. That deceased king had a son, who, on seeing these brothers become kings, never came to court, and was allowed to live in peace. I have seen him many a time, and his sister too. These two kings had great difficulty in maintaining their position, for they had risen from low estate, and there were some always on the point of revolt; but the kings never gave them time to do anything, for as soon as they got the slightest word or suspicion of their intentions, they took the proper measures. As it happened, the elder brother only had a son, while the younger had a daughter, who was of

1 The terms of the treaty as between the Portuguese and the Maldive princes *de facto*, do not appear in the Portuguese records. The tribute payable by the ex-king to the Portuguese treasury is frequently alluded to. From the King of Spain's despatch of the 10th January 1587, it appears that Dom Manoel (Hassan) engaged to pay, and did pay, to the Portuguese 500 bahars of coir (*Arch. Port. Or.*, Fasc. 3, No. 23). If Pyrard is right in saying that his tribute was one-third of what he received, the Maldive tribute would be 1,500 bahars of coir. In 1606 the ex-king Dom Filippe complained to the King of Spain that his revenue, which formerly amounted to 18,000 xerafins, had dwindled to 5,000 (*Liv. das Monç.*, i, 147).

2 *Bodu takuru;* the title shows that he was not of royal or even of high birth.

noble birth on her mother's side,—for in that land nobility passes by the mother as well as by the father. The son of the elder was the king we found there, who was not of lineage so good as the daughter (of the younger), for his mother was taken by the king for her beauty alone. And there they have many wives, but there is always one who is the chief, though all are lawful wives.

Subsequently, the younger of the two kings being fallen into a grievous sickness, it befell that his wife's brother, who was the greatest noble in the land, revolted against them. He bore the name of his island and fortress, to wit, *Misdoue Quilague.*[1] This island, which I have visited, is 30 leagues distant from Malé towards the south, in the atollon *Nilandoue.* Thither the elder brother proceeded in force with secrecy and despatch, bidding them say nothing to his brother, who was sick unto death. At length this lord was taken and put to death, and all his island pillaged. But when the news reached Malé, his sister, the younger's wife, had such sorrow that she wished for death, and they had some pains to prevent her laying hands on herself in her despair; whereupon her husband, all sick though he was, swore that if God should give him health again, his brother should rue it. For all that he died of that sickness, and men said that he was more valiant than his brother.

The reason why this elder brother despatched these great lords was, that he knew that his son would be king, and he misliked that such rivals should exist; for the son was still young, and was never like to be as valiant as his father. And so his humour turned out, as I to some extent saw, for he was in nowise inclined to war, but solely to letters, sciences, and manufactures, and he was also much given to women, as, indeed, was nothing remarkable in that land. It

[1] *Mídú*, the island of the *Mí* tree. It is omitted in the Adm. Chart, but lies on the N.E. of South Nilandu atoll, in lat. 3° N. It is inhabited. The revolt of this lord, *Midu kilage-fánu*, is still known in tradition.

is highly necessary to be valiant there, for the stronger wins the day, and they that would rule must slay the kings that be. Three were once slain in a year, the memory whereof keeps the kings in perpetual fear and apprehension. This elder brother lived three years after the death of the younger, and had his son acknowledged for king before his death, causing all his servants and subjects to swear allegiance to him.

During the lifetime of these two kings a great ship was wrecked on their island, in which were a great number of men, as well Indians as Portuguese, and among others a young boy, seven years of age, of Portuguese and Indian birth. For him the two brothers conceived an affection as great as though he were their own son, and had him brought up in like manner at the house of the elder; there he kept the king's son company, both being of the same age, and was made to adopt their faith. He was one of the finest boys one could see, of such high spirit, that, as I heard from all the natives, he attained in perfection to all their sciences and accomplishments.

The elder king caused him to be instructed in all kinds of exercises, in like manner and with like respect as his own son; while he, finding himself in this condition, believed himself to be brother to the young prince, going everywhere as his peer. But when he grew to years of discretion the kings bade tell him who he was, and advised him to be ever a good and faithful servant of the prince and future king. Moreover, after the death of the younger brother, the other made him marry his brother's daughter, the noblest and richest match in the kingdom; her he would like to have given in marriage to his own son, did not their law forbid the marriage of cousins-german; wherefore, for fear lest some other great lord of the realm should get her and make war upon his son, he preferred to give her to this young man, in whom he had perfect trust and confidence, as being his own creature; also he considered that, as a stranger, he could have no pretension to the throne.

After the death of his father the young prince peaceably succeeded; the young Mestif lord became daily more brave and gallant, more beloved and honoured of the people and all the foreigners. He was admiral, or *Vellanas,* and one of the six elders or *Mouscoulis*, and captain of a company, or, as they call it, a *Sardare.*[1] So then, seeing that the king was no warrior nor addicted to arms, while he himself was greatly esteemed for his valour, he became presumptuous, and began to despise the king and to pay him but little regard; wherefore the king entertained some jealousy, and feared lest the youth, enjoying all that favour and goodwill with the world, should take it into his head to dispossess him; so he took counsel with his friends, and resolved to put him to death rather than run the risk of greater troubles. Yet he could hardly bring his mind to do it, as well for the friendship he bore him as for the special trust regarding him wherewith his father on his death-bed had charged him, and further, that he was married to his cousin. Notwithstanding these considerations he continued his designs, being prompted by information brought to him daily, that this man was secretly treating with the Portuguese to make them masters of the kingdom and get himself made king under them. On his part he lacked not warning of the king's ill-will towards him, and could full well have saved himself had he been so minded; but he heeded not, saying that he was innocent of the charges against him. So one day, the king sending for him at an unwonted hour, though he doubted it would go ill with him, yet on that account he omitted not to go, nor indeed had he time to refuse. On his arrival in the great hall of the palace, where the king sat awaiting him with all his lords and guards, he made a profound reverence to the king, who saluted him in return, and bade him be seated in his proper

[1] M. *sarudáru*, Pers. *sardár*.

place. This he did, and forthwith issued from behind the tapestry, men with ropes and arms, who seized and bound him, and then dragging him along the ground, carried him to a place on the seashore, about a thousand paces off, where they put him into a boat and slew him, and then cast his body into the sea. When his wife heard of it she fell into such grief and sorrow that it was more than two years ere she would see the king or the queens, or even go to the palace. He left a son, who was fifteen years old when I left the Maldives, and was not at all like the Indians, being as fair as men of these parts. Such was the end of this unfortunate lord—an example to all foreigners who would rise above their condition in these lands and elsewhere.

Some time after this king lost his father, he began to ill-treat the wife that survived him, who was his own step-mother, and was called *Manaye Quilague*,[1] and whom his dying father had especially commended to his care; whereupon, in her indignation, she was resolved to be avenged. She had a brother who was one of the captains of the realm, very rich and valiant, named *Pammedery Calogue*,[2] whose son, a man of high breeding, was afterwards one of my greatest friends. This woman, then, and her brother conspired against the king's life, with design to make this boy king and his father lieutenant-general, and to divide all the offices of state among those of their faction. But their enterprise was discovered, and the king had them seized and forthwith given over to justice, swearing an oath that whatever justice should ordain should be carried out without hope of pardon. They had their hands cut off, this brother being the first to suffer, and were then exiled to *Souadou*. As for the step-mother, she was bereft of all she had, as also was her brother, and she was even tortured to make her dis-

[1] Perhaps a misprint for *Manike*, the fem. of *Maniku*.

[2] *Fámudéri kaloge-fánu*. Probably this *calogue* is a mistake for *quilague:* the former being an inferior title.

cover her treasure. So little security was there in the political estate of the Maldive king; treasons and attempts were practised upon him day by day, and the spoil remained to the stronger.

There was afterwards another revolt, which lasted a long time, during which this king was forced to quit the island of Malé, and retire to another called *Gouradou*,[1] ten leagues off. This revolt was raised by a great lord of the country, named *Parenae tacourou*,[2] who had a number of galleys and big ships, with which he pillaged and ravaged all the islands whereat he cast anchor. The king withdrew to this island of Gouradou because the access to it was narrow and exceeding difficult, and a very expert pilot was required to find the passage. This lord, then, became so strong and puissant that wheresoever he landed he caused to be borne over his head a white parasol, called *ou du ad*,[3] which is a mark of royalty; and in all other respects he made himself served and obeyed as king, distributing and granting to his followers the revenues and offices of the state. But after the king had sent against him many ships and men at arms, at length he was caught: for I shall say, in passing, this king never went to war himself, he only despatched forces; nor was he valiant like his father, who always went in person, and as soon as he heard of anyone bestirring himself, he gave him no time, but took measures at once.

As for this rebellious lord, the cause of his capture was that while his galleys were in the south of the islands, the currents then running east bore the greater part of them to Achen, in Sumatra, and the remnant of the force, thus weakened, were all taken. Most of the men were put to

[1] *Gurádú*, in S. Málé atoll, lat. 3° 53′ N. In this island, according to Pyrard, the Sultan afterwards found his grave.

[2] *I.e.*, the *Fárunā*, the minister next in rank to the *Quilague*.

[3] Now *hudu hai*; *i.e.*, *hudu* or *sudu*, "white" (as in Sin.), and *hai* = Sin. *sat*, "umbrella".

death with their leader, and the remainder only had a hand cut of, and were then sent into exile: for thus it is enacted by their law that those who conspire against their prince, or make attempts on his person, have their right hand cut off. Of those who were carried to Achen, some returned after a time, the king extending to them his grace and pardon.

With regard to these currents, of which I have just spoken, they run for six whole months (each way), so that if a vessel happens to be at the northern extremity of the islands it is no great matter, for then it is only carried to Cochin, on the coast of India, or thereabouts, about 150 leagues distance, or to some of the islands along that coast. But if they cannot make the island of Ceylon, they are carried to Sumatra, a distance of about 500 leagues; and if ill-luck has it that these currents carry them away at the close of the *Monsons*[1] or Seasons (when the current carries them, they call that *behigue*[2]), and before they make land anywhere, they are caught in the other current; as often happens, they are infallibly lost, as I have seen in a number of cases, when they were expecting to make land every night, and were without water and other provisions. If the current carries them to the west, they are borne straight to the Arabian coast, which is much further off than that of Sumatra; but most often they are dead before they get there. One day I saw a boat which had been carried off by these currents, and while it was a long way out, suddenly the currents changed and brought it back to these islands; but most of those on board were dead, and the rest only skin and bone, to such straits had they been reduced.

I have made mention above of Gouradou. I was at that

[1] *Monsoons.* As to the history of this word, see Dozy and Engelmann, *Gloss.*, and Yule, *Gloss.* Pyrard writes also *monssons*, *muesons*, and *muessons*.

[2] Correctly *behigeṇ gos*, "sailing with the wind and current"; *cf.* Sin. *bæhigana gos.* The old English phrase was "spooming along before the sea", as used by Drake.

island one day, and saw the mast and rudder of the ship that was lost there, wherein was the foreign queen who died in child-bed while I was about the king. I was told that it was the richest ship conceivable. It had on board some 500 persons, men, women, and children, for the Indians take the greater part of their household to sea with them. These 500 persons were nigh all drowned, and there remained but a hundred saved. This queen's father and mother, to whom the ship belonged, were among those that perished, and she, at that time but a child, was saved by chance. This ship came from Sunda, laden with all kinds of spices and other merchandize of China and Sunda. Judging merely from the mast of this vessel, I thought it the largest I had ever seen, for the mast was taller and thicker than those of Portuguese carracks; and the king of the Maldives built a shed of the length of the mast to keep it as a curiosity. I saw also another mast and a top much larger than those of Portugal. Thus was I led to believe that in the Indies they build vessels larger and of better material than in Portugal or anywhere else in the world. The greatest ships come from the coast of Arabia, Persia, and Mogor,[1] and some have as many as 2,000 persons on board. They build not their ships with as many decks as we, for they have but one, the main deck, and below they have none, not even a 'tween deck; as for their water, they keep it not in pipes and jars as we do; but on each side of the main-mast, which goes down to the ship's bottom, they fix two wooden cisterns, well joined and secured, so that the water is well preserved, and there are merely holes for drawing the water as from a well. These are of greater capacity than our pipes,

[1] *I.e.*, the coasts of the present Scinde and Guzerat, and such ports, including Surat, as were not in possession of the Portuguese. The application of the word *Mogor* to the territories of the Great Mogul is adopted by the author from Portuguese use. See Yule's *Glossary*, s. v. "Mogul".

and take up less room. But I observe that our system of pipes is better, for one reason, namely, that if any accident happens to these cisterns they lose all their water at once. It is not so with us, for in case of a cannon-shot, all that can happen is the loss of one or two pipes; or if any one goes bad, all the water is not spoiled. Throughout the whole of India they nowhere use our system of pipes. They use only certain handsome jars, of finer shape and lacquer than I have seen elsewhere. Some of these will hold as much as one pipe, or even more. They are made in the kingdom of *Martabane*,[1] whence they are exported, and take their name throughout all India. The water never goes bad in them, and the jars are kept shut by a key.

But to return to this ship of the queen, which was lost at the island of Gouradou, I would tell what, during the time I was there, befell an honorable, rich, and discreet merchant of Bengal, called *Mouhamede Oaca*, and his wife, also a foreigner, and very beautiful and fair-complexioned for those parts. She was called *Canboé Boubou*, *Canboé* being her personal name in the language of Bengal, and *Boubou*[2] signifying Mademoiselle. Both were wrecked with the queen; they were her slaves, and were about thirty years of age, and had no children. The queen had such an affection toward them that she made them

[1] Mr. Bell saw some large earthenware jars at Málé, some about two feet high, called *rumbá*, and others larger and barrel-shaped, called *mátabán*. The name seems to survive also on the Madras coast; *e.g.*, we find in Mr. P. Brown's *Zillah Dictionary* (1852), "Martaban—name of a place in Pegu: a black jar in which rice is imported from thence." Linschoten (i, 101) writes: "In this towne (Martaban) many of the great earthen pots are made, which in India are called *Martauanas*, and many of them carryed throughout all India of all sorts, both small and great: some are so great that they hold full two pipes of water." See also *op. cit.*, p. 268; and Yule's *Glossary*, s. v. "Martaban", where the quotation from Ibn Batuta shows that the term was current in the fourteenth century.

[2] *Búbú* is a Hind. term for lady, used in the same way as *bíbí*, though perhaps of different origin.

stewards of her household, and placed all her confidence in them, seeing that they had been about her in their youth; thus they rose to extraordinary wealth, to credit and favour with her majesty: but no sooner was their kind mistress dead, in manner already described, than every kind of misfortune and disaster overtook them. Theirs was the happiest home in the world, the fullest of concord and love; but, as misfortune would have it, their house adjoined the warehouse or lodging of the factor of the Christian king at Goa, who always has one such at these islands. This factor was a man of Cochin, of the race of Gentile Canarins, but baptised and naturalised as a Portuguese in dress and manners. He had been baptised as a child, and had a wife and children at Cochin; he was called Simon Rodrigue, and was at this time about twenty-seven years of age. It is customary not to leave these clerks or factors there, when they are Christians, for more than a year or two, so as they may come and render their duty to the Church, for in these islands there is no exercise of the Christian religion; but this fellow would not return so soon, and remained there four years. He learned exceedingly well the language and customs of the country, and made himself so agreeable to the king, and to all the inhabitants, that although he was recalled, and three other clerks one after another were sent to succeed him, yet he managed so cleverly, by making presents to the king, that he had not to budge. The king also, being written to, answered that he would not detain him, but could not and would not force him to go against his will. So this clerk and the merchant's wife being neighbours, fell into an intrigue of the closest kind, and indulged their amours at their ease, the merchant being often absent at his trading.

This continued for the space of two years without discovery; but at length the husband became aware of it, and getting certain information by means of spies, resolved to have his satisfaction. The more easily to attain his end, he made as though he were going abroad for a fortnight, according to his wont. He equipped a barque in the usual way, took leave of his wife, commending all his affairs to her keeping, and departed; but after nightfall he put back to land, and about eleven o'clock at night went straight to his wife's bedchamber, and finding her not in her bed, he presently went to the palace to find the king, who used never to retire till after midnight. The first person he met was the master of the galleys and all the king's ships, who was to all appearance an intimate friend of the factor; yet, as an instance of the faithlessness of these people, he was the first to apprise the king, and to assist the merchant in obtaining justice, as we shall see hereafter. The husband, on being introduced to the king's presence, made his complaint that his wife was abed with a Christian, whom they call *Caparou*,[1] and that he and his wife were Mahometans, whom they call *Mousseliman*,[2] that is, the faithful, and that his majesty should be pleased to have justice done. On hearing this, the king ordered the master of the galleys to take twelve soldiers of the guard, and to put the factor to death, and cast his body in the sea. These men forthwith surrounded his house, and knocked at his door to gain admittance. The poor factor was so astonished he knew not what to do, yet trusting to the king's friendship for him, and to the master, who cried out to him to open the door, with assurance of safety, he was so ill-advised as to open it, then throwing himself at his feet, prayed him to save his life; but he was slain on the spot, the other being the first to strike him. At this result those who had owed him money were well enough pleased, as also was the king, who wanted to be possessed of his great wealth, the which he seized incontinently. The Portuguese, too, were not annoyed; and thenceforth it was arranged that the

[1] Ar. *kafir*, "infidel".

[2] *I.e.*, *Muslimân*, the Persian plural of *Muslim*, but widely adopted as a singular, as in our form *Mussulman*.

factors should no longer be men of Cochin, but of the islands. The unfortunate man being thus slain, the husband went straight to his wife to do the like to her; but he was with difficulty restrained, and she was cast into prison, to come up for judgment thereafter. At first it was proposed to drown her, but seeing that the man was dead, and his goods seized, they were content to punish her in the usual manner, as all others are who are taken in adultery or lewd practices, but somewhat more rigorously. Her husband refused even to see her, and got married again, this time to a young girl of the country, as I shall tell hereafter,[1] with what came of that marriage.

To return to the king of the Maldives. Some years after the death of his father he became enamoured of a married woman, the fairest in complexion and beauty in all the land, and abandoned his first wife, whom his father had made him espouse, in order to get this woman, who had three daughters as fair as herself, all married to princes and great lords. I have often seen her arm, as she showed it to us out of coquetry, and it was as white as that of the fairest in our country here. Her husband was a pilot, the cleverest in the country in his profession and in trade, and a man of large means. The king and this woman loved each other much, and he was minded to marry her, while she daily strove to persuade her husband to consent to leave her, but he would do nothing; wherefore in her anger she advised the king to put him to death. This the king for the love of her resolved to do; and having sent for him one day to give him some information about navigation on the country chart, when the man came, and was making his obeisance, the king gave him a blow with a dagger, intending to plant it in his abdomen, but the man raised his hand to parry the stroke, and turned the dagger straight into his eye, which it put out. He was not otherwise hurt, for I saw him often afterwards. He

[1] P. 265.

was an agreeable companion, and he it was who gave me the news of our mate and comrades who escaped from the island of *Pouladou,* having himself seen them chained by the feet. So, to return to this woman, she got the king to marry her, but, after living together for a while, he fell in love with her who was the chief queen while we were there, and so got tired of the other,—who, in truth, was the lewdest woman in the world, abandoning herself indifferently to all sorts of men, slaves, as well as others. Yet that was not the sole cause why the king left her.

Now the king had two nephews, brothers, of whom the elder was married to the richest young lady in all the islands, the grand-daughter of the governor of the country under the Portuguese rule. She was also sister to the prince, who came to our ship, and with whom the king was so annoyed that he boxed his ears, as I have related above.[1] This lady was of noble birth, young and beautiful, and so the king became enamoured of her; but the mischief was that her husband would not leave her, nor she him: for she had no ambition to be queen, preferring her first condition and liberty. The husband and wife, then, aware of the king's intentions, resolved to escape in a barque along with a younger brother, who afterwards died with the king, as I shall tell hereafter; but while carrying out their plan they were unluckily surprised at their setting out: the king's galleys caught them and brought them back to Malé, where the poor husband was constrained to quit his wife, for sorrow whereof he was for a whole year without going beyond his house, and so died. It was also much against the will of the young lady,—as, indeed, she afterwards showed, for she never bore the king any goodwill, and always had other male friends.

Before marrying her, the king was constrained to leave his other wife, who would not by any means consent to quit

[1] P. 69.

him, for a separation must needs be by the free will and consent of both parties, otherwise the man restores her dowry to the woman, and then quits her whether she will or no; but it is dishonourable and scandalous for a woman to take it. This the king did in the case of this first queen, for he gave her her dowry and rank, and left her, and then married the other. The former remained unmarried ever after, for the king did not permit her to marry again, and without that none would dare to espouse her. Her first husband would not speak to her again, although they had had three daughters of their marriage. The king liked this man much, and did him many benefits. This lady was very gay in her dress, pearls, and jewels, and the king gave her a fine house in the island, where she resided at her ease in all respects, but without marrying again. She spent her time in pleasure, and was much visited, and had a large retinue of servants and slaves. As for the other, the king never afterwards abandoned her; and when he was killed she was still with him, with two foreign women; but she always maintained her regret for her first husband, who was, as it were, first prince of the blood, and lieutenant-general of the forces. The king being now well on in years, and having reared no children while he was young, saw that those he might now have would be still young when he came to die, and would be liable to be set aside and bereft of their inheritance; he therefore resolved to have no more: and accordingly, while I was there I heard that for four or five years he had no intercourse with this chief queen, because she was very prolific, and had already by him a son and a daughter, both of whom died at six or seven years of age. And yet these people have no scruples in killing the child in its mother's womb, deeming it better for them so to die than come into the world. But the queens had no great concern that the king went not to see them, for they were never in want of male friends, who used to visit them when they pleased.

But to return to the merchant of Bengal, that would not take back his wife, as related above. He married another woman, who was thought to be the most lovely in all the islands: and in truth she was no whit inferior to the fairest in these parts, save that her skin was not quite so white. She was eighteen or twenty years of age, and was chosen by him for her beauty alone, being neither noble nor rich: he, however, had plenty of means for both. Now a second misfortune befell him, for as he lived near the royal palace, no sooner did the king set eyes on this wife, than he became violently enamoured of her, and having attained his desire, even compelled her to separate from her husband, whom he threatened to cast into the sea, should he refuse to consent, insomuch that the unfortunate man was constrained to quit her with all possible regret; and, three months before the great Maldive disaster, the king took her to wife, because the Pandiare told him that, to free his conscience, it were better for him to marry her than to continue in the sin wherein he was. Such were the misfortunes that befell this poor merchant one upon another, which had never occurred but for the death of his kind mistress.

CHAPTER XIX.

The Maldives, when peopled.—Of many other memorable events which occurred at these islands and in the neighbourhood, during the sojourn of the author there.—Of a vessel of Tananor, and the story of a Malabar captain's dealing with the Maldive king, and his hapless fate; and the adventures of the king's nephew and brother-in-law.

Having described the Maldive polity, and the more remarkable events that happened before fortune cast us there, I now come to speak of the most singular and memorable occurrences during the space of five years I resided there. But first I must not forget to tell what I learned of the islanders concerning the first peopling of the Maldives, and how the inhabitants changed their religion.

They hold that the Maldives began to be inhabited only four hundred years ago, and that the first who came and peopled them were (as I have already said, in passing) the Cingalles[1] of the island of Ceylan,[2] which is not far distant, and were idolaters, but afterwards changed their religion, it being about one hundred and fifty or two hundred years at most since they received Mahometism, through the Moorish and Arabian navigators, who, while trading over all the continent and islands of the East Indies, brought there also their law, which has since remained in most of those parts. It also appears that it was then that the Tartars, who extended their dominion throughout the East, and even to these islands,[3] became infected with this accursed and false doctrine of Mahomet, which has wasted three-fourths of the world. The Maldive people have ever since retained this law, as I have fully described in my treatment of their religion and ceremonies.

I come now to what happened at the islands in my time, and to these facts my testimony will be good and sufficient, for I either witnessed or was personally acquainted with the greater part of them.

I will begin with what happened to a vessel of Tananor,[4] which came to trade there a year after our arrival at the

[1] From the Port. form *Chingalas*. The native adjectival form is *Sinhala*.

[2] All the earlier writers spell Ceylon with an *a*, as the French do still; the native name is *Lankâva*. For the evolution of the name Ceylon, see Yule's *Glossary*.

[3] This, of course, is a mistake. The Maldives were never in subjection to the Tartars, by whom he means the Moguls, nor indeed to any Indian power except, perhaps, to the Raja of Cananor.

[4] *Tanur*.

islands. This vessel was about five hundred tons burthen, and belonged to the king of Tananor, a kingdom situate between Calicut and Cochin. This king was a Gentile, and of the race of Nairs. There may have been aboard some five or six hundred men, well armed, good Malabar soldiers, and they came there to trade. Their principal cargo was rice, but they had much other merchandise, such as pepper, areca (which is eaten with betel), cotton, butter, oils for rubbing the body after washing, a quantity of white cotton cloths, pottery, iron and copper utensils: so that it was very rich, and their purpose was to barter all these for the merchandise of the country. But the Maldive king would not let them tarry in the roadstead of Malé more than three days, and then sent them to cast anchor at an island called *Bandos*, where I had been sick, distant about two leagues north from Malé. The reason of this was that he was afraid they meditated some treasonable surprise. He caused all their fighting men to disembark, all well armed and equipped, in good health and ready for action. But they had not been there more than two months ere they were all dying of the fever, although the air and water of that island Bandos is better than at Malé. Most of the men remained at Malé, all their goods being placed in cellars and *banquesalles*, constructed for the purpose. They were there six months and more, bargaining and selling and loading their ship; but during that time the island fever wasted them so cruelly, that there remained no more than a hundred of them alive, and those enfeebled in such wise that they were constrained to engage another crew of the islanders to work the ship back to Tananor. It was a most experienced pilot of these islands who brought them there, wherefore they bore him much ill-will, saying that he had brought them there on purpose to make his king heir to all their riches. At the islands they lost the chief of their captains, whom they regretted much. The rule is, when the captain or master of a vessel dies there, the vessel and cargo go to the king, who seizes them; but this was not so in this case, because it belonged to the king of Tananor.

As for the private property of the deceased captain, it was not taken by the king, although it appertained to him; but this was for the reason following. That captain had brought with him his son, a young man of twenty-five, called *Houssains Caca*,[1] the bravest soldier, the most noble gentleman in address and figure, and the most skilful gunner in all the coast of Malabar. Desiring that he should stay with him, the king worked him with the fairest promises, wherewith the young man was satisfied, as well in order to save the goods which the king gave over to him in their entirety for so consenting, as by reason of a difference he had with the second captain, who was then in command of the vessel. Moreover, the king caused to be delivered to him all his goods that were on board, which he had never otherwise got out; besides which, by remaining there, he became heir to all his father's goods, which he must have shared with his other brothers had he returned to his own country, and would have had to pay for most of what his father had got on credit. He was thus welcomed and esteemed by the king, who moreover granted to him a high dignity, viz., that of master of arms, called by them *Esdru*,[2] one of the most honourable offices in the land, requiring great capacity and experience. The king had only one such in his islands, and he was a great lord, as, indeed, the like officers are considered among the nobles and soldiers, as well in these

[1] Persian *kâkâ*, an uncle; used also among the Mâppiḷḷar of Malabar as a term of respect, and sometimes by other classes when addressing respectable Mâppiḷḷar.

[2] M. *eduru*, or, according to the fuller title, *eduru maniku*. Though the office has no doubt lost its importance since the Maldives came within the *pax Britannica*, and the profession of arms became a mere pastime, there are still four of these fencing-masters at Málé, who are held in some respect (Bell).

islands as on the continent. But this appointment caused the death of the young man, by reason of the jealousy which ensued between him and the former master, who was a native of the country, and the son of a previous master, and was much respected by all the lords and soldiers.

With these people there is no greater mark of dishonour and disgrace than the loss of respect between their masters and them. And since arms are held in such high honour, they respect masters in arms more than all others, and exalt them to the rank of princes and lords, for they give instruction to the king and the chief prince. Aforetime there was but one academy, so, when this new master came, there were two, and many of all ranks quitted the old master for the new, seeing that he knew the use of arms according to the system of the Nairs and Malabars, which is esteemed the best in the Indies.[1] And the king, in order that he should be recognised as a master, presented to him, in the presence of all the court, a bracelet, which he placed on his arm with his own hands, that being the badge of this office. This bracelet was a link of gold with buttons of the same, round, and hollow within, containing the royal sign and cipher written on paper.

These two masters, then, being jealous of one another, it came to pass on the day of a great festival, such as Easter is with us, that after dinner, according to custom, all the princes, lords, gentlemen, and soldiers went to the king's palace for an assault of arms, and to challenge one another, whereby it is seen who are most adroit in the use of arms. This lasts for three days. These two masters stood on opposite sides with their scholars beside them, and these went forth to fence one with another. The elder master had more scholars, and was more popular than the other, against whom he got up an idle brawl, setting one of his

[1] The *paṇikan*, or fencing-master, was held in great respect on the Malabar coast. See Yule's *Glossary*, s. v.

scholars against one of the other,—for there, to lay the blame on a scholar, is to attack the master. So arose a great *mêlée* between the two parties, and some soldiers were wounded. When the king heard of it, he wanted to know who was to blame, and being informed that it was the elder, he reprimanded him severely, and said aloud that the first of them that should cause any mischief should have his hand cut off: this he often caused to be done, even for trifles, when he was in anger; and both masters he ordered to live peaceably, themselves and their scholars. Nevertheless, the friendship which the king bore to the new master was ever increasing, in such wise that he gave him all the titles of honour he could confer on the greatest in the realm, among others, that of *Darade Tacourou*,[1] as who should say "Count" or "Duke". Further, he made him change his former Malabar name, by proclamation throughout the island, as the custom is, and made him captain of a company, and caused him to walk with the highest grandees as their equal. These latter conceived such envy towards him, that they resolved, in concert with the elder master, to work his death any way they could. In truth, the man did not know how to steer in his course of prosperity, for he abused it, and often started a quarrel with the chief men, and even with the highest grandees of the islands; but the king supported him in everything. He took in marriage such women as he pleased, and they thought themselves highly honoured in being married to him, as much for his personal merit as for his dignity and favour with the king. And what was a further advantage to him, he had for his comrade and scholar the king's brother-in-

[1] M. *Dáhará Takuru* (*fanu*). As above indicated, this was a mere title in Pyrard's time, and so it remained down to Christopher's time, by whom it is assigned to the sixth vizier, without special duties (*T. Bom. Geo. Soc.*, i, 71). In Ibn Batuta's day the *deherd*, as he calls him, was commander-in-chief. The title seems to have fallen into abeyance now.

law, the brother of the chief queen, of whom I have frequently spoken; these two held each other in such friendship, that this was at length the cause of his downfall: for, at the end of two years, during which this favour lasted, they resolved to go away together, and he (the master), the better to conceal his enterprise, took in marriage a widow of the grand Pandiare, who resided at the southern end of the islands, in the atollon called *Souadou*. For this purpose he took occasion to depart from Malé; but he was no sooner gone, than his enemies, feeling that the game was now won, went and told the king, giving him to understand the nature of his enterprise with the prince. The king forthwith took counsel with his principal advisers, the six Mouscoulis, and sent a captain with forty soldiers in a barque to bring him back, at the same time ordering them to do him no harm. But all the chiefs then about the king, and among others the former master, gave secret instructions that they should put him to death, and then say that he had opposed his arrest by force of arms, so should they make their peace with the king. All which they carried out, for they found him at the first halting-place, without arms, and there they slew him, and brought back word to the king that they were forced to do it, seeing he would not render himself up at the king's command. The king was grievously vexed, but took no further steps in the matter.

Having spoken of the fortunes of this stranger, I shall now tell of what I saw befall some of the princes of the country. At the time of our arrival there, the king had no children, but only a nephew, aged twenty-two, and called, like himself, *Ibraim Callam*.[1] This prince ought to have succeeded him. At that time he was in disgrace, and absent from the court, because he had gone to Arabia without taking

[1] *Callam* is probably the Pers. *Kalân*, "great": this is the only place in the text where the title is applied to an individual. The word, however, appears in the Vocabulary for "prince"; and see above, p. 209.

or getting leave of the king, and before going had pillaged some of the islands. Three years after our coming he returned, but dared not come to Malé at the first for fear of the king, who was presently apprised of his arrival at some islands in the north, which belonged to him, and at which he was married. The king received the news with joy, for he loved him and treated him as his son. But false news was brought to his ears daily, that his nephew had designs against him; and this was done by those who wished him ill, and by flatterers, of whom this court was full. Notwithstanding this, the king delayed not to send an armed galley to fetch him, while he, being innocent, made no scruples about coming to the king with only ten or a dozen of a body-guard, and some servants and slaves. But as soon as he arrived at the court, all his soldiers were cast into prison, with their feet passed through two pieces of wood in which holes were cut, which is their mode of securing prisoners. They also use chains and irons for this purpose. As for the prince, he suffered nothing, but that he was two months without seeing the king, though he came day by day to the palace, and sat in the place assigned to the public in general. One of the queens, the first of them, sent him a single leaf of betel, and that was a great honour, and the highest he could hope for: for that is done to the royal children alone, and this distinction of itself showed him to be sole heir to the throne, and chief prince. It is the custom of the country, when one is in disgrace, to go every day to the palace and to wait in the court there until the king speaks to him, and takes him again into favour. The nephew was at length received into favour by means of the grand Pandiare, who was of the Cherife[1] race, that is, of the race of Mahomet. For, being sent for by the king to preach before him as usual, before beginning his sermon, he made a

[1] Sherif, a descendant of Hassan through either of his sons, Zaid and Hassan el-Musanna.

humble request and petition to the king that he would be pleased to permit his nephew to come and hear the sermon, the which the king granted, for the friendship and respect he had for the Pandiare: nor would any but he have dared to make the request. The nephew came, and from a distance catching sight of the king, made a most profound reverence, like the lowest subject of the realm; whereupon the king said but two words, *Ana poute iringua*,[1] which is to say, "My son, be seated." This he did, everyone rising to yield him the highest place. While the sermon lasted, which was more than an hour, the young prince lifted not his eyes nor his head; and the same day all his attendants were set free, and he was forthwith received into favour, and treated with the honour and dignity proper to the heir to the crown. The king made him his lieutenant-general, and commander of all his men-at-arms, or as they call it, *Dorimesnas*.[2]

After he was restored to the king's good graces, there was always great jealousy between him and the king's brother-in-law, the chief queen's brother, who had been well enough pleased at the absence and disgrace of this prince, seeing that thereby he was nearest to the king's favour, and held the highest offices, which were now taken from him on the return of the prince. The king always called him his son, to the end that all the world should honour him as his true and legitimate heir. This prince, once, being enamoured of a certain lord's wife, who was of extreme beauty, he carried her off with her own consent, and kept her a long while, whereof the husband made complaint to the king, but got not any satisfaction; indeed, the young prince had

[1] Mr. Bell thinks this should be *Anádé futá irindé*, "Come, son, be seated". *Futá*, "son" (Sin. *puta*), is now used only in the southern atolls; in the north and at Málé, the word is *darifulá*.

[2] At present the *Doriméná kilage-fanu* and the *Doriméná maniku-fanu* have nothing to do with the soldiers; and, indeed, no such appointment has been made during the present reign.

him beaten in such wise that he was fain to give his wife up altogether. Such is the way of them in that country.

As for the king's brother-in-law, the rival of this prince, he was a young lord, aged about twenty-five years, one of the handsomest men in figure and accomplishments in the islands, resembling more those of Europe, as he was fair, though slightly olive in complexion. He was learned in all the sciences, as mathematics, astrology, navigation, etc., and in the exercise of arms. I taught him to cipher and write in French; and in truth I never found any difference between those people and ourselves, whether in mind or body, save that they are slightly olive, yet withal there are many fair persons, both men and women. His sister and he were of the best family in the country, being of nobler birth than the king himself. So this lord, in chagrin for the loss of his offices at the nephew's return, began to take counsel with his sister, the queen, as to the means of avenging himself; and her anger against the prince was greater than his. The first means they took was by charms and sorceries, which are very frequently employed, to work both good and evil. In this business they employed many to work sorceries, which they call *Quenuery*,[1] against both the king and his nephew, who were made very sick thereby, and had to get other sorcerers to cure them. The king ever after this was exceeding wroth with the queen and her brother. But she hated the king to the death, and had long wished to put an end to him, if she had had the opportunity, for she was tired of being kept by force as a captive, and she was never satisfied; and being so rich and noble in her own right, she cared nothing for the honour of being queen, and would have liked a husband of her own choice. So her brother and she, seeing that their first measures had not succeeded, resolved to try another, viz., to escape secretly by night in a barque, with all her trinkets, jewels, and wealth,—for all the rest of her property was in

[1] M. *kanveri-kan*.

another island belonging to her, called *Maspillaspoury,*[1] forty leagues to the north of Malé, where her mother, a widow, resided.

The prince, having framed his project, communicated the enterprise to the foreign master of arms of whom I have spoken above, and to another lord, whose father the king's father had in former days put to death, for fear lest he should rise against him, being as he was one of the most valiant lords in the kingdom: he was called *Cassin Tacourou.* So, too, this young lord his son was very brave, and very ill content that he was but a simple soldier, and had not the rank of his ancestors, wherefore he gave ear to the prince, who was in other respects his great friend, and promised him the queen in marriage; while to the foreign master he promised another sister that he had. Their design was that the prince and the young lord should remain in the island to carry off the queen, while the master should go on before, as he did. Now it is a custom of the islands that the soldiers carry no arms when they go forth from Malé to the other islands; all must be left in the magazine of the king, to whom they belong. They carry, indeed, daggers and other small-arms, but not fire-arms; but when they go anywhither by command of the king, they may carry all sorts of arms. This is to prevent revolt; also, a certain number of soldiers only are allowed to go at the same time, and the return of these is awaited ere others are allowed to go; and this leave is given only during the westerly winds, which is their winter, and they have to return before the easterly winds, which is their summer time.

In the conduct of this enterprise they won over to their party thirteen of the best soldiers in the country, but one of the thirteen discovered them, and gave warning to the

[1] *Máfilâfurhi*, in Fadiffolu atoll (*Marfile-foori* in the Adm. Ch.), in lat. 5° 20′ N., apparently not inhabited now. The name would seem to mean, the island of the *Mâpillar*.

king, who bade keep all secret: for he was hardly able to believe it, and wished to see what it really was. So he commissioned that lord who had brought me from the island where we were lost, and in whom he had most confidence, to take a certain number of soldiers and to find out the truth. This being done, the barque was seized, with the prince and his soldiers, who were all punished in the usual manner. As for him, he got no more than a severe reprimand from the king, and was kept in disgrace more than six months. It is to be noted that during their disgrace they have no care to dress themselves, or to deport themselves in the proper style, and they take no more part in affairs than if they were dead to the world. As for the queen, though the king was very angry with her, she said but four words to him, and he was at once appeased. What befell the master of arms I have already related. After this, on the day of the feast of the dead, when the king with his three wives went to visit the sepulchres of his ancestors, the queen caused her brother to be at a place where they had to pass, and there he came, plainly attired and without arms, as the custom was, and saluted the king, who returned his salutation and took him back into favour, and conferred upon him again all his offices and dignities. He was one of the six chief *Mouscoulis*. All the soldiers that were in this affair were at once set free, and restored to their former position. Albeit, this prince, being a man of spirit, as he afterwards showed himself, finding that he was not restored to all his offices, nor held in the same consideration as before the return of the king's nephew, continued in displeasure and discontent, and being no longer able to bear it, he resolved to betake him to Arabia, along with the husband of his other sister, who was at the time the grand Pandiare. They went off in secret, without taking leave of the king, who was exceeding wroth with them and with the queen, who had given them as much gold and silver as they wanted. The king was especially astonished at the Pandiare, who had quitted so worthy an office; but the latter chose rather to obey the queen and the brother-in-law than him. They went to Mecca, in Arabia, where the Pandiare died, and the prince, after a voyage of eighteen months, came back in a Cananor ship to Cananor, where he was well received of the king, who was very desirous to have him stay there, promising him armed support in case he wished to make war against the Maldive king.[1] But the king of the Maldives, on hearing of this, wrote to him at once, and made the queen write too, to beg him to return, with promises of new dignities. The letter of his sister was of more avail than that of the king. So he returned, and had all that was promised to him, and the country remained in peace until the death of the king and his nephew, the manner whereof I shall relate hereafter.

CHAPTER XX.

Accidents and casualties to ships at the Maldives.—Arrival of Hollanders.—A wandering Jew.—A captain of Mogor and his adventures; and of some ships wrecked there.

When I was at the Maldives, the king of Mangalore, an idolater, once upon a time sent to the king of the Maldives a galley fully laden with rice as a present, and to renew and confirm their ancient friendship through an ambassador who

[1] Âḷi Raja of Cananor turned the visit of Ranabandery Tacourou to good account, for, on the death of Sultan Ibrahim in 1607, this prince succeeded to the throne as his vassal. That Âḷi Raja already had designs upon the Maldives, if not possession of some of them, appears from the journals of Steven van der Hagen's voyage. That Dutch captain was at Cananor in 1604, but could not get the Raja to take the Dutch side against the Portuguese. He warned the Dutch not to make any attempt upon "his Maldive islands" (*Rec. des Voy.*, iii, 17).

accompanied the gift. The Maldive king received him well, and sent in return a present of the rarest and choicest things to be found in his kingdom.

About the same time the Hollanders[1] were guarding Point de Galle, in the island of Ceylon (of which I shall speak more fully hereafter in its proper place), with two or three ships only, it happened that two large vessels passed there on a voyage from Achen in Sumatra, and other places in Sunda, laden with the produce of China and other countries, and were on their way to Arabia. The Hollanders soon made them lower their sails, but seeing they were not friends of the Portuguese, they received them kindly, and they were for two or three days enjoying good cheer together. The larger of the two ships was going, as they said, to Mogor, Surrate, and Cambaye, the other was going to the opposite coast. The captain of the large vessel was quite young, and a native of the Mogor country. The king of Achen had killed his father in order to acquire his wealth, for he was the richest man in all the Indies, and was called *Chamy*.[2] He had much property in Sumatra, and that was the cause of his death. His only son, who was of the same name, and resided in his youth with his mother at Surrate, was very handsome, fair, and well to do, and may have been then about seventeen or eighteen years of age. The other captain was a Turk, aged twenty-five years. He was the strongest

[1] As will be seen, the Dutchmen on board the native vessels mentioned in the following passage, told Pyrard of the death of Queen Elizabeth. It is, therefore, probable that the *rencontre* off the coast of Ceylon took place sometime in 1604. I do not find it mentioned in the Dutch Collection. The Zeelanders had, in 1602, sent a factor to Cambay on board a Turkish vessel from Achin (*Rec. des Voy.*, ii, 525). And in January 1604, some Turks came to the Dutch at Bantam, and thanked them for the kindly treatment of their countrymen and their goods by the Dutch cruisers off Ceylon (*ib.*, p. 673). See further in the following chapter as to the determined efforts of the Dutch to open trade with Cambay.

[2] Perhaps *Shámi*, a Syrian or Western.

man I ever saw, and was renowned throughout all India for his great valour.

So, when the general of the Hollanders heard all this, and that the young captain was going to Cambaye or Surrate, between which places there is only an intervening river, he called together this captain and all the merchants, numbering about thirty or forty men of wealth and position, along with the ship's officers, and bade them tell the truth and say without fear where they were going; to which they replied as before. But this was out of fear, for their intention was to go to Arabia; but they durst not say so, for the Grand Mogor and the Hollanders were good friends, and the Hollanders also had factors at Cambaye and Surrate, which are in the country of the Mogor. At length the general bade bring him the book of the law and a piece of biscuit, upon which he made them swear, according to their custom, that they were speaking the truth. This they did, whereupon the Hollanders requested them to take two of their factors, with a quantity of goods, to Cambaye, with some presents for the Grand Mogor, and for the lords of Cambaye and Surrate. This they promised to do, and the general gave handsome presents to the captain and to the merchants, together with a stock of victuals.

So, taking the two Hollanders and the goods, they departed in great friendship, and the two vessels made straight for the Maldives, which was their course to take, either by the north end of the islands or through them. This is the cause of the prosperity of that country; for the islands are situate halfway between Sunda and the coast of Arabia and Persia, and there are no other islands between whereat provisions can be had. Every year upwards of five-and-twenty or thirty ships pass there, of which not two go there of deliberate purpose, on account of the dangers there; and but for the necessity of passing through them, they would not go there at all, and the islanders would be constrained to go elsewhere to purchase their necessary supplies. The passage is feared as well on account of the currents and reefs as of the fever which is peculiar to the islands, the Malé fevers being known everywhere. Most of the vessels are brought there by the currents, so that they are obliged to sojourn and do some traffic there, by reason of the *Monssons*, which change from one quarter to the other.

These *Monssons*, or *Muessons*, are winds which change for the summer and winter, every six months. They most frequently cheat the sailors who start too late, for the wind comes on to blow contrarily while they are out; they also cheat them by sometimes blowing for a shorter or a longer period one way than the other; and a favourable wind will sometimes cease too soon, and a contrary wind will continue too long, sometimes a month or six weeks, and even two months, beyond expectation. This obliges them to stay seven or eight weeks longer than they like, as I have frequently seen happen. I have also known them put to sea at the close of these Monssons, believing that they would last long enough for the voyage, and when they have got within fifty leagues of Arabia, they have been obliged by the contrary wind to return and make the Maldives again, or even the coasts of Sunda. In these return journeys some of them get lost. On some occasions, when they have passed the northern end of the islands, sailing on the current from the east, and are thinking they have escaped the reefs, one morning the current changes, and the western current carries them away to the islands of the south, where they are wrecked among the reefs. This is what happened to the large vessel in which the queen was, which, as I have related, was lost in the south.

But to return to the two ships voyaging to Arabia: when they arrived at the islands they were not minded to stay there, yet they were forced to await the other Monssons, which did not come for seven or eight months,—for the

Monsson which was then blowing was not yet over. They did not come to land at Malé, so not much was seen of them, because of the sickness which prevailed there; but, as was usual, they chose another island, thirty or forty leagues to the north, called Maspillaspoury, belonging to the chief queen, because it is the most healthy of all. The two ships cast anchor and remained there. The custom in such cases was that on their arrival they came to salute the king with presents. The king liked these casual arrivals much, and received the unfortunate men with the kindest face in the world; but his smile was a deceit, and was worth nothing in the long run.

For his usual plan was to endeavour to get the vessels to come to his island, which they never would; and when he found them to be too strong, he ceased to importune them, fearing to lose their goods and traffic; but when he saw that they were weak, he made them come, under one pretext or another, pretending to be angry with them, so that at length they fell into his power, if perchance the captain of the vessel came to die; in short, nothing passed through his hands without a part sticking to them. When a vessel or merchant happened to arrive at his island, he caused a *banquesalle*, or storehouse, to be assigned to it or him for depositing the goods, and the admiral took an account of everything in writing, and had the sails hauled down and took them and the rudder into his possession. The king was heir to such as died there, whether they left ship or goods behind them, wherefore most ships would not go there, or, as soon as their captain died, they sailed off as soon as possible.

While these two vessels were awaiting the other Monssons all the chiefs and principal men went to salute the king with fine presents. All were rich men, some of them Mahometans, and the rest Banians of Cambaye. The king received them in great state, and for their entertainment had a large bullock killed, and also gave each a cow or bullock, that being a mark of great goodwill. He treated the young captain with exceptional honour, saying that he had known his father well, and on that account was glad to see him. The captain replied that this was the first voyage he and his ship were making, and that he had been to the king of Achen, who had killed his father, to see if he could get from him some recompense; that he had been well received by that king, who had given him many slaves, a ship, and merchandise, and he had promised to return to him. After the Maldive king had thus given him a cordial reception, surrounded by all his court, in the usual fashion, he bade give them lodging, wherewith they were all well pleased. I went to see them in the evening, and they gave me good cheer, and told me they had on board their ship two Hollanders on their way to Surrate, at which news I was overjoyed, and had hopes of hearing some news from France; but they told me that the Hollanders did not want to come to Malé, as much from fear of sickness as that they had nothing to do there; besides that, they had heard tell of the king's humour, concerning which I sent them in writing a few words of advice in French.

Nevertheless, the king was informed that they were there, and what merchandise they were carrying, principally woollen cloth, which they had taken from the Portuguese, elephants' teeth and other things, and some silver. The king sent word that he had great desire to have a fine bit of cloth, and the captain said that he would have to send one of his own people to choose it, which he did; but the chief factor sent his companion to the king to settle the price, and to show him different sorts, so that was a good occasion for me to see him. He brought me the compliments of his companion, who sent me a fine piece of white cotton cloth, there being no white cloth in these islands, but all coloured. He brought to the king as a present an exceedingly beautiful matchlock, with its furniture, and a handsome sword, with which the king was well pleased. In exchange, the king gave some mats, and I did the same, for these are the rarest things manufactured at the island.[1] This factor was eight days at Malé, and the king took two pieces of his cloth, one red and the other violet, for which he paid in silver.[2] The factor then took his departure, and I saw him no more. He could speak French, and I acted as interpreter. The king would never give me leave to go where they were, and they frequently sent us letters, accompanied with some little presents.

As I am on the subject of the two Hollanders, I will tell what happened to them. The captain and merchants who had promised to take them to Cambaye told them frankly that they were going to Arabia, and that what they had told the general was said through fear of being thwarted in their design. The two factors therefore began to unload all their goods; whereupon the captain of the other vessel, who was a Turk, told them that if they wished he would carry them to Cambaye or Surrate in all safety. They accepted the offer, and went with him. Since then I have heard that before they got there one of them died. It was good luck for them to have had the opportunity of proceeding, for otherwise they had been forced to remain at the islands, and been lost, both themselves and their goods: for the king would never have let them go, so as at the last he should get possession of their merchandise.

About the same time came to Malé a man who was a Jew in faith and race, and knew a large number of languages; among others, he spoke Arabic and the Indian tongues well. He was a man of Barbary, and the greatest scoundrel in the world. The English had taken him to England, where he

[1] See above, p. 241.

[2] Above (at p. 242), he says that the Maldivians never allowed gold or silver to go out of the country. Probably the Dutchmen here would take nothing else; and, as will be seen, the king had designs upon the whole ship.

had learnt English well. About the same time that we left France four ships also left England, and the general took this fellow as his body-servant; and he was with him in the Indies.[1] He was already at Achen when our general arrived there, and he it was who informed me that the general had been poisoned by the Portuguese.[2] As for the English general, when he saw that he could not load with pepper at Achen, he went to Bantan in Java, where this Jew robbed him of twelve or fifteen hundred pieces of forty sols Spanish, and made his escape. With the English he was of their religion; with the Mahometans, of theirs; whereas he was all the while a Jew. He married a wife wherever he happened to be, and thus had four or five wives in India. He

[1] The English general here alluded to is Captain James Lancaster, who left Tor Bay on the 20th April 1601, with four ships—the *Dragon*, *Hector*, *Ascension*, and the *Susan*. The journal of the voyage is printed in *Lancaster's Voyages*, Hak. Soc., pp. 57-107. Lancaster arrived at Achin on the 5th June 1602, and at Bantam on the 16th December 1602. This Jew is mentioned as having been with Lancaster at Achin. The conferences with the Sultan's ministers were carried on in Arabic, and the chronicler notes, "Now the general (before his going out of England) intertained a Jew who spake that language perfectly, which stood him in good steed at that time" (p. 81). There is no mention of his having robbed him at Bantam. The character, as drawn by Pyrard, is of a not uncommon type, found a little later at Mocha, where, on the 8th May 1609, some of Captain Sharpeigh's men were lodged in the house of "a talkative lyenge Jewe w'ch spake Spanishe" (*ib.*, p. 123). A hundred years before this we find Jews playing the same *rôle*. In 1510, two Castilian Jews were taken by Simão Martinsz in a vessel going from Mecca to Calicut. "These Jews turned Christians: to the one was given the name of Francisco Dalboquerque, and to the other Alexandre Dataide. And Afonso Dalboquerque, as long as he lived, employed them as interpreters especially Alexandre Dataide, because he knew many languages, and had a great aptitude for business. And after the death of Afonso Dalboquerque they went to Portugal, in the time of King D. Manoel, and from that country returned to India, and from India they proceeded to Cairo, where they again became Jews" (*Comm. of Af. Dalboquerque*, Hak. Soc., ii, 230).

[2] Below, the author says that he had this information from the two Hollanders.

embarked at Achen in a ship of Surrate, which had lately passed by the head of the Maldives, and was so ill-advised as to land with all his goods. He had still left about one hundred and fifty crowns, for he had spent all the rest. After stealing the money he had gone to Surrate, where he married. At length, on this last voyage, being arrived at Malé, he came to make offer of his services to the king, under the pretext that he was a good gunner; but he knew nothing about it. He was well received at first, but when it was seen that he was a liar, no further notice was taken of him. Soon after he fell sick, and begged me to get his leave of the king; and I, making the request through the lord with whom I resided obtained it with great difficulty. He said that he was married in Guzeratte, and had a child there, which was partly the cause why his leave was granted; though after he got it he remained three or four months longer, and spent the remainder of his money, and then embarked with the richest merchant of Cananor, a Malabar Mahometan, and the greatest man of that place next to the king, Ali Radia. This merchant had a wife at the Maldives, and did a large business there, there not being an atollon whereat he had not factors and merchandise. Some of his ships and barques were always at the island: his name was *Poecaca*. So the Jew went with him to Cananor.

As for the young captain of whom I have spoken, I will now tell of the adversity which befell him and his crew. He sojourned at the islands some six months, doing much traffic the while. Though this was contrary to their purpose, they were obliged to do it for the need they had of the island commodities: thus, they took in exchange coco-cord, called *Cairo*,[1] and cocos themselves. But the merchandise they most eagerly desired was *Cambe*,[2] or tortoise-shell, which comes from these islands. The best are the largest and

[1] Tam. *kayiru*.

[2] M. *kahabu*, or *kahambu*. See above, p. 252, *note*.

thickest, a *Gaut,*[1] or quarter of a pound, being worth a larin at least. But as the commodity is in great request elsewhere, they will only take gold or silver in exchange, whereas for other things they will take merchandise. They sold me pepper at no more than two sols the pound, and four pounds of silk for a crown, while the natives bought it (of me) at a higher price; for the strangers used to like me much, and gave me many presents, in order that I should assist them in selling their goods. Our intercourse was in the Portuguese language, and I acted as their factor there. Many a time they have entrusted me with more than two hundred crowns' worth of merchandise on credit; in all cases giving me a quarter of the profit on the sales, so that I made considerable gain through them. It was the young captain who liked me best, and put the greatest confidence in me, wherefore I the more deeply regretted the misfortune which overtook him; for many of his chief men and richest merchants of his ship died, and the custom there is, as I said, that the king inherits the property of foreigners that die there. The king had prevented the captain and his merchants from proceeding to the island where their ship was, and had taken a quantity of their merchandise on credit, for he never used to pay until ships were on the point of sailing, thus thwarting them in their departure at their own time, and preventing any designs against his government. So they were bereft of all means of getting away; for as soon as a vessel arrives, the *Miruaire,* or admiral's sergeant, presently has the rudder carried off to the king's palace, whence it cannot be regained without the admiral's permission.

One day the king sent for this captain to get from him by soft speeches and flattery an account of his vessel's cargo, the amount of it, and the names of the owners: all which the other told him in good faith, for he was the best man for a Mahometan I have ever met, and showed his whole manifest.

[1] See above, p. 189, where it is spelt *gaux.*

When the king had looked over this, he told him that he was heir of all that had died, and that the captain had no interest therein, but should have his freight paid for all of it. This was agreed to, as also that the king should send his own people to get out this merchandise, which was of great bulk. The person sent for this purpose was the lord with whom I had resided so long,[1] seeing that in him the king placed most confidence. He took with him forty or fifty soldiers and mariners in barques; but the party was not as had been intended, for all the merchants of the ships went with this lord; and there remained with the king as hostages only the captain, two of the chief merchants, and the pilot, who was a brave fellow. When they were all arrived at the island where the ship lay at anchor, it being then late, the natives went ashore, while the merchants went on board to await the morrow; but at night they took counsel together that they would sooner die, every man of them, than let this merchandise be taken; and they resolved that, in order to get back their hostages, they would have to seize this great lord, whom the king loved so well that he would not have lost him for all the world's goods. So in the morning, when this lord was walking along the strand with two followers, suspecting nothing, the ship's folk of a sudden seized and carried him by force into their boat, wherein they had plenty fire-arms, and so held him prisoner; then they send word to the king that as soon as he shall send back their hostages, his people will be delivered up. When the news reached Malé, it was the most pitiful case in the world to hear every man crying aloud with his neighbour; nor was there any man but did so, and thus displayed, at least in appearance, his sorrow for the king's sake: the which I felt in real earnest, for this lord was the best friend I had in all that land. It was about midnight when the news came, and at once everybody arose in as great hurry and trouble as if the king himself had been seized. On

[1] *I.e.*, the lord named *Assant Caounas calogue.*

the other hand, the sad consequence was that the captain and his people were forthwith bound and laid by the feet in irons. This caused me many a heartache, for he was so warm a friend to me that I knew not for which of the two I mourned the most. Everyone pitied this captain, but none durst open his mouth on his behalf, for the king was in the greatest passion that ever was, and was terrified lest they should carry off that lord, insomuch that of a sudden he had three galleys armed and launched for the pursuit; but if he had had twenty, they could have done nothing, for the vessel set sail as if to go. Seeing this, the king's nephew, who commanded the galleys, with all speed sent a boat to parley and to arrange for delivering up the men on each side. This was accordingly effected, and war was thus avoided. Meanwhile, these poor Hollanders who had been witnesses of this disturbance were in great difficulty what they should do; and when the folk of the vessel asked them if they would re-embark in that ship with their merchandise, they replied they would not, nor would have aught more to do with men of such treachery, and preferred to go with the Turk captain, which they did; albeit one of them died on the way. As for the large vessel, when it came near the Arabian coast it sank to the bottom, and was lost with all on board, as we heard a year after. Many of the islanders made a large profit out of this quarrel, and I most of all, for I owed more than thirty crowns to the captain and the merchants, and I refused to pay that over to the soldiers, as it would have been for their own advantage, and not for that of the king, because the greatest men in the island owed as much, and they durst not ask it of them. Several times more than two hundred soldiers came to get it, for they had an account of all such as were indebted to the people of the ship; but I held out firmly that I owed nothing, and had paid for all I had taken. At length they sent word to the king (for they never dare speak to him themselves, unless he so orders or himself raises the question), but he replied that there was good security for what I owed, and he would answer for it, but not for all that such and such men owed, naming some of the chief men, as I said just now; that they should themselves pay their debts, if they could, and that I should pay anon. This stopped them short, for they would not have dared to open their mouths against these other lords that owed anything; and I heard nothing more of it.

The lord who had been seized by that vessel died a year after his deliverance, and I never saw the king weep as he did then: for three days he attended him and never left his bedside. He had him buried with the like ceremonies as if he had been his own brother or son, and ever after showed affection to his three sons who survived him, taking them to himself and giving them offices in his household. It is a rule in that country that when such men as he, that have acted as stewards, come to die, the king calls for a statement of his affairs; he then takes all their property, giving to the wife and children as much as he thinks fit. So, two days after the death of this lord, his widow and his four children, three sons and a daughter, came to the palace with all their accounts and papers, and a great array of servants, carrying gold, silver, and other valuables, according to the practice of those that have had the management of the king's affairs; but the king took the accounts and destroyed them without looking at them or taking any of the property, and said aloud and clearly that he gave it all to them, bidding them serve him as faithfully as their father had. One of the sons, as soon as his father died, brought and hid in my house property of more than five hundred crowns' worth, of which no one knew anything but he and I; and all his secrets he confided to me. The chief queen loved him dearly, wherefore the king prohibited him from coming to the palace; but he ceased not to go in such secrecy that none was aware of it.

By the way, the two Hollanders who came in the large vessel told me some news of France, and what had happened during the five years since my departure; among other things, the happy birth of Monseigneur the Dauphin, the king that now is,[1] whereat my companions and I were greatly rejoiced; next, of the death of the queen of England,[2] and of the Mareschal de Biron.[3] They told me also what had become of our admiral[4] the Croissant, and how our general, Monsieur de la Bardelière, being at Achen in Sumatra, was poisoned by the Portuguese, and feeling himself mortally struck, embarked forthwith and set sail, for fear lest the king of Achen, according to the custom of all Oriental countries, should seize his ship in case he died there. But he died ere he rounded the Cape of Good Hope.[5]

[1] Louis XIII, born at Fontainebleau, 27th September 1601; succeeded to the throne on the murder of his father, Henri IV, 14th May 1610; his mother, Marie de Medicis, being regent.

[2] Elizabeth died 24th March 1603.

[3] Charles de Gontaut, Duc de Biron, born 1561, celebrated for his valour at the battles of Arques and Ivry, and at the sieges of Paris and Rouen; and for his friendship with Henri IV, whom he afterwards sought to betray by treasonable correspondence with Spain and Savoy. He was beheaded at the Bastille, 31st July 1602.

[4] Here used, as by numerous French and English writers of the period, for the chief ship of a fleet. See *Hawkins' Voy.*, passim; *Linschoten* (Hak. Soc., i, 9), and *New Eng. Dict.*, s. v. Milton alone, in his well-known lines, "the mast of some great ammiral", affects the Italian form. At this time it was the common word, and the commander was almost invariably, as here, designated "general".

[5] The *Croissant* arrived at Achin, 24th July 1602, and left 20th November of the same year, "apres avoir sejourné", says Martin, "aux Indes l'espace de 5 mois ou environ, où avions eu le trafic libre, de plusieurs sortes d'epiceries et de quelques autres singularitez naissantes au pays" (Martin, *Voy.*, 90). It was there again met by Spilberg, whose chronicler says that the French had not done much business (*Rec. des Voy.*, ii, 516, 526). The Sieur de la Bardelière died as they passed the line, on the 1st December, after an illness of four months, attributed by the French chronicler to the climate and country, and not in any way to his having been poisoned by the Portuguese. Following his last wishes, the Sieur de la Villeschar was elected to fill his place (*ib.*, p. 91). See also Cunat, *St. Malo illustré par ses Marins*, 78; and an article on Bardelière by Cunat, in Lovet, *Biographie Bretonne*.

His ship, which was not half laden, got as far as athwart the Cape Finisterre, when the sailors were nearly all dead, and the remainder so ill that they could hardly walk, while the ship was so full of leaks that she was making water on all sides, and was sinking. Then by good fortune they fell in with two Hollanders' ships, who salved the merchandise and took the remaining men to England, and had the third part of all they salved for their pains. The men of the Croissant had taken ten Indians at Achen, at wages, to assist them in the return voyage, but most of them died going or returning Those who escaped were paid and sent back by the Hollanders. There was also an Indian who came to Holland and remained there three years, where he learned to speak Flemish and a little French, for that the mate with whom he lived in Holland was a Frenchman; and on his return to the Indies he recounted to all the Indian kings the marvellous grandeur and magnificence of Holland; but he spoke also of the great esteem and regard the Hollanders had for the kingdom of France.[1]

[1] The *Croissant*, after a terrible storm, rounded the Cape in January 1603, and reached St. Helena 3rd March. Leaving that island on the 19th, she reached Ascension on the 25th. On the 15th May the wearied remnant of the crew, who were suffering the extremities of hunger, and eating dogs and rats, sighted Terceira (Azores), and on the 21st fell in with three Flemish ships coming from Venice. The end of their sad story had better be told in Martin's own words:—"Nous les priasmes de nous recevoir en leurs vaisseaux et que nous leurs ferions part de nos marchandises selon la coustume de la mer, surquoy ils nous firent quelques offres generalles, nous promettant nous venir trouver le lendemain, ce qu'ils firent demandant quelques uns de nostres. pour traicter particulierement sur ce subject ; à la fin nous fusmes contrains transporter en leurs vaisseaux, ce que chacun avoit de particulier, et leur donner le pillage de nostre navire : lequel, peu de temps apres, s'emplissant d'eau, coula de luy mesme a fond à nostre veue. Demeurasmes sur lesdits navires Flamens, du 23 jour du mois de May, jusques au 11 jour de Juin, qu'eusmes la cognoissance de l'isle d'Angleterre, et le 13 posasmes l'ancre en la radde de Plemurs [Plymouth] (Martin, *Voy.*, pp. 100, 101). Estancelin says that eight Indians brought home by the *Croissant* were still at St. Malo in 1604 (*Voy.*, *etc.*, *des Norm.*, 54).

CHAPTER XXI.

Of a captured Portuguese vessel that was wrecked.—An ambassador from the king of the Maldive Islands.—A vessel of Achen.—A Malay native.—A Maldive confession.—The discovery of a strange island; and other events.

While I was at the Maldives the Hollanders had captured from the Portuguese a fine and good ship, and brought it, with all its cargo, to Achen, where they had discharged it into their magazine for sale there. They then found by chance a ship-captain and sixty sailors, who had lost their ship on the coast of Sumatra, and were men of Guzerate and Cambaye. The Hollanders asked them if they would serve them faithfully, and on their so promising, and giving such and such security at Achen, the Hollanders gave them this Portuguese vessel, victualled and equipped in all necessary respects, on a contract to carry one of their factors with merchandise to Cambaye, after which the master should dispose of the ship as he liked. The master and his crew, well enough pleased with this windfall, accepted the offer gladly. The Hollanders loaded the ship with more than 60,000 crowns' worth of goods, consisting of cloth, ivory, lead, iron, steel, sulphur, silver, precious stones, and other valuables. This ship made sail straight to Cambaye, but they were unable to pass the Maldives without paying forfeit like ourselves: for one fine night she went upon the reefs of the island and was wrecked. They saved their cargo in like manner as we did. I saw the Dutch clerk and factor, named Martin Dombe, a native of Zeeland, and a man of fine presence and education. He and the master and mariners remained about two months at Malé, after which the king gave them a barque to take them off. The master, who was a Mahometan, and well known at the islands, begged the king to treat the factor kindly, which he did. I saw this Martin Dombe afterwards at Cochin, as I shall relate in the proper place.[1]

It is impossible to describe the cruelty and tyranny exercised by the king towards the mate of this ship, a man of about thirty-five, and his son, a boy of twelve or thirteen, and two of their men, who were accused of having concealed some of the ship's treasure,—to wit, gold, silver, and precious stones; for he kept them upwards of a month in prison, beaten and whipped every day, and bound with their faces to the ground, without anything to eat, save such as was given them in small quantities in secret. But I may say also that I never saw such constancy and courage as was theirs, for they could never be got to avow anything, until at length they had to be liberated, when it was evident that they would not die. I was never astonished at anything so much as at that, that they did not die a thousand times over, with all the ills they endured. They were nothing but skin and bone when they came out of prison; but what I admired most of all was the resolution of the little boy, to undergo all that suffering with patience so great. When, then, the king saw that he could draw nothing from them, he had them doctored and nursed, and gave them some money to get home withal. Yet true it is that they had hidden this money whereof they were suspected.

About a year before we left the Maldives, there came to the king an ambassador from the Christian king of these islands, who lived at Goa, of whom I have already spoken. This ambassador was a Portuguese, and told me he had been at Rochelle in France. He was about fifty years of age, and was named Dom Adrien de Gouia.[2] He came in considerable state, accompanied by some other Portuguese and Christian Indians. The subject of his visit was a certain dispute

[1] His name was Martin Domburgh. For his subsequent history, see below, ch. xxviii, and vol. II, ch. vi.

[2] Adrian de Gouveia.

which existed between that young Christian king and his uncle, Dom Paulo,[1] who resided at Cochin, the latter wanting to take part of the tribute coming to the said king. A suit was pending about it in the Parliament at Goa for a long time, during which this Dom Paulo enjoyed the receipt of it, —for, under the treaty of peace, the Maldivians were not obliged to pay the tribute elsewhere than at Cochin, where the uncle was. At length, the Parliament of Goa having ordained that the Christian king, Dom Philippe, should have of the Maldive king and all the chiefs of the country a certificate to the effect that they recognised him as the king, he therefore sent this embassy with a quantity of presents. But the Maldive king took but little notice of it, and the ambassador waited there for two months without getting an audience, such was the pride and haughtiness of this king in a matter wherein he perceived no gain for himself; and when he was got to do business with them, his demeanour was exceeding proud. In fine, it was four months ere the ambassador got his despatch, which was granted, when he asked it, with offerings of the rarest gifts, as well from his master as from himself.

About the same time was wrecked there a ship belonging to the king of Achen. It had not intended to come there, but to Masulipatan or to Bengal, yet the calms and currents brought it there perforce. The king got all this merchandise, which accrued to him by law. The captain saved much gold, silver, and precious stones, and was well treated by the king, who gave him a barque well furnished with provisions to go away in. But I will tell what happened to one of these Malays (for so they call all the people of Sunda and the parts about Malaca). Having saved a large amount of property,

[1] This seems to be a slip: the name should be Dom Pedro. See vol. II, ch. ix, where the lawsuit is again referred to, and the name of the uncle given as Pedro. In the royal despatches, too, where frequent mention is made of the Maldive princes, only one brother of Dom João is mentioned, and he under this name (see App. B).

the captain and some of the chief men wanted to dole it to the others according to their own notions; but three of the men resolved to have their share or die in the attempt. So one day, espying the captain as he was taking a walk by himself, they attacked him in such wise that but for the succour of the inhabitants he must have been killed, or forced to surrender his booty; but he was saved for the nonce. Being a brave and courageous man, and knowing the natural temper of the Malays,—to wit that they are irreconcilable in their enmities, and never swerve when once resolved upon anything, and make no more ado about the life of a man than of a chicken,—he bethought him to be beforehand with them. So, with the assistance of some of his own party, he lay in wait, arms in hand, for the three men as they came out of their temple or mesquite, and attacked them with such vigour, that the most valiant of them, and the author of the quarrel, was laid low, and the two others were wounded, and only saved by the people of the island. They defended themselves bravely, and he that was killed received many wounds; for they are a cruel and vindictive race. The king was very angry, and ordered the Pandiare to do justice in the matter, which he did in this wise. He summoned the captain and the two survivors before him, and after inquiring all that had passed, he found that the dead man had come by his death justly, for having tried to kill his captain. But he could hardly make the others come to any agreement, for the captain was by no means willing to pardon the two others, and would do nothing but at the express command of the king. Finally an agreement was come to, the Pandiare ordering the two men to kiss the feet of the captain, and to ask his pardon, which they willingly did. He also made them recite aloud a confession in Arabic—as, according to their law, all have to do who have committed any fault: for criminals and convicts are not allowed to have speech of or intercourse with the rest until they have first made confession of their fault before the Pandiare, or others deputed by him to receive it (these being the Naibes, and no others), and are thus absolved. The Pandiare made the captain do the like, because he had slain a man, and all were afterwards good friends. Yet the two men would not embark with the captain when he went, saying that he would throw them overboard: for that race put no confidence in one another, whatever reconciliation they may have come to; so that they preferred to wait until the next Maldive ship should be sailing for Achen. When the captain went, the king of the islands wrote to the king of Achen, and sent him some presents; for they were good friends, and often sent letters and presents to each other. As for the wrecked ship, it is the general custom that all belongs to the lord of the country where the wreck is; and another lord would take it for an insult if the merchandise of a ship of his that was wrecked were restored to him.

Some time afterwards, the king sent on two occasions a very expert pilot to discover a certain island named *Pollouoys*,[1]

[1] M. *Fólávahi;* the first part of the word is, perhaps, the Malay *pulo*, "island". There can be little doubt that this island, around which so much fable had circled, was one of the Chagos archipelago. A very small island of the Peros Banhos group is still called *Poule;* but as most of the names of these islands are French, the identification is doubtful. The northernmost of that archipelago is in 4° 44′ S., and the southernmost of the Maldives (Addu) in 0° 44′ S. It is not surprising that the Maldivians knew little or nothing of islands so comparatively near, when we bear in mind that they were at the mercy of monsoons and currents, whose direction is east and west alternately, and that the Chagos Islands lie almost due south. More of them seems to have been known to the Maldivians than Pyrard was aware; for in the letters patent of 1560, issued by the ex-king Dom Manoel from Cochin, he describes himself as king not only of the Maldives, but also of the "seven islands of *Pullobay*" (see App. B). As for the devils, all we need say is that an island inhabited by them was a commodity which any respectable Mahomedan community of those days could hardly do without. See Lane's *Arabian Nights* (1877), i, 323; iii, 84, as to the demons called *Sealáh* and *Dahlán*, and the island *Bartáil*. The island of *Pollouoys* seems to have been famed beyond the Maldives. Vincent

which is still almost unknown to them, except that they say that long ago one of their barques landed there by chance (so they find it stated in their histories), but were forced to leave

le Blanc, while in Pegu, picked up the following story, where the legend is obviously mixed up with references to the cannibalism of the Battas of Sumatra or of some of the wild tribes of Arakan (see *Cathay*, pp. 100-1), and the mention of the kings of Achen and Bengal would seem to identify the island with *Pulowé*, to the north of Sumatra, rather than with the far-off Chagos. Geographical difficulties, however, did not trouble the great traveller of Marseilles:—"South-west of the isle of Seilan are the Maldives, many in number and very dangerous for their shelves of sand and rocks; but I will say no more of them, because my knowledge is but small; besides, they have amply and exactly been described by others; but I will say something of a wonderful island beyond the Maldives towards the south, some 12 degrees from the Line, and called *Polouis* or *Polouois*, now desert, though formerly inhabited and flourishing, which (as I since learnt at Pegu) was governed by a prince called *Argiac*, a potent king of many islands and kingdoms; he having many children by several wives, gave this island to one of the gallantest of them, named *Abdenac*, for his portion, with several treasures. This *Abdenac* was possest of it peaceably for five years space: his elder brother, called *Argiac* after his father, the king of Achen in Sumatra, refused him the share of treasure his father had left him, whereupon the other, enraged, craved the assistance of the king of Bengale, who furnished him with ships, wherewith he invaded his brother, burnt his towns, and put to death most of his followers, but received a mortal wound himself. Returning to his island of *Polouis* with the treasures he had regained of his brother, and finding himself near death, he distributed all his wealth among his own people, and bequeathed his island to his *Dume* or evil spirit, as his heir, intreating him to preserve it to the Day of Judgment, when he hoped to return to the world.

"This will made, he died, and had no other sepulchre than the bowels of his kinsmen and friends, according to the custom of that region, where in many places they eat the dead flesh of their kindred and near relations, persuading themselves the soul to be sooner at rest than if they permitted the corpses to putrify in the earth, and that no sepulchre is so honourable as the bowels of a dear friend.

"This island falling to the evil spirit's share, he became so turbulent that, from the time he took possession, the island was no longer habitable nor approachable; and all the inhabitants forced to retire into the adjacent isles. Ever since, this place remained desert; yet there are great store of birds and beasts. Sometimes the Maldivians have landed there by chance, but have been forced immediately to retreat, the evil

by reason of the great miseries wrought by the devils who, as it is said, possess the island, and cause the great, horrible, and perpetual storms, which rage with such fury in the seas there that ships cannot remain at anchor. They said also that the devil visibly tormented them. As for the island, it is said to be very fertile in all sorts of fruits; and the large medicinal coconuts which are so dear at the Maldives are believed to come from thence; others, however, think that they come from the bottom of the sea. I did not hear whether there was any betel or not. The island is under the tenth degree beyond the line, and about 120 leagues from the Maldives. The Maldive kings have many a time sent vessels to discover it, but they have never known where to find it; and such as have landed there have done so by chance. Had this pilot who was sent discovered it, it was intended to try and people it. They took with them some sorcerers and magicians to treat with the devil and come to terms with him, for they know not how to conjure him: they only pray him to do something, and promise him their vows, and offer gifts and banquets. But this pilot could not find the island, and was unable to return straight to the Maldives; in such case all that can be done

spirits do so perplex them, raising great tempests on that sea. Being at Pegu, I heard a famous magician had promised the king to bring him some animals from his island, and also the treasures of *Abdenac*; but the demons did so perturb him, he could not effect his purpose; for as he was taking footing in the island, and beginning his conjurations he had writ upon a leaf and put into the hands of one of his boldest disciples, they were, by the illusions of Satan, so suddenly terrified, that the miserable disciple fell dead upon the place, and the master magician was so horribly beaten and dragged by the devils to the ship side, that his companions had time only to re-embark him and hoist sail for Pegu. All the rest were strangely tormented and beaten, except the master's mate and the seamen, who were wiser, for, knowing the condition of the place, they would not put foot on land, which afterwards they were glad of. Thus was the magician served, and 'twas almost past his skill to recover himself" (*V. le Blanc*, i, 106-7).

Pyrard's story of the island will be found summarised in the *Quarterly Review* of 1814, p. 57.

is to make Achen, or, better, Ceylan, or the Cape of Comory. Both times that the pilot went he lost the greater part of his men by death. He used to say that he would pursue the discovery or die in the attempt. The reason why they always met with storms was that they every time went in the winter, while the winds and currents from the west prevail; and that was for the cause that had they gone during the east winds, and had not fetched the island,—as, indeed, was a matter of great uncertainty,—they had been borne towards the Ethiopian coast, and had perished there. This pilot was vastly keen to take me with him on this voyage, and I was as anxious to go; but the king would not permit it, knowing that if ever I reached the coast I would never return to the island. But while I remained there I witnessed the arrival of a tall ship of Bengal, laden with the merchandise of that country. It came to the islands solely to load the *bolits* or shells of which I have spoken so much. The captain of that ship died, and the king inherited all; and but a little thereafter another captain from Guzerate died also, and the king succeeded to his property too: wherein may be seen the great profits and revenues of the king arising from these casualties.

There was also a king of Ceylan, who, out of desire to make a present to the king of Cochin, equipped a galley and loaded her with cinnamon of the finest, and with areca, but after her setting out the calms and currents brought her to the Maldives, into a channel where the current was not strong enough to carry her beyond the islands. Yot those on board were unable to fetch land, till the islanders went out with their barques, and with plenty of ropes, anchors, and oars, and so salved the ship and brought her to anchor. Those on board, thinking to coast along and to make land every day, had not taken much provision, wherefore, after being a long while at sea ere they reached the island, they were so feeble and worn with hunger and thirst, that they could do nothing, having nought to eat but cinnamon and areca. If, indeed, they had not made land at these islands, they had made none nearer than the coasts of Arabia or Melinde, upwards of 900 leagues off, and so full soon had died. The island where they anchored is called *Itadou*,[1] to the south of Malé, from which it is distant about 50 leagues, in the atoll *Adoumatie*. The merchandise carried by them was in great request at the islands, and more the areca than the cinnamon: for they can no more want this areca than we bread and wine. They were constrained to sell their goods for the wherewithal to live. But the custom of these islands is, that none dare do business with strangers without permission of the king; yet they omit not to trade in secret, only when that is known they pay a fine, and all the merchandise is forfeited: it is allowed, however, to give some fruits, and to give food and drink. The strangers, too, must give their merchandise in barter without fixing the price, for it is the province of the king and the elders to fix the prices of foreign merchandise, that is, of all that comes not in the usual way of trade; for they use not so with what comes in the ordinary way, and is brought by the Malabars that come there frequently with their wives, children, and servants. These are permitted to traffic everywhere, like the folk of the country, and are subject to the same police and regulations.

This Cingala captain of the vessel of Ceylan had not brought any money, expecting to find at Cochin all commodities and credit. So, having no money to buy food, he made an offer to the king of all his merchandise for a supply of victuals, that so he should get away. But the king, well knowing that all the merchandise would fall into his hands, paid no attention, and only caused provisions to be supplied from day to day. Then arose the question of discharging the goods and getting the galley on dry land in order to refit her. But the islanders, who are a mischievous race, and seek only

[1] *Hitadú*, in Haddumati atoll, lat. 1° 46′ N., wrongly named Henadu-Adu in the Admiralty charts.

the ruin of the poor strangers, while they were assembled from all the neighbouring parts, and were receiving good pay for hauling the galley on shore, out of malice drove her on a sand-bank, where she broke up; and the poor captain and his men, thus left without a ship, were obliged to remain there for some time. Then they fell sick, and nearly all died, and among these the captain, whereby the king became heir to all the cinnamon, which they call *Poniembous Thory*,[1] and the areca, called *Poua*.[2] If the Cochin king had written for it, he would have sent it all to him. He afterwards thought to send it to Arabia, and at the time when he was killed there was a large vessel all laden to convey it thither; but that was taken, with everything else, as I shall relate hereafter.[3]

Shortly after this, arrived another vessel from Massulipatan, laden with rice, white cloths, oils, and other goods suitable to the island market. The captain was sixty years of age, and had hair as white as cotton and as long as that of women. His ship came to anchor 30 leagues south of Malé, and had come there to load fish for Achen. This captain took a great fancy for me, but he died at Malé, so the king forthwith sent to fetch the ship; but as they were bringing it by night it struck a reef, and all was lost. There was also a tall vessel of Cambaye, which cheated him cleverly; for the captain, casting anchor at an island 40 leagues to the north from Malé, sent four of his chief men to salute the king with presents. Their object was not to remain there, but only to get some ropes, victuals, and other commodities. So, when they feigned a desire to traffic, the king was well enough pleased, and waited to get his share; to this end he desired not that the four men should return, and told them to write word to their

[1] In the Vocab. Pyrard writes *ponianboutory*. Chr., more correctly, *fonitori*, and Bell, *fonitorhi*. *Foni* = Sin. *pæni*, "sweet", as in *pæni-dodan*, "sweet orange"; and *torhi*, "bark" or "skin". Pyrard introduces *anbu*, "mango", and makes it the "bark of the sweet mango".

[2] Sin. *puwa*.

[3] *Post*, ch. xxiii.

captain to come to Malé with his vessel. But they, knowing that their captain desired to be off, and fearing that he would leave them there, and so save their wages, got the king to permit them to return, under promise to bring the vessel, for which purpose he gave them a body of soldiers. But when once they set foot upon their own ship, they full soon sent back the soldiers with rounds of shot from their cannon and arquebuses, and flights of arrows. The king was much annoyed, and threatened punishment to some strangers who were residing in the said island, and likewise to the inhabitants of it, as being the parties who had caused the ship's people to abandon the notion of coming to Malé for traffic. He would have liked nothing better than to see them come and anchor at his own island, seeing that when they were so far off he could not make such dispositions as suited his purpose. But it would be impossible to describe in detail all the vessels that came to these islands while I was there. I have only made mention of those to which some misfortune or other notable accident happened. All the aim and object of the king and his subjects was but to bring about some mischief, for he used to give some portion of the wrecked ships to his ministers, and among others to the soldiers. But he gave nothing out of the ships whose captains died there: of these none but he drew any advantage.

CHAPTER XXII.

Divers judgments passed for adultery, lewdness, and other crimes. —Amorous humour of the Indian women.—Of the Grand Pandiare; and the strange resolution of a Mulatto.

I shall now relate divers occurrences that happened during my time to particular inhabitants of the island; among others, to a Gentile Canarin of Cochin, a man of great means and position. For eight whole years he had come and gone about the islands, having everywhere houses, factors, and domestics, speaking the language quite well, and being, in fact, naturalised. One day this man was surprised lying with a woman of the islands. He had kept her for six months, and she was but a poor servant-girl. He was presently haled with her before the Grand Pandiare, to whom he protested that he had done her no manner of harm; that he desired to become of their faith, and would marry the woman. This was done, and he became a Mahometan; and it appeared that he had for a long time desired this end, for that he owed much money at Cochin, as to which he became bankrupt. He espoused this woman and made a great lady of her: for there, strangers, both men and women, can wear whatever they please. When he made the promise he was set free, but upon her judgment was passed according to the law: all her hair was shaved, then she was bathed in old and stinking oil, her head put in an old sack of sail-cloth, and then she was beaten at all the cross-roads and round the island. This is their manner of punishing all men and women taken in adultery or fornication. But there, as here, money does everything and saves from everything. As for the conversion of the man, he was borne in triumph through the streets and round the island, accompanied by the greatest lords, and by the people of all sorts and conditions; he was presented with much money and raiment and a new name: for there, names are given at pleasure and by whomsoever, be it father, mother, kindred, or even the first comer; and also at any time, and not only at birth or circumcision, insomuch that it seemed to me they give names as we do here to dogs and horses: for the name first given by whomsoever is the one that sticks to a man.

The king likewise granted dignities to the new convert, making him purveyor and distributor of all the rice and other provisions and merchandise wherein the king trafficked.

It is a highly honourable office, and he had other men under him.

The Pandiare that passed the said judgment was a Cherife of Arabia, that is, one of a family the most respected and noble among these people, as being of the race of Mahomet. He was a very good man, and was greatly beloved of the king. He had great goodwill toward strangers, and blamed the king for, among other things, his evil treatment of us, seeing that we were their friends, and enemies of the Portuguese, and that the kings of Achen, Java, and other countries gave a cordial reception to all Europeans, such as the French, English, and Hollanders, as he had observed in those countries which he had visited. To which the king replied that he was much displeased with him; that such counsel came not well from him, but from the lords and elders of the island. This Pandiare was returning to Arabia from Achen, where he had been well received, and, loaded with much wealth, was returning with it; but on passing through the islands the king heard of it, and so besought him to remain, that he at length consented,[1] and became so familiar with the king as to be permitted to eat with him, an honour never done to any other person.

While this Pandiare was in office I saw him one day do examplary justice on a large number of women. They were about twenty-five or thirty in number, some of the greatest ladies in the land, who were accused of a crime whereof I never heard tell before; it is practised only at the Maldives, and is called *Pouy tallan.*[2] In truth, the women of all India are naturally much addicted to every kind of ordinary lewdness;

[1] Very much Ibn Batuta's case. See App. A.

[2] M. *fú* vel *fui*, "pudenda". et *talaṅ*, Sin. *talaṇḍa*, "percutere". Pyrard addit hæc, "scilicet pomo quodam utuntur ibi crescente, apud illos *Quela* apud nos *Banana* vocato, quod tam longum quam palma plerumque est, tam crassum quam brachium pueri decem annos nati. Quem vero ad modum hoc abutuntur tam fœdus tam turpis tam immanis est ut plura de illo pudeat me referre."

but those of the Maldives in particular are so tainted with this vice that they have no other talk or occupation, and hold it a boast and a virtue one with another to have some bravo or gallant, upon whom they lavish all such favours and tokens of love as a man could wish of a woman. Among other things, they never let them want for betel, prepared and served in some elaborate and extraordinary style, with some cloves put inside, or else a little black seed, the most tasty, odoriferous, and pleasant to the mouth that can be conceived. As for the men, they cull flowers and arrange them neatly in the manner of bouquets, and send them to the ladies out of gallantry. There are certain white flowers[1] of a full scent on which they can write and grave what they will with the point of a knife, and thereon they write three or four verses on the subject of their passion. Money and other valuable things they give not much to one another; and when these are given, it is more on the part of the women than of the men. To the women the men are exceedingly courteous and obliging.

Many reasons may be assigned for the fact that the women are of a disposition so hot and amorous; but the principal seem to me to be that they are exceedingly lazy, and do nothing but ever lie rocked in daintiness. Next, that they are continually eating betel, a very heating herb; and in their ordinary fare use so many spices that sometimes I could hardly put the food to my mouth; also garlic, onions, and other such heating things. Add to this, that the climate is directly under the line, a condition which renders the men more sluggish and less capable; yet for all that, most have two or three wives apiece,—I mean such as can afford to keep them. They are also lazy, idle fellows, more like women, their chiefest exercise being to lie abed with them, and then more often with desire than effect.

[1] Probably the *champaka* (*Michelia Champaka*), or "temple flower", as it is called in Ceylon.

But to return to the justice done upon those women: two at first were taken in the act, one of whom was married to one of the king's chief officers, and he loved her dearly. Now, their law and custom obtains that when a king's officer or any of his family is a delinquent, before proceeding to justice the Grand Pandiare sends word to the king, asking if it be his pleasure that the process be according to the ordinary forms. This the king never refuses. So the Grand Pandiare, having informed the king of the conduct of the two women, the king replied that he willed justice to be done, not only upon these two, but upon many others, who, as he had heard, had for a long while been engaged in this business, and that a strict inquisition should be made. Forthwith, too, he sent the husband of one of the women, with two of his most intimate advisers, to assist at the inquiry and trial, and bade them expressly tell the Pandiare to omit no part of his orders, for that if any remained unpunished, he would take the law into his own hands; insomuch that all the people incontinently assembled from all parts of the island, and even the highest grandees came, many of whom to prosecute their own wives. During this procedure the king had all the doors of his palace closed, so that none should enter to beg the royal favour towards his wife: thus was equal justice done. The poor wretches all accused one another, and even the men who had personal or hearsay knowledge of it, brought them forward, and named aloud whose wives they were. About thirty of these women were publicly punished; first they had their hair cut,—a mark of great infamy with them; then they were beaten with thick thonged whips of leather, in such wise that two or three died. Thereafter all were absolved, with a warning that if they returned to these practices they should be drowned. Subsequently, however, I saw certain of the same party who were again arrested, and were not drowned, but only beaten with those whips which are called *gleau*.[1] The sin of man and man is very common, and though the book of their law prescribes the penalty of death, yet they heed not that; and nowhere in the world are these enormities more common and less punished; wherein may be seen the curse and wrath of God upon these wretches, who are led by the falsity and unrighteousness of their law to fall into the abyss of these horrible vices.

About the same time I saw justice done upon a youth of seventeen years of age. He was the son of an Ethiopian Cafre and of a woman of the islands, such a one being called Mulastre.[2] He had the greatest resolution and courage that I was ever witness of, for alone he had the assurance to attack six or seven other men. He became so mischievous, that with a single companion he went about the islands in a boat, thieving and harrying whatever he could, and assaulting the poor folk in cruel fashion. But at length he was caught, and had his right-hand cut off. While he was being punished, I saw no change upon his countenance, nor did he utter the slightest cry, no more than if he was feeling nothing. This punishment in no way changed his humour, for he was no sooner healed than he returned to his former courses, insomuch than when he was caught again they were constrained to cut off his left-foot, whereof he made no more account than of his fist: for his resolution was such that he himself taught the man that was cutting him how he ought to do it, without ever showing any trace of pain. He had by him a vessel full of boiling coco-nut oil, into which he himself thrust his leg, all as though it had been cold water. I think that such determined courage has never been seen in a boy. Withal, his evil nature so led him to larceny that no sooner was his leg healed than he took to

[1] Mr. Bell has not traced this word; the ordinary term for whip is *durrá*.

[2] Mulatto, properly applied, as here, only when one parent is a negro.

crawling out at night to commit robberies. He was also horribly addicted to sodomy; so at length the king was forced to send him into exile, and to put him to death.

But to return to the Grand Pandiare who carried out so many executions. After remaining a short time longer at the island, he got leave to go to Arabia, with a ship laden with great riches; but his departure was not without much sorrow on the part of the king and all the people, who regretted him extremely, for he was there regarded as a saint. He made fair promises of returning, but for all that had no mind thereto. His successor in the office was one who had espoused the sister of the chief queen, and was a great noble and of good family: he died in Arabia, as I have said.[1]

Such is what I have been able to note and remember of the most memorable events which took place at the Maldive islands during the time I was there; and before finishing this chapter I shall further say that during the five or six years I was at that king's court I saw nearly his whole government changed, and the greater part of the officers of his household and court come by their deaths in various ways. This ofttimes gave me a foreboding that the end and period of his government was drawing nigh.

Also I must not forget to mention that I saw happen there a great eclipse of the sun at high noon (this was in the year 1605), which lasted three hours.[2] All the people were greatly astonished, and cried and howled in strange fashion, saying that it was an evil omen, and signified that they should lose the greatest of them. And, indeed, in the same year, one of the king's wives died in childbed, and soon after the king himself was vanquished and slain, and all his estate was overthrown, as I shall relate in the chapter following.

[1] *Ante*, p. 277.

[2] This eclipse took place on the 12th October 1605; total at 1 P.M., Paris time; visible in Europe, Asia, and Africa (*L'Art de Vérifier des Dates, etc.*; Paris, 1770).

They all carefully observed the day, hour, and minute of the eclipse, and it was recorded in the public archives.[1]

CHAPTER XXIII.

Of the expedition of the king of Bengal to the Maldives.—The taking of Malé island.—Death of the Maldive king, and voyage of the author to Bengal, with a description of the islands of Malicut and Divandurou.

Having then resided at these islands for the space of five years, or thereabouts, but sorely against my will, this long sojourn gave me a knowledge of the country, and an acquaintance with the language, manners, and customs of the inhabitants, greater, perhaps, and I may say it without vanity, than any other European has ever had. Wherefore I have been led to enlarge with so much particularity and exactness my description of the islands, well knowing that none before me has written to the same effect: and perhaps it will be long ere another will make so long a sojourn; for, indeed, men go there but rarely, and then against their will, by reason of the great hazard and peril attending the voyage, which induce them to avoid the islands as much as they can. In the next place, they have been little known up to now; and if misfortune should carry any other person there as it carried me, it is unlikely he should meet with the same favourable treatment and liberty that I experienced. This will gain me an excuse with my readers if I have been somewhat lengthy and tedious in this description of the Maldives; but I have

[1] "In the Sultan's palace at Mâlé is said to be preserved a national record styled *Târikhu* (Ar. *Târikh*, "history"), or *Muskuli foi*, in which all important events and matters of State have been faithfully noted for centuries, in the old Maldive character (*dives akuru*), in Arabic, and in the modern native character (*gabali tâna*)" (Bell, *Rep.*, 41). We may in time hear more of these archives.

thought that since God had granted me grace through the means of my misfortunes to learn so many particular things, I was obliged to share my knowledge with the public and my country, to whom my good intentions at least will be acceptable, showing that I am not ungrateful for the favours of God in that He hath granted me to know all these things, and at the last hath been pleased to deliver me miraculously, in such wise as I shall now relate.

But first I must not omit a dream I had while asleep at night at the islands two days before my deliverance, for it is worthy to be known. I dreamed that I was gone forth of that country, and was in full liberty in a Christian land. I was infinitely overjoyed, but at my awakening I was full sorely astonished to find my dream false. Nevertheless, though I was exceeding sad, I arose, and falling on my knees prayed God with all my heart and soul that He would be pleased of His grace to deliver me out of this Mahometan servitude, and to set me again on Christian soil, where I could resume the free exercise of my religion, which I had been constrained to discontinue for so long a time. Then I made a vow to make a voyage to St. James in Galicia,[1] there to render thanks to God. Two nights after that (it was in the month of February, in the year 1607) the king had warning of the coming of an armada of sixteen galleys or galleots, which were already preparing to enter the islands. The news greatly astonished both the king and his people, for they had no word of it before, and the suddenness of it surprised them. He commanded at once to put in the sea such galleys as he had, to the number of seven, let alone other vessels, barques, and boats, which were there in great number: and everyone set to this work with all his might; but they could not get it done speedily enough ere the enemy's sails came in sight.

[1] Santiago Compostella, the famous shrine in Galicia of the patron saint of Spain. As will be seen hereafter, Pyrard was enabled to perform his vow.

His consternation was then the greater, wherefore he commanded his people forthwith to ship all the most valuable riches he was possessed of, and so to save himself and his wives in the more distant islands of the south, where the enemy could not land because of the difficulties of the passages.

At first sight of the galleys all the people were greatly taken up, some with attending to the galleys and vessels of the king, others to their own barques and boats, so as to ship themselves and their goods and seek safety in the other islands. As for me, as soon as I saw the alarm was real, I called to mind my dream and the prayer I had made to God but a while before, and began to take some hope: and chiefly, when I perceived at a great distance the enemy's sails, I resolved, with my three companions, to seek an opportunity of safety and a deliverance from captivity, as we had so far found grace with God. But I leave you to imagine in what apprehension we were lest they should seek to prevent us from embarking, the which we had to manage or die in the attempt. But our good luck would have it that the alarm was so hot and sudden that they had no time to recover themselves, far less to think of us. So we had to save ourselves that day or never, and what happened was a true miracle for us. Meanwhile, during the great tumult which ensued at the sight and approach of the enemy, we made as though we were as greatly distressed and distracted as the rest, and made the same hurry; insomuch that the country folk, seeing us to be of like action and countenance with themselves, entertained no distrust of us. But I certainly believe that if the enemy's galleys had not appeared before the king had embarked (as I shall relate presently), and had we remained in the island without embarking with them, the king would not have failed on his return to have put us to death, all four,—that is, if the enemy had not cared to land, or the alarm had proved false. But God, having pity upon us, permitted the enemy to appear before the king and his people were ready, and this was the sole cause of our liberty. Meanwhile the enemy was ever approaching, and the king perceiving this, came forth of his palace and took to flight with the three queens, his wives, who were borne in the arms of some gentlemen, as a nurse carries her infant. They were covered each with veils and taffetas of divers colours, figured in the Chinese style, and as large as shrouds. They did not come forth from the palace till the king did, and he embarked with them. I was at the moment burdened with arms and other goods, which I was carrying to put on board the galleys, and being all soaked and in mean attire, the king met me and told me I was an honest man, and should take courage, using a word to me which is common throughout all India, namely, *Sabatz*,[1] that is to say, "Grammercy"; it is used also to praise a man for something he has done well. When he said this word to me tears of pity came into my eyes, for he wept and made the greatest lamentation to see himself obliged to quit all, and to see them thus bear away his wives, who on their part were bathed in tears, while all the people were in the saddest plight throughout the streets, and one heard naught but groans, cries, and howling of women and children. The king, having embarked for his safety in his royal galley, called by them *Ogate Gourabe*[2] (*gourabe* means "galley", and *ogate*, "royal"), along with his wives and his nephew, was constrained to leave behind the greatest part of his wealth, and all his arms and cannon, of which he had a great store in the island, for he had no time to arm himself or to ship them; and then, at the same moment when all the rest were on board, he gave the word to use sail and oars, and to take the route for the south and the atollons of Souadou. When all the galleys were gone saving the smallest, which

[1] Pers. *Shābāsh!* "Bravo! well done!" (Yule, *Gloss.*).

[2] M. *gurábu*, Ar. *ghurāb* (Yule, *Gloss.* s. v. *Grab*). Mr. Bell has not been able to trace the word *ogate* in the modern language.

was tarrying to load some goods, then said I to my companions that it was time to seek safety in the wood, fearing lest they should compel us to embark with them. Nevertheless, I made another journey to the king's palace with the islanders, and let them all take their loads first and go ahead towards the galley, while I, in place of following them, took a path aside and gained the wood, as did two of my companions from another quarter,—the third was got on board I know not how, though he had the same designs as we; but the galley was soon taken. Afterwards I learnt from him that he had been impressed on board by the islanders. So on that day we all four were borne on the same course of fortune, without knowing anything of one another. We were for more than four hours in the island along with some poor folk, all the rest having gone. I wandered about the king's palace, where there were all sorts of things, gold, silver, and jewellery, lying about; but I never dreamed of touching any, nor even of hiding the silver that I had, the which I gave to a friend, along with the trees, a boat, and a house I had purchased: that was to the son of the lord who had brought me out of the island Peindoüé, whereof I have spoken; to him I gave all I had. My companions saved some stuff they had hidden.

As soon as the captain of the enemy's armada discovered that the king was fled, he ordered eight galleys to the pursuit, while the other eight anchored at the island whereon I was. I gave myself up to the first that landed, and implored them to save me. At the first, not recognising me as a Frenchman, and believing me to be a Portuguese, they were about to kill me, and, stripping me naked, took from me all I had. But when they found that in truth I was not a Portuguese, they treated me more humanely, and conducted me to their captain, who took me under his protection, assuring me that I should suffer no evil; then he had me clad in other garments, and bade me remain in his galleys for my safety, at least for that day and night. Afterwards I was allowed to go where I liked throughout the island, without anyone saying a word.

The eight galleys that were bidden to go after the king came up with him and to close quarters, whereupon the king, attempting to defend himself, was slain by a pike-thrust, followed by sword-cuts; his wives were taken prisoners, and his nephew was drowned. No harm, however, was done to the wives, save that they lost all their trinkets, which were seized by the soldiers and mariners, these being the most dangerous fellows at pillage: these mariners are called *Moucois*.[1]

The cause of the taking and death of the king was that there was no wind, but the greatest calm possible, and that the enemy's galleys were better for rowing than those of the king, which were only good for sailing, and of no use for oars. Had there been but a little wind they could not have caught him; but his ill-fortune cast him into this fate, which he fully merited for the great cruelties he had used. Not one of the island vessels was taken in this chase; and had the king and his wives embarked in them, they would have had a chance of escape; but his hour was come, and for my part I hold that it was by the mercy of God he was thus slain at the first shock, so that he saw not the sad and piteous spectacle, which met my eyes, of the condition of his wives and state. There was, however, no great massacre, for except the king and two or three others slain with him, and as many wounded—among others, a young soldier, the son of a Portuguese *metiz*, who had aforetime been wrecked in his

[1] The *Mukkavar* are a fisher caste of Malabar, as Pyrard himself describes them later. But there is no doubt that the present expedition came from Bengal, as there were rejoicings when they returned home to Chittagong. Possibly there may have been some Mukkavar on board, but more likely the author thought he was justified in giving the Malabar name to people of the same class in Bengal.

ship at these islands[1]—there was no one harmed, except, also, his nephew, who, thinking to save himself by swimming, was drowned by reason of weakness, sickness, and of the melancholy and sorrow that he had for his wife, who had died in child-bed but a while before. He had abducted this woman from her husband, as I have related above.[2]

The enemy having thus seized and pillaged all the king's galleys, they collected them together, except two that were lost upon the shallows and reefs. They brought back, too, the three queens in a miserable plight, and lodged them in the house of the king's nephew, adjoining the royal palace. This house was also called palace, being enclosed by walls, and of the same form as the king's, only smaller: all the other houses of princes and princesses are called *Gandhouere*,[3] that is, " palace", while other houses are called *Gué*.[4]

The queens were put in that palace, for all day and night the men were ransacking the king's palace and carrying off everything that was of value. In his nephew's there was nothing to take, because all his property had been shipped off in good time; besides, this nephew had not much goods, no more indeed than what the king gave him, in addition to a small patrimony. Had he been richer, the king would have been afraid lest he should wage war against himself. Soldiers were placed on guard over these poor queens, who were kept in the semblance of prisoners, that so they might be led to discover the king's treasures; but this they could not do, for they knew nothing about any such; and I well know that the king let none know of these, except a certain secretary who had escaped among the first. Each of the queens was allowed a female servant to wait upon her, also three gentlemen of the king's household; but neither these nor the women durst go without the house, and the three gentlemen entered not

[1] See above, p. 255. [2] See above, p. 273.
[3] M. *gaḍuvaru*; see above, p. 219, *note*.
[4] M. and Sin. *gé*.

the queens' apartments, nor even saw them, but tarried with the soldiers to see what good or ill-fortune should befall their mistresses. All this was done according to the General's command. As for me, I went to see them often, the natives not being allowed to enter. I used to go in as often as I liked, and gave them what advice and consolation I could, for I heard all that was said about them. With tears in their eyes they asked me again and again if I sorrowed greatly for the death of the king, who had such affection for me. I answered I did, and now that he was dead I was minded to go away and remain no more at the islands, having no longer a master there. Had he not been slain I should never have gone away. All this was very far from my desire and thoughts. Nevertheless, I assured them that I would not withdraw without taking their advice and leave: this they highly approved, and promised they would never desert me. As they asked me what was being said of them, I told them they were held prisoners to point out the king's treasures (as they had already been informed), but that they should do nothing, for all threats of carrying them off were but to terrify them. I had myself heard from the chief men that they would not carry them off, with which news they were greatly pleased, and they besought me not to leave them.

They begged me also to go to and fro among the enemy, to bring word of all that was said and done, the which I did willingly enough, and discovered to them all I could glean from every quarter. The queens also told me in private a great deal about each other,—viz., the chief queen, the foreigner from Bengal, who was as fair and white as the women of this country; and the young one, whom the king had but recently taken, in manner already described.[1] She told me with sorrow that she brought misfortune wherever she was (this they call *sompas*[2]), and that since the king had taken her, every

[1] See *supra*, p. 265.

[2] Mr. Bell has not been able to explain this word.

disaster had befallen them. I was deeply grieved to see them in the state they were, having aforetime seen them so richly and luxuriously apparelled; they were indeed but poorly dressed, and had hardly anything but their own gowns left them, and everything was searched. But saving that, there was no harm or violence done to their persons, nor to their honour; not even a lewd word was passed; and all the girls and women of the island were treated in like manner. Their food was brought from the house of the Pandiare, who remained in the island along with the other clergy and many beside; but these did not for all that escape the general sack. The Pandiare did indeed save somewhat, for his house was the refuge of all, men and women alike, for personal security only, their goods being pillaged there as elsewhere. Yet he managed to appease in some degree the fury of the enemy, being held by them in some respect. I, too, though in the hands of the General and his army, was treated with much favour and courtesy, the reason whereof was our cannons, which indeed were the object of their enterprise and coming to the islands. They had not been used to see such pieces, and were in great straits how to mount and get them on board, not knowing by which end to take them. Therefore they took me with them to show them all the tackle and the way to use it; and they were well pleased with all I told them, for I gave them information as well in that respect as concerning the other equipment of our ships, and also the affairs of the islands, whereof I had good understanding. For all this they valued me much, and were exceeding kindly towards me. Another thing was that the pilot who had brought them thither was a native of the islands, though a resident of the continent, and I had often seen him at Malé. He well knew what regard the king and the lords of the country had for me, and this, rumoured among them, won for me the more respect. Yet did this vile fellow for gold betray his king and country, for all that the king had a great affection toward him, and gave him no cause of complaint; for the landing on these coasts is so difficult and dangerous, that the rest of the party had never dared come without him to guide them, and so was he the cause of the whole disaster. At this juncture I often went to the Pandiare's house to visit a number of my friends that were there, not daring to venture abroad; amongst others, the three sons of the lord with whom I resided so long. They counselled me to be gone, saying that the king their master was dead, nor were they nor I under any protection now; but all the others advised contrarywise, that if they had but one coco-nut, they would give me half; yet I took the advice of the three, one of whom had a gunshot wound. They were severely put to the torture, and all had to pay a ransom.

Three or four days after the arrival of this army there came to Malé a barque sent by the dead king's people, to ask leave of the General to convey some rice and other commodities for the funeral ceremonies of the late king, who was buried at the island *Gouradou*,[1] where that great master was of whom I have already spoken. It had been his fixed intention and desire to be buried at Malé, as I shall now tell; but they never keep their corpses, and have no custom of embalming them, or of conveying them from island to island. At length the General gave permission to take all that was required for the purpose, and so they did, and would even have taken me along with them, as they strongly suspected that I was minded to escape.

Had the king been slain by others than of his own faith, they say he had been blessed and sanctified (such a one

[1] The tradition is that Sultan Ibrahim was buried, not at *Guradú*, but at *Kanimídú*. When he escaped from Málé he took a course towards Huvadu, and the island Guradú in S. Málé atoll would lie directly in that course.

they call *Chayde*[1]); then had they made no ceremony, but buried him as he died, without washing the body or performing any other customary act; but though he did not die in defence of the faith, they did not perform the ceremony wont to be observed at the obsequies of a king, but buried him as any ordinary countryman of the islands, albeit this was to their great sorrow. They were even at much pains to get a white cloth for a winding-sheet, and a coffin to put him in—him who in his lifetime had so lavishly given to all the poor of his kingdom when they were in need. He had always by him more than thirty coffins ready made, for himself, his queens, and court, for use when occasion was. He had also caused to be built a magnificent shrine, and a burial-ground entirely enclosed, in Malé, with a view to being buried there. It was the best constructed of all, but God willed not that he should be laid there. Such are the common results of war, and so was it here, where all the wealth that he had collected was involved in havoc and useless waste; for whatsoever the soldiers could not carry off they utterly destroyed.

It was most pitiful to see the ravages committed in the island, and especially at the king's palace; for all the private citizens had secured their goods in their boats, and lost nothing: the boats being small, escaped in all directions, and sailed faster than the galleys. All that belonged to the king and queens, however, was pillaged, and nothing was saved either of what was in the galleys or on shore. Moreover, as the misfortune of these poor islanders would have it, there was a large ship belonging to the king all laden and ready to sail eight days before, but their magicians and astrologers had put it off to this very day, as being a lucky day for weighing,—so had they made it out by their reckoning and

[1] M. *Sáhidu*, Ar. *Shahid*, "martyr".

ephemerides; but they had made a sad mistake. The voyage was to be to Arabia, and she could not get away from the islands by reason of the great calm which befell, whereby she was seized, like everything else. The cargo of this vessel consisted, among other things, of the cinnamon that the king had of the ship of Ceylon, which a while before had been wrecked at the islands, as I have said[1]; the rest was merchandise of the islands, the greater part being coco produce. The enemy, in sacking the ship, took only the island stuff; for as for the cinnamon, they left it to its fate, with the vessel, which never made another voyage, as I afterwards learnt at Goa, and as I shall relate in the proper place.

At length, when the enemy had tarried in the island for the space of ten days, gathering their booty and loading their ships with all the valuables they found, and five or six pieces of cannon, large and small, that were there, they withdrew, and set the queens and all the rest of the people at liberty. They took no prisoners with them, except the chief queen's brother, brother-in-law to the late king. At first I believed they took him in order to get a ransom; but afterwards I learnt, on the contrary, that it was with his own consent, as he wished to go to visit *Ali Rhadia*, the king of Cananor, for a purpose I shall explain hereafter. On my part, I went and took farewell of the queens and my friends, not without tears, indeed—theirs of sorrow and chagrin, but mine of joy. When it came to embarking, all the captains got a-quarrelling which should have my companions and me in his galley. At length I embarked in one, and my three companions severally in three others, and we did not see each other for a long time.

As for what followed at the Maldives, I heard afterwards, while at Goa, that the natives fell into a bitter civil war. The king had died without children or nephews, and the kingdom there never goes to females, no more than in

[1] See above, pp. 299-301.

France.[1] Four of the greatest lords in the country banded themselves one against another who should be king; and this war continuing a long time, the king of Cananor, *Ali Rhadia*, had despatched a goodly armament of galleys, under the guidance of *Rana Banduy Tacourou*, the chief queen's brother, whom the Bengal galleys had taken prisoner, as has been said. By means of this army he had at length established that prince upon the throne,—who was, indeed, as next of kin, the lawful heir,—but on condition that he should hold it of him, and regard him as his suzerain. He scattered all who were causing trouble, and so restored peace to the islands.[2] Such is what I heard at Goa. But to return to what befell us: we embarked, as already said, at the Maldives, intending to make our course up the Gulf of Bengal. The

[1] Pyrard has fallen into an error exactly the converse to that of Masudi, who, visiting Ceylon (and? the Maldives) in A.D. 916, records that the islands were governed by a queen, "for from the most ancient times the inhabitants have a rule never to let themselves be governed by a man" (*Masudi*, by Sprenger, i, 335). We have little knowledge of the rule of succession in pre-Mahommedan times, though we are informed by Ibn Batuta, corroborated by tradition, that at the time of the conversion a king was on the throne. Since the Mahomedan conversion female sovereigns have been exceptional. Thus, in Ibn Batuta's time at the island, a queen was on the throne, in default of male heirs. And later, the islands were ruled, for two or three years prior to 1759, by or in the name of a queen Aminá (Bell, *Rep.*, 33).

[2] As will be remembered, this chief, on his return from Arabia, paid a visit to Âli Raja at Cananor, and was with difficulty induced to return to the Maldives. At that time a treaty seems to have been negotiated, whereby the aid of Âli Raja was secured, to obtain for Rana Banda the possession, and for Âli Raja the suzerainty, of the islands. As will be seen hereafter, the Bengal fleet, which took away this prince as well as Pyrard, touched at Minicoy and at the Laccadives, but proceeded to Chittagong without touching land on the Malabar coast. When Pyrard afterwards leaves Chittagong for the Malabar coast, he makes no mention of the Maldive prince; it may be conjectured that he was left at the Laccadives to make his own way across to Cananor. According to tradition gleaned by Mr. Bell, he was afterwards known as *Máfilafurhi Rasgefánu*, from the name of his family island.

passage between the islands is very dangerous, by reason of the reefs and banks, which are exceeding numerous; and no one would dare to steer through them without having native pilots, as we then had. The island from which the dead king came, by name *Oustisme*,[1] being at the head of the others, and quite the last, they cast anchor there, and set themselves to slay, sack, and pillage, carrying off everything they could find. We saw by day a wonderful number of barques and boats sailing away in all directions. Having refreshed themselves with a half-day's sojourn at this island, they passed orders as to their course, in case they should happen to separate,—as, indeed, they did, by reason of the great calm. At length we got out of the islands, by God's grace. The calm was such that we were about three days in reaching a little island named *Malicut*,[2] which is only thirty-five leagues to the north of the Maldives.

[1] M. *Utímu:* Tiladummati atoll, in lat. 6° 52′ N. It is noteworthy that our two great authorities on the Maldive islands, Ibn Batuta and Pyrard, both landed here, the one on his coming to, the other on his departure from, the islands. The fact of landing at it seems to have led the former to give its name to the atoll, of which it was but a unit, *Teeim*, according to this traveller, being one of the provinces or climates. It is not quite at the head of the others, as Pyrard states here: indeed, he says, but a few lines below, that after leaving it "at length we got out of the islands". The northernmost island of the Maldives proper is *Turacun*, in Heawandu atoll, in lat. 7° 7′ N.

[2] Minicoy, called *Maliku* by the natives, lies in lat. 8° 14′ N., being separated from the Maldives by the Eight-Degree Channel, the distance being about 68 miles. This channel is the course generally adopted by steamers proceeding to Ceylon during the S.W. monsoon. The island is about 7 miles by half a mile broad; it still belongs to Cananor. Pyrard is right in his statement that the people of Minicoy are of Maldive race and language. The population, according to the last census (1881), is 3,915. The majority follow a seafaring life, the island possessing six large vessels fit for the Bengal trade, four coasting vessels, and eight fishing-boats. Their trade is with the Maldives, the Malabar coast, Ceylon, and Calcutta. Minicoy has thriven to a great extent, owing to being free of the restrictions which require the Laccadive natives to carry all their produce to particular Malabar ports. Recently a lighthouse

This island is surrounded with very dangerous banks, which have to be carefully watched. Three of our galiots that had kept together cast anchor there; the others had separated. This island of Malicut is only four leagues in circumference; it is wonderfully fertile in coco-trees, bananas, millet, and other products of the Maldives; all sorts of fruit are abundant. The fishery is very good; the climate more healthy and temperate than at the Maldives; the people have the same customs, manners, and language as those of the Maldives. This island was at one time part of the Maldive realm; but a king gave it to his brother as a portion. It is now governed by a lady, who holds it of the king of Cananor, for the sake of greater security. This queen gave me a very good reception, for she had often seen me at the court of the king of the Maldives, her near relative. When she saw me she began to weep, as did most of the inhabitants, with sorrow for the death of the king, the story of which I have told.

After tarrying about two days at this island we set sail and made for the islands of *Divandurou*,[1] thirty leagues from

has been erected on the island by the British Government. One of the staff employed in its erection has written an interesting though short account of the island and its inhabitants (*Minicoy, etc.*, by Bartholomeusz; London, 1885). For further information, see Report by E. G. Thomas, in *Mad. Journ. of Lit. and Sci.*; Hunter, *Imp. Gaz. of India*, art. "Laccadives"; and *Encyc. Brit.* (9th edition), art. "Laccadives"; Bell, *Rep.*, 41.

[1] *I.e.*, the *Anduru* islands, from the chief of them, generally called *Androt*, which contains the tomb of the apostle of local Mahommedanism. The name *Laccadives* (*Laksha Dwípa*, "the Hundred Thousand Isles"), by which they are generally known, is that applied by the people of India, and was evidently meant to include the Maldives. Albirúni speaks of the Maldives and Laccadives as *Divah Kuzah* and *Divah Kanbar*, the "cowrie" and the "coir" islands. By the natives they are called *Amendivi*, from the island *Amini*, or simply *divi*. Barbosa says they are four in number, and were called *Malandiva* (*Barbosa*, Hak. Soc., p. 164). The Portuguese generally called these the *Mammale* islands, from the great Cananor merchant who controlled their trade; and the same name survives in Lancaster (*Voy.*, Hak. Soc., p. 10). The Lacca-

Malicut to the north; they are five in number, and vary from six to seven leagues in circumference; they are eighty leagues distant from the Malabar coast, right opposite Cananor. They are under the rule of the king of Cananor, who also possesses thirty of the Maldive islands, that were ceded to him about fifty years before by a king of the Maldives, to whom he had given succour against a revolt of his own people.[1]

These islands of *Divandurou* are inhabited by Mahometan Malabars, most of them rich merchants, who drive a great trade throughout India, and especially at the Maldives, whence they export much merchandise, and where they keep resident factors. They have the same customs and languages as the people of Cananor, Calecut, Cochin, and the rest of Malabar: their soil is very fertile, and the climate good. The Malabar corsairs, when on their voyages, often come there to refresh, and in most cases, being quite like natives, marry there. Albeit they fail not betimes to pillage them too, for all the friendship that is between them: for they do hold gain above all the friendship in the world, and when they cannot reap any booty from their enemies,

dives consist of ten islands,—Amini, Chetlat, Kadamat, and Kiltan (with Bitra, which is uninhabited) are British; Agathi, Kawrati, Androt, and Kalpéni (with Suheli, uninhabited) are the property of the Cananor Raja, but since 1877 have been sequestrated for non-payment of tribute, and are at present also under British administration. Another classification obtains:—Amini, Kalpéni, Androt, and Kawrati are *tarwat* islands, in which alone the high-caste natives reside; the rest are *melacheri*, or low-caste islands. The total population in 1881 (excluding Minicoy, which is the personal property of the Raja) was 11,287. See further the authorities cited in the preceding note, and also the valuable account, from a naturalist's point of view, by Mr. Allan Hume, in *Stray Feathers*, vol. iv; Calcutta, 1876.

[1] It must remain uncertain which were the thirty Maldive islands ceded by the Maldive king, and who was the king who ceded them. They could only have been ceded during a very serious revolt, such as that which ended in the abdication of Sultan Hassan (Dom Manoel), A.D. 1552, so that we may believe that the islands were given up by that Sultan, rather than by his rival Ali, who succeeded him.

being anxious not to return empty-handed, they fall upon their friends. These islands are, as it were, a half-way house for merchandise between the mainland and the Maldives and Malicut.

Having refreshed ourselves four or five days at these islands, we again set sail, now towards the south, in order to double Point de Galle, which is a cape at the end of the island of Ceylon. On our way we fell in with a great number of whales, which thought to upset our galiots; but those on board, with drums, pans, and kettles, set up such a din as caused them to make off.

We also fell in with some galleys or *padoes*[1] of the Malabars, on one occasion just at daybreak when the sky was cloudy and thick, so that we did not perceive them till they were close upon us. I was never more astonished than to see the perfect order of their sailors, all armed and ready to charge. We were taken unawares, while they had been the first to sight us; but being friendly, they only passed by. They numbered three galiots, and we the same. For the rest, before closing this chapter, I would say, for the better understanding of what has been described above, that this army, which thus attacked and sacked the Maldives, was sent on behalf of the king of Bengal, a kingdom lying beyond these islands, on the mainland, under the tropic of Cancer. The principal motive which had induced him to make the enterprise was to seize the cannon that the king of the Maldives had gotten out of our wrecked ship, and the many others he had obtained in like manner. The cannon in question was the most beautiful example to be seen anywhere, and had great renown in the Indies, many kings and princes having been continually on the point of coming to see it.

[1] Malayâlam *patak*, a country craft not now in use, frequently mentioned by the Portuguese writers.

CHAPTER XXIV.

The kingdom of Bengal, and some observations thereon.

After a month's voyage we arrived at Chartican,[1] a port of the kingdom of Bengal, where we were received by the inhabitants with much rejoicing. On landing, they took me with them to salute the king, who is not, however, the great king of Bengal, but a petty king of this province, or rather a governor, with the title of king,[2] as is generally the case in those parts. The great king of Bengal lives higher up the country, thirty or forty leagues off. On being presented to this petty king, he received me with great kindness, and gave me my full liberty, saying that if I would remain with him he would do great things for me: and, indeed, he bade bring me raiment and food day by day in great abundance. But after a month's sojourn there I found a ship of Calecut, whose master asked if I would go with him, saying that the Hollanders' ships often came to Calecut, and there might be some in which I could get a passage to France, since I was minded to return thither; whereto I gladly agreed, seeing I had no other aim but that, and on that score I declined all other favours. I therefore took my leave of the king, which was granted me without difficulty.

I was so short a time in Bengal, that I cannot record many of its characteristics; however, here is what I picked up.

[1] Chittagong, properly *Chatigam;* in the Portuguese books, *Chatigão* and *Porto Grande;* to be distinguished from *Sātgāuw*, or *Porto Pequeno*, the two ports being regarded as the eastern and western limits of the Ganges' mouth. See *Linschoten*, Hak. Soc.; Correa, *Lendas*, iii, 649; and Yule, *Glossary*, s. v. *Chittagong*, *Porto Pequeno*, and (in Supplt.) *Satigam.*

[2] This petty Raja was probably the "Mugg" (*Magh*), or king of Arakan (Yule, *Gloss.*, s. v.); the Portuguese called him *o mogo*, and the people *os mogos* (*Livro das Monç.*, i, 348, 350, 353; ii, 226, 392.)

The kingdom of Bengal is of great extent; it lies in the middle country of the Indies, and is said to be 400 leagues in length, so the king is the most puissant prince in India, after the grand Mogor. About the time I left, the Mogor had declared war against him, and the king was preparing to receive him with more than 200,000 men and 10,000 elephants.[1] He has many tributary kings: for instance, the kings of Aracan, of Chaul,[2] and other great lords, as well Mahometan as Gentile, who are bound to furnish him, when he goes out to war, with a certain number of men, elephants, and horses. They also pay him tribute for such harbours as they have in their territories; and at all of these a great trade is carried on in all sorts of merchandise, the merchants exporting large quantities of goods, by reason whereof they dare not risk the loss of this king's goodwill.

The country is healthy and temperate, and so wondrous fertile that one lives there for almost nothing; and there is such a quantity of rice, that, besides supplying the whole country, it is exported to all parts of India, as well to Goa and Malabar, as to Sumatra, the Moluccas, and all the islands of Sunda, to all of which lands Bengal is a very nursing mother, who supplies them with their entire subsistence and food. Thus, one sees arrive there every day an infinite number of vessels from all parts of India for these provisions; and I believe it would be still greater, were not the navigation so perilous by reason of the banks and shallows wherewith all this Gulf of Bengal is full. So it happens that when the Bengal ships are behind their time, or are lost, rice is fabulously dear, and there is a cry, as it were, of the extremity

[1] The preparations for, and the progress of this invasion, and the policy of the Portuguese, are given at some length in the King of Spain's despatches of the 19th March 1612, and 15th March 1613 (*Liv. das Monç.*, ii, 226, 391-4).

[2] As pointed out by Mr. Rivara, this is a palpable error, Chaul being on the other side of India.

of famine. On the contrary, when the navigation is good, the rice is as cheap as if it grew in the country, and fetches no more than four deniers the pound. The country is well supplied with animals, such as oxen, cows, and sheep; flesh is accordingly very cheap, let alone milk-foods and butter, whereof they have such an abundance that they supply the rest of India; and pile carpets of various kinds, which they weave with great skill. There are many good fruits,—not, however, cocos or bananas; plenty of citrons, limes, oranges, pomegranates, cajus, pineapples, etc., ginger, long pepper,[1] of which, in the green state they make a great variety of preserves, as also of lemons and oranges. The country abounds with sugar-cane, which they eat green; or else make into excellent sugar, for a cargo to their ships, the like not being made in any part of India except in Cambaye and the other countries of the Mogor adjacent to Bengal, these countries being of the same climate, language, and fertility. There is likewise exported from Bengal much scented oils, got from a certain grain, and divers flowers: these are used by all the Indians after bathing to rub their bodies withal. Cotton is so plentiful, that, after providing for the uses and clothing of the natives, and besides exporting the raw material, they make such a quantity of cotton cloths, and so excellently woven, that these articles are exported, and thence only, to all India, but chiefly to the parts about Sunda. Likewise is there plenty of silk, as well that of the silkworm as of the (silk) herb,[2] which is of the brightest yellow colour,

[1] Long-pepper is derived from two shrubby plants, *Piper officinarum* and *Piper longum*, and is to be distinguished from black and white pepper, both of which are obtained from *Piper nigrum*. Calcutta is still one of the chief ports for the export of long-pepper, the other regions being Malabar and the Archipelago. See Yule, *Glossary*, s. v. "Pepper".

[2] This grass-silk is referred to by Linschoten as a kind of linen: "It is yealowish, and is called the hearbe of Bengalen, wherewith they do most cunningly stitch their coverlits, pavilions, pillowes, carpets and

and brighter than silk itself: of this they make many stuffs of divers colours, and export them to all parts. The inhabitants, both men and women, are wondrously adroit in all manufactures, such as of cotton cloth and silks, and in needlework, such as embroideries, which are worked so skilfully, down to the smallest stitches, that nothing prettier is to be seen anywhere. Some of these cottons and silks are so fine that it is difficult to say whether a person so attired be clothed or nude. Many other kinds of work, such as furniture and vessels, are constructed with extraordinary delicacy, which, if brought here, would be said to come from China.

In this country is made a large quantity of small black and red pottery, like the finest and most delicate *terre sigillée;* in this they do a great trade, chiefly in *gargoulettes*[1] and drinking-vessels, and other utensils. There is a great quantity, too, of huge reeds or canes, as big as a man's thigh, and six or seven fathoms high, hollow inside, and knotted like those here. They are harder to break than any wood in the world; of these, levers and rods are made to carry over the heaviest weights, and are used throughout India, even at Goa and elsewhere: so much so, that the Portuguese and the Indians use no other poles for their palanquins and litters: these are

mantles, ... likewise they make whole peeces or webbes of this hearbe, sometimes mixed and woven with silke, although those of the hearbe it selfe are dearer and more esteemed, and is much fairer than the silke. These webbes are named Sarrijn, and it is much used and worne in India" (*Hak. Soc.*, i, 96).

[1] Port. *gargoleta.* For a fuller description, see vol. ii. It was an earthenware vessel with a spout, whereby the liquid was poured into the mouth from a distance, to avoid contact. The manner of so drinking is shown in a cut in Knox (*Ceylon*, opposite p. 87). The word is used and the practice described by several travellers in Portuguese India, this mode of drinking being adopted by the Portuguese themselves. To be clumsy in the use of a *gargoleta* at once proclaimed a person to be a *reinol*, or "griffin", fresh from Europe (*Linschoten*, Hak. Soc., i, 207; *Mandelslo*, Eng. trans., p. 105; *Fryer*, "gurgulets", p. 47). The word remains current both in India and Ceylon as "goglet", a water-bottle. See Yule, *Glossary*, s. v. The Sinhalese, I believe, call it *gurulota.*

everywhere called *Bambou.*[1] When one of these is bent into any required curve and heated, it remains so always, and will sooner break than lose its curve. Of these, too, are made their measures for measuring all their goods, such as rice, grain, oil, butter, and the like. Measures of all sizes are made of them. These reeds grow in quantity elsewhere in India; but this is their original home, and here they are found in greatest plenty. These canes will not bend double; and they are mottled black and white. There is another kind,[2] of a different shape and thickness, the largest of this sort being no more than four thumbs' girth, and very tall. It is porous, hard, and very pliant, so that you can bring the two ends together without its breaking, and yet it is very strong: of this are made walking-sticks and canes for chastisement; they raise the skin

[1] There is some doubt whether the word *bambu* is Malay or Canarese. The question is discussed by Col. Yule (*Glossary*, s. v.), who remarks that, while Marsden gives it as good Malay, Crawfurd, on the other hand, says that it is only used on the west coast of Sumatra. Col. Yule believes the true origin to be the Canarese *baṇwu*. In the Portuguese writers of the latter half of the sixteenth century, it generally appears as *mambu* (*e.g.*, De Orta and Acosta). I do not find it mentioned in the statistical works of 1525 contained in the *Subsidios, etc.* The author seems here to refer to the giant bambu, of which it is believed Bengal is the true habitat. It has been planted at the Botanic Gardens at Peradeniya, Ceylon; and there, Dr. Haeckel says, it attains a thickness of two feet. Col. Yule would seem to require corroboration of this statement. I have seen, though not actually measured, these magnificent specimens, and have been assured that in Ceylon the plant attains greater dimensions than in its native regions.

[2] This would seem to be the Malacca cane. Linschoten, in his account of Bengal, describes its appearance and use in much the same terms:—"There groweth likewise marble-coloured reedes, whereof you may see many sortes in the custodie of Paludanus, which the Portingalles call Canas de Bengala, that is, Reedes of Bengala. Within they are full of pith, and are about the thickness of Spanish reedes, but somewhat thinner, and when they are greene they bowe and bend like willow twigges. They are outwardly of divers colours, and speckled as if they were painted. They use them in Portingall for olde women to beare in their handes when they goe abroad or uppon the stones" (*Linschoten*, Hak. Soc., i, 97).

wherever they fall, but never break it, however tender it may be. They are neatly shaped, and are naturally of a mottled colour, white, yellow, and black: there is great trade in them to all parts of India, for they are found nowhere else. By rubbing hard two sticks of this cane together, fire is produced as from a match: and they are used for this purpose. There is yet another sort of cane, which never grows thicker than the little finger, of the same form and growth as the other; it is as pliant as an osier, and is called *Rotan*.[1] Ships' cables are made of it, and many kinds of neatly plaited baskets, and other wicker things. In short, it is used as cord, and can be split into any number of strips. It is a fathom and a half in length. It is trafficked in everywhere, and is in great demand for its use in manufacture; it is white, and not mottled.

This country abounds with elephants, which are exported hence to all parts of India. There are rhinoceros[2] also, and some say unicorns, too, which are said to be found in this land only. They say other animals will not drink at a well until a female unicorn has steeped her horn in the water, so they all wait on the bank till she comes and does so.[3]

[1] Malay, *Rotan;* Correa, De Orta, and Linschoten all write *rota*. The English form *rattan* appears in Fryer (1673).

[2] I use the word as a plural, as in orig. and in the English version of *Linschoten*.

[3] The unicorn localised in those parts was no doubt the rhinoceros itself: see *Marco Polo*, bk. III, ch. ix, and *note* by Col. Yule, and the following passage from Linschoten:—"Some thinke it (the rhinoceros) is the right unicorne, because that as yet there hath no other bin found, but only by hearsay, and by the pictures of them. The Portingales and those of Bengala affirme, that by the river Ganges, in the kingdome of Bengala, are many of these rhinoceros, which when they will drinke, the other beasts stand and waite upon them, till the rhinoceros hath drunke, and thrust his horn into the water, for he cannot drink but his horne must be under the water, because it standeth so close unto his nose and muzzle; and then after him all the other beastes doe drinke" (*Linsch.*, ii, 9). As to the right of first drinking, Pyrard's myth pictures

In short, I find no country in all the East Indies more abundantly supplied with all things needful for food, with the riches of nature and art; and were not the navigation so dangerous, it would be the fairest, most pleasant, fertile, and profitable in the whole world. They usually keep an ambassador at Goa; but when I was preparing to leave Goa to come home, there arrived an ambassador extraordinary at the court of the viceroy, and it was said that he had come to ask some assistance.[1]

One of the greatest trades in Bengal is in slaves; for there is a certain land subject to this king where fathers sell their children, and give them to the king as tribute; so most of the slaves in India are got from hence. Many of the merchants castrate them, cutting them when they are young, and not only the testicles, but also the entire organ.[2] I have seen many of this kind, who appeared to have but a little hole for the passage of water. This is in order to put them in charge of the women, and of the keys of the house; they trust them in all things, and never their wives. Such is the custom among Mahometans, for they quit their wives very frequently. Nowhere in India are slaves of so little value, for they are all old and knavish villains, both men and women.

The people are well formed in body, the women are pretty, but more shameless than elsewhere in India. The men are much given to trafficking in merchandise, and not to war or arms,—a soft, courteous, clever people, but having the repute of great cheats, thieves, and liars. They trade in

as a polite gallantry on the part of the other animals (*place aux dames!*) what in Linschoten appears as subservience to a male tyrant. I have no space here to discuss the unicorn generally; those who are disposed to entertain his existence may consult the note of Mr. Badger (*Varthema*, Hak. Soc., pp. 46-8).

[1] This embassy is not mentioned in the royal despatches, and perhaps was not reported by the viceroy.

[2] See *Barbosa* (Hak. Soc., p. 180); *Varthema* (Hak. Soc., p. 258); Beckmann (*Litt. der Alt. Besch.*, ii, 132).

many places, making long voyages; so do many strangers frequent their country: for example, Persians, Arabs, and the Portuguese merchants of Goa and Cochin. Under the government of this king are men of many religions, viz., Jews, Mahometans, and Gentiles, or pagans, these latter showing as great a diversity of ceremonies as of countries and provinces. The great king is a pagan; he of Chartican, whom I saw, was a Mahometan.

The Gentile people of this Bengal country have for their pagoda,[1] or idol, a white elephant; it is but rarely met with, and is deemed sacred. The kings worship it, and even go to war to get it from their neighbours, not having one themselves, and sometimes grand battles are fought on this score.[2]

As for dress, the men attire themselves bravely with very

[1] For a dissertation upon this perplexing word, see Yule's *Glossary*, s. v. There can be little doubt that it comes from *bhagavat*, "the holy" or "blessed", *i.e.*, god. Col. Yule gives a series of quotations in which the word is used, as here, of an idol; the application to a temple is of course more common.

[2] As need hardly be said nowadays, the white elephant is merely an albino, and with blotches of pink, which rarely extend over the whole body. I do not know an earlier mention of it than that by Horace (*Ep. II*, i, 196): "Sive elephas albus volgi converteret ora." The king of Ceylon had one at Anuradhapura in the fifth century A.D. (*Mahavanso*, c. xxxviii, p. 254). In the fifteenth century, Abd-er-Razzak saw one at Bisnagar. "The king possesses one white elephant of an extremely great size, on whose body are scattered here and there grey spots like freckles" (*India in Fifteenth Cent.*, i, 27). The references to white elephants in the books of the Portuguese and Dutch period are too frequent to be mentioned. Such animals were prized as rarities in all the countries of India, but received special veneration in Buddhist lands As to Ceylon, see Tennent (*Ceylon*, ii, 285), and Knox (*Hist. Relation*, p. 21). The white elephant cult attained its greatest proportions in Burma, Pegu, and Siam, and the reference in the text to wars for the possession of the white elephant is probably to the great struggle in 1568 between the kings of Pegu and Siam, as to which see *Linschoten*, (Hak. Soc., i, 98, 102); *Mandelslo* (Eng. trans., p. 127); Pallegoix (*Siam*, i, 152; ii, 2, 85).

large cotton shirts, which fall to the ground; over it is worn a silk mantle, and on the head a turban of very fine linen. The women wear little chemisettes of cotton or silk, reaching to the waist; round the rest of the body is thrown a cloth or taffetas; when they go abroad, they wear about that a large piece of silk, with one end brought over the head.

They are disorderly and very barbarous in their eating and drinking; they have many servants, and have each three or four wives, very richly adorned with gold chains and pearls.

They make wines of sugar and other materials, and get drunk therewith.

A large number of Portuguese dwell in freedom at the ports on this coast of Bengal; they are also very free in their lives, being like exiles. They do only traffic, without any fort, order, or police, and live like natives of the country; they durst not return to India,[1] for certain misdeeds they have committed, and they have no clergy among them. There is one of them named Jean Garie,[2] who is greatly obeyed by the rest; he commands more than ten thousand men for the king of Bengal, yet he makes not war against the Portuguese, seeing they are friends.[3]

[1] Here used in the Portuguese sense, meaning the western coast of the peninsula dominated by the Portuguese fortresses. Linschoten, in the same way, describes India as extending from Daman to Cape Comorin inclusive (i, 62-65); and in another place says that the rhinoceros is not found "in India, but only in Bengala and Patane" (ii, 8).

[2] Perhaps a misprint for *Garcie*, i.e., *Garcia*. I do not find this renegade mentioned in the Portuguese despatches.

[3] The Portuguese at this time settled in Bengal were chiefly men exiled for crime (*homisiados por delitos*), who occupied themselves partly with piracy, and partly in leading armies of rival Rajas (Hunter, *Stat. Acct. of Bengal*, vii, 110-1; *Livro das Monç.*, ii, 393). One of these, Nicote, had shortly before this time practically usurped the throne of Pegu. Another, Sebastian Gonzales Tibão, a man of low birth, rose to eminence in the invasion of Bengal and Arracan by the Mogul, to which allusion is made above. After engaging to support the king of Arracan, he turned traitor, and with his fleet harried the whole coast of that state (*Faria y Souza*, III, ch. viii). The king of Spain was con-

In this land is the great river *Ganga*, otherwise called the Ganges, the most renowned in the world. The natives hold that it comes from the Earthly Paradise; their kings have been curious to have its source discovered, but they have never discovered it, for all their journeys and expense. Its mouth is at twenty-three degrees from the equinoctial, towards our pole; but whether this is the famous Ganges of the ancients, or that of Canton in China, as some will have it nowadays, I leave to the discussion and decision of the learned in such things; any how, the common opinion of the Portuguese and many others is that this is the true Ganges; if its situation does not correspond, at least its name does.[1] From this river comes that excellent wood called *Calamba*,[2] which is believed to come from the Earthly Paradise. It is very dear throughout India, and more esteemed than any other, being more rare and odoriferous; very little of it is found, and then it comes floating to the seashore, or the banks of the river; it is also found on the shores of the Maldives, and I have met with it there many a time.

tinually urging the viceroys to reduce Portuguese affairs in Bengal to a more settled and satisfactory condition; but, owing to the greater urgency of matters in Ceylon and elsewhere, this region was left a prey to lawless ruffians (*Livro das Monç.*, i, 350).

[1] This passage would seem to be an insertion by, or at the dictation of some of Pyrard's learned friends who had read the current literature (see *Linsch.*, i, 92). Mr. Rivara thinks it not impossible that Pyrard may have seen the first Decade of Barros at Goa, where there is a similar passage (liv. ix, cap. i); but he admits against this theory that De Couto, in his dedicatory epistle to his fourth Decade, states that at that time there was but a single copy of Barros in India. Some of Pyrard's patrons in Paris may have read either Barros himself, or Ulloa's Italian version of the first two Decades (published at Venice, 1562). But it is more likely that he or they had read Linschoten, whose work had appeared in French in 1610, this passage and those immediately following being a mere transcript of *Linsch.*, Hak. Soc., i, pp. 92 and 93.

[2] The finest kind of *lignum aloes*. See *Linschoten*, i, 120, 125, 150; *G. de Orta*, f. 122; Yule, *Gloss.*, s. v. "Calambac".

This river breeds also a large number of crocodiles, and is marvellously rich in fish; in short, it is the wealthiest in all produce in the East Indies, and after it comes the Indus, the river of Surate and Cambaye.

The Indians regard the Ganges as holy, and believe that when they have washed therein they are absolved of all their sins; and Mahometans as well as Gentiles deem the water to be blessed, and to wash away all offences, just as we regard confession. They, however, believe that, after bathing there, they are altogether sanctified, even saints.[1] And they come from afar to wash them there, as do the Mahometans at the sepulchre of Mahomet at Mecca.[2] This is all I was able to observe of this kingdom during the short time I was there.

CHAPTER XXV.

Voyage to Calecut by way of Moutingué, Badara, and Marquaire; also concerning the famous captain Cogni-aly.

As I have said, my companions and I embarked in a ship of Calecut: we were at sea for three weeks, and at length made land at the port of *Moutingué*,[3] which is situate between

[1] Dr. Burnell (*Linsch.*, i, 93, *note*) points out that the Ganges is not mentioned in Vedic literature as a sacred river, but assumes that character only in the much later Puranic books. As regards the superstitions about the Ganges, he refers to Goldstücker's article in Chambers's *Encyclopædia*, reprinted in his *Lit. Rem.*, i, 63, *et seq.*

[2] *I.e.*, in the water of the Zem-Zem well. See Burton's *Pilgrimage*, vol. iii.

[3] *Muttungal*, now Port No. 12 of the Malabar district. It lies almost midway between Chombaye on the north and Vadakkara on the south, all three being situate a short distance to the north of the Kōtta river. This port, at which Pyrard landed, has not found its way into the maps of the coast, nor into any catalogue of the Malabar ports, except that of De Couto (*Dec. XII*, cap. xviii), who mentions it as *Motangue*.

Cananor and Calecut: it is one of the harbours of refuge for the Malabar corsairs and pirates. The country is under the king of Moutingué, who is a Nair king.

I was never more astonished than on my arrival there to see so many men-at-arms: every one there carries arms, as well Mahometans as idolaters, from the age of ten or twelve, —that is, all the Nairs or Malabars, for the villain folk carry none at all. I was received with great courtesy by the Malabars while I sojourned there. I was conducted to the house of a great lord, a Mahometan Malabar. The Malabars have no nobility among them, either in distinction of names or orders, so far as I could discover.[1] I tarried at Moutingué for the space of three days with this lord, my companions being with another, and we were well entreated. The king himself came to see the lord with whom I was, and I was much surprised to see him thus. He was one of the handsomest men, and of the best figure I ever saw, save only that he was of a slightly olive and ruddy colour, as are all the Nairs; but his figure was of excellent proportions, and somewhat resembled that of his majesty of Calecut, beside whom this personage was but a petty kinglet; and when he spoke of him, it was with great respect and in terms of honour. When I entered his house, one of his attendants brought a stool a foot and a half square, and less than half a foot high, which he placed in the middle of the hall: upon this the king sat, while all the lords stood round about. They touched the furniture and walls of this house no more than they wished others to do to theirs, when they came to see them. The king questioned me much about France, when I told him I was of that country, and asked me the difference between the English, the Hollanders, and us. Next he inquired of the estate and greatness of the king (of France), and asked me to come and see him, and even begged

[1] Meaning probably the Mahomedans. There are at least eighteen different classes of Nâyars.

the lords to bring me there, which they did. His residence is more than a quarter of a league from the sea-shore, where my companions and I were lodged. The building is on a height, with drawbridges, which are used at all their castles and palaces[1]: these are fortified with good terraces and walls, and a careful watch is always kept. This king has a single elephant only, which is very tame.

Besides this port of Moutingué, there are two others of the corsairs close by, just two short leagues from one another: one is called *Chombais*,[2] on the Cananor side, and the other *Badara*,[3] towards Calecut: Moutingué is in the middle. All are on the coast, and well fortified with great entrenchments to protect them from the descents of the Portuguese, with whom they wage war to the death. Each of these ports hath its own king, but all are in some way under the Samory.[4]

[1] This description of a fort with drawbridges tallies with that of the existing fort at Vadakkara, which Pyrard describes below, p. 346.

[2] *Chombâye* or *Chombâl*, Port No. 11 of the Malabar district, about two miles north of Muṭṭungal, and five miles north of Vadakkara. This is a very old port: it is mentioned by Barbosa under the name *Chemobai* (Lisbon edition), or *Chemonbay* (Barcelona edition), as a town of the Moors, possessing shipping (Stanley's *Barbosa*, Hak. Soc., p. 152). It appears as *Camboa* in the *Sommario* of Ramusio; as *Chomba* in De Barros; as *Somba* in P. Vincenzo; and as *Chomamba* in De Couto (*Dec. XII*, cap. xviii). It is not, however, given in the tolerably full list of Malabar ports by Andrade.

[3] *Vadakkara*, Port No. 13 of the Malabar district. It appears in Keith Johnston's atlas as *Waddakurray*. De Couto mentions it as *Baregare*, along with another town, *Coriare* (not given by other authorities). P. Vincenzo calls it *Bergare* (lib. v, c. i). Alex. Hamilton (i, 301) visited the place, which he calls *Burgara*, and says it produced pepper and the best cardamoms. Dr. F. Buchanan (*Journey*, *etc.*, ii, 514), who also visited it, names it *Vadacurray*, "which by Europeans is commonly called *Barragurry*."

[4] The Samorin of Calicut, who derived most of his influence from the Mahomedans who flocked to his ports. At this time the corsairs of these northern ports carried on the war against the Portuguese with his secret favour: it therefore served his purpose with the Portuguese not to claim any direct control over them.

This king of Moutingué would have had us stay with him, and gratified us in all things; he even allowed the Mahometan lords to kill a cow to give us a banquet, a thing they are not wont to do. The captain in whose house I was was called *Moussey Caca*,[1] and he with whom my companions were had for his name *Mestar Cogni-aly*.[2] These two were the chief men of Moutingué.

We remained there four or five days. The king and the Malabar captains expected that we would remain altogether, and begged us hard to do so. For my part, I said I wanted to go to see the great king *Samory*; to this they made no answer, not daring to say me nay: they even counselled me to go thither. I then took leave of the king and of my companions who wished to remain there,—for one was going with a Malabar captain in another direction, four leagues off in the Calecut territory. I set out with another captain, the most valiant and brave on all that coast, who has the most galleys of his own: he is called *Cousty Hamede*. He took with him some *Jangay*,[3] who are Nair guides: they tarry

[1] *Mûssa Kâkka*; as to the latter appellative, see above, p. 268.

[2] *Kunhâli*, from *Kunhi*, a youth, a term of endearment, a title, as here; and *âli*. The title of a great Mâppilla family of corsairs, as to whom we hear more presently.

[3] These Nâyar guides or guards are mentioned by most of the travellers who have visited the Malabar coast. "Those who desire to proceed thither" (says Fah Hian of the Deccan) "should first pay a certain sum of money to the king of the country, who will then appoint people to accompany them and show them the way." The guards of the king of Bidjanagar are called *djandar* by Abd-er-Razzak (*Ind. in XV Cent.*, p. 34). Barbosa, after stating their general employment as mercenary troops, proceeds:—"And if anyone is in apprehension of another man, he takes some of these nairs, as many as he pleases, into his pay: and they accompany and guard him: and on their account he goes securely, since no one dares to molest him: because if he were molested they and all their lineage would take vengeance on him who should cause this molestation. These guards are called *Janguada*" (Stanley's *Barbosa*, p. 129). De Couto gives a full account of them, calling them *jangadas* (*Dec. IV*, liv. VII, cap. XIV). So does P. Vincenzo, under the name

about the gates of towns to escort for payment such as have need of them. All the great lords keep some of them on fixed wages, which the king gives them. Every one takes some, the weak for safety and protection; while great folks, who go with retinues of followers well armed, take them only to bear witness that they have not attacked the Nairs, in case it should happen some dispute arises between the Nairs and them, and this often befalls them: for the Nairs are much addicted to drunkenness, whereas the Malabars drink no wine, and are not at all quarrelsome or treacherous without cause: thus they have often some contention between them, but the king deals them indifferent justice. These Nairs are very thieves on land, and would for a petty consideration kill a man. They do rob the towns and markets privily, and none dare say anything against them. It is true that all are not of this sort, but only some discontented soldiers. 'Tis on the coast these do most prevail, one party of them robbing by land, the others by sea. So there be none that dare go anywhere without these soldier guides.

The Malabars do no robbery by land. When they have a quarrel among themselves, the king allots to each a Nair or Archer as a surety, and forbids them to attack one another. These Nairs are kept at the expense of the Malabars; and

Giancadas (*Viaggio*, liv. I, cap. xl). Among the items of revenue of the old Malabar princes, Burton mentions *Chungathum*, or "protection": "Whenever a person wished to place himself under the safeguard of a man of consequence, he paid from four to sixty-four *fanams* annually for the privilege. He might also make an assignment on particular lands for the payment. The sum was devoted to the maintenance of a kind of sentinel, similar to the belted peon of the Anglo-Indian settlements, furnished by the protector to his dependent. In cases of necessity, however, the former was bound to aid and assist the other with a stronger force" (*Goa and the Blue Mountains*, p. 198; see also pp. 224, 244). See also, as to travelling in India generally, *Tavernier*, pt. II, bk. i, cap. 8. The word is *changngâtam* "convoy, guard, income of Rajas from granting such guards, grants of land to persons liable to such service, companion".

while they are there, the Malabars durst not fight, otherwise the aggressor would be held guilty of high treason, and would have to answer for it before the king himself. It is said the Malabars maintain a feud for seven years.[1] These Nairs are so dreaded, that were a Malabar to wound one of them, and had no Nair witnesses to prove that he was not the aggressor, it would be ruin to all the Malabars in the town. All these Malabar towns along the coast are full of Nairs, armed in all fashions, so much so, that as I journeyed I seemed to be in a camp of 20,000 men. Sometimes one cannot walk in the streets; but in the evening all the world goes abroad, save only the Mahometans and Moucois, who have a separate quarter on the sea-shore, in front of the Malabar towns; and also the Gentile artisans, whose houses are usually near the town of the Malabars for whom they work.

So, although the country belongs to the Malabars, yet, in speaking of the Malabars, the Mahometans are more properly intended; they are but seldom artisans, almost all being merchants, robbers, or sea warriors. There is no class of nobles among them; their distinction is solely in valour and wealth, and all sorts of men are welcomed among them. They but seldom keep slaves, and none[2] are constrained to go to the wars with them. They are trustful towards all men, and care not to compel others to go where they go. They provide a free table for all comers, and each has his own dish: that is, all soldiers. All their people are employed, for such as are not brave enough for soldiers, they make mariners, or press them into service for hire, or use them for selling the produce of their robberies. Their galiots they

[1] Referring to the *Kuḍippaka* or *Kuḍuppu*, "house or family feud", about which much curious information exists. When a man was slain it was customary to burn his body in the house of the slayer, who was of course also burnt.

[2] That is, none of the Gentiles; a few lines lower he says they do press their own people to go to the wars.

call *Pados*.[1] All the merchants of the coast, when they hear that the galiots of the pirates are about to come in, hold themselves in readiness to buy their goods cheap, and then they have the assurance to go and sell them in the markets of the very merchants of whom they were taken. These latter frequently buy them back a second time; and though they recognise their own goods, that matters not, so long as they have the Portuguese passport. The priests of their religion, too, and the poor are on the look-out, and come distances of thirty leagues to get their share; for they well know that these Malabars have made vows, in case they make a good prize, to give so much to the poor, and never fail to acquit themselves therein. Likewise they have their holy places, or *Ziares*,[2] places and temples especially kept for the purpose, where they pay their vows as at the Maldives. These priests are employed only at marriages and at the temples. They have no hand in administering justice; and all are habited in the Arab fashion, that is, entirely in white. In their company are a sort of men called *Abedalles*,[3] who have taken a vow of poverty, and so go about the world. Sometimes there will be thirty or forty of them in one place, yet they travel not more than two or three together, most often alone. They have alms given them, and, indeed, are passing urgent in demanding the same. They all sleep in the temples. They are the best company in the world, for they know all languages, and it is a great pleasure to entertain them; they have traversed all parts of the East, carrying their bit of baggage upon them. Money, cotton cloth, and silk are what they mostly get, and as much to eat as they will have. Some of

[1] Portuguese form of the Malayâlam *paṭak*, a country craft not now in use. Mr. Logan says it was intermediate in size between a *manji* and a *pattimâr* (as to both which, see Yule, *Gloss.*, s. vv. *manchua* and *pattamar*). In vol. II, ch. ii, Pyrard calls the *manjis* of Goa also galiots.

[2] Ar. *Ziyârat*, a place of visitation; see above, p. 176.

[3] *Abd-Allah*, "Slave of God", a Mahomedan ascetic.

them live in great austerity, according to their faith. These tarry near the temples, and ask for nothing; they would sooner die of hunger. They are very solitary, and all hold the faith of Mahomet. The Gentiles have also their *Abcdalles*, which are like to our hermits, and are called *Joguies*.[1] They, too, do go about the country, but only among the Nairs and other Gentiles. They eat nothing that has had life. The king of Calecut has one by him, whom he treats with great respect: he is regarded as a saint. All the Joguies that pass that way go and lodge with him, as it were at a monastery or hospital set apart for the purpose. It is two musket-shots from the king's palace, and is exceeding well constructed; it was built and endowed by the king. The other Nair kings, who merely give these folks passing cheer, receive them at their palaces, where they may tarry as long as they please. They cover their bodies with some kind of powdered ash, made with water into a white paste. They commonly wear large sea-chestnuts[2] as pendants in their ears, which have holes large enough to admit the thumb; others, the greater among them, wear gold and silver gilt in the form of these. Their diet is like that of the Bramenis and Banians of Cambaye and other places, who taste not anything that has had life. There is another sort of folk that wander about, just as here: that is, the charlatans, who exhibit beasts, taking their wives and children about with them, and dance and tumble in all manner of ways. I never saw any such good mountebanks, nor any that did such juggling and tricks of legerdemain.

But to return to my departure from Moutingué. I took the road for Calecut by land, a distance of twelve leagues, taking for my escort and guidance a body of Nairs from town to town. These are very numerous, being only two leagues

[1] *Jogi*, a Hindu ascetic: see Yule, *Gloss.*

[2] *Chastiganes de mer;* Anglicè, "sea-urchins"; Italicè, *frutta di mare.*

or so apart. Each man receives four *tarents*,[1] which are small silver coins, each of the value of one-sixteenth of a larin.

So I arrived at *Badara*, two leagues from Moutingué, on the Calecut road. The lord[2] there gave me even a better reception than the other had. He had two palaces, one of which was for his wives, for he had several, according to the law of Mahomet. I sojourned there about fifteen days. These three ports, Chombaye, Moutingué, and Badara are within the ambit of a single bay. Cangelotte,[3] another harbour of the corsairs, who rule a great extent of countries and peoples, is at some eighteen leagues to the north, near Barcelor, and between those places no succour can be afforded by land. But as between these three they succour one another in this fashion: they have certain lofty buildings erected upon piles on the sea-shore; there they keep sentinels to scan the

[1] Malayâlam *târan*, an obsolete silver coin of Malabar and the Deccan. In 1443, six *taras* went to the *fanam* at Bijayanagar (Abd-er-Razzak, *India in XV Cent.*, i, 26); while in 1504 a fanam was worth fifteen taras (*Varthema*, Hak. Soc., p. 130). By this time, a century after Varthema, the depreciation had not gone far, as Pyrard assigns the value of a larin and also of a fanam at sixteen *tarents*. The fanam, be it remembered, was at this time always a gold coin. The târam was not adopted by the Portuguese. Elsewhere Pyrard gives the European value of the coin, viz., three deniers, or a quarter sou. P. Vincenzo says it was worth a *bajocco*. The name is probably from *târa*, a star.

[2] Formerly known as the *Vâḷunnavar* of Vadakkara, now as the *Kadattanâd Raja*. A. Hamilton gives an interesting account of his visits to this local potentate, who claimed to be the king of the corsairs: he calls him *Balanore Burgarie* (i, 301). He was also visited by Dr. Buchanan (ii, 514). The ruins of his castle still remain (Sewell, *List of Ant. of Madras*, p. 245).

[3] *Kâṇyirôṭu*, short for *Kâṇyiram Kôṭu*, the place of the *Strychnos nux vomica* trees, the modern Cassergode in S. Canara; one of the earliest Mahomedan settlements on the coast. It is called *Canharoto* by the Portuguese writers, and is mentioned in the royal despatch of 1st March 1613, as a place of robbers, under the control of the Samorin, where it was proposed to erect a fortress (*Liv. das Monç.*, ii, 352).

horizon. They know within a little when the Portuguese fleet may be expected, and have intrenchments ready on land to obstruct their landing.

While I was at Badara there passed by sixty sail, all galiots, and two galleys, on their way from Cochin to Goa. There was such a calm that all the Malabars there treated the matter lightly. Those of the other ports, however, set out to assemble themselves at that port, off which the fleet lay, and so give succour to their friends. The Portuguese call their own galiots *Navires*,[1] and those of the Malabars, *Pairaus*.[2] Most of these vessels were *Chetils*,[3] that is to say, merchantmen. Immediately on arrival the Malabars draw up their *Pados*, or galiots, on the beach. I was witness to the most gallant behaviour on the part of one of these Pados, which was returning from war. All the Portuguese fleet was lying at the entrance of this great bay; the Pados, not perceiving them, found itself of a sudden engaged with sixty sail. Retreat being impossible, she took the bold resolution to run through the midst of the fleet, and so to make her own port, which was *Chombaye*. The crew capsized her, and though hard pressed by the Portuguese, saved themselves by swimming. The Portuguese got nothing for their pains, and after the fleet had retired, the owners brought their Pados safely to shore.

These robbers and pirates must take great booty, for be-

[1] Port. *navios*.

[2] Port. *paráos*, borrowed, as Col. Yule suggests, either from the Malayâlam *páṛu*, a boat, or from the *práhú* of the Eastern Archipelago. The early use of the word *paráo* by Varthema, as a Malabar word, would seem to indicate the former as the correct source.

[3] Malayâlam *chet̤t̤i*, a trader, used all over South India and Ceylon, similarly to "Banyan", further north. The Portuguese wrote *Chetins* and *Chatis* (see Yule, *Gloss.*, s. v. *Chetty*). I do not know any other authority for the use of the word for merchant-ships, though it is analogous to our "merchantmen".

sides the cost and expenses of their *Pados* and galiots, they have to pay customs and passport duties to the Nair king of the land; then they are subjected to the giving of all sorts of gratifications and presents,—as, for instance, to the king of Calecut and to their own king. They were wont thus to make gifts to the late king *Cognialy;* they have to give to their allies; and finally, to their priests and the poor, and in fulfilment of vows made at their *Ziares.*

The lords there do the same, and they own their *pados* like the rest. For there is no privilege of nobility among them, and no respect of persons, saving the aged, the wealthy, and the brave. When they set out for war, and for a round of expeditions, they appoint a general of the whole fleet, whom they obey during that voyage only; when it is over he returns to his former position. If any prize is taken, they give him a present, as they may be minded, though he has no right thereto; the rest is equally divided.

During my sojourn at Badara I often made excursions on foot up the country, which I found to be of fair prospect, very productive, well timbered, and pleasant. The soil is red and sandy, and the country open. The Nairs near the ports gather themselves to the coasts and to the king's palace when the alarm is given that the Portuguese or others are coming to attack the Malabars.

As for the king's palace, it is unapproachable from the sea side: it is situated on the top of a hill, about three musket-shots distance from the sea, the Malabar town being between; the hill has been cut down like a four-square wall. The king hath another castle, a league and a half up the country, where he keeps his wife and all his family, and also his Pagoda, which he took me to see. He is about sixty years of age, not so handsome as the rest of his race, but of a fine figure. I went often to Moutingué to see my companions. One of them went thence to another town two leagues from Badara, towards Calecut, and in the Calecut country, ten leagues from that city. This town is called *Marcaire Costé*[1]; the Portuguese call it Cognialy's country.[2]

This lord with whom I was at Badara loved me as a brother. He had a wife residing at Marcaire Costé (which is a fortress), and took me there many times. I saw my companion there, and stayed with him awhile. This district of Marcaire belongs to the king of Calecut, and, like the rest of the Calecut realm, is at peace with the Portuguese. The pirates and corsairs dare not land and equip their *pados* there,[3] but all the men of the place go a-robbing like the rest. The rich have their *pados,* which they keep at places under the king of Badara, and at the other pirate ports, and bring their booty, the proceeds of their robberies, home by land. The Malabar Indians make no distinction, until it be explained to them, between the English, Hollanders, and French. This is what made them like us so much, viz., that they saw we were hostile to the Portuguese. They asked me if I was of the same religion as the Portuguese; and when I answered yes,—why, then, said they, do you make war upon them? When I replied that they did the same upon other Mahometans, they remarked that that should not be deemed strange as to them, who were all robbers and pirates, a trade that was no dishonour to them, seeing they practised it from father to son. A man who would be welcomed among them must be always talking of warring against the Portuguese, and always speaking ill of them,—for, in truth, I never heard a good word said for them.

The real cause why this lord liked me so much and

[1] That is, the *kôtta*, or fort, of the *Mârakkâr*. Although Pyrard is aware that the latter is only a personal title, he presently calls the place by the names *Marcaire* and *Costé* successively.

[2] Throughout the eleventh and twelfth *Decades* of De Couto, the fort and town, as well as its ruler, are called *Cunhale*.

[3] That is, since the destruction of the place in 1600 (see App. C), and because of the stringent treaty made between the Samorin and the Portuguese after that event.

caressed me so greatly beyond the others, was that he had a mind to go to the Maldives the next year with a fleet, and seeing that I had acquaintance of the language and the country, and being informed by many merchants and Malabar pilots who had seen me there, how I had been entertained by the late king, he held me to no other talk but of the Maldives, inquiring closely which were the best islands, the richest individuals, and if I knew where the king and his queens kept their treasure, insomuch that he was like to have detained me by main force. The other lords were of the same mind, and made me the most flattering offers, so that I had had much pains to escape, but for the use I made of the name of the great *Samory*, whom I told them I was minded to visit. That alone restrained and silenced them, and by this means I got out of the mess, to their great chagrin. So with this purpose I bade them farewell, and took the road straight for *Marcaire Costé*.

Going from Badara to the Calecut country one has to pass a river, and there is a king also between, called *Auriole*.[1] He has no port, so he bides ashore. He is a friend to the Portuguese, and an enemy to the Malabars in his heart; but he makes no concealment of this: for though they do business together, they do not themselves pass or repass the border. Through his land flows a river that hath its mouth at Mar-

[1] De Couto, in his description of the attack on Kunhâli's fort, mentions a territory up the river, exactly as here placed by Pyrard, but calls the people *Arioles*, and the territory *Ariole* (*Dec. XII*, liv. I, cap. xviii, and liv. II, cap. v). On the other hand, the king, in a despatch dated 12th January 1591, speaks of the *Arioles* as "lords of powerful vassals, neighbours of Cunhale, who could give him aid or prevent him being assisted" (*Arch. Port. Or.*, Fasc. 3). The word is probably a title, namely, *Âyirôn*, *i.e.*, lord of one thousand Nâyars (*âyiram* = 1000); the "king" was probably a Nâyar chief, who at the time had made himself independent (of the Kôlattiri), for Pyrard, further down (p. 375), says his territory lay across the river from *Kôṭṭakkal*. It would seem therefore that this *Âyirôn* was at this time in possession of the *Putu paṭṭanam* country of *Kôlattanâd*.

caire, and carries boats afloat for more than five-and-twe leagues of its course.

It is impossible to describe in detail the welcome and good friendship extended to us by the Malabar Mahometans and Nairs. They counted themselves lucky when they got us under their roofs, saying that God had greatly blessed them; and most of them put in writing the day and hour of our coming in, and told their children to remember the day they saw us. All ran out upon the road to see us, when they heard tell of our name, and how that we were enemies to the Portuguese.

Having spent fifteen days or more at Badara, I went to Marcaire to find my companion, and we made up our minds to go together to the Samory, with the king's leave and that of Cousty Hamede, who was loth to give it, like the rest: for I used to go at my pleasure to *Costé*, to his wife's house, for meat and drink and sleep. Receivers, clerks, and other officers of the king of Calecut are always stationed at the town of Costé: they have a customs-house there, and examine all vessels and goods arriving at the port; in the evening they return to their lodging, half a league out of the town. The Portuguese have done all they know to conquer these four towns and ports, but always without effect, and to their own loss and discredit, chiefly so at Badara, where they have lost many of their men; for it is an exceeding strong port, all surrounded with water. They got soundly beaten there only a month before my arrival.[1]

I tarried ten or twelve days at Marcaire before going on to Calecut, and while I was there the lord *Cousty Hamede* came many a time, saying it was to see me, though the truth was he had his wife there. He would not let me quit him, or take another lodging than his, whether for sleeping, eating, or drinking. On the other hand, the king's receivers, who are

[1] Mr. Rivara notes that, owing to the want of historical documents relating to this period, he has not been able to trace the details of this expedition.

held in high honour there, gave us an allowance, saying it was a great indignity, as well for the king as for us, if we were fed by any but him, seeing we were in his country, and minded to go and visit him. Besides this allowance, they gave great entertainments in our honour, as did all the other lords, as well Nair as Mahometan, and were desirous to accompany us toward the king. They gave us every day a *Panan* each, which is a piece of gold money of the king, in value about four sous and a half. It was more than double what we could spend. All this Marcaire country, which I went far up, is very good soil; for about four[1] [forty] years it has been the principal retreat of all the pirates, and their king resided there.

Here dwell most of the Malabars, owing to the strength of the place; and here the king of Calecut sets a governor to rule all the Malabars of his realm, including those of the other towns and ports of the pirates and corsairs; which governor they acknowledge as their king, but subject to the Samory, for they must needs be ruled by one of their own faith and race. One such he gave them named *Cognialy*,[2] with the title of lieutenant-general: he was called Cognialy Marcaire, for Marcaire means lieutenant or viceroy.[3] This Cognialy was chosen for the post on account of his valour, and retained it for thirty or forty years; and by his robberies in all directions he became very powerful. He was the grandest corsair ever seen in those parts, and his district being large, men came from all sides to reside there. The fortress is small; past it flows a fine river, navigable for boats for

[1] I agree with Mr. Rivara that the *quatre* here is a misprint for *quarante*. De Couto dates the rise of the elder Kunhâli from 1572, and the place had been destroyed as a fortress seven years before the time of which Pyrard is writing. See further, App. C.

[2] *Kunhâli*, a family title borne both by the founder of the fortress and the corsair whose fortunes are here told, whom Pyrard confuses.

[3] It is really *Mârakkâr*, for *Mârggakâran*, from *mârggan*, "a way or law", and *kâran*, "a doer". There were Marakkars at all the pirate ports. It is still a common honorific title among the Moormen of Ceylon.

more than twenty leagues, down which are borne all kinds of goods. At the mouth of this river he erected, by leave of the king, a large fortress, in the fashion of ours, of strong walls, built with lime and sand, and having a supply of fresh water within. Beyond this, he constructed two large forts to guard the mouth of the river, so that all vessels came in to safe moorings under the fortress, and abode there out of all danger and trouble. The fortress protected the town, which was also fortified as well on the sea as on the land side; it was almost surrounded by the sea and the river. It is a large town, well peopled, with great buildings, streets, and shops, all well planned, as at Calecut and elsewhere on the Malabar coast: even among these towns it is one of the most beautiful, wealthy, and strong. It is built on an eminence, and the fortress towers above; while down below, on either side of the river, next the sea, are the two forts which protect the whole haven and the river's mouth. This town is reduced to half its importance in all respects since the death of *Cognialy Marcaire,* the manner whereof I shall now relate.[1]

This Cognialy was obedient in all things to his king, under whose favour and goodwill he had made himself so strong: and the king, who up to that time had warred against the Portuguese, was well content to have so redoubted a champion. The port and the town were worth as much to the king as those of Calecut itself. Down the river are borne much pepper and other produce, enhancing the wealth of the town and port. In a hall of the mansion of a great Malabar lord of this place, I saw all the adventures and victories of Cognialy, as well by land as by sea, very well painted and

[1] The Portuguese expeditions against Kunhâli in 1599 and 1600, which are here narrated at some length, though eclipsed in importance by the Ceylon wars, vie in tragic interest with any conducted by the Portuguese in India. Although they form the central subject of the eleventh and twelfth *Decades* of De Couto, they have been little regarded in modern historical notices of the period. The site of the fortress is shown, with the main outlines of the story, in App. C.

coloured, with all the galliots, galleys, and other vessels that he had taken or sunk, very skilfully represented. His fame and terror were spread abroad from the Cape of Good Hope even to China; and I was assured that he had at a single blow cut a galley oar in two, and likewise had cut down a man with a sword by his side, hewing man and sword with a single cut. He had a brother as valiant as himself, named *Cousty Moussey.*[1] Their power was greater than that attained by any others in those parts: they took innumerable ships and galleys of China, Goa, and other places, as I observed in these paintings. This Cognialy was likewise one of the cruellest men in the world, and his great strength and power led him to despise his neighbours, even the king of Cananor,[2] who had formerly been his protector and suzerain, and had aided him in all his projects. He harried in all directions, and all men's goods. None could number the cruel barbarities practised by him and his against all sorts and conditions of men, without distinction: among others, against his own neighbour, the Nair king Auriole, already mentioned, whom he robbed and pillaged and drove from his kingdom: he cut off the nose and breasts of that prince's queen, and had himself acknowledged as king. At length, puffed up with prosperity, he would no longer recognise the Samory, and rebelled against him, refusing to deliver up some vessels of his subjects that he had taken; and when commanded so to do, he set all such commands at nought.

The Portuguese were well enough pleased with this revolt of Cognialy,—which, indeed, they had fomented, believing that his speedy ruin was certain, as well on account of the exces-

[1] De Couto mentions *Cutimuça* as the nephew and great general of Kunhâli, meaning nephew of the elder and, perhaps, brother of the younger Kunhâli: Pyrard knows only of the younger pirate chief (*Dec. XI*, cap. viii; and see App. C).

[2] *Âli Raja*, Sea King, or King of the Deep, who was the naval commodore of the Kôlattiris, and whose ancestor was the great Mammâli, known in connection with Maldive history (see App. A).

sive barbarity of his cruelties and robberies that he had practised, as for his presumption and revolt: insomuch that, without delay, they sought for peace with the king of Calecut, who, out of desire to chastise his faithless vassal, too gladly hearkened thereto. The next year, which was 1599, the viceroy of Goa equipped a powerful fleet, under the command of his own nephew, by name *Louys de Gusman*,[1] who, with a view to surprise the fortress by a *coup de main*, entered the country of king Auriole, a bitter enemy of Cognialy, for the reasons already stated. This territory lay across the river, over which the Portuguese threw a bridge of thirty or forty boats, lashed one to another. A captain, named *Louys de Sylva*, with 300 of the bravest men of the fleet, was appointed to effect a landing on the other side, upon the signal being given. That was to be done by night, and the Samory was to despatch at the same time a land force, aided by Portuguese. Cognialy and his brother, being well warned of all this, got themselves ready at all points, without any display of doing anything. The result was that the 300 men who had crossed were repulsed, and their captain, Louys de Sylva, killed with a musket-shot. Seeing this, the soldiers turned about, and thinking to find their boats where they had left them, discovered that they had been removed. Meantime, the garrison of the fortress sallied out, and cut them all down: the most of them were drowned, and only about twenty or thirty saved themselves by swimming, the rest being unable to swim on account of their armour. As for the Nairs and Portuguese, who were to make the land attack, Cognialy had prepared entrenchments on the road they had to traverse, held by a force of arquebusiers.

The bulk of the Portuguese army, on attempting to land, were completely repulsed, and for their folly sustained a loss of 500 men, and re-embarked in disorder. The king

[1] Dom Luiz da Gama was brother, not nephew, of the viceroy, Dom Francisco da Gama.

of Calecut afterwards told the Portuguese it ought not to have been done in this fashion, but with deliberation. So the general returned to Goa crestfallen, and with the loss of the best part of his army. The Portuguese that were with the Samory took great umbrage at this, saying that he had betrayed them, and had led them to the slaughter; for that the men he ought to have sent, as he had arranged with them, were not on the spot at the proper time to give the agreed signal. But the cause of the miscarriage, in fact, was the intrigues of Cognialy and his people, who had received good information, and had at once sent a force of armed men to bar the passage; and to such effect, that the others could not be at the agreed place at the agreed time.

The Portuguese, afterwards informed of the truth of the whole business, were little disheartened at having been beaten once, and resolved to make the attempt a second time, so as to make themselves masters of Cognialy and his territory, according to the assurance they had given to the king his master. So the following year, which was 1600, *André Furtado de Mendoce*,[1] an old and brave captain, and the most dreaded Portuguese soldier in India (he died coming from Goa to Lisbon, on the same voyage as that on which I returned, as I shall relate below), took measures with the Samory to entrap Cognialy, and arranged together that the king of Calecut should come in person by land, while the Portuguese army, under the command of the said André, should arrive by sea: this they did, and Cognialy was besieged. Some grand sorties were made, with great losses on both sides. There are said to have been 60,000 Nairs present. I afterwards heard the whole story, both from the Portuguese, and from the Malabars and Nairs of the fortress;

[1] André Furtado de Mendoça, the greatest Portuguese captain of the time. He succeeded to the government of India on the 27th May 1609, and ruled till the 5th September of the same year. See further, App. C, and vol. ii.

but these said that the cause of the taking of Cognialy was the lack of provisions; for that Cognialy, having so soundly beaten them on the first occasion, little thought they would return so soon, and so was taken by surprise. He had despatched two large ships under *Metar Cognialy*, a great captain of Moutingué, to get provisions; but they could not re-enter the harbour; and so, after a long siege, seeing himself reduced to extremities, and after proving his mettle on many occasions, at length somewhat basely surrendered. It was said that he did so owing to some charmed betel the king had sent him, whereby his courage failed him. Others said it was out of pity at seeing his men in such great straits, that he would sooner die himself than see so many men suffer on his behalf. Another reason was that his brother, Cousty Moussey, was dead, who would never have permitted a surrender in this sort. Yet the thing which most led him to it was his despair of succour; for he had insulted the kings and princes of whom he might have expected it. So it was that he asked a parley, saying he would surrender to the mercy of his king, of whom he asked pardon. But the king could no longer save him: for it had been agreed between him and André Furtado that the fortress should be rased to the ground, and the booty halved, and that all the people should go to the king and Cognialy to the Portuguese, or Cognialy to the king and the people to the Portuguese. The king demanded the people. The compact being concluded, all the Nairs were drawn up on one side, and the Portuguese on the other. Cognialy then came forth, and proceeded to salute the king and ask his pardon. The king called upon him to deliver up his sword, and taking it, struck him two or three light strokes on the shoulder, as if in jest, and then addressed him in these words: "Cognialy, you have given me much trouble and grief"; at the same time turned to the Seigneur André, saying, "Take Cognialy: he is yours." He was forthwith seized and placed in a galley; the fortress and the forts were entirely demolished, while the town was left in its former condition, albeit it was sacked, and the people sustained no further loss. The two armies then retired.

When the news of the capture reached Goa, bonfires were lighted, the bells were rung, and the *Te Deum* was sung, and two days[1] after the return of the army Cognialy was beheaded. He was first asked if he would become a Christian, to which he replied that he was willing, provided his life was spared; but if he was to die, he preferred to die in the faith of Mahomet. Such were the fortunes and the miserable end of king Cognialy. Yet did the Portuguese afterwards pay dearly for his head: for the Malabars, in revenge, put to death all the Portuguese they could lay hands on: and the king of Calecut had great regret for having delivered up so valiant a man (he had done so out of anger and revenge), for Cognialy and his brother were esteemed the bravest captains in all the East Indies.

As for Cognialy's fortress, I have seen it many a time: the walls were still standing, to the height of two men's stature, so that it were easy to fortify it, and it could soon be refitted in case the king went to war with the Portuguese. When we left Goa, the news had arrived that the king intended to break the peace, to build sixty galleys or pados, and to reconstruct the fortress; and when the Hollanders went to him, he promised to put the place in their hands. Wherefore the factor or agent of the Portuguese who was there went and complained to him that he had received these Hollanders, and other enemies of the king of Spain, and that he was therefore resolved to return to Goa. The king made no further reply, than that he might go at his pleasure, for that he would detain no one by force.

There is no king in India who can damage the Portuguese

[1] We know from De Couto that the interval was longer than this, but not the exact time; also that De Couto himself interviewed Kunhâli in prison (see App. C).

by sea so much as he: for the coasts of his realm can furnish an immense number of Malabars, and it is very rich in supplies. He has some very wealthy men in his kingdom, and all are courageous and loyal: he has also plenty Moucois to man his pados. These Moucois are in the position of slaves to the king and the Nairs (as I shall explain below): they call the king in their language *Tambiraine*,[1] meaning "God". I know for certain that the Samory has an understanding with all the Malabar pirates, that they give him money and pay a tribute underhand. I am aware of this, from having often accompanied the captain, *Cousty Hamede*, when he went to treat secretly with the king's officers, which he did only by night, for fear of being seen. All the other lords and captains of the Malabars do the same, as I have observed many a time, and as the king's own officers assured me: and there is good reason for it, for he assists them in all things, and provides them with money when they have none, which they repay in full, and with interest. Every year many thousand men leave the Samory's territory to do their robberies on the sea along with the rest. On land these corsairs are the most gallant and honourable gentlemen in the world, and they are daily endeavouring by presents and flattery to get the Samory to break the peace with the Portuguese, and to give them this fortress of Cognialy. This Cognialy has left a son, also called *Marcaire*, or Viceroy: I have often seen him, and have eaten and drunk in his house. He resides mostly at Costé and Chombaye, with one or other of his two wives; and although since the death of his father the king has appointed no one in his stead, and has not recognised this son as his successor, yet he is treated with greater respect than anyone else, and the title is preserved to him for his father's sake only. Many have aspired

[1] *Tamburân*, title of grown-up member of Malayâli Rajan families; it means "lord" or "master", also "god". The title of a junior member is *Tambân*.

to the post, for which very reason the king appoints none to it, and thus keeps the land in peace. All affairs go directly before the king, or the Nair lords commissioned for the purpose, and justice is done throughout the country in all matters by them alone.

My companion and I, having stayed more than twelve days in this Marcaire or Cognialy's country, took leave of our friends. The king's officers, whose permission we asked for our departure, told us that, if we were minded to go to the king, they would give us letters and money; but we had no need of money except for crossing the river and paying the Nair guides. Had we not been liable to find our Nairs drunk with *arac*[1] (which is a kind of *eau de vie* made with the wine of the coco-tree), we should, in fact, have had no need of it at all, by reason of our letter of commendation, which ran in the name of the king: but that must not always be trusted to. We made only four short leagues a day at the most, sometimes only two. They made us lodge in their houses, although others were provided for us. Indeed, I cannot describe all the hospitality and honour we received on the road. The question always was who should have us; but they did not dare to press us to stay against our will, however much they desired it, seeing we were going to the king; and our passport insured us a good reception on all hands. We were about eight days on our journey from *Costé* to Calecut, although we might well have done it in two. It was our halting at this place and that, and the hospitality and welcome accorded to us everywhere, which caused us to take all that time; and in truth it would be impossible to describe the universal welcome given us, so full of honour, courtesy, and affection was

[1] The Ar. *araḳ*, "perspiration, exudation, distilled spirit", has spread over all Asia. Throughout the tropics arrack is made from the coco-tree; arrack punch used to be a favourite beverage both in India and England, and then frequently shortened to "rack-punch"; but since the days of Jos. Sedley both the name and the drink have gone out of fashion.

it: for even the greatest folks disputed among themselves which should entertain us. But I must remark that these were the Malabar Mahometans, and not the Nairs; for the latter, though liberal with their money, fruits, and all else, like not that strangers should eat and sleep in their houses, if they can help it, except in case of great necessity: and those of them that are of the Brameny race are the most particular in this respect. Though the others make the same difficulty, they are not so scrupulous as the Bramenys.

For the rest, if it were not for the excessive heat of the sun in those parts, it would be impossible to tell the pleasure and satisfaction of travel in that land, which is the fairest and most agreeable ever seen or even imagined: for the country is all open and sandy, but the sand is hard and firm as sandstone; and by the road-side are houses and buildings always in sight, and towns every league or half league, the most distant being two short leagues apart. The whole country is well peopled, and covered with fruits, which are common property and free to passers-by; and these fruits are the finest in the world, there being none of the same kinds or so good in these parts. Moreover, all along the roads one meets with great numbers of people, Nairs and Malabars, men and women: for everyone goes about there in perfect safety, so long as he has a Nair or *Jangaye* in his company. For a party of twenty or thirty persons, one Nair suffices; and if a man goes alone he wants no less, though it costs him more; but the greater the party the greater is the Nair's profit. There are many marshes and salt-pits to cross between *Coté* and Calecut, and two rivers to cross by boat,[1] about a league from one of which is a very fine

[1] Pyrard must have struck somewhat inland on his way to Calicut, as there are certainly not two rivers to cross between Kôṭṭakal and Calicut, when the route lies along the sea-shore. He probably crossed the *Agalapuḷa* river or backwater, and afterwards the Ellattûr river, by some inland road.

town, where we passed a night, named *Coluotte*,[1] where the Portuguese once had a fortress and a residency, as at Calecut; but they have lost the one as the other. I saw it as I passed, for it is not altogether demolished; it was even stronger than that at Calecut. This is all that I remarked on the journey.

[1] This is the northern *Kollam*, inflected, it is *Kollaṭṭu*, written *Coulete* by Barros and Andrada. It is a very ancient seat of trade, about 1½ mile north of Koilandi, and locally called *Pantalâyini* Kollam; but foreign writers have generally omitted the *Kollam* (see Yule, *Gloss.*, s. v. "Pandarāni"). Mr. Logan has kindly supplied us with the following note, showing that it was here that Vasco da Gama first landed in India. "Following Correa, I think it is clear that da Gama's fleet first anchored at *Kâppaṭṭ*" [the *Capogatto* of the Portuguese writers; see Yule, *Gloss.*, s. v. "Capucat".—Ed.], "the position of which is well known, about ten or eleven miles north of Calicut. Correa does not say that the fleet was moved after thus casting anchor at Kappaṭṭ, but the fact is mentioned by other writers, who, moreover, give the name of the place to which it was moved, viz., *Pandarane*. Now *Pandarane* is undoubtedly *Pantalâyini*, one of the *Desams* (small hamlets) of the *Amsam* (parish) in which Kollam is situate. It is the *Fandarina* of Edrisi, the *Fandaraina* of Ibn Batuta and Rashíduddín, the *Fundaraina* of the Tohfat, the *Flandrina* of Friar Odoric, etc." [see Yule, *Gloss.*, s. v. "Pandarāni"]; "and to go further back, it is probably the *Patale* of Pliny. The place has long been known because of its trade facilities. Off it, is one of those curious mud-banks, as at Calicut, Narakal, and Alpey, which protect shipping under shelter. Even at the present day, ships from the Red Sea and the Gulf almost invariably make for it when running over to India at the close of the south-west monsoon. The tradition, that da Gama's ships spent the monsoon season of 1498 at this place, has been current on the coast from the very commencement of the British administration. Da Gama sighted Mount Deli on the 26th August, and even at that time of year a country vessel would nowadays make for North Kollam for protection against occasional squalls. In 1793 the cruiser *Morning Star*, used by the settlement commissioners, took shelter here during the monsoon, they reporting, among their reasons for so doing, that da Gama's fleet had sheltered there. The tradition had probably come from the Portuguese themselves, and as it is consistent with all the accounts, I have little hesitation in accepting it."

CHAPTER XXVI.

Arrival of the author at Calecut, and a description of that kingdom.—The king and people: their manners, religion, and ways of life.

Having at length arrived at the town of Calecut, the first officers of the king whom we met with were the receivers of the king's dues, who have a house on the seashore, erected on piles, where they remain by day only: for the town and harbour are more than a league in length, and there are three of these buildings, for the watching of all the goods that are landed, for the taking of the number and quantities in writing, and for the conveyance of them thence to the *Alfandigue.*[1] This is a great square building of stone, with galleries above and below, and vaulted with stone arcades like those of our Place Royale,[2] but not so grand or so elegant, with a large number of rooms and warehouses for keeping all the different sorts of goods separate. Over the door is written the name of the goods kept in each warehouse; an officer of the king has one key, while the owner of the goods has another, and neither can enter without the other. The goods remain there till they have paid the dues and the customs, and the exports have to pay as well as the imports. This *Alfandigue* is two or three hundred paces from the sea, between the town and the port: it is strong and well guarded, all the the doors being well locked, and none may enter but on business, for the guards are always stationed there. Mistakes

[1] Port. *alfandega*, from *fondoc*, the Arabic form of the Greek πανδοχεῖον, a magazine; *cf.* Sp. *fundago*, Ital. *fondaco*, Fr. *fondeque* or *fondique*. See Littré (s. v. *fondique*), Ducange (s. v. *funda*), Dozy and Engelmann (s. v. *alfandega*); and Yule, *Cathay*, p. 355.

[2] The Place Royale, now Place des Vosges, remarkable for its arcaded galleries, was begun by Henri IV in 1604, and completed in 1612. It was the great new feature of Paris when Pyrard was preparing his second edition.

cannot well be made in the charging and discharging of goods, and in levying the king's dues, by reason of the number of clerks and officers who have to pass them, and these are all Nairs or Bramenis. And there is no port in all the kingdom so small but has its clerks, who, when the goods belong to merchants of the country, merely take a note of them; and at the end of six months or a year the merchants come and pay the gross amount. These officers are all men of quality, and highly respected. They have their offices and Alfandigues at the ports, where they pass the day; in the evening they return from the towns, and pass the night at their homes, which are usually not far from the town, half a league or so: they do not forgather with the crowd.[1]

When these officers saw us, and had heard whence we came, they were greatly joyed to have the presenting of us to the king; yet, by reason of the heat, they made us accept a lodging in the town, where we spent the hot hours of the day.

This town is not like the others of the Malabar coast, for it has its inns and drinking-shops, where food and lodging have their price. In the evening the officers gave us over to the soldiers of the guard, who conducted us to the king, whose palace is a half league from the town of Calecut. The

[1] The excellent management of the customs department at Calicut has been remarked by many travellers. In strong contrast to that of the Portuguese alfandega, it was characterised by a high degree of commercial honesty, which must account, in great measure, for the greatness of the port in the palmy days of the pre-Portuguese period. Thus, Abder-Razzak (*India in XV Cent.*, i, 14), says: "Security and justice are so firmly established in this city, that the most wealthy merchants bring thither from maritime countries considerable cargoes, which they unload, and unhesitatingly send into the markets and bazaars, without thinking in the meantime of any necessity of checking the account, or of keeping watch over the goods. The officers of the custom-house take upon themselves the charge of looking after the merchandize, over which they keep watch day and night. When a sale is effected, they levy a duty on the goods of one-fortieth part; if they are not sold, they make no charge on them whatsoever." See, too, *Barbosa*, Hak. Soc., pp. 110-111.

soldiers escorted us thither with all honour and respect. The king, aware of our coming, came down to the lower hall of his palace, because it was night. He was accompanied by ten or twelve Nair pages, all gentlemen, with large gold or silver gilt lamps, full of oil, for they use not candles or torches. Each lamp had six wicks, with snuffers as large as the finger, also of gold or silver gilt, and a large vessel of the same full of oil, so that the lamps should always be supplied. These lamps are hung from a great silver gilt rod, the end of which is fixed in the ground, while above it is curved outwards, so that the lamp does not inconvenience or soil the person who holds it, neither does it run over. The seats in the hall were of wood, well polished and handsome. They use also large black polished stones, like marble, for sitting upon. The king never sits in public, but remains standing.

The king held in his arms his little nephew, the prettiest and best bred child that could be, aged about three years, whom he greatly caressed as the heir to his throne: for there, the children never succeed, but only the nephews, the sons of sisters. He made a show of us to the little nephew, and asked him who we were, and made him approach and touch us to see if he was afraid of us, but he was not at all. After having questioned my companion and me for more than three hours he bade his interpreter in Portuguese ask us, amongst other things, what was the difference between the Hollanders and us (knowing, as he did, that we were not Hollanders), and which was the more puissant prince, Count Maurice, or the king of France. I told him that without comparison it was the king of France; but he replied that the Hollanders said the same of their Count Maurice, and the Portuguese of their king, and that he knew not what he ought to believe; whereto I answered according to the truth. At length, having asked how I had come to Calecut, and with what mind, and I having recounted all my adventures, and telling him that my only intention in coming there was to find the Hollanders (who were the more welcome strangers, as I had been told), he informed me that in truth, some three weeks or a month before, thirteen ships had come there and remained for nine or ten days; that he had given them permission to trade, and promised his friendship; and that the Hollanders had made him a present of two large cast-metal cannon (which had been taken from some Portuguese ships, and with which he was on that account less well pleased when he came to know it), and some other things that Count Maurice had sent him: that in return he had given them divers presents, such as jewels and gold chains, and had also given them leave to build a fortress; and that they had forthwith departed, promising to come again the following year.[1] He added that we were most welcome, and that we should want nothing while we were his guests.

The interpreter who interrogated us was a *Banian*,[2] and

[1] It is somewhat difficult to identify the Dutch fleet here spoken of. Van der Hagen arrived at Calicut with thirteen ships on the 27th October 1604, and had an interview with the Samorin, at which a treaty was concluded, and remained till after the 8th November (*Rec. des Voy.*, iii, 17). The Dutch chronicler does not say that he presented any guns. The next Dutch visit was that of Verhœven, who arrived, also with thirteen ships, on the 8th October 1608, and remained till the 16th. He, also, had an interview with the Samorin, at which the Van der Hagen treaty was confirmed; and at this meeting Verhœven presented to the Samorin two guns, which the Dutch had taken in a Portuguese ship, the *Bom Jesus*, at Mozambique (*Rec. des Voy.*, iv, 47-59). This incident is illustrated in *De Bry*, pt. IX, icon iv. Now Pyrard himself arrived at Calicut about the end of June 1607, some fifteen months before Verhœven. The conclusion is that the Samorin spoke to him of the visit of Van der Hagen, and that in writing his book some years after, the author inserted the details about the guns from what he had heard, probably at Goa, of the visit of Verhœven.

[2] Banyan, from *vaṇiya*, a Gujaráti trader. The name came to be applied to all Hindu merchants and brokers. The author, when he says, "and Brahman", does not mean that the Banyans were Brahmans by caste, nor, probably, that this individual was of Brahman caste, but merely that a Banyan was a Hindu. For illustrations of the use of the word, see Yule's *Gloss.* s. v.

Brameny, by race and religion, and spoke good Portuguese. He called himself broker (*courratier*) of the Flemings, or Hollanders,—that is, one who buys and sells merchandise, and acts as interpreter also, and is paid both by the vendor and purchaser. The king bade him to lodge us, and to take all care of us: he was called *Maniassa*.[1] He gave us a lodging at the house of a great Pandiare[2] and Mahometan Cherife, one of the greatest nobles of Calecut: it was at some distance from the town and the palace, and was one of the finest houses at Calecut. We had hardly established ourselves there ere we were told by him and other friends that the Portuguese were minded to do us a bad turn, and had conspired against us,—as, indeed, was the fact, and as we came to know afterwards. Whereupon the interpreter, fearing that we should come to harm, took us from that house after a stay of two or three days, and prepared us a lodging in the *Alfandegue*. This man was a kind of factor and agent to the king, in regard to the vessels despatched by the king to different parts. The Moucois commonly called him Marcaire,[3] or king's lieutenant; but that was merely to flatter him, as indeed they do to all the king's officers: albeit, he has the superintendence of all vessels used by the king in trade. We had also a servant given us, and each of us received daily two *panants*,[4] which are pieces of gold, in value four sols apiece, and also cloths for raiment, and all else

[1] Malayâlam *Maṇiâṇi*, an agent or manager.

[2] Probably used in the Maldive sense, of a cadi or judge.

[3] See above, p. 350.

[4] The value here given to the *fanam*, *i.e.*, 4 sous, leads me to believe that the *larin* of Malabar was of inferior value to that of the Maldives. In Malabar, the larin and the fanam were, according to the author, of the same value, 16 taras; therefore the *larin* of Malabar = 4 sous. The Maldive larin, Pyrard more than once says, was equal to 7 or 8 sous, *i.e.*, nearly twice the value of the Malabar *larin* and *fanam*.

The Old Virây fanam = 4 to a rupee.
" New " " = 3½ " "

that was necessary: for this man was so careful of us that he never quitted us, for fear we should complain of him to the king. Moreover, he was greatly desirous of being in the good graces of the Hollanders, who had given him such fair promises; and I know that the Portuguese bore him a deadly grudge on that score. When we had been there some fortnight or three weeks our companions who had remained at Moutingué arrived thence. They were treated as we were, and we all lodged together. In this way we resided at Calecut for about eight months, and I thus had the means to learn and observe both the country itself and the manners and character of the inhabitants.

Between the town and the king's palace there is nothing but houses, and there is no place in all India where contentment is more universal than at Calecut, both on account of the beauty and fertility of the country, and of the intercourse with men of all races, who live there in free exercise of their own religions. It is indeed a marvellous sight to see the great multitudes that are there, principally around the king's palace, where you will see a vast crowd of men, all in arms. All the greatest lords go every day to salute the king, who is greatly esteemed as a man of high spirit, albeit of a changeable humour: for he will greatly love, and then as greatly hate the same person, and afterwards of a sudden receive him again into his friendship. Wherefore no one puts his trust in him: he will take from any hand that gives, and himself confessed that he was a friend to those who gave him the best presents. He is very affable and pleasant, as well to strangers as to his own people, yet is he very choleric also, and is greatly feared by all his Nairs, who are ever apprehensive of his anger.

On one day, amongst others, I saw a female acrobat, one of the best dancers and tumblers that could be seen: for I have in my time seen many such, both men and women, but none to compare with her in the strange things she did, so that I could not but believe she employed some kind of diabolical art. This woman having come to do her perilous feats, the king and his wife were in a gallery to witness them, together with one other princess. There were some Nairs who obstructed the queen's view, and the king cried out to them once to keep back; but I believe that, owing to the great crush and noise of the crowd, they did not hear him; whereupon he, out of anger, himself stepped down with the fan-screen which his page was holding, and began to lay about him without respect of persons. It was the most pitiful sight in the world to see all the lords, soldiers, and others there fleeing hither and thither, and putting their hands to their heads in token of obedience: all of them would have quitted the scene of the exhibition, had he not himself commanded them to remain.

While I was at Calecut, all the lords used to bid us eat and drink with them, and to make us presents of gold pieces, silk and cotton cloths, and fruits. Among these was one of greater authority than all others,[1] for in the absence of the king he used to govern the city of Calecut. His house was about a league from the royal palace, situate upon a lake, and built of stone, of about a half-league in circumference, as all their other tanks are.

On a certain holiday (though it is far from easy to know when the Nairs' holidays are, for they never work) this lord had asked us to dine with him, my companion and myself, —a thing rarely done; but he was not very scrupulous. He was not of the Brameny race, and except the flesh of the ox and cow, he ate anything. So he went to bathe, for it is a custom with them when they come from among the crowd, considering themselves polluted, to bathe in these tanks.

[1] The Talachchennôr, or Nâyar of Calicut, is here alluded to. To the present day he signs for the Samorin during an interregnum. The house referred to is probably that which used to stand on a tank lying to the east of the public road to Beypore, beyond Mînchanda.

Now, two other great lords came to bathe at the same time in this large tank, one of whom was a relative of the king—I believe his nephew—for the king has a large number of them; the other was a man of high authority, having the command of a large body of Nairs, and was deemed a very valiant fellow. The king's nephew bearing the other a grudge, sent word to ask how it was he dared bathe at the same time with him, and threatening to drive him off. The lord, not wanting in courage, made no other reply, save that he boxed the ears of him who brought the message from the prince, bidding him to take that to his master. The prince, informed of this affront, forthwith assembles all his men, as also does the other on his side, so that there arose a great hubbub and affray between the two parties. The lord who had asked us to dine made haste to see what was afoot, and was never so astonished as to see such hosts of men assembled in arms in so short a time, and sought to put the matter straight. The king, on being informed of all that had passed, straightway ordered his nephew—who was his brother's son, and not his sister's—to be seized and put to death. The bell was rung at the royal palace, which at once became full of people waiting his commands. There were a number of people wounded in this affray, and the nephew of the king, fearing his wrath, took to flight, and with great expedition crossed the river which separates the Calecut kingdom from that of a king named *Chaly*.[1] This nephew was a great friend and protector to the Portuguese. It was five or six weeks ere he was allowed to return to favour. I saw him when he came back on his way to salute the king, along with a hundred of his followers, who had been in the same disgrace.

[1] Châliyam, which stood where the Beypore railway station now is (see plate in *Correa*, and *Linschoten*, Hak. Soc., i, 73, *note*). It was one of the earliest Mahomedan settlements, and probably gave its name to the piece-goods called *Shalceats* (see citation from Ibn Bat. in Yule's *Gloss.*). The Portuguese form was *Chale*, which our author follows.

This example shows what the sudden anger of the king means, and how he was slow to pardon even his next of kin; yet was his wrath always with some measure of justice.

The whole coast from Barcelor to the Cape Comorin is called *Malabar*[1]; and though there be many provinces and divers countries there, yet are they all of one language, law, and religion, of like government, classes, and ranks of men, according to their respective races, and above all of the same manners. There be many kings, such as those of *Cananor*, *Moutingué*, *Badara*, *Calecut*, *Tananor*,[2] *Cochin*, *Coilan*,[3] and many other kinglets too numerous to mention. But the greatest and most puissant king is he of Calecut, who is called *Samory*.[4] This is the distinguishing mark of his grandeur above all the rest, this word having the same meaning as Emperor with us. The king of Cochin is the greatest next to him, and assumes to be his peer, and this

[1] The limits usually assigned to Malabar are Mount Dely on the north, and Cape Comorin on the south (Yule, *Cathay*, 450; *Barbosa*, Hak. Soc., 101; *Fra Bart.*, Eng. trans., 103). Barros (*Dec. I*, liv. IV, cap. vii) puts the northern boundary at Carnate, near Dely; De Couto (*Dec. XII*, liv. I, cap. xviii) puts it at Cananor; others, erroneously, as high as Goa. Linschoten (i, 65) and Mandelslo (p. 87) agree with Pyrard in assigning Barcelor (*Bârkûr*), in S. Canara, as the northern limit; and if we go by language, as Pyrard does, they are right, as this is the northern boundary of Malayâḷam.

[2] Tanur.

[3] Quilon (*Kollam*). For references to the mediæval history of this place, see Yule, *Cathay*, 455; and *Gloss.*, s. v. "Quilon".

[4] One of the titles of the king of Calicut is *Kunnalakôn*, *i.e.*, King of the Hills (*kunnu*) and Waves (*ala*). The Sanskrit equivalent is *Samudragiri raja*, or shortly, *Samudri raja*, whence the Samorin, or Zamorin, of the Portuguese and other European writers. "This king became greater and more powerful than all the others; he took the name of *Zomodri*, which is a point of honour above all other kings" (*Barbosa*, Hak. Soc., p. 103). "The town of Calicut he (Cheramân Perumâl) gave to one of his best beloved servants, together with the title of Samoriin, which is as much to say as Emperour and chief of all the rest" (*Linschoten*, i, 72). As to the last quotation, the probability is that the first Samorin was a Home Ruler, and rebelled against the last of the Perumâls.

is why they are so frequently at war.[1] The others are petty kings of petty territories, who, though they be all kings with sovereign power in their own lands, yet revere and respect the greatness of Samory, speaking of him as their lord, and daring not to disobey him. This I say with assurance, for I have heard it from the mouths of many of these kings themselves. The king of *Coilan*[2] being so remote, at the very point of Cape Comorin, maintains more of his sovereignty than the rest; when I left India he was holding the Portuguese in siege on land.[3]

The kingdom of Calecut is of very great extent, and of a temperate sky. It is situate between Cochin and Cananor, at nine and a half degrees from the equinoctial, towards the Arctic Pole. The principal town, which is on the sea-coast, bears the name of the kingdom. The country is flat and without mountains, fertile in all the necessaries of life, such as fruits, grain, beasts, and pasture, save that for the bulk of the inhabitants rice has to be procured elsewhere, that grown in the country not being sufficient[4]: they take no other

[1] Before the Portuguese time the greatest Malabar prince was undoubtedly the Samorin. The Raja of Cochin, supported by the Portuguese, throve so much in trade, that Linschoten, only a few years before this time, considered him the greatest king of the coast. But Linschoten did not know much of Calicut, and in Pyrard's time the Samorin had the scale again turned in his favour by the waning of the Portuguese power and the organised system of piracy of which he was patron. The Samorins, however, never regained their earlier supremacy; and, a few years later, the Padre Vincenzo Maria accounts the Raja of Cananor the first, the Raja of Travancore the second, and the Samorin only the third in importance, of the Malabar princes.

[2] So called from the Portuguese *Coulão:* we call it *Quilon*. Its native name is *Kollam*. This very ancient port of Travancore was known to the Arabs as *Kaulam;* it is the *Columbum* of which Friar Jordanus was appointed bishop. It is mentioned in the Chinese annals as *Kiu-lan*.

[3] This expedition of the Portuguese is referred to in the king's letter of 17th February 1611 (see *Liv. das Monç.*, ii, 36), where it seems Quilon was then under a queen. Pyrard did not visit the place.

[4] This is true of the present day. Malabar pays for its rice by exporting coffee, ginger, coco-nuts, areca-nuts, and other palm-produce.

merchandise from their neighbours. There is abundance of pepper, which is the principal source of the country's wealth; of gems, which are very plentiful there; and of cotton, whereof they make a very fine white cloth,[1] and divers kinds of painted and patterned tapestry.

CHAPTER XXVII.

More of Calecut.—Classes of the people: Bramenis, Nairs, Moucois, and others, and characteristics of the country.

The kingdom of Calecut, like all the rest of the Malabar country, is inhabited by two sorts of people, foreigners and natives. The foreigners are those properly called *Mahometan Malabars,* who long ago came from elsewhere to inhabit this country, but only the sea-coasts. The natives are Gentiles and pagans, of the same religion as those of the greater part of Southern India.

They are divided into three ranks of life, Bramenis,[2] Nairs, and the common people. Among the Malabar Nairs, as among the Canarins of Goa, there are some Bramenis, but all are fundamentally of but one and the same faith,—that is, they are idolaters.

The Bramenis are of the most noble race, honoured and respected of all others; they have their peculiar habits of life, and practise a more religious and austere observance of their faith; for besides living scrupulously according to their religion, they have this peculiarity, that they never eat

[1] Whence our word *calico*, as to which, see Yule, *Gloss.*, s. v.

[2] Pyrard writes the sing. *Brameny* and the plur. *Bramenis.* The Port. wrote *Bramenes*, and the earlier English, *Brachmanes.* All the European forms seem to have come through the Greek Βραχμᾶνες, from the Sansk. *Brahmana.* The Brahmans of Malabar are called *Nambûtiris*, *i.e.*, trusted persons.

flesh or fish, or anything that has had life, or drink aught but water, and they preserve this austerity from father to son for all generations, never mingling or allying themselves with other people. They preserve an inviolable rule that the daughters of Bramenis never marry but with Bramenis, and the same with the men, who also may never marry a second time. Their habit is a frock of cotton cloth, with a white turban on the head, and red slippers on the feet. This frock or cassock, which they call *Libasse*[1] or *Cabaye*,[2] is of very white cotton, reaching to the heels; under it is a large white cloth hanging down to the mid thigh, which they fold twice or thrice, and pass between the legs in front and then fasten behind at the waist. Round the waist they wear a pretty scarf of fine white cloth, like that of the turban. Over the shoulders they are wont to carry a piece of white or coloured cloth, of silk or cotton, in the style we wear our mantles. All wear their hair long, and all the Bramenis, Banians, and Canarins wear pendants in their ears.

The only mark distinguishing them from other people is a cord of three strands of cotton, which they wear next the skin. It is a kind of order given to them at their temples, with great display and solemnity; and one could not do a Brameny a greater injury than to break his cord: in that

[1] The Ar. *libās* means a garment in general. Lane (*Mod. Egypt.*) uses the same word for "drawers". The author probably brought the term from the Maldives, where, as Mr. Bell now informs us, the word is applied to the loose-fitting over-chemise worn by the women there, and described above, pp. 166-7.

[2] French form of the Port. *cabáya*, itself taken from the Ar. *ḳabá*, a vesture. Col. Yule suggests that the word was taken to India by the Portuguese. But the following passages from Correa and the Albuquerque *Comm.* rather point to its prior existence in Eastern parlance, and to its being previously unknown to the Portuguese. "Cabaya is a garment such as a pelote is with us" (Correa, in Stanley's *Three Voyages*, p. 132); "Cabayas, or native dresses of silk" (Alb., *Comm.*, iv, 95). *Kabáya* is still a common word in Ceylon for a coat or jacket, worn by a European or native.

case he would have to get another with like ceremony, otherwise he would no longer be a Brameny. So also if one is punished, he is first degraded and his cord removed; likewise, if he intermits any of his ceremonies he is deprived of it, and is then no longer of this order. They are of divers professions, according as they are inclined: some serve in arms with the Nairs, performing the same duties and wearing the same dress as the latter, except that they maintain always their rules of living and abstinence from flesh, and are always distinguished by the said cord. The rest are either priests and sacrificers to their idols (for it is from this race alone these may be taken), or else they live as they will, as merchants, of which class there is a great and very wealthy body, both in this kingdom and in the rest of India. They are an industrious people, learned in astrology and other sciences, of great experience in all matters, and exceedingly adroit, besides being soft and pacific in temper, and men who keep inviolate their faith and word.

In short, they are held in the same honour and repute as here the clergy, philosophers, and doctors. Some of them in Goa practise medicine and the apothecary's art, after the mode of the Portuguese and of Europe. They are of all other vocations too, and the highest honour that a gentleman could desire would be to be of this race. They excel both in learning and wit, and are very judicious in all things. The king of Calecut himself is a Brameny, and wears the cord. When they go about the town with their *Cabaye*, or white cotton garment, and meet some stranger, they at once tell who they are and their race, in order to be acknowledged for what they are (for their cord, being worn next the skin, is not seen). Among all the Christian Indians[1] they rank next after the Portuguese and the Indian Metifs. Moreover, Metifs whose mothers are of a lower caste are not

[1] *Sic.* He probably means the Indians who inhabit the Portuguese territories.

esteemed equal to those born of a Brameny mother, for these latter hold their heads as high as the Portuguese themselves. When a Brameny would swear, he puts his hand on his cord, and then he must be believed. However poor they may be they maintain their rank and rules of life, and other folk in passing salute them by bowing the head as a mark of respect. Kings put their entire trust in them, and always keep some of the chiefest of them about their persons, both for religious purposes and as counsellors, and follow their advice in all things. They are not all equal, but there is one greater than all the rest.[1]

I have heard it said that the cause of the expelling of the Portuguese and the ruin of their towns and fortresses was this, that they had spoken slander of the Bramenis and their law, and that the Bramenis had complained to the king, and had demanded vengeance for it, exclaiming that if he drove not out that race, he and his house would come to a miserable end. Whereupon the king bade sound the bell and assemble his council, whereat it was resolved to drive them forth; and the king gave out that for as many stones as were brought to him from their fortress, he would give so many pieces of gold. So in but a short time this fortress was razed, and the garrison pillaged of most of their property. The Portuguese have had two fortresses[2] there, one after the other; both are in ruins and the garrisons expelled, and now they have none.

1 This account of the Brahmans is coloured by the author's knowledge of Brahmans elsewhere. The *Nambûtiris* of Malabar do not engage in trade, nor do they carry arms.

2 The fortresses at Calicut and Châliyam are probably meant. The former was built in 1513 (Barros, *Dec. II*, liv. VIII, cap. vi), and destroyed by order of D. Henrique de Menezes in 1525 (*ib.*, liv. IX, cap. x). The latter was built in 1531 (*Dec. IV*, liv. IV, cap. xviii), and taken by the Samorin, 4th November 1571 (Couto, *Dec. IX*, cap. ii). This was the first fortress lost by the Portuguese in India. As Châliyam was not in Calicut proper, the author may have had in his mind the fortress begun to be built at Ponani, 21st December 1585 (*Dec. X*, liv. VII, cap. v), but never finished; or that at Kollam, *c. s.*, p. 360.

It would seem that the king of Calecut has done well to drive them out, for they would have done to him even as they have done at Cochin and other places. They come in under colour of friendship and suavity towards the kings, and then by their encroachments endeavour to subdue them. He of Calecut had given them free admittance, but when he saw that they took more than he gave, he took prompt measures ere they made their position stronger. The king of Cochin, not having been so well advised, now has to receive at their hands a thousand insults, in such wise that when the viceroy of Goa went to the succour of Malaca, as I shall relate hereafter, and passed by Goa, the king sent him a number of almadies, or boats, laden with provisions, fruits, and other refreshments; but the viceroy, by name *Don Martin Alphonse*,[1] would not so much as look at or receive them, and had them all cast into the sea, bidding tell the king with proud words that on his return from Sunda he would visit him to his cost. This was because the king had been unwilling to deliver up something that he had demanded; but he was happily prevented from seeing him again on his return, for the viceroy died at Malaca.

Another time, when the Hollanders were before the harbour of Cochin, the Portuguese would not allow the king to enter their town. This shows the pride of these fellows, and with what insolence they scold any that give them the smallest occasion. But the king of Calecut, having been more prudent, now laughs at the other kings, who thus find themselves under the curb of the Portuguese.

But to return to the Bramenis, who were the cause of the expelling of the Portuguese: those who reside among the Banians and Canarins are all the same. As for the Canarins,[2]

[1] Dom Martim Affonso de Castro, eighteenth viceroy, assumed office January 1605, and died at Malacca, 3rd June 1607.

[2] The Portuguese form, so written by Garcia de Orta, though Barros writes *Canarijs*. The name was applied to the natives of the coast and

they differ not at all in their dress, but the Banians wear red slippers, much pointed in front, the point being raised somewhat high, with a knob of the same leather. The Canarins of Goa and the neighbourhood wear *Alparcas*,[1] which are a kind of sandals with several leather soles, and a number of little leather straps above, which pass between the toes and over the foot, and so hold it. These straps are of gilt leather, with little gilded buckles and fastenings.

These white dresses worn by the Indians of Goa are not at all convenient, because the soil of Goa is red, like bolarmeny,[2] insomuch that, whether in summer or winter, the dust or mud stains and soils all their garments. They change them, however, every day, and sometimes oftener. The greatest of these Bramenis and other Gentiles have always many men with them; one carries the parasol, another a silver box full of betel, a third, a silver flagon of water for washing. After obeying the calls of nature they wash the private parts; they also carry some water in their palan-

interior north of Malabar, as far as and including Goa district, *i.e.*, all that is now comprised in the Konkan (Bom. Pres.) and South Kanara (Madras Pres.). But, as Dr. Hunter says, the very name is a misnomer, for but a small part of the population of this region are Kanarese. If applied to the Kanarese people and language, it should be used of Mysore and other districts above the western ghâts. The other form of the name, *Karnatic*, has, "by one of the strange processes of history", come to be applied to the Tamil country on the other side of the peninsula, below the eastern ghâts (*Imp. Gaz. of India;* and see Yule, *Gloss.*, s. vv. *Canara* and *Carnatic*, and in Supplement, *Canarin*).

[1] *Alparca*, "hempen shoe", contraction of *alpargata*, from Ar. *pargat*, "sandals"; Vieira, *Dict.*, s. v. Ces. Federici calls them *alperche* (Hak., ii, pt. II, 222). Linschoten (Hak. Soc., i, 257) says that the Canaras and Decanins differ from the Guzeratis and Banians in their shoes, "which they wear like antiques with cut toes, and fastned above upon their naked feete, which they call *alparcas*." Mandelslo (p. 93) says that the Deccanis dress like the other Banians, "save that their shoes, which they call *alparcas*, are of wood, tyed up over the instep with straps of leather."

[2] *I.e.*, "Armenian bole", or *terra sigillata* (Cotgrave). Vincent le Blanc describes it in like terms (i, 77).

quins—that is, the rich. None of them eat ere they have washed and bathed: and then they use simply a cloth to cover their private parts, leaving off the rest of their clothes while they eat. Their food must be prepared by those of their own race, or even by themselves, no matter how great folks they be: for after food is touched, whether cooked or during the cooking, none durst touch the man who has or carries it; if they had to die, they would not eat anything that had been touched by a man or woman who was not of their race and faith. But the other Gentiles may well eat that which has been touched and prepared by the Bramenis, yet in no case do superiors prepare food for those who are beneath them.

All their women have the nose pierced, and wear therein trinkets of gold, silver, and jewels. They also wear rings of gold and silver on their toes, and in their ears large round plates of the same, as large as little saucers, with many gems set round the edge and in the middle. All these are worn by the wives of Bramenis, Banians, and Canarins, not by those of the Nairs, nor of the Moucois or other Malabars. They wear also bracelets, called *Manile*,[1] from the hand up to the elbow: of these, some are of gold and silver, others of glass or of tortoise-shell, which is much prized, and is worked up with all colours and in all patterns. All the fingers are also covered with trinkets and rings.

All these Gentiles abstain from the flesh of the cow, just as the Mahometans from pork; and they are so bound to this superstition, that most of them, when they become Christians, enter into a bargain that they shall not be compelled to eat it. Nor do they ever eat the flesh of oxen, bulls, or buffaloes. They dislike also to quit their own style of dress, and this

[1] *I.e.*, Port. *manilhas*, "bracelets". Pyrard seems to have taken it to be a native word. It occurs in Sir Thos. Herbert (edit. 1677, p. 114), "manilios and armolets of silver", and in Alex. Hamilton (*New Acc.*, i, 303) as "*manila*, or wrist jewel".

they are allowed to keep, along with many other superstitions; which leads to the belief that they are not by any means good Christians—and the fact is, most of them become Christians of necessity. The Mahometans of Cambaye, Surratte, and Guzerate, countries of the great Mogor, and the Banian Gentiles, have amongst them no superior or inferior race, though they have classes of various qualities and means, according to which they win respect and honour: and except the Nairs, all these Gentiles are artizans and merchants, and not men of war. The first thing they meet when they go out of their houses, whether birds or quadrupeds, they honour and worship the whole day, and ask of their priests and sorcerers, in whom they put their trust, what they have to tell of these things.[1]

The *Ioguies* are hermits that wander about the country, and are treated much as the religious orders in these parts. One sees also a large number of charlatans and sorcerers, who charm serpents, so that they can do no harm: some of these one sees of 22 or 23 feet in length. These Gentiles drink only out of copper pots, except the great, who use gold and silver gilt; and it is to be remarked that they never touch the vessel with their mouths while they drink, but only pour the water into their mouths from above. The Portuguese themselves have adopted this custom, as also that of never eating with spoons, and numberless other fashions, from the Indians, who never change theirs.

They marry very young, most often at seven and eight years of age, both men and women. The Gentile women, who burn themselves after the death of their husbands, first take off all their trinkets, and give them to whom they will. As for widowers, they make no other sort of mourning for

[1] This is a notion commonly entertained at this period of the Hindu religions; see *Linschoten*, i, 248. It arose from the practice of the natives drawing their omens from what they first saw in the morning or on commencing a journey, etc.

the death of their wives, except that they cannot marry again.

When they fast, which is but seldom, they go for a day, or at most two, without eating or drinking more than they are obliged. They believe that after death their souls pass into the bodies of cows, buffaloes, or bulls, and that when the cow or bull dies, they take to other bodies; and I believe that to be the reason why they will not eat the flesh of these, viz., on account of their notion of the passage of souls from one body to another. They have received this from the ancient tradition of the Brachmanes and Indian Gymnosophists, who were instructed in the doctrine of Pythagoras, for he was the first author of this Metempsychosis.[1] They have places of retreat for wandering beasts, and are mindful to give food and drink to birds and all other animals. They would not for anything in the world willingly permit the slaughter of any animal, and would sooner redeem it with money. But the Nairs eat of everything, except of the cow, bull, and buffalo, and use swine's flesh freely. All these Gentiles are badly off when they go a sea voyage, or get into gaol, or among a crowd of strangers: then most of them put up with dried and preserved fruits, or with a kind of rice, half cooked and then dried, which keeps two or three years. It is greatly used for provisioning all the Indian vessels, and serves them as biscuit does us; they eat it in handfuls, as the Brazilians do the *Mandoc*[2] flour, though it has a better taste than that. They eat it usually with sugar, dates, and other native fruits: they call it *Aualu*.[3]

The wives of these Bramenis, Banians, and Canarins of

[1] This is evidently not Pyrard. One cannot think that he of his own learning knew much of Pythagoras and metempsychosis; the spelling *Brachmanes*, too, differs from his usual *Bramenis*.

[2] See vol. ii.

[3] Mal. *avil*, Tam. *aval*, "unhusked rice steeped in water and then dried and bruised" (Winslow, *Tam. Dict.*). De Couto (*Dec. VII*, liv. x, cap. xi) writes *avéla*. Rivara says it is now vulgarly known as *fôvo*.

Goa and Guzerate are very pretty and of good figure, and some are as fair as the Portuguese. The men commonly wear the beard broad, rounded and thick, and shave it under the chin; others use another style,—that is, the Turkish. All the Indian ladies—that is, the rich—wear a massive collar of gold, set with precious stones, of two or three fingers' width. All the men, Gentiles as well as Mahometans, anoint the body and smear it with sandal and other odoriferous drugs; while the Gentiles, at the entrances to their pagodes, in lieu of holy water, present to those who enter pounded ashes of burned corpses, among them considered a very sacred thing.

As for the Nairs, they are all nobles,[1] and meddle with neither handicraft nor trade, nor any other exercise but that of arms, which they always carry: and in these they do exercise themselves continually from the time they can wield them, and when out of their houses are never without them. They are all lords of the country, and live upon their revenues, and upon the pensions which the king gives them. They are the most handsome men, of the best figure and proportion I have ever seen. In complexion they are tawny, in height slim and tall; the best soldiers in the world; hardy and courageous, exceedingly adroit in the use of arms, with such dexterous suppleness of limb that they can bend in all possible postures, and can parry and avoid with subtlety all blows aimed at them, and at the same time make lunges at their antagonists. Yet they never go to sea, and are of competency only on land. The greatest lords amongst them, and the most honoured, are those who keep schools for teach-

[1] They are of the *Sudra* caste, but are on the footing of the *Kshatriya*. Their functions in the State organisation are pithily described in the Kêralalpatti as *kaṇ*, *kei*, *kalpana*, "the eye" (they were the overseers, or supervisors), "the hand" (emblem of power), and "the order" (the givers and carriers of orders)—"so as to prevent the rights" of all classes "from being curtailed or suffered to fall into disuse."

ing the use of arms[1]: for they do greatly honour and revere their masters in arms; and none durst undertake this mastership without the express permission of the king,—as, in fact, is the case throughout all the East Indies, as well among the Mahometans as among the Gentiles. These masters are distinguished from the rest by wearing on the right-arm a thick gold ring[2]; the great lords, too, wear the same, but of a different pattern; the rest, who are soldiers of the middle class, wear one of buffalo or bull horn. The Nairs go quite naked, and march abroad so, covered only from the waist down with a large cloth of fine silk or cotton, very white, which reaches to the knees, and is then passed between the thighs; the feet are bare, and so is the head, only they let their hair grow without ever cutting it, and this distinguishes them from the vulgar herd. They wear the hair long without cutting it, and tie it neatly on the head, carefully arranged in a bunch, and they are careful to dress and wash the head every day. Those of the Brameny race are habited the same, only they wear their cord, which serves to distinguish them. They carry always a shield on one hand and a sword in the other, or else a javelin, or muskets, matchlocks, or pikes. Their women are dressed in the same style, without other accessories, saving the arms: insomuch that it is impossible to distinguish a boy from a girl, unless she is of age, and the breasts are seen.

When the girls are grown, there is another thing by which you discern them from the boys, and that is the rich ornaments they wear of gold and precious stones: for their necks

[1] These masters were on the Malabar coast called *Paṇikar* (see Yule, *Gloss.*, s. v.).

[2] "The principallest or chiefest of those Nayros, which are leaders or Captaines of certaine numbers of Nayros, weare a Gold or Silver bracelet, or ring about their armes, above their elbowes: as also their Governours, Ambassadours, and Kings, whereby they are knowne from other men, for otherwise they goe all naked" (*Linsch.*, Hak. Soc., i, 283). As to the use of these official rings at the Maldives, see above, p. 189.

are laden with necklets, carkanets, and chains of gold, pearls, and stones: their large ears are the same, a fourth part of the ear drooping on each side. Then they have bracelets and heavy rings up to the elbow, and on the fingers, both hands and feet being all covered with jewels, and thick rings on the legs, everything being of gold or silver gilt. Be it noticed that I have never seen plain silver used for ornament by the Nairs or their women, so it is a wondrous sight to see the ladies of quality so richly adorned and dressed, each according to her means.

The ordinary residence of these Nairs is not in the towns but in the country, except that by day they assemble in large numbers to attend upon the king, wherever he may be, even in the towns of the Mahometan Malabars, as I have already said. They employ themselves in the hunting of tigers, which are exceeding savage beasts, very plentiful in that country. I have seen some that without aid did attack and kill tigers, and among others, one which dragged the body of a tiger before the presence of the king, his own face and ears being sorely torn. Very frequently, and upon any pretext, they will draw upon each other with naked swords and shields. Many of them, besides the exercise and ordinary profession of arms, are given to the sciences. I have known many of them very learned in mathematics, but chiefly in astrology.

Although all are educated to arms, and are exceedingly valiant and resolute, and take no thought for their lives, yet are they most gentle and humane in their conversation, most courteous and cultivated, according to their notions. Such was my experience while I was among them, and mixed with them familiarly, and had most of them for my friends. Yet there are in the country districts some soldiers that are highwaymen and robbers, who attack passers-by and kill them without mercy, if they be not on their guard. But all strangers, and even the Mahometan Malabars who live among them, are wont to take a Nair escort, as I have said, when they journey even to the next town, giving him a piece of money, and changing their guard at every town. By this means one can travel securely throughout the whole Malabar country without coming to any harm, passing amid thousands of Nairs; and this may be done by the most feeble old man or the youngest boy among them.

They have similar ceremonies and superstitions to those of the Bramenis (and even among these are the Bramenis the most respected), save that their manner of life is less austere. They are allowed to eat anything; but they must use frequent ablutions, and must not associate, eat, or drink with any but of their race. To the same intent, they never marry or eat with such as are not of their faith, nor use anything that belongs to them, or that they have touched: it must first be washed, if it is a thing that can be washed, otherwise they go and wash themselves after using it; if they did not, they would consider themselves polluted. Only with the Bramenis do they live without difference or ceremony, as the Bramenis with them; yet do these not ally themselves in marriage, but a Nair with a Nair. Should it happen that a Nair woman kept company with any but a Nair man, they would kill her soon enough: so, if Nair men were to go with other women, they would be punished with death. This rule is observed inviolably, in order to preserve their race from pollution with strangers or the villain stock, towards whom they bear themselves in such sort that these will not dare to approach them: and, in fact, when the Nairs go about the town and come across the villains, they cry, *Popo*,[1]

[1] Malayâlam *Po! Po!* "Go! Go!" "For as the Nayros go on the streetes, and they (the common people) heare them call, they step aside, bowing their armes and stooping with their heades down to the ground, not daring so much as once looke up before the Nayros be past" (*Linsch.*, Hak. Soc., i, 284). So Mandelslo, later:—"They (Nairs) always go with sword and buckler, wherewith they make a noise in the streets as they go, and perpetually cry out *Po*, *Po*, that people should make way

—that is, that they should get out of the way; otherwise, if they should chance to touch them, they would resent it, and would strike them.

All the Nairs like to have their ears large, which they acquire by an artifice; for they pierce the lobes of their children's ears, as well males as females, and stuff the hole with little rolls of palm-leaves: this causes them to dilate, and from time to time they insert larger rolls to make them dilate the more, until they will extend no further. They esteem it a great beauty to have their ears thus large, and then they load them with gold and precious stones for ornament, and to bear them down. Amông others, I have seen the queen of Calecut, and many other ladies and lords, who had them so extended as to reach to the breast and further.

The Nairs may have but one wife at the time; but it is not so with the women: for every woman may have as many as three husbands at once if she likes (but a Nair woman of the Brameny race may have one only), and all contribute to support and maintain the wife and children, without any quarrel or jealousy on this score. And when one of the men is in the house with the wife, which is allowed only for a day and a night at a time, when she has other husbands, he leaves his arms or some other signal at the door, and the others will not dare to enter until he be gone forth.[1] The advantage they derive from this custom is, that one who hath not means himself to maintain a wife, may have a third part

for them" (p. 109). Varthema's account is the converse; he says that the common folk "always go crying out with a loud voice, and this they do in order that they may not meet the Naeri or the Brahmins"; for if a Nair should, for want of this precaution, come across a low-caste man, he might instantly kill him (*Varthema*, Hak. Soc., p. 142; and so *Barbosa*, Hak. Soc., p. 143; *Thevenot*, Eng. trans., iii, 89).

[1] The signal at the door is deposed to by most of the witnesses (*Linsch.*, Hak. Soc., i, 280; Conti, in *India in XV Cent.*, ii, 20; cf. Abd-er-Razzak, *ib.*, i, 17; *Barbosa*, Hak. Soc., p. 126).

of one, and the cost of her maintenance is only in this proportion. Nevertheless, for this cause is there an uncertainty of blood, and whose the children are cannot be truly known; wherefore fathers are not succeeded by their children, but by their nephews, the sons of their sisters, this being a more certain line. Their uprightness of conversation between men and women is most admirable; for although girls and boys live together, these as naked as those, yet there will never escape them a lascivious word or glance, nor any indecent act. They hardly ever laugh, regarding laughter as a great incivility and indiscretion, never to be indulged in without good reason, and then they observe in whose presence they are.[1] For the rest, they are by no means depraved; sodomy and incest are never heard of.

The true and original Malabars may be considered to be the Nairs, for, as I have said, they are the lords of the country, and the nobles are they who keep schools of arms, whither all the other Malabars go to be taught: and [? but] when one speaks of the Malabars without saying more, one means the Mahometans of this coast. The Malabars keep up great state in their towns, and consider themselves all nobles and men of honour, none of whom would do any toilsome or vile thing: all such work they make the *Moucois* and other villains do for them for hire. All their time is taken up with soldiering, and they all know the use of arms, as well merchants as pirates and the rest; for after going through this training they become merchants or corsairs, esteeming the one profession as good as the other, without any distinction. As for the artizans, they are all Gentiles, either native born or strangers. A Malabar, of whatever quality, never goes abroad through the streets without carrying arms like the Nairs. Their

[1] When simple natives are in the presence of a European official, and cannot restrain their laughter, they hide the face with their hands. Mr. Hartshorne goes so far as to say that the Veddas of Ceylon *never laugh* (*Fort. Rev.*, vol. xix, p. 410); but I am aware that this is doubted.

name and quality are according to their estate and profession, besides which they have honours peculiar to their race. They only marry with the poorer women of their own calling. Of the Nairs, those who stand about the town gates to escort travellers are the poorest of them, and they love to do this rather than any handicraft or other unworthy work. This condition is in no wise disgraceful to them. They would not be permitted to do aught in derogation of their nobility, and, indeed, would rather suffer every kind of hardship. The attire of the Nairs is fair white cloth, over which they wear round the waist a large scarf of red tafetas, with a fringe half a foot wide, half gold and half silk, of the same colour.

The third class of the inhabitants of Calecut and Malabar are the common people, who throughout all these countries are much despised, vile and abject beings, just like slaves. They are called *Moucois* or *Poulia.*[1] They have a quarter to themselves without the towns, next to the sea, and in other remoter places. They are of divers conditions; some live on the sea coast, and durst not venture to reside inland; these are properly called *Moucois.* They are all fishers or makers of salt, and on all the Malabar coast none others are employed as oarsmen and seamen, for which service they are hired. Their wives and daughters do all kinds of service on land, taking all sorts of work, and even carrying burdens, like the porters here. They scruple not to yield themselves for hire to any men whatever, no matter of what birth, race, or religion, having nothing to fear from their husbands, who durst not say a word, and meekly suffer it. And there are none other concubines or public girls but the wives and daughters of these *Moucois* and *Tiua,*[2] or artizan class; for the other

[1] These are by no means identical, as Pyrard (*infra*) seems to be aware. *The Mukkuvar* are the fisher caste, and are higher than the *Pulayar*, who are predial slaves (*pula* = pollution). See *Varthema*, Hak. Soc., p. 142; *Linsch.*, Hak. Soc., i, 279, and Dr. Burnell's note there.

[2] *Tiyar* or *Tivar.* These are, properly speaking, and as Pyrard pre-

women abandon themselves only to those of their own caste. The Moucois women lack not beauty, and some are fairer than the other women; their mothers prostitute them for money at the earliest age they can. The fairest and youngest of them may be enjoyed for seven or eight *tarans*,—that is, equal to two sols; and the mothers are not bashful in coming and offering them. This is a commoner practice there than anywhere in the world. All the Moucois, as well men as women, have much trouble in going about the streets when they meet the Nairs in any narrow passage, for they are constrained sometimes to wait a long while till they have passed, even when they are carrying a load.

In the country there are others of like condition, but of different offices and professions. One class they call *Tiua*, who gather the produce of the coco-tree; others are artizans; others, who till the soil, are called *Coulombin*,[1] and yet these are all of the same caste, who marry one with another, albeit there are certain grades and distinctions among them. Thus, the tillers of the soil are the most honourable, next the artizans, then the *Tiua*, and the last, the most vile and abject, are the *Moucois* fishers.[2] All these common people are attired in the same fashion; that is, they are naked, except for a little cord girdle, whereto is hung a bit of cloth, or a leaf, or a

sently indicates, toddy drawers, and are said to have come from Ceylon, hence their name *Tivar* = islanders (*Linsch.*, Hak. Soc., i, 279, *note*).

[1] Probably the *Kurumbar*, an extensive low-caste tribe of the ghâts, though Mr. Logan thinks he cannot have seen any of these so near the coast, and that he may mean the *Kollanmâr* (blacksmiths or artizans). The *Kurumbar* are referred to by P. Vincenzo as *corombini*, a middle form, which leaves little doubt as to the identity of Pyrard's *coulombin*.

[2] The castes below the Nâyars are thus classified by Dr. Burnell: (i) *Tîvar;* (ii) *Mukkuvar;* (iii) *Pulayar*, or, as in Malabar proper, *Cherumar*, who are "the ruling tribe of the fourteen castes of jungle-dwellers" (Gundert, *s. v.*). But, as Mr. Logan points out, there are other well-distinguished castes; *e.g.*, between the Nâyars and Tîvar come the professional schoolmasters and astrologers, and below the Tîvar, the basket-makers, etc.

piece of bark, to cover their shame; the women use a cloth round the waist, reaching to the knees, and wear the hair long. The men durst not wear long hair, like the Nairs, so they cut it all round the head, except that they leave on the crown a thick bunch of a hand's length; they durst not shave it altogether, for that is their mark of distinction.

Also they may not have their ears long, like the Nairs, but only three fingers' length at most. Both men and women have them bored and opened, but the pendants they wear are only of silver or copper or other material, and not of gold, like the Nairs. The king appoints certain of their chiefs and headmen to rule over them, and these, with their wives and children, have permission to wear gold and jewels; but there is always a difference in the weight and size between theirs and those of the Bramenis and Nairs. Thus are they distinguished from the Nairs: in form and colour they are less comely, being blacker and of lower stature, and ill-proportioned; they would not dare approach or touch the others,[1] nor enter their houses, as already mentioned; they have even their own separate temples. For the Nairs employ them solely to do their hard work; while in their houses they employ only Nairs and gentlemen of their own class who happen to be very poor.

These Moucois fishers catch a large quantity of a sort of little fish which is no longer than the hand, and as broad as a little bream; the Portuguese call it *pesche cauallo*,[2] and it

[1] That is, the Brahmans and Nâyars.

[2] The *cavalla*, or *cavala*, a name given by the Portuguese to perhaps more than one species of fish of the size of sardines. Bluteau describes it "peixe do mar: he quasi sarda grande assim como sarda parece Cavalla pequena." It is mentioned by several travellers on the Malabar coast. P. Vincenzo says: "A kind of sardines, which they salt and dry in the sun; the largest are thrown away as noxious, wherefore all the beach of Malabar is often strewn with them. In some places they are so plentiful that waggons are laden with them. They serve for food to the dogs and crows. Frequently, too, they extract from them a thick black oil, called *sciffia*, for oiling their ships" (lib. I, cap. xxxiii). Phil. à S. Trin.,

is the most common fish on all that coast, wherefore there is very great traffic in it, the method being to cut it in half, salt it, and dry it in the sun. They fish also for another kind, which is not eaten fresh; they use only nets and lines, and most of their boats are of a single piece of wood, and are called by them *Tonny*,[1] and by the Portuguese *Almedies*.[2] The largest are made of many timbers: these they call *Thaury*. They are all of the same build, flat-bottomed, and speed well to the oars. Order was given by the king to catch a certain number of fish every day, which the chief of the Moucois was charged to supply to us free of cost.

There is one religion only, common to all the natives of Malabar, as well Bramenis and Nairs as the Poulia or Moucois. They are all Gentiles,[3] and worship the rising sun. In

writing of Goa, says, "There is another very small fish vulgarly called *cavalle*, which is good enough to the taste, but not very wholesome" (Fr. trans., p. 383). Fra Bart. writes of "the *ayla*, called in Portuguese *cavala*" (Eng. trans., p. 240). Sir T. Herbert writes *cavalloes* (p. 28). The fish above described may, perhaps, belong to the genus *Equula*, two species of which are named *E. caballa*, by different zoologists (see Yule, *Gloss.*, and *Suppt.*, s. v. *Cavally*; Day, *Fishes of India*). Pyrard, when he reaches St. Helena on his way home, mentions a little fish there under the same name. This fish, still called *cavalley*, is identified by Mr. Melliss with the *Caranx denter* (Bl. Schn.) (*St. Helena*, p. 106).

[1] Malayâlam and Tamil *tōṇi*, from Sansk. *drōni*, "a trough", hence a boat, or, as the Canadians would say, a "dug-out". In Anglo-Indian it becomes *doney*; *vide* Yule, *Gloss.*

[2] Port. *almadia*, from Ar. *Al ma'diyah*, properly a raft. "*Almadias*, whereof some are hewen out of a peece of wood, and so narrow that a man can hardly sit in them, etc." (*Linsch.*, Hak. Soc., i, 262). They would seem, however, to have been of considerable size, as Pietro della Valle says that they were similar in all respects to the *manchuas* of Goa, having as many as twenty to twenty-four oars, except that the latter had "a large covered room in the poop" (Della Valle, Eng. ed., p. 102).

[3] At this time, no doubt, the Mukkuvar were all or nearly all Hindus; but the social advantages of the Moslem religion, proceeding from its non-acknowledgment of caste, have tended to convert large bodies of the lower castes; and now the Mukkuvar are mostly Mahomedans (Burton, *Goa and the Blue Mountains*, p. 241). Such is one explanation; Mr. Logan gives another: "To keep up a supply of sailors for

their temples is an image of a cow or other figure, which they worship; they have the like respect to the same animal alive, insomuch that they would not think of killing it or eating the flesh. This rule is observed with great strictness, not only by the Bramenis, but also by the Nairs, who eat everything but that, and by the Moucois.

When by chance a Gentile becomes Christian, as happens frequently, if his wife will not become of the same faith, she must act in all respects as if her husband were dead, except that she does not burn herself alive: she only cuts her hair, separates herself from all society, and lives the rest of her days in solitude. These Gentile kings put not any restraint on liberty of conscience in their territories; for every day one sees at Calecut and other places a mixing of Christians and Moors or Mahometans, and these Mahometans rival each other in assisting those who are converted to their faith. If a Mahometan becomes Christian, and his wife cares not to do so, she is not obliged to perform the same ceremonies as the others: she can marry again three months afterwards, which is the prescribed interval.

They recognise that there is a God, but say that as he is good there is no need to pray to him or worship him, since he does no evil. The Bramenis, as I have said, observe more peculiar ceremonies than the Nairs; and the Nairs, like the Bramenis, have some customs of their own which they most religiously maintain (which is not the case with the Moucois or common folk), for they hold intercourse only with the Bramenis, and consider themselves polluted by intercourse with others. They take their food seated on the ground, and eat off Banana leaves, which serve them for plates, even though they have or could have others, and these are used but once. They never eat without first washing the whole

the pirate crafts, the Zamorin established a rule that a certain proportion of children born to Mukkuvar should become Muhammadans." The custom is still kept up.

body. They are so superstitious, as I have said, that when their servants bring them their food or drink, should it happen that one not of their faith did but touch the servant as he passed, he must cast all the food upon the ground, and so the dinner is lost. So, if such a one entered their house and touched their furniture, the walls, or the door, they would not eat in that house ere they had washed it and performed certain ceremonies. In short, they touch no one of another religion without being polluted; and they observe this rule in such wise, that if some of them were sitting together upon a bench or other seat, and a man of another religion came to sit by them, they would incontinently rise; and if he had seated himself before they were aware, they would go and wash the whole body: this I have often seen happen in my own case, when I have sat by them without thinking of it. Thus have I seen, if they would hand something—as, for instance, a stick or a sword—to one of another religion, they toss it into the hand of the other, so as not to touch him when he would put out his hand to receive it. I have observed, too, that the soldiers of the king's body-guard, who lie upon mats and *esteres*,[1] warned me in good time to take care not to step upon or touch with my feet these mats and *esteres*. If they give such a one to drink, they allow him not to touch the vessel, but make him open his mouth, and pour therein from a distance; they often treated me in this fashion. For all that, I took note that the Nairs make not so much ado, save that on being polluted they must take the trouble to go and wash themselves entirely, and so all the Nairs that live among the Mahometan Malabars, who associated with me, made no scruple to touch me, or to let me touch them, after they were once polluted and before they went to wash. They were wont to advise us, when they had just bathed, that we should not touch them, so as not to give them the trouble to go and

[1] Port. *esteira*, "rush-mat".

bathe again; but, after being polluted by the merest contact, they would make no more ado or ceremony about the matter.

Among the Nairs are some men and women that have the feet and legs as thick as the body of an ordinary man. There is nothing hurtful in this: it is born with them. Some have only one thus large, while others have both, and you see plenty of them with this infirmity; I have seen even the greatest lords have it. The thickness is more or less in different cases, and the leg is hard and coarse like a wart; nevertheless, they suffer no pain from it, and are ready for everything, and are good soldiers. It is inherited with their blood. I have seen others in the Indies besides the Nairs who had these thick legs, but nowhere so many.[1]

At their marriages they make much ceremony, with feasting and rejoicings. At the commencement, when matters are arranged, they proceed to the temple or pagode, where they go through some ceremonies before their parents, who are Bramenis; but what they are I cannot describe, as I was not allowed to enter. Next, for a space of fifteen days, the kindred and friends of the parties, both men and women, conduct the bride daily to the house of the bridegroom; there they pass the day in rejoicings. The women, in gay attire, sing and play upon divers instruments, such as little drums like tambourines, flutes and hautboys, and to this

[1] Elephantiasis, in India commonly called "Cochin leg", or "St. Thomas's leg", from its prevalence in the south of the peninsula, mediæval travellers seeing in it the hereditary punishment of the apostle's murderers. "Here are also those elephant-legged St. Thomeans", writes quaint old Dr. Fryer, who had heard the disease attributed to snake-bite, and also (more reasonably) to "drinking bad water (to which, as we to the air, they attribute all diseases), when they travel over the sands, and then lying down when they are hot till the earth at night is in a cold sweat, which penetrating the rarified cuticle, fixes the humours by intercepting their free concourse on that side, not to be remedied by any *panacea* of their *Esculapian Sectators*" (*New Account of East India*, p. 53). The ailment is common also in Ceylon (see Cordiner's *Ceylon*, i, 182; Davy's *Ceylon*, p. 485; Pridham's *Ceylon*, p. 690).

music they dance, while the men spend the time in looking on. To all present, even to strangers, are presented a portion of betel, and very sweet-smelling scents dissolved in water, to rub the body withal, and so to perfume it. The betrothed are always present there, seated on a higher place, and very richly attired and adorned. I have seen some so loaded with gold trinkets and precious stones that they could hardly carry them; and I believe that they had borrowed them, for I have seen many wearing as much as the value of 200,000 crowns—indeed, the worth was not to be estimated. The hall where these festivals are held is nicely hung and adorned with tapestries of silver and gold. There the table is spread twice a day for the whole assembly, and that at the expense of the bridegroom; in the evening the women conduct the bride back to her own house. At length, at the close of the fifteen days, the betrothed are magnificently dressed and mounted upon an elephant richly adorned with trappings, each upon a seat facing the other, and joining hands. With which ceremony the kinsmen and friends, surrounding them with great pomp, conduct them in procession through the whole town, to the sound of music, tarrying awhile only before the houses of the kinsfolk and friends. Then do some come out to receive them, presenting betel, fruits, flowers, and comfits in the native style, rubbing and sprinkling the elephant on which they are mounted with scents, such as sandal and other perfumed woods, and drugs dissolved in scented water, wherewith they bathe his head and trunk; nor durst they omit this, for otherwise the elephant would resent it. Then they proceed forward and do the same at the next halt. The kinsmen and friends consider it an insult if they be not visited in this fashion. So at length they descend at the Pagode, where they remain for awhile; thence to the house of the bride, where the marriage ceremony is concluded. There every one presents a coco-nut, which the Nair in charge of the elephants takes for himself, and everyone residing in every house where the elephant stops must give a coco-nut, besides all those who assist at the nuptials. For the rest, on all this coast they do commonly marry very young,—that is, about the age of nine or ten years.

As for funeral ceremonies, in the first place, all the Gentiles, the Bramenis, Nairs, and Moucois burn the body; and to this end assiduously collect during their lives scented woods and other materials, and expensive odorous drugs, to burn their own bodies after death. The ashes are divided among the kinsfolk, who preserve them in great honour, and mix some with water on their feast days, and smear their faces withal, as already said. On the death of a Brameny, his wife is bound to show in what affection she holds him, by burning herself alive, leaping into the fire which consumes the corpse of the deceased: this is done with great solemnity in presence of the relatives, and to the sound of music. I have seen the burning of five or six in this sort while I was at Calecut.[1] If they like not to be burned, they may avoid it, but then they are infamous; they have their hair cut, they no longer hold up their heads, and are driven from the society of ladies of honour, without being able to marry again. Yet do most of them prefer to undergo this infamy rather than to be burned. The wives of the Nairs are not required to do this, although 'tis said that one will sometimes cast herself upon the fire out of affection, and of her own free will. But they are not bound to do it, and are even free to marry again without dishonour, provided they are not of the Brameny caste. This rule does not obtain among the common people. I have never seen them to wear mourning for their relations, albeit, when the king dies, all the men of the kingdom shave their beards and hair entirely.

[1] As to the rite of suttee, or *satí*, which is here referred to, see Dr. Burnell's note to Linschoten, i, 247, and Yule, *Gloss.*, s. v. But Mr. Logan informs me that Pyrard is in error, if he means that those whom he saw at Calicut were *Nambûtiris* or Malayâli Brahmans. The custom does not obtain among these. The women must therefore have been from the Konkan, or elsewhere.

As for their sicknesses, they have no medicines or cures but sorcerers,[1] which are equipped like very devils, and come only by night to see the sick, with fire in their mouths, at the ears, feet, and hands, and are all covered with a false skin, and having upon them an endless number of bells that make a strange and horrible din. They also perform divers gestures, grimaces, and superstitious tricks, and make offers and promises to the devil, and all this in the presence of the sick person, who deems himself much relieved thereby. Likewise, when they desire to know the issue of anything, they have recourse to these sorcerers and soothsayers, who are in the pay of the king, the princes, and the lords, as well Gentile as Mahometan. While I was there, the king, having a great affair against the king of Cochin, as I afterwards came to know, wanted to consult one of his sorcerers about it, and made him appear before all the people. I saw a most hideous man appear, all covered with a false skin, the hair of his head so long as to touch the ground, tall man as he was: he had also bells at his neck, on his arms and legs, and round his waist, which did make a wondrous jingling din. He ran five or six paces forward, then as many back, and kept roaring unceasingly all the time he was before the king, who did not descend from his gallery to the place where the sorcerer and all the people were gathered. He spoke some words to the king, and I believed that he was a sorcerer, but everyone told me he was a devil. It was said that this sorcerer had come more than sixty leagues during the night without a halt; afterwards, when he was ready to depart, he was seen to run like lightning, and to enter their Pagode or

[1] The practices here described are those of the *shamans*, or devil-dancers, which reappear with curious identity in the most various regions (see Tylor, *Prim. Cult.*). The local reference is to the *Velichchapâdo*, "enlighteners", the oracles of the various temples, who fall into trances, and whose frenzied utterances are still to the present day accepted as divine commands.

temple, whither the people followed him: he was there a long time, making a great noise as with bells and kettles. This sorcerer made the most fearful cry I ever heard; he did many magic tricks, and had two swords in his hands which he brandished continually. These were of a different fashion from the ordinary swords, being more edged; with these he struck himself on the bare head, and fell on his belly upon the points of them, without injuring himself.

They all complain of the apparitions of demons, and the harm they suffer from them, as at the Maldives, and in all those parts where are the Gentiles and Mahometans, which things, I believe, happen to them for their not believing in the Christian faith, and so being still under the power of the demons. As for me (thanks be to God!), I experienced nothing of the kind, except that on the night of my arrival at Badara, having no place to retire to, I went and lay me down in a Mosque for the sake of company, and because these places are more commodious and fresh for sleep and repose, as well by day as by night; they are all well matted and carpeted, instead of being paved. While there, my spirit was so burdened with illusions, and I heard so many noises, that I could not rest. I also felt myself to be so oppressed that I could neither speak nor breathe. The noise which I heard all the night was as if one were rolling a number of balls all over the ceiling and wainscotting of the Mosque, and I thought every minute that it would give way and fall upon me. During the evening there had been a goodly number of strangers, travellers, and wayfarers resting there; but having some distance yet to travel, they took to the road at midnight in the cool, while the moon was shining bright. Thus had I been left alone, and it was then that fear seized me in good earnest. All I could do was to pray to God, and so remain for the night; for there was no visible way to escape, this temple being outside the town, and distant from the houses: it is one of the largest temples they have there. At length, at break of day, when I began to recover myself a little, behold, two or three *Moucois*, who set a crying and yelling like very devils, with voices that were frightful and fearsome indeed. They were at the summit of the Mosque, where I could not see them before, nor tell what was the cause. It is their custom to call the people, as I have already said in speaking of the Maldives; but day being now come, I went forth without saying a word to them. This is all I saw and heard in that country of their apparitions and devilries. For the rest, these Mosques, wherein wayfarers repose and obtain a common refuge, are those of the Mahometans only, and not of the Nairs. In these great temples they cook every day, at the king's expense, a great quantity of rice, and distribute it to the poor and to all comers, who receive it with great solemnity. They give this rice a violet colour, and the ceremony is part of the service of the pagode, and there is as much ado about taking this rice as about the consecrated bread with us. When they are in their Pagodes, which are very dark and obscure, there are numerous lamps burning, and a terrible din of tinkling prevails from the sound of the bells wherewith the sorcerers there are covered. These fellows make frequent leaps and grimaces, crying and yelling at the entrance of the door. Within the court is a great well for bathing, and within the Pagode at the door are some ashes of the dead, whereof they take a little and rub it upon their forehead and breasts, as we do the holy water. The Moucois have their Pagodes apart, which are of a horrible darkness; they enter them more rarely than the Nairs; in fact, they never go but once a month at the new moon (save also when they celebrate a marriage, which is done in their Pagode, with the festivities pertaining to it); they are always occupied at their work. As for the Nairs, besides their solemn festivals, which are very frequent, they never pass a day without going to the Pagode, each by himself, to say his prayers, short though they be. They have some of these Pagodes in certain places which they visit on certain days of the year, and they will come thither for their devotions from a distance of thirty or forty leagues. There are two or three annual festivals, principally that of New Year's Day, which is in the month of April, when all the Nairs, the courtiers, and their attendants come to visit and salute the king, while he from the window of a high gallery receives their salutations, and tosses to each a packet of betel, which he gives by way of largess, and some pieces of gold, to some more, to others less; and this is a present which they value extravagantly, as coming from the king's hand. He gives these presents not only to the Nairs, but also to all sorts and conditions, for he gave to us as well, and also to some Christian Indians, who were habited in the Portuguese fashion.[1]

For the rest, the kingdom of Calecut is a very powerful state, and of great extent: it is the state which has given the greatest trouble and caused most of their reverses to the Portuguese, ay, and does so daily still; that is by reason of the authority and puissance of the king, who is held in wondrous affection, being feared and obeyed by all his subjects and dreaded by all his neighbours. His country is thickly peopled; it has great and beautiful cities, whereof the chief is Calecut, which gives its name to the whole realm. The second is *Panany*,[2] which is inland; it is a great city, and a

[1] For a description of one of these festivals which the Samorin left the siege of Kunhâli to attend, see De Couto, *Dec. XII*, liv. IV, cap. iv. The feast in April is called *Vishu*. It is called the vernal equinox. The Malayâli year is too long, and the equinox has shifted in consequence.

[2] *Panane*, or *Ponani*, twenty-eight miles south of Calicut, and forty-eight miles north of Cochin. Barbosa says it was in his time "a city of the Moors amongst whom a few Gentiles live". "The Moors are very rich merchants, and own much shipping. The King of Calicut collects much revenue from this city" (*Barbosa*, Hak. Soc., p. 153). Although Pyrard says the river at Ponani was only navigable for boats, it would seem to have been fit to carry sea-going ships at an earlier period. Varthema talks of a fleet issuing from it (Hak. Soc., p. 275);

fortress on the frontier of the kingdom of Cochin, and has always an ample garrison. The king resides most part of his time at these two towns, and chiefly at *Panany*, because of the perpetual war that he wages with the king of Cochin, as also because it is the pleasantest residence in his country. But it is not a seaport; it has only a river navigable for boats, which falls into the sea twenty-five or thirty leagues off, and forms the boundary of the two kingdoms. Besides these there are a great number of other towns and villages throughout the country, whither the king betakes himself frequently when he goes to visit his domains, all of which are everywhere so peopled that they could not be more so, and the houses and closes are very near together, viz., about a gunshot apart. What causes the country to be so thickly peopled is its most excellent and temperate climate: the seasons are the same as at the Maldives. They have their crops—that is, they sow and reap—twice in the year; and all the year long there are fruits in great abundance, and of the most excellent quality in the world. Moreover, the country is very pleasant and agreeable, being watered by many fine rivers and streams, and everywhere by springs of the most excellent water. No country in all the Indies is better furnished with all commodities. The whole country is covered with fruit-trees, cocos, jack, mangos, bananas, pineapples, cajus, lemons, oranges, pomegranates, mirabolans, Indian pears (which do not resemble ours), and cotton-trees; plenty of melons and water-melons (*patêques*), which are a kind of pumpkins of prodigious size, eaten raw, like melons; ginger, peas, beans, and other good fruits, which anyone passing by

and in November 1506 the place was stormed by the Portuguese fleet under the Viceroy F. de Almeida (*Varthema*, p. 286; Stevens' *Faria y Souza*, i, 124-5). Under a treaty made with the Samorin in 1584, a Portuguese fort was begun to be built at Ponani in December 1585, but soon after abandoned (De Couto, *Dec. IX*, cap. ii; *Dec. X*, liv. VII, cap. v; *Linschoten*, Hak. Soc., ii, 169). It is a seaport, and not "inland", as Pyrard erroneously describes it.

may pluck and eat without any preventing him: all neighbours, too, use their fruits in common. But the greatest wealth of the country, and that which alone is exported, is pepper, which abounds marvellously there. A tax is paid on it to the king, besides which he buys it all, and despatches it in his own ships to the Straits of Mecca or the Arabian Gulf, the port of the Arabs, whence he receives in return many commodities, and principally gold: in a word, it is the principal wealth of the country. So, too, there is great store of precious stones of all sorts, excepting diamonds; but plenty of emeralds, rubies, sapphires, cat's-eyes, etc.; the remaining source of wealth is cotton cloth.

Among animals native to the country are elephants, which they domesticate when young, and employ in war, and in carrying and drawing burdens. All belong to the king, and no private person may possess one. If anyone hath need of one for any purpose, even to ride, he addresses the king's officer that hath the care of them, and on payment of a piece of money he receives one without difficulty, either for one day or for more, the hire being according to the time he is kept. There are a great number of tigers, which are very savage, and the most common occupation of the Nairs is to chase and slay them. You see, also, wild pigs, like our wild boars, roebucks, cows, buffaloes, goats, dogs like ours, and monkeys innumerable. There are quantities of parrakeets, wild pea-fowl, poultry, and very large pigeons. The serpents are of great size and very dangerous, but for all that none is so bold as to kill one, for that the king, the Bramenis, and the Nairs worship them with great superstition, believing them to be spirits of God, created to afflict man and to chastise him for his sins: some there are of 22 feet in length and more. All the country is also full of foxes,[1] that come by night even into the towns and enclosures of the houses, and course about like the dogs here, and all night one hears

[1] *I.e.*, jackals.

nothing but the noise of them in the gardens and ways. There are also quantities of monkeys, which do much harm, and are very big, insomuch that all the inhabitants, as well of the towns as of the country, are constrained to put trellises to all their windows to keep these creatures out; for they are exceedingly importunate and cunning, and the reason why they are so numerous is that it is not lawful to kill them: the king forbids it. The skin is of a greyish colour: it is a pastime to see them leap from tree to tree. One day, among others, while one of my companions and I were on our way from the town to the king's palace (except at some places there are houses and shops all the way between), we were met by three of these monkeys, the largest and most fearsome I ever saw. They stood on their hind feet, at ten or twelve paces from us, grinding their teeth as though they would do us some injury. We had neither rod nor stick, and there were no stones about, so that, owing to our ignorance at that time of the nature of these animals, we were in great straits; however, we showed no sign of fear, and pretended to take up stones to cast at them, whereupon they at once took to flight and leapt into the trees.

The town of Calecut is the court, and, as it were, a summary of the whole kingdom. I resided there much, and I can say that it is a very fair and great city, situate on the sea-shore, in extent from one end to the other more than a league and a half of beach, and along the whole of that distance between the town and the sea are only the houses of the Moucois, the fishermen, and other poor folks, who also have there their Pagode and temples. All the beach or strand is covered with *almedies*, or little fishing barques, and other vessels. The circuit of the town is more than five leagues, but what is called Calecut is, in fact, a large district covered with handsome, large, and magnificent buildings and spacious enclosures, in such wise that a single house requires a very large space for all its gardens, orchards, fish-ponds, and plantations. And all around are mansions of this sort only, full of people, as well Nairs, Malabars, and Mahometans, as all manner of foreigners, who are welcomed there. For it is not as in the other towns of the Malabars, which are only occupied by the Malabars: here you see all sorts of temples and Pagodes, large and well built, for all the several religions, of which I shall speak anon.

There are many public tanks, which are very large, well paved, and furnished with balustrades of stone work, and are well cleaned and maintained. Each religion has its own; and there is one such that is a quarter of a league in ambit of the square. These are very necessary, owing to the excessive heat of the climate. The walls of this town are not very strong: it is only enclosed with earth-works and low walls. The houses are not built in order or arranged in streets as in Europe, but are scattered about in confusion: but in one part of the town, that next to the sea, and near to the great magazine of the king called *Alfandeque*, there is a quarter of about a half league in circuit, which is built and arranged in streets, as in these parts. In that part of the town are only shops, of all manner of trades, artizans and merchants, which are necessary for the public weal. All this quarter has a barrier round about, although it is within the enclosure of the whole city. In these houses they keep only such furniture and utensils as are necessary.

Their markets, which they call *Bazar*, or little towns, are so full of people all the day long that it is difficult to pass them. These people are of all races, from the Cape of Good Hope to Japan. At nightfall everyone shuts his warehouse and shop securely with bars and heavy iron padlocks, and goes home with his family to his dwelling-house, which is as I have described, with its gardens and enclosures. The buildings of this *Bazar* are very large and well constructed of stone and wood, and supplied with shops, warehouses, and yards, all securely enclosed: these serve only to keep their merchandise and goods, or for the purposes of their crafts, and there they spend the day only. There are three large spaces in these enclosures, where the market is held every day of the week. This market is surrounded with gates and walls, and the gatekeepers let none pass the night in these warehouses containing the merchandise; and yet nothing is ever lost, so excellent is their judicature and police. In these enclosures remain only officers and gatekeepers, whose duty it is to keep watch and ward throughout the night. There is not a single temple there. The vessels which enter and anchor at Calecut, bringing all that merchandise, ride there with no great security, for there is no proper port or harbour, but only a roadstead, so that when the wind is from the sea they are in great peril. The land is low, and there is a little cape or promontory jutting out into the sea.

As for the fashion and form of the buildings of the country, it is to be noted that the common people build with earth, and thatch their houses with coco-leaves, but not with such care and skill as the Maldive people. Taking some earth, they mix it with water, and mould it into large squares, which they dry in the sun, and then use for their walls; but the rich and well-to-do build with good stone, and roof with tiles. All their buildings are square, like four arcaded pavilions with a court in the middle. Their carpentry and joinery is the handsomest and prettiest it is possible to see: it is worked of divers agreeable designs, as we do our finest side-boards and tables, and all painted. Their houses have stories, but not so many as ours. Some have two or three buildings of this style in the midst of others; that in the midst has a smaller court and arcade; the others are round about it in a square. They construct their houses and courts in this fashion, to avoid spilling or casting a drop of water or any dirt upon their floors, which are as clean as a table of highly polished wood.

All the houses of the Malabars are of this sort. They have large porches at the entrance to their houses, as well poor as rich, within the enclosure: for all their houses are enclosed with walls,—that is, those of the rich; the rest have ditches and good strong palisades of wood, and note that these are so high that when one wants to go from one house to another one must ascend a ladder of five or six steps, and so descend, while on both sides are wooden barriers which close with locks. You never see there any house but has its garden and orchard, small or large. These porches or *Auiards* in front of the houses are for receiving passing strangers, both for giving them meat and drink, and also a place to rest and sleep; they take them not inside their houses, so that they may depart during the night when they will, and whenever their boats, or if they be wayfarers, their fellow-travellers, are ready to depart.

But to return to what concerns this town of Calecut in general: it is the busiest and most full of all traffic and commerce in the whole of India; it has merchants from all parts of the world, and of all nations and religions, by reason of the liberty and security accorded to them there[1]: for the king permits the exercise of every kind of religion, and yet it is strictly forbidden to talk, dispute, or quarrel on that subject; so there never arises any contention on that score, every one living in great liberty of conscience under the favour and authority of the king, who holds that to be a cardinal maxim of government, with a view to making his

[1] One particular feature of the freedom enjoyed by the merchants at Calicut may be noticed. The law of wreck of the sea, by which a wrecked vessel and its cargo went to the king as a casualty, prevailed all over India, and at the Maldives, as Pyrard has frequently said. Similar law applied to vessels whose captains died at the islands. And in other parts of Malabar, in the old days, a vessel taking refuge in a port to which she was not bound, was liable to be plundered by the inhabitants. But according to Ibn Batuta (iv, 97) and Abd-er-Razzak (*India in XV Cent.*, i, 14), these barbarous prerogatives had no place in the law of Calicut.

kingdom very rich and of great intercourse. If by chance there should arise any difference or disturbance on that subject, he who began it would receive corporal punishment, as being guilty of treason, without hope of pardon or remission of sentence. This is why everyone lives there in great peace and concord, notwithstanding the great diversity of races and religions of the inhabitants, and of strangers and sojourners: for besides the native Gentiles and Mahometans, there are many Christians. In former times the Portuguese lived there, and had two towns and fortresses, which they had permission of the king to build near the sea, yet was there never friendship or any good understanding between the two; in so much that these towns and fortresses were captured and razed by the native kings and the Portuguese driven out, and at the present day they have neither town nor fortress there, as I have remarked already. At present, however, they are at peace, and the Portuguese by divers presents cultivate as best they can the friendship of this king, whom they fear more than any other. For the purposes of trade, there is at Calecut a factor on behalf of the Viceroy of Goa, assisted by a clerk, along with their wives and families. This factor is a kind of agent or ambassador, having also the power of issuing passports to the Indian merchants; for at all the harbours and ports of India, which are at peace with the Portuguese, the latter have these factors for this purpose, otherwise the merchants would have much trouble in going for passports to the Portuguese towns.

There reside also two Jesuit fathers, the one an Italian, the other a Portuguese,[1] who are well received of the king, and get from him a pension of a hundred crowns a year, worth more than five hundred in Spain, besides what they have from

[1] The Italian was Padre Jacomo Fenicio (Guerreiro, *Relaçam Annual*, Lisboa, 1607, f. 118*a*). The Portuguese, Pyrard says below, was Father Hilaire.

the king of Portugal for their living and maintenance. They have builded a very handsome and large church,[1] with an enclosure and cemetery attached, near the sea-shore, on ground presented by the king; and they have the king's leave and licence to convert the people to Christianity, so long as they use no constraint. Their labours had borne good fruit at the time of my departure, for there were already a good number of new Christians.[2] They preached publicly in their church, and not elsewhere. They are very well housed, and have very fine gardens, and before their church is a large cross. The Christians all have their houses in the same quarter near to one another, which they have themselves built. There are, however, some among them that are not Christians, and even in the same house will sometimes be found inmates of different religions. Among these new Christians none, I believe, will be found to eat the flesh of cows, bulls, or buffaloes, as I have already said. These Jesuit fathers had the ear of the king, who liked them much, and they took great care to do nothing displeasing to him. They used to go often to the palace of the king to treat of affairs, assisted by Portuguese, Indian Christians, and Mestifs. We enjoyed their society sometimes, and they gave us a good reception. But the king and all the men of Calecut frequently gave us warning not to eat or drink with them, for fear lest they should poison us; also not to go abroad at night, lest they should do us some injury,—that is, the Portuguese in general; for they were extremely jealous and concerned at

[1] This was probably the church of which the Samorin himself laid the foundation stone in 1591, under the provisional treaty made with the Jesuit, Francisco da Costa. The Samorin's endowment of the church was continued by Hyder Ali, and is still paid by the British Government at Rs. 50 per month.

[2] The term "new Christians", properly, as here, applied to all converts, had at this time, as will be seen in other parts of this book, come to be used in Spain, Portugal, and their colonies as a synonym for Jews, who were required to observe an outward conformity with Christianity.

our presence there, and at the king's favour towards us. This jealousy they did afterwards openly discover, as I shall tell anon. Having spoken of the Christians resident at Calecut, I shall proceed with what concerns the other religions that are practised there. Among others, the Jews have their own quarter and synagogue, which none enter but they. The Mahometans, although they be of divers races and countries, yet have no difference of religion (except the Persians), and frequent the temple of the Mahometan Malabars. There is also another race of Gentiles besides the natives, who, albeit of the same religion, make no alliances with them, nor go to their temples, but have their own Pagode, using none other: of such are the *Banians* of Cambaye and Diu, who have their own Bramenis, and hold them in the greatest honour. Yet the Bramenis of Malabar may freely enter their Pagode, as having common rights with them. This leads me to say that they are the one race in India who are throughout all the countries held in the highest esteem, for there are some of them among all the Gentile Indians. These Banians observe the same austerities as the Bramenis, and all the same rules, but are inferior to them, and do not intermarry with them. In all other respects they agree, in dress, manners, and customs.

As for justice, it proceeds from the king alone, and throughout all his kingdom there is no other judge but he. For all that, justice is well administered and awarded to all gratuitously; for if anyone commits a crime, or will not pay his creditors, complaint is made to the king, who, after inquiry into the truth of the matter, accords such judgment and satisfaction as the case requires. In his absence the chief officers of state administer it. If it is some foreigner or Moucois who has a suit against another, he addresses his plaint to the first Nair he meets, and the Nair gives judgment and execution on the spot, without being paid anything for it, unless the complainant gives of his mere motion and liberality. That is the procedure only in cases of lesser consequence; as for great crimes, no step is taken without the knowledge and pleasure of the king, to whom must be addressed every claim of right. The punishments are imprisonment for a term, mutilation of members, or death, if the crime be of that gravity. In such case the criminal is delivered over to elephants or tigers, who incontinently tear him in pieces at the word of command: they have no other form of execution. The prisons are all at the king's palace; and the Malabars and all manner of foreigners are subject to the jurisdiction of the Nair kings, albeit one hears of but few lawsuits among them.

With regard to the language[1] of the whole Malabar country, it is peculiar to these people; the character and letters also are peculiar. They write with iron bodkins upon palm-leaves, which are yellow in colour, and very thick. Such is all I was able to observe in the kingdom, town, and people of Calecut. I now come to what concerns the grandeur and power, the manners and life of the king, the queen his wife, and of their court and palace.

The greatness of the king will be recognised from what has already been said of his state and kingdom. He is called *Samory* by all the Indians, a word of great weight in their language, and equivalent to Emperor, for he is one of the greatest and richest princes of India. He can put under arms 150,000 Nairs, without counting the Malabars and Mahometans of his own kingdom, and the innumerable pirates and corsairs of the coast, whose services he can command.

All the Nair kings of this coast are his vassals, obeying him and yielding to his majesty, except the king of Cochin, with whom, although a prince of the same faith, manners, and customs, he is almost always at war: that, however, is only since the Portuguese have been at Cochin, for it is

[1] *I.e.*, Malayâlam.

they who foster and maintain this hostility. In former days the king of Cochin recognised him as others do, but now makes himself out to be equal with him, not yielding on any point, the cause being that he trusts to the support of the Portuguese, without which he would not long survive.[1]

This prince, when I was there, was about fifty years of age, and had reigned about thirty-five.[2] He is handsome, tall, and erect; nimble, slim, and well proportioned in limb. He loves his people, and is beloved and obeyed by them, feared and dreaded by his neighbours and enemies. He has but one wife, like the other *Brameny Nairs*,[3] and at this time had no children. He resides, as I have said, sometimes at *Panany*, sometimes at Calecut; but often makes a tour of his kingdom. When he travels he does so with a very great company, having always about 3,000 men in his following. He rides upon an elephant, of which animals he hath a great number. Wherever he passes all assemble in arms to accompany him, insomuch that sometimes he hath more than 10,000 persons. His principal seat is at Calecut, where he hath a very handsome and well-built palace, all enclosed with good walls and moats, with drawbridge to the gates, and water all around in the moats. A large number of soldiers day and night guard the gates, which are four in number. They admit no one unless he is well known, nor such a one without questioning him, and conducting him or having him conducted to the part of the interior whither he desires to pro-

[1] As to the former subjection of Cochin to Calicut, see *Barbosa*, Hak. Soc., p. 156, where it is said that every new Samorin made entry into Cochin and exacted a tribute of elephants; also that Cochin had no right of coinage.

[2] His age is probably overstated here. In 1600, only seven years before, Couto says he was a little over thirty. "This king was a tall man, well proportioned, a little over thirty years of age, and among his followers was well seen to be a king" (*Dec. XII*, liv. IV, cap. i).

[3] The Samorin is of *Sâmanta* caste, as are some other Malayâli rajas. The ladies of his family have Brahman or Kshatriya husbands.

ceed. If he wishes to speak with the king, he is passed from one guard to another until he arrives at the door of the apartments where is stationed what you might call the body-guard, and these gain him speech of the king. I have said there are four gates at the four great entrances; but before reaching the apartments of the king you have to pass three gates on each avenue, and at all points soldiers are on guard, without counting those at the doors of the king's apartments. Besides all these guards, there is a strong body in the middle of the palace, in a covered place built expressly for the purpose, and all the other guards take their orders from this one. Overhead is a great bell, which only sounds for the assembling of men-at-arms at the palace, and about the king when he hath need of them. At all the gates of the palace there are spaces with closed barriers and palisades round about, for fear lest the crowd should approach the gates. Outside these barriers, and near the gates, are men whose only duty it is to give fresh water to all the thirsty that ask it; and when anyone wants a drink, whatever his quality or religion, they give it him in the manner described.

These men deputed by the king to give drink in this way are mounted upon benches or tables, of the height of four feet, under the shade of the trees, which is very pleasant and agreeable.

They have large vessels in the form of pitchers, with a tube or pipe a span and a half long, and made of gilded copper. Those who are athirst approach these men without entering the enclosure, and offer their mouths without touching the vessel in any way; the water is then poured into their mouths from above, and all the while the pipe or vessel must be more than a span from contact with them. But before they give them to drink, they give them one or two pieces of coco to eat, instead of bread. This mode has been ordained by the king, by reason of the fierce and excessive heat of that country, and the great multitude of people that throng to the palace every day. The Portuguese in India have adopted this manner of drinking. There are plenty of wells in the country districts, and even at the king's palace; but it is not permitted to drink at them, for they are guarded, and only certain priests may draw water there for their superstitious observances.

All the avenues of the palace are marvellously beautiful and delightful. All the roads are straight, like pall-mall alleys, and relieved on both sides by high terraces and palisades covered with trees of all sorts, among others, many of the trees they call *tristes*,[1] of which they make saffron. Throughout all the country their roads are of this fashion, or nearly so.

Between the town and the palace is about a quarter of a league, the road being as described, with fine mansions on either side; in front of the gate of the palace is a great square, where the market is held every day in the morning of all kinds of merchandise of the country, but not foreign. It is opened at seven o'clock, and one of the king's officers has the duty of sounding a bell to warn the king's servants

[1] *Nyctanthes arbor tristis*, thus called "the sorrowful tree", as Linschoten says, "because it never beareth blossoms but in the night time, and so it doeth and continueth all the yeare long: it is a thing to be wondred at; for that so soon as the sun setteth, there is not one blossome seene upon the tree, but presently within halfe an houre after, there are as many blossomes uppon it, as the Tree can beare . . . the flowre being white and in the bottome somewhat yellow and reddish, which in India they use for saffron" (*Linsch.*, Hak. Soc., ii, 58-62). According to De Orta, who had not found it anywhere in India except at Goa, this shrub had been brought from Malacca (f. 17*b*), but it is now known to be indigenous in sub-Himalayan forests (see Brande's *Forest Flora*, 314). A fine but transient buff or orange dye is made from the flowers. For a picture and another account of it, see Acosta, *Tractado*, p. 224; also P. Vincenzo, lib. IV, cap. ix. Dr. Fryer (p. 143) speaks of "the *arbor tristis* at St. Thomas his Mount", but this would seem to be a kind of passion flower, distinguished by P. Vincenzo as "il fiore di S. Tomaso" (cap. x). Mandelslo describes the *arbor tristis* as belonging to Sumatra (p. 137).

and purveyors to go buy what is necessary for his house, for none would dare buy anything ere the king's household was supplied. That done, the bell is sounded a second time to call the merchants; but before the merchants enter, the tax-farmers take their dues off even the smallest of the goods. Before the king's officers have taken what is due to them, no one would dare to go near or touch any goods, least of all anything eatable. Even after that, unless they be Bramenis or Nairs, they would not dare so much as touch any goods that are for sale ere a price has been made, and then they are obliged to take them. Care has to be taken also in going through the market, where all those that sell are seated, not to touch either their persons or their goods, unless they be of the same caste and religion. This market lasts only about three hours or more, and they come from all parts of the town and elsewhere to buy, in order afterwards to sell at the great market or *Bajar*, which is held every day and all day. After ten o'clock you see no one in the market near the palace, and everyone goes about freely. At that place, too, besides the shops and warehouses of particular trades, there are three or four large spaces for the people, wherein to bargain and sell their goods. All these houses and shops are used solely to hold the merchandise, yet throughout all the rest of the town there are great and rich merchants, who never come to this Bajar, having their own warehouses full of goods, which they sell not by retail, but wholesale.

Near this large square where the market is held is a large building where the king's money is struck, which is current on all the Malabar coast. This consists of gold pieces with his effigy on one side and a pagoda or idol on the other. These pieces are of the value of about four sols, and are called *Phanans*. Another sort of small silver coin is made of the same form and design, worth three deniers each, and called *Tarens*, of which sixteen go to a Phanan.[1]

[1] As to the *fanam* and *tara*, *v. s.*, p. 344.

Foreign money, too, is used, provided it be gold or silver. Amongst others, there are quantities of silver larins, which come from abroad, and of which I have already spoken in my discourse of the Maldives. This kind of money is current throughout all the Indies, and is made in many places, but the best is coined at Ormuz.

But to return to the king's palace: it is a very large enclosure, and contains many blocks of houses, all detached and well built, of many stories and galleries, with flower-beds, and orchards, tanks, fish-ponds, and canals, all fitted and paved with stone, and constructed on all sides of stone steps leading to the bottom. Add to these many springs and fountains, whose water is cold and excellent to drink. In the palace, too, is a magazine or arsenal, full of arms, cannon, powder, and munitions of war. But the great and chief arsenal of the king is at *Panany*, for that is his chief war town.

Hard by there is a block of buildings allotted to the secretary and clerk to the king, for keeping all the registers. The order and system is most admirable herein, and I have ofttimes wondered to see the great number of men with no other duty or work all day but writing and registering. These posts are of much honour; the clerks all reside in the palace, but in different apartments, and they have different duties. Some make entry of all goods arriving for the king; others, the dues and taxes paid day by day; others, the expenditure of the king's household; others, the most notable incidents of each day, both what happens at court and in the rest of the kingdom; in short, all news, for he has everything registered; and each clerk has his separate room. They keep also a register of all strangers who come there, taking their names and nationalities, the time of their arrival, and the business that has brought them, and so they did with us. It is a wondrous thing to observe their number and the perfect order that exists among them, and how fast they write on their palm-leaves, as described: these are of the length and breadth of the leaves of coco-trees, but thicker and stiffer. They make of them a kind of book, by means of holes in the thicker ends of the leaves, through which they pass a fillet, and thus bind together as many as are required.

The king hath the like writers in all towns, ports, harbours, and frontier passages of his kingdom, who render account to those of the palace, all being well organised and in obedience one to another, each having his proper superior. Throughout the whole Malabar coast there is the same manner of writing and the same ordering thereof.

About five hundred paces from the palace and the enclosure of the king's residence is the great *Pagode* or temple of the king (though he hath also a small one in his palace): that is the principal of all the many temples in the country. Inside is the figure of the idol which they worship, and also call *Pagode*. This figure, which is placed in the inmost part of the temple, has the head of a man, but exceeding hideous and frightful, of the same fashion as we are wont to figure devils. I have observed this temple and *Pagode* of the king at leisure. It is all covered in, the walls lined on the inside with bright and polished copper, and with doors of the same. Before the entrance there is a large porch and a close, like a churchyard, well secluded and near the gate of the temple; next there is a little pond or bathing-place, where they bathe, and at the door on the inside are some burnt ashes of the dead, as at the other pagodes. Proceeding further, one meets a copper figure in the form of a cow, and that is only seen through a grill; further on is another figure, of which I have spoken, which is of gold, enriched with precious stones. The whole temple is of itself very dark, but there are a great number of lamps burning within, which makes it quite clear. The Gentile Nairs on their way to the king fail not all to go in and worship this idol; albeit they tarry not long over their prayers. This idol, too, I could only see through bars, for none is allowed to enter there unless he be of their religion, caste, and quality.

With regard to the person of the king, I may say in the first place that in accoutrements and dress he differs in no way from the other Nairs, being no more clothed than they, except that he wears not so many ornaments, valuables, or precious stones as the other lords. But on a day of festival or solemnity it is not possible to see (anywhere) more gold or gems than he carries; but this happens rarely, and at the great ceremonies only[1]; for ordinarily he wears only a little gold chain round his waist, having a jewelled clasp in front. When he takes a walk he is always accompanied by Nairs, as well within as without his palace: he never employs others. The great lords go before and behind, but none by his side, while his guards line the way on both sides as he passes. When they salute him, it is their fashion, both gentle and simple, to put their shields or bucklers under one armpit, and their swords under the other, joining both hands over their heads, thrice separating and closing them, and thrice saying *Tabiran*,[2] and once *Samory*, meaning thereby that after God, whom they call *Tabiran*, the Samory comes next.

When the king rises in the morning, as soon as he sees the sun he prostrates himself before it with a fixed regard, as also

[1] According to De Couto, this description is not overdrawn. That historian thus pictures him as he came to meet Furtado de Mendoça at the siege of Kunhâli's fort:—"He wore so many ornaments, and on his arms such a quantity of jewelled bracelets, that they extended from the bend of his elbows down to his thumbs, wherewith he was so weighted that he was obliged to have two pages each sustaining one arm. From his neck hung a collar of inestimable value. In his ears, earrings of the same assay, set with beautiful rubies and diamonds, whose weight extended the ears down to the shoulders, so that the value of what he carried upon him was indeed great. He was naked from the waist to the head, while round the head was bound a cloth of gold and silk in many folds, the ends reaching half-way down the leg, and round the head a jewelled coronet of four fingers' width, very richly set and of great value" (*Dec. XII*, liv. IV, cap. i).

[2] *Tamburān*, "lord".

do all the Nairs, and addresses his prayers to it, holding his hands over his head and opening and shutting them three times. After that he straightway rubs his body all over with odoriferous oil; this lasts about an hour, and then he goes to bathe in one of the ponds within the palace close. To get there he passes along a lengthy covered way leading to it. Standing in the water, is a closet or pavilion of trellis-work to which he betakes himself; at the brink is another, with a covered passage between. While he is in the water the lords and officers rub him and tend him, and everyone there does what he can to assist; but it must be taken for granted that none of those present gets into the water, however great a lord he be. After being well bathed and rubbed he enters the other closet on the brink, where he gets well dried; after this he has his whole body slightly rubbed with a more precious and sweet-smelling oil than before, this being done with the hands until all the oil has been rubbed in, and none appears on the skin. This done, his valet takes some colours and powdered wood, with other odorous drugs mixed with scented water, and applies the same to his forehead and to his body above the waist, together with some leaves and flowers of different sorts, which they paste on wherever they have put these scented stuffs, and particularly on the forehead and breast.[1] It is only the king and great lords who may deck themselves out with such show and curiosity, and so preserve themselves more carefully than the rest from pollution: the reason being that it would take much time and trouble to be always washing and dressing again and again. After all this they moisten a little of the ashes of their ancestors, and smear that on the forehead and breast: the rest of the people do this too, but all that other dressing is indulged in only by the king and grandees, and by the king more than all: it is his chief manner of adornment.

While the king is at his bath, every morning, without

[1] Similarly to the Maldive custom, see above, p. 165.

fail, some dozen or fifteen of the prettiest girls in the country, of whom the eldest is not twenty years of age, all beautifully adorned with gold and jewels, and dressed in white in the native style, some bearing large basins, others vessels of gold or silver gilt full of water, take some fresh dung of cow or bull and mix it with water in these vessels, while others dash some water upon the walls and pavements of the palace; they then with both hands rub the dung thus mixed upon the pavements and walls. All the Gentiles in general do the same in their own houses, deeming it both a very good and a very righteous practice. This washing is done twice a day in the king's apartments; all the pavements and walls of the halls and courts and passages used by the king when he goes to the pagode, or to his other apartments for dinner, are thus cleaned; and notice is previously given whither he intends to proceed, in order that there be no omission of what is proper.

When he comes forth of his bath he most often goes to the temple, and thence to his food in another palace within the same enclosure, which is a part of the grand palace, devoted entirely to that purpose. While he takes his repast he sits upon a piece of well-polished wood, and eats off balsam leaves, like the other Bramenis. He never eats either flesh, fish, or anything that has had life, for he is of the Brameny caste, and wears the cord like the rest. He eats nothing but rice, cooked with milk, butter, and sugar, and divers kinds of broths made of vegetables, herbs, melons, cucumbers, and other fruits, such as water-melons (*Pasteques*), etc. What remains of his meal is cast to the crows and other birds, as I have seen done in the case of the other Nair kings, who are all of the same law.

This prince is magnificently served by his officers, of whom he has a vast number. He takes his food at noon, and eats but once a day, and is three hours at table. He goes to bed very late, and after a collation of some fruit or preserves of the native sort. After his dinner he despatches his business, and then changes his apartment, going to another prepared for him to receive all comers; and it is not that wherein he sleeps, takes his leisure, or eats. Here he is, as it were, exposed to public view, and if any would speak with him he may; if no affairs present themselves, he passes the time with his lords, and is much amused with buffoons and mountebanks, whereof he has always a goodly number. The Nair kings and lords often play a game of chance, which is a kind of chess, played with dice. He takes pleasure also in seeing the Nairs fence with one another with sword and buckler, whereat they sometimes get wounded; others, again, use pikes.

When a lord or Nair has been a-hunting, he delights in being able to present his game in public to the king, who is much pleased thereby. About the king are always a number of the children of the great Nair lords, who serve him as pages, one carrying his sword and buckler, another his parasol, another his gold box filled with betel—which he chews continually, according to the custom of all the Indians of the East—another his fan, wherewith he is fanned unceasingly, while another bears a gold basin into which he spits, for never in any place wherever he may be does he spit upon the ground: and no one would dare to spit upon the pavement of the halls, chambers, or galleries, but only in the courts and places where it is allowed.

As for the queen, she lives in a separate palace, yet within the same enclosure as the great palace. She never eats with the king, and is seen but rarely, and then only at the windows and galleries of her palace or of the king's, whither she frequently proceeds by a gallery which communicates between the two, and there they see each other in private. She bathes in the same manner and with the same ceremony as the king, and in the same pond; but they cannot see each other, for they each have their own end of the pond with a space covered in. She has ordinarily her ladies about her, who pass the time for her. The pond where they bathe is well enclosed and locked, and none but the king and queen do bathe there; there is a gallery whereby the queen descends on her side, and another for the king on his side. The ladies who are present to wash the queen do not enter the water, but remain in the closets and pavilions that are upon the pond, where the oiling, drying, and perfuming is done; and these ladies use all the same artifice and ceremony towards her as the lords use towards the king. The queen is of the Brameny race as well as he. She has her own Pagode, where she betakes herself with her ladies, then to her own apartments to take her food, and so on, as with the king. Only great ladies are about her person, and she has the pavements or boards, and the walls and passages where she goes, cleaned with this cow-dung of which I have spoken. I must not forget to mention, in passing, and as the opportunity arises, the great honour rendered by these people to cows, however low-bred, filthy, and all covered with dirt and dung they may be. They are allowed to enter the king's palace, and whithersoever their way leads, without anyone disputing their passage; even the king himself, and all the greatest lords, give place to them with the utmost respect and reverence, and the same with bulls and oxen.

But to return to the queen: in her dress and attire she differs in no respect from the other Nair wives and ladies, or even from the princesses and great ladies, except that their ornaments are a little more charged with pearls and jewels. The mark of the greatest honour and grandeur with them is to have their ears large, as already described, and this queen had them so large that they reached the nipples. She is nude from the waist upwards, like all the other women, but covered all over with divers trinkets, pearls, and jewels, as are all other women of every rank, as I have frequently remarked in speaking of them. These ladies had as much curiosity in seeing and speaking with me as I with them. For during all the time I resided in this state of Calecut, I always lived at the court, where I was much beloved and caressed by the king, and by all the lords and other Gentiles about the court. They had been very glad if I had remained always with them; not only the lords, but the king himself was anxious by all expedients to get me to *Panany* or Cognialy's *Costé*, in case I should get tired of Calecut, telling me that he would come there in a few days if I would go and await him there, or that he would take me there himself, that so I should not leave him. But I could never bring myself to accept his offers, for the great desire I had to return to a Christian land, and also because the two Jesuit fathers there were at me every day, persuading me to go thence to Cochin or any other territory of theirs. One of these fathers behaved very roughly and cruelly toward us; he was an Italian, but I forget his name.[1] The other, a Portuguese, named Father Hilaire, was very pleasant and agreeable, and consoled us unceasingly, assuring us always that we should be exceedingly welcome among his people.

So, after sojourning there all that time, we took resolution to depart, in manner and with the fortune to be described in the following chapter.

CHAPTER XXVIII.

Of the kingdoms of Chaly, Tananor, and Cochin.—Imprisonment of the author, and other occurrences.

We had remained about eight months at Calecut, my companions and I, waiting always for some Hollander ship to take us back to France. Seeing at length that none arrived, the Jesuit fathers of whom I have spoken counselled us to go to Cochin, and put ourselves in the hands of the Portuguese, as being the best means of returning home. To this end they gave us letters of introduction and recommendation, that so we should come to no harm. We believed them

[1] See above, p. 405.

at the time, accepting their offers and trusting their words, insomuch that we took the letters, with their instructions as to the conduct we should observe when we reached their [*i.e.*, the Portuguese] territory. We then settled our little affairs and took leave of the king, and the lords our friends. All were grieved at our departure, and chiefly the king, who made us even fairer offers than ever before. He told us we were free to go or to stay; if we were resolved to go, he would not prevent us,[1] but above all we should take especial heed not to trust ourselves too much to the Portuguese. He bade give us money, and a passport containing orders that wheresoever we passed throughout his territory his officers and receivers were to furnish us with everything we needed. Only three of us desired to go, for our other companion was a Hollander and a Protestant, and said he would not budge from Calecut, or ever put himself at the mercy of the Portuguese, who had treated him ill on a former occasion.[2]

Having, then, completed our preparations, which lasted some days, we took the final step of departing and taking to the road, to the great regret of all the people, Gentiles, Mahometans, and the rest; all but the Portuguese, who desired nothing better. The man who had attended us on behalf of the king, named *Manjassa*, a bitter enemy to the Portuguese, well forewarned us that we should suffer for it; but that he had nothing to gain by keeping us. We bargained with some sailors to take us in their *Almedie* or barque as far

[1] The immemorial parting speech of a noble host to his honoured guest: so Alcinous to Odysseus:—

οἶκον δέ τ' ἐγὼ καὶ κτήματα δοίην,
εἴ κ' ἐθέλων γε μένοις· ἀέκοντα δέ σ' οὔ τις ἐρύξει
Φαιήκων. (*Od.*, vii, 314-5.)

[2] Pyrard and his two companions, whose fortunes are henceforward followed, were French Catholics; the fourth, who escaped from the Maldives, is here described as a Hollander, but above (p. 91) as a Fleming, who was a clever worker in wood. Below, it seems he was a gunner.

as Cochin, which is but twenty leagues from Calecut. It was now towards the end of February 1608; but we were betrayed by our boatmen, who were Mahometans and Moucois, for they told us they would set out at night when the tide was high, that then they would come and fetch us, and that we should hold ourselves in readiness with our goods. We believed their word; but they came about midnight and called us; they told us that they were going forward to the *Almedie* or boat, which was at a distance about half a league from where we were. The day before they had showed us where we had to embark, right in front of the Portuguese quarters, or rather a little further off; we were then lodged at the king's *Alfandigue.* We took the road with our bundles all along the sea-shore to find the boat, and the moon was shining brightly. When we got near the place where we believed them to be, we were accosted by twenty or thirty Portuguese, Metifs and Indian Christians, all well armed. They were in ambush under the shadow of the Almedies of the Moucois, which are all on dry land (for when they return from the fishing they haul them ashore with their cargo, in such wise that the whole beach is covered with them). These Portuguese fell upon us, crying "*Matar, matar*"; that is to say, "Kill, kill", and gave us some blows to frighten us the more. They seized us and bound our hands tightly behind our backs, threatening that if we spoke a word we were dead men. They held swords to our throats in this fashion for more than an hour without stirring from the spot, while some of them went to their quarter to speak with the fathers and their factor, and to take counsel what should be done with us. We begged them on our knees not to put us to death without confession, for that we were Catholics; but they mocked at all that, and called us *Luteranos.*[1] He who had

[1] Boullaye-le-Gouz says that before the Spanish domination many French resided amongst the Portuguese in India, but since then the Inquisition had been very severe, and the French were frequently arrested as *Louteranos* (p. 200).

carried out this manœuvre was not the factor, but a captain of Cochin, who had been at Calecut for some time, to get back a ship that had been captured by the Malabar corsairs, which the king caused to be restored to him on payment of money at a good bargain. This captain was a metif named *Joan Furtado*,[1] a cruel and wicked man, and we could not well make out whether the fathers and the factor were in the plot or not.

While they were taking counsel with the fathers and their factor or agent, we were under guard of some soldiers, still crying for mercy. They then returned, and threw us, bound and throttled, into an Almedie, from which we thought we were to be cast overboard and drowned. When the Almedie put out to sea she half filled with water, in the which we lay, believing we were going to the bottom, so many people had she aboard. They had stripped us quite naked, and taken from us everything we had. When on board they freed our arms a whit, and presently the captain asked us what counsel and advice had been given to us by *Manjassa*, the man who had charge of us, and said he would kill him, but upon his word and honour we should take no harm. So we went coasting along till we had passed the territory of the king of Calecut, and were athwart that of the king of *Chaly*,[2] a friend of the Portuguese. He it was who harboured

[1] Not identified.

[2] Châliyam; see notes above, pp. 368, 374. The town is mentioned by Ibn Batuta (*Cháliyát*), by Barbosa (Lisbon MS., *Chiliate*; Barceloni MS., *Chaliani*), "where there are numerous Moors, natives of the country, and much shipping"; in the *Sommario* of Ramusio (*Chalia* and *Calia*); by Barros and Linschoten (*Chale*); by Andrada (*Charé*). The Portuguese fort (see above, p. 374) perhaps gave it the name *Cinacotta* (*qu.* "little fort"). "We passed *Cinacotta*", says P. Vincenzo, "at the mouth of the river *Ciali*, where the Portuguese formerly had a fortress" (liv. I, cap. xxxiii). The same writer speaks of "the kingdom of *Sale*, so called from its situation among the lagoons" (liv. III, cap. iii). G. de Orta thought *Chinacota* (as he writes it) meant "fort of the Chinese" (ff. 58*b*, 188). Camoens, perhaps with poetic licence, speaks of the "lofty towers of *Chale*", built by Nuno da Cunha (*Lusiadas*, x, 61).

the nephew of the king of Calecut when he was in disgrace with his uncle, as related above. There they landed, taking us with them. No houses were to be seen. After taking counsel afresh among themselves, they bound us still more strongly, and sent some of their fellows to Calecut to hear what was said about us. What annoyed them most was that our other comrade, the Hollander, was not with us, as they thought he must be; the fact being that he would have accompanied us as far as the boat, had he not by good fortune been taken sick. They regretted the loss of him much, as he was a gunner by craft. I know not how it happened, but the king and all the people of Calecut knew all about it the same day: for, as I afterwards learned, our comrade who remained, when he heard the news, went straightway to the king, exclaiming that he would remain no longer, and, in fact, returned to Moutingué, to the Malabar corsairs there, who received him gladly, because, as I said, he was a good gunner. But as soon as the king of Calecut was advised of this, he sent for the Jesuit fathers, the factor, the writer, and all the other Portuguese there, and was hot in his anger against them, telling them he would have them answer for us, for it was currently believed we were killed. The fathers and the rest made their excuses, as to which the king made them swear upon the Jesuit fathers' book; they put all the blame upon him that had seized us. Forthwith the king sent and burned that ship of his that was there, and the fellow has never dared return there since, as I was informed some time afterwards at Goa.

Having thus landed in the Chaly country, they consulted together for about half an hour. This we thought meant judgment of death for us; but presently the captain returned and told us we were in perfect safety in his hands, swearing to us by the Holy Gospels that nothing should harm us, and bidding us be of good cheer. We, however, put no trust in his word, and remained praying on our knees, so that they were at the greatest pains to reassure us. We could not make him believe that we were Catholics, for he always called us *Lutheranos,* although we went so far as to ask for even their beads and books to pray to God withal, and said the service along with them; but they kept saying that all this was but a make-believe. They led us about a league and a half across country, and then concealed us so well that none of the neighbouring village discovered us. They gave us good enough cheer, but that did not raise our spirits, for we deemed ourselves adjudged to death, and as men who await only the appointed hour. The shed in which we were was always well closed and barred, for fear lest any should perceive us. They remained there for a whole day, awaiting the return of the messengers to Calecut. They brought us Portuguese clothes, which they made us put on, in order that none might recognise us. We had till now carefully preserved the passport of the king of Calecut; so, when his messenger had returned, the captain came and asked if we had not a passport from the Samory. We answered yes, and gave it to him. We never saw it again, and all this was done of design, and they made us march by night and not by day. So at nightfall they took the road to Tananor,[1] and we marched all night by the light of the moon, and came to a halt at daybreak at the town of *Chaly,* which is four or five leagues from Tananor: there we spent another day. In the evening they took from us also the letter the Jesuit fathers had given us, and during that night we arrived at Tananor,

[1] *Tânûr.* I don't know where Pyrard gets the extra syllable. The king was the Raja of *Vettatt Putiyangâdi*, known to Malayâlis as the *Vettatt Raja.* The family became extinct in 1793, after the British occupation. Tânûr is a very ancient place. Barbosa (ed. Hak. Soc., p. 153) says it belonged to a lord who dwelt inland, and had "much shipping and trade, for these Moors are great merchants". It appears in the *Sommario*, in Barros, Andrada, etc., as *Tanor.* P. Vincenzo says it was in his time incorporated with the kingdom of Cochin (liv. III, cap. iii); but this is probably erroneous.

the king of which place was the same who had delivered over the two Hollander merchants or factors to the Portuguese of Cochin, as I have told above. The Portuguese have a church there, also a Jesuit father, a factor, and some other Christians, as at Calecut. Before entering the town, the captain sent word to the priest and the factor to give them notice of our coming. It so happened that one of the Jesuit fathers of Calecut had already arrived there, and while we were waiting in a little wood, the boy who had been sent returned with a letter which made them all very sad and anxious, and to all appearance they were hampered with us, and regretted they had ever captured us; for neither the Jesuit father of Calecut, the one named Father Hilaire, nor he of Tananor, nor even the factor, wished to be mixed up in the affair,—at least they so pretended. They required that we should be taken to some place remote from the town, for fear of being discovered by anyone. The Calecut father went back forthwith, lest it should be said that he was a consenting party. After two days there they resolved to have done with us, and to send us to Cochin, twelve leagues off, and put us on board a large Almedie manned by Moucois, and two soldiers and their servants. But before despatching us they took from us the Portuguese clothes they had given us, and left us each with nothing but a cotton cloth of the size of a shroud, wherewithal to clothe us, and cover us by night as well as day. They assured us we should be well received at Cochin, and should come to no harm, and that they had written a letter to the captain of Cochin, and to the Jesuit fathers, and had also sent on the letters we had of the Calecut fathers, which would be of use to us. But, in fact, they acted quite otherwise, for they sent word that they had taken us at sea, and had slain all the Malabar corsairs and the Moucois of the ship; and further, that we were coming with a design to rebuild the fortress of Cognialy, which the king of Calecut had promised to the Hollanders, as, in fact, the rumour went at Calecut; indeed, they told us to say that we had been taken prisoners at sea. All that was said with two intentions, the one to make an open avowal of our capture, the other, the hope of reward for having achieved so good an enterprise.

These Moucois who escorted us make no fires in their Almedie, wherefore they cook beforehand large pots of rice, and keep it steeped in cold water, so that it does not go bad. Moreover, they fry a large quantity of salt fish of the small kind the Portuguese call *Cavalle*[1]; they also carry a quantity of fruit and cocos: upon this fare they supported themselves, as we did, too. We sailed nearly all day and all night, and about ten o'clock in the morning arrived at Cochin. We were left for a considerable time before being put on shore, because the soldiers of our guard went to seek the governor with their letter. It was astonishing the great crowd of people who came to look at us.

It was about an hour and a half ere we landed; everyone was telling us we were to be hung, at the same time pointing out to us a large square on the right hand as you enter the town from the river. This square is called by the name of St. John, and has a fine church. They showed us a gallows-tree, whereon two or three Hollanders had been hung. On the other side of the river was the very handsome residence of the bishop. All this gave us but a poor hope for our future. We were then landed, and a miserable sight we were, all naked, save only for the covering of a mere rag of cotton. We were forthwith taken in charge by a Portuguese sergeant, whom they call a *Merigne*,[2] who was accompanied by seven or eight slaves, Christian Caffres of Mozambique, each with his halbert or partisan. These are bumbailiffs,

[1] *V. s.*, p. 388. Mr. Logan says this fish must be the sardine-like fish, common on the coast, and called *matti* by the Malayâlis; it is perhaps the same as that called by Day *chupea longiceps*, which he says is called *mutthi* in Canara and North Malabar (*Fishes of India*, p. 637).

[2] Port. *meirinho*, a tipstaff or usher.

and are called *Pions*[1]; all the Portuguese sergeants have a great many always with them. These sergeants and all other officers of justice never go about without a stick (their mark of office), which is as thick as a musket-stock, and of the length of an arm and a half: this they call *Vara de Justicia.* They carry no arms except a sword, but at night they are well armed with a cuirass, and a morion on their heads. They go on their watch at eight or nine o'clock till a very late hour, and beat all the streets, and so cause all persons to retire.

This Merigne then took us to the captain of Cochin, that is, the governor; for at all the Portuguese places in India they call their governors captains.[2]

This captain was a great noble, and questioned us of divers things. His daughters and wife had a curiosity to see us as a rarity, for in those parts wives and daughters are never in the society of men. He accordingly sent us to their chamber, where they eyed us all over, and were amazed at our condition, and mocked the Portuguese, that let themselves be so often beaten by the Hollanders, English, and French; for they make no distinction between these three nations. The daughters were very pretty, and regarded us with some pity; I believe they would have done us a good turn if they could or durst, but they had no means of so doing. They were Mestifves, and as pretty and fair as girls here. After they had asked us questions of one sort and another, the captain ordered the Merigne to take us to the *Oydor de Cidade*,[3] as being robbers and his proper game. As we were marched through the streets, it was a marvel to see the immense

[1] Port. *peão*, Sp. *peon*, from *pé*, "foot"; orig. a foot soldier, then an orderly, and now used all over India for a messenger on the staff of an official (see Yule, *Gloss.*, s. v.). The badge of office of the Anglo-Indian peon is a brass plate, fixed on a shoulder-belt of cloth.

[2] The governor of a Portuguese town is called *capitão de cidade.*

[3] *Ouvidor de cidade*, *i.e.*, "town's magistrate".

crowd that followed us, some taking pity upon us and telling us to have no fear, but to put our trust in God; others calling us *Lutherano* robbers, that should be hung. This Oydor, or criminal judge, after interrogating us and getting our answers, sent us back to the captain, saying that he was our proper judge, for that we were prisoners of war, and came under his cognizance. Whereupon the captain, seeing that the Oydor would not take charge of us, and himself having no desire for the job, commanded the Merigne (who also was much bothered, as he had nothing to gain in the business) to take us to the prison, to await an opportunity of being sent on to Goa, to be there judged by the viceroy, for that he would not take any cognizance of us. Indeed, we were no more questioned thenceforward, but were at once cast into prison; and there was none who offered us even a glass of water or a morsel to eat during all this time, that is to say, for more than four days.

This prison is the only one in all the town of Cochin, and is called the *Tronco*.[1] It is built in the form of a large and lofty square tower, and high above, in the middle of the floor, is a large square hole, like a very trap or the hatches of a ship, which is closed and locked; there they let down the prisoners in a scale or wooden table, which they lower with a rope, and draw up again by a pulley. It is six or seven fathoms in depth, like a well, and below there is no door, but only a large square window in the wall, of an arm and a half's length in thickness, to admit some light. This hole or window is trellised with thick, square-cut bars of iron, through which you can pass a two-pound loaf of bread, and through which the gaoler does pass whatever he gives to the prisoners, just as one would put bread into an oven with a long-hafted shovel. This grill is triple, for there is one within, one without, and one betwixt. This prison is verily the most frightful

[1] The name of the chief prison at Lisbon, and thence applied to similar prisons at Goa, Cochin, and elsewhere.

and cruel, I think, that exists in any part of the world, and yet some have been in it for five or six years. While we were on the upper floor, they wrote down the names of all three of us on paper. That upper prison is set apart for such as give a good sum of money to the gaoler, who notwithstanding puts their feet in irons, however great folks they be. Up there they keep also such as are sick, by leave of the judges and magistrates. The first man we met there was a Hollander, named *Martin Dombé*, who lost his ship on the Maldives, as I have related.[1] The sight of him assured us a little, but when we saw they were going to put us below, we began to be greatly saddened. This Hollander told us he had been there a very long time, and that it was only recently he had been brought above, and that the Jesuit fathers were the cause of his being badly treated. I will tell hereafter what happened to him. We found there also a gentleman who had been at Marseilles, and spoke French well. He asked me for news of Monsieur de Guise,[2] having seen much of him at Marseilles, and also been in his service. He also inquired if we had anything to live upon, and learning we had not, he gave us a gold piece of the value of a croisade. At length they lowered us down into the prison with the

[1] Martin Domburgh; see above, pp. 292-3, and in vol. ii.

[2] Charles de Lorraine, fourth Duc de Guise, born 20th August 1571. After the assassination of his father, Henry, the third duke, in 1587, he was kept a prisoner in the castle of Tours, until he made his escape in 1591. He took a prominent part on the side of the League during the next three years, but at length submitted to Henry IV, under treaty arrangements effected by Sully. The allusion in the text is to his capture of Marseilles in 1596, when it was on the point of being handed over to the king of Spain, an enterprise which he conducted with admirable skill and courage. In 1617 he led the royal army of Champagne against the leagued princes, and it 1622 achieved a naval victory over the insurgents of Rochelle. In the disputes between Louis XIII and Marie de Medicis he adopted the side of the queen-mother, and in 1631 was constrained by Richelieu to leave the kingdom. He chose Florence as his place of exile, and died at Cuna, in the Siennese district, in 1640 (*Nouv. Biog. Gén.*; Michaud, *Biog. Univ.*).

rest. There were there about six or seven score prisoners —Portuguese, Metifs, and Indians, Christians, Mahometans, and Gentiles, of all sorts and conditions. Among these we were treated with some courtesy.

Among the prisoners there was an elderly person that was a kind of judge over the rest, who obeyed him.[1] Everyone gives him an entrance fee, for his goodwill, half of which he gives to the gaoler. He is a Portuguese or Metif, and it is his duty to maintain the lamp before the image of Our Lady. Mass is said on all festivals and on Sundays at the outside near the grill, where it can be heard within. This prison is the most filthy, stinking, and noisome place imaginable, for the prisoners perform all their necessities one after another in vessels, which are voided only in the evening. This engenders such an infection, and an atmosphere so stinking and stifling, that one can hardly breathe. For at night the grill is shut with a trap-door from above, so that the heat of the climate, added to that of the place where so many people are huddled up pell-mell, engenders a close and stifling atmosphere, wherein it is impossible to survive long without becoming sick. A lamp is allowed to hang there alight all night, yet even that full often for want of air goes out. Gaolers are always on the watch to guard against any enterprises, and every night they search the goods and clothes of every inmate: and there is a great iron chain reaching from one end of the prison to the other, to which is fastened the foot of everyone imprisoned for crime: they did not, however, subject us to this treatment. Everyone is constrained to remain naked, both day and night, by reason of the heat; and one has even to lie sideways for want of room, and because of the great number of persons there; yet for all that one must perforce touch one's neighbour, in such wise

[1] Such a *doyen* of the inmates of a prison was a well-recognised personage in England,—*e.g.*, Mr. Melopoyn at the Marshalsea (*Roderick Random*, ch. lxi).

that the sweat exudes in large drops. Some slaves and paupers were employed in refreshing the company with a large fan, both day and night, for which service the elder or judge of the prison gives them something: without that it were impossible to live through it. We were the most pitiful sight in the world to witness after we had been there four or five days.

It was a great consolation that every day there was given out of pity a *demy tengue*,[1] equal to five sols here [*i.e.*, in France], to every Portuguese or Metif; and to the rest, once a day, some cooked rice and badly prepared fish, about as much as would serve one for a single meal, with some water to drink: this was given every morning, to last till the next day at the same hour. Water was also given for washing and bathing, and everyone washed all naked with the rest. One thing I remarked throughout all India, that the Gentiles and Mahometans, at their washing and bathing, never discovered their private parts, but always kept them covered with a cloth. It was only the Christians that had no shame in the matter, and even took pleasure in exposing them in a vile and disgusting manner. While we were in this miserable plight no one without was minded to aid us, because of our betrayer who had captured us, and of the false letter he had written against us: that was the cause of our being so cruelly entreated. There we remained nine or ten days, and I believe if we had remained there longer we had been all dead men: for the heat and infection were insupportable, and caused our whole bodies to be covered with large boils and eruptions, which gave us very grievous pain.

[1] Port. *meia tanga*. Mr. Da Cunha (*Indo-Port. Num.*) states that half tangas were coined a few years later than this, under the viceroy, J. Azavedo. The author seems to indicate the existence of the coin here. It is no doubt overstated in value, as in vol. ii he gives the value of the silver tanga of Goa as 7½ sous in India, and 5 sous in France. The current Portuguese value was 60 to 62 reis (see Yule, *Gloss.*, s. v. "tangha", and in Supplt., "pardao").

At length, by the advice of certain of the Portuguese prisoners, we wrote a letter to the Jesuit fathers of the Cochin college. The superior presently came to visit us, and recognising us to be Frenchmen and Catholics, went to request the governor to order our release. The governor replied that he could not do so absolutely, but that he would send us to Goa, to the Viceroy, and that meantime we should be enlarged in the town, on condition that he would answer for us at all times, and especially when called upon to produce us. This was effected, and during all that time, about six weeks, we were fairly treated, being well received by some and badly by others. We had but little time and opportunity to learn all the particulars of this kingdom and town of Cochin, which is one of the finest districts and most healthy towns of the Portuguese in India; yet I will shortly describe what I was able to note during my sojourn.

The kingdom of Cochin is situate under the altitude of eight degrees from the equinoctial, towards the latitude of the Arctic pole. It is one of the kingdoms of Malabar. The country has the same climate as Calecut, and is equally fertile in the same trees, herbs, and fruits; indeed, the two states are contiguous. Living is cheap, except that bread is dearer than at Goa, because the wheat comes from Cambaye to Goa, and is carried thence throughout all India. The orders and distinctions of the people—that is, of the Nairs and Moucois—are the same; the manners and customs are similar to those of Calecut, wherefore it would be wearisome and superfluous to repeat a description of their manners, customs, and police, seeing it would be all the same as is set forth above. The country, in like manner, abounds with pepper and with precious stones; but all the pepper is taken by the Portuguese, to whom the king of Cochin sells it: he collects it from all parts of his realm, stores it in his granaries, and sells it when he thinks fit, and not otherwise.

This king is not so puissant as he of Calecut. The Portuguese have always assisted him, and even now assist and succour him, albeit in a secret and underhand fashion: but for that the king of Calecut had long ere this subdued him. Indeed, it is said that in former days the kingdom of Cochin was subject and tributary to him of Calecut.[1] At the present day, however, he is no longer so, and that is owing to the Portuguese, as I have said. He is sovereign over his own territory, and holds himself equal with the king of Calecut; and on this account they are always at war and on bad terms. Wherefore, according as the Portuguese support the king of chin, so does the Samory support the Malabars and the other enemies of the Portuguese. The latter have never had so good a friend in the Indies as the king of Cochin, nor has anyone given them so much trouble as the Samory: ay, and he does so still every day.

There are two towns of Cochin, the one being the old town, distant from the sea about a league and a half, where the king resides; the other only a league from the sea, at the mouth of a large river, upon which also the old town is. The new town belongs to the Portuguese, and is fortified with good walls and a citadel.[2] The kings of Cochin have given them this place, and some land round about, over which they exercise full dominion. The bay and mouth of the river is large; in it appear three great rocks in a line, lying, like the coast toward the north, between a quarter N.W. and a quarter S.S.E.

[1] Pyrard is quite correct. The Samorins, with Mahomedan assistance, had made all the Malabar chiefs their dependents, except perhaps the Kôlattiris in the extreme north, and their cousins, the Travancore family, in the extreme south. To the disaffected the coming of the Portuguese was a godsend (as to Cochin, see *Barbosa*, Hak. Soc., p. 156). Hence the favourable reception of the Portuguese at Cannanore, Cochin, and Quilon.

[2] Excellent plans of Cochin will be found in Baldæus, and in Ressende (*Sloane MS.* No. 197).

After Goa, the Portuguese have no town so fine and large as Cochin. It is built of very handsome houses, churches, and monasteries; and the Portuguese and Christians there have the same order of government as at Goa, whereof I shall speak at large hereafter. They have a bishop, many churches and convents, a Jesuits' college, and a royal hospital for the Portuguese, as in their other towns. The river is a fair broad stream, and affords good harbourage. At the entrance from the north—that is, on the left side—is a little island, containing the handsome and splendid mansion of the bishop, which they call *Vaypin*.[1] The town is very populous, as well with Portuguese as Indians, both Christian (of whom there are a large number) and infidel, who, however, are not permitted to exercise their paganism in the town, but have to go without, to places depending upon the king of Cochin. There is great traffic and shipping there, and vessels come and enter this river from all parts: in short, for traffic and affluence of all the necessaries of life, it is a second Goa. This great shipping has rendered the country of the Cochin king busy, rich, and opulent; the king himself has become more wealthy and powerful, because he sells promptly all the produce of his country, and receives in return all that his country has need of, besides the tribute and presents that he gets daily from the Christian, Moor, and Gentile merchants. The king and the inhabitants, as well Nairs as Moucois and other Malabars, Gentiles and Mahometans, agree well with the Portuguese, and live in peace. There is a vast number of Jews there that are very rich, and all the other different nations live in perfect liberty as to religion, each having its own temple,

[1] *I.e.*, Vypeen island point. The formation of this island between the backwater and the sea (and it is still an island, as Mr. Logan informs me, contrary to Dr. Burnell's note in *Linschoten*, i, 69) is said to have taken place in A.D. 1341. Its name, *Putu Veppu* (*i.e.*, new deposit), is given to an era still in limited use among the people about Cochin.

except in the Portuguese town, which is reserved to that nation. The town where the king resides is called by the Portuguese *Cochin de riba*, or *Dacyma*,[1] that is, the upper, because it is higher up on the river than that of the Portuguese. The Cochin country is flat, very fertile, and well wooded, like the rest of the Malabar coast. Between the two Cochins are continuous houses, like suburbs, and it is the same all round. The country is well peopled and rich; and in the old Cochin is a market, where there is great traffic, and the king takes his dues there, as he does upon all merchandise coming from abroad. Certain tribute is levied on behalf of the king of Cochin in the Portuguese town, while the Portuguese levy dues on all goods for the king of Spain. There is also at Cochin a vast number of elephants and horses. The Nairs in the Portuguese town give place to the Portuguese, and let them pass when they meet them; in the old Cochin the Portuguese do the same to the Nairs: so the king has ordained, in order to avoid all disputes; but this is done only there. When the Nairs and Malabars walk in the streets, they clang their shields against their sides without ceasing, so loud as to be heard afar off, and so the rest of the people retire to their dwellings.[2] This clanging is also a kind of brag, and he who makes the most noise is the most esteemed. These shields and arms are made by the Gentile artizans, and are very beautiful, being worked in designs of all colours, gold, silver, and azure, varnish and lacquer. They are studded, too, with large gilt nails. The beautiful workmanship of these idolater Indians is indeed wonderful. Their children are taught to work from the age of five or six, and they have the keenest aptitude possible, understanding in but a short time all they see done. It may be remarked, however, that they follow their crafts from father to son, and marry their children to others of the same condition.

[1] Port. *da riba*, "of the river"; or *da cima*, "upper".

[2] *V. s.*, p. 383.

Justice is administered between them [*i.e.*, the Portuguese] and the traders or inhabitants, of whatever nation or religion, according to the laws and regulations of Portugal, and the king of Cochin has no jurisdiction except over his own subjects and criminals who take refuge with him. So also in like case the Portuguese cannot follow their criminals into the territory of the king of Cochin, or any further than the limits of the assigned territory.

For the space of six months from the month of May or April, sometimes earlier, sometimes later, until the month of November or thereabouts, no ships or barques enter the Cochin river. The reason is that the west wind comes from the sea, and the heavy and continual rains throw up from the land side such a quantity of sand at the mouth of the river, that banks are formed of such a height that it is impossible for either ships or barques to pass them. But when the rains cease there comes a contrary wind from the east, which drives the sand into the sea, and renders the river navigable for all manner of large craft.[1] This happens not only at Cochin, but all over India, at the mouths of rivers, which the Portuguese call *barre*[2]—that is, entrance.

The principal trade of Cochin is in pepper, and only the kings of Calecut and Cochin exercise it. The king of Cochin

[1] Mr. Logan informs me that this theory is not correct. The sand-banks are formed, not in the monsoon, but in the fair season (Sept.-May). The bar is cleared by the tidal scour during the monsoon, and the river is then closed for navigation, owing not so much to the state of the banks as to the heavy surf on the bar. Our engineers use every effort to promote the tidal scour, which, with the river current, clears the bar. A year or two ago the river forced a new passage for itself through the Vypeen island; and this, the *Cruz Milagre* gap, had to be closed at considerable expense.

[2] Port. *barra;* Bluteau defines the term as "the entrance of a port by which alone ships can enter or leave it; or, the entrance of a port where between the two shores the tide ebbs and flows; the bar of Goa is one of the best ports (*sic*) in the world, but you cannot enter or leave it without the tide."

stores it, buys it, and collects it; he has some of his own, and also takes tribute of others who have it, and the rest he buys through his factors, and has magazines for storing it. He keeps it sometimes two or three years before he sells it. Nowhere in all the Malabar Indies is there so much pepper as there and at Calecut, for the Portuguese, who trade everywhere, cause it all to be brought there. The next greatest trade is carried on with Bengal, and the merchandise carried there most frequently is the little shells of the Maldives, wherewith every year many vessels are laden. The Maldive people call them *Boly*, but the other Indians call them *Caury*[1]: in these they make a marvellous profit all over India. Where the Portuguese are well received, they associate with the natives and join in their voyages; yet all the mariners and pilots are Indians, either Gentiles or Mahometans. All these seamen are called *Lascar*, and the soldiers *Lascarits*.[2] All this trade between Cambaye and the Cape of Comorin is subject to much peril, because of the Malabar corsairs. When the fleet leaves Goa a large number of private galiots go with it for safety. These galiots are called *Navis de Chetie*, and the men-of-war *Navis d'Armade*[3]; in such wise that sometimes you see a hundred and fifty sail together, both at their setting out and return.[4] Nor is it only Goa which supplies these galiots: they come also from all the other Portuguese towns in India. All the ships of the Armadas are equipped at the expense of the king of Portugal, for they never speak there

[1] Hind. *kauri*, hence our "cowry" (see Yule's *Glossary*).

[2] For the history of these words see Yule's *Glossary*. The distinction made here (and here alone, in books of this period) is preserved in modern times. Throughout the East, *lascar* is applied to a native seaman; in Ceylon *lascoreen* means a native gunner, or a trooper of the Governor's native body-guard.

[3] Port. *Navios de Chatins*, and *navios da armada*.

[4] Such a fleet of merchant vessels under convoy was called a *Cafila* (see vol. ii, and Yule, *Gloss.*, s. v.).

of Spain or the Spaniards, but of Portugal, Goa, and the Indies only.[1] The arms of the Indian Government are a sphere; they put that on one side of their money, and the arms of Portugal on the other.[2]

CHAPTER XXIX.

Voyage from Cochin to Goa.—Of the kingdom of Cananor and the estate of the Malabars.—An accident which happened to the author.

We remained at Cochin, imprisoned and at liberty, about two months. In the meantime there arrived a fleet of fifty Portuguese galiots, under the command of a Portuguese lord. He was on his way from the coast of Cape Comorin and from Point de Galle in the island of Ceylon, and came to Cochin for refreshment in passing. This is their ordinary practice; for the Portuguese and the viceroy of Goa are wont every year at the beginning of summer, which is in the month of September, to equip two fleets[3] of a hundred

[1] It will be remembered here, as elsewhere, that Pyrard's sojourn in India was during the "captivity" or subjection to Spain (1580-1640). During this period India was governed entirely through the *Casa da India* at Lisbon, and altogether in the interests of Portugal and the Portuguese officials, who, as will be seen in vol. ii, jealously excluded Spanish interference.

[2] I have not observed any of the Portuguese Indian coins to have both the sphere and the arms: some have one and some the other. Some, such as the *roda* and the *vintem*, have the wheel of St. Catherine, which perhaps Pyrard mistakes for the sphere.

[3] These armadas, which are the subjects of frequent description and reference in the histories and despatches, were called respectively *Armada do Norte* and *Armada do Sud*, or *do Malavar*. The chief captain of the latter was called *Capitão Mór da Costa do Malavar:* and his vice-admiral sometimes bore the patent of *Capitão Mór do Cabo de Comorim* (De Couto, *Dec. XII*, liv. I, cap. viii).

galiots, along with three or four large galleys. Half of this fleet they send to the north, as far as Diu or Cambaye, and thereabouts, to guard the coast, and hold their power over the sea, and prevent any from sailing there without their passport. The other half they send to the south, as far as Cape Comorin, for the same purpose, but principally to purge the sea of the Malabar corsairs, who wage war with them and with all traders. So it is, that in those parts of India none dare navigate the seas without a passport from the Portuguese, unless they feel themselves sufficiently strong to resist, as do the Arabs and the men of Sumatra and others, who are always at war with them.

So while this fleet was refreshed for the space of five days, being about to return to Goa, which is distant from Cochin 100 leagues to the north, we employed the Jesuit fathers to get us a passage to Goa; this they did, using their offices with the governor of Cochin, who delivered me to the general of the fleet, to be put into the hands of the viceroy.

The governor, by name *Don Francisco de Meneiso*,[1] a near relative of the general, who bore the same name, put us back into prison two days before, with irons on our feet of more than thirty or forty pounds weight; thus were we escorted to the galley by two Merignes, assisted by their pions or tipstaffs. We were so loaded that we could hardly walk; these irons were only a foot in length, but, being very thick, they wounded our feet and legs sorely. The general of the fleet having received us, incontinently placed us in a galiot,

[1] Don Francisco de Menezes. In the royal despatch of 5th March 1612, the king says he is informed that this captain, while governor of Cochin, took some goods from the citizens and did not restore them, also that he prevented a neighbouring raja from paying a visit to the bishop of Cochin; and gives order for an inquiry to be made, and in case the charges be found proved, he is to be deprived of his office (*Liv. das Monç.*, i, 198).

with the irons on our feet, and thus set out from Cochin at the beginning of May 1608.

As ill-luck would have it, I fell into the hands of the cruellest fellow in the world, the captain of the galiot wherein I was placed, by name *Pedro de Poderoso*,[1] for neither he nor his men had any more pity for me than for a dog. Having these irons on my feet, I could not move from one place, so that everyone in going to and fro stepped upon me. This galiot was a very small one, and yet had such a number on board, that there was hardly room to lie down at full length. The crew insulted us in a thousand ways, exclaiming that as soon as we got to Goa we should be hung all three. The only consolation I got was from a religious of the order of St. Dominic, who, with a comrade, was with us. In these galiots they have a number of drinking vessels like glass water-bottles, but made of *cally*,[2] a white metal like tin, but much harder. As I have said, they never touch the vessel with the mouth while drinking. One day, when I was not taking care, I happened to touch it when I was taking a drink. A soldier observing me, forthwith came and gave me a violent cuff, which I bore without saying a word. The reason why the captain was so cruel towards me was that he had been taken prisoner and badly treated by the Hollanders, and thought we were of that nation. During our voyage we had contrary winds and rain all the way to Goa, for it was already the beginning of winter, so we were twenty days in going from Cochin to Goa, a voyage which with a good wind we could have done in two or three days. Moreover, on the evening of the first day after we set sail, we had the misfortune to meet a large merchant vessel of Malabar. Our galiot was anxious to board her (they are always anxious to be the first on board, as well for the profit

[1] Probably *Pedroso*: several officers of this name were serving in India about this time, but I do not trace a *Pedro*.

[2] Malay tin, elsewhere spelt *calin* and *callin*; *v. s.* p. 235.

as for the honour), and we ran into her with such violence with our prow, that the *dasoure*,[1] one end of which extends beyond the prow, struck the ship with that end of it, the other end being lashed to the galiot's mast. The shock of the two vessels was so great that the cable which held this *dasoure* (and which was so heavy that it required ten or a dozen men to lift it) snapped asunder. I was then on the deck, with my feet in the irons; it fell upon my back, and so remained for some time, and it was with great difficulty that ten men got me out. I was like dead, and could not speak, while they threw water upon me to bring me round. There was no surgeon on board, save some miserable barber, whose only skill was to bleed or to dress a slight wound. I was promptly bled, and had some kind of plaster clapped upon my back, which caused a high inflammation. I received the greatest assistance from this good Dominican monk, and I cannot tell you all his good treatment of me, for he supplied me with a clean shirt, stockings, clothes, a mattress, a pillow, a sheet, and other necessaries; and as for food, with his own hands he brought me in secret everything he could lay hands on, and left his own meal untouched to give it to me. He begged the captain to take off my irons, which he allowed, but from one foot only. In fine, this good monk brought me everything he could for my cure, and I believe that, without God's grace and his, I had been dead a hundred

[1] ? Spritsail boom. I cannot trace the word; it is not in the Port. Dictionaries of Vieyra, D. Vieira, or Roquete. Rivara, in his edition of Pyrard, translates it *verga*, "yard"; but this is not in accordance with the text, which speaks of the other *end* being lashed to the mast. The nearest approach to the word I can find is *ceuadera vela*, "voile ceuadere ou civadière, qui est la voile plus petite du navire, le beaupré du navire" (Oudin, *Tresor*, 1645, s. v.); *cevadere*, "the spritsail of a ship" (Cotgrave). Pyrard may have heard this word used with the genitive *da* before it. In the first edition (1611) he does not describe the accident in detail, but in recording his arrival at Goa, says: "j'estois lors fort malade à cause que le mast de la galliote étoit tombé sur mon dos, et m'avoit tellement blessé, que je fus en danger de mort."

times over. In fact, all who saw me get the blow and survive it, said it was a miracle, as it was the severest blow a man could receive without being killed; yet had I been cured at once, the wonder would not have been so manifest. The captain, seeing me thus wounded, put me in the forecastle, which is the most uncomfortable place in the ship; for it is there that everyone does his necessities, and the waves come in the most; where, too, if they wanted to cast or heave the anchor, I was always in the way. Add to this, I was always in either sun or rain, and was all the while suffering the greatest pain, believing that the spine of my back was broken; and I was more than a month ere I could do more than drag one leg after the other. I ate well, but without power of digestion, and became so wizen, thin, and pale, that on arrival at Goa I was a very mummy, or like a corpse dried in the sun. The captain had been content if I had died, so as to have me thrown overboard forthwith. If I was turned on one side I could not turn to the other. I even ate and drank lying, with the greatest discomfort and incredible pain; and if I so much as raised my head, I felt the most extreme thirst, while every hour the ship's water was failing. Throughout all this I got no aid but from the good monk and from the cook, who was a Canarin of Goa, and a Christian; for the place where I lay was where they did the cooking, in such wise that the heat and smoke tormented me sorely; and, to complete the picture of my condition, they kept threatening me that I was to be hung at Goa.

As for our voyage, we coasted along the Malabar country, passed in sight of Calecut, and cast anchor at Cananor, which is forty leagues distant from Cochin. There we sojourned three or four days.

Cananor[1] is a handsome town, situate on the sea-shore, and

[1] Properly *Kannanûr*, *i.e.*, the village (*ûr*) of *Kannan* (a common Malayâli name). It was the chief seaport of the kingdom of the Kôlattiri family, cousins of the Travancore rajas. Before Pyrard's time the

has a good harbour: it is one of the Malabar kingdoms. Of its condition it will not be out of place here to note what I observed (although I have already touched the subject, but not in detail), both on this occasion when I was at Cananor, and formerly when I arrived from Moutingué and Badara, and departed thence for Calecut, as well as on other occasions. The Malabar coast is inhabited, as I have said, by two sorts of peoples, natives and foreigners. The natives are Gentiles—that is, the Nairs, who alone inhabit the inner country; the foreigners, those of whom I am now speaking, are properly called the Malabars, as being the inhabitants of the seacoast of Malabar. It is quite certain they came from elsewhere, some say from Arabia; but that is a long time ago. They speak the same language and none other; they obey the Nair kings, and pay them tribute for the land they occupy; they are extended over the whole length of the coast, and their towns are for the most part densely peopled. Their religion is the law of Mahomet. They are kindly people, and are also rich merchants, and well skilled in trade, and the best soldiers in India, both on land and sea, and make as much profession of arms as do the Nairs. In their hands is the whole shipping and trade of the country. In their ships and galleys, and in all their business and work by land, they make use of the Moucois and Tiua, and other villein folk, paying them wages. They agree well, and are very good friends with the Nairs, but in their presence they do not sit down, nor even touch the walls or furniture: this comes from the ceremony and superstition of the Nairs, for the Malabars have no scruples of the kind. The king of Cananor is a Malabar, and one of the kings of Malabar: in his territory the Malabars are not subject to the Nairs, although there is a Nair king in the Cananor country. The latter, however, has no authority nowadays, and the Mala-

Mahomedan chieftain of Cannanor (Ali Raja) had become independent of the Kôlattiri.

bars of the whole coast, both merchants and corsairs, respect and honour this king. The people of the country have told me that it is not long since the Malabars of Cananor were in like condition with the rest of their race, and obeyed that Nair king, but that they became so strong that they made a king for themselves, and no longer recognised the Nair king nor paid him any tribute: he resides far in the interior, and is often at war with the king of Cananor. This king of Cananor is very rich and powerful, for he has plenty of men subject to him, besides the other Malabars of the whole coast, whom he calls upon in time of need. He is called *Aly Ragea*,[1] and is a Mahometan, like the other Malabars. He is powerful on the sea, has a large number of ships, trades all over India, and for this purpose has a number of factors at different places. The islands of Diuandurou belong to him, and the Maldives are at present held of him.[2] He is very courteous, humane, and affable, and, more than any of the other kings, is fond of the society of foreigners. The Portuguese are at peace with him, and by his permission hold a small fort[3] in Cananor, containing a church and a Jesuits' college. Nevertheless, the other Indian kings call

[1] *Âli Raja* ("Sea King"). The family of this chieftain was originally Nâyar, and dependent on the Kôlattiri rajas. One of the family embraced Islam, and was made captain of the Kôlattiri fleet, with the title of *Mammâli Kitavu* ("Muhammad, Chieftain of the Sea"). As captain of the fleet he was admitted to all the important counsels of the Kôlattiri, and ultimately became independent about the year 1525. The Âli Rajas were regarded as the heads of the Mâppilla community on the coast down to the end of last century. They played an important part in history after the establishment of the English factory at Tellicherry.

[2] See App. A.

[3] The Portuguese got this fort originally from the Kôlattiri, not from Âli Raja. It was named Fort Angelo. Falling into the hands of the Dutch in 1662, it so remained till 1771, when the Dutch sold it to Âli Raja. During the wars with Tippu it was twice taken by the British, and at the present time is garrisoned by our troops. Linschoten (i, 67) says it was "the best fortresse that the Portingalles have in all Malabar". A plan will be found in Ressende's *Livro do Estado* (Sloane MS. No. 197).

not this king of Cananor a king, saying that he is not so of right, but only by force.

Of these Malabars, too, some are corsairs and pirates, who for the six summer months, when the navigation is good, sweep the seas for more than two hundred leagues of coast, so to harry all the ships they find, as well Portuguese as Indian, and even those of their own brethren, the Malabars (who carry their merchandise at that season alone); this often happens. While at sea they are no respecters of persons further than this: they choose a chief when they set sail; when they return the chief is so no longer, and has no more power; they usually have as many as eighty or one hundred galiots well equipped. Moreover, they make the best soldiers in the world, being exceedingly brave and courageous. They are always at war with the Portuguese, to whom they give great trouble. The Portuguese have not seen their way to put an end to them from the time when they first came to the Indies to the present, and they have been oftener defeated by the Malabars than victorious over them. The war between them is very cruel and merciless, for the Malabars are so courageous that they never surrender, and prefer death. I have seen them, when in battle with the Portuguese, on perceiving that they were the weaker side, and could not avoid being taken, all come to one side of their galiot, and go down with their booty, galiot and all, and even sometimes to wait till some Portuguese had boarded their vessel, so as they should perish with them. When taken prisoners by the Portuguese, they remain at forced labour in the king's galleys all their lives, none being able to ransom them. When they take any of the Portuguese, they usually put them to death, or keep them for some time, to see if any will come and redeem them; if not redeemed they are put to death.

To him that takes one of them prisoner the king of Portugal gives ten *pardos*[1] in reward, and the prisoner is his slave all his

[1] As to the *pardão*, see vol. ii, and Col. Yule's valuable article in the Supplement to his *Glossary*.

life. To the Indians, of whatever race they may be, the pirates do no harm beyond pillaging them, for they let them go with their vessels and more bulky goods. What is passing strange is, that at sea they let not off even their own fathers, saying that it is their trade and custom to be sea-rovers, and they must seize every opportunity when it presents itself. For all that, they are by land the best folks in the world, the most humane and tractable. They have four harbours of refuge in the realms of the Nair kings, where they build their galleys, whence they sally forth, and whither they return with their booty. These harbours are well fortified on the sea side only, for with the Nair kings who have given them these refuges they have a good understanding, being subject to their judicature and paying them tribute. This understanding is highly profitable to these petty Nair kings, who are inaccessible by land. These ports are Moutingué, Badara, Chombaye, and Cangelotte, which these kings have given them permission to build. When in the winter time they return from sea they become good merchants, going hither and thither among the neighbouring places to sell their goods, both by land and by sea, using then merchant ships that also belong to them. They often go to Goa and Cochin to sell their merchandise and trade with the Portuguese, obtaining Portuguese passports, though in the previous summer they may have been at war. It is not only the Malabars of these ports who lead this kind of life, but also all others of the whole coast, when they are minded thereto, as indeed they usually are; but inasmuch as they durst not embark at other places, they come overland to these ports and there take ship; they afterwards return home to resume their ordinary life, and then only when they think fit. It is a thing worthy of admiration how these people, whether at sea or in their towns, although they have no masters, nevertheless agree so well together that no dispute, quarrel, or discord arises among them. In these towns they have indeed some very rich and great Malabar lords, who build and equip these galiots, pay the soldiers and pressed hands, and send them to sea without budging from home themselves, except to be chiefs of a large expedition, on which occasion the booty belongs to them. These lords have a most commendable custom, observed among all the Malabars, which is that every wayfarer, of whatsoever religion, and whether rich or poor, coming for a lodging to their houses, gets good cheer at no cost to himself.

When the Hollanders with their fleet passed by Cananor they fired some cannon-shots, and the king sent them a quantity of presents; they made as though they would blockade the place, but he begged them off, promising that when he took some other place he would give it to them.[1] Thus is this king friendly to all, and a lover of peace. In the town of Cananor is a fine market every day, called *Basar*. The country is fertile in all kinds of produce: there is great quantity of pepper, and much trade done therein: the Portuguese have not the upper hand there, as elsewhere. They (the Cananor people) send many vessels laden with pepper to Arabia. The corsairs nowadays respect this king; but while they had their *Coginay Marquaire*[2] they took but little account of him. The town of Cananor is situate under the eleventh and a half degree towards the north.[3]

All the Malabars of Cananor and the neighbourhood have but two professions, those of merchant and corsair; the merchants buy the goods filched by the others to sell at a higher price, even though they have been taken from their own

[1] The reference is probably to the fleet of Steven Van der Hagen, which arrived at Cannanor on the 26th October 1604. There was some firing, but it was at some Portuguese, who attacked the Dutch boat at its landing from an ambuscade. The Cannanor people took no part in this; and soon after the raja sent a deputation on board with a letter, in which he gave the Dutch to understand that he intended to maintain a strict neutrality as between them and the Portuguese (*Rec. des Voy.*, iii, 16).

[2] *Kunhâli Marakkâr.*

[3] More precisely, 12° N.

relatives and friends. They have no nobility but that of valour and riches. The Malabar merchants are recognised by their dress, and not otherwise; for while both merchants and corsairs usually carry arms, the merchants do not wear their hair long; they have a bonnet of red scarlet, in the form of a skull-cap, and most frequently a kerchief wound round it in the fashion of a turban, and called *Mondou*[1]; these kerchiefs are of gold embroidery and coloured silk. They wear the beard half shaved, but without moustaches. Also they have a little skirt of silk or cotton reaching three finger-lengths below the waist, and below that a cloth down to the knees. Then they have other pretty kerchiefs wherein they tie up and conceal their money. It is the habit of these merchants, as well as those of the Maldives and other places, to carry everything with them when they go to sea, both their petty baggage and their beds for sleeping on, for they will never sleep on other folk's beds if they can help it. The corsairs wear their hair long like women, and never cut it; they tie it in a bunch, like all the other Indians, and cover it with one of these pretty kerchiefs; they go quite naked, except that they are covered with a silk cloth as far as the knees, and have another handkerchief round the waist. All the Malabars, as well corsairs as merchants, carry knives with hafts and sheaths of silver—that is, such as can afford it; these are all beautifully fitted with little pendants, such as tooth-picks, earpicks, and other instruments. The corsairs wear the beard shaved, but never shave over the mouth nor the moustaches: these they wear like the Turks, in such wise that some have moustaches so long that they tie them behind the head. All the Malabars are covered with thick hair over the stomach and elsewhere; they wear no slippers. Their women are dressed like the other natives, and wear nothing upon their hair; they carry a quantity of gold earrings and rings and trinkets on their fingers and toes. They have a

[1] Malayâlam *mundu*, which means simply a cloth.

little light jacket of cotton down to the waist, and another silk or cotton cloth which reaches from the waist down to the feet. They go barefooted, and are very fair in complexion, and most of them are short of stature: the men are of middle height. The women are pretty, and addicted to licentious practices like the other Indian women, but not to the same extent as in other places.

When they find a stranger at one of these Malabar corsairs' ports, who is willing to go to the wars with them, they feed and maintain him all the winter, him and his wife, for they marry as soon as they settle awhile in any place. They engage in good time some soldiers and Moucois at high wages, which they advance to them to bind the bargain. When they are ready for the fray they take some betel, and some *Amfian*[1] or poppy juice, which most of the Indians use. They take this betel and *amfian*, or *afeon*, and swear fidelity thereupon. After making a prize, and before coming ashore, they search every man on board and the whole ship. The captain and chief men lay hands on everything, and account conscientiously to the owner of the galiot or pados. It is incredible the fatigues these fellows will undergo at sea, and how they endure hunger and thirst. They have plenty of cannon and other arms; but of money and other valuables they carry with them not so much as five sols' worth: all that they leave on shore. As soon as they have taken a prize they come in to discharge, and return to sea at once, if there seems a likelihood of other booty; if not, they remain at home for that year and consume the produce of their theft and rapine for the next six months. This is all I was able to observe of the Malabar coast and polity.

[1] Opium. The form *amfian* is the Port. *amfião*; *afeon* is the Ar. *afyun*. This Port. form is a corruption of the Arabic, and only came into use after the Portuguese went to India: this is seen from the passage in De Orta, where his interlocutor says: "Queria saber a certeza do *amfião*, que é o que a gente desta terra uza, se é o que chamamos *opio*" (f. 153*b*). The Ar. form came from the Greek ὄπιον.

But to return to Cananor: we sojourned there three or four days waiting for a favourable wind, but seeing it did not come, and there was no hope of it, owing to the commencement of winter, as I have said, we set sail and resumed our course for Goa, I being ill all the while. Meanwhile, that good father the monk was doing all he could with the general of the fleet and the captain of our galiot to get me left at the hospital of Cananor; but he (the captain) would not permit it, giving all sorts of reasons, and saying that if I died he would have me thrown overboard for a *Luterano* dog as I was. Whereupon the monk comforted me, and bade me to be of good courage, and even brought me from the town some drugs and sweetmeats, and all else he considered needful or useful to me. In this way we made our way to Goa, where we arrived in the month of June following. I was then very ill with my wound and the hardships I had endured on board, by reason of the inhumanity of the captain, who treated me, as I have said, with the utmost indignity and barbarity, and would have done worse but for the succour and charity of the monk, who comforted me on every occasion and resisted his harsh conduct. I must not omit to mention here the name of this good monk of whom I received so much favour; he was called *frere Manuel de Christ.*[1] As soon as the galiots were anchored at Goa, I was carried to the hospital, where I was well treated and cured of my sickness. It is verily a royal hospital, excellent and magnificent in all respects, where the sick, both rich and poor, are served with the utmost care, propriety, and kindliness. I will describe it more particularly hereafter, as also the town of Goa, the surrounding country, the police arrangements, and all else that is noticeable, as well as what happened to me while I sojourned there. But the size of this volume constrains me to conclude here the story of the first part of my voyage, and

[1] I have not found this good Dominican mentioned elsewhere; it may be hoped that the rest of his life was as praiseworthy as is this episode.

to leave the rest for a second, where, with God's help, I shall relate in detail my voyage to Sunda and the Moluccas; the navigation of the Portuguese, with whom I afterwards sailed, and their arrival in Brazil; and finally my return to France.

END OF VOL. I.

THE VOYAGE
OF
FRANCOIS PYRARD

THE VOYAGE
OF
FRANCOIS PYRARD
OF LAVAL

TO THE EAST INDIES, THE MALDIVES THE MOLUCCAS AND BRAZIL

TRANSLATED INTO ENGLISH FROM THE THIRD FRENCH EDITION OF 1619, AND EDITED, WITH NOTES,

BY ALBERT GRAY,

FORMERLY OF THE CEYLON CIVIL SERVICE

ASSISTED

BY H. C. P. BELL

OF THE CYLON CIVIL SERVICE

IN TWO VOLUMES—VOL II, PART II.

GYAN

Published by

Gyan Publishing House
5, Ansari Road
Daryaganj, New Delhi-110002
Phone: 011-47034999, 9811692060
E-mail: books@gyanbooks.com

Distribution Network
gyanbooks.com
India, USA, Canada, UK, Australia, France

ISBN : 978-81-212-4200-4 (Set)
ISBN : 978-81-212-4737-5 (HB)
First Published, 1890

2nd Impression 2020

Printed at: Gyan Press, Delhi.

The Voyage of Francois Pyrard
Author: Albert Gray

THE VOYAGE

OF

FRANÇOIS PYRARD

OF LAVAL

TO THE EAST INDIES, THE MALDIVES, THE MOLUCCAS AND BRAZIL.

TRANSLATED INTO ENGLISH FROM THE THIRD FRENCH EDITION OF 1619, AND EDITED, WITH NOTES,

BY ALBERT GRAY,

FORMERLY OF THE CEYLON CIVIL SERVICE.

ASSISTED

BY H. C. P. BELL,

OF THE CEYLON CIVIL SERVICE.

IN TWO VOLUMES.—VOL. II, PART II.

LONDON:

PRINTED FOR THE HAKLUYT SOCIETY,

4, LINCOLN'S INN FIELDS, W.C.

M.DCCC.XC.

COUNCIL

OF

THE HAKLUYT SOCIETY.

CONTENTS OF THE SECOND VOLUME.

(PART II.)

ADDENDA ET CORRIGENDA - - - - ix

HEADINGS OF CHAPTERS - - - - xi

VOYAGE : PART THE SECOND (*continued*) - - 289-339

TREATISE OF ANIMALS, TREES, AND FRUITS - 341-386

ADVICE FOR THE VOYAGE TO THE EAST INDIES - 387-403

DICTIONARY OF SOME WORDS OF THE MALDIVE LANGUAGE 405-422

APPENDIX :—

A. Early Notices of the Maldives - - - 423

B. Notices of the Exiled Kings of the Maldives - - 493

C. The History of Kunhâli, the Great Malabar Corsair - 509

D. List of Kings of the Maldive Islands since the Conversion to Mahomedanism - - - 528

E. Dedicatory Epistle to M. Guillaume - - - 535

GENERAL INDEX - - - - - 537

LIST OF ILLUSTRATIONS.

Porte Beucheresse, Laval - - - - 339

Maldive Chart of the Coasts of South India and Ceylon *to face page* 423

Attack on Mâlé by the Portuguese under Dom Ferreira Belliago in 1631 (from the Resende MS.) - *to face page* 507

Kottakkal, the Town and Fortress of Kunhâli, the Malabar Corsair (from the Resende MS.) - *to face page* 510

ADDENDA ET CORRIGENDA.

VOL. I.

P. 160, Note 1, for "A.D. 1677" read "A.D. 1585-6".

P. 347, Note 2. Here and elsewhere the 11th Decade of De Couto is referred to. As is well-known, this Decade is lost, and the reference should be to the volume substituted from contemporaneous sources by the editor of the edition of 1778. (See also vol. ii, p. 509, note 1.)

VOL. II, PART 1.

P. 22, line 12 from bottom, after "Father", read "by name Gaspar Aleman".

VOL. II, PART 2.

P. 305, line 17 from top, after "Corbin", read "a man of St. Malo".

P. 306, line 8 from top, after "When", read "after six days".

P. 322, line 13 from bottom, for "the Bay", read "this condition".

P. 324, line 16 from top, after "sons", read "the one 25 and the other 20 years of age".

P. 332, first line, the text reads "Teretra", for "Terceira".

P. 336, line 11 from top, for "being", read "lying".

P. 348, line 2 from top, for "wherein to", read "whereinto".

P. 355, Heading to Chap. V, for "*Musk*", read "*Nutmegs*".

P. 363, Note 1, for "*inda*", read "*iṇḍa*".

P. 369, Note 2, for "*aha-gaha*", read "*ahu-gaha*".

P. 372. This chapter is not numbered in the original text.

P. 406, Note 1, for "1821", read "1835-6".

P. 407, line 23 from top, for "*furana*", read "*furána*".

„ „ 28 from top, for "*gahá*", read "*gaha*".

„ „ 33 from top, for "*nahat*", read "*nahaṭ*".

„ „ 34 from top, after "mute", read "with sound of short *i*".

„ „ 4 from bottom, for "*elipan*", read "*elipán*".

P. 408, line 10 from top, after "*vaharé*", read "also *váré*".

„ „ 12 from top, for "visári", read "*visarí*".

„ „ 16 from top, for "*rœ*", read "*rǽ*".

„ „ 19 from top, for "*rœ-baga*", read "*rǽ-bage*".

„ „ 23 from top, for "*maddhyama*", read "*madhyana*".

„ „ 18 from bottom, for "*iyé*", read "*íyé*".

„ „ 8 from bottom, for "*Aditiya*", read "*Áditiya*".

P. 409, line 4 from top, after "*eli-velá*", read "*eli-vechcha*".

„ „ 6 from top, after "*rǽ-velá*", read "*rǽ-vejja* and *rǽ-vechcha*".

b

P. 409, line 25 from top, for "*rajya*", read "*rájya*".
„ „ 26 from top, for "*ho*", read "*hó*".
„ „ 15 from bottom, for "*miripœnna*", read "*miripœn*".
„ „ 11 from bottom, for "*varu-diya*", read "*vœhi-diya*".
„ „ 9 from bottom, for "*múdé-kara*", read "*mudu-kara*".
P. 410, line 22 from bottom, for "*bakalaya*", read "*bakalayá*, a bandy-legged animal".
„ „ 20 from bottom, for "*míyá*", read "*míya*".
„ „ 19 from bottom, after "civet-cat", read "cf. Sin. *yabáduva*".
P. 411, line 6 from top, after "*karhi*", add in last col. "cf. Sansk. *nárikela* and *nálikera*".
„ „ 16 from bottom, for "*pœnidodan*", read "*pœnidoḍan*".
„ „ 9 from bottom, for "*naran-gedi*", read "*náran-gedi*".
„ „ 5 from bottom, for "*raṇ*", in last col., read "*ran*".
P. 412, first line, last col., add "cf. Sansk. *tamara*".
„ line 17 from top, for "*mangi*", read "*nangi*".
„ „ 19 from top, last col., insert "cf. Sin. *Ambu*".
„ „ 20 from top, after "*pirimi*" add "also *puris*".
P. 413, line 3 from top, for "*kóllá, kellá, kellí*", read "*kollá, kella, keli*", and *dele* rest of note.
„ „ 7-8 from top, Sin. *tamun* prop. = themselves.
„ line 17 from bottom, for "*rodra*", read "*raudra*".
„ „ 12 from bottom, for "*Wastadu*", read "*Wastádu*"
P. 414, line 9 from top, for "*Hœmini*", read "*Hamini*".
„ „ 21 from bottom, for "*anga*", read "*añga*".
„ „ 16 from bottom, for "*vedi*", read "*veḍi*".
P. 415, line 7 from top, Sin. petta = leaf or slice.
„ „ 11 from top, for "*néfat*", read "*néfai*".
„ „ 20 from bottom, in 3rd col., for "*dat*", read "*dai*".
„ „ 4 from bottom, for "heart", read "breast".
P. 416, line 3 from top, for "*puduva*", read "*puḍuva*".
„ „ 5 from top, after "*hada*", read "also *hita*".
„ „ 15 from top, for "*pili*", read "*piḷi*".
„ „ 15 from bottom, add "also Sin. *kittan*".
P. 417, line 14 from top, for "*góma*", read "*goma*".
„ „ 19 from top, dele "Cf. Sin. *kasá*, sulphur".
„ „ 21 from top, add "also Sin. *rasa*, quicksilver".
„ „ 17 from bottom, in last col., read "Sin. *niyamurá*, pilot".
P. 418, line 4 from bottom, for "tail", read "plough".
P. 421, for "*eka-vis*", read "*eká-vís*".
„ „ "*ba-vis*", read "*bá-vís*".
„ „ "*ona-tiris*", read "*ona-tirís*".
„ „ "*et-tiris*", read "*et-tirís*".
„ against 42, read "*ba-yális*", then "etc."
„ against 47, read "*hat-ális*".
P. 444, Note 1, for "*Kotté*", read "*Koṭṭé*".
P. 509, Note 1, for "the above reference is", read "the subsequent references are".

CONTENTS OF THE SECOND VOLUME.

(PART II.)

CHAPTER XXIII.

Return of the Author.—The Island of Diego Rodrigue sighted. —Fearful storm.—Pitiable Occurrences.—The land of Natal. —The Cape of Good Hope.—Tempests and calms - 289

CHAPTER XXIV.

The Island of Saint Helena; a description thereof, and what befell us there - - - - - - 296

CHAPTER XXV.

Departure from Saint Helena.—Accident to the ship.—A French Diver.—Arrival at Brazil, and loss of the ship - - 303

CHAPTER XXVI.

Of Brazil, and the singularities thereof, and what befell during the sojourn of the Author there - - - 309

CHAPTER XXVII.

Departure from Brazil; of Fernambuq; Islands of the Açores; Brelingue in Portugal; great storm; the Islands of Bayonne; journey to St. James; return of the Author, and his arrival in France - - - - - - 327

TREATISE OF ANIMALS, TREES, AND FRUITS.

CHAPTER I.

Of Elephants and Tigers - - - - - 343

CHAPTER II.

Of Crocodiles and Turtles - - - - 347

CHAPTER III.

Of the Fish of the Indian Sea, and more particularly those of the Maldives - - - - - - - 349

CHAPTER IV.

Of Parrots, and a wondrous Bird that is bred in China - 352

CHAPTER V.

Of Pepper and Ginger, Mace and Nutmegs, Cloves and Cinnamon 355

CHAPTER VI.

Of Anil or Indigo, Musk, Ambergris, Benjoin, Sandal, and Aloes-wood - - - - - - - 359

CHAPTER VII.

Of Tamarinds, Cassia, and Mirabolans - - - 361

CHAPTER VIII.

Of the Arbre Triste, Ebony, Betel, and the Cotton-tree - 362

CHAPTER IX.

Of Bananas, or Indian Figs and Pine Apples - - 364

CHAPTER X.

Of Darions, Ramboutans, Jacks, and Mangos - - 366

CHAPTER XI.

Of numerous Trees and Plants that grow at the Maldives - 367

CHAPTER XII.

A most particular description of the admirable tree that bears the Indian nut, called Cocos, and alone produces all commodities and things necessary for the life of man - - 372

Advice to those who would undertake the Voyage to the East Indies. The order and police observed by the French in their navigation, the great faults and excesses committed by them, with examples thereof, and a word of caution against the like - - - - - - 387

Dictionary of some Words of the Maldive Language - - 405

CONTINUATION OF THE

SECOND PART

OF THE

VOYAGE OF FRANÇOIS PYRARD,

FROM HIS ARRIVAL AT GOA TO HIS RETURN TO FRANCE.

CHAPTER XXIII.

Return of the author.—The island of Diego Rodrigue sighted.—Fearful storm.—Pitiable occurrences.—The land of Natal.—The Cape of Good Hope.—Tempests and calms.

NINE or ten days after leaving port we sighted three sail coming from the direction of Arabia towards the Maldives; we were then in the latitude of the head of these islands, which is about 8 degrees this side the line toward the north. The Portuguese, at sight of these vessels, took fright, believing them to be Hollanders. Nor were we ourselves without grave qualms, being in the company of these fellows, some of whom said that if the sail proved to be Hollanders they should throw us overboard; others, however, with more pity, said that it was no fault of ours. Those who had been in the Hollanders' hands, and had been badly treated, as the majority had, were so much the more incensed against us, and were with difficulty appeased. In the event, we failed to make out what the ships were, though I judged they belonged to the Maldives, and were coming from Arabia, or perhaps were Arabs going to Sunda,

Sumatra, and Java. And so the Portuguese were again at ease, and we also.

On the 15th March 1610 we sighted the island of *Diego Rodrigue*,[1] which is at the altitude of 20 degrees south of the equinoctial line, and about 40 leagues east from the island of St. Lawrence. We sighted it at break of day; it is uninhabited.

While in view of this island we experienced so heavy and violent a storm that we could hardly carry our lower sails. The wind was dead against us and drove us on the island, so that we had some difficulty in weathering it. And much did we apprehend to meet our end there, and with good reason, seeing that the sea was so heavy and tempestuous, the wind so violent and contrary, and we driven so close upon an unknown island. Most of the shrouds both of the mainmast and of the foremast began to give, thereby causing us great anxiety, for these shrouds are the cordage and tackling that hold and stay the mast, which without them would not stand upright and steady a single hour. In this storm a good mariner fell overboard, and it being impossible to save him, he was drowned.

The storm, after raging for the space of five days, at length passed away and left our ship leaking badly. Our master, fearing that as we coasted the land of Natal and rounded the Cape of Good Hope we should meet other storms, as is usual in those parts, ordered all the cannon, as also the boat, to be taken below, and the ship to be girt with cables in three places, viz., at the poop, midships, and bows. These

[1] Diego Rodriguez, in lat. 19° 41′ S., long. 63° 23′ E., is now a British possession, as a dependency of Mauritius; pop. in 1881, 1,436, chiefly descendants of slaves. It is chiefly famous as the habitat of the extinct bird, the solitaire (*Pezophaps solitarius*), which died out with its Mauritius cousin, the dodo, about the end of the seventeenth century. The only representation of it is in a cut in Leguat, a copy of which is given in the *Encyc. Brit.* (9th edition, art. "Birds"). Recently a good many skeletons have been discovered in the limestone.

cables grip the ship all round on the outside and under the keel, and, being brought up, are joined with two or three turns and then made fast by capstans: they hold the vessel well together. It is with these cables belayed to the anchors that the vessel rides when at anchor: this method of lashing the ship is called *Vater*.[1] Some days after this storm an Indian Metice lady, the wife of a Portuguese lord, who was also on board, a handsome woman aged about thirty, was brought to bed; both she and her child died, and got no other burial but to be cast overboard. Soon after I saw another piteous accident befall one of the apprentices, who was, one fine day, as usual on the main-top. There being a heavy swell but no wind, the vessel was rolling from side to side as though she would capsize, and this poor boy, in a heedless moment, falling upon the deck was dashed to pieces and killed in a moment.

At length we skirted the land of Natal, and met with no storm until on the 8th of April 1610 we sighted the Cape of Good Hope.

As we neared the Cape it became bitterly cold, with much snow, frost, and thick fogs. These caused us intolerable distress, for we had been so long in India that we had forgotten what it was to be cold; moreover, we had only light garments of cotton and silk, with nothing to keep out the cold and rain; and the seas so continually and in such volume swept in upon us that frequently I was as thoroughly soaked as if I had just emerged from the deep sea: and though these cold and wet garments chilled us to the bone, we had to let them dry upon us. Nor had I a place to get under cover, nor any change of clothes or linen. At times indeed we got fairly warmed by working at the pumps and the buckets, and by doing other services; otherwise we had died of cold. Nor had we too much to eat—that is, we foreigners;

[1] Perhaps the Fr. *bâter*, to put a pack-saddle on an animal; the word is not given in Jal's *Gloss. Naut.*

on the other hand, in the matter of thirst we were a trifle better off in the cold weather, for the water was like ice to the mouth and teeth, and so far was better to the palate. But I cannot describe all the hardships and misery we endured in that Cape passage. Among others, one day, near the Cape, a strong and violent gale struck us and split our great yard in twain: this gave us much trouble and labour, for the Portuguese are not properly equipped with rigging, materials, or with good tackling, or with ropes and other furniture, as are the French and Hollanders, so that when any accident happens to their ships they are grievously thwarted.

During this gale also there fell out a great quarrel and dispute, for it being resolved to jettison all boxes, baggage, and goods that were on deck, so as to lighten the ship and save us from peril, they began with the first and nearest that came to hand, whereupon arose such an uproar and mutiny among the ship's company that they came to blows with their cutlasses, and the captain was at length constrained to lay many by the heels and put them in irons. This storm lasted well-nigh two whole months, which time we took to double the Cape, accompanied with many other misfortunes and hardships. When we first sighted it, if the fair wind had continued for but six hours more, we should have doubled it with good success; but, when quite close to it, we were driven far away. Thus we remained till the end of May, unable to make headway against the heavy gales and contrary winds during all that time. The cause of this misfortune was that we were too late in leaving Goa, it being customary always to set out towards the end of December or beginning of January. Verily we were in dire peril, for gales so heavy and furious, and of so long duration, had never been seen before, as one of our pilots said who had made the voyage many a time. Our great yard was broken asunder twice, our sails were torn more than thirty times, and three mariners and two slaves fell overboard and were drowned.

The ship was so shattered by the sea and leaked in such sort that for the remainder of the voyage we could not leave the two pumps night or day. And even so, the sea came in in such quantity that we could not manage to empty her with the buckets, though every one, even the captain, worked.

In this extremity, being without remedy, the captain, gentlemen, and merchants took counsel and resolved to return to India, seeing we could make no way, and that the King of Spain forbade any to tarry there attempting to double the Cape after the 20th of May. But the master-pilots, mariners, and other sailors were not of this thinking, saying that our ship was not fit to return and repass the Natal coast, where storms are constant. Upon which advice we took resolve to hold on and, awaiting the mercy of God, to battle with the sea. We had on board a goodly number of officers of ships which had been captured or lost, and these preferred rather to die than to return to India, and of the same mind were we; indeed, the general voice was to get to Portugal or perish in the attempt. Another argument was that it is impossible for the great Portuguese ships, on account of their size, to take the land at the Cape of Good Hope, as do the smaller vessels used by the French and Hollanders in their navigations.

Then did another grievous mischance befall us: for, being quite close to the shore, a calm overtook us, in such wise that our sails served us nought to get us back into the deep sea. So were we borne by the current toward the shore and within a great bay, called by the Portuguese *Enseada*, or, as we say, *ance*.[1] We were then so close to the shore that we saw no prospect of being able to get out or to double the two headlands, and our only hope was in the mercy of God and in the compassion of the inhabitants. Everyone got his arms and other things ready, with the intention of attempting to reach the land in case the vessel broke up: which event the

[1] Fr. *anse*, a little bay or creek.

savage natives all along the shore awaited in keen expectation, and I believe all the composition we should have been able to make with them would have been to be a meal for them, so eagerly, to judge from their appearance, did they await us. The crowd on the beach was vast beyond counting. Thereupon, however, it pleased the Divine goodness to save us from this peril by means of a little wind which then arose and carried us outside the bay, and so preserved us and our ship.

The coast of this Cape is very dangerous by reason of the contrary winds that vessels usually encounter. You see great and high mountains all of bare rock, with precipices, and lofty peaks which seem to touch the clouds.

The first sign of the Cape on coming from India is that, at thirty or forty leagues from land, you see a vast number of sea-wolves moving in bands; also numbers of great birds, white, like swans, but with the tips of the tail and wings black, and on that account called by the Portuguese *Manouas de Vellado,* that is, "velvet sleeves".[1] These wolves and birds are, as it were, the sentinels which God has been pleased to place there, as also are the *Trombas,* or reeds, whereof I have spoken elsewhere.[2] The poor mariners are much consoled thereby, for these animals never fail to come and salute the vessels. And when they are seen, the lead is at once taken in hand and sounding proceeds without ceasing until the Cape is sighted. Also, when the Portuguese mariners think themselves near, incontinently they run to get ready their lines for the fishing: for it is impossible to conceive a greater quantity of fish than exist in this sea, all excellent and of all kinds, amongst them one called *Cauallo.* They cast their lines sometimes to the depth of 80 and 100 fathoms to catch these fish; and on this occasion some were caught that four men could hardly carry. This Cape

[1] See vol. i, p. 21. [2] See vol. i, p. 20.

of Good Hope is called the Lion of the Sea, because it is so furious.

This Cape, or rather that of the Needles (*Aiguilles*), which projects still farther, is at 35 degrees from the equinoctial line towards the Antarctic Pole; that which is properly called the Cape of Good Hope, is at 34½ degrees. The people which inhabit this coast, and as far as Mozambic, are exceeding brutish and uncivilised, utterly dull and without intelligence, black and misshapen, with no hair upon their heads, and with eyes always bleared.

They cover their shame with beasts' skins in their natural state. Their backs are covered with a large whole skin, joined at the neck in front; from it hang the beasts' tails in such wise that from a distance the men themselves seem to have tails. The women have long breasts, and dress in the same style. They eat human flesh and beasts' flesh all raw, also guts and entrails without washing them, like very dogs.

The men have no other arms but certain sharp javelins with iron heads. For the rest, they live without law or religion, and just like beasts.

At length, having endured the travail of so many storms, it pleased God to send us a favouring wind, that so, on the last day of May 1610, we had the good fortune to double the Cape. On the morrow, finding we had passed it, we indulged the hope of reaching Portugal and returning to the Indies no more: for on the return voyage none entertain this hope till they have passed the Cape, ever expecting to be obliged to retrace their way; and in like manner do those proceeding from Portugal to the Indies. On that day, in token of our rejoicing, we sang a Mass with a *Te Deum*, so to render thanks to God. And on the Sunday following was represented a very pretty comedy that had been got ready and rehearsed during the voyage from Goa to the Cape, to be played when we passed it; thus had we good entertainment for three days after passing the Cape.

It was indeed an almost impossible and unhoped-for event for a ship to pass the Cape so late in the season on the return voyage; and had not a fair wind come we had met our deaths there without hope of safety, for it was altogether out of the question to return to India, or to survive that passage of Natal, with a ship leaking as did ours. Three days later—that is, about the 5th of June—a council was assembled to determine whether we ought to make straight for Portugal, that is, if we had fresh water enough, and if our ship was fit for the voyage, or whether we should go to St. Helena or the Kingdom of Angola in Africa for refreshment. At length, after much discussion, it was resolved to make land at St. Helena for refreshment and for refitting the ship. That island was the nearest land, and the wind was fair for reaching it, though it was distant from the Cape 600 leagues. Another reason was that it lay on our way, whilst Angola did not.

This resolution taken, a fear arose lest we should meet the Hollanders at this island; wherefore all the cannon that had been put below were remounted and the ship put in order for fighting. We had in all forty pieces of heavy iron cannon.

CHAPTER XXIV.

The Island of Saint Helena; a description thereof, and what befell us there.

On the 25th of the same month of June we arrived at the island of St. Helena, where we found no ships, but only some letters in the chapel, left by the three other carracks that had passed there in company. We also found some letters left by a caravel sent by the King of Spain to get news of us; having given up hope of our coming, she had gone home.

On landing, I was astonished to find in what state the chapel was, for when I passed there on my way to the Indies, as I have related above,[1] this chapel was adorned with a fair altar and handsome images and pictures, while above in front was a fine large cross of freestone, white as marble and well carved, which the Portuguese had brought from Portugal.[2] Now on my return all had been broken by the Hollanders, who touch there frequently, because the Portuguese used to take away all the drawings, letters, and writings that the Hollanders had left there, on which account the latter left a note for the Portuguese to this effect: "Leave our drawings, writings, and notes, and we will leave yours"; but the Portuguese consented not thereto, and so, out of the hatred these nations have for one another, everything is broken and spoiled, and even the greater part of the trees have not been spared.[3]

We repaired afresh the door of the chapel and the altar, and replaced the ornaments. Then, having taken in water and refreshments, and refitted our ship as best we could, we re-embarked after a sojourn of nine days. We were much afraid that our ship was shattered and had bad leaks,

[1] Vol. i, p. 18.

[2] This cross was probably sent out to replace the one destroyed by Cavendish's men in 1588. Linschoten (ii, 253) relates that the Englishmen "beate downe the Alter and the Crosse that stoode in the Church, and left behind them a Ketle and a Sword, which the Portingales at our arrival found there. Yet could they not conceive what they might meane."

[3] Mr. A. Wallace attributes the denudation of the island principally to the goats, which cut off all the young seedlings and thus prevent the natural restoration of the forest. This destruction was aided by the reckless waste of the native red-wood and ebony. In 1810 the island was so denuded that English, American, and Australian flora had to be introduced. These importations have had the effect, in Sir J. Hooker's opinion, of rendering it impossible to restore the native flora, which exists only in the inaccessible heights. (*Island Life*, pp. 282-6. See also *St. Helena*, by J. C. Melliss, London, 1875, 8vo.)

although she was not making so much water. The cause of that was that the leaks were stopped with sand, and we were afraid lest, when she got out into deep sea and began to strain, the leaks would reopen and we should thus go to the bottom. Nevertheless, in this state of fear and uncertainty, we made up our minds to weigh anchor and set sail for Portugal, as our resolution was; but, as it pleased God, we were hindered therein by a strange misfortune that befell us, as I shall describe hereafter.

But before leaving the island of St. Helena I will tell what I learnt more particularly of it on my return voyage; for on my first voyage we had not the same leisure or opportunity.

This island is, as I have already remarked, at some 600 leagues from the Cape of Good Hope, in a westerly direction, and some sixteen degrees beyond the equinoctial. It is very difficult to fetch on the way to India, and many have sought it in vain: for they take not this route on the voyage to the East, but only on the return, wherefore it was a mere chance that we fell in with it on our voyage out, and the Portuguese and Hollanders were much surprised. It was also contrary to the opinion and notions of our pilot; for, when we got close upon it, our general asked him if he had ever been there before, and being answered yes, inquired in what roadstead he ought to cast his anchor. The pilot did not know where he was, and the information was got from his valet, a Hollander lad, who had also been there. This caused our general to have great distrust of this pilot, as being a bad bargain, and this afterwards proved to be too true. And all the while he had his wages of 100 crowns a month, his bellyful at the captain's table, and his allowance of bread and a quart of wine a day, with a valet that was rated and fed as a mariner; besides all he had already cost for his keeping at St. Malo, for six or seven months, him and his wife.[1]

[1] This bad bargain was an Englishman. (See vol. i, pp. 49, 79.)

This shows how carefully the pilots should be chosen for so important a voyage.

But to return to this island;—it has a very good roadstead, and ships, even carracks, can approach quite close to the land. The island is about five or six leagues in circuit. The air is good and healthy, the water very excellent, descending from the mountains in many abundant streams that fall into the sea. On the heights of the mountain are many ebony and red-wood trees. There are many sorts of animals, such as goats, hogs, white and red partridges, wood-pigeons, turkeys, pheasants,[1] etc. Of fruits there are lemons, oranges, and figs in great quantity. All around the island there is an abundant fishery; among others is one sort of fish called by the Portuguese *Quculo*, which is of the shape of our breams; it is salted and pickled for use at sea. There are also plenty sea-eels, and of many kinds.

When the Portuguese approach this island they prepare their lines for a general fishing; and while some go a-fishing others go a-hunting on the mountain, and so they lack not flesh nor fish. The flesh cannot be kept for long in salt; but must be eaten promptly, or carefully protected from the flies, otherwise it is soon all covered with worms. Some of us that knew not this, and laid some pieces of meat aside for an hour or two, found them afterwards all full of worms. Fish, however, keeps well in salt.

All the island is surrounded by great rocks against which the sea ever beats furiously, and chiefly when the tide rises; and there are some grottoes, too, where the water is thus driven in and from time to time spouts out from a higher vent, and sometimes it is long ere it is spurted forth; so it befalls that, while it is held there, the sun, which is continually beating on the rocks, forms a very white and excellent salt; no great quantity, indeed, but enough for the nonce.

[1] The partridge is the *Caccabis chullar* (Gray); the pheasant, *P. orquatus;* the turkey, *Meleagris gallopavo* (Linn.) (*Melliss*, pp. 94, 95.)

This island is exceeding small, but has great commodities, and is very convenient for the East India voyage, which it were very difficult, nay, almost impossible, to make without fetching it. So I think that God has been pleased to fix it in this place as a halfway house in the midst of the great ocean, that so we should give to all the Indian peoples a knowledge of the faith, and obtain knowledge of all the wondrous things to be seen in those far-distant lands. To this end has Providence bestowed upon it all that is best of air, earth, and water; and nowhere in the world, I believe, will you find an island of its size to compare with it. Before the Portuguese went to the Indies there were in this island no animals nor fruits, but only fresh water, and the trees which the soil naturally produces.

The island is very dry of itself, yet it rains often. The mountains are exceeding high and difficult to climb, and were it not that the vast number of goats and pigs, by trampling, wear the hill-sides into paths, it would be impossible to ascend, and still more to descend. I have often seen men in such difficulties that they cried pity, and but for timely succour had never been able to get away. In the valleys the heat is excessive, while on the mountain-tops, by reason of the chilling winds, it is wondrous cold. We were constrained to get to the lee of the wind, and to make fires, though the sun was at the time right overhead. Most frequently we had to ascend crawling upon hands and knees, and to descend sliding on our backs. But for these difficulties there had remained no animals in the place, for all the passing ships would have taken what they listed, and the Hollanders, now that they go there regularly, would soon make a clean sweep. The consequence is that now fruits are found only by chance, and most of the trees are broken down or cut to pieces: for the passing ships take away the fruits, though still in flower, on the plea that 'tis better thus than to leave them for the Hollanders and

English; which peoples act in like sort toward the Portuguese. So is the land changed since others than the Portuguese have resorted there. It was a wondrous fair prospect at the time of our arrival in 1601, compared with the scene of ruin—to wit, of the chapel and the cross, the trees and cottages —that met my eyes on my return in 1610. Now there is no cultivation of fruits; and whereas in former days I observed infinite store of mustard, now there is hardly any at all. The Portuguese are wont to leave their sick there, and at present the Hollanders do the like. Provisions are left for them, such as biscuit and other ship's victuals; as for flesh and fish, they have no lack. The animals have become so used to it, that when they see the ships come in they all go off to the mountains, and when they see them depart they return to the valleys, and especially to that where the chapel is, which is the fairest and most spacious ground, and has always some plants growing, which they come to eat. The men that are left to sojourn there then catch these animals in this crafty wise: these gardens are enclosed with walls and doors, which they leave open, and, when the animals have entered, a man concealed at a distance draws a cord fastened to the door and shuts them in: thus they catch as many as they please and let the rest go. These sick folks remain there till other ships come and take them off, for without fail they recover their health in that excellent climate, nor has a single man been known to die there, so far as I could learn. But they must not leave there any except the sick, the King of Spain having expressly forbidden it, for fear lest they should make themselves masters and take possession of the island: which would in truth be a grievous hardship to the poor voyagers that come there worn out with the travail of ship-life; for either they would find no refreshment and no materials for their refitting, or else they would have to pay dearly for the same, and so they would be obliged to leave part of the profits of their voyage behind them there. I have heard the Portuguese tell how that once upon a time a certain hermit took up his abode there for some years, but the King of Spain ordered that he be brought back to Portugal, because he drove a great trade in goats' skins, having killed so great a number that in time he had certainly cleared the island.[1] They told me also that at another time two men and two women, all of them slaves, escaped and hid themselves in this island, and were there a long while ere they could be found, for when they saw any ships in the offing they went and hid themselves in the boskiest and most inaccessible places. There they increased and multiplied even to the number of twenty, and made the island one great waste ere they could be caught; but at last they were taken, and since then there has been no inhabitant. When the vessels arrive there all go ashore, some to the chase, some a-fishing, others to get water, to wash linen, to gather fruits, herbs, mustard, etc., everyone for himself. Mass is celebrated every day, and every man receives the sacrament. All that land there out of conceit cut their names on the bark of a fig-tree, which endure as long as the tree itself; the letters are scored across each other sometimes half a foot in length. Some of these inscriptions are of the years 1515 and 1520.[2]

Two Portuguese men and two slaves along with an Indian woman of our ship had made a secret design to remain at this island, and had even got ashore all their baggage, and had concealed themselves in the mountains, with some provision of arquebuses, ammunition, and fishing-lines, but they were discovered and brought back to the ship.

[1] Linschoten says this hermit sold at least five hundred or six hundred skins a year.

[2] All this description of St. Helena follows closely that of Linschoten, which Pyrard or his patrons must have read.

CHAPTER XXV.

Departure from Saint Helena.—Accident to the ship.—A French diver.—Arrival at Brazil, and loss of the ship.

On the point of our departure from the island of St. Helena an accident happened that was like to ruin us. We had weighed our anchor at the shore end, and were about to weigh that toward the sea, when by ill-luck this latter was found to be fouled with an old cable which had been at the bottom of the sea a long while. This cable had been left, as was said, by some Hollander ships: it caused our anchor to run along its whole length, while we thought it was still holding to the bottom, and so the mischief arose.

The consequence was that the more force we applied the nearer our ship approached the shore. This we did not notice till we were quite close in; then the captain, perceiving the cause, gave order to cut the cable forthwith, and to leave the anchor behind and to set sail at once. The foresail and spritsail were immediately set; but this we had hardly managed ere the wind, which had till now been off shore, suddenly changed, and, coming from the sea, drove the ship on the ground, where she lay bedded in shallow water for the space of five hours. We were at our wits' end, especially when we saw some of the planks and boards of our hull come off, and, indeed, we gave ourselves up for lost. However, we lightened the ship of the fresh water we had obtained at the island, and of some other things of small value, and then sent some anchors far out to sea, so as to work the ship out by hauling. So, after many prayers to God, and after much travail, at length she began to float, and was worked out to sea.

They had brought to the foot of the mainmast the image of Notre Dame de Jesus, from whom the ship was named, and all the company invoked her with prayers. The Franciscans, too, that were on board brought the image of St. Francis and his girdle, and so, after much hard work and easing the ship, we began to take heart. There were many who said they had observed a fish all the time at the rudder, and that as soon as the image and girdle of St. Francis were brought it made off. Some did therefore believe that St. Francis had done this miracle; others, however, held that it was Notre Dame de Jesus; but in this dispute I thought our preservation was due to the hand of the Almighty alone.[1]

Meanwhile the ship was making much more water than usual, and we doubted whether we ought not to remain at the island: and what is more, we had no fresh water, nor any casks to obtain it withal. Hereupon a council being assembled, it was settled that we should remain, discharge the ship on the island, and make a pinnace of the galion, which was to make for the Bay *de Todos Santos,* on the Brazil coast, with some of our crew; they were to look out for other ships and get them to come and take off the rest of us, and the merchandise, cannon, and furniture of the carrack, which was to be left where it was. But at a subsequent council it was resolved to venture to reach the said Bay of All Saints, which is the capital town of Brazil, and where the Portuguese viceroy resides, a distance of 550 leagues.

This resolution taken, it was deemed unadvisable to leave behind a little image in relief of the child Jesus, which a Portuguese gentleman had presented to the chapel of the island. Everyone said that had been the cause of our misfortune, and that the image of Our Lady, which we had, was not willing to leave her son behind her. Having determined

[1] P. Della Valle relates that when he was on a Portuguese ship, wanting a good wind, the sailors, as was their last resort in such circumstances, *bound* the image of St. Anthony, as it were to imprison him till he should grant their prayer.

to fetch it, they set out with the cross and banner, chanting hymns and litanies, and made procession all round the chapel: then, before coming on board, they made another procession all round the vessel with the boat. In the chapel they left only the pictures of Our Lady and of St. Helena.

To return to our mishap, I must add that during our travail we had to get a man who could dive, and the captain sang out that if there were any that could and would do it, he would give him a hundred cruzados, and a *certidon* or certificate to be further recompensed by the king. But although some made the attempt, none could do it, for it was necessary to remain a long while under the water, and to go right under the ship seven or eight fathoms and more; and also it was very cold, seeing the sun was in the tropic of Cancer, which is the winter in those parts. There was, however, one man, the carpenter of our ship, the *Corbin*, who had shared my fortunes, that essayed to attempt it, though he did not believe he could succeed. The captain and chief officers made him many fair promises. Whereupon, seeing he could no longer refuse, and having already given some proof of his skill, he went several times under the ship and discovered her leaks, finding that many of the planks and boards of her outer sheathing were burst and useless. And though he reported some to be held by only one or two bolts, he judged that the keel (the most important part of the ship) was nowise damaged. All were well pleased to have found such a man, and made much more account of him than before.

For the rest, we believed that God had inflicted this trouble upon us to save us from a greater. For if our ship had not taken the ground, we had set out for Portugal, and been swamped, by reason that the rudder was but barely fixed, as was discovered during that survey. Of the nine bolts and hinges by which it was fixed, six of the most necessary were broken or loose, so that, had we encountered but a moderate gale we should have been lost. The rudder had been thus badly injured by the storms at the Cape of Good Hope. When its condition was discovered, we had to unfix it with great trouble, which was all we could do with the two capstans and all hands, so heavy and unwieldy was it. By good fortune, some suitable bolts and hinges were found handy; for the Portuguese carry no armourer or blacksmith as we do. When it was mended and refitted, a collection was made throughout the ship on behalf of our St. Malo diver; he got no money, but Indian merchandise, such as cotton, cloths, and cinnamon, amounting in all to twelve or fifteen crowns' worth.

All this done, and the ship being refitted, after a delay of ten days since the accident, we took in as much fresh water as we could, and at length set sail from St. Helena, with the intention to make straight for Brazil. It was now the 14th of July, and by God's grace we had the wind fair, otherwise we had without doubt been lost. We were also obliged to tow our boat or galion behind us with a heavy cable, though this is against the ordinances of the King of Spain, and indeed, except for taking in water and refreshments at St. Helena, they would have left it at Goa. The custom and the express orders are to sink it, or break it up at that island, because sometimes the boat is the cause of a vessel's loss, inasmuch as it makes the captains, officers, and chief men of a ship careless, out of the confidence they have of escaping in the boat, as soon as they see the ship in danger, instead of using all their energies to save the ship. We thus made a good voyage from St. Helena to the land of Brazil, crossing over in about twenty-four days: yet was it not without much fear and apprehension, for we never left the pumps the whole time, so shattered and leaky was our vessel.

On the 8th August we began to sight the coast of Brazil, which is very white, like sheets, or bleached cloths, or snow; wherefore the Portuguese call it the land of sheets. When we first sighted it we were yet twelve leagues off.

On the 9th of the said month we cast anchor at four leagues distance from the entrance of the bay, which we dared not enter, as we did not know it, our pilot saying he had never been there. The galion was therefore despatched with seven or eight hands to give word of our coming to the viceroy, and to get pilots to take us in. Meanwhile, as we awaited the return of the galion, the cable of our anchor by misfortune broke through wearing upon a rock in the sea; the wind was then from the sea, and was like to drive us ashore, and we were in great peril. As soon as it was perceived that we were nearing the shore, we set sail, and thus got out to sea again, and there awaited the galion's return. The following night we saw signal-fires, which were to inform us that three caravels were on their way to succour us with refreshments, and pilots to take us in. When these at length arrived we were all greatly rejoiced, seeing it was now six months since we had left Goa, and we were accordingly utterly exhausted with the labours of the sea. There remained of our company about 550 persons, men and women, whereof the most part were sick.

On the 10th, in the morning, we entered the bay on the north side. On the shore on the right-hand is a fortress and a fine church of St. Anthony, where are a number of monks, whom we saluted with a volley of cannon. The entrance of the bay is about ten leagues in width. About midway across is a little island, four leagues or so in circuit, and vessels can enter on either side of it. We took the northern course, the safer of the two, and proceeding up three leagues we cast anchor, and again with our cannon saluted the town and the viceroy, whereto the viceroy responded with a salute of all his cannon. This was followed by much cannonading and fireworks, which lasted all the night long.

The next day, the 11th, the Council ordered that the ship be got nearer in, because we were not safe where we were, both on account of the English and Hollanders, and of the weather; wherefore we weighed our anchors, so as to get nearer the town; and while we were under sail, the viceroy and some of the chief men of the town were coming to visit us. But just as they were about to board us, by mischance our ship took the ground on one of the many sand-banks which are a great danger in this bay. This we could not have foreseen, though we had two good pilots of the country.

There appearing no means whatever of saving the ship, although we worked hard for the space of six hours, we were advised, in order to save the merchandise and the company, to cut down the mainmast, which was done forthwith. The viceroy incontinently despatched thirty or forty caravels and other small craft, which clustered round the carrack, to receive the company and the goods. When the goods were got into the caravels, and the ship thus lightened, she began to float, and approached within cannon-shot of the town, which is called *Sainct Salvador*.

Meanwhile our ship was in worse state than ever, and was making water at such a rate that there was no hope of moving her from where she was, still less of getting her to Portugal. So it was resolved to discharge her entirely, and to land the remainder of the goods. Upon our arrival, a despatch caravel had been sent off to Lisbon, to take the news of our coming to Brazil, and the condition we were in. Whereupon the King of Spain sent out a number of galions and caravels to bring home all the cannon and munitions of war, along with the crew and merchandise, for it was found that the ship was useless by reason of the heavy storms she had encountered, let alone the fact that she had taken the ground two or three times, and had her mainmast cut. Our French carpenter did good service also on this occasion, for he was required again to dive in order to get the cables down to the bottom of the sea, so as to recover the anchors, rudder, and other things needed: for this service the viceroy gave him fifteen crowns, and told him if he went to Portugal he would get the equivalent of 150 crowns: to ensure which the viceroy and the captain gave him a *certidon* or certificate. They told us that had he been a Portuguese he would have got more than 300 ducats, and would, moreover, have obtained an office on board a Portuguese ship bound for India.

As soon as we set foot on land in this bay, and at the city of *S. Salvador*, my companions and I sought the viceroy, and showed him our passport, granted by the viceroy and the *Viador de fasienda* of Goa; on sight whereof he received us with much courtesy, and bade us come and eat, drink, and sleep at his house. This we did, and, fortunately for us, this viceroy had a Florentine *maître d'hôtel* who had been in Paris, and proved a good friend to us all the time we were there. But I will postpone for the next chapter all that I remarked of this land of Brazil during our sojourn there.

CHAPTER XXVI.

Of Brazil, and the singularities thereof, and what befell during the sojourn of the Author there.

The Bay of All Saints in Brazil is 50 or 60 leagues broad, situate in the altitude of 13 degrees from the equinoctial toward the south. In this bay are many little islands; among others, one they call *l'Isle des François*, because the French were the first to discover Brazil, and here they retired for security from the ambuscades of the savages.

Into this bay fall many fine rivers, which are navigable far inland for boats and barques, and serve to supply the country with commodities.

The city of St. Salvador[1] is high-pitched on the summit of a mountain of difficult ascent, which on the seaside is sheer. Everything brought to the town or exported in gross has to be raised or lowered by a certain engine. No waggons are used, because it were too troublesome and expensive, whereas by this machine the cost is slight.

At the foot of this mountain, for more than a quarter of a league, are well-built houses on both hands, forming a long and handsome street, well crowded with all manner of merchants, craftsmen, and artisans. There also are the cellars and warehouses for the receipt and despatch of merchandise, whether of the king or of private persons. And

[1] The following description of modern Bahia is perhaps the best commentary on the above:—

"Along the shore is the Cidade Baixa, or lower town, the more ancient portion of the city. Here are the lofty stone houses of the old colonists, with antique churches of massive and quaint architecture. . . . The lower city is built on a narrow strip of land along the water at the foot of a steep black cliff some 240 feet high. One great street stretches along the beach, known as the Praya; it is four miles long, with a tramway running down its entire length. This Praya presents a very animated appearance, for here are the huge stores, magazines, and warehouses, and along the quays are moored the native craft, the queerest imaginable, with their gaudy paint, lofty sterns, strange rig, and semi-nude negro crews. . . . Behind this Praya, as I said, rises a cliff, not a smooth bare cliff, but rugged, with quaint houses let into it, and rich vegetation filling every crevice. On the summit of this cliff is the plain, on which is built the Cidade Alta, or upper city, with its narrow streets, nearly each with its tramway-line, its broad squares, and the cathedral. A steep road winds from the Praya to the upper city; but there is also another means of ascent prepared for an indolent population, that will not walk ten yards if such exertion can be avoided. From the sea an imposing-looking tower is observable, built from the lower town to the upper, along the cliff-side, and terminating in a broad platform on the summit. This is the Elevator, or *parafusa*, as it is called, being merely one of our now common hydraulic hotel-lifts on a large scale. A smart Yankee hit upon this speculation, and it has proved successful." (E. F. Knight, *Cruise of the Falcon*, pp. 57-8.) Pyrard shows that the smart Yankee's notion must be considerably antedated.

by this engine whereof I have spoken the merchandise is raised up into the town, according as it is sold for distribution. To lift a cask of wine costs 20 sols, and the same to lower it: that is, 40 sols a turn; for every time a cask or other weighty thing is raised, another of the same weight is lowered. It is like the two weights that ascend and descend in a well, and is in the fashion of a crane.

The city is walled and well built; it is a bishopric, and contains one college of Jesuits[1] (besides others in the country), a monastery of Franciscans, another of Benedictines, another of Carmelites: all these have handsomely built churches. Great numbers are continually converted to the Christian religion, albeit they are not so firm in the faith as are the East Indians after their baptism, but remain as fickle and hare-brained as before.

There is a hospital in the town, ordered after the manner of Spain and France. Also a Misericordia, and a very fine cathedral church or *Assee*, with a dean and canons, but no Inquisition,[2] for which cause there are there great numbers of *Christianos nuevos*—that is, Jews, or Jews turned Christian. It was said the King of Spain desired to establish it, whereat all these Jews took great fright. For the rest, the Portuguese in Brazil conduct themselves in all respects as in Portugal, and not as in the East Indies. The King of Spain maintains in the town of St. Salvador three companies of infantry of 100 men each, whereof one is on guard every day at the residence of the viceroy, or Governor of Brazil.

The coast of Brazil extends about 800 or 900 leagues. It is a rough and savage country, well-nigh all covered with woods; and even about and around the towns it is all forest, swarming with apes and monkeys, which work much mischief; also other animals and birds.

[1] Now used as a hospital.

[2] Bahia largely owed its prosperity to this fact.

The soil is unfruitful, and suffices not to maintain the Portuguese, all kinds of provisions being imported from Portugal, the Azores, and the Canary Islands; insomuch that, were it not for the quantity of sugar made in Brazil, it were useless to live there. The pound of sugar is sold there at two sols six deniers; and what in the way of provisions or clothes we can buy in France for five sols, is worth forty in Brazil. The country's riches lie principally in sugars, wherewith, as I have said elsewhere, the Portuguese lade their ships. I believe there is no place in all the world where sugar grows in such abundance as there. In France we hear only of the sugars of Madeira and of the island of St. Thomas; but these are nothing in comparison with that of Brazil, for in the island of Madeira there are but seven or eight sugar-engines, and but four or five in St. Thomas. There is indeed a large quantity refined in those two islands, being carried there for the purpose. But in 150 leagues of the coast of Brazil there are to my knowledge nearly 400,[1] and the whole coast is nearly 800 leagues. Yet is not all the rest of the coast like these 150 leagues, whereby I mean from 25 leagues this side of *Fernambuq* to the distance of 25 leagues beyond the *Baya de Todos Santos.* Each of these engines or mills turns out yearly about 100,000 *arrobes* of sugar (an arrobe weighs 32 pounds, and four arrobes go to a quintal, which fetches 15 francs on the spot). It is sold to us in France for Madeira sugar, and is as good; but it is refined and made into shape here, it having been necessary, in order to pack it in chests, to break it up and pound it; whereas, as loaf, it could not be packed, and half had been lost. For these reasons it is refined afterwards. Nevertheless, the sugar itself, if brought over in loaf, would be better, being purer, for the refiners here add an equal portion of alum and lime.

[1] Lopez Vaz, some twenty years before this, states that there were forty sugar-mills in the town of Bahia itself.

From these countries the Portuguese export silver, sugar, conserves, and comfits, both dried and liquid, of oranges, limes, citrons, and other fruits, chiefly green ginger, whereof there is marvellous plenty in those parts; but it is forbidden to dry it or import it to Spain otherwise than as a conserve, for the reason stated elsewhere. Also from thence is brought balsam and *petun*,[1] which the Portuguese call *tabaquo*, but no Brazil-wood: for this the King of Spain retains to himself, as I have said, because, owing to the unwholesomeness of the country for residence, he draws no subsidies therefrom. His farmers collect all that wood and send it across here. There is vast store of it there, yet none durst traffic in it; for if any quantities, great or small, were found in a ship, the whole ship would be confiscated, unless it were bought of the king or were being carried under a licence in writing.

This Brazil is so sorry a country that it would be impossible to reside there for long but for the traffic in sugar and wood; and even the making of the sugar entails great toil and trouble. The Portuguese, admitting that the French were the first discoverers and settlers, say that they could not put up with it, life being there too full of hardship and toilsome labour for men who like to have their tables spread for them. Yet of the Portuguese themselves the most part there are exiles, bankrupts, or convicts. When the King of Spain builds a town there, for the space of sixty years he

[1] The Brazilian word for tobacco. Burton (*Hans Stade*, Hak. Soc., p. 147) says it is properly written *P'ty* or *Pytýma*: it appears as *Bittin* in Hans Stade, *Betum* in Damião Goes, and *Betume* in Piso. As will be seen from the text, Pyrard uses it as the word which his readers will understand, while *tabaquo* is cited as Portuguese and foreign. It bade fair to become naturalised in French. Thus Scarron writes:

> "S'il avait l'haleine importune
> Comme d'un homme qui petune."

It still survives in Breton as *butun:* otherwise the name has been assigned to the well-known plant, the *petunia*.

levies no dues, subsidies, or imposts upon any manner of merchandise sold retail in the country. Moreover, the sites for their mansions cost them nothing, for they pay neither rent nor tax. Imports and exports pay but three per cent., and all goods, whether sugars or fruits, the produce of the country, pay only the tithe, which the King of Spain has obtained of the Pope for the following cause. Some countries are rich and others poor: thus the ecclesiastics would be in the one case rich and in the other poor, though their cures might be the same.[1] Wherefore they are all paid alike, that is, according to their rank and office, so that none hath ground of complaint.

In no country that I have seen is silver so common as in this land of Brazil; it comes from the river of *la Plata*, 500 leagues from this bay. You never see small money there, but only pieces of eight, four, and two reals; also of one real, which is worth five of our sols. They bring these pieces of five sols and of six blanks to Portugal to sell there for small money, and make profit thereby. There they use little other money than silver.

The Portuguese lack men to people this land of Brazil; they hold all the coast, along which are a number of towns, fortresses, and noble mansions, and about 20 or 30 leagues of the country inland. Some of the lords have great domains, with many sugar-mills, which the King of Spain has given them in recompense for some particular service. These domains carry with them a title of some dignity, such as baron, count, etc. The said lords demise these lands to others, who are willing to live upon them and plant the sugar-cane, on condition of bringing the cane to the mills or engines of the said lords, and receiving its price. They also

[1] A different reason is assigned by the Carmelite Philippus à Sanctiss. Trin.: "In India the king collects the tithe through his ministers; for inasmuch as the greater part of his subjects are Gentiles, the king's officers can perform that task more easily than the ecclesiastics." (French trans., p. 284.)

give them licence to cut timber for the use of the mill-furnaces, and pay them the same price as if it had been got elsewhere. They build fine mansions on their domains, with gardens and all manner of fruit-trees, and rear much cattle, poultry, etc., as do our farmers here. They also plant rice, millet, maize, the *Mandoc* root, batatas, and other vegetables. For the rest, the revenues of Brazil are more than sufficient to maintain all the garrisons, the viceroy, governors, captains, soldiers, and judiciary—indeed, all the royal officers; nor is there any need to send money from Portugal for these purposes. On the contrary, the King of Spain draws large annual profits as well from the Brazil-wood as from dues on sugars and other merchandises.

The Brazilians and likewise the Portuguese there, for their sustenance (inasmuch as bread is very scarce and dear, and flour has to be imported ready-made from Portugal) make a kind of flour of the root of a tree called *Mandoc*,[1] which they

[1] The well-known cassava-plant (*Manihot utilissima*). The reference in the text to the nutritive and poisonous qualities of this plant will best be explained by a description of its preparation by the Indians of Guiana. The roots are first peeled and then scraped upon a grater. The cassava then, in the form of pulp, is collected and placed in a "matapie", or cassava-squeezer, which hangs from the roof. This is a cylinder eight feet long and five or six inches in diameter, made of closely woven strips of pliant bark. Through a loop at the lower end of the "matapie" is thrust a heavy pole, one end of which is allowed to rest on the ground, fastened by a heavy stone; the other end, passed through the loop, being in air. A woman then sits upon the raised end of the pole, and by her weight stretches the "matapie" downwards. The pressure thus exercised forces the poisonous juice of the cassava through the walls of the "matapie". This juice, collected in a pot on the ground, is boiled, and becomes *cassareep*, a thick, treacle-like liquid which is no longer poisonous. The cassava, now dry and free from juice, is taken from the "matapie", broken into a sieve and sifted, so that it becomes a coarse flour. This is either wrapped in leaves and put away for future use, or is at once made into bread. When made into thin cakes, done upon a griddle or flat plate, and then sun-dried, the cassava bread is described, by the traveller from whom this account is borrowed, as having the flavour of freshly-gathered nuts. (E. F. im Thurn, *Among the Indians of Guiana*, London, 1883, 8vo., pp. 260-2.)

eat and live upon; it eats well crummed with meat, being like dried chestnuts bruised. I have lived upon this fare in lieu of bread for six months—that is, in the country and aboard ship—on my return home, when we had no other biscuit. This root has a strange property: eaten in a dry powder it is very wholesome, whereas eaten green it will kill you. There is such store of it that they lade cargoes of it for the kingdom of Angola, on the Guinea coast, whence come the slaves for the West Indies.

As for flesh, the commonest is pork, which is exceeding good, so much so that the physicians order it for the sick rather than mutton, chicken, or other. For all that, living is vastly dear in Brazil. A pound of pork costs 10 sols, of beef 7 sols 6 deniers, of mutton 10 sols; a fowl like ours a crown. There are numbers of turkeys,[1] which the Portuguese call *Perou;* they cost two crowns apiece. You get a couple of eggs for five sols, and a pot of Canary wine for 40. They make also a cheap kind of wine from the sugar-cane, but that is only for the slaves and natives. There is abundance of fruit, such as oranges, lemons, bananas, cocos, etc.

The Portuguese have fine gardens well stocked with excellent vegetables, such as lettuces, cabbages, capital melons, cucumbers, radishes, etc. The vine does not succeed there, because of the innumerable ants which eat the fruit. There is a kind of rice, like *maiz* or Turkey wheat[2]; but it is only

[1] In orig. *poulles d'Inde.* The Portuguese is *Peru.* The turkey is an American bird. Our name "turkey" is as erroneous as the names given in other languages than ours to maize (see below); but De Candolle (*Orig. of Cult. Plants*, Intern. Sc. Ser., p. 389) goes too far in ascribing a similar error to the French "poule d'Inde": has he forgotten that there are two Indies?

[2] No doubt maize itself: the passage is curious as showing the effect of an erroneous nomenclature. Maize—the plant as well as the name—is indigenous to America, and was unknown in Europe before the discovery of the New World. It was introduced into the several countries of Southern Europe and took divers names, the most widespread being that given by the French, *blé de Turquie.* The first

given to cattle. The Spaniards in the West Indies do not so, for they mix it with corn and make bread of it. There is a very profitable fishery of whales, from which oil is drawn in such great abundance that they lade ships with it and drive a very great commerce therein.

The Brazilian natives who live among the Portuguese subsist more upon fish than on aught else. They do but little in the way of hunting, the country being so woody and full of wild beasts that they seldom venture there for fear of being eaten.

The country is thickly peopled; the natives are of middle stature, big-headed, large-shouldered, and of a reddish complexion. The women are equally well-proportioned; they wear the hair long, whereas the men wear theirs short. The men have no pride in beards, wherefore the women pluck them out for them. They go as naked as when they came from their mother's wombs: naked are they born, naked they live, and naked they die; only their private parts they cover. Such as are in the service of the Portuguese wear a white shirt.

They have neither flax nor silk. Be it added, that they have all things in common, having no property of patrimonial lands. Nor have they any form of marriage, all manner of lewdness being permitted; and it is the women that are most addicted to lechery. They can have as many wives as they list, and in their intercourse are regardless of kinship, and that as publicly and shamelessly as if they were brute beasts. This I heard from residents in the inner country, for those that live among the Portuguese are

occurrence of this name is in Ruellius, *De Nat. Stirpium* (1536). By the end of the century people had grown up to regard it as Turkish wheat; and Pyrard, when he goes to Brazil, finds "a kind of rice like maiz". De Candolle notes some of the other erroneous assignments of origin: thus, in Lorraine, maize is called Roman corn; in Tuscany, Sicilian corn; in the Pyrenees, Spanish corn. In Sicily, as in England, it is more correctly called Indian corn.

more civilised. They have no temples or religion, worshipping neither god nor idol. They carry on no commerce, nor are acquainted with money. Yet are they given to war, for their arms using bows and arrows and massive clubs of Brazil-wood, wherewith they slay one another, tearing the flesh of their enemies, and roasting and eating it as dainty food; and white men's flesh they relish more than others. I have heard it said by some that were baptised (a great number having been converted by the Jesuits), that they had eaten many men, and that the most delicate parts were the hands and feet.[1]

The Portuguese never go without the towns save with arms, for fear of meeting these savages in the forests. These people live long by reason of the excellent air; 'tis said they live to full 150 years. They are also very healthy; you never see any sick, and when any fall ill they cure themselves with the juice of certain herbs which they know to be suitable to them; nor have they any physicians or surgeons.[2]

All about this bay they are much subject to the small-pox, but, forasmuch as they possess the Gayac,[3] which promptly cures them, they think little of this ailment.

[1] For a similar statement see Hans Stade, *Journal*, p. 93, where Burton quotes a horrible anecdote from Vasconellos (i, § 49). In modern times the same appears in St. John's *Hayti, or the Black Republic.*

[2] Much the same account of the Brazilians was given a hundred years before Pyrard's time :—"Women and men appear either entirely naked or clad with interwoven leaves and the feathers of birds of various colours. They live together in common, without any religion or king. They are continually at war among themselves. They eat the human flesh of captives. They exercise so much in the salubrious air that they live more than one hundred and fifty years. They are rarely sick, and then they cure themselves solely with the roots of plants." (Note on Ruysch's map contained in Ptolemy's *Geography*, Rome, 1508, quoted in Weise's *Discoveries of America*, 1884, p. 216.)

[3] *Gaiacum officinale*, L.

There is another malady, called by the Portuguese *Bische*,[1] which causes headache and pains in the limbs, resulting, if not promptly remedied, in an ulcer at the anus, and in death. When one is seized with it, forthwith for remedy he applies a quarter of a lime or citron to that part three or four times, and so cures it speedily. One of my companions fell ill of this complaint, and cured himself with this recipe.

There come also a manner of worms[2] on the feet, which with time grow as big as the tips of the fingers; and if they be not extracted, produce large ulcers and gangrene, but without pain. I have seen some lose their feet by them, yet are they easy to extract if one knows the method. For this cause every four days everyone examines his feet and casts out these creatures. They live on the ground, and attach themselves to the feet of such as go barefooted, who are the most liable; for these worms leap like fleas and bite folk's legs. I was myself much afflicted with them, and bear their marks on my legs and feet to this day.

The property whereof the Portuguese in Brazil make most account is that of slaves from the coast of Africa and the East Indies, because they durst not attempt to escape, seeing they would be caught and eaten by the natives of the country. The natives are not at all prized as slaves, inasmuch as they work neither well not willingly. It is a great pleasure on feast-days and Sundays to see all the slaves,

[1] In this paragraph he seems to be describing dysentery, though the name seems to belong to the next. Vieyra thus explains the Port. *bicho:*—"A worm: also a small insect in Brazil, as big as a flea, bred in the dust, which creeps in between the nails and the flesh of the feet, etc., and, if not taken out immediately, grows as big as a pea, and is then very troublesome to get out." He may, however, have intended to use the Port. *bichoca*, "a boil, a blotch" (*Vieyra*).

[2] This is the far-famed jigger or chigoe (*Pulex penetrans*). A recent traveller describes the swelling caused by the flea, which increases with eggs, as about the size of a pea; further, that it is easily extracted by raising the skin and pulling it out with a needle. (E. F. im Thurn, *Among the Indians of Guiana*, 1883, p. 153.)

men and women, assembled, dancing and enjoying themselves in the public places and streets, for on those days they are not subject to their masters. But I need say no more of the characteristics of this country, both because I have already spoken of it in the chapter of the Portuguese traffic there, and because it has been much written of by our own countrymen who have visited it.[1]

I must, however, describe how, at the time of our arrival, all the Portuguese were in great fear and trembling on account of the report that our King Henry the Great was preparing a naval armada, most of the vessels of which were being equipped in Holland to make war upon them. The alarm reached not only to the Bay of All Saints, but to all the other places of the Indies where were any subjects of the King of Spain. And wonderful it was to observe the great esteem wherein our king was held of all brave men of war, and the admiration they had for his consummate valour and other qualities. But, to our misfortune, at the beginning of September arrived a small vessel despatched express from Seville, bearing the sad and deplorable news of the disastrous death of our most great and noble king, whom God absolve.[2] By this news the Portuguese were put again at their ease, and told us the news in a style of mockery, as though they despised us, while we knew not what to think or believe. Yet did others make demonstration of great sorrow, and the brave captains and soldiers and all men of judgment said that he was a great loss, for that he was the bravest and most valiant prince in the world; and, indeed, the Jesuits and other ecclesiastics in their sermons and services bade all the people to pray for him, saying that he was a most Christian and Catholic king.[3]

[1] Probably referring to the works of Lery and Thevet.

[2] Henry IV was assassinated by Ravaillac on the 14th May 1610.

[3] The praise bestowed upon Henry IV by the Jesuits after his death may be ascribed to the liberty which he had given them shortly before

I found also in Brazil a Frenchman named Julian Michel, a native of Nantes, a very rich merchant, and a man of intelligence. He was in partnership with a Portuguese, who had, either by purchase or favour, obtained the right of whale-fishery for seven years in this bay. It is the richest in the matter of oil in the whole world, and is a very great business.[1] This French merchant was attired as a Spaniard, and passed for such, having been well received at the court of the King of Spain, to whom he had been sent as ambassador by Monsieur de Mercure during the League. Afterwards he had taken up his residence at Bilbao in Biscay, and I think it was in return for his good services to the king that he had this grant of the fishery; for so far from such a licence being given to French, English, Hollanders, or other foreigners, they are even prohibited from navigating those seas under pain of death. Thus, then, did these partners carry on the fishery, which is a pretty sight to see, for their liberty to hunt and catch the whales extends over all the coast near the town. One day, amongst others, one of these great whales, seeing its little one caught, came with such fury against the fishers and their barque, that she capsized it entirely, and so saved her young, while the men with difficulty escaped. I had never believed this animal to be possessed of this temper, astuteness, and skill. The profits of this fishery consist of the oil extracted from the whales, for none of the flesh of this fish is eaten, save that of the little ones, which is very delicate.

For the purpose of this fishery, every year come two ships of Biscay with some Basque men, who are reputed to be

to teach in Paris, and also to his having written an autograph letter to the Pope (July 1609), demanding the canonisation of Loyola Francis Xavier (see *Cretineau-Joly*, iii, p. 152, where the letter is given). These acts, again, are probably due to his having had a Jesuit at his elbow during his latter years (see Motley, *Un. Neth.*, vol. iii).

[1] At the end of the seventeenth century it was rented by the Crown for 30,000 dollars (Watson, *Sp. and Port. America*, ii, 119).

best for this work. When we arrived there one of the two ships that had come that year had left the Bay two months before, and we found there only the smaller one, whereof most of the crew were from Bayonne and other places in the Basque country of France. I made great friends with them, and went to visit them often. As for M. Julian Michel, he lived in the town during the fishing, just like a burgher of the place. Each of these ships had a captain who was in command for the voyage. One night, the captain, who happened to be there, was minded to weigh anchor and set sail, though his ship was but half laden with whale-oil. He was going to start secretly, without cocket or passport of the viceroy, which is contrary to the ordinance, and entails confiscation and corporal punishment. The occasion of this conduct was that he had a secret treaty with a merchant, who was to sell and deliver him a large quantity of red wood, that being expressly prohibited, and was to load it at a place 200 leagues to the south of the Bay. But the viceroy got wind of it, and straightway sent overland to seize the ship and take all the men prisoners. This was done; the ship was brought back to the Bay, where the captain and chief officers were cast into prison in irons. The vessel was dismantled of all her rigging and apparel, and was still in the Bay when we left. Many of these prisoners and others that were at liberty gave me letters to bring to their kindred and friends, if peradventure I should happen to pass through their country, or meet with any that were to do so; this I did, as I shall relate hereafter.

Julian Michel was not made prisoner with the others, for he disavowed the captain, saying that he had not acted upon his orders. He treated us with great courtesy and much kindness, and when we were ready to embark, he made us presents of some provisions, such as meal of *mandoc*, and among other things some salt beef from the river of La Plata, than which no meat can be more rich, tender, or better flavoured. The oxen are the finest and largest in existence; they come from Peru. A large trade is done in their hides, and the herds are so vast, that most of them are killed for the hides alone. They salt the flesh, cutting it in broad but thin strips, of the thickness of two inches at most. After being in the salt it is taken out without washing, and well dried in the sun, and in this condition will keep for long without spoiling, provided it be kept dry; for if allowed to get wet without being thoroughly dried again in the sun, it goes bad and breeds worms.

While I was in this Bay I made the acquaintance also of a Frenchman, a native of Provence, near Marseilles, who was servant to one of the greatest lords of the country, called *Mangue la botte*,[1] that being the name given him by the negroes of Angola, meaning the great and valiant captain, because he had been viceroy. In a war against these negroes this lord had quitted himself so valiantly that he was greatly feared among them. He was also said to be worth more than 300,000 crowns, drawing large revenues from many sugar-mills which he had. This Frenchman who lived with him was a musician and player of instruments, and that lord had engaged him to teach 20 or 30 slaves, who together made a concert of voices and instruments whenever required. This lord prayed and besought me to remain with him, promising me an appointment of 100 crowns and good provisions, if only I would take command of a certain number of slaves at their work. He also said that a year later he was going to Portugal, and indeed was building a very fine large vessel of 500 tons burthen for the purpose. He was also making a collection of all the strange animals and other rareties he could find, to make a present to the King of Spain. Among others, he had two of the animal

[1] Mr. Rivara thinks that the person here referred to was perhaps João Furtado de Mendoça, who was governor of Angola from 1594 to 1602. I do not understand the meaning of the sobriquet.

called *esure*,[1] whereof I make mention in my treatise of animals. I should willingly have accepted his conditions, but the mischief is, that after one is engaged with these lords, when one wants to come home they will not allow you.

I also met there an innkeeper and his wife, natives of the ditch of Nantes. They were well disposed towards us, but themselves were by no means well off: they kept a tavern and sold goods. They lost no opportunity of assisting us so far as their means permitted. They had been in Brazil upwards of 35 years, and were of great age. There were other Frenchmen resident here and there about the country.

Now having discussed sufficiently of this Bay, I must not forget to say a word about the viceroy, who was so good and gracious a friend to us, as indeed to every one he was a most kindly and courteous gentleman. This lord was a widower, and had with him his two sons, who were both held in high esteem. The father was called *Don Francisco de Menaissa.* While I was there his elder son was found abed with a Portuguese lady and surprised by the husband, who wounded him slightly; he, however, escaped. The wife had five or six sword-cuts, which, strange to say, did not prove mortal. I know not how the affair ended.

Nor must I forget to mention an adventure that befell myself there. One day, as I was walking in the town quite alone, habited in silk in the Portuguese mode of Goa, which is different from that of the Portuguese of Lisbon and Brazil, I met a slave girl, a negress of Angola, who, without further introduction or ceremony, bade me follow her with all assurance, saying she would lead me to a kindly gentleman who desired to speak with me. Thereupon, I paused to reflect awhile whether I ought to go, and trust to her words. At length I resolved to follow her and see what transpired. She led me by a thousand turnings and windings of the

[1] The zebra.

narrow lanes, every step increasing my fear and raising in me a resolve to go no further. She, however, gave me courage, and at length brought me to a large and handsome house, nobly furnished and carpeted, where I saw none but a young Portuguese lady, who gave me a warm reception, and incontinently bade prepare an agreeable repast. Seeing that my hat was but a sorry one, she took it off my head with her own hand, and gave me a new one of Spanish wool, with a handsome cord, and made me promise I would come and see her again, for that she would assist me and provide me with amusement so far as she could. The which I failed not to do, and went to see her often while I was there, and she did me a thousand good offices.

I made the acquaintance and friendship also of another young Portuguese lady, a native of *Porto* in Portugal, by name *Marie Mena*, who kept one of the best taverns in the town, and I lacked not meat and drink, for she gave me both when I was in need, with her husband's knowledge, supplying me with money to pay over to her. She called me her "Camarade". I made her presents of the little store I had brought from the Indies; such things they highly esteem in those parts, more so than at Lisbon itself. The women there are far more affable and friendly towards strangers than the men, who are usually exceeding jealous.

I will now relate another affair that befell us there. As I have said, the viceroy, on our first arrival, bade us come for our victuals and bed to his house, which we failed not to do for some ten or twelve days. But seeing that we were not well accommodated there, and had bad sleeping-room, we spoke to that Italian of Florence who had the control of the house, and he ordered a woman who lived hard by the viceroy's mansion to take us in. Thither we caused to be conveyed all our baggage and the small store of provisions that remained to us, amongst others two large parcels of

Indian rice, of the description called *Girasal*,[1] which is small, but the best in the world. This had been given us by the master pilot of our ship for our assistance on the voyage; each parcel weighed full one hundred pounds. Nevertheless, we used to go for our meals at the viceroy's house when we were so minded. This woman, our hostess, having a great fancy to possess this rice, which is greatly valued there, would not let us take it with us when we were about to leave, saying that she had bought it for a certain price—half, indeed, of what it was worth—and wanted us to pay at that rate; but we refusing, and she insisting to the contrary, we were constrained to carry our complaint to the *Oydor*, or town's magistrate. Everyone said we should take nothing by going to law with this woman, for that she was in great credit and favour by reason of certain good offices rendered by her to the viceroy, his sons, and others, in their amours. Nevertheless, these availed her not against our word. She was adjudged to restore us our rice, and to pay the costs. This she promptly did without more ado, out of fear lest she should be attached and taken before the magistrate, who knew full well what trade she had been driving. In this affair we had some good friends, who recounted to the Oydor all the life of this good lady, and he forthwith sent one of his officers with us to see the judgment carried out.

The Portuguese of this country also showed me a gallows-tree, upon which, some years before, thirteen Frenchmen had been hanged. They were men of Rochelle, who were taken with their ship. One of the captains was named *Pain de mil*, and the other *Brifaut*. I saw there also an Englishman that was seized with them, who was led to the gallows

[1] This rice is mentioned by Linschoten as being of the best quality. "It is broght in round bundels, wrapped in strawe, and bounde about with cordes. . . . . . This rice is better then that which commeth not in Fardens, and is called Girasall Rice, which is the best, and beareth the highest price." Dr. Burnell notes that it is the Mahr. jiresāl = cummin (like) rice, so called from its smell (*Linsch.*, i, 245).

with the rope round his neck ready to be hung with the rest, but was spared because the Frenchmen protested that he had been forced to come with them, having been taken at sea in an English ship: as indeed the truth was. This Englishman was worth more than a thousand crowns, and lived with a Portuguese lord, whom he served at his sugar-mills.

CHAPTER XXVII.

Departure from Brazil; of Fernambuq; Islands of the Açores; Brelingue in Portugal; great storm; the islands of Bayonne; journey to St. James; return of the Author, and his arrival in France.

At length, when I had been in Brazil for the space of two months, and was longing to return to Portugal, three brave and gallant Portuguese gentlemen, who bore me much affection, promised to get me on board with them. These three gentlemen were a certain *Don Fernando de Sylva de Menaissa* (who had been, as I have already said, general of the galiots of the North at Goa[1]), and his two brothers-in-law, who had been on board the same ship with me, the one[2] having been captain and governor of the island and

[1] See p. 264. This is the captain who captured one of the *Hector's* boats at Surat with seventeen Englishmen, and who on that occasion exchanged eloquent messages of defiance with Capt. William Hawkins (Hawkins' *Voy.*, p. 393).

[2] His name was Pedro Alvarez de Abreu. Tidoré was captured by Van der Hagen on the 19th May 1605, after several unsuccessful assaults, in which the Portuguese fought with determined valour. The fort was finally taken by reason of the explosion of the magazine by a Dutch shell, seventy lives being lost by this accident (*Rec. des Voy.*, pp. 79-85). Prior to the siege, Middleton had been the guest of Capt. de Abreu, and on the surrender interceded effectually with V. der Hagen for the lives of the prisoners (Middleton's *Voyage*, Hak Soc.). The Dutch captain promised to send them to the Manillas. De Abreu,

fortress of *Tidore*, when the Hollanders took it (and they hold it still); the other, being younger, had only had command of a galiot.

During the voyage these three lords had often given me testimony of their great affection, and all the way from Goa to Brazil had frequently assisted me in little ways, such as with clothes and wine, and many a time had we foregathered for a chat. And even in Brazil I considered myself as one of their household, their house being open to me at all hours, when I cared to go there.

They had chartered a caravel to carry them, their suite, baggage, and merchandise, straight to Portugal, to obtain there of the King of Spain the rewards and recompense due for their good service in the Indies, with the intention afterwards to return there, for they were all married in India.

I had been looking for some favourable opportunity of returning, but the difficulty was that a passage costs in all more than a hundred or a hundred and twenty livres; and our carrack being lost, I had no further claim upon the ship's officers—as, indeed, my passport stated; so that every person had to shift for himself. At this juncture these kindly gentlemen offered to pay my passage, which was ten crowns, and to feed me at their table free of all charge. With these assurances, when the caravel was ready I was about to embark with my baggage, but the master of the vessel refused to take me, saying he had once carried a Frenchman who had been taken in a Hollander prize, and this Frenchman had been more trouble than all the rest, wherefore he had made an oath he would never carry another. Hereupon a great dispute arose between the vice-admiral and the master on account of me. For the viceroy

after his return to Portuguese India, and before leaving with Pyrard, was captain of the fort of Mombasa (*Bocarro*, p. 112). What is known of his further history appears below.

had sent the vice-admiral to get me taken on board, and these gentlemen had spoken to the viceroy, who was of the same mind and intention, and had themselves done what they could in the matter. But the misfortune was that it was already night, and the vessel was all ready to sail. The vice-admiral told him angrily that he was sorry these gentlemen should go with a fellow that would never come safely to port. In short, he used dire threats of what would befall if he ever showed face again in that bay. Yet this refusal of the master was my salvation; for when I arrived in Portugal, the first news I got was that these three poor lords had been taken with the caravel by the pirates and carried to Barbary.[1] This intelligence caused me the utmost

[1] These unfortunate gentlemen were probably ransomed in ordinary course. Pedro Alvares de Abreu, alone of the three (his brother not being identified), can be traced after this point in the official documents. On the 13th March 1613 the king despatches an *alvará* to the viceroy, in which he recites that Pedralvares de Albreu, "fidalgo of my house", who served the office of captain of *Tidore* at the time of its loss, when the fortress was destroyed by the explosion of the gunpowder magazine while besieged by the Hollanders and Ternatese, and was oblige to retire without any receipts from his franchise of cloves and other things to which he was so entitled. The king therefore directs that the viceroy shall supply him "with two covered galiots, staunch and capacious, equipped with soldiers and mariners, and provided with all necessaries for the voyage, and supplied with all the apparel of war, offensive as well as defensive, at the cost of my treasury, in which galiots he may go, or which he may send to the Moluccas to obtain all the cloves due to him under his franchise for all the time during which he served the office of captain of Tidore." He does not seem to have gone out to India in 1613, for the *alvará* is endorsed with a further order, dated the 10th March 1614, directing that he is to be supplied with these galiots at the first monsoon after he reaches India. Of the same date (10th March 1614) are two other *alvarás*. The first, after reciting de Abreu's services as above, proceeds:—"I am pleased to direct that in case of his not entering upon the captaincy of the fortress of Chaul, to which I have appointed him, he may bequeath it to any one legitimate son or daughter, that is, to whomsoever she may marry, to serve the said office for the term of three years, upon any vacancy among those appointed before the 8th April 1611, the date of his

regret and sorrow, by reason of the good friendship they bore me.

Frustrate in this quarter, and in great trouble for my return home, I had the good fortune to meet with two Flemings, naturalised Portuguese, who were also glad enough to find us. They were in partnership, and possessed a very fine hulk built at Dunkirk, whose arms she bore; she was of 250 tons burthen. They asked us if we had a mind to go with one of them, for the other was remaining at St. Salvador. This proposal we gladly accepted, offering to go as the other sailors, but without wages. We considered ourselves lucky enough to be allowed to work our passage; while they were pleased to have found us, for we supplied them with three hands without pay. When we were thus come to terms, they bade us get our passport and license in writing from the viceroy. This obtained, we went on board the hulk, which was laden with sugar, and well equipped with cannon and all other provision of arms and munitions. We numbered about sixty persons on board, including my two companions and myself, and also the Fleming,

nomination; provided, however, such person be satisfactory to me or to my viceroy of India." He is also to have the habit of Christ, with 20 mil-reis allowance; he must, however, proceed to India by the ships of this present year, and not otherwise; if he wills the office to a son, that son must be fit for the office, and must prove the bequest, producing the will; if to a daughter, the person she is about to marry must, before the marriage, present himself before the President and Councillors (of the India Council) and prove his fitness for the office, and after the marriage, must prove the marriage according to the form of the Sacred Council of Trent. The second *alvarā* authorises de Abreu, in case he leaves no legitimate issue, to bequeath the office to whomsoever he will, on condition of paying his debts. The nominee must, however, be a fidalgo, and approved by the king. De Abreu did not, in fact, proceed to India till 1616, on the 19th March of which year the king gave him a letter of recommendation to the viceroy, requesting the latter (besides obeying his orders as to the galiots) to employ de Abreu in any services, as occasion may offer (*Arch. Port. Or.*, Fasc. 6, Nos. 208, 321, 322, 416).

who had been in our carrack. We left the Bay on the 7th October, 1610.

We had the wind contrary at the first, whereby we were delayed five-and-twenty hours ere we could double the Cape of St. Augustine, which is 100 leagues from the Bay, in the altitude of eight degrees south of the equinoctial. On the 3rd November we doubled the Cape in great peril, because of the shallows and reefs, which we approached quite close. The same day we sighted the town of Fernambuq,[1] which belongs to the Portuguese of Brazil: it is a very well-built town, and has some fine churches.

Two days afterwards we observed a caravel under sail, which put all our people in great fear, as they believed she was a pirate, wherefore we all assumed our arms; afterwards, however, she was discovered to be a Portuguese.

The fifth of December we re-crossed the equinoctial line, coming toward the Arctic Pole. I have crossed it ten or twelve times during my voyage.

On the 25th of the same month we began to see floating on the sea some *goymon*, or green moss, which the Portuguese call *Sargasso*.[2] This herb grows at the bottom of the sea, and is a sign continually seen in those parts: the whole ocean is covered with it, and is as green as a meadow. It begins at the 21st degree, and extends to the 30th.

On the 5th January 1611 we sighted the Açores,[3] amongst

[1] Pernambuco. "It is the greatest town in all that coast", says Lopez Vaz in 1586, "and hath above three thousand houses in it, with seventy Ingenios for sugar, and great store of Brasill-wood, and abundance of cotton, yet are they in great want of victuals, for all their victuals come either from Portugal or from some places on the coast of Brasill" (*Hakluyt*, iii, 787). It is the chief town of the province of the same name, and has a population of nearly 40,000.

[2] Floating seaweed (*fucus natans*), which covers a large area of the Atlantic, off the current of the Gulf Stream.

[3] The Azores first appear on the Genoese map of 1351, now in the Laurentian Library at Florence. They were effectually rediscovered, or rather "found", by the navigators of Prince Henry in 1432. The

others the islands of *Corbo, Flores,* and *Terceira,* which is the chief one, in the altitude of 39½ degrees: here we began to feel the cold, to us a strange sensation.

On the 15th January we descried the coast of Portugal at *Brelingue,*[1] a place eight or ten leagues north of Lisbon; this was in the morning at day-break. We thought we were still sixty leagues off, because the wind was from the south, and it blew a strong gale.

Our design was to enter at Lisbon, but we could not by reason of the contrary winds; whereupon arose a great debate between the captain and a Jew merchant, or, as the Portuguese would call him, *Christiano Nuevo* (the ship was a Flemish hulk of 250 tons, as already described). The captain was a Hollander that had his residence at Lisbon, and was in partnership with another Hollander, to whom belonged the greater part of the goods. The Jew had more than 100,000 crowns' worth of merchandise, most of it his own, the rest put in his care by the principal merchant and others. There was also another Jew on board as rich as he, and four or five other Jew merchants. The profits they make after being nine or ten years in those lands are marvellous, for they all come back rich: many of these new Christians,

first two discovered were Santa Maria and San Miguel (from which we have our St. Michael oranges). The third, thus named Terceira, was originally called the Island of Jesu Christo; its town Angora ("bay") is the capital of the group. The other islands are Graciosa, Saõ Jorge, Fayal, Pico, Corvo, and Flores. On the rediscovery they were named *las ilhas dos Açores,* the "kite islands", from the number of those birds seen there. Terceira, Fayal, and Pico were colonised under grants from the Duchess of Burgundy, to whom the king had assigned them, by emigrants from Flanders, and the whole group thus got the name of the Flemish Islands, which has given rise to the erroneous statement that the first discoverers were from the Low Countries (Major's *Prince Henry the Navigator,* pp. 130-7). The Azores are still a Portuguese possession, and have a population of about 250,000.

[1] The Berlingas Islands in our charts, and by our sailors known as the Burlings. Their light is well known to all ships coasting Portugal.

Jews by race, but baptised, being worth sixty, eighty, and even over a hundred thousand crowns; yet are they slightly esteemed withal. It was, indeed, long since a vessel had arrived with so rich a freight as this had. So, being in view of Brelingue, we determined to make it, the contrary wind notwithstanding. We were thus tacking about continually, now to landward, now to seaward, when suddenly a violent squall overtook us, the wind being contrary, and we close ashore. This put us in great fear, insomuch that the Jew merchant came and said to the captain that, with such weather and wind, there was no likelihood of reaching Lisbon. The captain in reply bade him give him an act signed under his hand, containing a promise that he would bear his share of all expenses, damage, interest, and risks attending the delay; otherwise he (the captain) would remain out at sea where the weather was fine enough, and would await the subsiding of the storm and a fair wind. The merchant refused to give this assurance, and desired him to steer a course for the Bayonne Islands, which were distant some eighty leagues, off Galicia. So saying, he took the helm himself, and brought her round before the wind, whereupon arose a mighty contention, with much abuse and hard words on both sides; but at length peace was made, and the merchant signed the act, and we stood away for the Bayonne Islands off Galicia. Methinks the storm had most to do with appeasing their choler.

We took about five days from Brelingue to these islands, the gale heavy all the while, nay, rather increasing. Hereupon another mischance befell us, to wit, our vessel began to make water in such sort that it could not possibly be kept down, and we were driven so close in shore that we were in double apprehension. One day, among others, some of the mariners led us to believe we were on the right side of the bay, and said they knew it well: which belief was like to ruin us; for, as we were standing a course right up it with the wind fair, and quite close ashore, we found it was not the bay. It was a very miracle that saved us, for the wind was from the sea, and we were so close ashore that we had great difficulty in doubling the point and getting out. I believe more than 1,500 crowns' worth of vows were made, which were afterwards duly paid. The principal merchant made one of 800 cruzados: to wit, 400 for an orphan girl to marry withal, and 400 for a lamp and other utensils for a shrine of Our Lady that is hard by. As soon as he set foot on land he sought out an orphan girl, and fulfilled his promise to her, as also to the churchwardens of the said church. Many others, too, did the like; nor did any fail therein, according to his means and the extent of his vows. It is a custom of the Portuguese, when they are in peril, to make these vows; but the worst of it is that it makes them indolent and careless about working stoutly to save their lives.

In short, from Lisbon to these islands, we thought we were lost more than ten times on account of the unseaworthiness of our ship and the proximity of the shore, towards which the sea-wind was driving us with such violence that it tore all our sails: in such extreme peril was I placed at the end of my ten years' voyage. So indeed it oftens happens that, after many long, distressful, dangerous voyages, men come to be lost at the very port, as has been seen in the case of many viceroys, who, after their endless course of larceny and robbery in the Indies, at length come to be lost at the very port of Lisbon, themselves and all their gains.

When we were at last on the point of entering the bay of the Bayonne Islands,[1] on the coast of Galicia, we met a small vessel on the same course, the sight of which gave us great fear and apprehension, though we were well equipped with cannon and arms, and numbered sixty men; for I may say

[1] Islas de Bayona, at the entrance to the Bay of Vigo, which they protect as a breakwater, so called from the town of Bayona on the mainland. More properly they are called the *Cies*, *Ciccas*, the Cicæ of Pliny.

with truth that the Portuguese are not men of valour on the sea, nor, for the matter of that, on land either. They are good merchants, mariners, and pilots, and that is all. I am sure fifteen or twenty Frenchmen, English, or Hollanders could easily have taken us; and the vessel was worth more than 500,000 crowns. The day before, a cruizer had taken a caravel in the same place, and when we entered the two were at anchor there together, the caravel discharging. They were, however, on the one side, while we passed to the other and made for the town. There are three or four little towns in this bay.[1]

Thus happily landed, the 15th of January 1611, I remembered the vow I had made while yet in the Indies (as already told[2]), to wit, that if God gave me grace to come again to Spain, I would make the pilgrimage of St. James in Galicia. To this end did I continually with stout heart offer my prayers to God while at sea, and that it might please Him I should land at any other place than Lisbon, for the certain fear I had lest we should be held prisoners there. Indeed, all the other foreigners that had come from the Indies had been given in charge to the captains of the ships by the Viceroy of Goa; yet, forasmuch as our ship was lost in the Bay of All Saints, our captain was no longer responsible for us, and we were free. Nevertheless, had we landed at Lisbon, we should have been arrested as prisoners all the same. But the Divine Providence was pleased to bring us in safety to these Bayonne Islands, where, casting anchor, we found a number of French ships riding there for purposes of traffic. As soon as their crews were aware of our arrival, they all came out of wonder to see us, and it was then we learnt all that had passed in France. It was now ten years since we had had certain news.

We went ashore, and spent some days in refreshing our-

[1] It does not appear whether he landed at Bayona, Vigo, or at Cangas.

[2] See vol. i, p. 310.

selves with the French and Portuguese there, and then bade good-bye to the Portuguese of our ship, returning them our thanks, and especially to the captain, who out of kindness gave me some pieces of money. I then resolved to accomplish my vow, so, leaving there my two companions, who were unwilling yet to leave the place, and whom I have never seen again, I took my journey straight for St. James, which is ten leagues off, passing by the way the town of *Ponte-Vedra*,[1] a handsome and busy place.

There were some vessels of Bayonne and St. Jean de Lutz[2] being at anchor at the time, and I then remembered that I had some letters of my countrymen who were detained at the Bay of all Saints in Brazil. I got information of the various persons to whom the letters were addressed, and by good fortune meeting them there, delivered to them the letters, and told them all the news of their friends, whereof they were exceeding glad. They gave me good cheer on board their ships, keeping me to spend the night; and on the morrow, after good entertainment, they made me presents of some money, and came to escort me a full quarter of a league out of the town. I then took my leave, thanking them warmly for the benefits and honour I had received of them, and then took my way towards *Campostelle*[3] to pay my vow;

[1] Pontevedra, a picturesque old town, now of 21,000 inhabitants, at the head of the next *ria*, or bay, north of that of Vigo.

[2] Bayonne and St. Jean de Luz, the French towns of the department of the Basses Pyrénées.

[3] The bones of St. James were discovered near the site of the present city in A.D. 835 by Bishop Theodomir, and a cathedral-shrine was finished in 874. Compostella (Jacom' hospitella) rapidly became one of the two or three chief places of pilgrimage in Christendom. In the Maritime Ordinances of Trani (A.D. 1063) it is mentioned along with the Holy Sepulchre and Rome. With Englishmen it was the favourite foreign pilgrimage, "à Saint James en pelerinage ou à aucun autre lieu" (*Black Book of the Admiralty*, Rolls Series, i, 157). It was one of the chief places on the Wife of Bath's list:—

"At Rome sche hadde ben, and at Boloyne,
In Galice at seynt Jame, and at Coloyne."
(Chaucer, *Prol.*, 467.)

I arrived there by God's grace the same day, and remained three days performing my devotions. There I met the Fleming or Hollander of whom I have already spoken somewhat, that came with us from Goa. I found him in the hospital grievously sick; but seeing me, he determined to take courage and try to come with me to France. Nevertheless, we had not marched a quarter of a league out of the town, when he was constrained out of weakness to halt and return, and I have not heard any news of him since.

Having thus paid my vows to St. James, I went to *la Corugne*, or *Crugne*,[1] one of the best towns and seaports in all the coast of Galicia, a distance of ten leagues, there to endeavour to get a passage to France.

After a sojourn of three days at this place, I found no opportunity or means of taking ship, but got word that at a little port about ten leagues off, between *Corugne* and

The cathedral above-mentioned was destroyed by the Moor Al-Mansúr in 997; the present one dates from 1078. It is a very fine church, built on the model of St. Sernin at Toulouse, and probably by the same architect. The exceptionally grand west door is figured in Street's *Gothic Architecture in Spain*, and is represented by a cast in the South Kensington Museum. The objects of the pilgrimage were the statue of the saint, and the box which was supposed to have contained his bones; but for centuries the relics themselves had disappeared. In 1884 a workman discovered some bones, which have been authenticated by the Committee of Relics at Rome as those of the Apostle; but it may be feared that the shrine, though thus supplemented, will not again attract any such stream of pilgrims as in the ages of faith when the box sufficed.

[1] La Coruña, in French *Corogne*, in English Corunna, but in Elizabethan days "the Groyne". Few regions are so notable in English history as this corner of Spain. At Corunna John of Gaunt landed to claim the Castilian crown; and Philip II embarked to marry our English queen. From this port the Armada sailed in July 1588; nine months later the tables were turned, and Corunna was destroyed by Drake and Norris. Vigo and Finisterre recall the victories of Rooke in 1702, and of Hawke and Anson in 1747. Lastly, the retreat and death of Sir John Moore at Corunna in 1807 gave to that town an English fame which poetry has rendered imperishable.

another town called *Betance*,[1] there was a small Rochelle barque of 35 tons, laden with oranges, and ready to sail. I took the road forthwith ; but, on arriving at the place, found it quite otherwise, for the barque was not half laden, nor was she fully so for twelve days thereafter. However, seeing no other means, I resolved to wait, praying the master to give me a passage when he should go. This he promised most willingly, regretting that he could not leave for fifteen days. This news afflicted me sorely on account of the expense, my purse having but small store of money. Yet was it well for me that living was not so dear there as in a big town, and also that at the time there was one of the greatest catches of fish I have ever seen, chiefly sardines of the finest and largest description, insomuch that you got them for almost nothing ; for a sou I got more than I could eat in a whole day. Moreover, I used frequently to go with the skipper to the country, and accompanied him in his buying and collecting of oranges and lemons. We went twice or thrice to *Betance* together, and he would not have me pay for anything when in his company.

I also lodged with a kind host and hostess, who treated me with much civility, and did not make me pay half the cost of my living. Having thus waited ten or twelve days, I was one evening notified by the master of the barque that he would be ready to take me on board the following day, and that I should make some provision for my victuals, for as to my passage, he would take nothing. When he heard all my adventures and fortunes he was much pleased at this *rencontre*. Having thus embarked, we had the wind so fair that we were but six-and-thirty hours in crossing over to Rochelle, where, thanks to God, we happily arrived the 5th of February. Then praising God with all my heart, I had assurance of seeing once again the land of France, for which I had prayed with so much desire. The master

[1] Betanzos.

who gave me this passage was named *Jean Arnoul*, and was of the island of Oleron.[1] He deemed himself lucky to have brought me, and gave me good cheer at La Rochelle, willing not that I should take lodging elsewhere than at his house, and took great pride in showing me the sights of the town, and presenting me to his friends, who greatly caressed me and did me much honour. After some days I bade him farewell, and took the road to the town of Niort,[2] where the fair must be held. Here I met with many merchants of my native place, which is the town of Laval in Brittany, and thither I returned with them the 16th day of February, in the year 1611, for which God be praised!

[1] A small island opposite the mouths of the Charente and Seudre, chiefly famous for its ancient maritime court, which gave its name to the celebrated code of mediæval sea-laws known as the "Laws of Oleron". The earliest known manuscript (early 14th cent.) is preserved in the Guildhall archives of the City of London. (See the laws themselves, in the *Black Book of the Admiralty*, Rolls Series.)

[2] On the river Sèvre, chief town of the department of the Deux Sèvres.

Louange à Dieu.

Porte Beucheresse, Laval.

TREATISE

OF

ANIMALS, TREES, AND FRUITS.

Treatise and Description of the animals, trees, and fruits of the East Indies, observed by the Author.

ALTHOUGH many have written amply of the nature, forms, and habits of many animals to us unknown, and of the trees and fruits of the East Indies; nevertheless, having seen and known them so thoroughly and for so long, and having handled them not once but countless times, and having lived upon them, I have felt myself constrained to put in writing the results of my long experience, assuring myself that none, perhaps, will have observed their nature with the same particularity.

CHAPTER I.

Of the Elephants and Tigers.

THE elephant is the largest of all animals, with the most judgment and intelligence; one might even say he possesses the use of reason; he is also of vast profit and service to man. If it be desired to mount him, this animal is so supple, obedient, and disciplined to the service of man, to wit, of such as he is willing to serve, that he will bend low and himself assist one to mount with the aid of his trunk.

This animal loves of all things to be praised and caressed; this done, he is humble and obedient; nevertheless, his strength is so great that without experience none can know it. I have seen one with his tusks carry two metal cannons, tied and bound round about with ropes, and weighing each three thousand weight. He lifted them all alone, and carried them some 500 paces. I have also seen an elephant draw ships and galleys ashore, or launch them afloat.[1] These elephants are of a wonderful nature, seeing they will obediently do whatever they are required, provided only they be treated with kindness.

Throughout all the Malabar country, and even in the realm of Dealcan or Decan, I have remarked that only the Nairs tame and train this animal; and at Calecut I have seen little Nair boys caressing little elephants, and leading them hither and thither, and so becoming familiar with them. Only Nairs control them, give them their food, and lead them about the town or elsewhere, and none others would dare to come near them. Led by his Nair, no animal is more docile or tractable; he does all that is told him, caresses any one pointed out to him, admits all sorts of persons to mount him, extends his trunk, which serves him as a hand, and assists them to mount, or, in the case of a child, lifts it with his trunk and places it on his back. But if the Nair is not there, none is so bold as to touch him; such a one he would kill. On his nose he carries a great trunk, which is very long and like a gut (*boyau*), which he sways about; it serves him for a hand to convey his food to his mouth, and for other uses; yet is it so strong that with it he will seize a man, lift him high in air, and then dash him to the ground; thus indeed are malefactors executed at Calecut.[2] I was also told of one at Goa that some time ago killed many

[1] Varthema, a century before this time, describes the beaching of vessels at Cannanor: "They put the side of the vessel foremost, and under the said ship they put three pieces of wood, and on the side next the sea I saw three elephants kneel down and with their heads push the ship on to dry land" (p. 127).

[2] The employment of elephants as executioners dates from very early times. Tennent quotes 3 *Maccabees*, v, 42, and Ælian, *Hist. Anim.*, viii, 10.

persons in this manner as he went about the town, although he had a conductor; and, indeed, I have seen some that could not be approached, though they had their Nairs: these were of a more cruel nature.

When they lead them to war, they attach to their trunks a sword, wherewith they strike their enemies. I have seen some with these swords attached for parade, and they brandished them about in furious style.[1] These animals eat no flesh, not even when wild, but live only on branches and leaves of trees, which they break off with their trunks, and they will chew even thick wood. In captivity they are more delicate in their living, and must have their rice well cooked, and served with butter and sugar, and made up into big balls; they require full a hundred pounds of rice a day, besides leaves of trees, chiefly of the Indian fig, which we call *Bananes*, and the Turks[2] *Plantenes*. The reason why only

[1] This was a very ancient practice; but we have no good testimony as to the dexterity of these armed trunks. Mas'ûdi (10th century) says that the Prince of Mansura, south of the Indus, "maintained eighty elephants trained for war, each of which bore in his trunk a bent scymitar, with which he was taught to cut and thrust at all confronting him. The trunk itself was effectively protected by a coat of mail, and the rest of the body enveloped in a covering composed jointly of iron and horn." The Russian, Nikitin, thus writes of the Deccan: "Elephants are greatly used in battle. The men on foot are sent first, the Khorassanians being mounted in full armour, man as well as horse. Large scythes are attached to the trunks and tusks of the elephants, and the animals are clad in ornamental plates of steel. They carry a citadel, and in the citadel twelve men in armour, with guns and arrows" (*India in 15th Century*, iii, 12).

[2] I cannot account for this notion. The word "plantain" is the Spanish *platano* or *plantano;* while the Turks, in all probability, know the fruit by its Arabic name, *mauz*, whence its botanical generic *Musa*. Col. Yule remarks (*Gloss.*, s. v. *Plantain*), that many authors have distinguished the banana and the plantain, identifying the former with the smaller fruit, the *Musa paradisaica*, and the latter with the larger, the *Musa sapientum;* but this distinction cannot be supported. The name banana (and Indian fig) was applied to all varieties of the *Musa*, as well by the Portuguese as by most Oriental travellers of the 16th and 17th

kings keep them is because of the cost of their maintenance,[1] and in the keeping of many is shown their magnificence and power; for this animal is of great service, even in war. I have seen a number in possession of the King of Calecut. The King of Bengala has 10,000; and the Grand Mogor, otherwise called *Acoubar* (which means "the Great King"), as I heard from many Indians and others who had been at his court, maintains as many as 30,000.[2]

Further, it is a remarkable fact that this animal never covers the female, in whatever heat he be, while any one is by. Some will have it they have no joints in their legs,[3] and that they never lie down; but this is false, for they bend themselves and lie down at their pleasure. I need say no more, seeing that many have already written of them.

Of tigers there are a vast number in the Indies; indeed, they are commoner than wolves here. It is a most ferocious and mischievous animal, which will not flee from men except they be in great numbers, but, on the contrary, will pursue,

centuries: 'plantain' was more general in the Spanish West Indies. Curiously enough, 'plantain' is the common word in Anglo-India, probably because English connection with the West Indies preceded that with the East; while 'banana' is now the prevailing term in the London fruit market. The plant is of Asiatic origin; but the statement of its existence in Peru before the Conquest, made by so high an authority as Garcilasso, has given rise to some doubt. The subject is discussed by De Candolle (*Origin of Cult. Plants*, pp. 304-311).

[1] Emerson Tennent says that an ordinary elephant engrosses the attention of three men, and that the daily cost of his keeping amounts to about 3*s*. 6*d*. (*Ceylon*, ii, 396).

[2] See vol. i, p. 327, and above, p. 251.

[3] This fallacy, as Sir Thomas Browne says, is "not the daughter of latter times, but an old and grey-headed errour, even in the days of Aristotle" (*De Anim.*, lib. II, c. i), who got it from Ctesias. The text above shows that the notion was still current, requiring personal testimony to confute it. About the same time Shakespeare is only half convinced—

> "The elephant hath joints; but none for courtesy:
> His legs are for necessity, not flexure."
>
> (*Troilus and Cressida*, Act ii, sc. 3.)

attack, and devour them. The kings take great pleasure in hunting tigers, both for the purpose of ridding the country of them and saving the poor people, and also because therein are the valour and bravery of their noblesse shown forth and proved. The Nayres are continually hunting them, engaging them with sword and buckler; nor is this without danger, for the beast is bold and savage. The Nayres having slain him, drag him before the king with great honour and triumph. I have seen many bring their spoil before him thus, and many too that were grievously wounded in the encounter.[1] These tigers are of the height of a mastiff, but longer, with big heads resembling that of a cat. The skin is passing fair, all marked with white, black, and red. They live by hunting their prey, and are especially fond of fowls.

CHAPTER II.

Of Crocodiles and Turtles.

There are vast numbers of crocodiles in the rivers of the Island of St. Lawrence, of the Bengal coast, the Malabar country, and of Guinea and Angola.

The crocodiles live in fresh water; they are of great size, and being covered with scales, are therefore very difficult to kill, but the belly is tender and easy to pierce. They have an odour of musk, as we perceived from those we killed at the Island of St. Lawrence[2]; for as soon as they were struck all the air was, as it were, perfumed with musk, and even the banks had the same odour. They who have eaten the flesh say it is very delicate and good; but, for my part, I never tasted it, and had no fancy to try it.[3] The mouth is garnished with very sharp teeth, those of the lower jaw overlapping and

[1] See vol. i, pp. 382, 400. [2] See vol. i, p. 37.

[3] "To my taste", says Sir S. Baker, "nothing can be more disgusting than crocodile flesh. I have tasted almost everything, but

transpiercing the upper jaw, which is all marked with the cavities wherein to the teeth pass, and it is the upper jaw that works.[1]

The turtles float on the surface of the water in order to bask in the sun; some are of such a size that the shell of one would suffice to roof a little hut or cot, and to cover ten or more persons sitting.[2] There are vast numbers of them at the Maldives, and some little islands you may see inhabited by no other animals than these great turtles, but covered with them. On our arrival at the Maldives we caught a great one with 500 or 600 large eggs, like yellow hen's eggs. We boiled them in fresh water, and ate them; indeed, we lived upon them for three or four days, our company numbering forty persons, and with nothing else to eat. The flesh is very rich and delicate, like veal; but as we ate it without bread, salt, or other dressing, many fell sick, and for my case, I was very ill, vomiting continually, and sometimes spitting blood.[3] The islanders make use of the shell for their bucklers and other utensils and commodities.

At the Maldives there is another smaller kind,[4] but even these are three or four feet in diameter, more or less. The shell is brown, part of it running to black, part to red, very smooth and shining, and so wonderfully patterned that when polished it is an article of great beauty. The reason why it is greatly sought after by all the kings, lords, and rich people in the Indies, and chiefly by those of Cambaye and Surat, is that it is made into boxes and caskets garnished with gold and silver, also into bracelets and other ornaments.[5] It is

although I have tasted crocodile, I could never succeed in swallowing it. The combined flavour of bad fish, rotten flesh, and musk is the *carte de dîner* offered to the epicure."

[1] This is an old belief—unfounded, of course.

[2] This is the loggerhead turtle (*Couanea olivacea*), Maldive *musimbi*. As to its size, see Tennent's *Ceylon*, ii, 190.

[3] Repeated from vol. i, pp. 65, 66.

[4] Probably the hawksbill turtle (*Caretta imbricata*), which supplies the tortoiseshell of commerce.

[5] See above, p. 248.

found only at the Maldives and at the Philippines or Manillas, and is one of the most valued articles of merchandise exported thence. The nature of this animal and its tenacity of life are indeed remarkable; for the islanders, when they catch one, put it near the fire, and then take off the shell, separating it from the turtle in pieces, the largest being the best, and fetching the best prices. They do not remove the whole in one piece, as in the case of the common tortoises. Next they put back the turtle all alive into the sea, where it grows a fresh shell, it being prohibited to kill them.[1] Furthermore, they never eat any kind of tortoise, because, say they, this animal has some kind of conformity and kinship with man.[2]

CHAPTER III.

Of the Fish of the Indian Sea, and more particularly those of the Maldives.

The sea under the Torrid Zone bears some strange fish, very different from those of our seas. Amongst others, strange to say, are certain fish that eat and devour men. At the Maldives are many of these, for they love the shallow water there, and roam in great numbers. The fish is very large, nine or ten feet in length, and big in proportion, *i.e.* more than a man's armful; it has no scales, but is covered with a kind of hide of a dark hue, albeit white under the belly, though not of the same

[1] "If taken from the animal after death and decomposition, the colour of the shell becomes cloudy and milky, and hence the cruel expedient is resorted to of seizing the turtles as they repair to the shore to deposit their eggs, and suspending them over fires till heat makes the plate on the dorsal shields start from the bones of the carapace, after which the creature is permitted to escape to the water." (Tennent, *Ceylon*, ii, 190.)

[2] This is not quite true of the Maldivians; Mr. Bell informs me that they eat certain varieties.

thickness or toughness as that of the whale. The head is round, high, and somewhat broad, garnished with a number of great pointed teeth set in many rows. The inhabitants of the Maldives are much incommoded by these animals, for they come and devour them as they fish and bathe, or, at least, dock their arms or legs. You see there many of the people that have lost a leg or an arm, or a hand, or have been wounded elsewhere in their bodies by the bites of these fish. I have seen many at the Maldives thus maimed; indeed, I have seen some of these fish caught with whole limbs of men in their bellies. Every day some accident happens, because it is the usual custom of the people to bathe and wash in the sea. One day I was like to have been seized by them as I passed from one island to another by a narrow ferry. The Maldivians have assured me that these fish go in troops, and have many a time attacked little boats and fishers' wherries, and capsizing these, have devoured the men. This never happened while I was there, but every one described the affair as a thing certain: they say that God sends these animals to punish them for their sins. They call these fish *Paimones.*[1] There is also another smaller kind, called by the Portuguese *Tuberons,*[2] which have the head broad and round, the mouth exceedingly large, with a number of teeth in several rows, and also covered with a skin instead of scales, just like the former; they also eat human flesh, and devour or maim such as they find bathing or swimming in the sea. They are found in all those seas, and sometimes follow ships in search of their prey, even eating shirts and sheets that are left to soak in the water. And it is a wondrous thing to relate that they have always about them certain little fish of a dark skin, and rough under the belly, which by means of this roughness fasten themselves to the tuberon, and cannot be eaten by him.

[1] M. *femunu;* see vol. i, p. 96.

[2] Port. *tuberão*, M. *miyaru.* Sir R. Hawkins gives a good description of the "shark or tiberune" (*Hawk. Voy.*, pp. 250-1).

The Maldives abound in fish more than any place in the world. The natives are exceedingly dainty, and eat only the best and most delicate, despising the rest. There is a little fish about a foot or thereabouts in length, square at the four corners, and covered with a shell of one piece, so hard that it requires a hatchet to break it, with only the point of its tail turned back to serve it for a helm; the shell is of a yellowish colour, and marked with dark stars. On this score some call it the star-fish.[1] It is the most delicate eating imaginable; the flesh is white, firm, and without any bones. You would say it was chicken, so good is it. You see there, too, many rays of vast size, some from six to seven feet broad; the natives, however, take no count of them, and never eat them, considering this fish not to be good. I have, however, eaten it, and found it as good as it is here. But, as I have said, they are so dainty and nice, and have so abundant a supply, that they disdain to eat most of the fish that are like ours, finding them not good enough for their tastes. The larger rays, however, they skin, and with the dried skin, after it is well stretched, they make their drums, using none other.[2] A number of their fishes have a hard shell; thus there are crustaceans of all sorts, and some of great size; some I have seen whose shells blazed out into divers colours, and were very beautiful to see.[3] Of these there is one kind like that called by the sailors *crabes*, which abounds at the Maldives, and is of extraordinary size; it frequents both sea and land, where it hollows out great holes for its retreat. I have seen some with claws bigger than the two fists. Some islands are full of them, to the great annoyance and inconvenience of the inhabitants, who often get wounds through being caught in their claws; and in some of the islands none durst go about at night, because these creatures are then abroad, and swarm every-

[1] Probably one of the skates or rays (M. *maḍi*, Sin. *maḍu*).

[2] The Maldive *tari* or tambourine is still made of this skin. Mr. Bell has given a specimen to the Colombo Museum.

[3] The Maldives, like the Laccadives, are a "perfect paradise for crabs", as Mr. Allen Hume says in *Stray Feathers*, iv, p. 435.

where. Thus did it happen to me once to be wounded by them as I was walking about by night. The people suffer annoyance also from another large fish,[1] all covered with hard, pointed spikes like awls, four inches in length; nor is there any part of its body that is without them. When the people go a-fishing betimes, one treads upon one of them, and runs his feet upon these spikes, the wounds of which are considered venomous.

The sea in those parts is full of vipers or sea serpents,[2] which bite those they meet. As for flying fish,[3] they are met with everywhere under the Torrid Zone, and chiefly near the equinoctial line. Besides those I saw at sea during our voyage, I have seen many at the Maldives; but having spoken of them in my relation of our voyage, I will not repeat here what I have there written.

Moreover, I have been astonished to see so many different kinds of fish to us unknown, small and great, and of all shapes, whereof some are attired in gaudy colours, others glitter as if they were covered with gold; in short, a diversity so multitudinous that one can only wonder and confess that the marvels of our Creator are more apparent in the sea than in any other portion of His handiwork.

CHAPTER IV.

Of the Parrots, and a wondrous Bird that is bred in China.

All India, Africa, Brazil, and the islands adjacent thereto abound (amongst many other sorts of birds) with vast numbers of parrots of all kinds. Some are of a grey and

[1] The sea-hedgehog, M. *Kaḍu-burafati* (Kaḍu = sea; burafati = anything with points that turns round, *e.g.*, a weathercock).

[2] Mr. Bell, in his Report, mentions two kinds, *Hydrophis spiralis* (M. *fen-harufá*) and *Pelamis bicolor* (M. *máridá*), as being much dreaded by the natives.

[3] See vol. i, p. 9.

violet plumage: these are found in the island of St. Lawrence, and are good eating, of the same flavour as wood pigeons; we ate many of them during our sojourn there.[1] The largest green parrots brought home here come from Guinea, Cape Verd, and Brazil. Those of the Indies are green too, but smaller, more tractable, and speak passing well. There is another kind, very large and all white. You see also little parrots no bigger than sparrows. In Brazil, some are all red, some all yellow, and of many other single colours: these are all much bigger than the others. As for herons, they frequent the sea, and are to be seen in great numbers under the Torrid Zone.

While I was at the Maldives a bird landed upon one of the islands, of prodigious form and size. This bird is three feet in height, the body exceedingly thick, more than a man could embrace; the plumage is all white, like a swan's; the feet are flat, as with birds that swim; the neck is half a fathom, and the beak half an ell in length; at the end of the beak above is a kind of crooked hook; the lower jaw is much larger than the upper, and has a large pocket depending therefrom, very capacious, and of a yellowish golden colour, like parchment. The king was greatly astonished to think whence this animal could have come, and what was its nature, and inquired of all who had come from foreign parts, but none could resolve the matter. At length arrived certain strangers, who informed him that this animal was peculiar to China, being bred only there, and that the Chinese use it for catching fish, inasmuch as this animal swims in the water like other water-fowl, and for long whiles at a time. It catches fish industriously, filling the great creel or pocket which hangs beneath its beak, and is so large and capacious as to carry therein many fish of two feet in length each. The king hearing of this bird, wondered exceedingly how it was possible for it to have come alone from China, a

[1] See vol. i, p. 37.

distance of more than 1,200 leagues. He then wished to see it tried, and sometimes had its neck tied and bound round, leaving only enough room for breathing, so that it should not swallow the fish, but should come back with its pocket full: this is the artifice employed in China. I have seen it in this manner go into the sea for a long space, and return laden with fish. It used to go out to sea for a considerable time, sometimes remaining away a whole day, which leads me to believe it not impossible that it had come from China, for it loves the sea and tarries there a long time, catching fish for its food. In addition to this, I have been assured by numberless Indians of all parts that fowls of this kind are bred in China alone.[1]

In Brazil, on my arrival there, I saw two very rare animals. They were of the form, height, and proportions of a small mule, but not of the same nature, for this species of animal is distinct, engendering and bringing forth young after his kind. The skin is wondrously fair to see, being smooth and shiny like velvet; the hair is short, and, what is more strange, it is composed in bands of pure white and deep black, so orderly arranged, even to the ears, the tail, and other extremities, that one can only say of its whole aspect that the art of man could hardly effect the like. Moreover, this beast is very wild, and is never quite domes-

[1] Buffon refers to this passage, *Hist. Nat. des Oiseaux*, ix, p. 171. With respect to the pelican fishing for its masters he quotes Labat (*Nouv. Voy. aux îles d'Amérique*, tom. viii, p. 296), who states, on the authority of Father Raimond, that the bird was so trained by the Caribs. There is no ground for discrediting Pyrard's testimony as an eye-witness, and there is no improbability in the fact. I am not aware, however, of any authority corroborating him as regards this use of the bird in China, where the employment of cormorants in the same capacity is common enough. Mr. P. L. Sclater, F.R.S., informs me that the bird described as visiting the Maldives was probably a *P. onocrotalus*, which, as Jerdon states (*Birds of India*, iii, 856), "is a regular visitant to India during the cold weather, sometimes appearing in considerable flocks."

ticated; in the natural state they are passing savage, and devour men. They are called by the name given them in their own country, that is, *esures*.[1] They are bred at Angola, in Africa, whence they had been brought to Brazil to be afterward presented to the King of Spain; they were taken quite young and small, and had been tamed a little; nevertheless, there was but one man who tended them, or durst approach them. In fact, just a little while before my arrival, one of them, that had by chance got loose, killed a groom, and would have devoured the body, had it not been torn from between his teeth. The keeper, too, showed me a number of marks where they had bitten him, though they were tied with a very short halter. The skin of this animal is certainly one of the most beautiful things imaginable.

CHAPTER V.

Of Pepper and Ginger, Mace and Musk, Cloves and Cinnamon.

Pepper[2] grows in abundance at Cochin, Calecut, Cananor, Barcelor, and all along the Malabar coast. It is thence only the Portuguese take it, and none others dare buy it in those parts. There is also great store of it in the islands of Sumatra and Java, whence the Arabs and all other Indians, and latterly

[1] Probably for *sevres* = *zebres*. The word zebra is said by Littré to be of Ethiopian origin.

[2] These paragraphs on the varieties of pepper are very accurate. Both black and white pepper are obtained from the same climbing plant, *Piper nigrum*, which is indigenous in Malabar. The white is obtained by removing the dark outer layer of pericarp, thereby depriving it of a part of its pungency (Yule, *Gloss.*). As to long pepper, which is the fruit-spike of the shrubs *Piper officinarum* and *Piper longum*, see above, vol. i, p. 328. In the African trade it seems to have gone under the name of *manigueta* (see above, p. 221).

the Hollanders, English, and others that voyage thither, in despite of the King of Spain, supply themselves withal; it is bigger and heavier than that of Malabar, and the Indians prize it more; the Portuguese, however, boast theirs to be the best, saying it has more strength. There are three kinds, black, white, and long. The long grows in Bengala, Brazil, and Guinea.

The black and white pepper (these being the same) comes from a plant or tree like ivy, which is planted at the foot of another tree; as it grows it entwines itself and climbs up to the top of the tree, just like the vine, the hop, the ivy, or any other climber. The leaf resembles that of the orange. The fruit grows in little bunches, rather long, in fact, resembling red currants. At first it is green, when nearly ripe it becomes red, and when dried, black. It is gathered in the months of December and January.

Ginger[1] is commoner than pepper, and is found all over India, also in Brazil and at the island of St. Lawrence. I have not been at any place in the Indies that I did not find ginger. The King of Spain prohibits the export of it in bulk, because otherwise it would interfere with the sale of his pepper, inasmuch as many would content themselves with the former. It is a root that grows in the ground like the iris plant. The Indians make of it a great variety of conserves.

[1] The root of *Zingiber officinale*, the word being the Arabic *zănjabīl* (Yule, *Gloss.*). The cultivation of this plant was very wide-spread in the old world even in classical times, but it does not seem to have been found in its wild state. De Candolle, curiously, does not discuss the plant at all in his *Origin of Cult. Plants.* It was introduced into Brazil after the discovery, and, as stated above (p. 313), throve greatly there. The apprehension that the export of ginger would interfere with the sale of pepper is curious. The reason was that the virtues of both were similar, Paludanus observing of pepper, "it warmeth the mawe, and consumeth the cold slymenes thereof"; and of ginger, "it heateth a cold mawe, and is good against humours" (*Linschoten*, ii, pp. 75, 80).

Nutmegs[1] and mace grow only in the island of Banda, which is distant twenty-four leagues from the Moluccas, but in such quantity there that this island supplies the world. The nutmeg ripens thrice a year, namely, in April, August, and December, the April crop being the best. The tree is most like the peach; the fruit is covered with a rind or very thick skin; when ripe it opens like a nut, and the nutmeg is discovered with another rind, which is the mace: this is of a red colour, but as it dries it comes away, and the colour turns to orange. This mace is of great virtue in fortifying and warming the stomach, in expelling wind, and in digesting food.

Cloves[2] grow only at the Moluccas. The leaves of the tree resemble those of the laurel; the wood, and even the leaves, have almost the same taste as the fruit, or but slightly different. All around the tree grows no other herb, because the roots are so hot that they attract all the humidity. This is proved by placing a sack of cloves over a vessel full of water; the water is consumed and diminished, while the cloves are increased in bulk.

While the flower of the clove is blooming it is white; then it turns to yellow, and at length to red, and it is then the clove is begotten in the flower, and the scent is strongest and best. The odour is the sweetest and most delightful that can be imagined; and one standing within the full force of these flowers would say the whole air was perfumed with the scent.

[1] The nutmeg does grow at the Moluccas, but not so luxuriantly as at Banda.

[2] *Caryophyllus aromaticus*, L. The clove is probably indigenous in the Moluccas, where alone it was found to exist three centuries ago (*De Candolle*, p. 161). It is curious that this spice seems not to have been known to the Romans, nor to any Europeans till the discovery of the Moluccas by the Portuguese. The clove itself is the calix or flower-bud of the plant.

When the clove is ripe it falls to the ground. They are gathered and steeped in sea-water, then dried upon wicker-trays under which fire is placed, the fumes turning the clove black, which before was red.

Cinnamon grows only in the island of Ceylon, and there in so great abundance that the most part of the country is covered with it,[1] as ours here is with underwood and forest. The tree is like the olive, the leaves like those of the laurel; it bears a white flower, and a fruit like a ripe olive. It has two barks; the first is worthless, the second is the true cinnamon, which is stripped on the tree, and allowed to dry there; afterwards, when dry, it is gathered. In other two or three years it grows again, without the tree suffering any harm.[2]

This tree will not grow without being planted. In that country is so great a store of cinnamon that a pound of it is worth on the spot no more than six deniers.

[1] A mistake: the cinnamon (*Cinnamonum zeylanicum*) grows only on the western coast of Ceylon, between Chilaw and Matura, and chiefly in a small area around Colombo. The author probably argues from what he saw of the cinnamon gardens of Colombo. For a full account of the history of cinnamon as an article of commerce, see Flückiger and Hanbury, *Pharmacographia*, p. 467.

[2] This may have been the former method of gathering the bark, but it is not the modern practice. The finest growth of bark is that of the younger shoots of about three years. The branches of this age are lopped, and the bark then removed in strips (see full accounts of the cultivation and preparation in Percival's *Ceylon*, p. 340; Cordiner, *Ceylon*, ii, p. 405; Thunberg, *Travels*, iv, pp. 194-204).

CHAPTER VI.

Of Anil or Indigo, Musk, Ambergris, Benjoin, Sandal, and Aloes-wood.

The *Anil*, otherwise called *Indigo*,[1] is found only in the kingdom of Cambaye and Surat.[2] It is a herb that grows like rosemary, and comes up from seed; when gathered it is dried, then steeped and dried again several times until it becomes blue. It is greatly prized as a dye, and is one of the best commodities of the Indies.

Ambergris[3] is produced from the sea, and chiefly under the Torrid Zone; I have seen great quantities of it at the Maldives, where it is found on the sea-beach. None of the natives of the countries visited by me know for certain whence it comes or how it grows. It is only known that it comes from the sea.

Musk[4] comes from China alone. It proceeds from a little animal of the size of a cat. To get the musk they kill this animal, and beat it all over in its skin, and so let it rot; when rotten they make little purses of the skin, and fill them with the flesh, minced small, and thus sell it. The Chinese drive a great trade in this commodity, but they mix and adulterate it, like everything else that comes from their

[1] *Anil* is the Portuguese name, from the Ar. *al nīl*, which itself is the Sansk. *nīla*, "blue". *Indigo* is from the Greek 'Ινδικόν, and the Latin *Indicum*, probably through the Italian (see Yule, *Gloss.*, under both names). The native place of the cultivated variety (*Indigofera tinctoria*) is unknown, several wild species being found in India, but not in the parts where the former is cultivated. (*De Candolle*, p. 136.)

[2] Incorrect: much was then, and is still, grown in Agra province.

[3] See vol. i, p. 229.

[4] The musk deer (*Moschus moschiferus*) is found in the Himālayas and northwards to Tartary, at a high elevation, generally over 8,000 feet. (Yule, *Gloss.*) It is at least as large as a roebuck. The process described is also quite erroneous.

hands. Wherefore it is never seen in its pure and natural state.

Civets[1] are found in great quantity throughout all the Indies.

Benjoin[2] proceeds, like every other gum, from a very lofty tree; it is highly aromatic. It is produced chiefly at Malacca and in Sumatra.

White Sandal[3] is a tree that grows in the Indies, and in great abundance at the island of St. Lawrence; red sandal is also found there. The Indians use it to rub their bodies, to give them a pleasant scent, and to refresh the skin when they are hot. The tree bears no fruit.

There are two sorts of aloes-wood[4] in the Indies; one the Indians call *Calamba,* the other *Garoa.* They use these woods to rub their bodies, and for perfumes.

[1] *Viverra Indica.*

[2] A kind of incense derived from the resin of *Styrax benzoin.* The name is a corruption of the Ar. *lubān-jāwi*, Java frankincense. Another common form was *benjamin.* (Yule, *Gloss.*)

[3] White sandal is the fragrant wood of the *Santalum album*, L. The old English name was *Sanders wood.* It is doubtful whether the red sandal of the middle ages was a variety of the *Santalum*, or was another species, the *Pterocarpus santalina,* a South Indian tree of inodorous wood, to which the term "red sandal" has also been applied. The latter wood was used largely for its colouring properties. (Yule, *Gloss.*)

[4] The eagle wood of commerce. Calamba or Calambak is given by Crawfurd as Javanese, but probably belongs to the language of Champa (or S. Cochin-China), from the kingdom *Champa*, whence the wood was obtained. This is the finest kind. The name *garoa* seems to come through the Malay *gahru*, from the Sansk. *ayuru.* The Malayālam form is aγil, whence the Portuguese *aguila*, which led to *aquila,* and finally to the French *bois d'aigle*, and the Eng. eagle-wood. The best incense is obtained from the wood of the *Aloexylon agallochum* in a diseased condition. (Yule, *Gloss.*, under names "Aloes", "Champa", "Calambac", and "Eagle-wood".)

CHAPTER VII.

Of Tamarinds, Cassia, and Mirabolans.

There are tamarinds[1] everywhere in India in great quantity; the trees are very high, like pear-trees, and higher, with a fruit resembling a peascod, which the Indians use for verjuice to put in soup; the wood they burn. It is also highly laxative.

The cassia-tree[2] resembles the pear-tree, but with a longer leaf; it bears a yellow, sweet-smelling flower. It blooms in the month of September, then it produces long cods of a green colour, which blacken as they ripen. The Indians make small account of it. It grows of itself without being sown or tended. When the cassia is ripe—that is, in the month of January—it falls; and at this season the people abstain from eating the flesh of animals such as cows and sheep, which then causes fluxes and dysenteries, by reason of the laxative powers of the cassia, which these beasts eat, finding it lying on the ground. The Dealcan country is full of it; I have seen it only round about Goa.

In the Indies are also found mirabolans,[3] which are like plum-trees; there are great numbers at Cochin and Calecut. The fruit also is like a plum; it is very delicate, and is made into conserves and comfits.

[1] *Tamarindus indica*, L. The word is the Ar. *tamar-u'l-Hind*, "date of India".

[2] *I.e.*, here *Cassia fistula*.

[3] A name applied to a number of nuts or kernels used from very early times for medicinal purposes. Mirabolans are now used chiefly for dyeing and tanning. As to the different products to which the name was applied, and the early authorities, see De Orta, *Coll*, f. 148; Yule, *Gloss.*; and *Linschoten*, ii, 123.

CHAPTER VIII.

Of the Arbre Triste, Ebony, Betel, and the Cotton-tree.

That tree called *Triste,*[1] which is produced in the East Indies, is so named because it blooms only by night. As the sun sets you see no flowers upon the tree, then, half-an-hour after the sun is below the horizon, the tree flowers all over; and when the sun rises, incontinently all the flowers fall off, nor does one abide. The tree is of the size of a pear-tree; the leaf resembles that of the laurel, save that it is somewhat slashed. The seeds are useful for soups, for they colour it like saffron; and the water distilled from the flowers is useful against the eye-disease.

The ebony-tree is of the size of the olive, having a leaf of the form of sage, and bearing a white flower like a rose. The wood is exceeding hard; it is found in great quantity at Mozambic,[2] and that is the best; also at the island of St. Helena, but there it is not so good, being full of knots.

Betel is a plant set at the foot of other trees, which it clasps like as does pepper or ivy: the leaf is about as big as that of the rib-wort (*plantain*), but harder and thicker, and full of little nerves or filaments. There is great store of it in the East Indies, and chiefly at the Maldive islands, for there they cultivate it with extreme care. The Indians make great use of it, everybody chewing this leaf almost perpetually: they mingle it with a little lime (in default of oyster or other sea shell), which they call *onny,*[3] and a fruit they call *arequa,*[4] in order to temper its bitterness. It is this which causes the

[1] See vol. i, p. 411.

[2] The Portuguese therefore called it *páo de Moçambique* (see above, p. 224).

[3] Maldive *uni*, Sin. *hunu*, the chunam of India.

[4] The seed of the *Areca catechu* palm.

red colour produced in the chewing. They say they use it for their health, and that they could not otherwise live,[1] for that this leaf is hot, and aids digestion; wherefore they chew it at all hours, having some of it in their mouths at all times, except when they sleep. Moreover, it is of good taste and pleasant odour, and perfumes the breath; in such wise, that a man would not kiss a woman unless her mouth savoured of betel, nor would a woman a man. In truth, its odour is pleasant and agreeable; and, furthermore, it provokes and incites the passions of love.[2] And though it is thus hot, nevertheless it is refreshing to the mouth, quenches the thirst, and saves them from continually drinking, whereto the great heat would otherwise compel them. Having sucked the juice, they spit out the remnant. I made use of it while I was among them, and found it salutary. It dries the brain and the evil humours of the body. Also it preserves the teeth so well, that I never knew one that used it who had toothache, or had lost a single tooth; it makes the teeth as red as coral, indeed, but that they deem a beauty.[3] They think so much of it, that were one to enter a house without being offered some betel, he would take it for an affront and a disgrace; and so, when friends meet by the way, out of politeness and in token of good will, they offer one another betel. In a word, at all feasts, banquets, and rejoicings, it is the first and chiefest item of all good cheer, as good wine is with us.

[1] Probably the Maldivians' own words, just as the Sinhalese would say, *bulat nokaevot inda bae*, "one couldn't live without chewing betel". Linschoten says that the Portuguese ladies expressed themselves to the like effect (ii, 64).

[2] So *De Orta*, f. 37*d*.

[3] Mr. Bell informs me that the Sinhalese have a proverb, *Gilimalet aeti data suddó*, "even in Gilimale (a village famed for its betel) there are people with white teeth", as we speak of every flock having its black sheep.

The plant which bears the cotton is of the height of rose-trees here. The leaf is like that of the maple, the flowers like rose-buds. Within the flower, as it fades, expands a pod, which throws out the cotton, and amid this is the seed, which the people sow as we do in nurseries, thus getting a continual supply of cotton, wherewith they make their cloth, having no other material, neither flax nor hemp, as we have here. And of these cotton cloths they make no account except of the very finest. There is also another kind of cotton[1] that comes from a tree larger than the preceding, like an ash; this tree produces certain pods full of cotton, which, by reason of its short staple, is good for nothing but to make pillows for their beds.

CHAPTER IX.

Of Bananas, or Indian Figs and Pine Apples.

The banana is a tree nine to ten feet high, very common in India, and wondrous tender, like a cabbage-stalk, and yet as big as a man's thigh. It is all covered with several sheathings one over the other, like our leeks; when these are removed the heart remains, of the thickness of the arm, which is used for making soup; the leaves are of an ell and a half in length and half an ell in width. The Gentile Indians use these leaves in place of table-cloths and plates in taking their meals, and the same leaves never serve twice. The fruit is very delicate and precious; little children are fed upon it as pap. Each tree produces but once, and is then cut down; but soon it casts forth new shoots, each of which produces the same fruit once a year. The tree exists in great quantity. The fruit grows in a bunch containing

[1] The silk cotton-tree (*Bombax Malabaricum*), Hind. *semal.*

as many as 200 or 300; each is as thick as the arm, and a foot long, and very good and well-flavoured to eat; it is to be got at all seasons; at first it is green, afterwards it becomes yellow, and then is ripe. The Maldivians have large orchards full of it.

Pine-apples[1] grow upon a very low plant which never exceeds three or four feet in height. Beneath it is like a bush; the leaves are narrow, long, and pointed, and spread out all round. The fruit resembles an artichoke, or rather a pine-cone, save that it is somewhat bigger. When the fruit is ripe it is yellow; the inside is very tender and very good to eat. Atop of the fruit is a bunch of leaves, which if planted produces new fruit, and this may be left fifteen days out of the earth without decaying, by reason of its great power of keeping moist. If, after cutting the fruit, you leave the knife without wiping it, it will become all rusty in a single night, so biting and penetrating is the juice. Some Indians betimes make of it a kind of wine like our cider, but better, being stronger and more exhilarating.

[1] He does not seem to be aware that the pine-apple was a recent importation into India from America. The name *Ananas*, by which the Portuguese introduced it (probably, as Col. Yule says, from the Brazilian *nana*), has been naturalised in all the Indian dialects, as well as in all European languages, except English, although Thomson did his best:—

> "Witness, thou best Anana, thou the pride
> Of vegetable life, beyond whate'er
> The poets imaged in the golden age." (*Summer.*)

CHAPTER X.

Of Darions, Ramboutans, Jacks, and Mangos.

The Darion-tree[1] nearly resembles a pear-tree in size; the fruit is as big as a melon. The Indians esteem this fruit to be one of the best and daintiest in the Indies. To those who are unaccustomed to it, it is disagreeable, having a stink like that of our onions, but the taste is far more excellent.

Ramboutans[2] are fruits with a thorny husk like the chestnut. Their colour is red, the inside of the size of a walnut, furnished with a kernel like an almond and of similar taste; over this is a flesh or pulp of a very agreeable taste, which melts in the mouth. This fruit is greatly esteemed in the Indies.

The Jaques[3] is a tree of the height of a chestnut, which produces a fruit as big as a pumpkin. It is attached all round the trunk of the tree, not at the end of the branches, as all other fruits are; at a distance one might say they were big pumpkins fastened to the tree. The outside is like a pine-cone of a yellow colour. When ripe it is very sweet to the taste, yet over-laxative. Within and about the fruit, in place of a nut or pip, you find a number of chestnuts as good and tasty as those of France; and these, contrary to the nature of the fruit, are of a binding quality. So that

[1] The Durian is a native of the Malay peninsula and islands. The lovers of this extraordinary fruit are generally at a loss to describe its virtues to those who have not tasted it: it is a combination of all the most excellent flavours in the world. Its enemies have less difficulty in expressing their opinions: it is like rotten onions, rotten eggs, carrion, etc.

[2] *Nephelium longana*, the Malay *rambūtan*. It is commonest in the Malay countries, but grows well in Ceylon.

[3] Full notes on the jack (Port. *jaca*, from the Malayālan *chakka*) will be found in Yule's *Glossary*.

after having eaten some of the fruit, in order to avoid evil effects, one has but to eat a raw and uncooked kernel.

Mangos grow in trees which are of the height of walnuts in these parts, albeit the leaves are smaller and narrower. The fruit is of the shape of plums, as big as the fist. Within is a stone which is not by any means easily separated from the fruit; when ripe the latter is yellow. There are vast quantities of this fruit in the Indies, not however at the Maldives.[1] While they are still green the natives salt them as we do olives, and thus are they kept the year round. For this fruit, like the jaques, ramboutans, darions, and pine-apples, has its certain season, and does not bear all the year round, like the banana and countless others.

CHAPTER XI.

Of numerous Trees and Plants that grow at the Maldives.

The Maldives are very fertile in all manner of fruits, and beside those already described, which grow there, are many others, whereof I should wish to mention some, as well because they are altogether alien to the species here, as that I have myself made use of them and observed them more narrowly at the Maldives than elsewhere. I would not say that some of them may not grow elsewhere in India, nor that I may not have seen them there.

In the first place, I did much marvel to observe the very remarkable nature of a kind of root, peculiar to the Maldives, which they use much with their food, and dress very cunningly. It grows as big as a man's thigh. It is sown and cultivated ; and what is astonishing is, that they cut the root alone into a number of exceeding small pieces

[1] Mr. Bell says this is not quite accurate ; though scarce, the mango is not unknown at the Maldives.

and plant these, insomuch that it grows not from seed but from a morsel of the root—a strange fact, and contrary to the nature of other plants.[1]

There are many sorts of trees, some bearing fruits, others only flowers. Among those bearing fruits are cocos, bananas, pomegranates, limes, and orange. Of trees less known that bear fruit, here are some observed by me. There are, for example, *moranque gasts*,[2] as they are called in their language; it is a very great tree, with extensive branches and leaves quite round and small; the fruit is of the form of long bean-pods. The leaves and fruit serve to season their broth, and they are tasty enough.

The tree called *congnare*[3] is another, with widely extended branches. Its leaves are round, with little spikes; the fruit is like small plums, and very delicious eating. It is much esteemed at the Maldives, and even at Goa. This tree bears fruit at all times, and, just as with oranges, you see it in flower as well as with fruit, some just set, some half ripe, and others ripe, all at the same time.

The *papos*[4] is of middling height, with leaves like the fig; its fruit grows like the cocos, not attached to the branches

[1] The reference is to the Maldive *hitala* (Sin. *hiritala*), the yam (*Dioscorea oppositifolia*). Ibn Batuta refers to its great value as a diet of the islands (see below, App. A). The flour made from this yam is referred to above (vol. i, p. 111) as *itelpoul* (= hitala-fu). Pyrard's astonishment at the method of growing the yam seems to show that he had never seen the potato, though it had been introduced into France some years before he left.

[2] M. *moraga-gas* (the muraga-tree); Sin. *mora* (the *Asclepias acida*).

[3] M. *kunnāru*, the Sinhalese *masan* (*Zizyphus jujuba*).

[4] The papaya or papaw (*Carica Papaya*, L.). This nasty, insipid fruit, which in taste bears no comparison with the melon, is a native of America. The name is said by Oviedo to be Cuban; it travelled to most countries of the East Indies with the fruit, but at the Maldives, as Mr. Bell informs me, its name is *falo*. Linschoten (ii, 35) says that "this fruit at the first for the strangeness thereof was much esteemed, but now they account not of it".

like other trees, but proceeding from the summit of the trunk at the spring of the branches. The fruit is very like the fig, only much bigger, of the size of a melon, which it resembles inside, having divisions marked on the rind, the seeds in the same place, and a very similar taste. When green, they use it in their broth as they use the pumpkin. The Portuguese grow some of it, and esteem it to be very delicious.

There is another tree of a strange nature, called *Ambou*[1]: it resembles a medlar. The fruit is like a white plum, and passing sweet and well-flavoured; it has a stone like a big nut or filbert, which is good to the taste, but, if you eat ever so little of it, disorders the senses, and if you were to take much of it, would cause a strange sickness, leading to death. This I can well understand, for I happened, out of necessity, at the beginning of my residence at the Maldives, to taste it, and had my senses disordered thereby for the space of twenty-four hours.

There is a tree called *Ahegasts*,[2] producing a fruit which is left to the birds; the roots, however, the people use for dyeing a beautiful carnation colour; and to get the roots they cut not down the tree, but only the roots on one side, and afterwards on the other, the tree being none the worse.

The *Macarequeau*[3] is another fine tree, being both lofty and wide-spreading: it is also of great service. Its roots are above ground, long, thick, and of a polished surface; the roots are run into the ground only by their tips, so that the tree seems supported on piles and arcades, and you can see daylight through them. When they want some wood of very fine grain they cut some of these roots, leaving the tree supported

[1] Apparently a misprint for *jambou*, the jamboo or rose-apple (*Eugenia jambos*, L.); M. *jabu*. Mr. Bell considers that the author refers to a small species known at the Maldives as *jaburol*.

[2] M. *ahi-gas*; Sin. *aha-gaha* (*Morinda citrofolia*).

[3] M. *mā-karhi-keyo*, the Pandanus.

on four only; this does the tree no harm, for it incontinently puts forth others. The flower is a foot long, big, white, and bent back, and casts an excellent odour. The fruit is as large as a pumpkin, and quite round; the rind is somewhat hard, and divided into partitions which reach the heart, in the manner of a pine-cone; but the difference is that these portions are of fruit, and very excellent. It is of a deep carnation colour; the bulk of the fruit is not eaten, but it is full of kernels, which are passing sweet and much better than those (of our pines) here. The leaves are an ell and a half in length, and a span broad. They divide them into two strips, and write upon them as upon parchment with ink. The timber is good for nothing, being too sappy, porous, and full of filaments.

At the Maldives there is great store of the tree which the Portuguese call the wild Indian fig[1]; it has a leaf like a walnut, and bears a small fruit which is used for nothing save that they burn it and produce a dark oil, which they use to blacken their ships in place of pitch and tallow. What is wonderful in the nature of this tree is that the branches, after they have spread aloft, cast forth little roots at their ends; these bend naturally and enter the ground, whence they produce other branches, and so on to infinity, in such wise that this tree would soon fill a whole country unless it were cut down. The timber is used only for firewood.

As for flowering trees, some are of great size, producing only flowers, which, however, are most sweet and odoriferous. Such is the *Innapa*,[2] the leaves of which the Maldivians bruise, and then rub upon their feet and hands to make them red, which

[1] M. *nika;* Sin. *nuga*, the banyan (*Ficus indica*). The Portuguese also called it *arvore de ráiz*, "the tree of roots". The poetical descriptions of the banyan tree by Milton and others are given by Col. Yule in his *Glossary*.

[2] M. *híná* (*Lawsonia inermis*). The *innapa* of the text is *híná-fai*, híná leaf. The *innamaus*, below, is *híná má* = híná flower. It is the *henna* of writers on the East.

they esteem a great beauty. This colour does not yield to any washing, nor until the nails grow, or a fresh skin comes over the flesh, and then (that is, at the end of five or six months) they rub them again. The flower is called *Innamaus;* it is very small but of a strong smell. The same is true of the tree called *Onnimaus,*[1] which bears no other fruit than white flowers of a very sweet and agreeable smell. They last but four-and-twenty hours upon the tree and then fall; but the tree produces them unceasingly all the year round. There is another tree of a very singular nature; it is called *Iroudemaus,*[2] which in their language means "sun-flower"; it comes out and appears only at the rising of the sun in the morning, and at sunset it falls, which is contrary to the nature of the "arbre triste". This flower is the most excellent of all, and has the best smell, and is ordinarily served to the kings and queens. There are endless other sorts of flowers that bloom at all seasons of the year, and of so excellent odour and perfume that the best of ours, or of our neighbouring countries, are not to be compared with them; the reason is that they are nigher to that which gives flowers their chiefest lustre; and this is more the case at the Maldives than elsewhere. The country folk there are exceedingly fond of flowers, binding them in their hair, and every day covering their beds and garments with them; they are also wonderfully cunning in the making of pretty bouquets, chaplets, wreaths, and garlands.

[1] M. *Uni-má*, the flower of the *uni* tree. This tree is identified by Mr. W. Ferguson as the *Guettarda speciosa*, the St. Thomé flower tree.

[2] M. *irude-má;* not, however, the Sin. *suriya kántá*, nor the "four o'clock flower" (*Mirabilis jalappa*), but one of the jasmines, probably either *Jasminum grandiflorum*, or *Jasminum pubescens*.

CHAPTER XII.

A most particular description of the admirable tree that bears the Indian nut, called Cocos, and alone produces all commodities and things necessary for the life of man.

In all the Indies there is no tree which serves so many purposes of the nourishment and convenience of man as the tree which produces the cocos or Indian nut.

The Portuguese call this tree *Palmero*,[1] and the fruit *Cocos*.[2] The Maldivians call it *Roul*,[3] and the fruit *Caré*.[4] The Malabars call it *Tengua*,[5] and the Guzerats *Narquilly*.[6] It grows only in countries that are within the two Tropics, because it requires nothing but a warm and humid soil; and yet it is not found throughout the whole Torrid Zone, but only in certain places, where it is a marvel to see it growing all naturally and without cultivation[7]; and one of its chief

[1] More correctly *palmeira*.

[2] The origin of the word *coco* is involved in some obscurity. Col. Yule gives three choices,—(i) the Sp. and Port. *coco*, a mask or bogey: "e nós os Portuguezes, por ter aquelles tres buracos, lhe pozemos o nome de *coco*: porque parece rosto de bugio ou d'outro animal", says Garcia de Orta (f. 66*b*): "and we Portuguese, because of those three eyelets, give it the name of *coco*, as resembling the face of a monkey or other animal": this is the accepted Sp. and Port. derivation. (ii) the old Sp. *coca*, a shell = Lat. *concha* and Fr. *coque*: this is Col. Yule's own suggestion, and, except as to gender, seems probable enough; (iii) the ancient Egyptian *kuku*, found by Goodwin as applied in particular to the fruit; this word seems to appear again in the *κύκας* of Theophrastus, applied to a palm of Ethiopia.

[3] M. *ru'*, Sin. *ruk* or *ruka*, "tree"; the ordinary M. word for tree is *gas* (Sin. *gaha*), but the coconut is *karhi-ru'*, "the nut-tree".

[4] M. *kárhi*, cf. Greek *κάρυον*, "nut"; Cosmas describes coconuts as *κάρυα Ἰνδικά*.

[5] Tam. *tengku* or *tengka-maram* (*maram* = tree).

[6] Sansk. *narikela*; whence Pers. *nargīl*.

[7] This may be so as regards the Maldives, but in Ceylon the coconut tree is rarely seen far from human habitations:—"The natives have a

places is the Maldives, where it is more abundant than in all the rest of the world together. Such, indeed, is its increase there that the natives have to cut it down to make room for their houses and buildings. Usually, they do not allow these trees to stand too close to their houses, both because the trees are frequently blown down by the wind, thereby ruining the houses and killing the occupants, and because great quantities of nuts are falling every day owing to the rats,[1] and they often cause the death of men by reason both of the height of the tree and the weight of the fruit. I have seen a green fruit to weigh full six pounds. The rats attack them only when green, both because when dry they are too hard to gnaw, and because the chief desire of these creatures is to drink the water. They are clever enough to make a hole on the upper side, so that the water shall not escape, and they make it of their own size, so that they can enter in to eat and drink. When the fruit is thus empty within, it rots and falls in such wise that in the uninhabited islands the ground is all covered with them; for in inhabited places the people diligently collect them, when dry, for firewood, which purpose they serve better than any other wood. The people are much troubled by the destruction and ravages of these rats, and even more so by those of the bats whereof I

superstition that the coconut will not grow out of the sound of the human voice, and will die if the village where it had previously thriven becomes deserted; the solution of the mystery being in all probability the superior care and manuring which it receives in such localities" (Tennent, *Ceylon*, i, 119). The fact is, as De Candolle shows, that the coconut palm is not indigenous to India and Ceylon; it was not known to the writers of the *Mahavanso*. In connection with this it may be noted that, thanks to this wonderful tree, the seaboard of Ceylon now supports a teeming population, whereas in the days of the *Mahavanso* the mass of the population was centred in the interior, where rice was the staple.

[1] The rats are a terrible plague at the Maldives and Laccadives. At the latter the islanders have instituted periodical rat-hunts (Allan Hume, *Stray Feathers*, vol. iv).

have spoken, which are so big, and a great annoyance both in regard to this tree and to wine-jars, and other vessels used for catching and drawing the wine. These creatures will break and crack the vessels in their desire to drink the wine, most frequently spilling it entirely. The people are also much molested in all the islands by ants, which make their tunnels beneath these trees, traversing all the roots, and displenishing them of earth so much as to cause them to fall.

This tree is loftier not only than any tree of these parts, but even than any of the Indian trees, being about twenty fathoms high.[1] It is quite straight, without any branches up to the summit; it is not of proportionate thickness, but very smooth, thicker towards the roots, and diminishing up to the top. I have never seen one quite straight, nor any but was without branches up to the top. It has but little root, and so has no strong foothold, and a high wind is sure to blow some down; and, as I said, these sometimes fall upon the houses, in whose ruins the people within are overwhelmed, the houses being low and little able to resist so great a weight. The bark is light in colour, and the trunk very pithy, and full of filament. The timber is used for building houses, yet but half the tree can be used for the purpose, that is, the lower or thick half, for the rest is only pith, and too tender. Of the lower part of the tree where it is thickest a length of about three feet is cut, and then hollowed out to make buckets for keeping honey, water, and other commodities. The best of the timber is used for making ships, which are altogether composed of it; no other is used, nor is a particle of iron employed.

The branches are all aloft, in a bunch at the top of the tree. They are exceeding long, flat, and straight. The leaves grow equally on both sides, and close together, with

[1] The question as to the greatest height attained by the coconut palm has recently been raised in the *Ceylon Observer*; the loftiest tree measured was found to be 117 feet.

only the interval of an inch between. They are half a fathom or more in length, finishing in a point, two inches broad on each side; for they are folded in two at the middle, where there is a stalk of wood, very slender, but very strong, giving support to the leaf. They are of a white colour when the leaf first opens, afterwards they become green, and latterly, when dry, brown. The fruit never grows upon the branches, but only on the trunk of the tree at the spring of the branches. There it grows, and waxes in clusters, each cluster hanging from the tree by a stalk as thick as the arm, of a due length, and very strong. By this stalk hang the nuts or cocos, usually to the number of fifty or sixty, more or less; and what is more wonderful than all, the tree produces a cluster of cocos every month, in such wise that sometimes it is charged with ten or twelve clusters of nuts, some ripe, others half ripe, and others just beginning to set, all in the order of their growth; and they become perfectly ripe in six months. Thus it has ripe fruit all the year round, and is always in season.[1]

This tree requires low, humid, and watery ground, and marshy or sandy places; wherefore it grows well at the Maldives, the ground being low, and water being found at three or four feet deep, so that these trees are always kept fresh and nourished. On the other hand, on the mainland it is some trouble to get them reared, and it is necessary to use water-channels, or to irrigate them by the hand-labour of slaves night and morning. For planting, the fruit must be taken when naturally ripe upon the tree, nor too much so, for if too ripe and dry, the water inside will have dried up; and it is

[1] "The produce of the tree in full health and properly tended is much dependent on soil and climate. The average may be put down at 120 nuts in the twelve months, while in a low and sandy soil it will amount to 200, and when planted in gravel and laterite foundations not 60; the most productive months are from January to June, that is for ripe nuts, the heat bringing them quickly to maturity" (*All About the Coconut Palm*, Colombo, 1885, p. 27).

the water alone which germinates, and not the kernel. The whole fruit must be laid in humid soil, with its shell and husk, and it suffices to cover it with earth. Without the husk the tree cannot possibly grow, because otherwise the earth would rot the shell ere the germ and root were nourished, and the plant had sprung above the ground. It bears fruit at six or seven years. They that would gather this fruit can, by rapping the fingers or other thing against the husk, judge in what condition it is, whether hard or soft, ripe or unripe. When it is becoming ripe the water joggles and stirs within, but when not ripe, or only beginning to ripen, the water gives no sound; and in measure as it becomes over-ripe, the water dries up until it is exhausted; the kernel then becomes hard and dry, and when pressed, no longer yields milk, but only oil, and separates from the shell. In place of being white within it then becomes of a leaden hue, while the outer surface turns brown like the shell.

The trees growing near the close of the royal palace and other houses at the Maldives are ascended only by night: it is forbidden to do so by day, for the climbers would overlook the close, which hath not walls of the height of these trees. Indeed, the gatherers of this fruit, who are called *Ravery*,[1] dare not climb them by day at any place where they could overlook the close of the humblest dwelling, ere they have first given a loud shout three times, standing at the foot of the tree. This is done for the sake of the women who bathe and wash themselves, all naked, in their ponds and in the closes of their houses. This rule is observed very strictly amongst them, and it is forbidden to the *ravery* to climb the tree until the women have done their bathing and have withdrawn.

Marvellous indeed are the commodities drawn from this tree, of which there is no morsel or particle but serves some use. The branches are split in two and are made into laths

[1] M. *rá-veri*, "toddy-men".

for roofing the houses, and into close and well-fitted palisades, wherewith houses and gardens are enclosed. They are put to a thousand other uses which it were tedious to explain. With the leaves the houses are thatched; they are used for lining and closing up all fences and houses, being very neatly sewn together and plaited over, with several rows of cord run along the whole length to keep them firm.[1] No other material is used for their houses, fences, and screens; and it resists water so well that not a drop passes through: it must, however, be renewed at the end of three years. While the leaf is still green it is used like paper for writing letters, missives, verses, and ballads, and then is neatly folded up; this is done with knives and iron styles. Again, the leaves when dry are split into strips or tags, which are woven and interlaced in the fashion of a mat, exceeding well executed; these mats, sewn one to another, are made into sails for ships of any size required, and throughout all the Maldives no other sails are used. The same mats serve as ordinary carpets for sitting upon the ground in the country manner, and throughout all the coast of Malabar the people use no other, because there they have not the proper reed, as at Caël and the Maldives, of which other mats, much handsomer and prettier, are made. Also with these leaves, used whole, the people fashion, in very cunning plaited work, all manner of baskets and scuttles, and a thousand other such manufactures, such as we here fashion of osiers or willow; of the same they make sunshades or sombreros, and very pretty hats for use against the rain. I myself always wore the like.

In short, these leaves, when young and white, are worked into a thousand things: being fashioned in birds, fish, and all other animals, such as we here frame by the artful fold-

[1] These are the well-known *cadjans*, or plaited coconut leaves, which serve for walls, screens, cart shades, etc., in South India and Ceylon. At the Maldives, where they are called *fan̩*, they are still used for the sails of sea-going boats, as described by the author.

ing of linen. When they would make a present of flowers, betel, or the like, they put this in a kind of basket made of these leaves very neatly. When it is required to take out the contents, they cut an opening with a knife and cast away the basket. The slender stick in the middle of the dry leaf becomes very hard, insomuch that of it they make besoms[1] to sweep withal, and use none other. These slight stalks also serve to make boxes and cases; they are plaited together, and are quite strong, and such boxes are fastened with lock and key.

Of these stalks are also made the shafts of weapons, such as small spears, javelins, etc.; they bind together the little stems, which are no thicker than an iron spike, and about a half fathom in length, packing them together to the required thickness, and placing them end to end to the required length.[2] These sticks diminish in size from their thicker end, which is the lower end of the leaf, up to the point, which is no bigger than a little needle. They dispose these little sticks with such art, that the shaft constructed of them is no longer weak, nor stouter in one place than another. Next, when well polished, they cover these shafts with a varnish called by them *Las*,[3] which they possess in all colours, adorning them with numberless figures and patterns at their pleasure; these shafts are called *Ziconti*.[4] They are of the thickness of a good-sized thumb, and are staunch and strong, yet will bend sooner than break. They are made as thick and long as required, and are also used for making bows. When these people want needles they use none other than

[1] These brooms are called in M. *ilorhi-fati*, and in Sin. *ila paṭa*.

[2] Mr. Bell writes :—"I wondered much at the pliancy of their longer javelins; those used in the sports quivering strangely in the hand when ready for use."

[3] M. *lá*, Hind. *lákh*, Sansk. *lákshá*, "lac", the resinous incrustation produced on certain trees by the puncture of the Lac insect, *Coccus lacca* (Yule, *Gloss.*).

[4] Cf. Hind. *senti*, "javelin".

these little stems, fashioning and pointing them with their knives.

The nut is covered with a husk or shell; some are of the size of a man's head, and some less. The husk has a yellowish hue over the green when it is ripe, and is three or four inches thick. This husk is composed of fibre, whereof they make their rope. They remove the husk when green, as we should that of a nut, and lay it to steep in the sea, covering it with sand. After it has been there for the space of three weeks they take it out and beat it with wooden mallets, such as we here use for flax or hemp. Thus, having separated the fibres, they expose it to the sun. Next, the women twist and spin it into rope with the hand on the naked thigh, for the men take no part in the labour of rope-making. The rope[1] thus made serves for all uses, and none other is employed throughout all the Indies. The same husk, when dry, serves to caulk the ships withal.

Of the same substance, too, are made matches for arquebuses; it keeps alight well and makes good charcoal, better indeed than ours; but in making matches it is prepared differently from the rope: for the husk or shell must be dried with the fruit, and not plucked green, nor steeped, nor beaten, and the fibre is spun and twisted with the whole of the rind, and very finely twined. It is of the colour of tan, wherewith leather is tanned; and all about this fibre is a substance like sawdust. Moreover, in dwellings, at guard-houses, and elsewhere, they employ this dry husk for preserving fire, as it keeps alight for a long while, and a small spark applied to it will convey the fire, which will not go out so long as there is the least substance left. When they have made their match, they boil it with ashes, as we use here; then they fold it together into thick hanks, like rings, of the thickness of an arm; through these they thrust their arm when they are carrying their arquebuses. They never

[1] Coir-rope.

cut it, but merely snuff it as it burns away, as we do candles. They use no other manner of match, either in these islands or elsewhere in India; in some places, however, where cotton is common and cocos scarce, they make their matches of cotton.

The nut, when separated from the husk, or, as we call it, "shelled", is still so big that, empty and cleaned out, it will hold two or three pints of water or other liquid; for some of them are of divers smaller sizes, and the least are of the size of a lemon.

The shell is exceeding hard, and as thick as two testoons, or a whit more. The Indians use it to make their porringers, pots, pints, and other measures, and also utensils such as spoons and the like. Moreover, of this shell they make charcoal for their forges, and use none other.

All around the inside of this shell comes a thick and firm white substance, which is tasty like an almond, and very good; they use it in divers ways. First, the Indians eat it as we eat bread along with other viands, whether flesh or fish. Next, from this same white stuff they extract a milk which is as sweet as our milk sugared, or rather as our milk of almonds. To obtain this milk they pound the kernel into meal, then strain and squeeze it; the milk thus caused to flow is passed through a sieve. This milk is very laxative; it is served with honey or sugar, and drunk fasting; no other purgative is used.

From this same milk oil is obtained, for when boiled it changes and thickens into oil; it is very good for frying, and no other is used by the people, whether for seasoning their meats or mixing with their sauces. The same is used for lamps, and not only at the Maldives, but throughout all the East Indies; even the Portuguese use none other. It is also very good for wounds and ulcers, and is the principal recipe at the Maldives. I myself was cured by it. It is a sovereign remedy against the itch, which it consumes and causes to fall off a few days after it is rubbed on. The physicians and surgeons that are among the Portuguese use it with their medicines and unguents, though they might use that of Spain, holding this to be more medicinal and the best in certain ailments. This oil, when kept for about three months, thickens and congeals into a very white butter, though the oil was yellowish; this butter is not, however, delicate or fit to be eaten with bread as ours is. They use it in the same manner as the oil, that is, melted, and thereby it loses not its savour. Moreover, with this squeezed kernel, or compressed white, after the extraction of the milk, are made excellent comfits and conserves, prepared with the sugar that is produced from the same tree.

Inside the nut, and within this kernel or white, and at the very centre, is found a quantity of water, according to the size of the cocos: the largest have a good pint of very beautiful water, clear as that from the rock, and as good and of the same taste as sugared water, and the fresher the better. It is a very refreshing drink, principally when the fruit is half ripe; but the wine made of it is very fiery. Finally, the entire cocos, comprised within the husk and shell, can be eaten as we should eat a sweet apple.

When the tree begins to blossom and to put forth the bunch or cluster, a pod is produced, long and pointed, in the form of a gherkin, which, when fully extended, opens and expands into a yellow flower, and thence proceeds the fruit.

This pod when dry falls to the ground, or is cut off, and made into charcoal for drawing, and also into boxes or pails, also into bushel measures; so indeed that there is no part of this tree but is put to some use; even the flowers are made into most excellent conserves and comfits.

This cocos yields another commodity, viz., a certain tissue[1]

[1] Sin. *matulla*, a remarkable substance resembling coarse cloth or gauze, which arises at the base and outside of the fronds, especially in

found at the base of the branches between the trunk of the tree and the fruit cluster. This tissue the Indians employ to make their sacks. Also, being of fine mesh, it is very proper for strainers to pass any liquids through.

This tree also yields a liquor which serves in place of wine.[1] For when you cut the thick spathe of the cluster, leaving it only of a foot's length, there drops therefrom a liquor passing sweet and luscious, just like hypocras, saving that it is quite fresh. At the Maldives this liquor that flows from these cut branches is drunk instead of wine—for they dare not drink the other sort; but it will not keep sweet without turning sour for more than four-and-twenty hours. Each branch usually yields about a quart a day, though some will yield two or three or more, and this branch, dropping continually, lasts for the space of six months. To receive this liquor they attach a pot, also of cocos, to the branch or spathe, in such wise that the wind cannot carry the droppings away.

With this liquor they make honey and sugar. They collect it in a pan and boil it with certain white porous pebbles that are found in the sea. When boiled for some time it becomes converted into honey, as excellent as ordinary honey, or, rather, as the finest syrup imaginable; it is yellow like wax, but they make it clear or thick as they please.[2]

From this honey also is manufactured sugar, by boiling with other pebbles and then drying it: thus is produced a fine sugar, either white or candy, wherein is much traffic

young trees. "The length and evenness of the threads or fibres, the regular manner in which they cross each other at oblique angles, the extent of surface, and the thickness of the piece, corresponding with that of coarse cotton cloth, the singular manner in which the fibres are attached to each other, cause this curious substance, wove in the loom of nature, to represent to the eye a remarkable resemblance to cloth spun and woven by human ingenuity" (Ellis, *Polynesian Researches*). It is much used for sieves, and also in the South Sea for making cloths.

[1] *Sura*, *tārī*, or "toddy".

[2] The Maldivians make their jaggery in this manner still.

done, both at the Maldives and also at Cael and Ceylon. But this sugar is not by any means so white as cane sugar, though in some places it is whiter than at others.

Also if of this liquor they desire not to make honey or sugar, they put it on the fire and make an excellent brandy, called by them *Arac*,[1] which is quite as strong as ours here.

This brandy, or arac, the Portuguese use for a beverage, but they add thereto raisins from Persia, putting about 30 or 35 pounds of them in a cask, and mixing the whole together to redden and sweeten it. The Portuguese drink no other wine, and call this *vin de passe*[2]; it is very good and cheap. Great lords sometimes drink Spanish wine, which is very dear out there. If vinegar be wanted, this liquor is left for ten or twelve days to turn sour, and the vinegar so made is as strong as the best we have here.

Thus from the same tree can be obtained fruit and wine; but, to say truth, the fruit is in that case neither so good nor so plentiful. Wherefore at the Maldives, where these trees are so numerous, they set apart certain of them solely for the production of wine; and then, a single tree cannot have more than two or three of these distilling taps going at once. Nevertheless, some wine can be drawn from a tree which is left to bear fruit, but a small quantity only.

The tree has yet another commodity, viz., that at the top it throws out a tender shoot[3] about two or three feet long, which is very good eating, and as sweet as an almond. I have eaten it many a time. When the trees are felled for the purpose of building, this tendril is promptly cut, but never except then.

Another extraordinary thing is, that when the cocos is ripe

[1] From Ar. *'araḳ*, "perspiration". The toddy is twice distilled, giving one-eighth of its quantity in arrack.

[2] See above, p. 73, *note*.

[3] The so-called "coconut cabbage", M. *ruk-kuri*, Sin. *pol-bada*. When boiled it is very delicate, with a nutty flavour. The natives preserve it in vinegar and use it as a pickle.

and dry, if you put it in some damp place, or in the ground, for the space of three weeks or a month, the water within forms itself into a kind of apple, yellow on the surface and white beneath[1]; this is as tender and sweet as can be, and melts in the mouth. The dainty and curious among the inhabitants eat this often, esteeming it most delicate fare, and even give it to their little children. This apple is the germ of the cocos, which would shoot forthwith and engender a tree were it left a while longer, for the kernel that is all around the shell in manner described has naught to do with the germination of the cocos, but only the water within; this it is which furnishes the substance. The rest of the cocos rots, and is good for nothing more.

Further, the natives make a sort of merchandise out of the fruit of the cocos, which finds a market all over India, and fetches a high price too; they call it *suppara.*[2] They take the fruit, break it in two parts, and dry it in the sun, which causes it to shrink mightily; and it will thus keep as long as they wish. They pack it in sacks and send it to all parts. It is of good flavour, and serves for sauces and soups. It is carried in quantities to Arabia, and the oil extracted from it is much better and will keep longer than that drawn from quite fresh fruit.

Black dyes are obtained from the sawdust of cocos; it is steeped in the water and honey of this same tree, and left in the sun for some days; a very black and excellent dye is thus produced.[3]

Of the stalks of the fruit are made paint-brushes for

[1] M. *muḍi*, Sin. *paela madē.*

[2] Probably misprint for *kuppara;* M. *kufarā*, Sin. *kopara*, Eng. *copra.* Ceylon exports annually about 60,000 cwts. of copra, and a small quantity is sometimes exported from the Maldives to Ceylon.

[3] Mr. Bell says they make two kinds—(*a*) *bobi-deli*, charcoal burnt from the soft shell, mixed with coconut oil, and used for painting boats, etc.; (*b*) *nárhi-deli*, charcoal from the hard shell, mixed with water, and used as ink.

painting their boats, galleys, temples, and houses, which are painted all over, but never (as I have said before) with the figures of men.

I have oftentimes seen at the Maldives an infinite number of ships of 100 or 120 tons, built entirely of this timber, without any iron or other wood or material except what this tree produces. The anchors even are made of it, and are very excellent and handy. They have a cross-piece of wood of the same tree, hollowed out and packed with flints and little stones, and then firmly closed. This is to render the anchor heavier, so that it shall catch and keep a better hold. The planks are fastened with pins, and lashed and seamed within with cordage made of the fruit. Moreover, these ships, entirely built, fitted, and equipped with the timber or fruit of this tree, are loaded with merchandise proceeding from the same tree, to wit, cordage, mats, sails of cocos, comfits, oil, wine, sugar, and other goods, all the produce of this tree. And this is true also of the provisions of the ship, whether of meat or drink; and whether the voyage be to Arabia, 800 or 900 leagues distance, or to the coast of Malabar, Cambaye, Sumatra, or elsewhere. These vessels last four or five years, and with repairs and proper treatment will make many long voyages.

To make their drums they hollow a trunk of this tree till it be quite thin; then, when they have caught some of the fish, called by us the ray, which they never eat, they skin it, and cover their drums with the hide, as I have already said.[1] These rays are the largest to be seen anywhere.

They use this wood also as being the best for polishing and furbishing articles of iron or copper, whether arms or household utensils. They also employ powdered porcelain mingled with oil to scrub, clean, and polish their arms and other utensils.

For the rest, I have yet to say that there are two sorts of

[1] See above, p. 351.

these cocos trees; the fruit of the one when young being sweet and tender as an apple, that of the other not so. The tender and sweet are very rare, and held in great esteem, but when they are ripe they are not so good as the others.

I have given an extensive description of this tree, as being one of the greatest marvels of the Indies; also because I sojourned five years at the Maldives, where it is the chief source of wealth, food, and all commodities, and where they are better experienced in drawing its produce and in applying it to the divers petty amenities of life than elsewhere in India. Nor have I only seen all this a few times. I have eaten this fruit and lived upon it regularly. I myself possessed a great number of trees, and those of the very best, and myself produced all these commodities which I have described. Wherefore, I have thought it not otherwise than proper that I should describe with all particularity that which I have learnt by an experience so long and so well approved.

Advice to those who would undertake the voyage to the East Indies. The order and police observed by the French in their navigation, the great faults and excesses committed by them, with examples thereof, and a word of caution against the like.

INASMUCH as it is expedient and necessary for those who would undertake the voyage to the East Indies to know the proper times and seasons for setting out, both on the outward and the homeward voyage, the things whereof they ought to make provision, and the manner of their governance, whereby to avoid the accidents which hourly befall, as indeed I have myself experienced many and many a time—on these matters I will give a short discourse which may serve for a conclusion to my voyage, and will treat in some measure of the excesses and lack of order attending our navigation, and the means of remedying the same. I begin by saying that voyagers must above all things take care to set out in season in order to successfully weather the Cape of Good Hope and the coast of Natal, where the winds and storms are both very frequent and very dangerous, and the more so when the passage of these regions is made out of season.

It behoves them also to be provided with good and experienced sea-pilots, who have made the voyage several times, and have a practical knowledge of it, for it is certain that if we had had a good pilot our voyage had come to happy issue. They must make choice of good ships that are inured to the sea, and have already made some voyages; because, if on a long voyage any accident befalls a new ship that has not been proved at sea, it cannot be repaired. Further, for a complete voyage there must be a company of four or five ships at the least, one of these to carry victuals, ship's utensils, and other furniture and material for the repair of the other ships in case of need, and to make fitting distribution of her men and provisions as occasion may require: when she is thus emptied she may be abandoned. Also it is very desirable to have a small pinnace, which is of infinite service in approaching close to land and in reconnoitring.

I have not found it of use to sheath the ship with lead as ours was. For although this may be good against worms, preventing them from piercing the timbers, yet for all that it clogs the vessel overmuch. The Portuguese use it only at the seams and joinings of the timbers. For this purpose tin would seem to me the most suitable.[1]

Moreover, it is requisite to make good provision of fresh water rather than wine, seeing the heat is so vehement that the drinking of wine rather enhances than quenches the thirst; nevertheless, you must take some, and some brandy also, to drink when you approach the Cape of Good Hope, which is a cold neighbourhood, and also to keep for the return voyage when you begin to reach the altitude of Spain and

[1] The Portuguese had formerly used complete lead sheathing, but probably it had been given up for economical reasons. Sir R. Hawkins has some interesting remarks on this subject (*Hawkins' Voyages*, p. 203): "In Spaine and Portingall, some sheathe their shippes with lead; besides the cost and waight, although they use the thinnest sheet-lead that I have seene in any place, yet it is nothing durable, but subject to many casualties. Another manner is used with double plankes, as thicke without as within, after the manner of furring, which is little better than that with lead; for besides his waight, it dureth little, because the worme in small time passeth through the one and the other. A third manner of sheathing hath been used amongst some with fine canvas; which is of small continuance, and so not to be regarded. The fourth prevention, which now is most accompted of, is to burne the utter planke till it come to be every place like a cole, and after to pitch it; this is not bad." He then describes the Chinese method of varnishing, and lastly the English mode, viz., by thin sheathing boards over layers first of tar and then of hair. The most approved modern sheathing is copper over felt.

France. But it must be Spanish wine, for that of France will not keep under the Torrid Zone. We carried some that went bad before we reached the line. Then the candles to be carried must be of wax, for tallow melts, and olive oil must be carried for food, that being a most wholesome thing at sea, and at all times very useful for sauces and seasonings, while walnut oil should be carried for the lamps.

Above all, the provisions and refreshments must be carefully husbanded, for the reason that during this long and difficult voyage many accidents and diseases befall, and amongst others scurvy. In this matter not a few of our men had a sad experience, who, in the space of three or four months they were at sea, had without consideration eaten and wasted all their provisions. And then, when sundry ailments overtook them, they had nothing left for their sustenance, wherefore did many die that could not eat of the ships victuals, which consist of salt meat, biscuit, and salt fish.

Amongst other things it is necessary to be forewarned of the ailments which ordinarily occur on this voyage. The first is one very common under the Torrid Zone, and among the most cruel and painful, whether to witness or to endure. I speak with some knowledge, for I was twice attacked with it, the first time on the voyage out, when we reached the Island of St. Lawrence, and again at Goa, where it seized me when I was abed in the house of Don Diego Hurtado de Mendoza. This malady is a grievous pain in the stomach, which comes on only at night, but in manner so strange that one can hardly breathe, and the sufferer tosses and strains by reason of the extremity of the pain. It is most prevalent near the line, where the heats are the greatest and most violent; and yet it proceeds from cold, because the excessive heat of the day attracts all the natural heat of the body and causes it to exhale; then as night falls it becomes so faint and feeble that without feeling the night chill coming on, one falls asleep at sunset, and then the ensuing cold is attracted to the mouth of the stomach, which is thereby incontinently swollen with these throes. This illness sometimes lasts twenty-four hours; in my case the worst of the pain lasted only three or four hours. Yet does it make itself felt for three or four days thereafter, and the only remedy is heat, viz., by drinking good Spanish or Canary wine, or brandy, cinnamon water, or other ardent liquids.

For a protection against this disease one must be clad warmly, and well covered at nights, and above all care must be taken not to sleep in the dews of sundown and night. The head must be swathed, the legs well and warmly enclosed, and the stomach in like manner. For this purpose they wear broad bands sufficient to cover the stomach, quilted and stuffed with cotton,[1] and handsomely powdered with scents. It is indeed a strange thing that in the hottest places the body becomes quite cold and bereft of heat.

Now with regard to another malady, called *scurbut* by the Hollanders and the gum disease by the Portuguese;[2] we French call it "le mal de terre", I know not why, for it comes on at sea and is cured on land. It is a very common ailment in all parts of the voyage, and is contagious, even by approaching or breathing another's breath. It is ordinarily brought on by the great length of the voyage, and the long sojourning at sea, and also by the want of washing and cleanliness, and of changing linen and other clothes; by the sea air and water, by the corruption of the fresh water and the victuals, washing in sea water without washing afterwards in fresh; by cold, and sleeping in the night dews,—all these cause this disease. Those attacked become swollen as by dropsy, and the swelling is as hard as wood, chiefly on the thighs and legs, cheeks and throat, all the surface being suffused with dark blood, of a livid and leaden hue, as though it were all tumours and contusions, rendering the muscles and nerves

1 A description of the "Cummerbund".

2 Port. *Mal das gengivas*.

impotent and stiff. Besides this the gums are ulcerated and black, the flesh all swollen, the teeth displaced and loose, as though they had but a slight hold; indeed, most of them fall out. Add thereto a breath so fœtid and disgusting that one cannot approach; it can be smelt from one end of the vessel to the other. The appetite is not lost, but the distress of the teeth is such that one can only eat slops, wherewith the ship is but ill furnished; indeed, one becomes so famished and greedy that it would seem as if all the victuals in the world would not suffice to produce satiety. The discomfort is, in fact, greater than the pain, which is confined to the mouth and gums. So it is that full often a man dies at his talking, drinking, and eating, without knowledge of his approaching end. Then, too, this malady makes a man so opinionative and fractious that nothing pleases him. Some die in a few days, others endure a while longer ere they die. They become of a white or yellowish colour, and when first overtaken with the disease the thighs and legs are covered with little pustules and spots like flea-bites, which is the black blood issuing through the pores of the skin; the gums begin to rise, and to become cancerous. The patient is subject to syncope, fainting, convulsions, and nervous swoonings. While we were at the Island of St. Lawrence there died three or four of our men of this malady, and when their heads were opened all the brain was found to be black, tainted, and putrified. The lungs become dry and shrunk like parchment that is held near the fire. The liver and spleen wax immoderately large, and become black and covered with apostumes full of the most loathsome matter. During this sickness a sore never heals or closes up; on the contrary, it runs to gangrene and putrefaction. When a man is seized at sea, let him use what remedies he will, all are useless, and nothing avails but to get ashore wherever possible, and gain refreshment of sweet and fresh water and fruits, without which none can be cured, do what he will. It is a terrible thing to see the big lumps of foul flesh that have to be cut from the gums.[1]

Such are the maladies to which men are most subject on this voyage, and whereof they must be well advised so as to guard against them, or cure them as best they can.

But it is especially necessary before setting out to make provision of orange and lemon juice in order to their protection against this scurvy, because there is nothing more sovereign to resist it than the refreshments of the land, the which consist of fresh water, oranges, and lemons; this I have observed and experienced many a time.

Moreover, it behoves men to be sober as well in drinking as in eating, and when they happen upon some islands where they can obtain fresh viands, it is not good to eat overmuch thereof, nor even of the fruits.

One must not sleep too much, for that is unwholesome, especially sleeping by day. Moreover, as I said before, there is a proper time and season for setting out, to wit, at the beginning of March, for if you do not get away then you will find calms at the equinoctial line, and currents at the coast of Guinea, which bring about the loss of the voyage, as indeed was our case, for we did not set out till the month of May, nay, till the 18th of that month, and so were delayed by contrary winds off Guinea for more than four months. Had we started sooner we had made the passage easily enough. The coast of Guinea is intemperate and unhealthy, and those that go to the Indies must take care not to get out of their course on the Guinea coast, for it is the most unhealthy place in the world, and very difficult to get out of by reason of the calms. Furthermore, as they near the Cape of Good Hope they will usually fall in with violent storms and contrary winds.

Likewise they must take warning not to touch land on this

[1] Compare Sir Richard Hawkins' account of scurvy and its prevention in the *Hawkins' Voyages*, pp. 138-42.

side the Cape of Good Hope; on the return voyage only it is customary to touch at the island of St. Helena.

Coming home on the return voyage from the Indies, they must set out at the end of December or beginning of January, so as to avoid the same perils, for it is most necessary to double the Cape of Good Hope at the beginning of May, or sooner if possible. We did not leave Goa till the end of January, and for this reason were nearly lost, being two months in sight of the Cape ere we could double it, and all the time buffeted by contrary winds.

It were well also to have priests for the exercise of our religion, to console the sick, and to administer to them the Sacraments of the Church.

I come now to the matter of our order and police in navigation, to the great faults committed, as the same were observed by me in my voyage, and the means of remedying them.

When we set out from France we were two ships, whereof one was the *Admiral*, the other the *Vice-Admiral*. The general of both was on board the *Admiral*, while his lieutenant-general commanded the other. The general had on board his own ship his own lieutenant, and the lieutenant-general had also his own lieutenant with him; so that each vessel had her own captain and lieutenant; add a pilot, a second pilot, a mate, a second mate, a merchant, a second merchant, a clerk, two surgeons, two pursers, two cooks appointed by the captain, and two chief stewards. There was also a master gunner, assisted by five or six gunners. Such are the persons in command and the officers of a French ship.

The captain hath absolute command in all things; and the chief merchant hath power over the merchandise and trading only; for the second is only for his assistance, and to take his place if peradventure he should die. For this cause there be always two for each office, this being wisely ordained as a provision for the supply of vacancies. Nevertheless, there is no increase of pay hereby, but of honour only: for in our ships pay is never increased or diminished, and if a man should die the first day after going on board his heirs would be paid for the whole voyage. In our voyage wages were paid monthly, three months being advanced to each man before we sailed. The pay amounted to half as much again as the English or Hollanders (who observe the same order in their ships as we) give to their seamen.

So then the captain has power over all, and the factor or chief merchant has control over the merchandise, having under him a clerk, who is appointed, according to maritime practice, by the lords or burgesses to whom the ship belongs, and so with the other officers. But this clerk hath not the same trust and power as on the Portuguese ships. He merely registers the merchandise laden upon and discharged from the ship in the way of traffic, and has no other office. As for the pilot, his office is only in what concerns the navigation, and he is not held in the same awe as are the Portuguese pilots. The mate has command over all the seamen, and the care of the ship, and all her utensils and victuals. This I have found a bad arrangement, inasmuch as he appoints pursers that are at his beck.

The mate and second mate take a hand at jobs just like the mariners. There are also two stewards, chosen by the captain and the mate from among the best and most capable of the mariners. They are appointed to have charge of the ropes, sails, tackle, and other ship's furniture, and 'tis they who cut and mend all these when necessary. They are chiefs over all the seamen next after the mate and second mate, and are very necessary. They have command over all the young mariners and ship's boys, to whom they alone can give the lash. As for the surgeons and apothecaries, they have to do only what appertains to their own calling, having no rank in the ship's company like the other officers. For it is not with us as with the Portuguese, seeing that (with us) all the other men, whether gunners, pursers, cooks, coopers, carpenters, blacksmiths, sail-menders, and others are rated as mariners, and do all the like work. For, saving the captain and his lieutenant, the merchant, the clerk, and the surgeons, all the others take their turn at the night watches and work like the rest, whatever their birth. I have seen many scions of good family that came to sea solely for their pleasure, and drew no pay, yet were liable to the same labour and fatigues as the rest.

As for the pursers, there be two of them to assist each other, because they take night watches, and every four days serve out to each man a portion of bread, wine, and water, beginning with the captain, and ending with the boy or page, to all equally, viz., three pounds of biscuit, a pot of Spanish wine, and three pots of water only to each for four days. Other victuals are supplied by the two cooks to the whole company, the pursers distributing the same in platters equally, that is, on each platter a mess for six persons, and each one takes thence his own share of biscuit and drink. At the captain's table there is always something better and out of the ordinary. Also more than six persons are provided for at his mess, for all persons of honour and quality are received there. Neither the mate nor the pilot eats at the captain's table. Six persons of like quality are chosen to mess together. Such was our manner of living on board our ships; but there was, as I found, one default amongst others, which was this, that the burgesses and owners of the ship ought to have appointed a superintendent of the provisions, who should be under the command neither of the captain nor of the mate; inasmuch as they appointed to be pursers whom they would—ill-conducted fellows, who dared not refuse them anything they asked, for fear of being removed from their office. This was the cause that our victuals were full soon eaten up, and a clean sweep made of them, and every day arose perpetual bickerings and quarrels on this subject.

The next day after departure, the captain and mate call the whole ship's company to make the "matelotage", that is, to arrange the seamen in pairs, like comrades on shore, beginning with the captain and lieutenant down to the humblest boys; and thereafter these call each other only by the name of *matelot.*[1] This "matelotage" consists in these succouring and aiding one another like brothers, according to the custom of the sea, whensoever required. So, too, all the seamen are divided into two parties, the mate having one and the second mate the other, for purposes of relief. For, when one party is asleep, the other is on watch, and does the work for the space of four or five hours. On board our French ships there is no difference between the several mariners, as with the Portuguese; all are equal, though there be some of greater age and capacity than others, yet is there no difference made in name or quality, save only that the former receive a higher wage.

Further, I must in all candour mention one matter, which I have already touched, although it be little to the honour of the French, yet do I mention it as a warning, and to the end it may be corrected, and a better disposition made. It is this, that I have never seen mariners of such ill and vicious behaviour as ours. In our voyage the greater part of the officers and mariners were of St. Malo, and well-nigh all kinsmen; notwithstanding which there was ordinarily naught but strife and quarrel betwixt them, nor did I ever see any two men bear to one another any goodwill, friendship, or respect. None was willing to obey those that were in command. To this add—and herein is my chief complaint—that they were the greatest swearers and blasphemers of the name of God anywhere to be met with; insomuch that I ceased to feel surprise that our voyage succeeded so ill, seeing what great

[1] As our sailors say "messmate" and "mate".

sin was committed on board our ships day by day. The greater part of them were drunkards and very gluttons, for they had been well content to have eaten and drunk our whole substance in a single day, had that been possible, without any thought for the morrow. So it was that all the refreshments brought for their private use, to sustain them in sickness and necessity, were finished ere we had passed the Line; and when they fell sick, they had not wherewithal to comfort them, except the common sea fare of healthy men. The most of these fellows, too, were altogether lacking in devotion, and observed neither Lent nor Vigils; one would even rob another of his meat and drink. In good sooth, I candidly confess that I had rather make shift to do with the worst barbarians in the world than with them;—men whom oftentimes in the height of a storm I have observed to swear and blaspheme more than before. Nevertheless, they are very good soldiers and mariners, and capable beyond all other nations of the highest enterprises; albeit they will neither obey, nor deny their bellies aught, nor brook to be anywise corrected.

All these things from the beginning gave me a bad opinion of the success of our voyage; then, too, we delayed our departure too long, for in place of taking ship in the month of February, as arranged, we with difficulty got away at the end of May. This was a great fault, but the chiefest, and that which damnified us the most, was our long delay after doubling the Cape of Good Hope. Next, we did not take the course outside of the Island of St. Lawrence, the cause whereof was that we dallied too long with the Hollanders' ships. We had fine weather, and let the ships go at their will, for the most part under the lower sails; whereas the Hollanders, better sailors than we, held always to their course along the coast of Africa, and we only followed them. For the space of three or four days the matter was who should give the best cheer, with braying of trumpets, bands of music, and volleys of cannon: all this was an affair of honour with the captains. The ship which had given the feast fired off all its guns by way of adieu, when any returned to his own vessel. The Hollanders told us it was them we had sighted on the coast of Guinea off Serseylyonne.[1] In truth, it must be confessed they are worthier to make that voyage than we, for the French are more delicate, and less capable of fatigue, and worse husbands of their resources; also they eat too much, whereas the Hollanders keep what little refreshment they have until they fall in with their friends, or fall sick, while our men never care to eat the ship's victuals so long as they have any of their luxuries left. The Hollanders also make shift to do without wine, and drink water alone. Those we met had but one quart of wine in fifteen days, while we had four. Their biscuit was all black, while ours was like chapter-house bread. On this coast of Ethiopia we saw all night long many fires on the tops of the high mountains.

But I must not forget to mention that when ships are sailing in company or meet one another at sea, and are yet afar off, and those on board cannot speak by word of mouth, this default may be supplied on both sides by the use of trumpets, whereby intelligence may be given as well as by the voice. This is observed only on the ships of the French, English, and Hollanders.

But to return to the disorders of our voyage; that which gave me the worst presage was, as I have said, the great sins committed daily by our crew. The service of God was in nowise observed, as I have seen it observed as well among the Portuguese as the English and the Hollanders; and even among the Indians, who are more observant of their religion than we of ours. Among us was nothing but quarrelling, even among our chief men; as, for instance, between the captain and the chief merchant, who

[1] *I.e.*, Sierra Leone.

struck one another, and were for more than six months without speaking or eating together; and but for the storm that overtook us off the coast of Natal, which aroused their consciences, I believe they would not have spoken during the whole voyage: and when they did so, it was not out of apprehension of death, though we saw that to be as near as well could be. All we could do was to crave pardon of God and man, and pump the ship free of water; and for four days and four nights we were without sails, helm, and masts. But the cause of their being brought together again was that after the storm was over a council was held, and advice taken what we ought to do, and where we ought to go for our refreshment, and for the repair of the ship. To this council the merchant would not come; whereupon the other officers took an attestation of the whole ship's company, to make their report of the matter on the conclusion of the voyage to the Honourable Company, forasmuch as a private quarrel, quoth they, ought not to prejudice the general concern, nor to prevent them from doing the duties of their offices. This brought about their reconciliation.

Their quarrel arose out of nothing but the placing of a chest; for the captain's brother, seeing a place vacant, had his chest placed there without more ado, whereas the merchant's chest two days ago had been removed from the same spot, because, as I believe, it interfered with the whipstaff of the helm. Thereupon the merchant comes and removes the chest, and on his own authority replaces his own. Forthwith the two come to high words, and at length to blows, and with some difficulty they were separated. We being then at anchor at the island of Anobon, our captain straightway despatched our galion to the *Croissant* to give word to Monsieur de la Bardelière of the occurrence, and begging him to come and restore order. This he did, and when he had heard the pleas on either part, and taken counsel thereupon with all the chief officers of the two vessels, he ordered the chain to be fetched.

Hearing this, the merchant, without a word, ran to his cabin to prime and cock his pistol. When the chain was brought the general gave order that he be chained by the feet to the mainmast, which is the usual place for chaining misdemeanants; but first that he should be straitly reprimanded for having dared to attack his captain. But as they went to seize him he presented his pistol ready cocked, protesting he would kill the first man that laid a hand upon him. Whereupon the general, in great wrath, vowed he would not take his departure till he should be seized; but our captain, being of a mild and benign disposition, notwithstanding that he had been insulted, himself besought the general to pardon him, and so did both ships' companies. The general yielded to this request; the merchant, however, was not appeased, for he was the proudest and haughtiest man I ever saw, and the most revengeful, and had quarrels with everyone.

In short, to return to my discourse, it was very pitiable to see so much wrangling, to hear the utterance of so much blasphemy, and to witness so many larcenies and revengeful deeds as were done amongst us. Often out of revenge they would cast overboard one another's baggage by night, or cut the cords that kept their linen and shirts together; in a word, there was no wickedness or malice they were not guilty of. When one fell sick they mocked him with the utmost inhumanity, and when one died they rejoiced, and, instead of praying God for him, said there would be so much victuals to spare. They even cursed the voyage, and all who had a hand in the undertaking: insomuch that I altogether despaired of any success to an enterprise wherein was neither law, nor discipline, nor fear of God. But if I may be permitted to make a conjecture of the sinister nature of days, I will mention what I observed, viz., that I left St. Malo on a Friday, and that I left Goa, the Maldives, St. Helena, and Brazil all on the same day, and not one of my voyages was fortunate, as I have already told.

This was the first sea-voyage I ever made, and, as it proved in my case, it was a very luckless experience to have come across such barbarous, inhuman, and ill-conditioned fellows, for out of the whole crew of the *Corbin* I found not one that was courteous and gentle, or that had a spark of honour, except our captain, *Du Clos Neuf*, who was constable of St. Malo. He was a person of good morals, and very learned, especially in mathematics and in the knowledge of the globe and of sea-charts. In short, he manifested nothing of his St. Malo origin, yet was he quite unfit to make this voyage, and it was the first time he had been to sea. He was a man of letters, and had more of the mien of a courtier than of aught else. He was, indeed, too gentle and timid for a captain, and none of the St. Malo men, who, though they knew each other well, were quite without mutual respect, took any account of his orders. Neither of our captains had any authority from the king or the Court of Parliament to administer justice, therefore everyone encroached. Moreover, our captain was of a melancholic complexion, and somewhat delicate and weak in body, so that he was incapable of great fatigue, and had none of the qualities requisite in a soldier and a seaman. This may serve for an advertisement to all that would undertake great voyages, to choose their men well according to their qualities and natures. For it is necessary that the chiefs and leaders of such enterprises should be both well qualified and of good character; and I know full well, by the ill-conduct and government of our voyage, how dearly we paid for default in selection of a captain.

The captain must not only be a man of authority and of good birth, he must understand the sphere and navigation chart; he must be of soldierly temper, and of great endurance; above all, he must have absolute power over all beneath him, even to condemn them to death. For if he be a son of the soil, and of humble condition, he will not be feared; and if such an one attempts to inspire fear by use of force, there will be risk of revolt. Next, the men whom he chooses must be of proper quality, not given to wine, nor mutinous, nor quarrelsome, for a single mutineer in a ship infects the whole crew. Next let him appoint for pursers trustworthy men, and let him as little as possible hector his crew, especially those that hold responsible posts. Let him show favour to the well-deserving, and rather to good mariners than to good soldiers. To my knowledge, some of our men, in revenge for a single cuff which the mate gave to a Flemish gunner, made a plot, when we should be arrived at Sumatra, to lay a slow match to blow up all the powder in the ship before deserting; so they afterwards confessed to us, when we were wrecked at the Maldives. And notwithstanding that we were all in the like captivity, they spoke all the ill they could of us to the king of the Maldives, saying we were all robbers and pirates, and had brought them by force. This had not much effect, because the Maldivians could not have treated us worse than they did. But thus it is seen how the recklessness of a single man can sometimes ruin a whole community, and also how dangerous it is to give the command of a vessel to one that hath not skill to exercise it well.

More than all, a good mariner cannot be too highly prized and rewarded, for he is seldom to be had. You will find plenty of raw hands, that is, fellows to haul on the ropes, but the mariners are they who rig and handle the ship, and are always ready to go aloft to the mast-heads. A good mariner is much more able to save a ship than a good soldier is.

Finally, a captain ought to establish good order in his ship from the very first; he should be careful above all that prayers be duly said, and to this effect should take with him some ecclesiastics (as I said before), and should require respect to be paid to them, for the seamen will tender respect and honour to none unless constrained thereto. He must also rigorously punish all thefts, and chiefly those of meat and drink, wherein great robberies are most commonly practised.

Such are the disorders and troubles that most usually arise in our ships, and cause all our enterprises to succeed so ill. Let us, then, take warning to remedy the same, as, indeed, may easily be done by the means which I have described, so may these be of some material service to all who shall in the future undertake voyages of the like nature.

God be praised.

DICTIONARY

OF

SOME WORDS OF THE MALDIVE LANGUAGE.

In many parts of my book I have observed upon the diversity of languages which are current throughout the East Indies. I shall therefore content myself here, by merely repeating that about Goa and its neighbourhood, besides the Portuguese, which is the chief one in vogue, there is a native language called *Canarine.*[1] Next there is the Malabar, which extends along the whole Malabar coast, from Ceylon and Cape Comory as far as Goa; for on the opposite coast, toward the east, the language commonly spoken is that called *Guzerate,*[2] which extends far into the inner country of the mainland and the realm of the Grand Mogor. This language is also spoken in Cambaye, Bengal, Bisnagat, and elsewhere, differing only slightly in dialects and idioms. At Malacca there is a language called *Malaye,* which also prevails over a wide region, even to the Sunda Islands; for example, Sumatra, the Javas, the Moluccas, etc. As for the Maldives, they have their own separate language, which is spoken only at those islands. The best is spoken in the northern islands near the king's court, for towards the south they speak somewhat more rudely, being more remote from the court, and from inter-

[1] More properly *Konkaṇi;* the modern division of North Canara is part of the territory properly known as the Konkan, and the old Portuguese called the natives of their territory, both those of Goa and the North (properly the *Konkanis*), and also those to the southward, indiscriminately *Canarins.*

[2] A mistake: the languages on the east coast are chiefly Tamil and Telugu. He was probably thinking of Mahratti.

course with other nations. Besides this vulgar tongue, they use also the Arabic language for the affairs of religion and matters of science, just as Latin is employed with us; it is spoken and understood only by the priests and the learned. I might have made a complete dictionary of the native language, inasmuch as my long sojourn gave me a sufficiently large and exact acquaintance with it; but in order not to weary my readers, I will content myself with giving here some of the principal and more necessary words, which may, I trust, satisfy the keenest curiosity.[1]

[1] In the following vocabulary the modern forms and notes are, for convenience, placed side by side. The first two columns represent the text. The third column shows the words as now written and used. It will seen that, in many cases—such as *Kaláge* "God", *hulagu* "wind", *kaḍu* "sea", etc.—the *n* of Pyrard's time is no longer written: it is, however, still sounded in speech, giving the consonant, which formerly followed it, a slight nasal tone. The cases where this pronunciation occurs will be found by reference to the words in the first column.

The few instances in which Pyrard has misapprehended the exact meaning of words will be noted in the fourth column, where also are given the Sinhalese equivalents and some of the more obvious derivations.

Some years ago, before I had the advantage of Mr. Bell's assistance, I published this vocabulary in the *Journal* of the R. Asiatic Society (N. S., vol. x, p. 173). In testimony of Pyrard's accuracy, I then supplied the modern equivalents from the vocabulary compiled by Lieut. Christopher, in 1821, and published in the *J. R. A. S.*, vols. v, vi. This list, which is fuller than Pyrard's, and the only other as yet published, should be referred to by anyone desirous of further studying the Maldive dialect. As it coincides, with but few exceptions, with Mr. Bell's list of equivalents in the third column, it has been thought that special mention of it in the fourth column is hardly required except in cases of variance.

Some valuable suggestions as to cognate Sinhalese words have been supplied by B. Gunasekara Mudaliyar, Chief Government Translator at Colombo, and F. M. Wikramasiṇha, Assistant Librarian, Colombo Museum.

Pyrard's Vocabulary.		Modern.	Notes.
God	*Calangue*	(*Ma'*) *Kaláge*	Lit. the Great One; perhaps the same word as *callans*, v. infrà.
Paradise	*Souergue*	*suwaruge*	Sin. and Sansk. *swarga*.
Hell	*Narque*	*naraka*	Sin. *naraka*.
Angel	*Roüa*	*rúha*	Ar. *rúh*, soul, spirit. "Angel" is erroneous; the word is the Arabic equivalent of *furana*, infrà.
Devil	*Chaitanne*	*saitán*	Ar. *Shaitán*.
Lucifer	*Pourete*	*furéta*	Sin. *préta*, goblin, sprite.
Evil spirit	*Ybilis*	*ibilis*	Ar. *iblis*.
Good deed	*daroumant*	*daruma*	Sin. and Sansk. *dharmma*.
Prayer	*Aloquan Coura*	*aḷukan-kurán̥*	Perhaps the Sin. *aluyamchá-ra*, the observance during the morning watch.
Sin	*papa*	*fáfa*	Sin. *pápa*.
Love	*Niet*	*niyat*	*t* mute.
Will	*rohon*	*ruhun*	Sin. *rihi*, wish or desire.
Law, religion	*Dime*	*din*	Ar. *din*.
Understanding	*bouddy*	*buddi*	Sin. *buddhi*
Soul	*Pourane*	*furana*	Sin. *prána*.
World	*Donia*	*duniya*	Ar. *dunyá*.
Sky	*Ouddou*	*uḍu*	Sin. *uḍa*, above.
Sun	*Yrous*	*iru*	Sin. *iru*.
Star	*Tary*	*tari*	Sin. *taru*.
Star of the North	*Gaa*	*gahá*	Sin. *gaha* (Nám,) the North Star.
Star of the South or S. Cross	*Cally*	*káli*	Sin. *káli* (*see* Clough).
Planets	*Naquate*	*nakat*	Sin. *nakat*. In Maldive the final *t* is almost mute.
North	*Outourou*	*uturu*	Sin. *uturu*.
South	*Deconnou*	*dekunu*	Sin. *dakuṇu*.
East	*Yroüez*	*iruwá*	*I.e.*, the sun-rise quarter. *Iru*, sun; *wá*, coming.
West	*Olangou*	*hulagu*	*I.e.*, the windward quarter; cf. Sin. *sulanga* or *hulanga*, wind.
Fire	*alipan*	*alifán*	Cf. Sin. *eliya*, light, and *pána* for *pahana*, meaning also light or clear sight. The Sinhalese say *elipan velá*, "the light having appeared", *i.e.*, when it is dawn.

Pyrard's Vocabulary.		Modern.	Notes.
Water	*Penne*	*fen* or *fe̥n*	Sin. *pæn.*
Earth	*Bin*	*bin* or *biṇ*	Sin. *bima;* cf. also Sin. *gambiṇ*, landed property.
Sea	*Candoue*	*kaḍu*	Cf. Tam. *kaḍal.*
Clouds	*Vilas*	*vilá*	Sin. *valá.*
Thunder	*gougourou*	*guguri*	Sin. *gigiri*, *giguru*, or *gigiru;* and *guguranavá*, to thunder.
Lightning	*vidi*	*vidá*	Sin. *vidu.*
Rain	*varé*	*váré*	Sin. *vaharé.*
Wind	*vaé*	*vái*	Sin. *vá.*
Tempest	*vissare*	*vissára*	Cf. Sin. *vissára* or *visári*, the region of the wind.
Dew	*pini*	*fini*	Sin, *pini.*
Day	*Duale*	*duválu*	Sin. *daval* and *daváḷa.*
Night	*regande*	*ré* or *régaḍu*	Sin. *ræ.* The Maldivians say *ré-gaḍu*, the night part (of the day), just as the Sinhalese use *ræ-bága*, with the same meaning.
Noon	*medurou*	*menduru*	Prob. *meḍa iru*, the middle sun.
Midnight	*medan*	*mendamu*	Sin. *maddhyama* (*rátriya*), the middle (of the night).
Morning	*indunon*	*hedunu*	Cf. Pali *aha - udana;* Sin. *udǽsana*, morning.
Evening	*auire*	*haviru*	Perh.=*hava-iru*, wasted sun; cf. Sin. *havasa* or *savasa.*
To-day	*adu*	*adu*	Sin. *ada.*
Yesterday	*Yé*	*iyyé*	Sin. *iyé.*
To-morrow	*madaman*	*mádamá*	
Past time	*eyouduas*	*ihu duvas*	Sin. *iha* or *isa*, before; and *davas*, days. Cf. also, Sin. *ayu*, past.
Future	*paon duas*	*fahu duvas*	Cf. Sin. *pahu-dawas*, the following day, the morrow.
Hour	*dam*	*dama*	A space of three hours; Sin. *yáma.* An hour is *sáya* (Chr. *sahádu*), Ar. *sá'at.*
Sunday	*Adyta*	*Ádita*	Sin. *Aditiya*, the Sun (God).
Monday	*Homa*	*Hóma*	Sin. *Sóma* or *hóma*, the Moon.
Tuesday	*Engare*	*Aṇgára*	Sin. *Angaharuvá*, Mars.
Wednesday	*Bouda*	*Buda*	Sin. *Buda*, Mercury.
Thursday	*Bouraspaty*	*Burasfati*	Sin. *Brihaspati*, Jupiter.
Friday	*Oucourou*	*Hukuru*	Sin. *Sikurá*, Venus.
Saturday	*Onnyre*	*Honihiru*	Sin. *Senasurá*, Saturn.
Month	*masse*	*mas*	Sin. *mása* and *masa.*

Pyrard's Vocabulary.		Modern.	Notes.
Clear	*aly*	*ali*	Sin. *alu* and *eli*, light.
Dull	*endiry*	*adiri*	Sin. *andura*.
'Tis day	*aly viligué*	*ali-vilijje*	Cf. Sin. *eli-velá*, and *aluyam vélehi*.
'Tis night	*reuegué*	*ré-vejje*	Cf. Sin. *ræ-velá*. The *vejje* here, and the *vilijje* of the foregoing expression, seem to be the past participle, corresponding to the Sin. *vechcha*.
Life	*dyril*	*diri*	Sin. *divi*.
Death	*mare*	*maru*	Sin. *mara* (n.), and *maru*, death (m.).
Sickness	*bally*	*bali*	Cf. Sin. *bæri* in *bæri-kama*, inability, *i e.*, sickness.
Fever	*homan*	*huma*	Ar. *hummà;* but the word *huṇ* is also used (see vol. i, p. 83), which seems to be the Sin. *una*, or *huna*.

Country	*ral*	*rarha* or *ra'*	Cf. Sin. *raṭa*. Sansk. *rashtra*.
Beach or Sea-shore	*atiry*	*atiri*	Cf. Sin. *tira*, *tera*, and *addara*.
Island	*guesiral*	*jazira*	Ar. *jazirat*.
Kingdom	*ragué*	*rajje*	Sin. *rajya*.
River	*core*	*kóru*	Sin. *ho* and *oya*, river. *Kóru* is applied to any channel or drain.
Salt	*lone*	*lunu*	Sin. *luṇu*.
Sea- or Salt-water	*lonepene*	*lunu-fen*	The Sin. use *lunu-diya* (*diya* = water).
Fresh water	*mirepene*	*miru-fen*	Sin. *miripænna* (*mihiri*, or *miyuru*, sweet, and *pæn*).
Scented water	*pinipene*	*fini-fen*	Sin. *pini* (*pæn*), but here again the Sin. use *diya*.
Rain-water	*varepene*	*váre-fen*	Sin. *varu-diya*.
Sand	*vely*	*veli*	Sin. *væli*.
Coast	*caras*	*kara*	Cf. Sin. *kara* in *múdé kara*, and Tam. *karai*.
Cape	*capy*	*kafi*	Perhaps connected with Sin. *kæpu*, that which is cut off: cf. Lat. *caput*, Gr. *κεφαλή*, and English *cape*. The Maldivians use *de-kafi*, two headlands, but not *ek-kafi*, one headland.

Pyrard's Vocabulary.		Modern.	Notes.
Trees	*gats*	*gas*	Sin. *gas*, *gasa*, and *gaha*. In Mald. *gas*, sing. and pl., in Sin. only plural now.
Herbs	*pila*	*fila*	Sin. *pila*, tree, and *pili*, leaves.
Birds	*donny*	*dúni*	
Fishes	*masse*	*mas*	Sin. *mas*.
Beasts	*soupis*	*súfi*	Cf. Sin. *sivupárá*, quadruped.
Lion	*singa*	*singa*	Sin. *sinha*.
Elephant	*el*	*e'*	Sin. *ætá*.
Camel	*ol*	*o'*	Sin. *oturá;* Sansk. *otthaka*.
Horse	*asse*	*as*	Sin. *as* and *aswayá*.
Ox : cow	*guery*	*geri*	Sin. *geri*.
Pig	*oure*	*úru*	Sin. *úrá*.
Dog	*nagoubalou*	*balu*	Sin. *balu* and *ballá*. The *nagou balou* is an amusing mistake. There were no dogs at the Maldives (see vol. i, p. 116), but the expression *nagu-balu*, tailed dog (*nagu* = tail), was and is still a term of abuse.
Cat	*boulau*	*bulá*	Sin. *balalá;* Sansk. *bilála*.
Sheep (m., f.)	*bacary*	*bakari*	Ar. *bakara;* but cf. Sin. *bakalaya*, a strange or distorted animal.
Rat	*mida*	*midá*	Sin. *miyá*.
Civet	*zabade boulau*	*zabádu-bulá*	Lit. "civet-cat".
Leopard	*vagou*	*vagu*	Sin. *vaga*.
Stag	*poulla*	*fulla*	Cf. Sin. *pulli*, the spotted one.
Hen	*coucoulou*	*kukulu*	Sin. *kukulo*, fowls, but *kukulá*, cock, and *kikili*, hen.
Cock	*aule*	*há*	Sin. *sævul*.
Crow	*caule*	*kálu*	Sin. *ká*, the one that *caws;* though it may be "the black one", from *kalu*, black, the *a* being sometimes lengthened in Sin.; *e.g.*, *kála-gólayá*, the nickname of a black short man.
Pigeon	*cotaron*	*kottaru*	Mr. Bell thinks this too is onomatopoeic, and cites a Vedda song, in which the cooing of doves is represented "*kuturun, kuturun kiyannan*".

Pyrard's Vocabulary.		Modern.	Notes.
Parrot	*gouray*	*gurá*	Sin. *girá*.
Heron	*maoana*	*má-kaná*	Cf. Sin. *kana koká*, the paddy bird (*Loxia orizivora*).
Coconut tree	*roul*	*ru'*	Sin. *ruk* and *ruka*.
„ fruit	*carė*	*kárhi*	
„ timber	*ory*	*orhi*	Not the timber, but only the mid rib or stalk of the branches
„ leaves	*pan*	*fan, faŋ̥*	Sin. *paŋ̥*, leaves used for plaiting or thatching.
„ flower	*maoë*	*má*	Sin. *mala*.
„ root	*moul*	*mú*	Sin. *mula*.
„ top	*coury*	*kuri*	Sin. *kuru*.
Coco-honey	*acourou*	*hakuru*	Sin. *hakuru* and *sakuru*.
Bees'-honey	*ma mouy*	*mamuy*	
Sugar	*ous-courou*	*us-sakuru*	Sin. *uk*, sugar-cane, and *sakuru*.
Sugar-candy	*lone acourou*	*lunu-hakuru*	Lit. salt-sugar. It is lump-sugar, with some salt mixed with it.
Wine	*ras*	*rá*	The M. *rá* is sweet toddy; the Sin. *rá* is fermented.
Pepper	*mirou*	*mirus*	Sin. *miris*, chillies, *gam-miris*, pepper.
Cinnamon	*ponian boutory*	*fonitorhi*	Lit. the sweet (*foni*) bark (*torhi*). M. *foni* = Sin. *pæni* in *pænidodan*, sweet oranges. Pyrard inserts *anbu*, making it the bark of the sweet mango.
Nutmeg	*tacoua*	*takúva'*	
Cloves	*carampou*	*karaŋfú*	Sin. *karábu*, Tam. *káránpu*.
Ginger	*ingourou*	*in̥guru*	Sin. *inguru*.
Oranges	*narigue*	*nárigu*	Sin. *naran-gedi*. Ar. *náranj*.
Limes	*lomboy*	*lubó*	Cf. Hind.-Pers. *limú*.
Pomegranates	*anare*	*annáru*	Pers. *anár*.
Dates	*cadourou*	*kaduru*	Hind. *khajur*.
Gold	*rhan*	*ran, raŋ̥*	Sin. *raŋ̥*.
Silver	*rihi*	*rihi*	Sin. *ridi*.
Tin	*oudu timara*	*hudu-timara*	This is whitelead. Malay *tima*, and Sin. and Mald. *hudu*, white.

	Pyrard's Vocabulary.	Modern.	Notes.
Lead	*callothimara*	*kaḷu-timara*	Lead proper. Malay *tima*, and M. and Sin. *kaḷu*, black.
Iron	*dagande*	*dagaḍu*	Sin. *yakaḍa*.
Steel	*miellany*	*miyalani*	This is cast steel.
Brass	*taras*	*tará*	A mixture of metals.
Bronze	*loë*	*lo*	Sin. *ló*, and *lóha*, metal in general.
Copper	*ramvanloë*	*ranvan-lo*	The gold-like metal.

	Pyrard's Vocabulary.	Modern.	Notes.
Man (m.)	*pyrienne*	*firihenuṇ*	Sin. *pirimi*.
Woman	*anghaine*	*aṇhenuṇ*	Sin. *angana*.
Child	*dary*	*dari*	Sin. *daru*.
My son	*mapoutte*	*mage futá*	In the northern atolls they say *mage darifulu*; but *mage futá* is still used in the south. Sin. *mage putá* = my son.
My daughter	*mandié*	*manje*	Cf. Sin. *mangi*, younger sister: used to any young girl.
My wife	*ambye*	*abi*	
Husband	*piris*	*firi (miha)*	Sin. *pirimi*.
Full brother or sister	*heobande*	*eb-baḍu*	Lit. children of one womb. Half brothers and sisters on the father's side are *debaḍu*.
Son-in-law	*damy*	*dami*	Cf. Hind. *jamá'i*.
Father-in-law	*hours*		The ordinary expressions are *bafákalége*, father-in-law, and *mádáitá*, mother-in-law. The words given seem to be the Pâli *sasura* and *sassû*.
Mother-in-law	*housse*		
Male relative	*lien*	*liyan*	Really sister's husband or wife's brother.
Female relative	*pauery*	*fahaveri*	Really brother's wife or husband's sister.
Father	*bapa*	*bafá*	Sin. *bapa*.
Grandfather	*capaé*	*káfá*	In the southern atolls *káfá* = father's father, and *máfá*, mother's father.
Mother	*amaé*	*amá*	Sin. *ammá* and *ambá*.
Grandmother	*mamonia*	*munimámá*	In the southern atolls *mámá* = mother's mother, and *munná*, father's mother.
Daughter-in-law	*lis*	*li*	Sin. *léli*.
Elder brother	*bee*	*bébé*	

Pyrard's Vocabulary.		Modern.	Notes.
Elder sister	*daïtas*	*dáita*	
Younger brother	*coé*	*koyi*	Cf. Sin. *kòllá, kellá, kelli.* In both languages used irrespectively of actual relationship.
Younger sister	*coeas*	*koyá*	
Kinsmen	*timans*	*timan*	Lit. "I" or "mine" = Sin. *tamun.*
Cousins-german	*de bee dedary*	*de bé de-dari*	Lit. the two children of two (elder) brothers, or brothers' children. The Sinhalese do not use this dual, but with them parents are called *de-maw-piyo.*
Companions	*demitourou*	*de-mituru*	The dual is much used in Maldivian. See foregoing, also *de-mihun*, two men, *de-dúni*, two birds. The islanders do not, however, use the singular dual of the Sinhalese, *dennek*, a (party of) two persons. *Mituru* = Sin. *miturá.* Chr. gives *rahumaiteri*, friend.
Friends	*macelats*	*masalas*	*I.e.*, reconciled friends. Cf. Ar. *musálaha.* Chr. gives *masalas* = pleasure, amusement.
Enemies	*rouly*	*ruli*	Cf. Sin. *rodra*, wrath; *ruduru*, cruel.
My master	*manica*	*maniku*	Cf. Sin. *mænika.* A few persons, such as the Cazi, are styled *maniku-fánu.*
Teacher	*aydru*	*eduru*	Cf. Sin. *æduru. Wastaḍu* (Ar. *ustád*) is also used.
Mistress	*maniqué*	*manike*	

King *rascan* *raskan* This is probably not quite accurate. The ordinary term for king is *rasge-fánu* (*fánu* being merely honorific), which Christopher gives. The Sultan's letters to Ceylon use the word *ras* (= Sin. *rajan*, *rada*). *Rasge* is, therefore, genitival, *ge* being the genitive suffix common to Maldive and Sinhalese: *rasge-fánu* is thus our "King's Majesty". *Ras-kan* would seem = Sin. *raja-kama*, king's business, government; and Mr. Bell cites in favour of this view the following expressions used in the Sultan's letters:—

	Pyrard's Vocabulary.	Modern.	Notes.
			raskamugai vaḍaigen innavá, "he who is carrying on the government"; and *Divehi Rájé raskamu vadaigenvá*, "he who is carrying on the government of the Maldive realm".
Queen	*renequilague*	*rani-kilage-(fánu)*	The *kila* is probably of Persian origin.
Prince	*callans*	*kalá-(fánu)*	Cf. Pers. *kalán*, great.
Princess	*camenas*	*kamana-(fánu)*	Cf. Sin. *Hæmini*, lady; Sansk. *kamini*, woman.
Lord	*saibou*	*sáhibu*	Common to Pers., Hind., etc. Orig. Ar. *Ṣáhiḅ*, companion.
Lady	*saibas*	*sáhiba*	
Gentleman	*taocurou*	*takuru-(fánu)*	See vol. i, p. 58, *note*.
Young lady	*bibis*	*bibi*	Pers. *bíbí*, lady.
Well-born man	*calogue*	*kalóge-(fánu)*	
„ woman	*camulogue*	*kamulóge-(fánu)*	
Low-born man	*callo*	*kalo*	*I.e.*, without the honorific suffix as in the preceding terms.
„ woman	*camulo*	*kamulo*	

Captain	*sardare*	*sarudáru*	Pers. *sardár*.
Soldiers	*engou*	*hagu-bé-(kalun)*	Chr. writes *hanggube*: from Sansk. *anga*, an arm, a limb; hence *chatur-anga*, the four arms, an army.
Fighting	*engouran*	*haguráma*	
Arms	*sillia*	*siléha*	Cf. Sin. *sili*.
Cannon	*badi*	*baḍi*	Cf. Sin. *vedi*.
Gunpowder	*badi baise*	*baḍi-bés*	Sin. *vedi-bét*.
Arquebuze	*caytte*	*kaituva'*	The *-tuva'* is evidently the Sin. *tuvakkuva*, a gun. Mr. Bell suggests that the first syllable may represent *kála*, death.
Ball	*onda*	*uṇḍa*	Sin. *uṇḍiya* or *uṇḍé*.
Lance	*lancia*	*lonsi*	Port. *lança*.
Sword	*candye*	*kaḍi*	Sin. *kaḍuva*.
Shield	*addande*	*aḍḍana*	
Dagger	*creis*		Malay *kris*.
Knife	*piohy*	*fiyohi*	Sin. *pihiya*.
Javelin	*ziconty*		Cf. Hind. *senti*.
A person	*miou*	*mihu'*	Sin. *miniha*.
Head	*bolle*	*bo, boḷu*	Sin. *oḷuva*, but cf. *bola*.

Pyrard's Vocabulary.		Modern.	Notes.
Hair	*ystarin*	*istari*	Apparently = "head-tree"; Sin. *isa*, head, and *tura* or *turu*, tree; cf. *tará* (Nam.), canopy.
Ears	*campat*	*kaṉfat*	Sin. *kampetta*, ear = *kana*, *pata*, or *petta*.
Eyebrows	*bouman*	*buma*	Sin. *bæma*, Sansk. *bhamuka*.
Eyes	*lols*	*ló ; lólu*	Cf. Sansk. *lócana*, Pali *lóchana*, eyes.
Nose	*nepat*	*néfat*	Sin. *næhæ*, *nahaya*.
Moustaches	*naraualle*	*nuravá*	I had interpreted *naraualle* as the "manly hair", Sin. *nara*, male, and *wála*, hair; but the more correct *nuravá* contradicts this. Moreover, Mr. Bell states that the latter means not the moustaches themselves, but the bare space betwixt them. The hair of the moustaches is *matimas*, lit. upper- (*mati*=Sin. *matu*) beard (*mas*).
Beard	*tombouly*	*tubuli*	
Lips	*tombou*	*tubu*	
Mouth	*anga*	*aga*	
Teeth	*dat*	*dat*	Sin. *daṭ*.
Tongue	*douls*	*du*	Sin. *diva*, *divu*.
Cheeks	*cos*	*kó*	Sin. *kopula*.
Neck	*gandouras*	*kaḍerá*	
Shoulders	*condou*	*koḍu*	Sin. *kañda*.
Arms	*at*	*aṫ*	Sin. *at*.
Right arm	*canat*	*kanaṫ*	Lit. the eating hand; Sin. *kanavá*, to eat.
Left arm	*vaat*	*vaṫ*	Sin. *vamata* (*vama*, *ata*).
The side	*quibat*	*kiba*	Pesh. Sin. *kayé-bóge*, half or side of the body.
Fingers	*inguily*	*igili*	Sin. *æñgili*, *añguli*.
Nails	*niapaty*	*niyafati*	Sin. *niyapotu*.
Skin	*ans*	*han*, *haṉ*	Sin. *hama*, pl. *han*.
Nerves	*nare*	*náru*	Sin. *nahara*.
Blood	*lets*	*lé*	Sin. *lé*.
Chest	*oura*	*ura*-(*mati*)	Sin. *ura*, heart, and *mati*, over.
Navel	*poulou*	*fúḷu*	Sin. *buriya*.
Abdomen	*bande*	*baḍu*	Sin. *baḍa*.

Pyrard's Vocabulary.		Modern.	Notes.
Knees	*cacoulou*	*kakuḷa*	Sin. *kakul*, legs.
Buttocks	*boudou*	*buḍu*	Cf. Sin. *puduva*.
Feet	*paé*	*fá*	Sin. *pá*, *paya*, *piya*.
Heart	*il*	*hit*	Sin. *hada*.
Liver	*mee*	*mé*	
Cloth	*sacalas*		Pers. *saḳallát*, the *syklatoun* of Chaucer, perhaps the origin of our "scarlet": it appears sometimes applied to silk and sometimes to woollen stuffs. See Yule, *Gloss.*, s. v. *Suclát*, and *supra*, vol. i, p. 244.
Linen	*pellé*	*féli*	Sin. *pili*.
White	*houde*	*hudu*	Sin. *sudu*, *hudu*.
Black	*callo*	*kaḷu*	Sin. *kaḷu*.
Yellow	*rindou*	*ridú*	Sansk. *haridu*, yellow.
Red	*rat*	*ray*	Sin. *rata*, *ratu*, *rat*.
Blue	*bes*	*fehi*	Chr. gives *blue*=*nú*, ; Sansk. *nil*. Mr. Bell says *fehi*= green, as applied to green mould.
Silk	*farouy*	*farui*	Apparently = silk-thread.
Thread	*ouy*	*ui*	Sin. *huya*, thread.
Cotton	*capa*	*kafa*	Sin. *kapu*.
Wool	*cambali*	*kambaḷi*	Sansk. *kambala*, the Anglo-Indian "cumbly", a coarse woollen blanket. See Yule, *Gloss.*, under this head.
Hemp	*quitan*	*kittán*	Ar. *kattán*. Pers. *katán* ("cotton").
Velvet	*velouzy*		Port. *veludo*.
Satin	*sopy*	*súfi*	
Petticoat	*enqué*		
Turban	*caqué*	*kachche*	Cf. Tam. *kachchai ;* Chr. gives *fagudi*.
Gown	*libasse*	*libás*	Ar. *libás ;* see vol. i, pp. 167, 372.
Slippers	*paeuane*	*fairán*	Sin. *paya*, foot, and *rahan*, cover or dress.
Hat	*topye*		Sin. *topiya*, from Hind. *topí*. The fez is called *tákihá*.
Cloak	*caban*		Ar. *ḳabá*, and hence Port. *cabaya*. See vol. i, p. 372.
Shoes	*samboc*		

Pyrard's Vocabulary.		Modern.	Notes.
One	*heo*	*eke'; e'*	Sin. *eka*, and *é* as in *é-siyak* = 100.
Two	*dec*	*dé'*	Sin. *deka.*
Three	*tinet*	*tine'*	Sin. *tuna.*
Four	*ataret*	*hatare'*	Sin. *hatara*
Five	*pahet*	*fahe'*	Sin. *paha.*
Six	*ahet*	*haye'*	Sin. *haya.*
Seven	*ateo*	*hate'*	Sin. *hata.*
Eight	*aret*	*arhe'*	Sin. *aṭa.*
Nine	*nouahet*	*nuvaye'*	Sin. *nawaya.*
Ten	*diahet*	*dihaye'*	Sin. *daha.*
Eleven	*ecolohet*	*ekolohe'*	Sin. *ekoḷoha.*
Twelve	*dolohet*	*dolohe'*	Sin. *doḷaha.*

Note that they count up to twelve (as we do up to ten), then they go on by twelves, and their "hundred" is ninety-six, or eight times twelve.[1]

Twenty-four	*passee*	*fassehi*	Sin. *paswisi* = 25.
Thirty-six	*tindolos*	*tindolos*	*I.e.*, three dozen.
Forty-eight	*panas*	*fanas*	Sin. *panas* = 50.
Sixty	*passedolos*	*fas-dolos*	*I.e.*, five dozen.
Eighty-four	*addolos*	*had-dolos*	*I.e.*, seven dozen.
Ninety-six	*ya*	*hiya*	Sin. *siya* = 100.
Thousand, or ten times ninety-six	*assa*	*hás*	Sin. *dása* = 1,000.
Million, or ten times a thousand (*sic*)	*lacqua*	*lakka*	Sin. *ḷakshaya* = 100,000. It may be noted, however, that in Malay and nearly all the languages of the Archipelago *laksa* means 10,000.

House	*güé*	*gé*	Sin. *gé.*
Temple	*mesquite*	*miskit*	Ar. *masjid.*[2]
Kitchen	*vadique*	*badi-gé*	*I.e.*, fry-house; cf. Sin. *badi-navá.*
Door	*dore*	*doru*	Sin. *dora.*
"Compound" (of a house)	*gouety*		
Wall	*paore*	*fáru*	Sin. *pavura.*
Guest	*nasile*		Ar. *nazol.*

---

[1] See "Note on the Maldive Numerals", at the end of this Vocabulary.

[2] Col. Yule notes (*Gloss. s. v.* "Mosque"): "According to Pyrard *mesquite* is the word used in the Maldive Islands. It is difficult to suppose the people would adopt such a word from the Portuguese (*mesquita*). And probably the form both in east and west is to be accounted for by a hard pronunciation of the Arabic *j* as in Egypt now; the older and probably the most widely diffused."

Pyrard's Vocabulary.		Modern.	Notes.
Precious stones	*es*	*es*	Sin. *æs;* lit. "eyes".
Diamond	*alimas*	*alumas*	Pers. *almás.*
Ruby	*yacouth*	*yágutu*	Ar. *yakút.*
Emerald	*akika*	*agida*	Cf. Ar. *akika,* bloodstone.
Turquoise	*persi*	*firózu*	*I.e.,* the "Persian" stone, as we call it the "Turkish".[1]
Pearls	*moul*	*muy*	Sin. *mutu, mutya,* or *muttika.*
Ring	*moudi*	*mudi*	Sin. *mudu.*
Bracelet	*oula*	*ulá*	Sin. *valá, vala.*
Necklet	*guilli*	*giléfati*	
Chain	*partare*	*fattara*	Cf. Sin. *paṭṭa,* bandage, ligature.
Ambergris	*gomman*	*goma*	Sin. *góma,* cowdung; see vol i, p. 229.
Musk	*castury*	*kastúri*	Sin. and Sansk. *kastúri.*
Civet	*zabade*	*zabádu*	Ar. and Pers. *zabád.*
Storax	*comozane*	*kumunzáni*	"Incense."
Sulphur	*cassadoine*	*kassanduváni*	Cf. Sin. *kasá,* sulphur.
Quicksilver	*raha*	*raha*	Sin. *raha-diya,* lit. "moving-water".
Alum	*sabou*	*sabbu*	Ar. *shabb.*
Copperas	*tutia*	*tutiya*	Sin. Sansk. *tuttha, tutthaka.*
Compass	*samca*	*samugá*	Tam. *samukká,* Sansk. *chumbaka.*
Loadstone	*niamirgau*	(*niyamin-gau*)	Lit. "pilot-stone", but not used now.
Pilot	*niamyr*	*niyamin*	Prob. Sin. *næva,* ship, and Ar. *emir,* chief; Chr. gives *niyameng* = mate or lieutenant.
Mariner	*calassir*	*kalási*	Ar. *Khalási.*
Marine chart	*mouraban*	*murubbá*	
Cross-staff for taking height of the stars.	*pilagaha*		Chr. has *filá;* the *gaha* is tree or rod.
Ship	*ody*	*oḍi*	Cf. Tam. *odam.*
Galley	*gourrabe*	*gurábu*	Ar. Hind. *ghuráb;* see vol. i, p. 312.
Anchor	*naguilly*	*nagili*	Mr. Bell suggests = Sin. *nangurama,* anchor, or *nagula,* tail. It may, however, be ship-chain; cf. Sin. *næva,* ship, and *guilli,* above translated necklet.

[1] This may probably be the original form; but *firoza* = "victorious"; and that seems to be the transformed meaning.

NOTE ON THE MALDIVE NUMERALS.

It is clear, from the numbers given above, that the Maldivians, on their separation from the Sinhalese, took with them to their islands the decimal system of notation. Their numbers, not only up to 10, but also beyond (*ekolohe'* = *eko-laha* = 1 + 10, and *dolohe'* = *do-laha* = 2 + 10, etc.), were the same as the Sinhalese, and the common inheritance of Aryan races. Since the separation, the remote situation of the islanders has enabled them to evolve for themselves a complete duodecimal system, founded upon the words of the old decimal system. This native system, born of commercial convenience, after flourishing for several centuries, has in its turn been compelled to yield to the necessities of international intercourse, and a decimal system, in which the numbers after 10 are borrowed from the modern tongues of India, is said to be ousting the practice of counting by twelves.

A perusal of the chapter on the art of counting, in Mr. Tylor's *Primitive Culture*, shows clearly enough that if Nature had but endowed the human hand with an extra finger, the use of duodecimal counting would now be almost universal. As it is, digital counting obtained too strong a hold on the practice of primitive races to be displaced by a notation founded on the number "twelve", the advantages of which, in point of divisibility, would not become obvious until a race arrived at the commercial stage. The permanence of the decimal system is also largely due, no doubt, to the use of figures, or written symbols for numbers, and more especially to the discovery of the cipher. When this stage was reached, and numbers were employed in arithmetical calculations for a large diversity of purposes, it was thenceforth impossible to alter the common use.

The Maldivians, however, were favourably situated for making their gallant experiment in numbers. Their commerce consisted chiefly in cowries, their transactions in which would, in nearly all cases, be conducted orally. At an early period of their separate nationality they must have found the advantage of the number 12, though the growth of the new practice cannot be clearly traced. Ibn Batuta, our only Maldive authority before Pyrard, does not give us a list of numbers, and those stated may be inexact. Among them, however, is the word "cotta" (catty), which, he says, meant a parcel of 24,000 cowries. This is an indication of the use of twelve in transactions, though we cannot tell whether, in the Moorish traveller's time, the number thirteen was represented by 12 + 1, and no longer by 10 + 3. The title of the Sultan, as given by Pyrard (vol. i, p. 95), and evidently an ancient formula, shows the two systems in competition. He was called "Sultan of 12,000 islands and 13 atolls", the words being *dolos assa ral* (= 12,000 lands), and *tera atholon* (= 13 atolls). Now the assignment of the number 12,000 to the Maldives is merely evidence of the prevalence of the number 12, and indicative of a vast number, stated with conscious want of preciseness. The number *tera*, on the other hand, is the old Sinhalese for 13 (*tera* or *teles* = 3 + 10). It was probably obsolete in general usage in Pyrard's time, for the common word, as he intimates in his note following the number "twelve" in the vocabulary, must have been the duodecimal *dolos-eke'*.

Whatever were the steps in the transition, the duodecimal system, based on the decimal words, attained its completion with some curious anomalies. The Maldivians were probably as unconscious that *dolos* was *do-laha* = 2 + 10, as are most Englishmen who use the word, that dozen is "duo-decim"; and they proceeded with their second dozen, *dolos-eke'*, *dolos-de'*, etc., just as we, if we were to adopt the same system, should probably say "dozen-one", "dozen-two", etc. The first anomaly comes at 24, which, if Sinhalese were followed, should be *visi-hatara*; the word used is *fassehe*, which is the Sin. *paswisi*, 25. The next comes at 48, for which *fanas* (Sin. *panas*, *i.e.*, two more than the actual four dozen) = 50, was forced to do duty. So, too, 72 is represented by *fahiti* (Sin. *paha-hetté* = 75, *i.e.*, three more than the actual six dozen), and 96 by *hiya* (Sin. *siya* = 100, *i.e.*, four more than eight dozen). While thus 2, 4, 6, and 8 dozen are represented by the Sinhalese equivalents of numbers greater than these by 1, 2, 3, and 4 respectively, the alternate dozens, 12, 36, 60, and 84 are represented by correct duodecimal words, *dolohe'* (twelve); *tin-dolos* (three dozen), *fas-dolos* (five dozen), and *had-dolos* (seven dozen). The best explanation of these anomalies which occurs to me is, that on the adoption of the duodecimal system, the decimal words for 100, and its quarterly subdivisions 25, 50, and 75, had obtained too strong a hold to be easily displaced, and were accordingly transferred to the next respective multiples of twelve. The larger numbers, *hás* (960 or 1,000 = Sin. *dása*) and *lakka*, which should be neither a million nor ten times 1,000, but 100,000, are necessarily somewhat indeterminate.

We now arrive at the third stage of the history of Maldive numerals. Modern commerce with the mainland of India, involving the greater use of accounts and written calculations, has, in quite modern times, caused a return to the decimal system. "The inconvenient duodecimal mode of numeration", says Mr. Bell—though I would point out that its inconvenience arose solely from the use by other nations of the decimal system—"was formerly exclusively used by the Maldivians; but though still in vogue here and there, it is gradually dying out, and rarely employed in business calculations. Beyond 10 a modified form of the Hindústáni decimal numeration is that in common use. Some confusion, however, arises from the co-existence of the two systems; thus, *fanas* or *fansás* may be either 48 or 50; *hiya* or *satéka*, 96 or 100" (*The Maldive Islands*, p. 121).[1] The following list of the two sets of numbers, transcribed from a Maldive *tartib*, or commentary on the Kurán, is published by Mr. Bell in the *J. R. A. S.* (Ceylon Branch), vol. vii, pt. III, 1882:—

	Duodecimal.	Decimal.
1	*eke'*	*id.*
2	*de'*	
3	*tine'*	
4	*hatare'*	
5	*fahe*	
6	*haye'*	
7	*hate'*	
8	*arhe'*	
9	*nuvaye'*	
10	*dihaye'*	
11	*ekolohe'*	*egára*
12	*doloke'*	*bára*
13	*dolos-eke'*	*téra*
14	*etc.*	*sauda*
15		*fanara*
16		*sóla*
17		*satára*
18		*arhára*
19		*ona-vihi*
20		*vihi*
21		*eka-vís*
22		*ba-vís*
23		*té-vís*
24	*fassehi*	*sau-vís*
25	*fassehi-eke'*	*fansa-vís*
26	*etc.*	*sab-bís*
27		*hata-vís*
28		*árhá-vís*
29		*ona-tiris*
30		*tirís*
31		*et-tiris*
32		*etc.*
33		
34		
35		
36	*tin-dolos*	
37	*tin-dolos-eke'*	
38	*etc.*	
39		*ona-sális*
40		*sális*
41		*ek-ális*
42		*etc.*
43		
44		
45		
46		
47		
48	*fanas*	
49	*fanas-eke'*	*ona-fansás*
50	*etc.*	*fansás*
51		*eká-vanna*
52		*etc.*
53		
54		
55		
56		
57		
58		
59		*ona-hatti*
60	*fasdolos*	*hatti*
61	*fasdolos-eke'*	*eká-hatti*
62	*etc.*	*etc.*
63		
64		
65		
66		
67		
68		
69		*ona-hattiri*
70		*hattiri*
71		*eká-hattiri*
72	*fáhiti*	*etc.*
73	*fahiti-eke'*	
74	*etc.*	
75		

[1] When Mr. Bell says that the duodecimal system is rarely employed in business calculations, I take him to mean that this is so at business centres such as Málé. It is unlikely that the statement will hold good as to ordinary business among the islanders. A change of this magnitude is not likely to have fully developed in fifty years; and as to the state of things in 1835, we have to note that Christopher remarks, "They reckon by dozens as we do by tens" (*J. Bo. Geo. Soc.*, vol. i, p. 54), and makes no mention of a decimal system.

	Duodecimal.	Decimal.
76		
77		
78		
79		*ona-d́hi*
80		*d́hi*
81		*ek-d́hi*
82		*etc.*
83		
84	*had-dolos*	
85	*had-dolos-eke'*	
86	*etc.*	
87		
88		
89		*o-navai*
90		*navai*
91		*eká-navai*
92		*etc.*
93		
94		
95		
96	*hiya*	
97		
98		
99		*ona-satta*
100		*satéka*

APPENDIX.

A.

EARLY NOTICES OF THE MALDIVES.

THE race which now inhabits the Maldivian archipelago, and which has occupied it from the earliest times of which we have any record, is unquestionably of the same stock as the Sinhalese. This conclusion is borne out by evidence of language, physical traits, tradition, folk-lore, manners, and customs, which has been in part adduced or referred to in these volumes. It does not appear that the atolls were inhabited before they were colonised by the Sinhalese, no traces existing of any race, such as the Veddas of Ceylon, which the settlers may have conquered or gradually displaced; and the recognised admixture of foreign blood in the northern atolls being attributable to intercourse within the historical period with merchants from India and Arabia, and with negro slaves from Africa. While, as has been seen, the local tradition of Pyrard's time asserted a colonisation from Ceylon, it was silent as to any war accompanying the settlement, or any intermarriage of the conquerors with the daughters of the land.

The colonisation must be assigned to a period not anterior to that of Ceylon by the Sinhalese, an event which probably occurred about the fifth or sixth century B.C. It is improbable that the Maldives would have any attraction for the adventurers from Bengal at a time when the broad lands of Ceylon were still untilled, offering a more ample return to their enterprise than the tiny coral islets and lagoons of the West. On the other hand, it is more likely that the Maldives were discovered long after the settlement of Ceylon, and perhaps at first by some belated fishermen from Galle or elsewhere on the western coast. The first discoverers would be able to return to their villages on the change of the monsoon, bearing the intelligence of this strange cluster of islands, which, though presenting no attractions of an agricultural character, had riches of its own in fish, tortoise-shell, cowries, and ambergris. For a considerable time, it may be that the Galle fishermen made annual voyages, and maintained a dual home. If they sojourned at the Maldives for the period of a monsoon, the transportation of wives and families, which would be a condition of the system, would eventually lead to a permanent settlement of some portion at least of the adventurers.

But whether we assume a single original occupation in force, or a gradual settlement such as is surmised above, we are met by an argument which seems to tell, if at all, in favour of the latter hypothesis. Neither the Mahavanso nor any other Sinhalese record as yet discovered throws any light upon the original occupation of the Maldives or upon the early relations of the Maldivians with their Sinhalese cousins.[1] If the conquest had been effected by any warlike operations, it is only likely that the credit would have been attributed to the Sinhalese king of the period. On the other hand, we can imagine the gradual progress of a fisher colony from occasional visits to a permanent settlement, and latterly to the status of a constitutional government. Nor, considering the distance of the atolls, the troubled condition of Ceylon arising from periodical invasion, and the bijou character of the new possession, need we feel any surprise that this distant colony was allowed to work out its destiny unaided or unchecked by Sinhalese proconsuls. The Maldive tradition, as recorded by Pyrard, was that the atolls were colonised from Ceylon some 400 years before his time, *i.e.*, about the beginning of the thirteenth century A.D. No reliance can,

[1] "In the Sultan's palace at Málé is said to be preserved a national record styled *Tárikho* (Ar. *tárikh*) or *Muskuli foi*, in which all important events and matters of State have been faithfully noted for centuries in the old Maldive character (*dives akuru*), in Arabic, and in the modern native character (*gabali tana*)" (*Bell*, p. 41). These archives contain the list of the Sultans, which will be found on a subsequent page, but are believed to contain no information as to the pre-Mahommedan times.

however, be placed upon this traditional date, in the face of the evidence of Ibn Batuta, who, in the middle of the fourteenth century, found the present Maldivian race in full possession, with a well-developed and apparently ancient system of government. This traveller, as will be seen, while giving no traditional account of the colonisation, records as a historical fact that the islands were converted to Muhammadanism at a period synchronising with that assigned by Pyrard to the original settlement. The probability is that the present race were the first colonists, but if we are right in assuming that the Maldives were peopled by a gradual emigration of Sinhalese, it will be impossible to do more than approximately suggest the period at which the discovery was made; and that at which the Maldivians became independent of Ceylon in regard to population, government, and religion. Now, if the indications of Buddhism which are already described[1] are to be trusted—and I do not conceal my belief that an archæological survey of the Maldives will furnish further reliable evidences of the fact—we shall have to bear in mind that the Sinhalese themselves were only converted to Buddhism about the middle of the third century B.C. The conversion may have been rapid, but was probably not so rapid as the Sinhalese epics allege. If, therefore, the evidence justifies us in concluding that Buddhism flourished at the Maldives before the advent of Islam, either it was brought thither by the colonists, probably not before the first century B.C., or it was subsequently introduced by missionaries from Ceylon. If the latter had been the case, it would probably have been matter of record in the Sinhalese chronicles; and on this point, as has been said, the chronicles are silent. It is, therefore, safe to assume that the emigration was not concluded until after Ceylon was wholly converted, and that the Buddhist religion was part and parcel of the civilization conveyed by the colonists beyond the sea.

Of the notices extracted below, I do not myself regard any as furnishing clear proof of the peopling of the Maldives until we arrive at Suleiman, the Arab traveller of the ninth century. And if

[1] See vol. i, p. 123, *note*.

subsequent investigation of the islands leads to the discovery of Buddhist remains, the character of those remains may afford evidence that the colonisation took place so late perhaps as the fourth or fifth century A.D.

Periplus.

2. The author of the *Periplus* [A.D. 90?], in describing the trade of the Malabar coast, mentions "tortoise-shell, both that called *Chrysonesiotikè*, and the kind from the islands off Limurikè", the latter being the name given to Malabar, or a particular portion of it.

Ptolemy.

3. Ptolemy (*circa* A.D. 150) says:—"Over against Taprobane lie a multitude of islands, said to number 1,378. The following are some of the names given:—*Vangalia* (or *Vangana*), *Kanathra*, *Aigidion*, *Orneon*, *Monachè*, *Amminè*, *Garkos* (or *Karkos*), *Philikus* (or *Phelikus*), *Eirenè*, *Kalaiadua* (or *Kalandradrua*), *Abrana* (or *Arana*), *Bassa*, *Balaka*, *Alaba*, *Gumara*, *Zaba*, *Bizala* (or *Zibala*), *Nagadiba* (or *Nagadena*), and *Susuara*." The position assigned to the islands named shows that, according to his information, they lay round about Taprobane on all sides. Mr. Bell has bravely, and in some instances, I think, successfully, identified certain of these islands. In his view the list includes some of the group off the north-west coast of Ceylon, and some of the Laccadives, while none of the names can be satisfactorily assigned to the Maldives. The following suggestions have some appearance of probability: — Kanathra = Kavarathi; Aigidion = Agathi, or perhaps Angediva; Orneon = Underu; Monachè = Minikai; Amminè = Amini; Kalaiadua = Karativoe.

Ammianus Marcellinus.

4. Ammianus Marcellinus (A.D. 320-390) records that in the year 362, ambassadors came to the Emperor Julian from the *Divi* and the *Serendivi*. The passage[1] runs thus:—"Legationes undique solito ocius concurrebant; hinc Transtigritanis pacem obsecrantibus et Armeniis, inde nationibus Indicis certatim cum donis optimates mittentibus ante tempus, ab usque Divis et Serendivis." The name Serendivi—a form so similar to the *Serendib* of the long

[1] Lib. xxii, c. 3.

subsequent Arab period—is linked to it by the intermediary *Sielediba* of Cosmas. The Serendivi were no doubt the Sinhalese. But whether the Divi (*Divi* = Mald. *divehi-mihun*), "the islanders" (see above, vol. i, p. 83), were the Laccadivians or the Maldivians, or both, or neither, must remain uncertain. **Ammianus Marcellinus.**

Moses Chorenensis.

5. Moses Chorenensis, on the supposed information of one Pappus of Alexandria, writes[1]:—"Taprobane is the greatest of all islands . . . . it has also smaller islands round about it, to the number of 1,372." The number here is only six less than that given by Ptolemy, and is evidently a mere variation.

Fáh Hian.

6. Fáh Hian, the Chinese traveller, who visited Ceylon early in the fifth century, adds to his description of the island the following[2]:—"On every side are small islands, perhaps amounting to one hundred in number. They are distant from one another ten or twenty *li*, and as much as two hundred *li*. All of them depend on the great island. Most of them produce precious stones and pearls." This passage has been taken to refer to the Maldives, but the small number, the allusion to pearls, and the dependence upon Ceylon, would seem more applicable to the islands at the north and north-west of Ceylon, in the neighbourhood of the pearl fishery.

Cosmas.

7. Cosmas the monk, surnamed Indicopleustes (A.D. 535-550), who himself visited Ceylon, "called *Sielediba* by the Indians, and *Taprobane* by the Greeks," adds to his description[3]: "Round about it are a number of small islands, in all of which you find fresh water and coco-nuts (ἀργέλλια; corruption of Skt. *nârikeli*, Pers. *nárgíl*). These are almost all set close to one another." This is a clearer reference to the Maldives, being somewhat more characteristic, and, except as to the "round about it", correct.

1 *Geographia*, 367, Whiston's edition, London, 1736.

2 See Beal's *Buddhist Pilgrims*, London, 1869, 8vo.

3 Montfaucon, *Collectio Nova Patrum, etc.*, vol. ii; and see extracts in Yule's *Cathay*, p. clxvii.

Palladius. 8. Here may be entered a passage from the tract so-called of Palladius, *De Bragmanibus*, a work of uncertain date and origin. "This island (Taprobane) is the seat of the greatest Indian king, whom all the rest obey as satraps. So Scholasticus relates on the information of another, for he was not allowed himself to enter the island. Round about it (unless the report be false) lie a thousand other islands, through which the Red Sea flows. In these islands, which are called *Maniolæ*, the magnet-stone which attracts iron is produced; so that if any ship built with iron nails should approach these islands, it will by the virtue of this stone be drawn thither and stayed in its course. Wherefore those who sail to Taprobane employ ships built with wooden bolts specially for this voyage." This tract, though perhaps not genuine, is no doubt very ancient, and gives one of the earliest references to the ships of southern Asia built without the use of iron. This phenomenon had to be explained, and the fable of the magnetic rock served this purpose.

Suleiman. 9. The gap between Cosmas, the last of the classical authorities, in the sixth century, and the Arabs of the ninth, is still unbridged. In the collection of notes of Arabian travellers, published first by the Abbé Renaudot, and afterwards by Reinaud, occurs in the portion attributed to Suleiman a notice of the Sea of Herkend, which extended from the Díbajat,[1] *i.e.*, the Maldives, to Sumatra[2]:—

"The third Sea bears the name of the *Sea of Herkend.* Between this sea and that called *Al-larevy* there are a vast number of islands, amounting, so it is said, to 1,900. These islands separate the two seas, *Al-larevy* and *Herkend*; they are governed by a woman.[3] The sea throws up on the shore of these islands big lumps of

[1] Divehi-raja, "the island kingdom", the Maldivians' own name for the islands.

[2] See Reinaud, *Relation des Voyages, etc.*, Paris, 1845, 12mo., pp. 4, 5.

[3] The Maldivians, like the Sinhalese, allowed females to succeed in default of male heirs. So far as is known, only three women have in fact ruled, but the phenomenon was so strange to the Arab traveller that he inferred a regular succession of females. It will be seen that Suleiman is followed by Mas'udi, and partly by Edrisi.

amber: some of these pieces have the form of a plant, or nearly so. Amber grows at the bottom of the sea like the plants; when the sea is much disturbed, it throws up the amber in pieces like pumpkins or truffles. Suleiman.

"These islands, which are governed by a woman, are planted with coco-trees. The distance separating the islands from one another is two, three, or four parasangs. They are all inhabited, and all produce coco-trees. Their money consists of cowries. The queen stores these cowries in her treasuries. It is said that no people are so adroit as the natives of these islands. They make tunics woven of a single web, with sleeves, ornaments, and borders. They build their ships and houses, and load them with their produce in like manner. The cowries come up to the surface of the water, and contain a living creature. A coco-tree branch is thrown into the water, and the cowries attach themselves to it. The cowry is called *Al Kabtadj.*

"The last of these islands is Serendib, in the Sea of Herkend; it is the chief of all. To these islands is given the name *Díbaját.* Over against Serendib is the pearl fishery."

10. Abu'l Hasan Ali, called El Mas'udi, who himself visited Ceylon in A.D. 916, gives a detailed account of the Maldives[1]:— Mas'udi.

"Between the third sea, or that of Herkend, and the Sea of Lar, there are, as has been said, a great number of islands, forming, as it were, a separate group. There are counted of them 2,000, or more exactly, 1,900. They are all very well peopled, and are subject to a queen: for from the most ancient times the inhabitants have a rule never to allow themselves to be governed by a man. The amber (gris) found on these shores, thrown up by the sea, attains the size of large pieces of rock. Many navigators, and also the traders of Siraf and Oman, who have made the voyage to these islands, have assured me that the amber grows at the bottom of the sea, and is formed like the different kinds of white and black bitumen, as mushrooms and other substances of like sort. When

1 *Les Prairies d'Or*, trad. par de Meynard et de Courteille, 2 vols., Paris, 1861; also in English, *Meadows of Gold*, by Sprenger (Or. Trans. Fund), London, 1841.

Mas'udi. the sea is troubled, it throws up from its bosom fragments of rock and shingle, and at the same time pieces of amber. The inhabitants of these islands are all subject to one government. They are very numerous, and can put an innumerable army in the field. Each island is separated from its neighbour by a distance of a mile, or one, two, or three parasangs. Coco-nuts flourish there, but they have not the date palm."

[Here follows a discourse on the coco-tree.]

"To return to these islands: there are none whose natives are more skilful artisans, in the manufacture of stuffs, instruments, etc. The queen has no other money but cowries, which are a kind of molluscs. When she sees her treasure diminishing, she orders her islanders to cut coco-branches with their leaves, and to throw them upon the surface of the water. To these the creatures attach themselves, and are then collected and spread upon the sandy beach, where the sun rots them, and leaves only the empty shells, which are then carried to the treasury. From these islands, which are known by the name of *Dabihat*,[1] a large quantity of *Zandj* or coco is exported."

Alberuni. 11. Alberuni[2] (A.D. 1030) classifies the islands of the ocean which stretches from Africa to China in three groups:—

"The eastern islands in this ocean, which are nearer to China than to India, are the islands of the *Zábaj*, called by the Hindus Suvarṇa-Dvîpa, that is, the gold islands. The western islands in this ocean are those of the *Zanj* (Negros), and those in the middle are the islands *Ramm* and the *Dîva* islands, to which belong also the *Ḳumair* islands. It is peculiar to the *Dîva* islands that they rise slowly: first there appears a sandy tract above the surface of the ocean; it rises more and more, and extends in all directions, till at last it becomes a firm soil, whilst at the same time another island falls into decay and melts away, finally is submerged, and disappears in the ocean. As soon as the inhabitants become aware of this process, they search for a new island of increasing fertility, transport there their coco-nut palms, date palms, cereals, and

[1] More probably *Díbaját*.

[2] *Alberuni's India*, by Dr. Edward C. Sachau (Trübner's Or. Series), London, 1888, 2 vols.

household goods, and emigrate to it. These islands are, according to their products, divided into two classes—the *Dîva Kûdha*,[1] the islands of cowries, because there they gather cowries from the branches of the coco-nut palms, which they plant in the sea; and *Dîva-Kanbâr*,[2] the islands of the cords twisted from coco-nut fibre, and used for fastening together the planks of their ships." Alberuni.

This is a very accurate description of the Maldives and Laccadives, the groups being distinguished by their chief exports.

12. Our next authority is Edrisi [A.D. 1099-1186]. His account, which is altogether compiled from previous authorities and the information of others, is as follows[3]:— Edrisi.

"To this section belong the islands indicated in their place, amongst others, those called *El Roibahat* [read *Dîbajât*], which are very close to one another, and innumerable. The greater part of these islands are desert. The largest of them, however, which is called *Anberia*, is flourishing and peopled with a great number of inhabitants, who cultivate both it and the neighbouring islands, *El Comor*. All the inhabitants of these islands are subject to a chief, who convokes them, and protects and defends them to the best of his power. His wife administers justice, and speaks in public unveiled, after an established custom from which they never vary. The name of this queen is *Demhera;* she wears for ornaments a robe of gold tissue, and on her head a crown of the same metal, enriched with pearls and precious stones. She wears gold slippers, such as none other may use under pain of having their feet cut off. This queen, on solemn feasts and other great occasions, appears in public, along with her maids of honour, with a great array of elephants, trumpets, and flags. Her husband and the viziers follow her at a certain distance. This queen has wealth deposited in cellars, to be distributed in due course to the poor of her dominions. No

[1] Or *Kaudha*, cf. Hind. *Kaudí*, *Kaurí*. This passage is referred to above, vol. i, p. 237, but there the word is misprinted *Kandha*.

[2] This form, which appears also in Ibn Batuta and other Arab writers, is considered by Col. Yule (*Gloss.*, s. v. Coir) to arise from some misreading of the Indian term, Malayāl. *Kâyar*. The explanation is correct, *Kâyar* being from *Kayaru*, to be twisted.

[3] *Géographie d'Edrisi*, par P. A. Joubert, 2 vols., Paris, 1836.

Edrisi. distribution of alms is made but in her presence and under her eye. The inhabitants of the country suspend silk stuffs along her path, and at places which she is to pass, for she keeps up great state, as we have explained. The king and queen of these islands reside at *Anberia*.

"The principal production of these islands is the tortoise-shell called *zabl*,[1] which can be parted into seven pieces, of which four weigh a *mina*, that is, 260 drachmas. The heaviest weigh half a mina each. With these shells are made divers ornaments for the women's dress, also combs, seeing that it is thick, transparent, and very varied in colour.

"The women of this island wear the head uncovered and the hair plaited, and each of them uses ten combs (more or less) in her hair; it is their principal adornment, as with the women of *El Sahab*, whose inhabitants are without religious belief, as we shall tell hereafter.

"The islands known by the name *El Roibahat* [*Dibajat*] are peopled. They cultivate there the coco-tree and the sugar-cane. Commerce is carried on by means of shells. They are distant from one another about six miles. Their king preserves these shells in his treasury, and he possesses the greater portion of them. The inhabitants are industrious, adroit, and intelligent. They manufacture wide tunics, open at the neck and supplied with pockets. They build ships with very slender timber. Their houses and other important buildings are of very durable stone, but they also employ, in the construction of their dwellings, timber which comes over sea, and also scented woods. They say that the shells which compose the royal treasure are found on the surface of the water in calm weather. They throw into the sea pieces of coco-wood, and the shell-fish attach themselves thereto. They are called *El Kendj* [probably *Kaudha*]. In some of the islands is found a substance resembling liquid pitch-resin, which burns the fish at the bottom of the sea and is extinguished at the surface. The last of these islands is over against Serendib, on its most northern side, in a sea called *Herkend*."

[1] Mald. *Kahalu*, tortoise-shell.

13. Marco Polo does not speak of the Maldives by name, but the number which he assigns to the Indian islands collectively is evidently a mere variant of the Maldivians' traditional number of their own islands, of which Polo must have heard on the Malabar coast. Comparing Polo's few lines, and the equally vague notices of John of Montecorvino and Friar Jordanus (given below), with the accounts of Mas'udi and Edrisi, we see that while the knowledge of the Maldives attained by the Arab geographers and travellers had long been circumstantial, if not correct, that of the Christian travellers of this period showed no advance upon the information of Ptolemy. **Marco Polo.**

The passage from Polo[1] runs as follows :—

"You must understand that, in speaking of the Indian Islands, we have described only the most noble provinces and kingdoms among them; for no man on earth could give you a true account of the whole of the Islands of India. Still, what I have described are the best, and as it were the Flower of the Indies. For the greater part of the other Indian Islands that I have omitted are subject to those that I have described. It is a fact that in this Sea of India there are 12,700 Islands, inhabited and uninhabited, according to the charts and documents of experienced mariners who navigate the Indian Sea."

14. John of Montecorvino, in a letter dated 22 Dec. (?) 1292, writes[2]:— **John of Montecorvino.**

"The state of things in regard to the Sea of India is this. . . . Traversing it towards the South there is no continent found but islands alone, but in that sea the islands are many, more than 12,000 in number. And many of these are inhabited, and many are not. You can sail (upon that sea) between these islands and Ormes, and (from Ormes) to those parts which are called Minibar is a distance of 2,000 miles in a direction between south and south-east," etc.

The latter portion of this passage is somewhat obscure, and the

[1] Book III, ch. xxxiv.

[2] For particulars of this traveller and the context, see Yule's *Cathay, etc.*, p. 215.

John of Moutecorvino. extract is of no value except as giving fresh currency to the traditional Maldive number, 12,000.

Prince Hayton. 15. In the geographical work of Prince Hayton, the Armenian,[1] dictated to Nicholas Faulcon in 1307, occurs the following dubious reference to the Maldives:—

"To the south the Ocean extends a great way, and there is found therein a quantity of islands, whose inhabitants are black. They go naked by reason of the heat, and in their folly worship idols. In these islands are found precious stones, pearls, gold, and many kinds of simples useful in medicine to the human race. In this region also is situate an island called *Celan*," etc.

Friar Jordanus. 16. Friar Jordanus,[2] who visited the east twice, viz., in 1321-3, and again after 1330, is as vague as the early classical geographers:—

"In this India be many islands, and more than 10,000 of them inhabited, as I have heard; wherein are many world's wonders. For there is one called *Silem* (Ceylon), where are found the best precious stones in the whole world, and in the greatest quantity and number, and of all kinds."

Ibn Batuta. 17. With Abú Abd-Allah Muhammad, commonly called Ibn Batuta, the Moor of Tangier, we arrive at more interesting material. This prince of travellers was born at Tangier in 1304, and died at Fez in 1377. At the age of twenty he set out on his travels of thirty years, during which every part of the known East was explored. The following is a summary of his routes[3]:—

"From Tangier he travelled across Africa to Alexandra, and in Palestine, Syria, and Arabia : down to the east coast of Africa to Quiloa: across the Indian Ocean to Muscat, Ormuz, Kish, Bahrein and El Catif: through Central Arabia to Mecca and Jedda: and again in Egypt and Asia Minor, and across the

[1] Comprised in *Recueil des divers Voyages Curieux*, Leyden, Vander Aa, 1729.

[2] *Friar Jordanus*, by Yule (Hak. Soc.), p. 28.

[3] Abridged by Dr. Birdwood, in his *Report on the Misc. Old Records in the India Office*, from Yule's *Cathay*.

Black Sea to Caffa or Theodosia, and by Azov or Tana 'on past the hills of the Russians' to Bolgar on the Volga—but not daring to penetrate further northwards into 'the land of Darkness'. Returning south to Haj-Tarkhan (Astrakhan) he proceeded in the suite of the wife of the Khan of Kipchak, the daughter of the Greek Emperor Andronicus, westward to Soldaia and Constantiniah (Constantinople), whence returning to Bolgar he travelled on eastward to Bokhara, and through Khorassan to Cabul, Multan, and Delhi, where he remained eight years (1334-42). Being sent on an embassy to China, he embarked at Kinbaiat (Cambay), and after many adventures at Calicut (where he was honourably received by the 'Samari' or Zamorin) and Hunawar (Onore), at the Maldive Islands, and in Ceylon and Bengal, he at last took his passage toward China in a junk bound for Java, as he calls it, but in fact Sumatra. Returning from China he sailed direct from the coast of Malabar to Muscat and Ormuz: and travelling by Shiraz, Bagdad, Jerusalem, Damascus, and for the fourth time to Mecca, Egypt, Tunis, at last reached Fez again, after an absence of half his life-time. Subsequently he spent six years in Spain, and Central Africa, where he was the guest of the brother of a countryman of his own from Ceuta, whose guest he had been in China. 'What an enormous distance lay between these two?' he exclaims." Ibn Batuta.

Ibn Batuta visited the Maldives out of pure curiosity. He found himself, as he frequently did, quite at home among a Mahommedan people, and was pressed into their service as *kázi*. After a year-and-a-half at the Islands he crossed over to Ceylon, and thence to the Coromandel coast, whence, two years later, he returned to the Maldives to see a son who had been born to him after his departure. With perfect nonchalance he satisfies his sense of parental duty by a mere sight of his child, whose welfare he consults by leaving him with his mother, and proceeds to Bengal, concious that he will never see the boy again.

His first visit to the Maldives extended from the beginning of 1343 to the middle of 1344; his second took place about the end of 1346.

Nothing seems to have been known in Europe of Ibn Batuta

Ibn Batuta. till the end of last century, when a copy of the work was obtained at Fez. At the beginning of this century a MS. was brought from the East, of which an abstract in Latin was published at Jena in 1818 by Kosegarten. An incomplete Portuguese translation of the Fez MS. was issued by Moura in 1845. Dr. Lee's translation (*Or. Trans. Fund*) was made from a short abridgment brought from the East by Burckhardt. On the French conquest of Algeria many texts were acquired, of which five are in the National Library at Paris. These have been collated in the edition of MM. Defrémery and Sanguinetti (4 vols., Paris, 1st edit., 1853-9; 2nd edit., 1879), which is accompanied by a French translation, but with very inadequate notes. Other abridgments and extracts have been published in divers languages, for particulars of which the reader is referred to Col. Yule's *Cathay*, p. 430. The passages dealing with the Maldives, which are given below, it is hoped, are fairly expressive of the author's narrative; but it may be feared that certain of the Maldive names have been distorted by copyists, and I trust that the MSS. at Paris may some time or other be examined by some one competent to select the truest readings.

Ibn Batuta's account of the Maldives and his residence there is as follows[1]:—

"I resolved to go to the *Dhíbat Almahal*, of which I had heard much. Ten days after we had embarked at Calicut we arrived at the *Dhíbat Almahal* islands. *Dhíbat* is pronounced as the feminine of *Dhíb*.[2] These islands are among the wonders of the world: they number about 2,000.[3] A hundred or less of these islands lie together in a circle in the form of a ring: the group has an entrance as to a harbour, and ships get through by that alone. When a ship arrives near one of these islands it must of necessity have a pilot from among its natives, so that it may reach the other islands under his guidance. They are so close to

[1] *Voyages d'Ibn Batoutah*, par C. Defrémery et le Dr. B. R. Sanguinetti, 2nd edit., tom. iv, pp. 110-85, 191-2, 205-6, 207-10.

[2] Arabic for "wolf". It is really, of course, from the Sansk. *dvípa*, "island".

[3] *V. s.*, vol. i, p. 95.

each other that the tops of the palms which grow on one seem to belong to its neighbour.[1] If the vessel misses its way it cannot reach the islands, and is driven by the wind to *Ma'bar*[2] or towards Ceylon. **Ibn Batuta.**

"All the inhabitants of these islands are Musalmáns, pious and honest people. They are divided into regions or zones, each of which is ruled by a governor called *Kordúi.*[3] Among these zones the following are distinguished: 1st, the zone of *Bâlibúr;* 2nd, *Kannalús;* 3rd, *Mahal*, the province after which all the islands are called, and at which their sovereigns reside; 4th, *Tíládíb;* 5th, *Karáidú;* 6th, *Tím;* 7th, *Tiladummati;* 8th, *Haladummati*, a name differing from the preceding only by having for its first letter an *h*; 9th, *Baraidú;* 10th, *Kandakal;* 11th, *Molúk;* 12th, *Suwaid*. The last is the most distant of all.[4] All the Maldive

[1] So, too, more recent travellers:—"The Malabares say that heretofore they were joyn'd to the Continent, and were separated by the sea, which in some places hath left such narrow divisions that an active man might leap from one side to the other" (Mandelslo's *Travels into the Indies*, 1639, lib. ii, 116; London, 1662). "But that which makes them so numerous is the multitudes of canals that divide them; which are so narrow that the sprit-sails of the ships strike the leaves of the trees which are planted on both sides. And in some places a nimble man may leap into an island from the top of a bough that grows in another" (*Collection of Voyages of the Dutch East-India Company*, p. 131; London, 1703).

[2] Coast of Coromandel.

[3] Below, p. 443, written (probably more correctly) *Korduvéri*, though I suspect that in neither place has the best reading been given. The governor of an atoll is styled *Atoḷu-veri* or *Váru-veri;* the head-man of an island is *Rarhu-veri*.

[4] On comparison of this list of the provinces or administrative atolls with that of Pyrard at vol. i, p. 99, and with the more correct names at p. 97, *note*, some difficulties present themselves. The first observation to be made is that Ibn Batuta names twelve only, while the full number is thirteen. He does not, however, intimate that his list is complete. From his closing his list with places most distant toward the South, he might seem to be naming the atolls in order from the North; but as the most northern atoll, *Tiladummati*, comes only seventh in his list, it follows that the order of names, except in the case of the last, will not avail us in the process of identification. Coming now to the names themselves, we find only four to correspond palpably with the

Ibn Batuta. islands are destitute of grain, except that in the province of *Suwaid* there is a cereal like the *anly*, which is brought thence to *Mahal*.[1] The food of the natives consists of fish like the *lyroûn*, which they

atolls as named in later days, viz., *Mahal* (Málé), *Tiládummáti* (Tiladummati), *Molúk* (Mulaku), and *Suwaid* (Huvadu or Suadiva). Next we may observe that the Moorish traveller gives to his zones or provinces the names of particular islands. Thus *Kannalús*, the second province, is the island at which he lands on both his visits to the Maldives (see below), and may be identified with *Kinalos* in Málosmadulu atoll. *Karâidú* may be clearly identified as *Kárhidu* (the Cardiva of our charts), the large solitary island which gives its name to the channel north of the Málé atolls. *Tím*, which he visited after leaving *Kannalús*, and before reaching Málé, would seem to be *Utimu* in Tiladummati atoll, the *Oteeim* of the charts; but as to this two difficulties suggest themselves—(i) that it lies far to the north of Kinalos, and would not be taken on the way to Málé; (ii) that the atoll Tiladummati, in which it is, has already been named. *Kandakal*, the *Kaindecolu* of our charts, is Kedikolu in Miladummodulu atoll. There now remain the provinces named *Bálibúr*, *Tíládíb*, *Haladummati*, and *Baraidú*. The third of these has been, I think, satisfactorily identified by Mr. Bell with Haddummati, the first syllable being a contraction of Sin. *hela*, "white". In confirmation it may be noted that this province was, during Ibn Batuta's visit, assigned as a place of exile, and we know from Pyrard that the southern atolls were always used as penal settlements. *Bálibúr* has been identified by the French editors with *Fadiffolu* (the *Padyfolo* of Pyrard), and *Baraidú* with *Fulidu* (Pyrard's *Poulisdous*); but possibly better readings may produce more satisfactory conclusions. *Tíládíb* may perhaps be miscopied for *Níládíb*, and if this reading be adopted, the atoll intended to be referred to is probably *Nilandú*.

Even if Ibn Batuta is mistaken in attributing the names *Kannalús*, *Kandakal*, and *Tím* to atolls, he has probably named the most important islands in the atolls to which they belonged. In the earliest European maps of the sixteenth century these names appear against the Maldive atolls (see the *mappe monde* of Henry II of France, *circa* 1555, figured in the *Encyc. Brit.*, 9th edition, art. "Maldives"), but whether intended for atolls or islands is uncertain. It is difficult to say where the early European cosmographers got the Maldive names, though it is possible that Ibn Batuta's book may have been known in Spain and Portugal.

[1] Either the fine grain known to the Sinhalese as *tana hál* (*Setaria Italica*), M. *urá*, or *meneri* (*Panicum miliaceum*), M. *kudibai*—both of which are found on the southern atolls. Some nacheri or *kurakkan* (*Cynosurus corocanus*), M. *bimbi*, is grown on the northern atolls.

call *kulb almás*. Its flesh is red; it has no grease, but its smell resembles that of mutton. When caught at the fishing, each fish is cut up into four pieces, and then slightly cooked: it is then placed in baskets of coco leaves and suspended in smoke. It is eaten when perfectly dry. From this country it is exported to India, China, and Yemen. It is called *kulb almás*.[1] Ibn Batuta.

"*The Trees of the Maldives.*—Most of the trees on these islands are coconuts: they furnish the food of the inhabitants along with the fish, of which mention has been made. The nature of the coconut is marvellous. Each of these palms produces annually twelve crops, one a month. Some are small, others large: many are yellow; the rest are green, and remain always so. From the fruit are obtained milk, oil, and honey, as we have said in the first part of this book. With the honey is made pastry, which they eat with the dried coconut. All the food made from the coconut, and the fish eaten at the same time, effect an extraordinary and unequalled vigour in manhood. In this matter the inhabitants of the islands accomplish astonishing feats. As for me, I had in that country four legitimate wives, besides concubines. I visited them all every day, and spent the night with each in turn. I continued this course of life during the year and a half that I spent at the Maldives.

"Among the remarkable trees of these islands are the *jumún*,[2] the lemon, the lime, and the colocasia. From the root of the last named, the natives prepare a flour with which they make a kind of vermicelli, and this they cook in coco-milk; it is one of the most agreeable dishes in the world. I had a great taste for it and ate it often.[3]

"*Of the Inhabitants of these Islands and some of their Customs: Description of their Dwellings.*—The inhabitants of the Maldive islands are honest and pious people, sincere in good faith and of a strong will: they eat only what is lawful, and their prayers are granted. When one of them meets another, he says, 'God is my lord: Muhammad is my prophet: I am a poor ignorant being.' In body they are weak and have no aptitude for combat or for war,

[1] M. *kalu-bili-mas.*; *v. s.*, vol. i, p. 190.

[2] *Eugenia Jambu.*

[3] *V. s.*, vol. i, p. 111.

Ibn Batuta. and their arms are prayers. One day in that country, I ordered the right hand of a robber to be cut off; whereupon many of the natives in the audience-hall fainted away. The Indian pirates do not attack them, and cause them no alarm, for they have found that whoever takes anything of theirs is struck with a sudden calamity. When a hostile fleet comes to their shores, the marauders seize what strangers they find, but do no harm to the natives. If an idolater appropriates anything, if it be but a lime, the captain of the idolaters punishes him and beats him severely, so much does he fear the results of such an action. Were it otherwise, certainly these people would be a most contemptible foe in the eyes of their enemies, because of the weakness of their bodies. In each of their islands there are fine mosques, and most of their buildings are of wood.

"The islanders are good people: they abstain from what is foul, and most of them bathe twice a day, and properly too, on account of the extreme heat of the climate and the abundance of perspiration. They use a large quantity of scented oils, such as sandal-wood oil, etc., and they anoint themselves with musk from *Makdashau.*[1] It is one of their customs, when they have said the morning prayer, for every woman to go to meet her husband or son with the collyrium box, rose-water, and musk oil. He smears his eye-lashes with collyrium, and rubs himself with rose-water and musk oil, and so polishes the skin and removes from his face all trace of fatigue.

"The clothing of these people consists of cloths. They wrap one round their loins in place of drawers, while on their backs they wear the stuffs called *wilyán*,[2] which resemble the *iḥrám*. Some wear the turban, others supply its place with a little kerchief. When any one meets the *Kázi*, or the preacher, he takes his garment off his shoulders, and uncovers his back, and so accom-

[1] *Makdishu* or *Magadoxo*, on the Zanzibar coast, which Ibn Batuta had visited (tome ii, 181).

[2] A probable corruption of M. *fêliya* (cf. Sin. *pili*, "clothes"), the term for the waist-cloth worn by Maldivian women commonly, and by soldiers on special occasions. The Maldive equivalent for the *iḥrám*, the attire of the Muhammadan pilgrims, is known as *digu libás*.

panies the functionary, till he arrives at his place of abode. Another of their customs is this. When one of them marries, and goes to the house of his wife, she spreads cotton-cloths from the house-door to that of the nuptial chamber: on these cloths she places handfuls of cowries on the right and left of the path he has to follow, while she herself stands awaiting him at the door of the apartment. On his arrival she throws over his feet a cloth which his attendants take up. If it be the wife[1] who goes to the husband's house, that house is hung with cloths, and cowries are placed thereon; and the woman on her arrival throws the cloth over his feet. And this is also the custom of the islanders when they salute the sovereign; they must without fail be provided with a piece of cloth to cast down at the right moment,[2] as we shall hereafter describe. **Ibn Batuta.**

"Their buildings are of wood,[3] and they take care to raise the floor of their houses some height above the ground, by way of precaution against damp, owing to the humidity of the soil. This is the method they adopt: they dress the stones, each of which is of two or three cubits long, and place them in piles; across these they lay beams of the coco-tree, and afterwards raise the walls with boards. In this work they show marvellous skill. In the vestibule of the house they construct an apartment which they call *málam*[4], and there the master of the house sits with his friends.

[1] It appears from this passage that the two kinds of Sinhalese marriage, *bina* and *diga*, were in vogue at the Maldives. Both forms are said to be recognised still. A *bina* marriage takes place when the bride has a house and lands of her own. The bridegroom is conducted to her house, which becomes the domicile of the couple. In Ceylon, a *bina* wife had, and still has, a position of much freedom and dignity; she is mistress of the situation, and formerly could turn her husband out of doors at any time and in any weather. Thus, according to a Sinhalese proverbial saying, the whole "kit" of a *bina* husband consists of a *talipat*, a *chule*, and a lime—the talipat, or umbrella, to protect him from the rain, the chule, or torch, to light him on his way, and the lime-juice to protect his body from the leeches. In a *diga* marriage, on the other hand, the husband, being owner of house and lands, is master of his wife also.

[2] Cf. vol. i, p. 57.

[3] *V. s.*, vol. i, p. 118.

[4] This term does not seem to survive.

Ibn Batuta. This room has two doors, one opening on the vestibule, by which strangers are introduced, the other on the side of the house by which the owner enters. Near the room in question is a jar full of water, a bowl called *walendj*,[1] made of the coconut-shell. It has a handle of [only] two cubits, wherewith to draw the water from the wells, by reason of their little depth.

"All the inhabitants of the Maldives, be they nobles or the common folk, keep their feet bare. The streets are swept and well kept; they are shaded by trees, and the passenger walks as it were in an orchard. Albeit every person who enters a house is obliged to wash his feet with water from the jar placed near the *málam*, and rub them with a coarse fabric of *líf*[2] placed there, after which he enters the house. Every person entering a mosque does the same. It is a custom of the natives when a vessel arrives for the *kanádir*,[3] *i.e.*, the little boats, to go out to meet it, manned by the people of the island, and bearing some betel and *karanba*,[4] that is to say, green coconuts. Each presents some of these to whom he will of those on board the ship, and then becomes his host, carrying to his own house the goods belonging to him, as if he were one of his near relations. Any new-comer who wishes to marry is at liberty to do so. When the time comes for his departure he repudiates his wife, for the people of the Maldives do not leave their country. As for a man who does not marry, the woman of the house in which he is lodged prepares his food, serves it, and supplies him with provisions for his journey when he goes. In return she is content to receive from him a very small present. The revenue of the treasury, which is called

[1] The M. for these coconut bowls with long handles is *dáni* (as to *walendj*, cf. Sin. *valanda*, "chatty"). They are regularly used by the islanders for drawing water. The ordinary coconut ladle or spoon they call *uduli*.

[2] Persian for the *stipulæ* which envelope the base of the stalks of the date-palm leaves. Egyptian *loofahs* (the same word) are now sold in England for bath use.

[3] Plural of *kundura*. The old Portuguese historians speak of Maldive *gundras*, and the Sinhalese still call a Maldive boat *gundara*, and the Maldivians themselves *gundara-kárayó*, the "gundara-men".

[4] M. *kuruba*; S. *kurumba*.

bandar,[1] consists in the right of buying a certain portion of all cargo on board ship, at a fixed price, whether the commodity be worth just that or more; this is called the *bandar* law.[2] The *bandar* has in each island a house of wood, called *badjansár*,[3] where the governor, the *korduvéri*,[4] collects all such goods; he sells or barters them. The natives buy with chickens any pottery which may be brought; a pot fetches five or six chickens. Ibn Batuta.

"Ships export from the islands the fish of which I have spoken, coconuts, fabrics, the *wiliyán*, and turbans; these last are of cotton. They export also vessels of copper,[5] which are very common there, cowries (*wada'*),[6] and coir (*kanbar*); such is the name of the fibrous husk which envelopes the coconut. The natives make it undergo a preparation in pits dug near the shore; then they beat it with picks, after which the women work it into rope. This

[1] Pers. *bandar*, a landing-place or quay; a harbour; a seaport: probably connected with *bund* (Hind. *band*), an embankment. In the sense of quay we have the well-known *Apollo Bunder* of Bombay; in that of seaport, *Bunder Abbas* in the Persian Gulf. The meaning given in the text, *i.e.*, treasury, is probably derivative, the custom-house being usually at the quay-side; if it is not so to be explained, we might be led to derive it directly from the Sansk. *bhanḍára*, "treasury". Ibn Batuta, however, subsequently uses the word with respect to Chilaw in Ceylon, which he calls *Bandar Seluát*, probably implying only that the place was a seaport.

[2] The system of raising revenue here described was in force in Pyrard's day, and is so still (see vol. i, p. 228). It seems to be identical in principle with the "culture system", employed by the Dutch in Java, where it is supposed to have been invented by one of the Dutch governors subsequent to the English occupation.

[3] Now called *váru-gé* (see vol. i, p. 213, *note*). *Bajansár* (for *bagansár*) is evidently a form of the well-known word *bankshall*, as it is called in Anglo-Indian talk. See above, vol. i, p. 85; vol. ii, p. 48.

[4] Above spelt *kordúi*.

[5] It is hard to believe that "vessels of copper" ever formed one of the genuine exports from the Maldives. A few old copper pots are occasionally sent over to Ceylon for repair.

[6] Evidently an Arabic corruption of Sansk. *Kavaḍi*; cf. Sin. *Kavaḍiya*. The *Kabtadj* of Suleiman (*v.s.*, p. 428), and the *Kendj* of Edrisi (p. 431), are to be similarly explained. The Sansk. *Kavaḍi* becomes in Hind. *Kauḍi* or *Kauṛi*, hence our "cowry".

Ibn Batuta. cordage is used for joining the boards of their ships, and is also exported to China, India, and Yemen. *Kanbar* rope is worth more than hemp. With this cord the (timbers of) ships are joined in India and Yemen, for the Indian sea is full of rocks, and if a ship joined with iron bolts strikes a rock, it is broken up; but when it is fastened with this cord it has elasticity, and does not break.

"The money of the islanders consist of *wada'*. This is the name of a mollusc, collected in the sea and placed in pits dug out on the beach. Its flesh decays and only the white shell remains. A hundred of them is called *siya*, and 700 *fál*; 12,000 are called *kotta*, and 100,000 *bostú*.[1] Bargains are struck through the medium of these shells, at the rate of four *bostú* to a dînâr of gold. Often they are of less value, such as twelve *bostú* to a dínár. The islanders sell them for rice to the people of Bengal, where also they are used for money. They are sold in the same way to the people of Yemen, who use them for ballast in their ships in place of sand. These shells serve also as a medium of exchange with the negroes[2] in their native country. I have seen them sold, at *Máli* and at *Jújú*,[3] at the rate of 1,150 to a dînâr.

"*The Women of the Maldives.*—The women of these islands do not cover the head: the sovereign herself does not so. They comb their hair and tie it up on one side.[4] Most of them wear only a cloth, covering them from the navel to the ground: the rest of the body remains uncovered. Thus attired, they promenade the markets and elsewhere. While I was invested with the dignity of Kází in these islands, I made efforts to put an end to this custom, and to compel the women to clothe themselves: but I

[1] *Siya* = M. *hiya*, Sin. *siya*, 100. *Fál* = M. *fálé*, *fá*, or *fara*, Sin. *para*, a bushel. *Cotta* = M. *kottê*; cf. Tam. *kaḍḍu*, a bundle. *Bostú* = M. *bastá*, Pers. *bastá*, a bag or sack. Cowries are still sold in the Islands by the *hiya* = 96 or 100, the *falé* = 1,000, and the *kotté* = 12,000 (*bára-fá*).

[2] In later days they were used in exchange *for* the poor negroes; *see* vol. i, p. 238, *note*.

[3] Two places in the Soudan, afterwards visited by the traveller.

[4] Pyrard, on the contrary (vol. i, p. 108), mentions that this style distinguishes the men.

could not succeed. No woman was admitted to my presence in the trial of a case, unless she had her whole body covered: but, beyond that, I had no power over the usage.[1] Some women wear, besides the cloth, chemises with short and full sleeves. I had some young female slaves whose dress was the same as that of the women of Delhi. These girls covered the head: but that disfigured rather than embellished their appearance, as they were not used to it. Ibn Batuta.

"The ornaments of the Maldive women consist of bracelets: each has a certain number on both arms, indeed, so that the whole of the arm from the wrist to the elbow is covered. These trinkets are of silver; only the wives of the Sultan and his nearest relatives wear bracelets of gold. The Maldive women have also anklets, called by them *báil*,[2] and collars of gold round the neck, called *basdarad*.[3] One of their curious customs is to engage themselves as house servants, in consideration of a fixed sum, which does not exceed five pieces of gold. Their board is at the expense of those who hire them. They do not regard this as a disgrace, and most of the daughters of the inhabitants do it. You will find in the house of a rich man ten or twenty of them. The cost of all dishes broken by one of these maids is charged against her. When she wishes to go from one house to another, her new masters give her the amount of her debt, which she pays to the people of the house she is leaving; her new masters thenceforward become her creditors.[4] The principal occupation of these hired women is to twist the *kanbar*.

"It is easy to get married in these islands, owing to the smallness of the dowry, as well as by reason of the agreeable society of the women. Most of them say nothing about a nuptial gift, contenting themselves with declaring their profession of the Musalmán

[1] Pyrard (vol. i, p. 109) says that all women in his time carefully kept the breasts covered. It is still customary for the women in the remoter parts of Ceylon to go about their villages clothed only from the waist downwards.

[2] The mod. M. for anklet is *takaholi*.

[3] The mod. M. is *fa̤t̤taru*.

[4] See Pyrard's account of this institution, vol. i, pp. 202-4.

Ibn Batuta. faith, and a nuptial gift in conformity to the law is given. When foreign ships arrive there the crews take wives, whom they repudiate on their departure; it is a kind of temporary marriage. The Maldive women never leave their country. I have not seen in the whole world any women whose society is more agreeable. Among the islanders, the wife entrusts to no one the care of her husband's service; she it is who brings him his food, takes away when he has eaten, washes his hands, presents the water for his ablutions, and covers his feet when he wills to go to sleep. It is one of their customs that the wife never eats with her husband, and he does not even know what she eats. I married many wives in that country: some ate with me at my request, others did not; and I could not succeed in seeing these take their food, and no trick on my part to get a sight was of any avail.

"*The story of the motive for the conversion of the Inhabitants of these Islands to Islám: Description of the Evil Spirits who formerly wrought them harm every month.*—Trustworthy men among the inhabitants, such as the lawyer *'Iça al-Yamaní*,[1] the lawyer and schoolmaster *'Ali*, the Kází *'Abd Allah*, and others, related to me that the people of these islands used to be idolaters, and that there appeared to them every month an evil spirit, one of the Jinn, who came from the direction of the sea. He resembled a ship full of lamps. The custom of the natives, as soon as they perceived him, was to take a young virgin, to adorn her, and to conduct her to a *budkhána*,[2] that is to say, an idol temple,

[1] *I.e.*, Jesus of Yemen.

[2] Christopher gives *budu* as the modern Maldive for "image" (*J. R. A. S.*, vol. vi, O. S., p. 57). The word was probably borrowed from the Persian *bud* or *bod*, an idol, which is probably taken from *Budah*. *Bud-parast* = idolater. The word *bod*, too, is a general term for an image with the Arab Oriental travellers, and may only indicate that the Buddhist parts of India were the first visited by the Arabs (*Journ. As.*, 1845, p. 167). Ibn Batuta elsewhere says that the Jama Masjid of Delhi was built upon the site of a former *Budkhána;* he does not therefore mean to imply here that the word was Maldive. As to the question whether Buddhism prevailed at the Maldives, see vol. i, p. 123, *note*. The Cretan sacrifice here described had of course no connection with Buddhism, and, likely enough, is mere legend: though it is probable enough that the temple with which the legend was connected was Buddhist.

which was built on the sea-shore and had a window by which she **Ibn Batuta.** was visible. They left her there during the night and returned in the morning, at which time they were wont to find the young girl dishonoured and dead. Every month they drew lots, and he upon whom the lot fell gave up his daughter. At length arrived among them a Maghrabin[1] Berber, called *Abú'l-barakát*, who knew by heart the glorious Kurán. He was lodged in the house of an old woman of the island *Mahal*. One day he visited his hostess and found that she had assembled her relatives, and that the women were weeping as at a funeral. He questioned them upon the subject of their affliction, but they could not make him understand the cause, until an interpreter, who chanced to come in, informed him that the lot had fallen upon the old woman, and that she had an only daughter, who was now about to be slain by the evil Jinni. *Abú'l-barakát* said to the woman; 'I will go to-night in thy daughter's stead.' At that time he was entirely beardless. So, on the night following, after he had completed his ablutions, he was conducted to the idol temple. On arrival there he set himself to recite the Kurán. Presently, through the window, beholding the demon to approach, he continued his recitation. The Jinni, as soon as he came within hearing of the Kurán, plunged into the sea and disappeared; and so it was that, when the dawn was come, the Maghrabin was still occupied in reciting the Kurán. When the old woman, her relatives, and the people of the island, according to their custom, came to take away the girl and burn the corpse, they found the stranger reciting the Kurán. They conducted him to their King, by name *Shanúráza*,[2] whom they informed of this adventure. The King was astonished: and the Maghrabin both proposed to him to embrace the true faith, and inspired him with a desire for it. Then said *Shanúráza* to him: 'Remain with us till next month, and if you do again as you have now done and escape the evil Jinni, I will be converted.' Wherefore the stranger remained with the idolaters, and God disposed

[1] *I.e.*, of *Maghreb*; the name given by the Arabs to the Moorish principalities of North-West Africa, nearly corresponding with what we now call Morocco.

[2] Cf. Sin. *Senarat*, "King (Chief Commander) of the army", and *Seneviratna*, "the gem-like General".

Ibn Batuta. the heart of the King to receive the true faith. He became Mussalmán before the end of the month, as well as his wives, children, and courtiers. At the beginning of the following month the Maghrabin was conducted again to the idol-temple; but the Jinní came not, and the Berber recited the Kurán till the morning, when the Sultau and his subjects arrived and found him so employed. Then they broke the idols, and razed the temple to the ground. The people of the island embraced Islám, and sent messengers to the other islands, whose inhabitants were also converted. The Maghrabin remained among them, and enjoyed their high esteem. The natives made profession of his doctrine, which was that of the *Imám Málik.* Even at present they respect the Maghrabins for his sake. He built a mosque, which is known by his name. I have also read the following inscription graven in wood on the enclosed pulpit of the chief mosque: '*Sultan Ahmed Shanúráza has received the true faith at the hands of Abú'l-barakát the Berber, the Maghrabín.*' This Sultan assigned a third of the taxes of the islands as alms to travellers, in recognition of his reception of Islám through their agency. This share of the taxes still bears a name which recalls this event.

" Owing to the demon in question many of the Maldive islands were depopulated before their conversion to Islám. When I reached the country I was not aware of this matter. One night, while I was at one of my occupations, I heard of a sudden people crying with a loud voice the creeds, 'There is no God but God', and 'God is very great'. I saw children carrying Kuráns on their heads, and women rapping the insides of basins and vessels of copper.[1] I was astonished at their conduct, and asked, 'What is happening?' to which they replied, 'Do you not see the sea?' Whereupon I looked, and saw, as it were, a kind of large ship, seemingly full of lamps and chafing-dishes. 'That is the demon,' said they to me; 'he is wont to show himself once a month; but when once we have done as you have seen, he turns back and does us no harm.'[2]

[1] M. *Koli*; see vol. i, p. 130.

[2] Vestiges of this romantic legend of their conversion still live in the traditions of the islanders. Intercourse with Persia has, however,

"*Of the Queen of these Islands.*—One of the marvels of the Maldives is that they have for their Sovereign a woman, by name *Khadíja*, daughter of the Sultan *Jalál uddín 'Omar*, son of the Sultan *Saláh uddín Sálih al-banjálí*. The kingdom had at one time been possessed by her grandfather, then by her father, and when the latter died, her brother, *Shiháb uddín*, became King. He was a minor, and the Vizier *'Abd Allah*, son of *Mohammed Alhadhramí*, espoused his mother and assumed authority over him. He is the same personage who married the Sultana *Khadíja* after the death of her first husband, the Vizier *Jamál uddín*, as we shall describe hereafter. When *Shiháb uddín* attained full age he ousted his step-father, *'Abd Allah*, and banished him to the islands of *Suwaíd*. He was then left in sole possession, and chose as Vizier one of his freedmen, by name *'Alí Kalakí*,[1] whom he deposed at the end of three years and banished to *Suwaíd*. It is related of the Sultan *Shiháb uddín* that he consorted nightly with the wives of the public officers and with courtezans. On that account he was deposed and exiled to the province of *Haladutení*[2]; some time afterwards one was sent thither who put him to death. Ibn Batuta.

"There then remained of the royal family only the sisters of the deceased, *Khadíja*, who was the eldest, *Miryam*, and *Fathima*. The natives raised *Khadíja* to the throne, who was married to their preacher, *Jamál uddín*. The latter became Vizier and Prime Minister, and promoted his son *Mohammed* to the office of Preacher in his own stead; but orders were promulgated only in the name of *Khadíja*. These are traced on palm leaves by means of an iron [style] bent down and resembling a knife. Only the Kuráns and scientific treatises are written on paper. The Preacher makes

led them to assign to a Shaikh, *Yúsuf Shams-ud-dín* of *Tabríz*, the honour which Ibn Batuta claims for a Maghrabin, and the votaries of Hazrat Mirá Sáhib for the Nágúr saint (*C. A. S. Journ.*, No. 24, pp. 125-36, 1881). Their first Royal convert to Islam the Maldivians commonly know as *Darumavanta* (= S. *Dharmmavanta, i.e.*, "the Just") *Rasgefánu*. The mosque he built still stands, and continues to bear his name.

[1] *'Alí Kalége*. The title *Kalége-fánu* or *Kalóge-fánu* (Pyrard, *Callogue*) accrues by purchase, not by birth.

[2] Above spelt *Haladummati*.

Ibn Batuta. mention of the Sultana on Fridays and on other great days, in the following terms: 'O God, succour Thy servant, whom Thou hast in Thy wisdom preferred before other mortals, and whom Thou hast made the instrument of Thy mercy towards all Musalmáns, namely the Sultana *Khadíja*, daughter of Sultan *Jalál uddín*, son of Sultan *Saláh uddín*.'

"When a stranger comes among these people and repairs to the hall of audience, which is called *dár*,[1] custom requires that he should take with him two cloths. He makes obeisance before the Sultana, and throws down one of these cloths. Then he salutes her Vizier, who is also her husband, *Jamál uddín*, and throws down the other. The army of this Queen consists of about a thousand men of foreign birth, though some of them are natives. They come every day to the hall of audience to salute her and then go home. Their pay is in rice, supplied to them at the *bandar* every month. When the month is ended, they present themselves at the audience hall, and, saluting the Vizier, say, 'Convey our respects (to the Queen) and inform her that we have come to request our pay.' Thereupon the necessary orders are given in their favour. The Kází and ministers, who among the people are entitled Viziers, also present themselves every day at the audience hall. They make a salutation, and when the eunuchs have transmitted their respects to the Queen, they retire.

"*Of the Ministers and their conduct of Government.*—The people of the Maldives call the Grand Vizier, the Sultana's Lieutenant, *Kalakí*[2]; and the Kází, *Fandayarkálú*.[3] All judgments are in the jurisdiction of the Kází: he is more highly esteemed by the people than all other men, and his orders are executed as those of the Sultan, and even better. He sits upon a carpet in the audience hall: he possesses three islands,[4] whose revenue he places to his

[1] Ar. "house".

[2] *I.e.*, Pyrard's *Quilague*; *v. s.*, vol. i, p. 210.

[3] I.e., *Faḍiyáru Kalóge-fánu*, Pyrard's *Pandiare*.

[4] Corresponding with *nindagam* lands in Ceylon, the tenure of which is thus explained in Sir J. D'Oyley's MS., "Constitution of the Kandyan Kingdom": "*Nindagama*, a village which, for the time being, is the entire property of the grantee, or temporary chief; definitely granted by the king with *sannas*, it becomes *paraveny*," etc. (p. 144).

private account, after an ancient custom established by the Sultan *Ahmed Shanúráza*. The Preacher is called *Handíjarí;* the Chief of the Treasury, *Fámeldári;* the Receiver-General of Revenue, *Máfákalú;* the Minister of Police, *Fitnáyak;* and the Admiral, *Mánáyak.*[1] All these have the title of Vizier. There is no prison in these islands: criminals are shut up in wooden houses built to contain the merchants' goods. Each one is placed in a wooden cell, as we have (in Morocco) for the Christian prisoners. Ibn Batuta.

"*Of my arrival at these Islands, and of the vicissitudes which I experienced there.*—When I came to this country I landed at the island *Kannalús,* which is fair to behold, and contains many mosques. I was lodged at the house of one of the most pious inhabitants. The lawyer *'Alí* gave me a feast. He was a man of distinction, and had sons addicted to study. I saw there a man named *Mohammed,* a native of *Dhafár-ul Humúdh,* who entertained me and said to me, 'If you set foot on the island of *Mahal,* the Vizier will forcibly detain you, for the people have no Kází.'[2] My intention at the time was to proceed from that country to Ma'bar,[3] to Serendíb, to Bengal, and then to China. I had then arrived at the Maldives in a ship whose captain was *'Omar Alhinaúri,* who was of the number of virtuous pilgrims. When we had come into harbour at *Kannalús,* he remained there ten days; then he hired a little barque to take him thence to *Mahal,* bearing a present for the Queen and her Consort. I wished to go with him, but he said, 'The barque is not big enough for you and your companions; if you will embark without them, you are welcome.' I declined this proposal, and *'Omar* took his departure. But the wind played with him, and at the end of four days he

[1] As to these ministers, see vol. i, pp. 210-13, *note,* where the names are given according to the French editors' transliteration.

[2] Probably meaning no duly qualified Kází; the existing Kází is mentioned below.

[3] The name of *Ma'bar* ("passage" or "ferry") was given to the Coromandel coast by the Arabs during the thirteenth and fourteenth centuries. Col. Yule suggests that it referred to the communication with Ceylon, or, as is more probable, to its being at that age the coast most frequented by travellers from Arabia and the Gulf (*Marco Polo,* ii, p. 268). The tract of coast called *Ma'bar* extended from Cape Comorin to Nellore.

Ibn Batuta. came back to us, not without experience of travail. He made his excuses to me, and implored me to go with him, my companions and all. We set sail in the morning, and towards midday disembarked on a certain island; leaving that, we passed the night at another. After a four days' cruise, we arrived at the province of *Tím*, the governor whereof was one *Hilál*. He welcomed me, and gave me a feast; and afterwards came to visit me, accompanied by four men, two of whom had on their shoulders a rod[1] from which were suspended four chickens. The other two had a similar rod, to which were attached about ten coconuts. I was surprised that they thought so highly of these common objects; but was informed that they do this as a token of consideration and respect.[2]

"After leaving these people we landed on the sixth day at the island of *Othmán*, a man of great distinction and rectitude. He received us with honour, and entertained us. On the eighth day we put into an island belonging to a Vizier named *Talamdí*. On the tenth, we at length reached the island of *Mahal*, where the Sultana and her Consort reside, and cast anchor in the harbour. It is a custom of the country that no one may disembark without the permission of the inhabitants.[3] This was accorded to us; and I then desired to betake myself to some mosque, but the slaves on the beach prevented me, saying, 'It is necessary that you should first visit the Vizier.' I had requested the captain, when he should be questioned about me, to say, 'I know nothing of him,' for fear lest they should detain me; for I was then unaware that some ill-advised babbler had written out for them a full account of me, stating that I had been Kází at Delhi. On our arrival at the audience hall, we took our seats on benches at the third entrance door. The Kází *'Iça al-Yamaní* came up and welcomed me, while I saluted the Vizier. The ship captain *Ibráhím*[4] brought ten pieces of worked stuffs, made a salute before the Queen, and threw

[1] M. *daḍimáru*—the *katlíya* of the Sinhalese.

[2] The Sinhalese *penumkaḍa*, or pingo, of presents of sweetmeats, provisions, fruits, etc., is presented on like occasions.

[3] This rule is enforced to this day.

[4] Above he is called *'Omar*.

down one of them; then he bent the knee in honour of the Vizier, and threw down another, and so on to the last. He was questioned about me, and replied, 'I know nothing of him.' Ibn Batuta.

"We were then presented with betel and rose-water, which is a mark of honour with them. The Vizier gave us lodging in a house, and sent us a repast consisting of a large bowl full of rice and surrounded with dishes of salted meats dried in the sun, chickens, melted butter, and fish. On the morrow I set out with the captain and the Kázi *'Iça al-Yamaní* to visit a hermitage situated at the extremity of the island, and founded by the virtuous Shaikh *Najíb.*[1] We returned at night, and on the following morning the Vizier sent me some raiment, and a repast comprising rice, melted butter, salt, sun-dried meat, coconuts, and honey extracted from the same fruit, called by the natives *korbáni,*[2] signifying 'sugar-water'. They brought me also 100,000 cowries for my expenses. After ten days there arrived a ship from Ceylon, having on board some Persian and Arab fakírs who knew me and told the servants of the Vizier all about me. This enhanced the pleasure given by my coming. He sent for me at the commencement of Ramazán. I found the Chiefs and Viziers already assembled; food was served at the tables, each of which accommodated a certain number of guests. The Grand Vizier made me sit by his side, in company of the Kází *'Iça*, the *Fámeldári*, Vizier or Chief of the Treasury, and the Vizier *'Omar* the *Déherd*, or General of the army. The dinner of these islanders consists of rice, chickens, melted butter, fish, salt, sun-dried meat, and cooked bananas. After eating, they drink some coco-honey mingled with aromatics, which facilitates digestion.

"On the 9th of Ramazán, the son-in-law of the Vizier died. His wife, the daughter of that minister, had already been married to the Sultan *Shiháb uddín;* but neither of her husbands had cohabited with her, on account of her youth. Her father, the Vizier, took her back home, and gave me her house, which was an exceed-

[1] This old shrine (*Najíbu miskitu*), it is said, may still be seen at Málé.

[2] Probably ought to be *hakurpani* = Sin. *hakuru*, "jaggery", *peni*, "water" or "liquid", the former word appearing as *acourou* for "coco-honey", in Pyrard's vocabulary.

Ibn Batuta. ing fine one. I asked permission to entertain the fakírs on their return from visiting the Foot of Adam, in the island of Serendíb. This he granted, and sent me five sheep, a rare animal with the islanders, having to be brought from Ma'bar, Malabar, or Makdashau. The Vizier sent me also rice, chickens, melted butter, and spices. I had all these carried to the house of the Vizier *Suleïmán*, the *Mánáyak*, who took the greatest care in having them cooked, augmenting them in quantity, and sending me carpets and copper vessels. We broke the fast, according to custom, in the palace of the Sultana, with the Grand Vizier, and I requested him to permit some of the other Viziers to assist at my dinner. He said, 'I will come myself too.' I thanked him and returned home; but he had already arrived with the Viziers and grandees of the State. He seated himself in a raised pavilion of wood. All who came, whether Chiefs or Viziers, saluted the Grand Vizier, and threw down a piece of unworked stuff, in such numbers that the total reached to a hundred or thereabouts, all of which the fakírs appropriated. Dinner was then served and eaten; then the readers of the Kurán gave a recitation with sonorous voice, which was followed by singing and dancing. I had a fire prepared, and the fakírs then entered and trampled it under foot; some of them even ate the live embers, as one would devour sweetmeats, until the flame was extinguished.

"*The Story of some of the Vizier's benefactions to me.*— When the night was ended the Vizier went home and I accompanied him. We passed a garden belonging to the Treasury, and the Vizier said to me, 'This garden is for you; I will have a house built upon it to serve for your residence.' I praised his kind action, and made vows in his favour. Next day he sent me a young female slave, and his messenger said, 'The Vizier bids me say, if this girl pleases you she is yours; otherwise he will send a Mahratta slave.' I liked the young Mahratta girls, so I replied, 'I prefer the Mahratta.' The minister had one brought to me, by name *Gulistán*, which signifies 'the flower of the garden'.[1] She knew the Persian tongue, and pleased me highly. The Maldive inhabitants have a language which I did not understand.

[1] More exactly, "the parterre of flowers".

"The next day, the Vizier sent me a young female slave from Coromandel, by name *Anbéri*.[1] On the following evening he came to my house with some of his servants, and entered, attended by two little boy slaves. I saluted him, and he asked me how I did. I made vows for his welfare, and thanked him. One of the slaves put before him a *lokcha* (or *bokcha*),[2] that is, a kind of napkin, from which he drew some silk stuffs and a box containing pearls and trinkets. The Vizier made me a present of them, adding, 'If I had sent these with the young slave, she would have said, "This is my property; I brought it from the house of my master." Now that the things belong to you, make her a present of them.' I addressed prayers to God for the minister, and rendered to him expressions of my gratitude, of which he was worthy. Ibn Batuta.

"*Of the Vizier's change of disposition towards me; of the project which I formed to depart; and of my continued sojourn at the Maldives.*—The Vizier *Suleïmán*, the *Mándyak*, had proposed to me to espouse his daughter. I sent to ask the permission of the Vizier *Jamál uddín* to conclude the marriage. My messenger returned, saying, 'It does not please him; he wishes you to marry his own daughter when the legal term of her widowhood shall have expired.' I refused to consent to this union, fearing the sinister fortune attached to the daughter of the Vizier, since two husbands had already died without having consummated the marriage. In the midst of this a fever seized me, and I was very ill. Every person who goes to that island must inevitably catch the fever.[3] I then made a firm resolve to get out of the country; I sold a portion of my trinkets for cowries, and chartered a ship to take me to Bengal. When I went to take my leave of the Vizier, the Kází came out to meet me, addressing me in these terms, 'The Vizier,' said he, 'bids me tell you this, "If you wish to go away, give us back what we have given you, and begone."' I replied, 'With a part of my trinkets I have bought cowries; do with them what you will.' In a little while the Kází returned to

[1] *I.e.*, of the colour of ambergris.

[2] If the latter be the correct reading, it is perhaps the M. *burugá*, a cloth sometimes worn over the face by Maldive ladies.

[3] *V. s.*, vol. i, p. 83.

Ibn Batuta. me and said, 'The Vizier says, "We have given you gold, not cowries."' I replied, 'Very well; I will sell them and will pay you gold.' Accordingly, I sent to request the merchants to buy the shells from me. But the Vizier gave them orders not to deal with me; for his design in so conducting himself was to prevent me going away from him.

"Then he deputed one of his household, who had this conversation with me, 'The Vizier bids me request you to remain with us, and you shall have everything you desire.' So I said to myself, 'I am under their authority: if I do not stay with a good grace, I shall have to stay by constraint: a voluntary sojourn is preferable to that.' I therefore made reply to the envoy, 'Very well; I shall remain with him.' The messenger returned to his master, who was delighted with my reply, and sent for me. When I entered his presence, he got up and embraced me, saying, 'We wish you to remain with us, and you wish to go!' I made my excuses, which were accepted, and said, 'If you wish me to stay, I will impose upon you certain conditions.' The Vizier replied, 'We accept them: please to name them.' I answered, 'I am unable to walk on foot.' Now it is a custom of that country that no one rides on horseback save only the Vizier. So it was that when I had a horse given to me and was mounted, the whole population, men and children, began to follow me with astonishment, whereof I complained to the Vizier. Accordingly, a *donkora* was beaten, and it was proclaimed among the people that no one should follow me. The *donkora* is a kind of copper basin, which is struck with an iron or hammer, and gives a noise heard afar.[1] After it is struck, the crier makes then in public his proclamation.

"The Vizier said to me, 'If you wish to ride in a palanquin, well and good: otherwise we have a horse and a mare: choose which of these animals you prefer.' I chose the mare, which was brought to me at once. At the same time some garments were brought to me. I said to the Vizier, 'What shall I do with the cowries which I have bought?' He replied, 'Send one of your

[1] Probably intended for *koli*, "gong". The iron striker is called *dadigadu*.

companions to sell them for you in Bengal.' 'I will do so,' said I, 'on condition that you send someone to help him in the affair.' 'I will,' he replied. So I despatched my comrade *Abu Mahommed*, son of *Ferhán*, in whose company they sent one called the pilgrim *'Alí*. But it happened that a storm arose: the crew jettisoned the whole cargo, including even the mast, the water, and all the other provisions for the voyage. They remained for sixteen days without sail and rudder; and after the endurance of hunger, thirst, and toil, they arrived at the island of Ceylon. In a year's time my comrade, *Abu Mahommed*, came back to me. He had visited the Foot (*of Adam*), and he afterwards saw it again with me. Ibn Batuta.

"*Account of the Festival in which I took part with the Islanders.*—The month of Ramazán ended, the Vizier sent me some raiment, and we made our way to the place consecrated for prayer. The path which the minister had to traverse, between his residence and the place of prayer, had been decorated: stuffs had been spread, and cottas of cowries had been placed on the right and on the left. All the Emirs and grandees who had houses on the road had planted near them little coco-trees, arecas, and bananas. Ropes were strung from one tree to the next, and green nuts were suspended from the ropes. The master of each house was stationed at his gate, and when the Vizier passed, he threw before his feet a piece of silk or cotton. The slaves of the minister appropriated these, as well as the cowries placed by the way. The Vizier advanced on foot, covered with an ample robe of goat's hair of Egyptian manufacture, and a large turban. For a scarf he wore a kerchief of silk; four umbrellas shaded his head, and sandals covered his feet. All his attendants, without exception, had their feet bare. Trumpets, clarions, and drums[1] preceded him: the soldiers marched before and behind him, all shouting the cry, 'God is very great!' until they were arrived at the place of prayer.[2]

"Prayer ended, the son of the Vizier preached: then was

[1] M. *tálafili; dummárhi; beru.*

[2] Compare Pyrard's account of the festival at the close of Ramazán, vol. i, p. 140.

Ibn Batuta. brought a litter, which the Vizier mounted. The Emirs and the other grandees again saluted him, casting down pieces of stuffs, according to custom. Before this time the Grand Vizier used not to ride in a litter, for the Kings alone did so. The bearers then lifted it; I mounted my horse, and we entered the palace. The minister seated himself at a raised dais, having near him the Viziers and the Emirs. The slaves remained standing, bearing shields, swords, and staves.[1] Food was then served, and afterwards areca-nuts and betel, after which was brought a little dish containing sandal *mokassiri*.[2] As soon as one party of the guests had eaten, they rubbed themselves with sandal. That day I saw upon one of their dishes a fish of the species of sardines, salted and raw, which had been sent as a present from *Kaulam*.[3] This fish is very abundant on the Malabar Coast.[4] The Vizier took a sardine, and began to eat it, at the same time saying to me, 'Eat some of that; it is not found in our country.' I answered, 'How can I eat it? It is not cooked.' 'It is cooked,' said he. But I replied, 'I know this fish well, for it abounds in my native land.'

"*Of my Marriage, and of my nomination to the dignity of Kázi.*—On the 10th day of Shawwál I agreed with the Vizier *Suleïmán Mándyak* or Admiral, that I should espouse his daughter, and I sent to request the Vizier *Jamúl uddín* that the betrothal should take place in his presence at the palace. He agreed, and sent the customary betel, and also some sandal. The people were present for the ceremony. The Vizier *Suleïmán* delayed his coming. He was sent for: and yet he came not. He was sent for a second time, but he excused himself on account of the illness of his daughter; wherefore the Grand Vizier said to me in private, 'His daughter refuses to marry; and she is mistress of her own actions. But see! the people are assembled: would you like to espouse the step-mother of the Sultana, the widow of her father?' (The Grand Vizier's son was then married to this woman's

1 M. *addana; kadi; dadi.*

2 The latter part of the word is perhaps the M. *kasturi*, "musk".

3 Quilon.

4 It is probably the *pesche cavalle* of Pyrard; see vol. i, pp. 388, 427.

daughter.) I replied, 'Yes, by all means.' He then convoked the Kázi and the notaries. The profession of the Musalmán faith was then recited, and the Vizier paid the nuptial gift. After some days my wife was brought to me. She was one of the best women who ever lived. Her good manners were such that when I became her husband, she anointed me with scented oils and perfumed my clothes; during this operation she laughed, and allowed nothing disagreeable to be seen. Ibn Batuta.

"When I had married this lady, the Vizier constrained me to accept the functions of the Kází. The cause of my nomination was that I had reproached the Kází for taking the tenth part of inheritances, when he made partition among the heirs. I said to him, 'You ought to have only a fee, which you should agree for with the heirs.' This judge did nothing rightly. After I was invested with the dignity of Kází, I used all my efforts to have the precepts of the law observed. Disputes are not settled in that country as in ours. The first bad custom which I reformed concerned the sojourn of divorced women at the houses of those who had repudiated them; for these women did not cease to remain at the houses of their former husbands, until they got married to others. I forbade this to be done under any pretext. About five-and-twenty men were brought to me who had conducted themselves in this sort. I had them beaten with whips, and had them marched through the bazárs. As for the women, I compelled them to leave the homes of these men. Next I exerted myself to get prayers celebrated: I ordered some men to run down the streets and bazárs immediately after the Friday's prayers. If any were discovered who had not prayed, I caused him to be beaten and marched through the town. I compelled the *Imáms* and *Muazzins* in possession of fixed incumbencies to apply themselves assiduously to their duties. I sent orders in the same sense to all the other islands. Lastly, I essayed to make the women clothe themselves, but in this I did not succeed.

"*Of the arrival of the Vizier 'Abd Allah, son of Mohammed Alhadhramí, whom Sultan Shiháb uddín had banished to Suwaíd: account of what passed between us.*—I had espoused the step-daughter of this personage, and I loved this wife very dearly.

Ibn Batuta. When the Grand Vizier recalled him to the Island of *Mahal*, I sent him presents, went to meet him, and accompanied him to the palace. He saluted the Grand Vizier, who lodged him in a magnificent house, and there I often visited him. It happened, when I passed the month of Ramazán in prayer, that all the inhabitants visited me, except *'Abd-Allah.* The Vizier *Jamúl uddín* himself came to see me, and *'Abd-Allah* with him, but only bearing him company. Enmity arose between us. Afterwards, when I came out of my retreat, the maternal uncles of my wife, the step-daughter of *'Abd-Allah*, made a complaint to me. They were the sons of the Vizier *Jamúl uddín Assinjari.* Their father had appointed the Vizier *'Abd-Allah* to be their guardian, and their property was still in his hands, although they had by the law emerged from wardship. They demanded his appearance in Court. It was my custom, when I summoned one of the contending parties, to send him a slip of paper, either with or without writing. On delivery of that the party repaired to the Court; if he did not, I punished him. In this way I sent a paper to *'Abd-Allah.* This procedure raised his choler, and on account thereof he conceived a hatred for me. He concealed his enmity, and sent someone to plead for him. Some unseemly language was reported to me as having been used by him.

"The islanders, both gentle and simple, were accustomed to salute the Vizier *'Abd-Allah* in the same way as the Vizier *Jamúl uddín.* Their salutation consists in touching the ground with the forefinger, then kissing it, and placing it on the head. I issued orders to the public crier, and he proclaimed in the Queen's palace, in the presence of witnesses, that whoever should render homage to *'Abd-Allah* in like manner as to the Grand Vizier should incur severe chastisement. And I exacted from him a promise that he would not allow men to do so. His enmity against me was now increased. Meantime, I married another wife, daughter of a highly esteemed Vizier, whose grandfather was the Sultan *Dáud*, the grandson of the Sultan *Ahmed Shanúráza.*[1] Then I married

[1] This relationship fixes approximately the date of *Shanúráza* and of the Mahommedan conversion, which may have been as early as 1200 A.D., but—allowing for early marriages—perhaps more probably about 1220 or 1230 A.D.

one who had been married to the Sultan *Shihâb uddín*, and I had three houses built in the garden which the Vizier gave to me. My fourth wife, the step-daughter of *'Abd-Allah*, lived at her own house. She was the one of all my wives whom I cherished the most. Thus allied by marriage to the persons named, I was much feared by the Vizier and the people of the island, by reason of their own weakness. False reports were spread concerning me and the Grand Vizier, in great part by the zeal of the Vizier *'Abd-Allah*, so that our estrangement became final. Ibn Batuta.

" *Of my departure from these people, and of the motive thereof.*— It happened that one day the wife of a certain slave of the late Sultan *Jalál uddín* made a complaint of him to the Vizier, to the effect that he had an adulterous intrigue with one of the Sultan's concubines. The Vizier sent witnesses, who entered the girl's house and found the slave asleep with her upon the same carpet. Both were put in durance. In the morning, on being informed of this, I went to the audience hall and took my seat in my customary place. I made no reference to the affair. A courtier then approached me and said, 'The Vizier requests to know if you have any business with him.' I replied, 'No.' The design of the minister was that I should speak of the affair of the concubine and the slave; for it was my invariable rule to decide every case which he put before me. But as I was showing him my dissatisfaction and dislike, I omitted to do so then. I went straightway to my own house and took my seat where I delivered my judgments. Soon after came a Vizier, saying on behalf of the grand Vizier, 'Yesterday, such and such occurred in the matter of the concubine and slave; judge both of them conformably with the law.' I replied, 'It is a cause in which it is not fitting to deliver judgment save at the Sultan's palace.' I then repaired thither; the people assembled, and the concubine and the slave were summoned. I ordered that both should be beaten for their intrigue; then that the woman should be set at liberty and the slave kept in prison; after which I returned home.

"The Vizier sent several of his principal attendants to speak to me about setting the slave at liberty. I said to them, 'Intercession is made with me in favour of a negro slave, who has

Ibn Batuta. violated the respect which he owed to his master; while but yesterday you deposed the Sultan *Shiháb uddín* and slew him, because he entered the house of one of his slaves.' Thereupon I ordered the prisoner to be beaten with bambu switches, which produced more effect than the whip. I had him marched through the whole island with a rope round his neck. The messengers of the Vizier went and informed him of what passed, whereupon he discovered great agitation and was inflamed with anger. He assembled the other Viziers, the chiefs of the army, and sent for me. I obeyed the summons. It was my custom to pay him homage by bending the knee; but this time I did not do so, only saying, 'Peace be with you!' Then I said to those present, 'Be ye witnesses that I resign my functions as Kází, because I am rendered powerless to exercise them.' The Vizier then beckoning to me, I went up and took a seat in front of him, and then I answered in terms yet more severe. After this rencontre, the *Muazzin* made the call to prayer at sun-down, and the Grand Vizier entered his house, saying, ''Tis said, forsooth, that I am sovereign; but see! I have sent for this man in order to vent my wrath upon him, and he dares to be angry with me.' I was only respected by these islanders for the sake of the Sultan of India, for they knew the position I occupied under him. Although they are far removed from him, they fear him much in their hearts.

"When the Grand Vizier had returned to his house, he sent the deposed Kází, an eloquent speaker, who addressed me as follows: 'Our master requires to know why you have violated, in the presence of witnesses, the respect which is due to him, and why you have not rendered him homage?' I replied, 'I saluted him only when my heart was satisfied with him; but now that dissatisfaction has supervened, I have renounced the usage. The salutation of Mussulmans consists only of the *assélám*, and that I have pronounced.' Subsequently the Vizier sent this person a second time; he then said, 'You have no other aim but that of leaving us; pay the dowries of your wives, and what you owe to the men, and go when you will.' At this speech I bowed, and went to my house and paid such debts as I had contracted. Up to this time the Vizier had given me some carpets and household utensils, such as copper vessels, etc. He was wont to grant me anything I asked, loving me and treating me with all consideration; but his disposition changed and he became inspired with fear of me. Ibn Batuta.

"When he heard that I had paid my debts, and that I was intending to depart, he repented of what he had said, and put off granting me permission to go. I adjured him by the strongest oaths that I was under necessity to resume my voyage. I removed my belongings to a mosque upon the beach, and repudiated one of my wives. To another, who was with child, I gave a term of nine months, within which I might return; in default she was to be mistress of her own actions. I took with me that one of my wives who had been married to the Sultan *Shihâb uddîn*, in order to restore her to her father, who dwelt in the island of *Molúk*, and my first wife, whose daughter was half-sister to the Sultana. I agreed with the Vizier *'Omar*, the *Dêherd*, and the Vizier *Hasan*, the Admiral,[1] that I should go to the country of *Ma'bar*, the king of which was my brother-in-law, and that I should return with troops, to the end that the island might be reduced under his authority, and that I should then exercise the power in his name. I arranged that the signals between us were to be white flags hoisted on board the vessels. As soon as they should see these, those on shore were to rise in rebellion. I never had any such idea up to the day when I showed my displeasure. The Vizier was afraid of me, and said to the people, 'This man is determined to get the Vizierate, whether I live or die.' He made many inquiries about me, and added, 'I have heard that the King of India has sent him money, to use in raising trouble against me.' He dreaded my departure, lest I should return from the Coromandel Coast with troops. He bade me remain until he should get a ship ready for me: but I refused.

"The half-sister of the Queen complained to her of the departure of her mother with me. The Queen wished to prevent her, but did not succeed. When she saw her resolve to go, she said to her,

[1] Above, he calls the *mánáyak*, or admiral, by the name Suleimán.

Ibn Batuta. 'All the trinkets you possess were provided with money from the custom-house. If you have witnesses to swear that *Jalál uddín* gave them to you, good and well: otherwise restore them.' These trinkets were of considerable value; nevertheless, my wife gave them up to these people. The Viziers and Chiefs came to me while I was at the mosque, and prayed me to come back. I replied to them, 'Had I not sworn, I would assuredly return.' They said, 'Go then to some other island, so that your oath be kept, and then return.' 'Very well,' said I, to satisfy them. When the day of my departure was come, I went to bid adieu to the Vizier. He embraced me, and wept in such wise that his tears fell upon my feet. He passed the following night watching in the island, for fear lest my connections by marriage and my comrades should rise in rebellion against him.

"At length I got away and arrived at the island of the Vizier *'Alí*. My wife was in great distress, and wished to return. I repudiated her and left her there, and wrote this news to the Vizier, for she was the mother of his son's wife. I repudiated also the wife to whom I had fixed the term for my return, and sent for a slave girl I was fond of. Meanwhile, we sailed through the midst of the islands, from one group to another.

"*Of Women who have only one Breast.*—In one of the islands I saw a woman who had only one breast. She was mother of two daughters, of whom one resembled her exactly, and the other had two breasts, only that one was large and full of milk, the other small and contained none. I was astonished at the conformation of these women.

"We arrived in course at another of these islands, which was small, and had a solitary house, occupied by a weaver, a married man and father of a family. He possessed small coco-trees, and a little barque, which served him for fishing and visiting the other islands when he wished; on his islet were also small banana trees. We saw there none of the birds of the continent, except two crows, which flew in front of us on our arrival and circled round our ship. I truly envied the lot of this man, and made a vow that if his island should belong to me, I would retire to it until the inevitable term should arrive for me.

"I next arrived at the island of *Molúk*,[1] where I found the ship belonging to the captain *Ibráhím* in which I had resolved to sail to Ma'bar. That person came to visit me along with his companions, and they entertained me at a fine feast. The Vizier had written in my favour an order requiring them to give me at this island 120 *bostú* of cowries, 20 goblets of *atuán*[2] or coco-honey, and to add to that every day a certain quantity of betel, areca-nuts, and fish. I remained at *Molúk* 70 days, and married two wives there. *Molúk* is one of the fairest islands to see, being verdant and fertile. Among other marvellous things to be seen there, I remarked that a branch cut off one of the trees there, and planted in the ground or on a wall, will cover itself with leaves and become itself a tree.[3] I observed also that the pomegranate tree there ceases not to bear fruit the whole year round. The inhabitants of this island were afraid that the captain *Ibráhím* was going to harry them at his departure. They therefore wanted to seize the arms which his ship contained, and to keep them until the day of his departure. A dispute arose on this subject, and we returned to *Mahal*, but did not disembark. I wrote to the Vizier informing him of what had taken place. He sent a written order to the effect that there was no ground for seizing the arms of the crew. We then returned to *Molúk*, and left it again in the middle of the month of Rabí the second of the year 745.[4] In the month of Shabán, of the same year,[5] died the Vizier *Jumál uddín*. The Sultana was with child by him, and was delivered after his death. The Vizier *'Abd-Allah* then took her to wife. Ibn Batuta.

[1] Probably *Fua Mulaku* Island, which lies detached a little S.E. of the centre of the Equatorial Channel (lat. 0° 17′ S.) between Huvadú and Aḍḍú atolls. Ibn Batuta had already "sailed through the midst of the islands, from one group to another."

[2] Above, at p. 22, coco-honey is called *korbáni.*

[3] There are considerable remains of temples on this island; see above, vol. i, p. 124, *note;* and below, the account of the visit of the brothers Parmentier in 1529. The tree indicated seems to be the Bo-tree; were, then, the temples originally Buddhist?

[4] About the 26th August, A.D. 1344.

[5] December 1344.

Ibn Batuta. "As for us, we sailed on, though without an experienced pilot. The distance which separates the Maldives from the Coromandel Coast is three days' sail. We were for nine days under sail, and on the 9th we made land at the island of Serendib."

[Ibn Batuta landed in Ceylon at the port of *Batthála*, somewhere on the N.W. coast, and thence, after successfully performing the pilgrimage to the sacred footprint of our father Adam, he took ship for the coast of Coromandel. At Devipatam and Madura he was the guest of a Mahommedan prince, *Ghaiyáth-ud-dín*, who died during the visit. This raja was succeeded by his nephew, *Násir-ud-dín*, whom Ibn Batuta had previously known as a domestic servant at Delhi. The traveller had exacted from the deceased prince the promise of a fleet wherewith to subdue his enemies at the Maldives, and this promise was renewed by his nephew. While the fleet was being equipped, Batuta was attacked by a serious fever, which made him anxious to get away from the country without delay. Regardless alike of his revenge and his matrimonial connections he took ship at Devipatam for Yemen, but got himself put ashore at Quilon, where he remained three months. He then embarked in another, which was attacked by pirates near Hunáwar. He was robbed of the whole of his property, including some valuable gems presented to him by a raja in Ceylon, and even his clothes. He thus proceeds:—]

"I returned to Calicut and entered one of the Mosques. A lawyer sent me a suit of clothes; the Kází, a turban; and a merchant, another coat. I was here informed of the marriage of the Vizier *'Abd Allah* with the Queen *Khadíja*, after the death of the Vizier *Jumál uddín*, and I heard that my wife, whom I had left pregnant, was delivered of a male child. It came into my heart to go back to the Maldives, but I feared the enmity which existed between me and the Vizier *'Abd Allah*. In consequence, I opened the Kurán, and these words appeared before me: 'The angels shall descend unto them, and shall say, Fear not, neither be ye grieved.'[1] I implored the benediction of God, took my departure, and arrived in ten days at the Maldives, and landed at the island of *Kannalús*. The Governor of this island *'Abd-al-*

[1] *Kurán*, Sur. xii, 30.

'Azíz Al-Makdashawi,[1] welcomed me with respect, entertained me, and got a barque ready. I arrived in due course at *Hololi*,[2] an island to which the Queen and her sisters resort for their diversion and for bathing. The natives term these amusements *tetdjer* (?), and they then have games on board the vessels. The Vizier and chiefs send offerings to the Queen of such things as are found in the island. I met there the Queen's sister, wife of the preacher *Mohammed*, son of *Jumál uddín*, and his mother, who had been my wife. The preacher visited me, and he was served with food. Ibn Batuta.

"Meanwhile, some of the inhabitants went across to the Vizier *'Abd Allah* and announced my arrival. He put some questions about me and the persons who had come with me, and was informed that I had come to take my son, who was now about two years old.[3] The mother presented herself before the Vizier to complain of me, but he told her, 'I will not prevent him taking away his son.' He pressed me to go to the island (Málé), and lodged me in a house built opposite the tower of his palace, in order that he might be aware of my estate. He sent me a complete suit of clothes, betel, and rose-water, according to custom. I took to him two pieces of silk to throw down at the moment of saluting him. These were received from me, with the intimation that the Vizier would not come out to receive me that day. My son was brought to me, but it seemed to me that it would be better for him to remain among the islanders. I therefore sent him back, and remained five days in the island. I thought it best to hasten my departure, and asked the usual permission. The Vizier sent for me, and I repaired to his presence. They brought to me the two pieces of stuff they had previously taken from me, and I cast them before the Vizier and saluted him in the customary way. He made me sit by his side and questioned me of my condition. I ate in his company and washed my hands in the same basin with him, which thing he does with no one. Betel was then

[1] *I.e.*, of Makdashau, or Magadoxo.

[2] Probably *Oluveli* island in North Málé atoll.

[3] The son of Ibn Batuta here spoken of was probably born before the close of 1344. The traveller took his final departure from the Maldives about the close of the year 1346.

Ibn Batuta. brought, and I came away. The Vizier sent me cloths and *bostús* of cowries, and conducted himself towards me in the most perfect way. I took my departure, and after a voyage of forty-three days we arrived at Bengal."

Abd-er-Razzak. 18. For nearly a hundred years after the departure of Ibn Batuta nothing is recorded of the Maldives by traveller, friend or foe. De Barros' statement, that they were involved in the vassalage to China, to which Ceylon is said to have been subjected for the first half of the fifteenth century, is confessedly founded upon a mere rumour.[1] The next recorded allusion to the islanders, indeed, is against the hypothesis. In the year 1442 the traveller Abd-er-Razzak, in describing the various foreign merchants who frequented the great emporium of Ormuz, mentions those of "the islands of *Diwa-Mahal*".[2] Any suzerainty, therefore, to which the Chinese may have laid claim does not seem to have involved commercial monopoly.

The presence of the Maldivians at Ormuz on the occasion of Abd-er-Razzak's visit is to be regarded not as a solitary venture, but rather as indicative of a regular trade. We learn from Ibn Batuta that in the preceding century the islanders conducted a regular trade with Arabia, probably at Aden, in dried fish, coir, and cowries. Their more valuable products, ambergris and tortoise-shell, were, as we have seen, well known in the markets of the East from an early period. During the fifteenth century Ormuz was the market at which were collected the most precious products, suitable alike by their lightness and value for the long caravan journey through Persia and Syria to Europe. While, therefore, the Maldive coir and fish would find a ready sale as ship's provisions at such a port as Ormuz, we may conclude that the more substantial profits of the voyage proceeded from ambergris and tortoise-shell. Other indications also point to regular and long-continued commerce with Persia. The silver coinage of the

[1] See De Barros' *Asia*, Dec. III, liv. II, c. i, p. 111. The Maldives were, however, regularly visited by the Chinese in this century, and are marked and described in Chinese charts of the time. See Mr. Phillips' paper in *J. China Br. R. A. S.*, 1885 (vol. xx, N. S.).

[2] *India in Fifteenth Cent.* (Hak. Soc.), i, 6.

Maldives, the *larin*, was adopted from Persian use,[1] and probably for a long period the Persian coins taken in exchange for Maldive commodities were themselves current at the islands. It is also to be noted that the Maldivians of later days attributed, if not the introduction, at any rate the revival of the Mahommedan faith to the efforts of Persian missionaries. Abd-er-Razzak.

At the beginning of the next century the trade with Ormuz and Aden was at first thwarted by the Portuguese blockade of Western India, and, as to Ormuz, finally closed by the capture of that port. Although Maldive trade was temporarily enhanced at subsequent times—during the first years of the sixteenth century, and again during the Portuguese occupation of the islands,—we may regard the latter half of the fifteenth century as the period at which it attained its highest point of normal development.

19. The last glimpse of the Maldives before the irruption of the Portuguese is afforded us by the Genoese merchant, Hieronimo di Santo Stefano, who, returning from Pegu and Sumatra on his way to Cambay in 1497, was forced by weather to take refuge at the Maldives. It is to be regretted that his six months' residence produced no better result than the following paragraph[2]:— Hieronimo di Santo Stefano.

"After being twenty-five days at sea in unfavourable weather, we reached certain islands called the Maldives, which are from seven to eight thousand in number, all desert,[3] small and low, through which the sea for the most part enters, the space from one to another being about a mile and a half; and there were seen in them an infinite number of people, all black and naked, but in good condition, and courteous. They hold the faith of the Moors, and have a chief who rules over the whole of them. There are trees growing there which produce the coco-nuts of large size. The people live on fish and a little rice, which they import. We were obliged to stay here six months to wait for favourable weather for our departure."

[1] See vol. i, p. 232.

[2] *Op. cit.*, iv, p. 8.

[3] The text reads *dishabitate*, which may be a transcriber's error. Mr. Major translates as above, but "desert" is almost as contradictory to the latter part of the sentence as "uninhabited". I am inclined to think the author wrote *habitate*.

The Portuguese irruption.

20. In the following year, 1498, Vasco da Gama arrived at Calicut by way of the Cape, an event which, happening almost simultaneously with the discovery of America, had the effect of removing the centres of trade and civilisation from the Levant to Western Europe. Down to this time the luxuries of the world were enjoyed by the cities of Bagdad, Damascus, Cairo, and Constantinople, which had now attained the highest pitch of wealth, refinement, and civilisation possible under Moslem conditions. The most opulent of European cities, Venice and Genoa, flourished mainly by retailing the surplus commodities of those great marts among the countries of the West. To have merely named the above half-dozen cities is sufficient to recall to our imagination the magnitude of the Eastern trade of those days as compared with anything that Western Europe could show. The wealth of the Mahommedan merchant cities arose chiefly from the fact that they collected and disseminated the whole export produce of India and the Far East. The bulk of this produce was sea-borne, and a few words, with a mere glance at the map, will serve to explain the mode in which the Portuguese struck for the prize which fortune now displayed to their avarice.

The lines of maritime commerce from further India and China drew together until Ceylon was rounded, and then again diverged. Vessels bound for Aden and the Red Sea touched at Ceylon, the Maldives, or Calicut, thence striking across the Indian Ocean. The other main line proceeded by way of Calicut and the other flourishing ports of the Malabar coast to Cambay, and thence across to Ormuz. The produce carried by way of Aden was carried up the Red Sea to Jeddah, or further to Suez, for delivery to the merchants of Cairo. That landed at Ormuz, enhanced by the merchandise of all Western India, found its way to Bagdad or Damascus, and thence by the caravan routes to Europe.

A first preliminary observation is that free trade prevailed: a second, that all nations seem to have had a hand in it, no one race, as in later days, doing a disproportionate share of the carrying trade. "Calicut is a perfectly secure harbour", writes Abd-er-Razzak, whom we have already quoted, "which, like that of Ormuz, brings together merchants from every city and from every country: in it are to be found abundance of precious articles brought thither from maritime countries, and especially from Abyssinia, Zirbad, or Zanguebar: from time to time ships arrive there from the shores of the House of God [Mecca] and other parts of the Hedjaz, and abide at will, for a greater or longer space, in this harbour; the town is inhabited by infidels, and situated on a hostile shore. It contains a considerable number of Mussulmans, who are constant residents, and have built two mosques. . . . . Security and justice are so firmly established in this city, that the most wealthy merchants bring thither from maritime countries considerable cargoes, which they unload, and unhesitatingly send into the markets and the bazaars, without thinking in the meantime of any necessity of checking the account or of keeping watch over the goods. . . . . When a sale is effected, they levy a duty on the goods of one-fortieth part: if they are not sold, they make no charge on them whatsoever. . . . . At Calicut every ship, whatever place it may come from, or wherever it may be bound, when it puts into this port is treated like other vessels, and has no trouble of any kind to put up with."[1] Of Ormuz the same traveller speaks with equal wonder: as a port "it has not its equal on the surface of the globe. The merchants of seven climates . . . . all make their way to this port." Among those mentioned are the merchants of Egypt, Syria, Turkistan, China, Java, Pegu, Bengal, the Maldives, Malabar, Cambay, and Zanzibar. "Travellers from all countries resort hither, and, in exchange for the commodities they bring, they can without trouble or difficulty obtain all that they desire. Bargains are made either by money or by exchange. For all objects, with the exception of gold and silver, a tenth of their value is paid by way of duty.[2] Persons of all religions, and even idolaters, are found in great numbers in this city, and no injustice is permitted towards any person whatever."

The Portuguese Irruption.

This picture of Indian trade in the fifteenth century is here

[1] *India in the Fifteenth Century*, i, pp. 13, 14.

[2] The Russian Nikitin justly thought this ten per cent. duty rather high (*India in the Fifteenth Century*, iii, p. 19). There was, however, no favoured nation clause, and in effect it was not prohibitive.

The Portuguese irruption.

introduced as being illustrative of the commercial world in which the Maldivians moved and took their part. It will now be easy to understand what followed when the Portuguese swooped upon Calicut, and, by conduct not to be distinguished from common piracy, broke up link by link the commercial chain which had hitherto extended from Genoa and Venice to Malacca and Pekin.

Active operations were begun by the second expedition which left Lisbon under Cabral, in March 1500. The Zamorin of Calicut declared against the invaders, and entered upon the long struggle for free trade and independence, which lasted throughout the Portuguese domination, and reduced Calicut to commercial insignificance. The rivalry which existed between the Zamorin and the Raja of Cochin led the latter to accord the Portuguese a favourable reception. A factory was established, and from this coign of vantage the Portuguese commenced to harry the seas of Western India.

They found the largest share of the carrying trade in the hands of Mahommedans, to whom they transferred all the implacable hatred stored up in their European memories against the followers of the Prophet, and whom, regardless of race and distance, they designated by the common name of "Moors". Confiscation of goods and slavery were meted out to everyone seized on the immemorial route of Eastern commerce; nor was any prior notice or proclamation deemed necessary to justify the capture. Natives of Calicut, as will be seen, were specially dealt with.

The Maldivians got their first practical information of the new *régime* when, in the year 1503, four of their ships had the misfortune to be sighted by Chief Captain Vicente Sodré, then cruising off Calicut.[1]

"When he (Sodré) was off Calicut," Correa relates, "he sighted four sail, which he overhauled and took. They proved to be *gundras*, barques of the Maldive Islands, at which is made the *cairo* rope which serves the ships of all India for cables and shrouds, besides

[1] Vasco da Gama had just left for Europe after his second visit to India, and had appointed Sodré to carry on his work. The events at Calicut, preceding the episode of the Maldive ships, may be read in Lord Stanley's *Three Voyages of V. da Gama*, extracted from Correa.

being of great use on shore. *Gundras* are built of palm-timber, joined and fastened with pegs of wood without any bolts. The sails also are made of mats of the dry leaves of the palm. These vessels were laden with cairo and *caury*, which are small white shells found among the islands in such quantity that ships make their cargoes of them. In these a great trade is carried on with Bengal, where they are current as money. These *gundras* also carried some dried fish, called *moxama*, which consists of pieces of bonito fish dried in the sun, because there is no salt at these islands: yet are they made so dry that they never go bad. Such quantities of this, too, are made at the islands, that ships are laden with it; there is no better victuals for sailors, and all seamen are provisioned upon it during their voyages. The vessels also carried good store of silks, both coloured and white, of divers fabrics and qualities, and many brilliant tissues of gold, made by the islanders themselves, who get the silk, gold, and cotton-thread from the numerous ships that pass among the islands on their way from the coast of Bengal to the Straits of Meca. These ships buy these stuffs from the islanders, supplying them in exchange with the materials whereof they are made. Thus are these islands a great emporium for all parts, and the Moors of India frequent them, bartering their salt and earthenware, which are not made at the islands, and also rice and silver. In these *gundras* were many Moors of Calicut, who had gone thither to purchase goods, and were bringing them back in the vessels chartered by them.

The Portuguese irruption.

"On the capture of the *gundras* the chief captain bade the several masters of them point out the Moors of Calicut, otherwise he would burn the whole of them together; thereupon, in their fear, they did so. These were forthwith bound hand and foot, and placed in the hold of one of the *gundras*, which had been discharged of its cargo. Over them was heaped a quantity of *ola*,[1] all the *gundras* being fitted with packing-cases of *olas* for carrying

[1] Malayāl. *óla*, Tam. *olei*, the palm-leaf. Upon strips of the palmyra leaf all native letters, orders, and books are written, and these are in Anglo-Indian, as in Indo-Portuguese use, commonly called *olas*. Here, probably, ordinary coconut leaves are intended. See Yule, *Gloss.*, s. v. "Ollah".

The Portuguese irruption.

the goods. Fire was then applied, which, with the aid of the breeze, set the whole in a blaze. Some of the Moors took to the water, and succeeded in swimming ashore, and there related what had taken place. The Moors that were burnt numbered upwards of a hundred, and this event much increased the mischief at Calicut. As for the Moors of the islands that were in the other three *gundras*, the chief captain warned them never again to go to Calicut, for that if ever they were found carrying any goods there, they would be burned alive. He then sent them in to Cananor in charge of one of the caravellas to be unloaded at the factory. With them he also sent his fleet factor, and also his clerk, who appraised and sold the whole cargo," etc.

Thus began Portuguese intercourse with the Maldives. In the same year a Portuguese ship was driven by stress of weather to one of the Maldives, where, in the course of a few days, many died through drinking stagnant water, and over-indulgence in the fruit and fish diet of the place.

Up to this time the Maldives had not drawn upon them the personal attention of the Portuguese. The tactics of the Eastern traders now involved them in the general misfortune. Calicut being under blockade, the merchants were obliged to give Western India a wide berth. Thus, in 1506, the viceroy, Francisco de Almeida, "was informed that many ships from Pegu, Siam, and Bengal were passing through the Maldive Islands to Mecca. Therefore orders were given that Dom Lourenço [de Almeida, the viceroy's son] should proceed with the armada, and see what was going on at these islands, and whether ships could be seized."[1] Lourenço set sail, but was carried by the currents to Ceylon, where he laid the foundation of the Portuguese connection with that island. The Maldive expedition was not carried out.

The next mention of the Maldives is in the year 1509, when Affonso d'Albuquerque was repairing his fleet at Cochin, and sent orders to Cananor for a supply of coir. His information was that one Mamalle, a Moor of that place, "was trading with the Maldive Islands, under an agreement with the king of these islands,

[1] *Lendas*, tom. i, p. 643.

whereby the latter sold his goods at fixed prices, the Moor sending rice, salt, and earthenware, which the islands lacked, and receiving in exchange coir, dried fish, cowries, and very fine silks. The Moor had his own factors there, and as the islands were distant only three days' sail from Cananor, he was gaining great profit. Owing to his said agreement the other merchants could not buy or sell, and thus the Moor Mamalle was called Lord of the Maldive Islands. All the coir for the use of the whole of India was bought from this Moor, and thus he was master of great wealth." The Portuguese irruption.

Albuquerque sent for Mamalle, and ordered him to give up his trade with the islands, and to remove his factors from the place, "as the islands belonged to the King of Portugal, who would hinder no one from trading there". Mamalle not being convinced of the blessings of free trade, especially, perhaps, when preached by the Portuguese viceroy, begged earnestly to be allowed to keep his monopoly. He made the best terms he could, which were that he should deliver annually to the Portuguese factor at Cannanor 1,000 ropes of fine and 1,000 of coarse coir, each weighing a quintal and a half, and that he should place no hindrance in the way of the Portuguese if they should visit the Maldives for purposes of trade.

"The foregoing agreement," adds Correa, "was duly observed during the government of Affonso d'Albuquerque; but his successors, understanding how to profit themselves by the trade, gave it over to their servants and friends, and violated the contract. The ships and armadas sent by the factor of the King of Portugal reduced his profit to nothing, and did many robberies and mischief at the islands, as they are doing at the present day. These practices have cost the king much expense. The coir has also cost him much money, and has not been got without many difficulties and the deaths of many Portuguese, as will be related."

After the departure of Albuquerque the Maldives became the hunting ground of Portuguese pirates. In 1517 the third viceroy, Lopo Soares, was informed that one Jeronymo de Sousa was "playing the pirate" at the Maldives. An expedition was accordingly sent under Dom Fernando de Monroys and and João Gonçalves de Castello Branco, with orders to capture or

The Portuguese irruption.

kill the rebel. Whether they took Sousa or not does not appear: Correa merely relates that when they got to the Maldives they turned pirates themselves, and seized two rich ships of Cambay, which were sailing under Portuguese passports. "What!" cried the masters of the captured vessels, "you dare to seize these ships that are at peace with you, and you observe not the promises made in your own passports!"

In 1517, according to Faria, permission to build a factory was granted to the Portuguese by the Maldive king; and for this purpose the successor of Soares, Diogo Lopes de Sequeira, despatched an expedition in 1519, under João Gomes Cheiradinheiro, consisting of four small vessels carrying 120 men. This worthy also proceeded to play the pirate; for not only did he seize two rich ships of Tenasserin, the goods and crews of which he sold to the islanders, but he also harried the islanders themselves at his will. Collecting his booty, he landed at *Mafacelou* (? Málé), "where the king of the islands was dwelling", and there built himself a fort, into which he continued to draw compulsorily the produce of the islands, "paying for it according to his pleasure."

The Maldivians, in their distress, despatched a boat to Calicut to invoke the aid of Baleacem, a noted Malabar corsair. This personage was absent at the time, but the envoys found a friend in Pata-marakkâr, formerly a merchant of Cochin, who, having had two ships seized by the Portuguese, had taken to buccaneering. Twelve Malabar *paráos* were soon collected, manned, and despatched. Guided by the Maldive boat, they fell upon the Portuguese ships as they lay unmanned in the harbour, and then upon the fort, which was unprotected on the water-side. The islanders joined in the attack with the fury of revenge, and, after a short struggle, every Portuguese was put to the sword. The whole booty, which was considerable, was divided between the islanders and their allies.

Thus did the Maldivians regain the freedom of their territory. For the next thirty years no attempt was made by the Portuguese to establish a fort at the islands, though they continued to be the resort of cruisers, whose captains, while affecting to intercept the merchantmen on their way to and from the Red Sea, employed their leisure in piracy among the atolls.

In 1550 the abdication of King Hassan, and his subsequent conversion to Christianity, induced the Portuguese again to intervene actively in Maldive affairs. From this point Pyrard himself takes up the thread of Maldive history. (See vol. i, p. 244.) **The Portuguese irruption.**

21. There now remain three notices of the Maldives relating to the first half-century of the Portuguese period, the close of which will be assigned as the limit of this Appendix. The first of these is from the work of Duarte Barbosa, a Portuguese soldier, who saw much service in various parts of the East between 1501 and 1517. The book[1] deals but little with Portuguese affairs of State, and much with geography and native races; the author, indeed, writes hardly at all as a soldier, and more as a gazetteer than a traveller. Every place of importance on the coasts between the Cape and China has its paragraph or chapter, and among these are— **Barbosa.**

"*The Islands of Maldio.*—Over against this land of further Malabar,[2] forty leagues off, lies an archipelago of islands, said by the Moors to number 12,000. They begin opposite Mount Deli, at the shoals of Padua,[3] and extend to the parts opposite Malaca. The first are four small and very flat islands called *Maldio*[4]; these are peopled by Malabar Moors, and said to belong to the King of Cannanor.[5] They grow nothing but palm-trees, upon which the natives subsist, together with such rice as comes from Malabar in the ships which come there to load coir rope. [[6]*Islands of Palan-*

[1] Published in the *Noticias das Naç. Ultramarinas*, tom iii, p. 352, Lisbon, 1812. This edition shows the various readings of Ramusio and of the Lisbon MS.

[2] He has just described Cape Comorin.

[3] *Baixos de Padua*, in lat. 13° N. They are mentioned by De Barros (see below), and also in the *Albuquerque Comm.* (Hak. Soc.), vol. iii, p. 55, and figured in the Map of F. Vaz Dourado, *op. cit.*, vol. ii, p. 1.

[4] He misapplies the name to the Laccadives.

[5] As they do still; but see vol. i, p. 323.

[6] This passage is in Ramusio, but not in the Lisbon MS. It is evidently a paraphrase of the preceding paragraph by the Spanish translator whose text Ramusio used. Unfortunately, this has not been noted in the Hakluyt Society's translation of this work, and the author is thus made to describe two separate groups in strangely similar language; whereas it is tolerably clear, if we omit this passage in brackets, that he regards the Laccadives and Maldives as one group,

Barbosa. *dura.*—Over against Panani, Cochim, and Coulão (Quilon) are other islands, ten or twelve of which are inhabited by dusky Moors of small stature, who have a language of their own. The king, who is a Moor, has his residence at an island called *Mahaldiu.* To all these islands they give the name of *Palandura.* The natives do not bear arms, and are feeble folk, but very clever, and above all, great sorcerers. The king of these islands is elected by some Moor merchants, natives of Cananor, who change him at their will. The king of their choice pays them annually tribute of cordage, ropes of coir, and other produce of the place; and sometimes these Moors themselves come and load their ships without bringing any money, notwithstanding which, the natives, willingly or unwillingly, are constrained to give them all they ask.] At these islands is much dried fish (*moxama*), which is exported: as also some little shells, in which is great traffic with Cambay and Bengal, where they are used for petty cash, being considered better than copper. They make there also very rich cloths of cotton, silk, and gold, which fetch a high price among the Moors for their apparel, and . . . . [[1]The men of these islands wear very fine kerchiefs on their heads, so close-woven and beautiful that our workmen could not produce the like except with a wrong and a right side. In these islands, also, they collect tortoiseshell, which they call *Alquama;* this they cut into very thin pieces, and export largely to the kingdom of Guzerat.] Much amber(gris) is also found at these islands, and in large pieces, some white, some grey, and some black. I asked many of these Moors frequently what this amber was, and whence it came. They deem it to be the droppings of birds, saying that in this archipelago are some uninhabited islands, on the rocks and reefs of which some big birds perch, and there void this amber; there it is exposed to the action of the wind, sun, and rain, until by storm

some of the more northerly islands of which were occupied by Malabars. With these he seems to include Málé (*Mahal-diu*), probably on account of the close commercial relations of that island with Cannanor. It will be seen below that De Barros follows Barbosa in all his mistakes. *Palandura* (or, as Lord Stanley reads, *Palandiva*) is unintelligible.

[1] In the Lisbon MS., but not in Ramusio.

and tempest the sea sweeps over these rocks and reefs, and it is broken off in large and small pieces. Thence it floats on the sea till either it is found or cast up on some beach, or eaten by whales. They say that the amber found in the white state, which they call *Ponambar*, has been but a short time on the sea, and is by them esteemed the most precious. The grey has been a longer time in the water, and thence has this colour; it also is considered very good, but not so good as the white. That which is found black and bruised they say has been eaten by whales, and thus has been turned black. Its nature is such that the whales cannot digest it, and therefore eject it whole. This kind is called *Minambar*, and is of less value among them. **Barbosa.**

"In these islands of Maldio they build many large ships of palm-wood, held together with matting, because they have no other timber there. In these they voyage to the mainland. These ships have keels, and are of very considerable capacity. The islanders build also small rowing-crafts, like brigantines or fustas: these are of great strength, admirably built, and extremely light; they serve chiefly for going from one island to another, though they are also used for crossing over to Malabar.

To these islands come many ships of the Moors from China, Maluco, Peegu, Malaca, Çamatra, Benguala, and Ceilam, in their passage to the Red Sea. Here they take in water, provisions, and other necessaries for the voyage. Sometimes they arrive in such battered condition that they have to be discharged and abandoned. Among these islands are lost many rich vessels of the Moors, which in their passage of the Ocean dare not make the coast of Malabar for fear of our ships. [[1]From these the inhabitants of the islands get much rich merchandise, which they sell to the Malabars who come there to load coir, as has already been said.]"

22. João de Barros, the historian of Portuguese India, was a clerk or officer in the *Casa da India*, or India Office, at Lisbon. He had never himself visited the East, as had Gaspar Correa, whose *Lendas* cover nearly the same period, and Diogo de Couto, **J. de Barros.**

[1] In the Lisbon MS., but not in Ramusio.

J. de Barros. his continuator.[1] His materials were obtained in the course of his official duties. Uncorrected by personal observation, and lacking the picturesqueness of detail which Eastern experience imparts to the narratives of the other historians, his work is of the greatest value as a compendium of the information about India possessed by the authorities at Lisbon in the middle of the 16th century. De Barros died in 1570.

The expedition of João Gomes de Cheiradinheiro to the Maldives, which has been described above in the language of Correa, who was in India at the time, is more shortly and less correctly narrated by de Barros, but the opportunity is taken, by way of preface, to summarise all the information about the Maldives that was then current in Portugal. The passage here translated occurs in the 7th chapter of the 3rd book of the third *Decada*, first published in 1563:—

"Inasmuch as João Gomes de alcuna Cheiradinheiro was the first to build a fort on the Maldive Islands, it will be convenient, before describing his actions, to give here a general account of these Maldive islands, which we have referred to so often. This name *Maldiva*, though it is the distinctive name of a single island, as we shall see, etymologically is derived from the Malabar language, meaning 1,000 Islands—*mal*, a thousand, and *diva*, islands —there being upwards of that number all in a string. Others say that this word *Mal* is the proper name of the chief island, at which resides the king who is lord of all: that one is commonly called *Maldiva*, as though one should say the island of *Mal:* and as it is at the head of the group,[2] the rest are called after it.

"This string of islands, which runs like an extended diadem over against the coast of India, begins at the flats which we call

[1] Correa's *Lendas* extend from the first voyages of Diaz and da Gama to 1550; de Barros' *Decadas* from 1497 to 1539; de Couto's *Decadas* from 1529 to 1600; Castanheda's *History* from 1497 to 1550; Faria y Souza's *Asia Portugueza* from 1497 to 1640.

[2] Either de Barros was quite mistaken as to the situation of Málé, or believing the Maldives to extend to Java, as appears in the next sentence, he regards it as situate at the north end of the group. His observation below as to the language shows that he does not accurately distinguish the Maldives from the Laccadives.

the shoals of Padua, in the neighbourhood of Mount Delij, and ends at the land of Java and the coast of Sunda. This is seen in some of the sea charts of the Moors, for ours as yet describe them for only a distance of 300 leagues of their extent, beginning at those called by us the islands of Mamálle,[1] from the name of a Moor of Cannanor. This man was lord of the first section of them, distant from the Malabar coast about forty leagues, at the altitude of 12½ degrees north. The remainder, called *Candú* and *Adú*, 300 leagues off, are in 7½ degrees south. In the middle, as it were, of this 300 league diadem, is the capital island, Maldiva, as above stated, where resides the king, who is entitled lord of all the islands. The smaller islands are subordinate to the larger, so that some thirty or forty are governed by one, according to their situation: and this number of islands so grouped is called a *patána.*[2] And although the king, who is entitled lord of all, and the whole of the people are Gentiles, the governors are Moors—a circumstance which is a fruitful source of trouble; having secured the government of the mainland, by little and little, they have become lords of these islands too. They have managed this by first becoming farmers of the revenue on the mainland, and prin- J. de Barros.

[1] In the map referred to in the previous note the island *Mamale* appears as one of the Laccadives.

[2] In the note in vol. i, p. 94, it is stated, perhaps hastily, that *patana* is Sinhalese. It is in common use in Ceylon (middle *a* short), as I there state, for an open patch or stretch of grass among the hills. Mr. D. W. Ferguson of Colombo, in reviewing that vol. in the *Ceylon Observer*, has called my attention to the question. He quotes from Clough, *patan*, "a royal city, a town", and *patana*, "a town, a city, a seaport town", and other forms; also from Childers' *Páli Dict.*, *paṭṭanam*, "a port, a seaport". He suggests that the Ceylon use for a stretch of grass arose from a mistake of Dr. Davy, who writes thus of Nuwara Eliya: "We came to a great extent of open country . . . our guides called it Neuraelliya-pattan." Another suggestion, however, is that the word is a corruption of *piṭṭaniya*, a meadow or lawn. All this is beside the question of the Portuguese application of *patána* to an atoll. If it ever was so used by the Maldivians it is now obsolete: and if, as it seems, the middle *a* was long, it cannot be connected with the above Sinhalese words. It is used, as will be seen hereafter, by one of the Maldive exiled kings, but then only in a Portuguese document, for the wording of which he is perhaps not responsible.

J. de Barros. cipally at the seaports. To this farming of the revenue they have added the administration of justice, thus better securing the revenues of the prince of the country. This position the Moors have not as yet obtained so firmly in the islands as on the continent.

"As regards their situation, though some of the larger islands are distant apart some five, ten, fifteen, or twenty leagues, the great majority are so close-set that they look like an orchard half inundated by a flood, equal parts of which are visible and concealed; and you can leap from one to another without wetting the feet, or else swing across by means of the branches of the trees. The currents of water collecting in the channels are so strong that the natives, when overtaken by a tide, as sometimes happens, cannot make the crossing they desire. And while many of these channels are so deep as to carry very large vessels, yet are they so narrow in some places that the yards will strike the palm trees.

"These palm trees do not yield dates, as do those of Barbary and all Africa, but a fruit of the size of a man's head. Before reaching the kernel, it has two husks, after the manner of nuts. The first, although on the outside, is quite smooth; beneath this is another all of fibre, which excels the *esparto*. The rope made from this fibre supplies the whole of India, and chiefly for cables, because it is more secure and stands the sea better than any made from hemp. The reason is that it agrees with the salt water, and becomes so tough that it seems like hide, contracting and expanding with the strength of the sea; so that a good thick cable of this rope, when the ship is standing at her anchor in a heavy gale and straining upon it, draws out so thin that you would think it could not hold a boat; when the vessel is pitching in a mere swell, it keeps its usual thickness. This coir is also used instead of bolts, for such virtue hath it of swelling and shrinking in the sea that they join the timbers of their ships' ribs with it, and consider it quite secure. True it is, these ships are not sailed through the furious gales of the Cape of Good Hope. The islanders make their voyages in avoidance of the winds, navigating only in the summer time during the monsoons, which are seasons of fair winds, regular in their direction, for three months at a time; when the winter comes round, they do not go to sea. J. de Barros.

"This profitable fruit hath another shell of very hard substance, on the surface of which are seen the traces of the fibres and threads of the outer husk; it is like the pith of the cork tree, or, rather, like a nut shorn of its green shell. This shell, at the place where the fruit receives its vegetable nourishment—that is, at its lower end—is somewhat pointed, and resembles a nose between two round eyes. It is through these that the nut throws out its shoots when planted. Owing to this shape our countrymen call this nut *Coco*,[1] the name given by women to anything used to frighten their babes. This name has so stuck to it that no one knows it by any other. Its proper name, however, is *Tanga*[1] with the Malabars, and *Narle*[1] with the Canarins.

"The kernel within this second shell is about the size of a large quince, but of a different appearance, resembling the filbert in its outer surface and inner substance; it has, however, a hollow space within. It is of the same taste, but of greater bulk, and is more oily in its consistency than the filbert. Within the cavity is distilled some water, which is very sweet and cordial, principally when the nut is young. When the nut is planted, all this cavity in which the water was becomes a thick mass like cream, called *lanha*. It is very sweet and tasty, and better than almonds, when it thickens on the tree; and as this fruit in its substance and edibility is very like the almond or filbert, so, too, its outer surface is fawn-coloured, and its interior white.

"This nut and the palm which yields it have other profitable uses, ordained of God for the support and necessities of man, for besides those mentioned it supplies him with honey, vinegar, oil, and wine, and is itself a substantial food, either eaten alone or with rice, or served in other modes employed by the Indians in their cookery. Of the first outer husk is made coir, which, as we said, is in common and universal use for the ships of the whole East, after being soaked, beaten, and twisted like hempen rope. The palm trees also are used for timber, logs, and tiles, for the natives cover their houses with the leaves, which prevent any water getting in; these

[1] As to these names, see above, p. 372, *note*.

J. de Barros. also serve them for paper, and their *palmitos*[1] put them in no need of the *palmitos* of Barbary. In short, when a man of those parts has a pair of these palm trees he has everything necessary for existence; and when they wish to praise one for his benefactions, they are wont to say, 'He is more fruitful and profitable than a palm tree.'

"Besides these trees, which in those islands grow aboveground, it seems their seed is endowed by nature with such virtue that it has produced in some places beneath the salt water another species,[2] which yields a larger nut than the coco. The second shell of this nut is found by experience to be more efficacious against poison than the Bezoar[3] stone, which also comes from the East, growing in the stomach of an animal called by the Persians *Pazon*, whereof we have treated at large in the chapters of our *Commercio* upon antidotes.

"The commonest and most important merchandise at these islands, indeed, the cause of their being visited, is the coir; without it those seas cannot be navigated. There is also a kind of shellfish, as small as a snail, but differently shaped, with a hard, white, lustrous shell, some of them, however, being so highly coloured and lustrous that, when made into buttons and set in gold, they look like enamel. With these shells for ballast many ships are laden for Bengal and Siam, where they are used for

[1] The inner rind of the palm.

[2] The *coco de mer*. See vol. i, p. 230.

[3] The word *Bezòar* is a corruption of the Persian *pádzár*, "poison antidote", of which de Barros' *pazon* is a corruption: the animal referred to is the wild goat of Persia. For the history of the word see Yule's *Glossary*, and the *New Eng. Dict.* As an addition to the quotations given in these two works, I may observe that a false Bezoar stone gave occasion for the establishment of one of the great distinctions in our common law, viz., between actions founded upon contract, and those founded upon wrongs: *Chandelor* v. *Lopus* was decided in 1604 (reported in 2 *Croke*, and in Smith's *Leading Cases*). The headnote runs: "*The defendant sold to the plaintiff a stone, which he affirmed to be a Bezoar stone, but which proved not to be so. No action lies against him, unless he either knew that it was not a Bezoar stone, or warranted it to be a Bezoar stone.*" Chandelor, who was a goldsmith, "having skill in jewels and precious stones", had sold the worthless stone to Lopus for £100, a large sum in those days.

money, just as we use small copper money for buying things of little value. And even to this kingdom of Portugal, in some years as much as two or three thousand quintals are brought by way of ballast; they are then exported to Guinea, and the kingdoms of Benin and Congo, where also they are used for money, the Gentiles of the interior in those parts making their treasure of it. J. de Barros.

"Now the manner in which the islanders gather these shells is this:—they make large bushes of palm leaves tied together so as not to break, which they cast into the sea. To these the shell-fish attach themselves in quest of food; and when the bushes are all covered with them, they are hauled ashore and the creatures collected. All are then buried in the earth till the fish within have rotted away. The shells (*buzios* as we, and *Igovos* as the negroes, call them) are then washed in the sea, becoming quite white, and so dirtying the hands less than copper money. In this kingdom (Portugal) a quintal of them is worth from three to ten cruzados, according as the supply from India is large or small.

"These islands produce abundance of fish, of which great quantities of *moxama* are made. It is exported as merchandise to many quarters, and gives a good profit, as do also fish-oil, cocos, and jaggery, which last is made from the cocos in the same manner as sugar.

"The fabrics made by these islanders are silk and cotton, and no finer stuffs are made in all those parts. The principal manufactory is at the islands *Ceudú*[1] and *Cudú*,[2] where there are said to be better weavers than in Bengal or Coromandel. Yet all the silk and cotton, of which those stuffs are made, come to them from abroad, the islands lacking both these commodities, and also rice, whereof their whole supply is imported.

"They rear herds of sheep and cows,[3] but not sufficient for the supply of butter, which is brought from Ceylon and other parts, and yields the carriers a good profit.

"The people of these islands, with whom our countrymen have

[1] Hawadú or Suadiva Atoll, which is still famed for its weavers, both of cloth and mats. (Bell's *Report*, p. 88; and above, vol. i, p. 241.)

[2] Probably a printer's mistake for *Addú*.

[3] See above, vol. i, p. 116.

J. de Barros. come into contact, are dull, feeble, and malicious—qualities always found together, not only in the human race, but also in the brute creation, wherein is verified the paradox that a weak intellect is crafty in mischief.

"The higher classes dress in silk and cotton; the rest of the people make shift to weave themselves a clothing made from palmy leaves and herbs. They have a language of their own, though those nearest to the Malabar coast speak the language of that country; this is so chiefly at *Maldiva* island, where the king resides, because it is frequented by so many Malabars."

[The account of João de Cheira-Dinheiro at the Maldives, which here succeeds, has already been given above, at p. 476.]

The Brothers Parmentier.

23. The description of the Maldives by De Barros has been advisedly placed in immediate sequence to the sketch of Portuguese relations with the islands during the first half of the sixteenth century. We are thus enabled to conclude this Appendix with a more pleasing episode in the history of their intercourse with European races.

The voyage of the two French ships, the *Pensée*[1] and the *Sacre*,[2] under the brothers Jean and Raoul Parmentier, has already been referred to in the Introduction to vol. i (pp. x, xi), as the second, if not the first, voyage made to the East by way of the Cape, in defiance of the Portuguese claims of exclusive right. Jean Parmentier had already made long voyages, including (it seems certain) one to America. Besides being a classical scholar and a poet, he was also a first-rate seaman. The expedition was thus well planned, the ships well found, and the crews well handled. But for the sad death of the gallant and accomplished commander at Ticou, in Sumatra, it might have been hoped that Parmentier would have roused his countrymen to further efforts, and have led to an earlier destruction of the monopoly in ocean routes.

The French ships left Dieppe on the 28th March 1529. They

[1] The *Pansy*.

[2] Fr. and Port. *sacre*, Eng. *saker*, a peregrine hawk, *falco sacer*. This Lat. term is a misnomer, arising from a fancy that *sacre* was a translation of the Gr. *ἱέραξ*. It is really, as Dozy has pointed out, the Ar. *çaqr*.

The Brothers Parmentier.

rounded the Cape in safety, and towards the latter end of September were in the neighbourhood of the Maldives. Let the chronicler of the voyage now tell his own tale[1] :—

"On Sunday [19th September 1529] we made sail S.S.E. and S. with scant wind, believing these islands to be the archipelago near *Calecut* and *Commori*, which extends north and south.

"Monday, the 20th September, in the morning, were sighted six or seven islands on the W., the S.W. and the S. On taking our altitude at noon, it was found to be half a degree to the south of the Line. We endeavoured to fetch one of these islands, but the wind was contrary, and obliged us to stand off. Yet did we cease not until the Friday following [September 24th] to tack, so as to come up with some of them: but, when we approached, we found no anchorage. Then came contrary winds and rain. At length we found one green island, well planted with palms, about a league in length. Jean Masson in our little boat went ashore, as did also the boat of the *Sacre*. The people of the island gave them a good reception and presented some of their palm-fruits and long figs,[2] while the said Masson gave them some knives and mirrors, and other wares. They also gave him, as a present for the captain, a little chain artificially made of a single piece, which was bent double; and also sent to the captain, between two large leaves of trees, about two or three pounds of sugar-candy, called by them *Zagre*,[3] and made of the same palms, and also a quarter or half hundred balls of thick black sugar, which is made from the same sugar-candy, and the husk or envelope of the substance whereof the said sugar is composed.

"On the 25th died one of our mariners, by name *Jean François*. The same day our captain landed on the island with the two boats, well armed and equipped, and was honourably received by the

[1] The translation which follows is from the edition of M. Schefer, Paris, 1883. As will be seen, his reading of some of the names differs from the earlier edition of the voyage published in 1832 by M. Estancelin, in his *Navigateurs Normands*, and also from another copy, edited by M. Margry, in the *Bulletin of the Soc. Normande de Géographie for* 1883.

[2] Bananas, called by the Portuguese *figos da India*.

[3] Mald. *sakuru* or *hakuru*; *v. s.*, p. 411. Estancelin reads *lagre*, and Margry *sagre*.

The Brothers Parmentier.

chief or arch-priest of the island, who came towards him kneeling as though he would kiss his hands, and presented a fine large lemon, quite round, like a big orange. The captain hastened to raise and embrace him, and made him a present of two pairs of knives, which he esteemed highly. The islanders climbed a number of coco palm-trees, and gave our people to drink of the water. Two or three others presented a few of the island lemons to our captain.

"In this island was a temple or mosque, a very ancient structure, composed of massive stone. The captain desired to see the inside as well as the outside, whereupon the chief priest bade them open it and entered within. The work pleased him greatly, and chiefly a woodwork screen, of ancient mouldings, the best he had ever seen, with a balustrade so neatly turned that our ship's carpenter was surprised to see the fineness of the work. The temple had galleries all around, and at the end a secret enclosure shut off by a wooden screen, like a *Sanctum Sanctorum*. The captain bade them open it, to see what was within, and whether there were any idols there, but he perceived nothing but a lamp formed of the coconut. The roof or vault of this temple was round in form, with a wainscoted ceiling covered with ancient painting. Hard by the temple was a *piscina*, or lavatory, flat bottomed, and paved with a black stone like marble, finely cut with ancient mouldings, and having all the appearance of massive workmanship. In another place, a little apart, was a kind of square well or fountain, six or eight feet deep, having within it a number of poles, each with a gourd at the end, wherewith the natives drew their water. This well also was flat bottomed, and paved with the same stone as the lavatory. In this island were many other similar fountains or wells, and also many small chapels and oratories in the same style as the great temple.[1]

[1] The only information as to remains at Fua Mulaku, the island referred to (*v. i.*, p. 490), is that given to Mr. Bell by resident natives, to the effect that there are still to be seen there "the jungle-covered ruins of a tope or *dágaba*, and amid these the stone image of a Buddha in the *sthánamudrá* or standing position. This tope is described as resembling the solid bell-shaped *dágabas*, rising from platforms, usual in Ceylon"

"The dwelling houses are quite small and miserably built: the people are small and thin, and the only women our men saw were old and emaciated, bald and poor-looking creatures. There was The Brothers Parmentier.

(*Report*, p. 75). It will be noticed that Parmentier says nothing of the image, but, on the contrary, says that the building shown contained none. The temple to which the Frenchmen were admitted may have been originally a Buddhist *vihára* adapted to Moslem use; and so may the bathing-pond have been a Sinhalese *pokuna*, such as may be seen in great perfection of workmanship at Anurádhapura.

In further illustration of the objects of archæological interest which may still be found at the Maldives, I will insert here an extract from a MS. relation at Batavia of the voyage of Frederick de Houtman in 1598-9. The extract, headed "Short account of the adventures of Frederick de Houtman bound for action", was sent from Batavia by Mr. Van der Chys to Mr. Bell; it is translated by Mr. F. de Vos, of Galle, and has been revised (through the kind intervention of Mrs. Clements Markham) by Col. Jansen, of the Hague. If the MS. in its entirety (of which I have as yet no information) is a relation of the whole voyage of F. de Houtman, it is interesting on grounds hereafter stated. However that may be, the extract, so far as it goes, runs thus:—

"On the 1st June (1599) we fell among the Maldives . . . . the small island close to which we lay had many beautiful buildings, most in ruins, very artfully built after their fashion. There appeared to be all sorts of temples and altars, which were all there in that small space, fully from ten to twelve: among them one specially of an ancient structure, all of blue-stone (lazulite), and round it also mouldings, basements, capitals (pillars), friezes, and their groovings (*tandeerzel*), on the steps of the entrance breastways: and what surprised me most was that all this was put together without any lime or building material; yet was everything so closely bound together by means of hewn grooves that the point of a knife could not be put between them, while at each corner a keystone held the entire work together.

"Round this temple was a rectangular wall, constructed with a broad walk around it, and outside this walk were also some walls built of stone which were dry, and among these one which appeared to be a tank. It was — feet measured round, entirely built of white stone, with stone steps leading to it. There was also hard by a crumbled pyramid, of which the basement or foundation was still to be seen. It was 12 feet square, and appeared to have been a beautiful work, for it seemed to have been made with mouldings round and hollow and square, with groovings all in proportion.

"All the temples stood east and west, the entrance being at the east.

The Brothers Parmentier.

but little in the houses, whereby we judged that they had removed all their valuables, as also their young women and children, further into the interior of the island, fearing perhaps lest they

I thought it must have been a sacred place, as all these buildings stood close to each other. Moreover, we found nowhere on the whole of this island any buildings used as houses or showing any signs of having been used as habitations," etc.

If the island described is still uninhabited, there is good reason to hope that some of these interesting buildings may be preserved. It is, however, somewhat difficult—in the absence of any mention of names or bearings—to localise, much less to identify, the island. Some circumstantial evidence regarding the voyage may be of assistance, and this gives a peculiar interest to the passage extracted.

Frederick de Houtman left Flushing on the 15th March 1598, in command of the *Lioness*, his brother Cornelis, the leader of the expedition, being on board the *Lion*, on which ship also sailed our famous sailor, John Davis, as pilot.

Above, at vol. i, p. 31, I stated, before this extract came to hand, that no Dutch account of this voyage existed, and that Davis's letter to Lord Essex was the sole account of it extant. If the document from which the above passage is extracted proves to be a report of the voyage at large, that statement will no longer hold good.

Now, as Davis also mentions the visit to the Maldives, we should be able to localise the island described by F. de Houtman, if only we knew that the two vessels were in company at the time. But neither Davis nor F. de Houtman refers to the other's ship while at the Maldives: and the evidence points to the fact that they were not at this time in company. From Davis's account we gather that the *Lion* merely stood off an island, that the crew did not land, but that the island was inhabited, inasmuch as a pilot was obtained at it. There is also some difference in dates, Davis stating (*Voyages*, *Hak. Soc.*, p. 138) that his ship arrived at the Maldives on the 23rd May 1599, and left the island at which the pilot was taken on the 27th, while on the 3rd June she was off the coast of Cochin. Our extract above puts the arrival of the *Lioness* at the uninhabited island on the 1st June.

While, therefore, it seems that the two ships were not together at the Maldives, they may have been so nearly in company as to strike the same channel. As to the route of the *Lion*, Davis's letter leaves us in no doubt. In the passage of the channel he gives his latitude as 4° 15′ N., which identifies the channel as that of *Kardiva*. Possibly, therefore, F. de Houtman's island may be found somewhere on the borders of this channel. When the MS. in full comes to hand from Batavia, some reference to latitude in the context may decide.

should be seized by force. This was probably done at the advice of the chief priest, who was a man of much discretion and knowledge, as was seen by what ensued. For while we were there, a little strife had arisen between the captain and the Portuguese sailors of the *Sacre*, the said Portuguese asserting to the mariners that this island was one of the *Maldive* islands. This, however, could not be so, for we were then at ½ degree south, while the Maldive islands extend from the 7th to the 17th degree north of the equator: whereupon our captain told him that he was wrong. But the other, persisting in his opinion, said he was right, and proposed that they should enquire the fact of the chief priest, who replied that the name of the island was *Moluque*,[1] and that the *Maldive* islands were fully 200 leagues north of that island.[2] Nevertheless, I have since seen in a Portugal chart that these islands south of the line are called *Maldiva*. Moreover, this chief priest showed the captain in what quarters lay the countries of *Adam*,[3] *Persia*, *Ormus*, *Calicut*, *Zeilan*,[4] *Moluque*,[5] and *Sumatra*, and proved himself to be both learned and well travelled. He was very devout, modest, and amiable, of middle height, white-bearded, apparently about 45 to 50 years of age; his name was *Brearou Leacaru*.[6] Meanwhile, our people took supplies of water, and the captain paid the natives handsomely for their coco-nuts and long green figs, which were loaded in the boats. He then took his leave and withdrew his men to the boats in order to return to the ship, which was plying off and on, in default of any

The Brothers Parmentier.

1 *Fua Mulaku*, a solitary island in 0° 17′ S., not to be confounded with Mulaku Atoll, which is farther north. The chronicler above states that just before landing at this island they were in ½° S. latitude.

2 The chief must have understood the Frenchmen to ask for the Málé Atoll.

3 Estancelin and Margry read *Dam*.

4 Estancelin and Margry read *Zela*.

5 Probably the Moluccas; but Estancelin and Margry read *Meluque*, which would likely mean Malacca.

6 Estancelin and Margry read *Orquarou Leacarou*. Neither seems to be right. The second word, however, almost certainly should be *Tacarou*, for M. *Takuru*; see vol. i, pp. 96, 208.

The Brothers Parmentier.

anchorage at the island. The people there call God *Allah*.[1] The same evening after supper we sailed S.E. $\frac{1}{4}$ S., close-hauled to the wind.

"On the 26th our altitude, on being taken at noon, was found to be $\frac{2}{3}$ of a deg. south," etc.

[1] So Estancelin; Margry, however, states that the text reads *Aillat*.

B.

NOTICES OF THE EXILED KINGS OF THE MALDIVES.

In the course of his narrative Pyrard makes reference on several occasions to the family of titular Kings of the Maldives who resided in India under Portuguese protection. By the aid of the Portuguese archives at Lisbon and Goa, supplemented by other authorities, we are enabled to follow the fortunes of these exiled royalties during the century which elapsed between the revolution that cost them their throne and the death of the last representative of this legitimist line. They were in no sense Portuguese captives, for the first exile lost his throne fairly enough in an internal revolution, and threw himself upon the protection of the Portuguese. When he afterwards became a Christian and married a Portuguese wife, he forfeited any chances of restoration that might have been hoped from a counter-revolution. The Portuguese, after one endeavour to replace him, saw that it was impossible to impose a Christian king upon the Maldivians, and thereafter merely used the family claims as a lever to enforce the necessary supply of coir for their fleets. The individual princes on their part eked out inglorious, and not always reputable, lives as pensioners in the foreign land of which by intermarriages they became half-citizens. Somewhat similar cases have occurred in the history of British India; and the despatches quoted before would probably find their counterpart in many filed in the Foreign Departments of our Indian Presidencies.

Pyrard, whose account is founded upon the tradition of his time, relates that, about fifty years before, a certain King Hasan,[1] being hard pressed by a rival, was "inspired of God to quit all",

[1] According to tradition, still current, this Hasan, whose Maldive name was *Hasan Dobulá Fáruná*, was the son of a Sultan Yúsub; his rival's name was *Ali*.

and secretly departed to Cochin with his wife and certain of his family. From the date of his conversion, which took place in 1552, we shall be not far wrong in assuming that the revolution occurred in 1550 or 1551. When he became a Christian he was twenty years of age, a fact which seems to indicate that youth may have been his chief incapacity. However that may be, he was baptised a Christian under the name of Dom Manoel, and it is noteworthy that he was received into the Church by no less a personage than the Apostle of the Indies, St. Francis Xavier.

The Jesuit historian Bartoli, one of the people of importance in their day with whom Mr. Browning has "parleyings", thus relates the conversion (*Asia*, iii, 201-2) :—"There sprang up, I know not why, between the Maldivians and their Lord, a youth of twenty years, discord and war, and he, finding himself unable to withstand the force of the conspiracy, saved his life, though he could not his kingdom, by flight to Cochin, where he trusted to obtain his re-instatement by aid of the Portuguese arms. The fathers received him into their house; and, by the example of their living, which is ever a more potent influence than words, and by that which S. Francis Xavier, who opportunely arrived there, told him of God—and more, that which the saint told God of him, praying Him to give him that spirit whereby a new realm would be gained to the Church—at length the saint conquered, and having instructed him as far as needful in the divine mysteries, solemnly baptised him."[1] Padre Lucena says that this conversion "filled with joy the whole of India, exciting hopes that after the head, all the members would be converted."[2]

[1] St. Francis arrived at Cochin from Malacca on the 24th January 1552, and left for Goa at the beginning of February, and probably had little to do with the conversion and catechising of the Maldive king, which were managed by Padre Antonio Heredia (F. N. Xavier, *Res. Hist.*, p. 175). Bartoli and other Jesuit writers, however, claim for the Apostle of the Indies the lion's share of the credit. Crétineau-Joly goes so far as to say that St. Francis succeeded where Heredia had failed (*Hist. de la Comp. de Jésus*, i, 238). See also Bouhours, *Vie de S. François Xavier*, 1682, 4to., p. 462.

[2] *Vida de Fran. Xav.*, lib. ix, c. 15.

The Rev. H. Coleridge adds that "this king was a witness to one of Francis's miraculous elevations in the air while saying Mass" (*Life and Letters of S. Franc. Xav.*, ii, 65). It would seem that the king submitted to conversion as a means of gaining Portuguese support, the Jesuits of Cochin promising their aid. "Some of the fathers," continues Bartoli, "were then ready to sail with a Portuguese armada, and with the converted king, to the Maldives, and, as soon as he should be re-instated, to reduce the inhabitants to the Faith. But because in the interests of the Crown of Portugal it was not worth while to have these islands tributary, being poor in spices and gold, the Governors of India were not inclined to give the King effectual aid." The expedition was, nevertheless, sent, but on terms, as Pyrard states, that Dom Manoel should not accompany it.

The first expedition was, as Pyrard relates, disastrous to the Portuguese: but in the second, probably about 1554, they took Málé, after a battle in which the rival king Ali was slain. Experiencing the difficulties attending the subjection of the whole of the scattered kingdom, they prudently assembled the chiefs for a conference, at which it was arranged that the islands should be governed by a native regent, who should be subject to the control of the Portuguese commandant, and who should rule in the name of the exiled king, Dom Manoel. This condition of affairs was adhered to for upwards of ten years. At this period the Maldivians again rose in rebellion, and, under the leadership of the two noble brothers, the elder of whom was the father of the Sultan of Pyrard's time, succeeded, with the aid of a party of Malabars, in taking the Portuguese fort and putting its occupants to the sword (*supra*, vol. i, p. 248).

During the ten years of Portuguese occupation it seems that Dom Manoel was enabled, by the treaty arrived at with the native chiefs, to exercise to some extent his sovereign rights. In the archives of Goa is still preserved a copy of certain letters patent granted by him to Manoel da Silveira d'Araujo, bestowing upon him the privilege of three voyages to the Maldives as chief captain. The document, including the titles of the grantor, is couched in the approved language of Portuguese officialism:—

"Dom Manoel, by the grace of God King of the Maldive islands, and of the three *patanas* of Cuaydu, and of the seven islands of Pullobay, of the conquest and navigation of all the coasts of Sumatra, and of the Strait of Manacuma, etc.,—To all to whom this my letter shall be shown, I make known and give to understand that as of right I think fit and am hereby pleased to grant unto Manoel da Silveira d'Araujo, Cavalier fidalgo of the household of the King of Portugal, three voyages as chief captain to my Maldive islands, in like manner as to preceding chief captains, with the customary gains and profits thereof, which voyages he may enter upon after Jorge de Sousa Pereira, now captain of this city of Cochin, shall have made and concluded the two voyages which he purchased for money from Janebra de Torres, formerly wife of Bastião Rebelo, and now with God, and which he shall have in precedence of all others. I think fit, therefore, that the said Manoel da Silveira shall have these three, which I now grant, before any other person to whom the like grant shall be made (saving only the two purchased by Jorge de Sousa from the said widow, the same being within my grant), having respect to the fact that he slew the robber of Baura,[1] who assumed the title of king of the islands, and dispossessed me of my realm and estate, to which I should hardly have been restored, had not the said Manoel da Silveira killed him and dealt with him so valiantly as he did, as also all the rest concerned in the rebellion, whom also he slew: all which deeds cost him much trouble and blood of his own body with five deadly spear-wounds which crippled him, and which he received in battle with the said king and rebels:—as also for other services which he has done me and which I hope he may still in the future do. . . ." [He then proceeds to say that these three voyages and the two of Jorge de Sousa are to come at the end of the lease of the island trade which he has granted to one Anrique de Sousa, and concludes:]—"And I hereby command my regents and officers in the said islands that they receive and obey this letter without the exaction of any duty or tax whatever. Given in the city of Santa Cruz of Cochin under my seal. Ruy

[1] His rival Ali, who was a native or chief of the island *Bára*, in Tiladummati Atoll.

Correa wrote this the twenty-fifth of June, in the year of the birth of our Lord Jesu Christ one thousand five hundred and sixty years." The document is approved, sealed, and registered by the Viceroy at Goa, under date 24th Sept. 1561.[1]

Pyrard states that when Dom Manoel fled to Cochin he took his Maldive wife with him, and that she too became a Christian. According to Bartoli, he married "a noble Portuguese lady", whose name does not transpire. Nothing more is heard of the Maldive wife, and, whether she had any children or not, it is probable that the only children recognised by the Portuguese were those of the second marriage. His family consisted of three sons, Dom Francisco, Dom João, and Dom Pedro, and some daughters. The eldest son, Dom Francisco, seems to have resided at Cochin with his father till about the year 1581. We learn from a despatch of the King of Spain to the Viceroy, date 15th Feb. 1583,[2] that the Prince had written to request that his servants, Pero and João Garces, should be appointed respectively clerk of the factory and accountant of orphans at Cochin. The king directs that they should be so appointed for the space of three years from the next vacancies of those offices; but this is to be done only if the appointments do not of right belong to the town, and in that case some similar offices may be given to the applicants. It was probably soon after that letter to the King of Spain, or about the year 1582, that Dom Francisco proceeded to Europe, where he was stabbed to death in a street brawl at Lisbon,[3] but, owing to the loss of most of the royal despatches prior to 1585, we are without information as to the circumstances.

Dom Manoel seems to have made repeated requests to the King of Spain for his re-instatement,[4] but the viceroys set their

1 *Arch. Port. Or.*, Fasc. 5, No. 350.

2 *Op. cit.*, Fasc. 3, No. 2.

3 Bartoli, *loc. cit.;* Maffei (*Hist. Ind.*, lib. xv; F. de Sousa (*Or. Conq.*, C i, D i, § 67). The last-mentioned writer gives 1581 as the date of his death; but this must be an error, as the India Office at Lisbon evidently believed him to be alive in Feb. 1583.

4 *E.g.*, *Arch. Port. Or.*, Fasc. 3, No. 9.

faces against any further expeditions to the islands, and seem not to have communicated to him the king's replies to his letters. Thus, "ever hoping to regain his own, he lived and grew old in privacy at Cochin; and finally, after the disgraceful end of his son, who was stabbed to death at the Court of Spain, in great affliction died."[1] The death of Dom Manoel can only be approximately fixed as having taken place in 1583. Assuming that Bartoli and Pyrard are right as to his age when he came to Cochin, he was but little over fifty at his death. Whatever be the exact date of Dom Manoel's death, the news of it had reached Lisbon by the beginning of 1585, for on the 11th February of that year the King of Spain directs the viceroy, Dom Duarte de Menezes, to condole with the queen on the death of her husband, and to make proper provision for her and her daughters.[2]

The heir-apparent, Dom Francisco, having been killed at Lisbon, Dom Manoel was now succeeded in the titular sovereignty of the Maldives by his second son, Dom João. This prince gave the Portuguese much trouble. In a despatch dated the 10th Jan. 1587, the king thus addresses the viceroy: "I regret to be informed by your letter of the unruly behaviour of the King of the Maldives, and the trouble he has given in the city of Cochin, where he is. I recommend you to correct his follies as they may display themselves, and to give orders that he may gather his revenues, provided he pays into my treasury 500 *bahars* of coir, as his father always did. And as you say that it would be convenient for my service to collect the revenues of these islands through the controller of the treasury at Cochin, and for me to pay to the king his share, you will inform me what amount of coir you have taken into my treasury for the use of the navy, as well as for the ships repaired there, for which compensation should be made to him."[3]

Again, on the 28th Jan. 1588: "The king of the islands, in a letter he has written to me, complains of the inhabitants of the city of Cochin as not paying him due respect; and as I am

[1] Bartoli, *Asia*, *loc. cit.*

[2] *Arch. Port. Or.*, Fasc. 3, No. 9, § 22.

[3] *Op. cit.*, No. 23, § 24.

informed of his follies and unruly conduct, which perhaps may be the cause of his treatment, I recommend you to remedy this in such manner as may leave no ground for complaint, and to warn him as to his follies, so that he shall demean himself according to his duties. As to his applications, I gave orders last year, as well as this, that he must send them to you, that so, aided by your information, I may send such replies as may be conducive to my interests."[1]

As time went on the young prince did not improve his conduct, and on the 6th February 1589 the king writes as follows:—

"I am informed by you that the King of the Islands has married a sister of Antonio Teixeira de Macedo,[2] who went from this kingdom in your company with the orphans, and that he has done so against your opinion: further, that owing to his excesses and misconduct in the married state, you did not give him the letter I directed to him by the armada of 1587, and that you thought it would be prejudicial to my service to correspond with him, unless he greatly mended his ways. In view of what you write I think it well done on your part not to have delivered my letter, and that you ought to endeavour to train this king, who, as you know, is very young, in all the affairs of my service, and also in those which will be serviceable to himself, in order that he may know how to govern well."[3]

On the 22nd February of the same year, 1589, the king again

[1] *Op. cit.*, No. 34, § 12.

[2] This captain arrived at Goa in command of the *Sta. Cruz* in September 1591; he returned in command of the same ship on the 10th January 1592, but was attacked at the Azores by the English; his ship was burnt and the crew escaped on shore. He came out to India again in 1593, in command of the *S. Christovão*, and left in her again early in 1594. She reached Mozambique with great difficulty, but being unable either to proceed or put back to India, she was abandoned, the crew being saved by another ship. Teixeira was then put in command of a new ship, built at Bassein, the *Madre de Dios*, wherein he left Goa on the 15th January 1595: this was probably his last voyage, for this ill-fated vessel was lost near C. Delgado, on the coast of Mozambique, all except sixteen hands perishing in the sea or on the inhospitable shore. (De Couto, *Dec. XI*, ch. xiv, xxvii, xxxi, xxxiv.)

[3] *Arch. Port. Or.*, Fasc. 3, No. 57, § 22.

writes: "The King of the Islands wrote by the ships of the past year, complaining that the Moors of Cannanor are absolute lords of the said islands, and that they gather their whole produce: and that Nicolláo Petro, the Controller of the Treasury of Cochin, did not answer his protests with becoming respect, and in general complained that he was treated with scant courtesy. To this letter I thought it not fit to reply, seeing that you had informed me by letter of 23rd of November 1587 that he had married a sister of Antonio Teixeira de Macedo, who had gone from this kingdom in your company with the orphans, and was behaving in such manner and with such excesses that you had not thought it to my service to deliver to him the letter which I wrote to him that year. Wherefore I do not write to him by these despatches. And since I have already caused a despatch to be written to you requesting you to endeavour to train him in the affairs of my service, and the duties incumbent upon one in his position and of his name, I desire again to recommend this to you, and to request you to favour him when any reasonable opportunity occurs, at the same time giving him to understand that, owing to the bad reports which I have had of him, I do not think fit to reply to him, yet that I have given you instructions as above."[1]

This letter of paternal instruction is followed by another on the 8th March of the same year: "Dom João, King of the Maldive islands, has sent me a message to the effect that you have, in my name, awarded to Dona Francisca de Vasconellos,[2] his wife, who proceeded from this kingdom as one of the orphans in the year 1584, a pension of 500 pardáos annually for her life, to be received by her out of the tribute of the islands, which he is obliged to pay into my treasury, with a declaration that you will get this award confirmed by me within three years. He begs me that, having respect to his marriage with the said Dona Francisca, I shall be pleased to confirm the same, and further to increase the pension by 200 cruzados annually, in order to enable his wife to maintain herself suitably to her position. Inasmuch as in your

[1] *Arch. Port. Or.*, Fasc. 3, No. 62, § 10.

[2] She appears to have dropped the name of Vasconellos when she married: in one despatch the king calls her by both names.

letters of the past year, 1588, you do not mention the letter which I directed to be written to you, as to his misconduct towards his said wife, and as to his behaviour not being conformable to his duties and to the obligations of his rank, I deem it undesirable to yield to his request without information from you as to his present conduct; on receipt of such information I shall reply as befits my service. Until then, I think he should have the 500 pardáos which you have ordered to be paid for his wife's provision."[1]

There is no further reference to the Maldive family in the despatches until the 12th January 1591, by which time it seems the young princes had removed from Cochin to Goa. The king now writes to the viceroy, Mathias d'Albuquerque: "He (*i.e.*, the preceding governor, M. de Sousa Coutinho) also writes that he had recently caused to be arrested at Goa the King of the Islands [Dom João] and the prince his brother [Dom Pedro] for the commission at Cochin and elsewhere of great crimes, meriting exemplary punishment, wherewith he has scandalized the whole of India; and that for a long time that king had quitted his wife; and that when he [the governor] sought to proceed against them, and to carry into execution such judgment as the High Court (*Rellação*) of Goa should award, the judges intervened, saying that he could not do so before first giving me notice thereof, and that he therefore suspended proceedings until I gave such order as befitted my service: which was proper in consideration of the quality of the persons,—on which account, and on others, I approve of the suspension of execution on that king and his brother, although their misdeeds merit natural death, and I ordain that they be kept in prison separately and securely until my further pleasure be known, and that their indictments and the sentence upon them be sent to me with the despatches, that so I may see them and give such order as befits my service. I also confirm to the wife of the said king the 500 *pardáos* which the Viceroy Dom Duarte gave in my name, and direct you to give her as pension 200 more, making in all 700 *pardáos* a year on my account. This

[1] *Arch. Port. Or.*, Fasc. 3, No. 64, § 9.

I direct out of respect to the information which I have of her necessities and upon other grounds."[1]

What decision the Court of Spain, or, rather, the *Casa da India,* came to upon the case does not appear. By the next despatch referring to the princes, viz., that of 13th February 1597, it appears that during the intervening years they had been kept in honorary confinement at Goa, and that they were constantly demanding their freedom, and leave to return to Cochin. The King of Spain, however, directs that they be kept at Goa under the immediate surveillance of the viceroy.[2] The same orders are repeated in the despatch of 21st November 1598, addressed to the viceroy, Dom Francisco da Gama, wherein the king refers to the misdeeds of the brothers, formerly committed at Cochin, as having been "so outrageous and scandalous that it were better not to speak of them".[3]

Owing, perhaps, to the hiatus which exists between the royal despatches contained in the Goa collection (*Archivo Portuguez Oriental*) and the Lisbon collection (*Livro das Monções*), now in course of publication, which commences with the year 1605, we cannot fix the date of the death of the titular king, Dom João. It had occurred before the beginning of 1606, when the Portuguese, Dom Adrian de Gouveia, went to the Maldives: as we learn from Pyrard that this personage was the ambassador of the young king, Dom Filippe,[4] whom our traveller afterwards, 1608-9, met at Goa as a youth of fifteen. Gouveia's embassy bore no fruits, and its failure probably led the young king to write to the King of Spain a letter bearing date 18th December 1606, the contents of which we learn from the recital in the king's reply of 10th December 1607 (*Liv. das Monç*, i, 147). He complains that the revenues from the islands, which in the time of his grandfather, Dom Manoel, and his father, Dom João, had amounted to 18,000 xeraphins, were now, owing to the negligence of the viceroys, reduced to 5,000; he begs the king to give him an

[1] *Arch. Port. Or.*, Fasc. 3, No. 76, § 21.

[2] *Op. cit.*, No. 244, § 10.

[3] *Op. cit.*, No. 365, § 29.

[4] See vol. i, pp. 293-4; vol. ii, p. 139.

honorary office, with the pay thereof, in order to maintain his position, and asks for his retainers four habits of the Order of Christ, with such pension as may seem fit to the king; for a marriage portion to his sister Dona Inez, he asks one of the fortresses, Sofala or Ormuz.[1] He further seeks that orders be given that no captain or *vedor da fazenda* or other officials of Cochin, or elsewhere in Malabar, "under pain of chastisement and suspension from office", be permitted to enquire into the merchandise brought from the islands by his vassals, and that the viceroy should equip an armada to bring the islands into greater obedience, that so he may acquire a greater revenue, and otherwise that he may be excused from further paying tribute under the treaty made with his grandfather. His mother, at the same time, in consideration of the services of her father, Jeronymo Teixeira de Macedo, asks for a voyage (*i.e.*, the privilege of sending a ship on private account) from China to Japan. It is characteristic of the failure of the Portuguese to administer India effectively from Lisbon in those days, that the king's reply, dated a whole year after the petition, is simply a request for information as to the facts and for the viceroy's opinion as to the best course to adopt, and an instruction to keep the exiled prince quiet in the meantime.[2]

The petition referred to was ultimately answered by the despatch of 4th November 1609, after the receipt of the requisite information from the Archbishop Menezes, then Governor of India. Dom Filippe is to get one habit of Christ, and therewith a pension of 150 *pardáos*, payable out of the Courts of Ceylon. Dona Inez,

[1] See vol. ii, Introd., p. xxxi.

[2] The *Casa da India* at Lisbon had endeavoured to introduce the system maintained even in these more rapid times, in our India and Colonial offices, of requiring all letters and petitions to the Crown to come through the local government, by which they are forwarded home with all materials necessary for coming to a decision. But the Portuguese officials of those days, as indeed the correspondence shows, could not be trusted as a channel of communication. Petitioners were obliged to send their requests direct, or as best they could, and the chances were that some eighteen months afterwards a despatch would arrive at Goa, asking for information.

his sister, is to be married to a fidalgo of quality, and to have as her portion one of the Canara fortresses, that is to say, her appointed husband is to have the captaincy of such fortress for three years. As to his complaints about the revenue, the king recommends that the *vedor da fazenda* at Cochin be directed to take from the Maldive consignments only so much coir as is required for the public service, and to leave all the rest to the king, Dom Filippe, and that the viceroy should write to *Adarrajao* (Ali Raja of Cannanor) not to meddle with the islands and property belonging to Dom Filippe, and that if the viceroy thinks proper he may send two or three *fustas* to induce greater obedience on the part of Filippe's vassals, who at the same time are to be coaxed to do their duty rather than punished, as the latter course would only have the effect of estranging them. Lastly, the pension of the queen-mother, Dona Francisca, is to be raised from 700 *pardáos* per annum to 1,000, but without the grant of a voyage.[1]

As has been said, Pyrard made the acquaintance of Dom Filippe and his mother while at Goa (1608-10). They were then lodged in a fine house near the Jesuits' College, where he frequently visited them and entertained them with his talk about the Maldives. At that time, he says, there was a lawsuit pending in the Courts of Goa between the young king and his uncle, Dom Pedro, who resided at Cochin. This prince was married to a half-caste lady of good birth and considerable property; so that he was well off, irrespective of his share of the Maldive tribute, which seems, however, to have been the subject of the litigation.[2]

The king's despatch of November 1609 would, in ordinary course, arrive at Goa in May or June 1610, some months after Pyrard left. On being communicated to the young prince and his mother its terms were not acquiesced in. She pressed for the voyage to China, and he for a powerful armada to be sent to the Maldives. On these demands being made to Lisbon, the king replies on the 28th March 1612, that Dom Filippe is to have 200

[1] *Liv. das Monç*, i, 261-64.

[2] *V. s.*, vol. i, pp. 293-4; vol. ii, p. 139.

milreis pension with his habit of Christ; that the fortress of Daman, instead of one of Canara, is to be given for three years to the man who marries his sister, Dona Inez; that the pension of Dona Francisca is to be paid in silk, as she requests; that further pressure be put upon the Rája of Cannanor not to meddle with Dom Filippe's affairs; and that a trustworthy agent be sent to the *de facto* King of the Maldives to induce him, by threats of invasion, to a better fulfilment of the treaty; and, finally, that the captains and officials of Cochin and Malabar are not to issue passports on their own account for trade to the Maldives, as, by the queen-mother's complaint, has been done.[1]

The forthcoming volumes of the *Livro das Monções* may give some further particulars of the life of the young half-caste king. Meantime, the next notice of him at present available is found in the letters of the Roman traveller, Pietro della Valle, who, while at Goa in 1623, thus describes the feast of St. John the Baptist:—

"The 24th June. For the feast of St. John, according to annual custom, the Viceroy issued forth with many other Portuguese gentlemen on horseback, in masquerading dress, but without masques, two and two attired alike, or three and three. After hearing Mass at the Church of St. John, they proceeded down St. John's Street, which they are wont to call *La Carriera de' Cavalli*, it being the finest open space in Goa. Here, after many companies of Canarin Christians had passed with their banners, drums, and arms, many of them leaping and playing along the street, with their naked swords in their hands, all being on foot, at length all the cavaliers on horseback ran two careers, one downwards from St. Paul's Church toward the city, the other upwards; running matches, two and two or three and three, according to their similar attire, with their Moorish lances, and at last all came marching down from St. Paul in order. Which done, they all proceeded to the piazza of the Viceroy's palace, where the festival ended.

"I went to see this sight in the said street of St. Paul, at the

[1] *Livro das Monções*, ii, 258; *Arch. Port. Or.*, Fasc. 6, No. 451, 452. It appears from the documents directing the investiture at Goa, that the prince was not admitted to the order of Christ till June 1618.

house of one whom they call the King of the *Maldiva* or *Maladiva* islands, which are an innumerable number of very small islets, almost all in one long, wide belt, joined together on the western side, not very far from the coast of India. Of these islands an ancestor of this man was actually king, but being driven from his country by his own people, he betook him to the Portuguese, and became a Christian, in the hope of getting back to his own country and reigning there with their aid. But the Portuguese taking no steps in his behalf, he and his descendants remained thenceforth deprived of their kingdom, and with the empty title alone, which the Portuguese, having formed connections with them, still preserve to them; and since a number of merchant vessels come from these islands to the Portuguese ports, they compel them to pay a little tribute, as it were, to their legitimate lord, who thus (albeit the harbour officials, through whom the transaction is necessarily conducted, appropriate more than one-half) draws at the present day about 3,000 crowns, and therewith supports himself.

"Similar fortune has befallen many other princes in India, who, trusting to the Portuguese, have found themselves deluded. In this matter good policy has been but little observed by the Portuguese, because by this mode of conduct they have discouraged all the rest from having confidence in them; whereas, had they assisted and protected them in earnest, as they ought and might easily and cheaply have done on many fair opportunities, they would at this day have had the fealty and love of all India; while they themselves would in consequence, with the strength and aid of their friends, have been much more powerful than they are, and would have been incomparably more dreaded by their enemies."[1]

Dom Filippe seems to have gone on demanding from the Court of Spain active support towards, not his reinstatement, but the more punctual and full payment of his revenues. At length, in 1631, according to Resende,[2] or more probably in 1632, according to the letters which, prior to the despatch of the armada, passed between the Maldive prince and the viceroy,[3] the Spanish govern-

[1] Pietro della Valle, *Viaggi*, parte 3a, Lettera iii (Brighton ed., vol. ii, p. 606).

[2] *Sloane MS.* 197, fol. 377.

[3] Given in the notes to *Livro das Monções*, i, 148-54.

ment ordered the viceroy to send a force to the islands.[1] The armada, consisting of fifteen ships, under the command of Domingos Ferreyra Belliago, the chief captain of Canara, was despatched in the month of April, and sailed direct for Male. "But the King of the Maldives was advised of the coming of the armada, and when it arrived he was well fortified, and the only entrance to the island was stopped up with ships filled with stones, so that it was impossible for ships to enter by it, and more impossible to enter by any other way, because the whole island is encircled by rocks and reefs, as may be seen by the plan with the mode of the fortification. The said armada, for some days, fired upon it with cannon, and then seeing it was impossible to force an entrance, and that the time spent was all wasted, returned to Goa."[2]

Some member of the force made a drawing at Resende's request, and from that he prepared the coloured plan of which a copy is given opposite. Leave had been given to Dom Filippe to accompany this expedition, but he made various excuses, such as that he objected to be under the control of the chief captain, and that he could not bear to see the havoc that would be made among "his subjects" by the Portuguese soldiery.[3]

The last mention of Dom Filippe is made by the bare-footed Carmelite monk, Philippus a Sanctâ Trinitate, who was at Goa, 1631-1639:—"He was of a middling colour, that is, somewhat dark and tanned, after the black skin of his father, with some of the whiteness of his mother. I have often visited and talked with him, and it was arranged that he should come to Europe with me,

[1] The year is given by Resende, both at fol. 377 and in the writing upon the Maldive plan, as 1631. On the other hand, there can be no doubt that the letters given in the *Livro das Monções* are correctly dated, and in them there is no mention of any expedition in the previous year.

[2] Resende MS., *loc. cit.*

[3] The documents given in the *Liv. das Monç.*, i, 147, are as follows:— 20 Jan. 1632 (Dom Filippe to the Viceroy); same date (Viceroy's reply); 24 Jan. 1632 (Dom Filippe to the Viceroy); same date (Viceroy's reply); same date (certificate of Izidoro de Lemos da Mesquita, Secretary of State, to the effect that permission to accompany the expedition had been given under proper conditions).

for he believed that by his presence he could obtain of the King of Spain what he failed to get by letters, seeing, as he saw, that either the commands were not efficacious or that he was mocked in India. He had not much revenue, for only some of the islands persevered in acknowledging his sovereignty. He also died while yet young and unmarried, leaving as his successor a nephew on his sister's side; though his father's brother, in reliance upon the laws and customs of the kingdom and the acceptance of the people, claimed the throne as rightfully his. When I left Goa the law-suit was still afoot, and there was no settled king of these islands."[1]

The end of the family of exiled Maldive kings is related by F. de Sousa[2]:—"The last King of the Maldives was Dom Luis de Sousa,[3] who, on the 22nd October 1653, attempted, with other fidalgos, to depose the Viceroy, Dom Vasco Mascarenhas, Conde de Obidos; for which cause he was imprisoned at Mormugão until the 10th November 1655, in the viceroyalty of Dom Rodrigo Lobo da Silveyra, Conde de Sarzedas. For the same cause he was sent a prisoner to Portugal in the ship *Nossa S. da Graça*, in the year 1656. The ship was dismasted in a storm off the Cape of Good Hope; it put back to Mozambique, but, before reaching port, the king was dead. He left no legitimate successor, and named the King of Portugal as his heir to the 11,000 islands."

As has been stated above, we are without knowledge of the exact terms of the original treaty with the Maldives after the war described by Pyrard, and how far the Portuguese bound themselves to active support of the exiled king; but it would seem from the foregoing summary that the treatment of the exiled family at Cochin and Goa, for more than a century, was on the whole marked with forbearance and humanity.

[1] Lat. ed., 1649, p. 98; Fr. ed., 1652, p. 226.

[2] *Oriente Conquistado*, C. 1, D. 1, p. 67.

[3] Probably the son of the fidalgo who married Dom Filippe's sister, Dona Inez.

C.

THE HISTORY OF KUNHÁLI,[1] THE GREAT MALABAR CORSAIR.

ALTHOUGH the story of Kunháli, as shortly given by Pyrard,[2] is generally accurate, it differs in some respects from the fuller account given by the official historian, De Couto, and from that of Faria y Souza, and, as will naturally happen when a narrative is compiled from the reminiscences of casual informants, the dates are sometimes wrong. The detail in which De Couto recounts the operations against the great corsair attests the importance attributed by the Portuguese to the reduction of the fortress, and Pyrard's episodical account, in like manner, shows how the story of the brave Kunháli was in everyone's mouth, and how, with all his cruelties and robberies, he had achieved the posthumous fame of a hero. It may be advisable, therefore, to supplement the traveller's narrative with a *résumé* of this episode in Portuguese-Indian history, so far as it can be traced in the writings of the time.[3]

During the viceroyalty of Dom Antonio de Noronha (1571-3) Kunháli[4] the elder (uncle of the great corsair), who was then a

[1] The 11th *Decada* of De Couto being lost, the above reference is to the substituted volume compiled from contemporary historians by the editor of the Lisbon edition of 1778. The topographical information given below as to the condition of the Kunhâli's fort at the present day, and the details of the family, are drawn from notes of Mr. W. Logan, which he courteously wrote at Mr. Bell's invitation, having taken the trouble to visit the place for the purpose.

[2] See vol. i, pp. 351-56.

[3] See De Couto, *Dec. XI*, cap. xiii, xiv, xxxv; *Dec. XII*, liv. I, cap. i-iii, vii-x, xvii, xviii; liv. II, cap. ii-x; liv. III, cap. xi; liv. IV, cap. i-xi; Stevens' *Faria y Souza*, vol. iii, pp. 96-116.

[4] Kunháli, i.e., *Kunhi*, a youth, a term of endearment, a title as here, and '*Ali*. It is a title, not a proper name. This Mâppilla family set

native of Kuṛichchi,[1] cast his eyes upon the neighbouring port of Putu paṭṭanam[2] as a place well adapted for a rover's stronghold. The permission of the Samorin was obtained, and Kunhâli, with his kindred and associates, proceeded to build the fortress, afterwards known as "Kunháli's fort", and, according to Pyrard, Marcaire costè (*Márakkár Kóttá.*)[3]

Shortly before reaching the sea the *Koṭṭa* river takes a turn to the north, then again to the west, forming a peninsula of low-lying sand-dune, on which the fort was built. The mouth of the river, at the time of which we are speaking, was, at the point of the peninsula, guarded by the fort. That mouth is now silted up with sand, and the river finds its exit further south, through what was, in the Portuguese times, a salt-marsh. The fort and town stood only fifteen or twenty feet above the water's edge. De Couto describes the river as being a musket-shot wide in one place, and of volume sufficient to bear *catures* for three leagues up the country, and *almadias* much further.

The fortress, as described by De Couto, was square, each side

apart from the common stock two portions for the support of two *sthánams* or dignities. Kunháli was the title of the head of the family (*múppa sthánam*); Kuṭṭi assan (*Kuṭṭi*, child + Hassan) that of the second in rank (*eḷuma sthánam*). The original family-house was at Kollam (Pyrard's *Coluotte*, from the inflected form *Kollatta*). They moved up the coast to Trikkodi, probably about the year 1525.

[1] Commonly called Coriche, a place on the sea-shore, two miles north of Trikkodi, in Meladi Amsam, Kurumbranâd taluk.

[2] The town of Putu paṭṭanam ("new town") was at the mouth of the Kóṭṭa river on its northern bank. This was a place of great trade in early times, and the Portuguese gave its name to the river. De Couto probably speaks in general terms when he says that the fort was built here. It was actually built on the southern bank of the river mouth, and as the fort (*Kótta*) became more famous than the opposite town, it in time gave to the river the name which it has since borne. Dr. Burnell (*Linsch.*, i, 73) erroneously identifies Kunhâli's fort with Waddakuray (*Vadakarei*), which, as its name implies, was on the north bank.

[3] *I.e.*, the Márakkár's fort, *Márakkár* = *Márggakkáran*, from *Márgya*, "a way or law", and *Káran*, "a doer". The town was called *Kóṭṭakkal*, and the family name became *Kóttöl* (corruption of *Kóṭṭayil*, "of or belonging to the Fort"). *Kóttakkal* is in the Tringngal Desaṃ of Méladi Amsam, in Kurumbranád taluk.

being of 500 paces, ending with the usual bastions at the corners. The walls were four paces thick. In the middle was the citadel, with its dungeon, where Portuguese captives were immured, and which, as De Couto sadly adds, "for our sins was seldom vacant." The fort walls had their parapets, port-holes, and loop-holes, with much good artillery; but the strongest bastion was that which guarded the bar of the river on the north-west of the town.[1]

Such is the description of the fortress as it was at the time of the Portuguese attack, and though it was much strengthened by Kunháli the younger, it is expressly stated by De Couto that the square fort was built by the founder of the town.

On the death of the elder Kunháli he was succeeded by his nephew, Mahomet Kunháli Márakkár,[2] who proved himself the most active and enterprising enemy the Portuguese had yet met with in India. "All these great defences", says De Couto, "served not only to make him secure, but also to make him so proud as to forget that he was but a vassal, and to hold himself out for a king. He created offices agreeable to that dignity, with pageantry of arms, and rode upon a white elephant, which is part of the insignia of the chief sovereigns of Asia. He also bore himself toward the Portuguese as his uncle had, only with far greater success, for besides taking many of our *fustas* and other small craft, he also seized a ship on her way from China, and afterwards a galeot. He also assisted with captains and soldiers the Queen of Olala, when she rebelled against us, and also the Melique at Chaul. And not only against us, but against the Malabars he acted in like manner, in such wise that, by reason of the great wealth which he thus accumulated, he deemed himself invincible."

Towards the close of the year 1591, the viceroy, Mathias de Albuquerque, who had arrived in India in May of that year, despatched two armadas from Goa, one under André Furtado de Mendoza against the Raja of Jaffna, the other under Alvaro de

[1] Mr. Logan states that the only remains now discernible are those of a rectangular fort, with bastions at the four corners. It is but a small place, 48 yards by 28. The people could not point out any other remains.

[2] Mahomet Cunhale Marcà, as written by De Couto.

Abranches against Kunháli. Furtado, on approaching Ceylon found a fleet of Kunháli, of twenty-one galleys, under Cutimuza,[1] the nephew of Kunháli, "lording it over the whole Coromandel coast", as the historian expresses it. A battle was fought off the island Karativu, in which the corsairs were totally defeated, Cutimuza himself escaping on shore.[2]

Alvaro de Abranches meanwhile proceeded to the Malabar coast. At or before his arrival there, a Jesuit, Francisco da Costa, then a captive at Calicut, represented to the Samorin the advantages of a Portuguese alliance for the suppression of Kunháli. D. Alvaro was communicated with; the matter was referred to the viceroy, and at length a treaty was concluded, in pursuance of which all the Portuguese captives at Calicut were liberated, the Jesuits had free leave to preach in the Calicut dominions, and the Samorin himself laid the foundation of a Catholic church![3]

What happened between 1591 and 1597 does not clearly appear. The Portuguese were much occupied during this period with the war in Ceylon, and also on the Mozambique coast; and the next mention we have of the affairs of Kunháli is a repetition of the treaty negotiations a short time before the arrival of the viceroy, Francisco da Gama, when D. Alvaro de Abranches again appears as the Portuguese representative.

Francisco da Gama, Conde de Vidigueira, who arrived at Goa on the 22nd May 1597, and assumed office as sixteenth viceroy, was the grandson of the great Vasco, and a young man of thirty-one years of age. Faria y Souza says, and De Couto his official apologist admits, that he was unpopular from the first. The causes assigned are, first, that he was distant and haughty in his bearing, as, for instance, that he attended church concealed behind a curtain; secondly, that he was severe towards his official subordinates. It must, however, be pleaded on his behalf that he succeeded a notoriously lax governor, Mathias de Albuquerque, who "could not believe any man capable of lying". Da Gama's unpopularity pursued him to the close of his viceroyalty; but the fact that his government was on the whole deemed meritorious is

[1] The *Cousty Moussez* of Pyrard.

[2] *Dec. XI*, cap. xiii.

[3] *Dec. XI*, cap. xiv.

proved by his being, at a later period, appointed to a second term of office.[1]

Preparation was at once set on foot for several expeditions, and in particular an armada was equipped for the attack upon Kunhâli, in conjunction with the Samorin's land forces. The viceroy appointed to the command of this armada his own brother, Dom Luiz da Gama, a young man of thirty, already nominated to the government of Ormuz. This appointment was received with open discontent among the Portuguese captains, but is defended by de Couto.

The despatch of this fleet was delayed, first, by the news which then arrived at Goa of the fateful appearance of the Dutch on the Mozambique coast, and, afterwards, by the capture by the Malabars of two ships, under Simão de Abreu de Mello, off Cape Jaquete in the North. These ships were attacked by eight prahus, and, after a desperate encounter, the Portuguese were slain to a man. Both events were received with consternation at Goa, and necessitated the immediate despatch of a squadron to avenge the disaster in the North, and another to protect Malacca and the Archipelago, which were truly surmised to be the goal of the Dutch.

Luiz da Gama did not leave Goa till the 13th November 1597, and then with a fleet diminished to the extent of the above-mentioned squadrons. He proceeded to Calicut, and there held a conference with the Samorin. The raja had to decide between supporting the Portuguese arms against his own vassels and race, a course which would probably lead to his own subjection to Portugal, or to witness the further growth of Kunhâli's power, which along the whole coast was already overshadowing his own. He accordingly tried to better the terms previously made ; in consideration of his assistance he demanded of Luiz da Gama a sum of 30,000 *pataçoes*, some companies of Portuguese soldiers, and half the spoil. On being reported to Goa, these terms were deemed to be inadmissible, and the Samorin's good faith being impeached, he

[1] His first viceroyalty ended 25th Dec. 1600; his second extended from the 19th Dec. 1622, to the end of Jan. 1627.

was declared an enemy, and the whole Malabar coast was laid under blockade. Luiz da Gama himself returned to Goa in April 1598.

The Samorin now altered his mind, owing, as it is said, to fresh presumption on the part of Kunháli, and to the persuasion of a Jesuit, P. Antonio, and declared himself ready to give active aid with his land forces. The viceroy forthwith ordered fresh ships to be equipped, and amongst others caused six boats, specially adapted for work on the Koṭṭa river, to be built at Bassein. Twelve ships were sent to supplement the blockading fleet, and towards the end of 1598 the Samorin was encamped outside Kunháli's fort with a large army.

In December, Luiz da Gama again left Goa with three galleys and twenty fustas, which, added to the eighteen ships already at Koṭṭakkal,[1] and the six river boats from Bassein, contained a force of about 1,500 men. At this juncture Archbishop Menezes was leaving Goa on his celebrated mission to the Malabar Christians, and he was requested by the viceroy to call at Koṭṭakkal and to take counsel with the fleet and report the state of affairs. In January a council of the captains was held, at which the archbishop was present, and a vote was taken to attack the fort from the river by means of the boats. The results of the council were communicated to Goa, and were there approved. The archbishop proceeded to Cochin, whence he despatched three or four more ships to the assistance of the fleet, and did further service in restraining the Raja of Cochin from an invasion of the territories of an ally of the Samorin, which was intended to break the alliance of the latter with the Portuguese.

All was ready for the attack on the 3rd March 1599. Three hundred Portuguese, under Belchior Ferreira, were sent to join the Samorin, who was encamped on the landward side of the fortress; while Luiz da Sylva, a great and experienced captain, was assigned to lead the attacking force of six hundred Portuguese against the river front. The 4th March was passed in confession and prepara-

[1] The fort (and town) of *Koṭṭakkal* is erroneously named *Cunhale* by de Couto, and *Cogniały* by Pyrard.

tion. It was now found that obstructions had been placed in the river channel by Kunhâli, and after great efforts a narrow space was cleared, but only sufficient to allow one boat to pass. Doubts were entertained of the success of the plan adopted by the Council and endorsed at Goa, and on the night of the 4th some five or six captains sought an interview with the commander and induced him to advance the force under Luiz da Sylva, not by boats up the river, but by land from the Ariole[1] side, whence it was to cross by rafts (*jangádas*) to beneath the fort.

On that night a meteor was seen in the sky, which was deemed of evil presage to the Portuguese, and of good augury for Kunhâli. A fire-signal for the combined attack from the land and river sides had been arranged, but by mistake it was given soon after midnight instead of shortly before dawn. Belchior Ferreira and his three hundred men, along with six thousand Nairs of the Samorin's army, accordingly rushed to the attack without their scaling-ladders and other engineering implements. Luiz da Sylva crossed the river by the aid of sixty boats. His instructions were to extend his force round the base of the fort, and so to join hands with Belchior Ferreira. The besieged were, however, ready, and opened a heavy fire upon the landing parties. A disaster which gave special poignancy to the memories of that day came upon the Portuguese at this early hour, for among the first to fall was the gallant leader, Luiz da Sylva himself, who had hardly set foot on land when he was shot through the head. Two other captains who succeeded to the command soon after shared his fate. The force never got into formation, each party being separately engaged. Some rushed back to the boats, and, overcrowding them, met their deaths by drowning, though a few succeeded in swimming across the river or down to the fleet. Those for whom this mode of flight was impossible kept up a desperate resistance till noon, by which time the flower of the Portuguese army was destroyed. Belchior Ferreira, meanwhile, had delivered his attack in good order, but at length, seeing the day was gone,

[1] A small territory under a raja on the right bank of the river inland. It is mentioned by Pyrard (*supra*, vol. i, pp. 348, 352).

withdrew to his camp. All this time the obstructions in the river, and the deficiency of boats, had kept Luiz da Gama a mere spectator of the scene, unable either to direct or to succour. We have, from de Couto, a picture of him standing knee-deep in the mud of the river bar, endeavouring to embark succours in the boats, while ever and anon his attempts thus to rally his forces were frustrated by the sight of the fugitives, some in boats, some swimming down the river, and all shouting, "Treason! Treason!" The body of the brave Luiz da Sylva had been got into a boat, wrapped in his flag, which a captain had torn from its standard, in order to conceal the fact of his fall. This manœuvre, however, only added to the disorder of the soldiery, who found themselves of a sudden, and at the critical moment of the attack, without a competent leader and without colours. Thus ended the gravest disaster which had as yet befallen the Portuguese arms in India. De Couto gives a long list of noble fidalgos who fell that day, sacrificed by the incapacity of their leaders; and though he confidently asserts that the total loss was 230 men and no more, his own story of the events of the fight gives colour to the statement of Pyrard that the loss amounted to no less than 500 lives. It is further stated by de Couto, who talked the matter over with Kunhâli and his lieutenant, Chinale, when they were in the Goa prison, that the loss of the besieged exceeded 500 men.

The sorrow and vexation of Luiz da Gama at the death of his brave captain and the miscarriage of the whole enterprise were unbounded. His next measures, however, were dictated by good sense and humanity. Leaving a small force to blockade the fort under Francisco de Sousa, and despatching the body of da Sylva to Cannanor, where it was temporarily interred with all available pomp,[1] he withdrew his shattered forces to Cochin, where the wounded received attention at the hospital and in the houses of the citizens.

The blockading force was insufficient, and Kunhâli, who had thirteen galeots ready for action in his port, might easily have forced a way to sea, had not de Sousa, by a skilful ruse, led him

[1] It was afterwards conveyed to Portugal.

to believe that he was reinforced. The Samorin, on his side, said to have been at the head of 20,000 men, now thought he had an opportunity of seizing the fort by a *coup de main*, but the attempt proved fruitless.

The news of the disaster was not long in reaching Goa. "The Count Admiral (the Viceroy) was awaiting the news from Koṭṭakkal with intense interest, when a rumour began to circulate that D. Luiz da Gama was lost with all his men. He concealed his great sorrow without appearing sad or melancholy in the presence of the people, because the news was not yet certain; when on the 15th of March the certainty came by letters from the Chief Captain, brought by the D. Luiz Lobo. This caused so great a shock in the city that men rushed forth like madmen from their houses to hear the truth, while the women crowded the windows, shrieking for news of their husbands, sons, and brothers." The viceroy maintained his composure with great courage, and called his council to meet him three days later, when the first paroxysms of sorrow should have subsided. When the meeting took place, the viceroy's first proposal was that he should be allowed to go against Kunháli in person, and he expressed his confidence that he would succeed in capturing the fortress and restoring the credit of the State. Whether from disbelief in his capacity, or, as they alleged, because the viceroy's presence was required at the capital, the council voted against the project, and it was then unanimously decided that the blockade should be strictly maintained (it being known that the besieged were in want of supplies), that so the Samorin would be held steadfast in continuing the siege by land. Thus it was hoped at the close of the south-west monsoon, when active operations could be resumed, the beleagured fort would be half conquered by starvation. A fresh treaty of alliance was then drawn up and sworn between the Samorin and Luiz da Gama at Cochin.[1] The unfortunate Luiz da Gama returned to Goa, and his brother was, no doubt, glad enough to get him forthwith shipped off to Ormuz, the

[1] The articles of this treaty are given at length by de Couto (*Dec. XII*, liv. II, cap. x).

captain of which fortress had lately died. His enemies, however, did not let him rest there; his misconduct of the expedition was made the ground of a legal charge, which, after such adjournments and delay as are usual in State trials, resulted in an unvalued acquittal.

During the next few months preparations went busily forward at Goa. The annual armada arrived from Portugal with a large complement of raw recruits. "There were men enough," says Faria y Souza, "but they wanted a commander: neither was such a one wanting, but that the envy of the Portuguese endeavoured to rob André Furtado of that glory, or rather their country of that advantage."[1] André Furtado de Mendoça was accordingly appointed to the post of chief captain of Malabar, but, whether from jealousy of this great soldier, or merely from a desire to retrieve his family honour, F. da Gama, at a council held in November, again pressed his claim to lead the army in person. The Archbishop and a majority of the council strongly opposed, and the fleet departed under its nominated leader. Furtado's force consisted of two galleys, twenty-two ships, five *manchuas*, and eight *periches*, which, with a contingent from the Northern ports, and the blockading squadron already at the Kotta river, amounted to three galleys and fifty-four other ships, with a complement of about 2,000 men.

Furtado himself arrived at the Kotta river early in December, in advance of some portion of the expeditionary force. On the 16th the allied commanders held a ceremonial meeting at Kurichchi (*Coriche*), the ancestral home of Kunhâli's family, both Furtado and the Samorin being accompanied by large bodies of troops, who, drawn up in crescent formation around the place of meeting, fired salvos of artillery and musketry. The Samorin conducted Furtado to the seats prepared for them, and there, after the usual formal compliments, "they spoke of the mode of conducting the war, which the Samorin promised to prosecute with redoubled courage and vigour. He also told the chief captain that as soon as Kunhâli saw the power of the armada then at his river, and

[1] Stevens' *Faria y Sousa*, iii, p. 113.

learnt that he (Furtado) was its captain, a general so renowned and feared by the Moors, forthwith he sent word to offer to capitulate on condition that his life and those of all the Moors with him should be spared, and that he, the Samorin, should come to the gate of the fortress to receive his surrender, and thus secure him from violence at the hands of his Nairs : all which he had conceded with the intention of putting him to death as soon as he got him into his hands : because this is the proper policy in dealing with traitors, especially when they are such that it is impossible to expect that they will act otherwise on every available occasion. And that at the time fixed for the surrender, he (the Samorin) sent his fencing-master with some Nairs to receive Kunháli, but the latter seeing that he, the Samorin, was not there in person, that being a bad sign, sent out his Moors to the Nairs, between whom there arose a great strife, followed by a sharp conflict, in which many were wounded on both sides, and that now there was no confidence between them. Therefore it was necessary to continue the war against that tyrant, for which purpose he offered everything needful so far as his kingdom could afford, and that as an earnest of his goodwill and faith he would give whatever hostages the chief captain should require, because everything must be done according to his opinion and wishes. André Furtado de Mendoça thanked him for his offers, and made other suitable offers in return, whereupon they parted, the Samorin adding that he would send the Padre Francisco Rodrigues and his Regedores to his (Furtado's) galley, so that with them he might draw up such capitulations as he might deem necessary."

The first indication that Furtado was a party to the treachery and duplicity of the Samorin appears from the fact that he listened to the above speech of his ally without amazement or resentment; the second is the somewhat remarkable omission, in the settled capitulations (given in full by de Couto), of all mention of the mode in which the person of Kunháli was to be disposed of. One article, indeed, provided that the fortress is to be destroyed, and that the Samorin was to have one-half of all the money, merchandise, ships, artillery, and other arms which might be taken as loot ; but, to judge from what followed, it would seem to have been recognised that the intentions of the parties with regard to Kunháli himself were better to be understood than expressed.

Although Furtado himself had arrived in December, his entire force was not collected around the doomed fortress till the middle of February 1600. Meanwhile, in January, another cause of delay had arisen in the departure of the Samorin to attend a festival at Calicut. Time, however, was on the side of the besiegers, and desertions from the famine-stricken garrison began to be frequent. Although food was thereby saved to the remaining garrison, Furtado rather encouraged these desertions. As a commander he was careful of his men's lives, and as he felt assured of his chief prey, he desired to minimise his loss of life in case the capture should come about by assault.

During the absence of the Samorin, Furtado was by no means idle. His first task was to make a complete reconnaissance of the town from the landward side, for which purpose he landed on the shore to the south of the town, and marched on foot a distance of three leagues to the Samorin's camp. He then commenced active operations by taking measures to clear the river channel. In order to protect his boats engaged in this operation, he effected a landing on the northern or Ariole bank, and took up entrenched positions at several points, from which with heavy artillery he was able to bombard the town itself. In response to this move, Kunháli then advanced his works to the sands on his side of the river, but, before this counterwork could be made secure, Furtado crossed over and took it, throwing in a garrison of 300 men, who defied all attempts of the besieged to retake it. Meanwhile the heavy artillery on the Ariole bank, after playing for five days upon the bastion which guarded the town, had effectually destroyed it, and thus laid open the bazaar to assault. At this juncture the Samorin again appeared on the scene.

About the same time, viz., the beginning of March, letters arrived from the viceroy expressly forbidding the commander to attempt the town by assault; but Furtado, in view of the dubious conduct of the Samorin, foresaw that this might lead to difficulties, and, in case the garrison was in any way relieved, the capture might be delayed till after the coming monsoon. He therefore laid the viceroy's letter before his council, and deliberately obtained their vote to disregard the Goa instructions and to sanction an immediate assault.

As soon as the Samorin returned Kunháli began to open negotiations with him, accompanying his petitions with rich presents. It was agreed between them that, on his delivering himself and 250 of his men into the hands of the Samorin and Belchior Rodrigues, their lives should be spared. Whether this Portuguese captain was a party to these capitulations does not appear : but it is the fact that when Kunháli and his 250 followers came out of a stockade to present themselves to the Samorin, the Portuguese, under Rodrigues, took advantage of them, and rushing in, set fire to the stockade, and all the houses and ships that were in or about it. Kunháli, believing that the Samorin had deceived him, retired within his fort.

The final assault on the town was ordered for the 7th March. F. da Sousa was to lead the attack on the Eastern wall with 400 men. A. Rodrigues Palhota was to assault the bastion on the river bar with 600 men, while Furtado himself was to join the Samorin on the land side, and with 1,200 men to overawe his wavering allies and carry the place. The Calicut Nairs, to the number of 6,000, responded to the call with some misgiving, their prince having promised quarter to the besieged. The town was soon taken, and its bazaars burnt. The fortress, or citadel, now alone remained, in which Kunháli still stood at bay, supported by a mere handful of starved retainers.

So far as the narrative of de Couto enables us to judge of the motives of the chief participators in the bad business which was now to be transacted, it appears that the Samorin desired the death of Kunháli, who, whether as vassal or rebel, wielded a power on the coast inconsistent with his own. On the other hand, Kunháli and his adherents were Moplahs, and thus connected by the ties of religion and blood with a large and powerful section of the Samorin's subjects, who were regarding the affair with half-disguised sympathy towards the besieged. Had the Samorin obtained possession of Kunháli's person, he would have had some difficulty in knowing what to do with him, for to put to death the stoutest opponent of the Portuguese would have endangered his own throne. He could not depend on his own men to fight well enough to please the Portuguese, and if they did not, he feared that the Portuguese would take the whole spoil. He was, therefore, anxious to bring about a surrender, and while he would attain that end by promising quarter to Kunhāli, at the same time promising the Portuguese to deliver him over to them, he would save his credit with his own subjects by arranging that at the surrender the Portuguese should make a show of seizing Kunhāli by force. As for the Portuguese, it is sufficiently apparent that they were determined upon the death of the great corsair who had so long defied them, but were willing to accomplish that end by participation in the treachery of the Samorin, rather than expose their troops to the risks of an assault in which they might be deserted by their half-hearted allies. Their conduct in the matter would have extorted the warm approbation of their late master, Philip II.

How the event was in fact brought about had better be told in de Couto's own words:—"In his extremity of want Kunhāli sent envoys to the Samorin, heartily beseeching him to have mercy upon him, and inquiring whether, if he should deliver himself up, the Samorin would promise to spare the lives of him and his followers: this the Samorin conceded, and the agreement was ratified by the *olas* of the parties. This negotiation the Samorin communicated to the chief captain (Furtado), begging him to confirm it, in which case he (the Samorin) would promise to give over to him Kunhāli and some of his captains. Furtado made answer *that His Highness should act as he proposed, and that he was quite satisfied.*" Some days now elapsed during which the Samorin seems to have been seeking means of avoiding the *émeute* of his own troops which he expected would accompany the surrender of the brave man to whom he had made a worthless promise of life. At length, Furtado having threatened an assault, the Samorin and Kunhāli arranged for the surrender to take place on the 16th of March.

On this day the Portuguese and Calicut forces were drawn up opposite to each other. Down the broad way thus formed by the allied forces the remnants of the garrison marched forth. "First came 400 Moors, many of them wounded, with their children and wives, in such an impoverished condition that they seemed as dead. These the Samorin bade go where they pleased. Last of all came Kunháli with a black kerchief on his head, and a sword in his hand with the point lowered. He was at that time a man of fifty, of middle height, muscular and broad-shouldered. He walked between three of his chief Moors. One of these was Chinale, a Chinese, who had been a servant at Malacca, and said to have been the captive of a Portuguese, taken as a boy from a *fusta*, and afterwards brought to Kunháli, who conceived such an affection for him that he trusted him with everything. He was the greatest exponent of the Moorish superstition and enemy of the Christians in all Malabar, and for those taken captive at sea and brought thither he invented the most exquisite kinds of torture when he martyred them.

"Kunháli walked straight to the Samorin and delivered to him his sword in token of submission, throwing himself at his feet with much humility. Some say that the Samorin, inasmuch as he had promised him life, had secretly advised the Chief Captain, when Kunháli should deliver himself up, to lay hands upon him, as though he were taking him by force; and so the Chief Captain did. For, as the Samorin was standing by him, André Furtado advanced, and, seizing him by the arm, pulled him aside; while the other gave a great lurch so as to get free. As he was then at the brink of a hole, the Chief Captain was in risk of falling therein, had not his arm been seized by Padre Fr. Diogo Homen, a Religious of the Order of the Glorious Father S. Francisco, who stood on one side; Diogo Moniz Barreto, who was on the other, fell into the hole and skinned all his leg."

A tumult now arose among the Nairs, which the Samorin with difficulty suppressed. In the midst of it, Chinale and Cotiale, the pirate-chief's nephew, and the other captains, attempted to escape, but were seized and manacled by the Portuguese soldiery. Kunháli himself was led off under a strong guard to the Portuguese lines. Furtado, after entering the fort hand-in-hand with the Samorin, prudently gave up the place to be sacked by the

Nairs, and so diverted their minds from conscientious scruples. In return for this concession, a trivial one, as it turned out that all the valuables had been made away with, the Samorin gave over to the tender mercies of the Portuguese, besides the chief prisoner, forty of his chief adherents, all of whom afterwards suffered death in Goa prison by order of the viceroy. The artillery was divided between the captors, according to the previous engagements. Furtado's last act was to utterly destroy the fort, not leaving one stone upon another, and to burn the town, bazaars, and mosques to ashes.

On Saturday, the 25th March, Furtado set sail for Goa, and on his way put in to Cannanor. Here he was met by letters from the viceroy requiring him to proceed with his whole force to the destruction of Quilon, in the south. The enemies of da Gama suggest that he was animated by jealousy, and intended to deprive Furtado of his triumphal entry into Goa. A council of war was held, at which the captains unanimously refused to proceed to Quilon, and, for the second time in the course of the same expedition, the viceregal commands were set at naught.

On the 11th April Furtado appeared off the bar of Goa. Here he wrote to the Viceroy announcing his arrival, explaining that the condition of his fleet prevented him from proceeding forthwith to Quilon, but offering to proceed thither as soon as it could be refitted. Da Gama, though he may well have been jealous of one who had succeeded where his own brother had failed, was sufficiently prudent to conceal any such feelings, and himself directed the municipality to make preparations for the triumphal reception of the conqueror. A deputation of *vereadores* or aldermen waited upon him at Pangim and requested him to remain there for three or four days, until the preparations were complete.

A question now arose as to the part to be taken by Kunháli. The Viceroy, being informed that Furtado intended to have his illustrious captive marched in front of himself in the procession, requested the Archbishop, who was about to visit Furtado at Pangim, to state that this course would be inconvenient and contrary to precedent, all former captains, on like occasions, having sent their captives into the city from the bar before making their own entry. To this Furtado replied that he would bring him to the quay, where the prison authorities should take him in charge.

"This matter arranged, the armada made its entry all decked with flags, accompanied by many other boats from the city, and from Bardes, which were so decorated with branches of trees that the river was almost encumbered with them. In the middle-way came the ships, firing their guns amid much noise of instruments, as well martial as of lighter sorts, such as drums, fifes, bagpipes and trumpets. Before mooring in front of the gallery of the viceroy (from which point to the Cathedral, where they were to go in procession to give thanks to Our Lord for His mercy in giving the victory which had been obtained over Kunháli, the whole city was covered with green trees and branches, while at the city gates stood the vereador and the Archbishop in expectation), one of the ships of the armada advanced forward, conveying a servant of André Furtado, who, by his orders, landed on the quay four or five Moors, whom the mob there and then stoned to death, in defiance of all the authorities could do." The viceroy, fearing an outbreak when Kunháli himself should appear, sent the chief police magistrate (*Ouvidor Geral do Crime*) to Furtado's ship, with authority, as soon as the latter should land, to take Kunháli secretly off to the prison. To this demand Furtado made a reply which he desired to be conveyed to the viceroy, but the magistrate "behaved with so scant courtesy that, without returning to the Viceroy with Furtado's answer, he insisted upon compliance with his order." Furtado allowed his prisoner to be carried off, but he showed his indignation by refusing to land at the quay, or to take any further part in the triumph, and by proceeding to disembark privately at Madre de Dios, further up the river. De Couto says that he imagined, without any good cause, that the viceroy, out of envy, did not want to see him enter the city with his illustrious prisoner before him. The viceroy, on learning the cause of Furtado's behaviour, warmly reproved the magistrate for his discourteous conduct, and suspended him from office for two months. The people also were highly indignant at the treatment the popular hero had received, and the triumph for which the city had made so much preparation came to an abortive end by the mob tearing down all the decorations and erections that had been set up. The religious ceremony of thanksgiving was performed some considerable time afterwards, when the excitement of the people had subsided, but it is not stated whether Furtado took any part in it.

The captives remained some time in Goa prison.[1] The delay in the proceedings against them was caused by a sudden illness of the viceroy. His first act on his convalescence was to send word to the judges to sentence Kunháli off-hand, but though a fair trial was never contemplated, the judges preferred to mask the perfidy of the State with the semblance of a legal process. A formal indictment was prepared, upon which Kunháli was sentenced to be beheaded, his body to be quartered and exhibited on the beach at Bardes and Pangim, and his head to be salted and conveyed to Cannanor, there to be stuck on a standard for a terror to the Moors. Before his end, he "was many times invited and entreated to seek entrance within the fold of Our Lord Jesus Christ, by many of the Religious of all the Orders, who laboured heartily to gain that soul, and add it to the flock of the Lord. Kunháli, however, refused to yield." At the execution, which was carried out on a scaffold raised in the large square in front of the viceregal palace, and in view of an immense crowd of citizens, Kunháli bore himself with a dignity and courage which won the respect of his pitiless foes.

After some days Chinale was brought forth to share the fate of his leader. As the pious historian puts it, "a better lot awaited him," inasmuch as, before his execution, he yielded to the persuasion of the Fathers and became a Christian, and was baptised by the name of Bartholomew. After this ceremony, at which he "shewed pleasure and good will, he was conveyed to the scaffold, accompanied by the Holy Misericordia, and by the orphan children who were praying to God for him; and his body was buried in consecrated ground." Kunháli's nephew, and all the rest of the forty prisoners given over by the Samorin, some others of whom became Christians, were likewise put to death, "and not one that was taken escaped."

[1] More than for two days, as Pyrard was informed.

"So did the governor and rabble go hand in hand in murder and breach of faith," is the final comment of Faria y Souza.

By the murder of Kunháli and the destruction of his fortress, the privateering of the Malabars was no doubt for some time checked,[1] but the description of Pyrard and other travellers bears witness to the burning hatred of the Portuguese which pervaded the whole coast, and awaited only the advent of the Dutch and English to become a destroying flame. More than fifty years later a rock off the shore, perhaps that called in English times "Sacrifice Rock", was still known as "Kunháli's Rock",[2] and the Kóṭṭa river long continued to be the principal nest of the corsairs, who, friendly to the Dutch and English, continued to work havoc upon the waning commerce of Goa. The Malabar pirates were not finally extirpated until far on in the British period, when they had become pests indeed; but in their long struggle with the Portuguese it is impossible not to regard them as, to some extent, fighting the battle of free trade against monopoly, the battle of the whole coast against the Portuguese marts, and from this point of view to deny a certain measure of consideration, and even of sympathy. This sympathy may more freely be extended to Kunháli himself, notwithstanding his cruelties, which are probably much exaggerated by the Portuguese, as to one who, after a prolonged siege, the first stage of which closed with his conspicuous victory, was, at length, treacherously murdered in defiance of a well-understood capitulation.

The fame of Kunháli is still preserved in the neighbourhood of the Koṭṭa river. The natives there tell that he was taken captive by the Portuguese and made a martyr (*sahîd*) at Goa. In a building which is said to contain the ashes of his uncle and his mother, is pointed out a memorial tomb erected to the memory of the great corsair.[3]

[1] *Liv. das Monç.*, i, p. 26. Doc. 6 Mar. 1605.

[2] See P. Vicenzo, lib. III, cap. v, and lib. v, cap. i.

[3] In the Jamát Mosque, about one hundred yards from the fort, is carefully preserved an encaustic tile, said to have been taken in the loot of a Portuguese church, and now the sole remaining trophy of the wars with the Portuguese. The tile has a cream-coloured ground, and in the centre an ornamental design in different shades of blue, still brilliant in colour.

D.

LIST OF KINGS OF THE MALDIVE ISLANDS SINCE THE CONVERSION TO MAHOMEDANISM.

THE following list has been extracted from the *Tárikh*, or "Chronicles" of the Kings of the Maldives, which, as above stated (vol. i, p. 309), have been kept for many centuries at Málé. The work of extraction has been done by one of the Naibs, a man of intelligence and conversant with Arabic, under the direction of a near relative of Ibrahim Dídí, the Prime Minister.

The Naib informs Mr. Bell that he has done his best to obtain with accuracy the dates of the succession of each Sultan and the length of his reign, but he admits that there may be some mistakes, inasmuch as the present *Tárikh*, which is about 150 years old, is only a copy of a preceding one, which itself was probably a copy of one still earlier, and so on.

Even to us, whose knowledge of Maldive dynasties is confined to a few short periods of the national history, several errors appear on the surface; but these appear to be mere errors of detail, accessions being misdated by a few years. They may, perhaps, be due to the recopying above referred to; or, again, the record may have been left unsupplied during years of trouble, after which the precise year was forgotten. Inasmuch, however, as we find in the list all the names of kings of whom we have extrinsic information, we must regard the record as on the whole trustworthy, and as a quite remarkable proof of the continuity of Maldive civilisation and government.

The number of Maldive monarchs since A.D. 1141, here appearing as eighty-six, should properly be reduced, Nos. 30, 40, and 44 being represented as reigning during two distinct periods, and Nos. 19 and 50 during three. Moreover, the *Tárikh* enters princes-consort as separate kings, see Nos. 20, 22, 25, 27.

The date of accession in each case has been converted from A.H. to A.D.

The *Tárikh* is said to record distinctly the accession of the first Moslem Sultan as having taken place in A.D. 1141, and his conversion to Mahomedanism twelve years later, in 1153. This date, if reliable, puts the conversion about fifty years earlier than the date suggested above at p. 460. But it is probable that in successive copyings of the *Tárikh* more errors may have accumulated than in the later parts of it; and in particular it is to be noted that Sultan Dáúd (No. 16) is here entered as the grandson of No. 12, while Ibn Batuta (*v. s.*, p. 460) states that he was grandson of the first convert. The Moorish traveller, indeed, is not to be implicitly trusted in matters of genealogy. The date given to Dáúd, $130\frac{1}{2}$, corroborates his story to this extent, that the traveller may well have married that Sultan's grand-daughter in 1341, but he may be wrong in asserting that Dáúd was grandson, being, perhaps, a remoter descendant, of the first converted king.

Maldive Kings.

No.	Accession. A.D.		Reigned. Yrs.	Mns.
1	1141	Muhammad-ul-ádil[1] . . .	25	—
2	$116\frac{5}{6}$	Muti Kalaminja[2] [Nos. 1 and 2, sons of sisters]	19	—
3	$118\frac{4}{5}$	'Ali	8	—
4	$119\frac{2}{3}$	Dinai Kalaminja [son of Fahihiriyá Mavákilage]	7	—
5	$119\frac{8}{9}$	Dihai Kalaminja [son of Fahihiriyá Mavákilage]	15	—

[1] This is the Sultan whom Maldive tradition, now at least, regards as the first convert to Mahomedanism, and to whom is given the title *Darumavanta* (*Dharmmavanta*), "the religious", "the just". If he be not identical with Ibn Batuta's "Ahmed Shanuraza", I should be inclined to trust Ibn Batuta, whose account of the inscription in the mosque is circumstantial (*v. s.*, p. 448). The *Tárikh* fixes the date of the conversion at the year 1153-4.

[2] The honorific *kalaminja* is stated to imply more than our "royal highness", viz., descent from royalty through both parents.

No.	Accession. A.D.		Reigned. Yrs.	Mns.
6	$121\frac{3}{4}$	Vadi Kalaminja [son of Fahihiriyá Mavákilage]	20	—
7	$123\frac{2}{3}$	— Kalaminja [son of Fahihiriyá Mavákilage]	25	—
8	$125\frac{7}{8}$	Hudai Kalaminja [son of Hiriyá Mavákilage]	7	—
9	$126\frac{3}{4}$	Aim Kalaminja [son of Hirati Kabádikilage]	2	—
10	$126\frac{5}{6}$	Hili Kalaminja . . .	1	6
11	$126\frac{7}{8}$	— Kalaminja . . .	—	9
12	$126\frac{8}{9}$	Muhammad-údú Kalaminja . .	9	—
13	$127\frac{7}{8}$	'Ali Kalaminja [son of No. 12] . .	10	—
14	$128\frac{7}{8}$	Yusub Kalaminja [younger brother of No. 13]	7	—
15	$129\frac{3}{4}$	[1] [son of No. 14] . .	8	—
16	$130\frac{1}{2}$	Dáúd[2] [son of No. 14] . . .	5	—
17	$130\frac{6}{7}$	Umaru-víru[3]	35	—
18	$134\frac{0}{1}$	Shihab-ud-dín[4] [son of No. 17] . .	8	—
19	$134\frac{7}{8}$	Malaka Rehendi Kambádikilage[5] [daughter of No. 17]	17	—

[1] The course of succession from this point down to No. 23 being so fully corroborated by Ibn Batuta, we can have no difficulty in supplying this vacancy from his narrative, by the name Saláh-ud-dín Sálih-al-Banjáli, the father of No. 17 and the grandfather of No. 19 (*v. s.*, p. 449).

[2] Ibn Batuta married the great-granddaughter of this Sultan in 1343 or 1344 (*v. s.*, p. 460). Thus, either he succeeded somewhat late in life, or, as seems probable from the erroneous date given to No. 19, his accession is here post-dated. Possibly he ought to be No. 15, as Ibn Batuta seems to imply that Jálál-ud-dín 'Omar immediately succeeded Saláh-ud-dín (*v. s.*, p. 449).

[3] The Jalál-ud-dín 'Omar of Ibn Batuta (*v. s.*, p. 449), *Umaru* being the Maldivian form of 'Omar.

[4] Ibn Batuta, who here corroborates the *Tárikh* satisfactorily, says he succeeded as a minor, and that the Vizier Abd' Allah espoused his mother and governed in his name. The same vizier afterwards married the daughter and became Sultan No. 22. Shihab-ud-dín, who seems to have misbehaved himself, was deposed, exiled, and afterwards put to death (*v. s.*, p. 449).

[5] The *Khadíja* of Ibn Batuta (*v. s.*, p. 449), the name here given being probably her Maldivian name. As Ibn Batuta found her on the throne in A.D. 1343, her date of accession should be some half-dozen years ante-dated. All we know of this queen will be found in Ibn Batuta's account.

No.	Accession. A.D.		Reigned. Yrs.	Mns.
20	136$\frac{2}{3}$	Muhammad Jamil[1] [husband of No. 19] .	1	—
21	136$\frac{3}{4}$	Malaka Rehendi Kambádikilage[2] [No. 19] .	10	—
22	137$\frac{3}{4}$	Abdallah Kilage[3] [husband of preceding] .	3	—
23	137$\frac{6}{7}$	Malaka Rehendi Kambádikilage [No. 19] .	3	—
24	13$\frac{79}{80}$	Malaka radafati Kambádikilage[4] [daughter of No. 17] . . .	—	4
25	13$\frac{79}{80}$	Muhammad[5] [husband of No. 24] .	4	—
26	138$\frac{3}{4}$	Malaka dáyin Kambádikilage [daughter of No. 25]	4	—
27	138$\frac{7}{8}$	Abdullah [husband of No. 26] . .	—	—
28	1388	Usmán	—	—
29	1388	Hasan	10	—
30	139$\frac{7}{8}$	Ibráhim [son of No. 29] . .	—	4
31	139$\frac{8}{9}$	Husain	10	—
32	140$\frac{8}{9}$	Nasr-ud-dín . . .	3	—
33	141$\frac{0}{1}$	Hasan	—	9
34	141$\frac{1}{2}$	Ísá [younger brother of No. 33] . .	—	3
35	141$\frac{1}{2}$	Ibráhim [No. 30] . . .	8	9
36	14$\frac{19}{20}$	Usmán [son of No. 29] . .	—	3
37	142$\frac{0}{1}$	Muhammad álim [son of Házin (Boḍu baḍéri) Yúsub]	—	11

1 Jamúl-ud-dín, according to Ibn Batuta. The entry of this vizier-consort as a separate Sultan seems to imply that queens of the Maldives ceased both to reign and to govern on their marriage. See also Nos. 22, 25, and 27. But this is not confirmed by Ibn Batuta, who says distinctly that orders were promulgated in the name of the queen, and it seems that in the mosque service she alone was prayed for by name (*v. s.*, pp. 449-50).

2 If the date of re-accession here given is intended to coincide with the death of No. 20, it is wrong by some nineteen years, Jumál-ud-dín having died in December 1344 (*v. s.*, p. 465).

3 Here the discrepancy amounts to twenty-eight or twenty-nine years, Ibn Batuta representing this vizier as marrying the queen forthwith on the death of her previous consort.

4 As the *Tárikh* states this queen to be sister of the preceding queen, she may be identified with one of the two sisters mentioned by Ibn Batuta under their Arabic names Maryam and Fátimah (*v. s.*, p. 449).

5 Son of No. 20, according to Ibn Batuta, married to one of Queen Khadíja's sisters (*v. s.*, p. 467).

No.	Accession. A.D.		Reigned Yrs.	Reigned Mns.
38	$142\frac{0}{1}$	Yúsub [son of No. 29]	23	—
39	$144\frac{2}{3}$	Abú Bakr [son of No. 29]	—	7
40	$144\frac{2}{3}$	Háji Hasan [son of No. 39]	25	—
41	$146\frac{7}{8}$	Sayyid Muhammad	—	1
42	$146\frac{7}{8}$	Háji Hasan [No. 40]	1	—
43	$146\frac{7}{8}$	Muhammad [son of No. 40]	13	—
44	$148\frac{0}{1}$	Hasan [son of No. 43]	—	1
45	$148\frac{0}{1}$	Umaru [son of No. 38]	4	—
46	$148\frac{4}{5}$	Hasan [son of No. 45]	2	—
47	1486	Hasan [No. 44]	4	—
48	$14\frac{89}{90}$	Sheikh Hasan [nephew of No. 39]	1	9
49	$149\frac{1}{2}$	Ibráhim [son of No. 46]	—	8
50	$149\frac{2}{3}$	Muhammad [son of No. 45]	—	9
51	$149\frac{2}{3}$	Yúsub [son of No. 45]	—	—
52	$149\frac{2}{3}$	'Ali	2	3
53	$149\frac{4}{5}$	Muhammad [No. 50]	15	—
54	$15\frac{09}{10}$	Hasan [son of No. 51]	2	—
55	$151\frac{1}{2}$	Sherif Ahmad-ul-Makká[1]	2	9
56	$151\frac{3}{4}$	'Alí	—	9
57	$151\frac{3}{4}$	Muhammad [No. 50]	16	—
58	$152\frac{8}{9}$	Hasan [son of No. 57]	20	—
59	$154\frac{8}{9}$	Muhammad	2	4
60	$155\frac{0}{1}$	Hasan[2]	2	—
61	$155\frac{1}{2}$	Abú Bakr	4	—
62	$155\frac{5}{6}$	'Ali[3]	—	—
63	$155\frac{6}{7}$	Andiri-Andiri[4]	17	—
64	$157\frac{3}{4}$	Muhammad Takurufán-ul-álam[5]	12	6

[1] An Arab, who perhaps was appointed to the office of Kázi, and then seized the government.

[2] This is Pyrard's *Assan*, who on abdication and flight to Cochin became Dom Manoel, the first of the line of titular Christian kings.

[3] The rival of Hasan, slain by the Portuguese.

[4] The interim half-caste governor under the Portuguese. The *Tárikh* does not call him "Sultan", but "Captain", and adds after his name, Nasóra [? Nazarene].

[5] The elder of the two brothers who threw off the Portuguese yoke.

No.	Accession. A.D.		Reigned. Yrs.	Mns.
65	$158\frac{4}{5}$	Ibráhim[1] [son of No. 64]	14	—
66	$159\frac{8}{9}$	Husain Famudéri kilage[2]	22	—
67	$16\frac{19}{20}$	Muhammad Imád-ud-dín[3]	29	—
68	$164\frac{8}{9}$	Ibráhim Iskandar [son of No. 67]	39	6
69	$168\frac{6}{7}$	Muhammad [son of No. 68]	4	1
70	$169\frac{0}{1}$	Muhammad Moyiddín [nephew of No. 68]	1	—
71	$169\frac{1}{2}$	Muhammad Shams-ud-dín al-Hamávi[4]	—	5
72	$169\frac{1}{2}$	Muhammad [son of Hájí 'Alí]	8	5
73	$170\frac{0}{1}$	'Ali	—	9
74	$170\frac{1}{2}$	Hasan [son of No. 73]	—	—
75		Ibráhim Mulhír-ud-dín	—	—
76		Muhammad Imád-ud-dín[5]	17	4
77	$172\frac{0}{1}$	Ibráhim Iskandar [son of No. 76]	29	2
78	$17\frac{49}{50}$	Muhammad Mukarram Imád-ud-dín [son of No. 76]	2	10
	$175\frac{3}{4}$	[Málé taken by the Malabars: Interregnum of six years.]		
79	$17\frac{59}{60}$	Ghází Hasan Izz-ud-dín	7	—

[1] The Sultan of Pyrard's time. If the term of his reign is correct, his accession is antedated some eight years.

[2] The date here is wrong by about eight years. Ibrahim was killed in February 1607. It is somewhat difficult to explain from Pyrard's narrative who this No. 66 was, for the traveller states, on reports which reached him at Goa, that after the Bengal invasion four chiefs struggled for the throne, and that their pretensions were at length suppressed by Ali Raja of Cannanor, who placed Ranabaḍéri Takuru, otherwise called Máfilafurhi Rasgefánu, on the throne as his vassal (*v. s.*, vol. i, pp. 320-1). But according to Mr. Bell's information the Maldivian archives do not acknowledge that this prince ever ruled the Maldives as a whole, and, accordingly, he does not appear in this list. It would seem probable, therefore, that this No. 66 was the son of the chief called by Pyrard *Pammedery Calogue* (vol. i, p. 255), which son was a distinguished person in Pyrard's time, and very friendly towards him.

[3] Described as the son of a daughter (Aminá) of a daughter (Maryam) of 'Alí, the elder brother of Muhammad (No. 64).

[4] This king, like No. 55, was an Arab, of Hamaví in Yemen.

[5] His date of accession is probably 1704, as he died late in 1721, having reigned seventeen years.

No.	Accession. A.D.		Reigned. Yrs.	Mns.
80	$176\frac{6}{7}$	Muhammad Ghiyás-ud-dín [son of No. 77] .	7	—
81	$177\frac{3}{4}$	Muhammad Shams-ud-dín[1] . .	—	—
82		Muhammed Muiz-ud-dín [son of No. 79] .	—	—
83	$177\frac{8}{9}$	Hájí Hasan Nur-ud-dín [son of No. 79] .	21	—
84	$179\frac{8}{9}$	Muhammad Muín-ud-dín [son of No. 83]	37	—
85	$183\frac{4}{5}$	Muhammad Imád-ud-dín [son of No. 84] .	49	—
86	$188\frac{1}{2}$	Ibráhim Nur-ud-dín [son of No. 85] .	—	—

[1] The *Fáruna Kalegefana* of Christopher (*Trans. Bo. Geo. Soc.*, i, p. 73); but he is said to have been the son of a younger brother of No. 79, and therefore was cousin, not uncle (as Christopher says), of Nos. 82 and 83.

E.

DEDICATORY EPISTLE

Prefixed to the Treatise of the Animals, Trees, and Fruits, in a portion of the 3rd Edition of the original Voyages.[1]

TO

MR. GUILLAUME

LUSSON, COUNCILLOR OF THE KING,

In his Council of State and Privy Council, and First President in his Court of Money.

MONSEIGNEUR,

I may thank God for this, among other things, that after so many ills and calamities suffered in my voyage to the Indies, he hath vouchsafed to me one blessing on my return home, namely that I have thus had the opportunity of acquaintance with many persons distinguished for honour and merit. Among whom you are one of the first, for, being endowed with a mind inclined to all things praiseworthy and of good report, you have not only taken pleasure and commended the recital of my story which I made to you, but also have prompted and encouraged me to commit the same to writing, and approved the publication thereof. What is more, you have of your grace given me such assistance in my extreme

[1] It is in Mr. Bell's, but not in my copy. A transcript reached me after the sheets comprising the Treatise were already printed off. It adds another name to the list of Pyrard's patrons.

misery and affliction that I can say that, after God, you are the cause that I still live and breathe. This hath rendered me under such obligations to you that I could never acquit myself therein, did you not deign to accept my gratitude, goodwill, and affection in your service, the which I am resolved to testify in all places and at all times. Wherefore I offer to you this little treatise which I have separated from the rest of my story, to the end that here may appear to better advantage and with less confusion the rarities and singularities of those distant parts whereto my fortune hath led me. Herein, too, will be seen the admirable effects of God's Providence, which hath with such diversity distributed the good things of his favour, according to the diversity of countries. May it please you, therefore, to accept in good part this offering of mine, as proceeding from one who heartily, as well as by duty and obligation, acknowledges himself,

MONSEIGNEUR,

Your very humble and obedient servant,

FRANÇOIS PYRARD.

INDEX.

Abd-er-Razzak, his reference to the Maldives, II, 468
Abedalles (*Abdallah*), ascetics, I, 342, 343
Abexis (Abyssinia), II, 236
Ablutions, I, 128, 131; during Ramadan, 135; before and after meat, 149, 172; on entering mosque, 174
Abrolhos, I, xxi, 18, 19; II, 197
Abú Abd-Allah Muhammad. *See* **Ibn Batuta.**
Abú'l-barakat, the Maghrebin apostle, II, 447, 448
Abyssinia, II, 236
Achin, Maldive boats carried to, I, 256, 257; two ships of, met by the Dutch, 278; men of, taken in *Croissant*, 291; ship of, wrecked at Maldives, 294; presents sent to Sultan of, 296; description of, II, 158; embassy to Holland, 159
Acouraz, I, 210, 214
Acrobats at Calicut, I, 366, 367
Acuña, Pedro de, II, xv
Adam's Peak, pilgrimage to, II, 454, 457, 466
Adoumatis, atoll, I, 99, 300
Aḍḍu, atoll, I, 97, 99; II, 481; channel, I, 103; ruins at, I, 124
Admiral, or flagship, I, 290; II, 393
Adulteration, of sugar, II, 312; of musk, 359; general practice of the Chinese, *ib.*
Adultery (punishment of), I, 205
Afeon, I, 450. *See also* **Opium.**
Agalapuḷa backwater, I, 359
Agoada, fort, II, 29, 30, 31
Agoadas, watering-places, II, 30
Agra, II, 251
Agulhas, Cape, I, 21, 22; II, 295
Agy (hadji), I, 165
Ahegasts (*M. ahi-gas*), a tree, II, 369
Akbar, II, 250, 252
Alas (yams), I, 112
Alas Alas aquebar, I, 131
Albacores, I, 9, 189
Alberuni quoted, II, 430
Albuquerque, Affonso de, bust of, II, 51; his treaty with Mamale, 474, 475
Alcatif (carpet), II, 102, 103
Alcazar-quivir, battle of, II, xix, 278
Alcoran. *See* **Kuran.**
Aleman, Father Gaspar, II, 22, 269
Aleppo caravans, II, 245
Alexander VI, Pope, I, ix
Alfandega (custom-house), at Calecut, I, 361, 365, 402, 422; at Goa, II, 48, 177, 247
Alfange (scimitar), I, 43
Ali, King of the Maldives, I, 245; II, 532; death of, I, 246; II, 496; son and daughter of, I, 251
Ali Raja, of Cannanor, I, 277, 320, 321; 444, 445; II, 504
Aljabe, prison at Goa, II, 18
All Souls' Day, celebration, II, 97
Allo (slaves), I, 202
Almedia, a kind of boat, I, 389, 401, 421, 422
Almeida, Dom Lourenço de, II, 474
Almsgiving, I, 139, 145, 157
Aloes wood, I, 335; II, 237, 360
Alparcas (sandals), I, 376; II, 132
Alquama (tortoiseshell), II, 478
Alqueire, a Port. measure, II, 218
Alum, rock, II, 247
Aluya (Spanish white), II, 175

Aly alas Mahomedin, a cry, I, 148
Aly Pandio Atacourou, chief of island Fehendu, I, 64 ; his boat stolen, 67
Ambassadors, to Maldives from Goa, I, 293, 294; at Goa, I, 332 ; II, 27, 134, 135 ; Portuguese, at Deccan court, 134 ; Persian ambassador to Europe, 277
Ambergris, I, 229 ; II, 359
Ambou (for *jambu*), II, 369
Amboyna, II, v, xvi, xxxiv, 166, 167
Amfian, I, 450. *See* **Opium.**
Ammianus Marcellinus, quoted, II, 426
Amigos, II, 128
Ana poute iringua, I, 273
Anbéri, name of a slave, II, 455
Ance (bay), II, 293
Andoue (rice), I, 112
Angola, II, 197; trade with, 218-221; silver mine, 219; endeavour to join with Mozambique, 219, 235 ; question of making for, 296
Anil (indigo), II, 246, 359
Anly, a kind of grain, II, 438
Annobom ("Good New Year"), II, 98
Annobom, island, I, xx ; arrival and adventures at, 13-17 ; trade of, II, 221
Antennes (yards), I, 53
Antonio, Padre, a Jesuit, II, 514
Antonio, Dom, pretender, II, 278
Aphion, I, 195 ; *and see* **Opium.**
Apontador, II, 42
Apothecary, at Goa hospital, II, 6-9
Apprentices, on carracks, II, 187, 190
Aquiry (madrepore), I, 97
Arab prisoners at Goa, II, 24
Arabia, Maldive boats carried to, I, 257 ; large ships of, 258
Arabic language, I, 122 ; letters, 184
Arack, i, 358 ; II, 73, 383
Arakan, I, 326, 327
Arbaleste, I, 10
Arbor tristis, I, 411; II, 362
Arch of the Viceroys, II, xxxviii, 47
Archbishop of Goa, his house, II, 53. *See* **Menezes**
Archives, of the Maldives, I, 309; II, 528
Archivo Portuguez Oriental, II, xxiii, cited *passim*
Arco, a coin, II, 68
Areca, in Ceylon galley, I, 299-301 ; abundance of, in Ceylon, II, 141 ; used with betel, 362
Ari, atoll, I, 97, 99
Ariole. See Auriole.
Armadas of the North and South, I, 439, 440; II, 116, 117, 205; advance pay to the soldiers of, 122
Armenians, at Goa, II, 36
Arms worn at the Maldives, I, 197 ; practice in use of, 187 ; masters-in-arms, 187, 268 ; assault at, 269; must be left behind at Málé, 275
Arms (coat of), of Portugal and Portuguese India, I, 439 ; II, 3 ; of Spain, II, 3
Arnoul, Jean, a ship captain, II, 339
Aroba, a Port. weight, II, 194
Arosbay, II, 164
Arquebuses, manufacture of, in Ceylon, II, 142
Arsenal of Goa, II, 40-42
Ascension, ship, I, xiii, 45 ; II, 265 ; crew of, II, xviii, xix, 265
Ashes, human, use of, I, 390
Assa ("permit me"), I, 175
Assan, king. *See* **Hassan.**
Assan Quilogue. See **Hassan Kilagefánu.**
Assant Caounas Calogue, a commissioner, I, 69; gives Pyrard lodging, 77; referred to, 276, 287; death, 289; son referred to, 313; his three sons, 318
Assee. See Sé.
Assegais (javelins), I, 38
Astrolabe, I, 10
Astrology, at the Maldives, I, 186, 187, 319; by the Nairs, 382
Ataide, Dom Estevão de, II, 225-228, 234, 235

Atolls, group of Maldive islands, I, 93, 197; meaning of word, *ib.;* description of, 94, 99-103; names, 97, 99; openings in, 101-103; each governed by a Naib, 198; revenue collectors of, 200

Atolu-veri, I, 223

Atudn (? jaggery), II, 465

Aualu. *See Avil.*

Augustinians. *See* **St. Augustine.**

Auiards (porches), I, 404

Auriole (or *Ariole*), territory and people in Malabar, I, 348, 352, 353; II, 515, 520

Australia, discovery, I, x

Auto da fé, described, II, 95

Avil (half-cooked paddy), I, 379

Awnings, I, 12

Azevedo, Dom Hieronimo de, II, 143

Azores, exports to Brazil, II, 216; wine, *ib.*; sighted, 331

Bacalor, II, 273

Bachian, island, II, 166

Badara (Vadakkara, or Waddakurray), I, 336, 338, 369; arrival and reception at, 344-348; the raja's palace, 346; raja intends expedition to Maldives, 348; Portuguese beaten at, 349; author's nightmare at, 396; a man of, at the Goa galleys, II, 45, 46

Badjansár, II, 443; *and see Banquesalle*

Bahia, II, 197; arrival of author at, 307-309; description of, 309-311; elevator, 310; no inquisition at, 311; sugar-mills of, 312

Bahrein, island, II, 239

Bail, II, 445

Baixos de Judia (Europa shoals), II, 199

Bajus, II, 103, 112

Balagate or **Ballagate,** II, 79, 133, 136

Baleacem, a corsair, II, 476

Báli, island, II, 165

Ball games. *See* **Football.**

Balsam, from Brazil, II, 313

Bamboos, I, 329-331; II, 22, 45

Banana, I, 16, 113; price of fruit, 117; leaves of, used as plates, I, 70; food for elephants, II, 345; general description of tree, 364, 365

Banda, island, II, 167

Bandar, II, 443, 450

Bandicoy, vegetable, II, 9

Bandos (island), I, 85, 118, 267

Banguenim, fountain of, II, 7, 71, 72, 101

Banquesalle (warehouse), I, 85, 267, 281; II, 48

Bantam, description of, II, 160-164

Banyan tree, II, 370

Banyans (Hindu traders), I, 364; at Calicut, 407; at Goa, II, 38; at Cambay, 249

Baptism of native converts, II, 60, 61

Bára island, II, 496

Baratilla (petty auction), II, 69

Barato (misprinted *Barbo*), II, 111

Barbers at Goa, II, 70

Barbosa, Duarte, his account of the Maldives, II, 477-479

Barcelor, I, 369; II, 259, 273

Bardeliere, Michel Frotet de la, captain of the *Croissant,* I, xiv, 3, 5-7; blamed, 23; visits the *Corbin,* 43; death of, 290

Bardes, II, 30, 135

Bargaining, silent, II, 178

Baroso, Antonio, II, 281

Barre (*barra*), river bar, at Cochin, I, 437; II, 29; at Goa, *ib.;* of Surat, 106

Barricades, I, 6

Barros, J. de, his *Decadas,* II, xxiii; his description of the Maldives, II, 479-486

Bartoli, quoted, II, 494

Basaruco, coin, II, 33, 68, 69, 71, 72, 73

Basdarad (necklets), II, 445

Bassein (Wasái), stone brought from, II, 63, 257; ships built at, 182; timber, 257
Bastingues, I, 6
Batatas (potatos), II, 315
Bathing, ceremonial, I, 174; at Goa, II, 115
Bats, I, 115; II, 373
Battas, of Sumatra, I, 297
Batthála, port of Ceylon, II, 466
Batuta. *See* **Ibn Batuta.**
Bayona islands, II, 333-335
Bayonne, sailors and ships of, II, 322, 336
Bazar, at Calicut, I, 402; at Cannanor, 448
Bazar do peixe, at Goa, II, 44
Bazar grande, II, 48
Bazar pequeno, II, 54
Beards, how worn at the Maldives, I, 110
Bêche de mer, I, 63
Beds, at the Maldives, I, 222
Behigue (sailing with wind and current), I, 257
Bell, Mr. H. C. P., his Report on the Maldives, I, xliv, cited *passim*
Belliago, Dom Ferreira de, commands expedition against Maldives, I, 160
Benedictines, monastery at Bahia, II, 311
Bengal, a merchant of, I, 259; a ship of, at the Maldives, 297; expedition to the Maldives from, 310-320, 325; description of, 326-336; king of, 326, 327; war with Mogul, *ib.*; export of rice, *ib.*; characteristics of people, 329, 332-334; pottery, bamboos, *ib.*; elephants, rhinoceros, and unicorns, 331; slaves, 332; religion, 333; drunkenness, 334; Portuguese in, *ib.*; ambassador at Goa, 332; women of, *ib.*; dress of natives, 333, 334
Benjamin (*benzoin*), II, 169, 360
Bergeron, Pierre, I, xxxiv-xl
Berlingas islands (Burlings), II, 332, 333
Betance (Betanzos), II, 338
Betel, chewing, I, 71, 149, 174; II, 135; strengthens the gums, I, 183; used by the king, I, 223; used by Goa ladies, II, 113; general description of, II, 362, 363
Bezoar stone, II, 484
Bignon, Jerome, I, xxxiv, xxxv
Bimby (a grain), I, 111
Biron, Duc de, death, I, 290
Biscay, galions of, II, 180, 182; ships used in whale fishery, 34
Bische (? Port. *bicho*) II, 319
Biscuit, mode of swearing on, I, 279
Bishops in Port. India, II, 26, 27
Blanks (French coin), II, 73, 130, 314
Bleeders, II, 70
Bleeding, not resorted to by natives, II, 13
Blérancourt, Pyrard at, I, xxxv
Bo-trees, at Maldives, I, 124
Boats, cleanliness of, I, 178
Boat-stealing, I, 79, 87
Bode ta Courou, title of a king, I, 251
Bolarmeny, I, 376; II, 27, 63
Boly (cowry), I, 78, 157, 228, 236, 240, 438; *spelt also Bolits*, I, 299; *and Bollis*, I, 250; *and see* **Cowries.**
Bom Jesus, church and college of, at Goa, II, 54, 59, 97
Bom Jesus, carrack, I, 367; II, 263
Bonitos, I, 9, 189
Bonne guerre, terms of capitulation, II, 193, 200, 208
Borneo, II, 168, 169, 175
Bostú (measure), I, 237; II, 444, 465, 468
Boubou (lady), I, 259
Boues, a fruit, II, 9
Bouseruque. *See Basaruco.*
Boy, Anglo-Indian use of term, II, 45, *n.*
Boye (Port. *bóy*), II, 44, 45
Bracelet, a badge of office, at the

Maldives, I, 189, 269; in Malabar, 381
Bradshaw, Samuel, his account of the *Union's* voyage, I, 45, II, 264
Brahmans, I, 371; marks and characteristics of, 372-374; influence of, used against the Portuguese, 374, 375; customs of, 376-379
Brato (cockroach), II, 286
Brazil, produces no wine or wheat, II, 216; times for voyages from, 217; no foreigners trade with, 218; slaves of, compared with African, 221; appearance of, 306; description of, 311-320; import and export duties, 314; silver, *ib.*; mode of life in, 314-317; revenues of, 315
Brazil wood, II, 216, 217
Brazilians, conversion of, II, 311; described, 317, 318
Brearou Leacaru (?), II, 491
Brière, M. Louis, I, xlviii
Brifaut, a Frenchman, II, 326
Brokers, sworn, at Goa, II, 177
Brothels, none in Port. India, II, 115
Buddha's tooth, II, 145
Buddhism, at the Maldives, traces of, I, 123, 174
Budkhána, II, 446
Buffaloes, II, 45
Burgonets, II, 127
Burial, at the Maldives, I, 156-161; in Malabar, 394; at sea, French mode of, II, 202
Buttoncauters, I, 182
Buzios (shells, *i.e.,* cowries), I, 237, 238; II, 485
Bybis (ladies), I, 217

Cabaya, I, 372, 373
Cabexa de las Ilhas, I, 98
Cabo, fort, II, 29
Cacoué (crab), I, 97
Cadamosto, his discovery of C. Verd islands, I, 8
Cadjans, II, 377
Cady, I, 138, 199; *see also Pandiare and Kazi*
Caelle (Káyal), II, 108, 377, 383
Caerden, P. van, I, xiii
Caes da Santa Catherina, II, 44
Caffres, of Ethiopia, I, 307; at Cochin, I, 427; at Goa, II, 3, 17, 22; excellent slaves, 221, 222; description of, 232; stink of, *ib.*; war with Portuguese, II, 234
Cafila, fleet under convoy, I, 438; II, xxii
Cahoa. See **Coffee.**
Cairo, I, 250, 285; II, 108; *and see* **Coir.**
Cajus (fruit), I, 328
Calamba (*lignum aloes*), I, 335; II, 360
Calans (princes), I, 209, 271
Calbalolan (burial), I, 156
Caldera, Dom Francisco de, II, 278
Calico, I, 371
Calicut, P. embarks in ship of, I, 326; Dutch frequenting, *ib.*; arrival at, I, 361; custom-house at, 362-3; crowded population, 366; acrobats at, *ib.*; Portuguese driven out of, 374, 375; relations with Portuguese thereafter, 405; freedom of religion at, 390, 404, 405; description of the country, 399; of the city, 401-407; church at, 406; administration of justice, 407; palace at, 409-411, 413-414; daily market, 411, 412; mint, 412; secretariat, 413; in 15th century, II, 470-472
Calin, also *callin* and *cally* (Malay tin), I, 235, 441; II, 68, 176
Callo, I, 218
Calogue (*or Callogue*), I, 56, 69, 217
Camara da cidade (town hall), II, 53
Camara presidial, II, 49
Camarade, II, 325
Cambalis, II, 240
Cambay, ship of, I, 301, 302; visited by P., II, 23; tortoiseshell manufactures, II, 248, 348; trade

of, II, 245-249 ; people, language, etc., 250
Cambe (tortoiseshell), I, 240, 285
Camenaz (princesses), I, 209
Camlets, of Persia and Ormuz, II, 240
Campbell, Capt. C., I, 83
Camphor, II, 169
Campo do paço, II, 49
Camulo, I, 218
Camulloques, I, 217
Campveer, I, 22
Canada (pint measure), II, 73, 194
Canarese (*i.e.*, Konkáni) language, II, 405
Canarins, one turns Mussulman, I, 302, 303; description of, 375, 376 ; of Goa, II, 28, 35
Canary Islands, I, xx, 7; exports to Brazil, II, 216 ; wine, 316
Canboé Boubou, a Bengali woman, I, 259
Candis cacan, I, 145
Candou, I, 103, 247; *and see* **Channels.**
Candou (wood), used for raising stone, etc., I, 119-122 ; for coffins, 156
Candouepatis (raft), I, 67, 122, 191
Candú, islands, II, 481
Cangelotte (*Kányirótu* or *Cassergode*), a Malabar port, I, 344
Cannanor, raja of, welcomes Maldive prince, I, 277 ; expedition to and partial conquest of M., 320, 321; suzerainty over Minicoy, 323; over the Laccadives, 324
Cannanor, a Malabar kingdom, I, 369 ; description of, I, 443 446; relations of Mahommedans and Nairs at, 444; Portuguese fort at, 445 ; II, 259
Cannibalism, II, 318
Cannon, of the *Corbin*, the object of the Bengal invasion, I, 317, 325
Canton, I, 335
Caparou (Kafir or infidel), I, 261
Cape of Good Hope, I, 20, 21 ; II, 291-295 ; a Portuguese Lethe, II, 121
Capitão Mór, of Goa, II, 16, 33 ; of armada, II, 118, 200
Capitulation, terms of (*bonne guerre*), II, 193, 200, 208
Capon (funeral money), I, 157
Captain of a Portuguese ship, powers of, II, 188, 189
Captivos, II, 90
Capucines, monastery of, II, 31, 33
Carans (secretary), I, 210, 214
Caravels, as despatch boats, II, 180, 189 ; chiefly used for W. Indies, 215 ; tonnage of, *ib.*
Carceres (prisons of the Inquisition) II, 18
Cardaen, P. van, II, 29, 225
Cards, games of, II, 111
Caré (coco-nut), I, 113 ; II, 372
Caridou (*Karhidu* or *Kardiva*), island and channel, I, 130
Cariuadiri (small-pox), I, 181
Carmelites, monastery at Bahia, II, 311
Carpets, of Bengal, I, 328 ; of Persia, II, 239; of Cambay, 248
Carracks, description of, II, 180-184; how manned and officered, 184-197; berths sold, 185 ; service in, more esteemed than in other ships, 186 ; number of crew, 186, 187; prisons on, 191 ; kitchens and fires, 192 ; silver only exported on behalf of king, 193, 211 ; provisioning of, 194 ; pay and profits of officers and men, 195; filthy condition of, II, xxxiii, 196; religious rites on board, 197; rules as to touching land on voyage, 197; times of departure and arrival, 197-199 ; captains decline to sail together, 200 ; crews often unpaid, 201; tonnage of, 208; offices on, given to widows and orphans, 196, 209 ; goods carried on behalf of private merchants, 211 ; foreigners sometimes get aboard, 212; must make for Cochin

or Quilon, 213 ; sometimes laden at Cochin, *ib.* ; overtaken at Mozambique, 226. *See also names of particular carracks.*
Cartas (passports), II, 205
Carts, use of, at Goa, II, 63
Casa da India, II, xxiii; II, 119, 212
Casa do Arcebispo, II, 53
Casado, II, 125
Cassergode. *See Cangelotte.*
Cassia, II, 361
Cassin Tacourou, I, 275
Caste, remains of, at Maldives, I, 114, 170
Castello Branco, João de, II, 475
Castici (pure Portuguese born in India) II, 38
Castilian captain, II, 21
Castille, arms of, II, 3
Castro, João de, II, xxiii ; his cruelties, xxvi, xxvii ; memorial of his triumph, II, 13
Castro, Martim Affonso de, Viceroy, I, 375 ; proceeds to Achin and Malacca, II, xvi, 152, 266 ; death, xvii, 2, 155 ; failure of attack on Achin, 160
Catel, island, II, 166
Cathecuminos, II, 60
Cathedral of Goa, II, 53
Catherina, Donna, II, xiii
Catibe (priest), I, 70, 110, 125, 127, 212 ; may be also Naib, 186 ; of the King's island, 131-133 ; of other islands, I, 198
Cats, at the Maldives, I, 116
Caty (bill-hook), I, 79
Caueny (weddings), I, 150
Caury (cowry), I, 438
Cauuery (sorcery), I, 180. *See also Quenuery.*
Cavalleyro Fidalguo, II, 120
Cavallo, a fish, so called, I, 388, 427; II, 127, 294, 299
Caz (itch), I, 181
Cenes (or **Seine**), Father Jean de, II, 36, 270
Cemetery of the French, I, 34
Certidon (Port. *certidão*), II, 123, 305, 309
Ceylon, Maldives colonised from, I, 105, 266 ; a ship of, 299-301; her cinnamon, 320 ; visited by P., II, xiii, 23, 140 ; description of, 140-145 ; people, 142 ; precious stones, 143
Chaa (Shah), II, 253
Chagas, As, carrack, II, xx, 182, 183
Chagos (archipelago), referred to, I, 50, *n* ; I, 296, 297
Chains, silver waist, I, 164
Cháliyam, I, 368, 423-425
Chaly. *See* **Cháliyam.**
Cham, Great, of Tartary, II, 251
Chamy, a ship captain, I, 278
Changngdtam (guides), I, 340
Channels of the Maldives, I, 99-104
Chandelor *v.* **Lopus,** case of, II, 484
Chapins (or *chopins* ; Ital. *cioppino*), II, 102, 104
Chapter-bread, II, 286, 398
Charms, use of, I, 178-180
Chartican. *See* **Chittagong.**
Charts, Maldive, I, 65, 99
Chatigam. *See* **Chittagong.**
Chaul, erroneous reference to, I, 327; referred to, II, 2; described, II, 256-258 ; Englishmen at, 265
Chaydes (martyrs), I, 161, 319
Cheraffes (shroffs), II, 67
Cherife, I, 272, 304, 365
Chersonese, Golden, II, 233
Cherufins. *See* **Xerafim.**
Chess, I, 418
Chetils (or *chatie*), applied to merchant ships, I, 345 ; II, 117
Chigoe, II, 319
China, wares of, I, 329 ; goods for, shipped at Goa, II, 175
China-root, I, 182 ; II, 13
Chinale, lieutenant of Kunháli, II, 516, 523, 526
Chinese, said to have peopled Madagascar, I, 38
Chinese at Bantam, II, 163 ; cunning rogues, 171

Chittagong (*Chartican*), expedition from, to the M., I, xxv, xxvi, 310 *et seq.*; arrival of P. at, 326 ; raja of, *ib.*, 333 ; departure from, 336

Cholera, II, 13

Chombais (Chombaye), I, 336, 338, 344, 345

Christ, Order of, II, 503, 505

Christian king of the Maldives, I, 57; his factor at Málé, 85, 260 ; revenues of, 200 ; government in name of, 247; reference to, in treaty, 250 ; gave one-third of his revenue to Portugal, 250 ; his Portuguese ambassador, 293, 294

Christmas, celebration of, at Goa, II, 97, 98

Christopher, Lieut., his visit to the Maldives, I, xliv ; death, xlv-vi ; description of a funeral, 158

Chudders, I, 222

Chunan (chunam), II, 135

Church-going at Goa, II, 101-104

Cinco Chagas, church of, II, 41 ; carrack, so named, *see Chagas.*

Cingala (Sinhalese), captain, I, 300, 301

Cingalla (Sinhalese), characteristics of, II, 142

Cingalles (Sinhalese), I, 267

Cinnamon in Ceylon galley, I, 299-301, 320 ; grows wild in Ceylon, II, 141, 143 ; description of, 358

Circumcision, I, 128-130; day of the, II, 82

Cisdy (cook), I, 173

Civet, II, 172, 360

Clerigos, II, 96

Clerk, ships', II, 187, 188, 394

Cloves, II, 166, 167, 357

Cobolly mas (fish), I, 190, 194 ; II, 439

Cochin, a ship of, at Málé, I, 78; buys salvage of *Corbin*, 80; carracks load and discharge at, II, 213; relations of, with Calicut, 369; suffers affronts from the Portuguese, 375 ; a captain of, and his family, I, 428 ; prison of, 429-432 ; description of country and city, 433-438; formerly subject to Calicut, 434; two towns of, 434, 436 ; port closed by sand, 437; trade with Bengal in cowries, 438

Cochin, Bishop of, II, 27

Cock, sacrifice of, I, 178, 180; medical use of liver of, 181

Cock-fighting, II, 54

Cockroaches, II, 286

Cocks, Richard, II, xx

Coco, origin of name, II, 372, 483

Coconut, abundance of, at Maldives, I, 113 ; uses of, *ib.;* II, 324 *et seq.* ; price of, I, 117; drinking the young, I, 172; general description of tree, etc., II, 372-385 ; description of, by Ibn Batuta, II, 439 ; by de Barros 482. Sea-coconut, *see* **Coco-de-mer.**

Coconut cabbage, II, 383

Coco-de-mer, I, 230-232

Coco-sugar. *See* **Jaggery.**

Coco-wine, I, 71 ; *and see* **Arack** *and* **Toddy.**

Coffee, drunk at the Maldives, I, 172

Cognialy. See **Kunhāli.**

Coilan (Quilon), I, 369, 370 ; II, 107

Coin, of the Maldives, I, 232 ; of Portuguese India, II, 68, 69

Coir, dues of, I, 228, 250 ; trading in, 285 ; mode of preparation, II, 379 ; described by Batuta, 443, 444

Colchas (coverlets), II, 247

Collo madous atoll. *See* **Koḷumaḍulu.**

Colombo, II, 143

Coluotte (Kollam), I, 360

Coly (bell), I, 130, 138

Combolly masse, I, 194 ; *and see Cobolly mas.*

Comedy, performed on doubling the Cape, II, 295

Commeres (Port. *comadres*), II, 100

Communion, ticket or token for, II, 97

Comorro Islands, I, xxiii ; arrival

at, 42; description of natives, 42-48
Companions of Pyrard, I, 91, 92 *n.*; the three surviving, at time of Bengal invasion, 313; remain at Moutingué, 346; one goes to Koṭṭakal, 346, 347; Hollander remains at Calicut, 421, 424; the French carpenter, II, 305, 306, 308, 309
Compasses, three on carracks, II, 191
Comperes (Port. *compadres*), II, 100
Compostella, author's vow to make pilgrimage to, I, 310; performed, I, 335-337
Confession, a public, I, 295
Congnare (a tree), II, 368
Congo, trade with, II, 221
Conrart, founder of French Academy, I, xxxiv
Consent, ship, I, xiii
Consett, s.s., wrecked on the Maldives in 1880, I, 106
Constable (or master gunner), II, 187
Contador, II, 42
Contretador, II, 172
Converso, an erroneous term, II, 189, 190
Convez, mid-ship deck, II, 189
Convicts, of Portugal sent out as colonists to Angola, II, 218; garrison Ceylon, II, 143
Copper cups, I, 172
Copra, II, 384
Coquetees, I, 240
Coral, black, I, 232
Corbin (ship), I, xiv, xv; summary of voyage, xx-xxiii; tonnage, etc., 2; accident to, 5; misconduct of crew, 5, 27, 55, 62; II, 398-403; chief merchant of (*see* **Moreau**); condition of, at Madagascar, 40; total crew of, *ib.*; runs aground at the Maldives, 51; fortunes of the shipwrecked crew, 56 *et seq.* (*see special references*, 91, 92 *n.*); cannon of the, 58, 325; silver of, 60 *et seq.*, 72; ensign of the, 220; carpenter of, II, 304, 306, 308, 309
Coriche, II, 510, 518
Corpses, Portuguese fable as to floating, II, 202
Corpus Christi, anticipated in India, II, 35
Correa, Bras, II, xx, 279
Corunna, II, 337
Corvo, island, II, 332
Cosmas, quoted, II, 427
Costa, Francisco da, II, 512
Costé, I, 347, 357, 358, 359; *and see Marcaire Costé* and **Kunhâli.**
Cotignats, II, 261
Cotta, a measure, I, 237
Cotton bought raw and worked up by Maldivians, I, 241; export from Bengal, 228; cotton trees, II, 364
Cotton cloths, use of, as hangings, I, 146, 222; dues of, I, 228; fineness of Bengal, 328
Couelan. *See* **Quilon.**
Couesme (Cuama, *i.e.*, the Zambesi), II, 223-235
Coulombin (a low caste), I, 387; II, 35
Coulon, his part in the voyages of Le Blanc, I, xxxix
Couroan. *See* **Kuran.**
Cousty Hamede, a Malabar, I, 339, 349; II, 108; his brother, II, 46
Cousty Moussey (or *Cutimuça*), I, 352, 355; II, 512
Coutinho, Dom Diogo, II, 241, 262
Coutinho, Dom Pedro, II, 241, 242, 277
Couto, Diogo de, his description of the Samorin, I, 415; his *Decadas*, II, xxiii; his *Soldado Pratico*, xxix; on Portuguese gunners, 193; his account of siege of Kóṭṭakkal, II, 509-527; visits Kunhâli in prison, 516
Cowries, export of, from Maldives, I, 78, 236-240; II, 484, 485; values of, I, 236, 237; scattered at fune-

rals, I, 157; dues of, I, 228; mode of collection, I, 236, 237; as ornaments for furniture, I, 240; trade from Cochin to Bengal, 438; use in W. Africa, II, 219; mention by early travallers, II, 429-432, 443, 444

Cows, at the Maldives, I, 116; II, 485

Crabs, I, 97; II, 351

Cranganor, II, 259

Créadas (female servants), II, 103

Criados (servants), II, 89, 90

Crignon, Pierre, poet, I, xi

Cris, I, 164; II, 162, 170

Crocodile, musk smell of, I, 37, 38; II, 347; in Ganges, I, 336; description of, II, 347

Croisade (Southern Cross), I, 9

Croissant (ship), I, xiv, xv; summary of voyage to Maldives, xx-xxiii; tonnage, etc., 2; off Natal, 26; arrival at St. Augustine's Bay, 30; refitting there, 40; loses her boat, 48, 49; subsequent fortunes of, I, 290, 291; at St. Helena, II, 109

Cross of solid gold, II, 59

Crows, I, 115

Cruzado, II, 83

Cuama (Zambesi), II, 233-235

Cunat, quoted, I, 3, 7

Currents, at the Maldives, I, 101, 257

Dabul, II, 256, 259

Dáhará, I, 210, 211, 213

Daman, II, 256

Damascus raisins, II, 261

Dár, II, 450

Darada Tacourou, I, 270

Darumavanta, II, 449

Dasoure (?), I, 442

Dates, of Socotora, II, 237

Datura, use of, in India, II, 113, 114

Daugim, fort, II, 33

Dauphin, birth of (Louis XIII), I, 290

Davis, Captain John, I, 31; II, 490

Dead-pays, II, 42

Dealcan. *See* **Deccan.**

Debt slavery, I, 202-204; described by Ibn Batuta, II, 445

Deccan, kingdom of, II, 24, 25, 32, 131; king of, besieges Goa, 132, 134; treaty with Portuguese, 133; no extradition between Goa and, 133; description of, 133, 134, 136; ambassador at Goa, 134, 135; war with Great Mogul, 134; princes of, at Goa, 135-138; elephants, diamonds, etc., 136; dress of natives, *ib.*

Déherd, I, 210; II, 453; *and see Dáhará.*

Demy tengue (half tanga), I, 432

De La Croix. *See* **La Croix.**

Delhi (spelt *Dirly*), II, 251

Deli, Mount, II, 477

Della Valle, Pietro, quoted, II, 505

Denis, Ferdinand, mistake as to Pyrard, I, xviii

Deos de Misericordia, II, 100

Desambargador Mór, II, 49

Destrappes, Leonard, Archbishop, I, xxx

Deuanits (sergeants), I, 139, 150, 201, 206, 212

Devil, author of sickness, I, 180; worship of, *ib.*

Devil-dancers, I, 395

Dharmapála, king of Ceylon, II, xiv

Dhîbat Almahal, Ar. name of Maldives, II, 436

Diamonds, of the Deccan, II, 236

Dice, use of, at Goa, II, 111

Dida (flag), I, 129

Diego de Roys, supposed islands, I, xxiii, 49

Diego Rodriguez (island), erroneously called de Roys, I, 50; sighted, II, 290

Dieppe, I, x

Digga tree, bark of, I, 121

Dishes, banana leaves used for, I, 170; wooden, 171

Diu, II, 23 ; described, 254, 255
Diu matil (Friday), I, 130
Divandurou (Laccadive islands), I, 323-325 ; a ship of, II, 108
Dives (islander), I, 83
Dives (islands), I. 117
Divorce, I, 153-155
Dogs, hatred of, I, 116
Dombe. *See* **Domburgh**.
Domburgh, Martin, a factor, wrecked at the Maldives, I, 292 ; met at Cochin, 430 ; mysterious death, II, 108-110
Dominican monk, I, 441, 442, 451
Dominicans, church of, II, 49, 71
Donkora, II, 456
Donny (bird, and name of boat), I, 86
Dorados (fish), I, 189
Dorimenaz (general of militia), I, 210, 211, 214, 273
D'Oyly, Sir J., quoted, I, 203
Dragon, ship, II, 237
Dragons (heavy squalls), I, 11
Drinking, mode of, in India, I, 378, 410, 411; II, 72, 73
Drug, which kills on a day certain, II, 129
Drums, how made at Maldives, II, 385
Dugong, I, 47
Dunkirk, author ships in vessel of, II, 330
Dupleix, I, xi
Duret, Charles, dedication to, II, xliii
Durian tree, II, 366
Durries, II, 248
Dutch (or Hollanders), interdicted from Lisbon traffic, I, xii ; fleets of, xiii; nine ships met, 5-7; cruisers off Galle, 278; two Dutchmen come to Maldives, 281; frequent Calicut, 326; confused with French and English, 337, 347; thirteen ships at Calicut, 364; at Cannanor, 448; policy in the East, II, xxxv ; blockade Goa, II, 29 ; capture part of C. de Feira's fleet, 86; incidents of war with Portuguese, 148-150 ; relations with Achin, 158, 159 ; at Bantam, 164; traffic between India and the islands, 171 ; give good terms of capitulation, 149, 193, 200; effect of, on Portuguese, 201, 207, 208 ; six ships blockade Goa, 207 ; sieges of Mozambique, 225-229 ; attack Ormuz ship, 261
Dutroa. *See* **Datura**.
Du Vair, G. Bishop, I, xxx ; dedication to, liii
Du Val, P., editor of 4th edition, I, xxxi
Dyes, used at Maldives, I, 241, 242 ; made from coconut, II, 384

Ears, extension of, for ornaments, I, 167, 384, 419
Ear-rings, I, 167
Earthenware of the Maldives, I, 170
Earthly Paradise, I, 335 ; II, 140, 141
Easter, celebration of, at Goa, II, 98
Eau-de-vie (arack), I, 358
Ebony, of Mozambique, II, 224 ; generally, 362
Ecclesiastics, in India, II, 95, 96 ; on board P. ships, 127, 187; not allowed to return, 187, 284
Eclipse of the sun, I, 308
Edrisi, quoted, II, 431
Edwardes, Sir H., I, xlvi
Elephantiasis, I, 392
Elephants of Bengal, I, 331; white, 333 ; at Calicut, 400 ; at Goa, II, 41 ; description of, 343-346
Elevator, at Bahia, II, 310
Elizabeth, Queen, her death referred to, I, 278, 290
Ellattúr (river), I, 359
Elmina, fort, II, 221, 222
Emir-el-Bahr. *See Mirvaires.*
Endequery, I, 210, 213
Enganado el Rey, II, 212
English, first voyages of discovery, I, xii ; confused with French and Dutch, 337, 347; position in the

Far East, II, xvii; in India, xxxvi; some at Goa, 36; proud as compared with Dutch, 107; called Kings of the Sea, 203
Englishmen referred to (*see* **Pilot, Wickham, Stevens, Hawkins, Lancaster, Middleton**); one put to death by the Portuguese, II, 106; crew of *Hector* referred to, *ib.*; a gunner of the *Croissant*, 107; number of, at Goa, II, xviii, 269; some made prisoners at Lisbon, 276; a traveller from Tartary, 278; one nearly hanged at Bahia, 326, 327
English ships, at Comoros, I, 45; at Socotora, II, 237
Enseada (bay), II, 293
Escritorios, II, 177
Escuderi Fidalguo, II, 120
Esdru (fencing-master), I, 268
Esperes (small cannon), II, 183
Esquif (bed), II, 4
Essomerique, I, x
Estancelin, quoted, I, x, 2
Esteres (mats), I, 391; II, 103, 237
Esure (zebra), II, 324, 355
Ethiopian coast, I, 25
Eunuchs, references to, I, 173, 332
Europa shoals, II, 199
Exports, to India and profits on, II, 211; to Brazil, 216
Eyes, ailments of, I, 181; putting out of, II, 137, 242

Fádifolu (Padypolo) atoll, I, 97, 99
Faenza, I, 170
Fah Hian, quoted, II, 427
Fál, a number or measure, I, 237; ii, 444
False money, reference to charges of possessing, in France, I, 231; passing of, by Europeans in the East, II, 159
Falmeldari (treasurer), II, 451; *and see Pammedery.*
Fámudéri. See Pammedery.
Fandayarkalú, II, 450; *and see Pandiare.*
Farangui (Franks), I, 183, 243; II, 201
Farangui baescour (syphilis), I, 182
Farhind, I, 210; *and see Parenas.*
Faria y Souza, Manoel, historian, II, 518; comment on execution of Kunhâli, 527
Fayance. *See* **Faenza.**
Fehendu (island), author taken to, I, 59
Feira, Conde de, appointed viceroy, II, xx; dies on the voyage, 85, 86, 267, 275; fleet of, 86
Felidu (*Poulisdon*) atoll, I, 97, 99; channel, 104
Fencing, I, 141
Fencing-masters, I, 268-270, 380, 381
Fendu (island). *See* **Fehendu.**
Fernambucque. *See* **Pernambuco.**
Fernando, Manuel, II, 129, 283
Ferreira, Belchior, II, 514, 515
Ferreyra Belliago, Domingos, commands expedition to Maldives, II, 507
Festivities, on passing the Abrolhos, I, 19
Fever, the Maldive, I, 82, 83, 180-181, 267
Feynes, Henri (Count de Monfart), II, xx, 279, 280
Fiance, II, 100
Fidalgo, II, 78, 120
Fidalgo de la Casa del Rey nosso Señor, II, 120
Figs, Indian, bananas so called, I, 113
Filippe, Dom, exiled Maldive prince, I, 294; II, 138, 139, 502-508
Finisterre, Cape, I, 291
Fire, mode of generating, I, 122; regulation of, on ships, II, 192
Fish, at the Maldives, modes of fishing, I, 189-194; fish kraal, 192-194; greatly eaten at Goa, II, 105
Fish-kraal, I, 192-194
Fishes for splicing masts, II, 183

Fishing, modes of, at Maldives, I, 189-194
Flemings on board the French ships, I, xiv, xxvii; a gunner, 29; a truant, 39; survivors at Málé, 78, 80; escape and death of four, 85-87; a clever wood-carver, 91; two, at Bahia, 330
Flemings, some at Goa, II, 36
Flemish hulks, I, 5; II, 184
Florentine, at Bahia, II, 309, 325
Flores, island, II, 332
Flour, exported from the Azores, II, 216
Flying-fish, I, 9; II, 352
Flying-foxes, I, 115; II, 373
Football, I, 137, 138, 187
Formosa, bay, I, 23
Fortaleza del vice Rey, La, II, 47
Fougons, ships' kitchens, II, 192
France, neglect of navigation, I, 1; talk about, with Maldive king, 77, 242, 243; Samorin asks about king of, I, 363; treaty with Spain, II, 23
Franciscans, royal treasury at convent of, II, 50; convent of, 53; baptism in church of, 61; two embark without leave, 284; invoke St. Francis, 304; monastery at Bahia, 311
Francisco, Dom, Maldive prince, death of, II, 497
François, Isle de, at Bahia, II, 309
François, Jean, II, 487
Franqui (Franks), I, 183, 243; II, 201
French, confused with English and Dutch, I, 337, 347
Frenchmen, some at Goa, II, 36; in Brazil, 321-324; thirteen hanged at Bahia, 326
French ships, promotion in, I, 15; messmates in (*see* **Messmates**); manning and equipment of, II, 393-403
Frigates, II, 118
Friday, celebration of, I, 130-134, 224, 225; no business done on, 175; an unlucky day, II, 400
Frotet. *See* **Bardelière**.
Frotet de la Landelle, I, 3
Fua Mulaku island, ruins at, I, 124; II, 488-491
Fuladú island, I, xxiii; landing at, 55; party left at, 59; their condition, 61-68
Funeral ceremonies at the Maldives, I, 156-161; in Malabar, 394
Furadi. *See Pouraddé*.
Furtado, João, a captain, I, 423
Furtado de Mendoça, André, leads expedition against Kunhâli, I, 354; II, 518-526; his expedition to the Moluccas in 1601; II, xv; becomes Governor of India, xvii, 267; career of, xix; victories in Ceylon, 145, 512; his defence of Malacca, 151, 152; quarrel with Coutinho, 242; activity, 268; petition in his favour, 271; appointed general of homeward fleet, 273-276; general sorrow at departure of, 276; death, 277
Furtado de Mendoça, Diego, nephew of the preceding, II, 268, 389

Galetaire, a kind of bonnet, II, 112
Galicia, I, 310; II, 333, 335
Galion of the *Corbin*, I, 53-56; orders as to, on Portuguese ships, II, 306
Galiots, of the Malabars, I, 341, 342; one runs through a Portuguese fleet, 345; Portuguese oarsmen of, II, 117
Galle, Dutch ships off, I, 278; II, 140, 148; doubling, I, 325; a Portuguese fort, II, 143
Galley slaves, II, 45, 46
Galleys, rowed by convicts, II, 117
Gallows, at Cochin, I, 427; at Goa, II, 56; at Bahia, 326
Gama, Francisco da, viceroy, I, 353; causes memorial arch to be built,

II, xxxviii; character, 512; receives news of his brother's defeat, 517; conduct at Furtado's triumph, 524-526

Gama, Luiz da (misspelt *Louys de Gusman*), his expedition against Kunháli, I, 353-354; II, 513, 518

Gama, Vasco da, note on his first landing-place in India, I, 360; referred to, II, xxxii; statue of, xxxviii

Game, an island, I, 250

Gaming-houses, II, 111, 112

Gandoyre (palace), I, 218, 219; also written *Gandhouere*, 316

Ganga. *See* **Ganges**.

Ganges, I, 335, 336

Gardafui, Cape, II, 236

Gargoulettes (goglets), I, 329; II, 74

Garie, Jean (? Garcia), I, 334

Garoa (aloes wood), II, 360

Gas, an exclamation, I, 197

Gaspar Dias, fort, II, 25, 32

Gaspard Aleman, Father, II, 22, 269

Gaut or *Gaux* (a weight), I, 189, 286

Gayac, II, 318

Germans, some at Goa, II, 36, 51

Gerun (Ormuz), II, 238

Gilolo, island, II, 166

Ginger, Bengal, I, 328; of Brazil, II, 217, 313; competes with pepper in market, 217, 356; generally, 356

Girasal, a kind of rice, II, 326

Glass, Venetian, I, 43

Gleau (whip), I, 307

Goa, soil red, I, 376; II, 27; hospital, I, 451; administration of, II, xi, xii; inscription over gate, 3; common ailments at, 11; prisons of, 18; description of, 24 *et seq.*; river, 24, 28, 31, 32; proverb as to Lisbon and, 26; suffragan bishop of, *ib.*; forts of, 29-33; parishes of, 33; permits for the mainland, *ib.*; passages, 33, 34; inhabitants classified, 35-39; walls of, 39; esplanades and quays, 40-48; galleys, 45; palace (*see* **Viceroy**); streets, 51, 52, 57; churches, 32, 41, 49, 51, 53-61; celebration of capture of, 54; buildings, 63; condition of, in rains, 63, 64; markets, 69, 178; water-supply, 70-72; farmers of the revenue, 74, 174, 178; wealth of, 105; gaming saloons, 111, 112; life of soldiers at, 128-131; sieges of, 132-133; trade with Far East, 173-177; is the entrepôt for the whole East, 213; language spoken about, 405

Godam (wheat), I, 112

Goidú, island, I, xxiii

Gold, not exported from the Maldives, I, 242; worth less in India than in Spain, II, 69; brought from Far East, 176; of Sofala and the Zambesi, 233

Gold, ornaments, worn by king only, I, 164; and by women, 167, 168

Gomen (ambergris), I, 229

Gomes Cheiradinheiro, João, II, 476, 480, 486

Gonville, Paulmier de, I, x

Gonville, Abbé Binot Paulmier de, I, x

Gouia. *See* **Gouveia.**

Gouldrins (coverlets), II, 4

Gourabe (galley), I, 312

Gouradou (island), I, 256, 257, 259, 318

Gourmet, a ship's apprentice, II, 187

Gouveia, Dom Adrian de, ambassador to Maldives, I, 293, 294; II, 139, 502

Goymon (Sargasso weed), II, 331

Gram, referred to, II, 79

Grande, Ruo, II, 55

Grass-silk, I, 328

Gravestones, at the Maldives, I, 159

Grooms, at Goa, skill of, II, 79

Grotius, I, ix, x, 3

Grout, François, captain of the *Corbin*, i, xiv, 3; particulars of his family, *ib.*; quarrel with chief merchant, I, 17; II, 398; falls sick at

Madagascar, I, 34; dies at Málé, 59, 78; inhuman treatment of, on deathbed, 87; character of, II, 398-401
Grout de St. Georges, I, 3
Guardian, a ship's officer, II, 187, 189, 192
Gué (house), I, 315
Guinea, I, 10
Guise, Duc de, I, 430
Gulistán, name of a slave, II, 454
Gundara-karayó, the Maldives so-called by the Sinhalese, I, 83
Gundura, II, 442, 472
Gunners, incompetence of Portuguese, II, 193
Guzerat captain, dies, I, 299
Guzerati people, II, 249; language, II, 405
Gymnosophists, I, 379

Haddummati (*Adoumatis*) atoll, I, 97, 99, 300
Hadégiri (an officer of state), I, 210, 211; *and see Endequery.*
Hagen, Steven van der, I, 277, 364; II, xv, xvi, 29
Hair-oils, used at the M., I, 107
Hajji, privileges of, I, 165
Hakurá (an officer). *See Acouraz.*
Haly. See Ali.
Hammocks, beds like, at the Maldives, I, 222; in India, II, 248
Hangings, silk and cotton, I, 221, 222
Harmansen, W., I, xiii, 7
Hasan, king of the Maldives, I, 244, 245; II, 477, 493, 532; *see also* **Manoel.**
Hassan kilage-fánu, rebellion of, I, 247-250; becomes joint king, I, 249; death, 252
Hawkins, William, I, xiii; II, 253, 263, 264
Hayton, Prince, quoted, II, 434
Hector, ship, I, xiii; at Socotora, II, 237; crew of, at Goa, II, xviii, 237; how they were kidnapped, II, 263, 264
Heemskerk, J. van, I, xiii, xx, 7
Henry IV, news of death of, II, 320
Herons, II, 353
Hidalcan. *See* **Deccan.**
Hieronimo di Santo Stefano visits Maldives, II, 469
Hilaire, Father, a Jesuit, I, 420, 426
Hitadú, island, I, 300
Hollanders mentioned, chief carpenter of the *Corbin*, I, 28; a jeweller at Goa, II, 95. *See* **Domburgh.**
Hololi, island, II, 467
Homan (fever), I, 180
Homo branco, II, 12, 121
Honore. *See* **Onor.**
Honorifics, in use at Goa, II, 82
Honrado, II, 120
Hooks, fish, form of, I, 189
Horses, at Goa, II, 67, 75, 79; broken in the Deccan, 136; export from Ormuz, II, 239
Horta (garden), II, 28, 110
Hospital, at Goa, I, 451; II, xi, xii; inscription over gate, 3; description of, 3-15; administered by the Jesuits, 6; number of inmates, 7, 8; number of deaths, 11; property of the sick, *ib.*; none except Portuguese men admitted, 12; viceroy's physician appointed to charge of, 14
Hospitals for natives and women, II, 15
Hottentots, observed, II, 294; described, 295
Houssains Caca, a Malabar, I, 268; put to death, 271; had taken part in conspiracy, 275-276
Houtman, Cornelius de, I, xiii
Houtman, Frederik de, his sojourn at the Maldives, II, 489-490
Huadiva or **Huvadú** (atoll). *See* **Suadiva.**
Huet, Bishop of Avranches, I, xxxiv-xli

Hukuru. (Friday.) *See Oucourou.*
Hulks, I, 5
Hypocras, II, 382

Iader (chudders), I, 222
Ibn Batuta, quoted, summary of his travels, II, 434-435 ; editions of his book, 436 ; his description of the Maldives, II, 434-468 ; names of islands, 437; his marriages at, 439, 455, 458, 460 ; appointed kázi, 459; quarrels with ministry, 460-464 ; leaves Maldives, 466; returns, 466, 467; final departure, 468 ; sultans named by, 529, 531
Ibrahim, king of the Maldives, promise to send the crew to Achin, I, 59, 64, 66, 78, 81; anger towards his brother-in-law, 69; inquisitiveness of, 77, 224, 242-244; provides drugs for the sick, 84 ; care for Pyrard, 85, 89; fond of fishing, 188, 224 ; dress of, 222, 223 ; royal insignia, I, 223 ; mode of eating, 224 ; artistic taste, *ib.* ; his guards, *ib.* ; puts to death the young Mestif, 255 ; as a trader, 228 ; his genealogy, 244-256 ; not a warrior, 252, 256 ; frequent conspiracies against, 255, 266 ; attempts to murder a pilot, 262; and marries his wife, *ib.*; marries his nephew's wife, 263 ; favours a young Malabar, 268-271 ; receives his nephew into favour, 271-273 ; devices to capture ship, 286-289 ; cruelty towards Guzerati sailors, 293 ; pride towards ambassador from Goa, 294; sends presents to Achin, 296 ; conduct of the invasion, 312 ; death, 314 ; burial, 318, 319; place in list of kings, II, 533
Ibrahim Callane (nephew of the king), I, 271 ; received into favour, 273 ; abducts a wife, 273, 315; conducts exchange of hostages, 288; drowned, 314, 315
Ibrahim, lord of Tuladu Island, I, 56
Igovos, African name for cowries, II, 485
Images, Portuguese use of, II, 303, 304
India (meaning Western India), I, 334; II, 256
India, languages of, II, 405
India, Portuguese, arms of, I, 439 ; II, 3; sketch of history of, II, xxiv-xxxiv, xxxvi, xxxvii ; reasons for maintaining dominion, 88
India voyage, seasons to be observed, II, 386, 393 ; equipment necessary for, 386-388, 392
Indian fig, *i.e.*, banana, II, 345, 364
Indian fig, wild (*i.e.*, banyan), II, 370
Indian ships believed to be larger than European, I, 258; description of, *ib.*; built by Europeans, II, 181
Indian soldiers at Goa, II, 125
Indigo, II, 246, 359
Indus, I, 336
Inez, Dona, Maldive princess, II, 503, 505, 508
Infanticide at the Maldives, I, 264
Innamaus, flower, II, 371
Innan (bathing), I, 174
Innapa, tree, I, 169 ; II, 370
Inquisition of Goa, prisoners of, II, 18; house of the, 52, 53 ; its procedure, 92-95 ; condemns prince of Ormuz, 244
Inscriptions at the Maldives, I, 125, 159
Iris plant, ginger compared to, II, 356
Irmanos (of the Misericordia), II, 20
Irmanos em armas, II, 204
Iroudemaus (a jasmine), II, 371
Isa-al-Yamani, a lawyer and vizier, II, 446, 452, 453
Ispahan, II, 279
Itadou. *See* **Hitadú.**
Italians at Goa, II, 36, 51; are the best received in P. India, 212
Itch, i, 181

Itelpoul (a kind of flour), I, 111
Ivory, trade at the Congo, II, 221; from Mozambique coast, 224

Jack-tree, II, 366
Jackals in Malabar, I, 400
Jacobins. *See* **Dominicans.**
Jaggery (coco-sugar), a drink made of, I, 172; preparation of, II, 382, 383
Jambu-tree, II, 369, 439
Jamúl uddin, a vizier, II, 449, 455
Jangádas (rafts), II, 515
Jangay (Nair guides), I, 339, 359
Japan, trade with, II, 170-179; silver of, 174
Japanese, at Goa, II, 38; assist in defence of Malacca, 152; women whiten their bodies, 175
Java, II, 160
Jeannin, President, I, xxix
Jehangir, Emperor, II, 250, 253
Jerid, game of, referred to, II, 101, 110
Jesuits named. *See* **Seine, Stevens, La Croix, Trigaut, Ricci.**
Jesuits, at Calicut, I, 405, 406; persuade P. to go to Cochin, 420; of the Cochin college, 433; had a college at Cannanor, 445; conflict with archbishop, II, 18; their churches and colleges at Goa, 54, 55, 58-63, 96, 97; none but Portuguese can become, 61; keep the patents of succession, 77; as apothecaries, 83; disputes with archbishop, 92; conduct towards Domburgh, 109; at the Mogul court, 252; at Bahia, 311
Jesuit Father, appointed to superintend foreign and native Christians, II, xi, 20, 22
Jew, a wandering, I, 283-285
Jews in Bengal, I, 333; at Calicut, 407; of Cochin, 435; called New Christians, II, 93, 311; great numbers at Bahia, 311; Jew merchants on board ship, 332, 333
Jigger, II, 319
João, Dom, exiled Maldive prince, I, 294; II, 497-502
Joguies (Hindu ascetics), I, 343, 378
John of Montecorvino, quoted, II, 433
Johore, Raja of, alliance with Dutch, II, 151, 152
Jordanus, Friar, quoted, II, 434
Juan, Don, king of Ceylon, II, 144-147
Judia, Baixos da (Europa shoals), II, 199
Júјú (in the Soudan), II, 444

Kabtaj, I, 237; *and see* **Cowries.**
Kanádir, II, 442
Kanbar (coir), II, 443-445
Kannalus, island, II, 451, 466
Karamba (young coco-nut), II, 442
Karativu, sea-fight off, II, 512
Karhidu (*Caridou*), island and channel, I, 103
Katu (a billhook). *See* **Caty.**
Kauri. *See* **Cowries.**
Káyal, II, 108
Kazi, II, 440, *et seq.*
Keeling, voyage, I, xiii
Kenj, I, 237; II, 432; *and see* **Cowries.**
Khadija, queen, II, 449 *et seq.*
Killing animals, mode of, at the Maldives, I, 173, 174
King of Spain, draws no profit from India, II, 88; not mentioned in India, 205; considers question of abandoning India, 210, 211; edict against foreigners, II, 272
King of the Maldives, is absolute, I, 197; ennobles whom he will, 209, 215; sells titles of dignity, 217; his palace, I, 218-222; royal insignia, I, 223; revenues, I, 227 *See also* **Ibrahim**

King of the Sea (a divinity worshipped), I, 176; (a fish), I, 192
Kings of the Sea, applied to the Dutch, II, 149, 203; and to the English, 203
Knives worn at the Maldives, I, 163, 223
Kolumadulu (Collo madous) atoll, I, 97, 99
Konkani language, II, 405
Korbáni (? *Hakurpani*), II, 453
Kordui or *Korduveri*, II, 437, 443
Kotta, a measure, II, 444
Kotta, fort. *See Marcaire Costé* and **Kunháli.**
Kotta, river, 348
Kottakkal, fortress of Kunháli, visited by Pyrard, I, 349; then condition of, 356; negotiations with Dutch as to, *ib.*; referred to, I, 426; described, II, 510. *See also* **Kunháli,** *Marcaire Costé.*
Kulb-almas, II, 439; *and see Cobolly mas.*
Kunappa Bandar, II, 144
Kunháli (spelt *Cognialy*), Malabar corsair, shares booty, I, 346; history of, I, 350 356; II, 509 *et seq.*; description of his fortress, I, 350, 351; II, 509, 510; pictures of his achievements, I, 351; revolts against Samorin, I, 352; his victory over L. da Gama, I, 353, 354; II, 514-517; conquered by Furtado, I, 354-356; II, 518-523; death, I, 356; II, 526; his son, I, 357; referred to, II, 448; fame of, II, 527
Kuran, I, 130, 184, 186, 199; II, 447, 448

Laccadives, I, 323-325; belong to Cannanor, 445; barque of, arrives at Goa, II, 108; referred to, II, 477
La Croix, Father Etienne de, II, xii, xix, 22, 23, 36, 271, 281
La Fontaine, quoted, II, 87 *n*
Lagoa, pond at Goa, II, 35, 56
Lahore, II, 251
Lancaster, James, I, xlii, 284
Lanha, II, 483
Larins, description of, I, 232-234; fish-hook, form of, 234; as used in India, II, 68, 69; is made of the best silver, II, 174; brought from Ormuz, II, 239
Las (lac), II, 378
Lascar (seamen), I, 438; II, 3
Lascarits (soldiers), I, 438; II, 117
Laughter, an indiscretion, I, 385
Launching ships, ceremonies at, I, 178; lucky days for, 187
Laval, share in expedition, I, xiv, 2; description of, xv; a young man of, 26; author's return to, II, 339
Le Blanc, Vincent, his voyages, I, xxxix; quoted, I, 297
Le Fort, Guyon, I, xxi, 30, 31
Leilão (spelt *Laylon*), street at Goa II, 52, 64, 69
Lentils, II, 126
Leper hospital at Goa, II, 55
Lerma, Duke of, II, xxx, xxxiii
Liard (copper money), I, 61; II, 237
Libasse, I, 372
Lif, II, 442
Lime, made from shells, I, 122; used with betel, II, 362
Linhares, Conde de, II, 71 *n.*
Linschoten, influence traced in Pyrard's book, I, xli, 335
Livros das Monçoes, II, xxiii, cited *passim*
Lizards, great, at Madagascar, I, 35
Lobo, Dom Luiz, II, 517
Long ships, II, 118
Louesme, I, 12, 27, 54
Louis XIII, birth of, I, 290
Love-making among the Maldivians, I, 138
Lusson, Guillaume, dedication to, II, 535
Luteranos, I, 422, 425, 429, 451; II, 283
Luzon, II, 171
Lyroun, a fish, II, 438

Ma'bar (Coromandel coast), II, 437, 451, 454
Macao, II, 172, 173
Macarequeau (the Pandanus tree), II, 369
Mace, II, 167, 169, 357
Maconnodou, island, I, 76
Madagascar, sighted, I, 26; arrival at, 29 (*and see* **St. Augustine's Bay**); description of, 36; strange habit of cattle, 37; considered the greatest Indian island, II, 168
Madeira, sugar of, II, 312
Madre de Dios, fort at Goa, II, 33, 525
Madre de Dios, carrack, I, xii
Madrepore, I, 96, 97
Madura, island, II, 164
Maé dau da elle (captain of king's ships), I, 90
Mafacelou (?) island, II, 476
Mafai and *Máfácalou*, I, 210; *and see Manpas*
Magadoxo, II, 440
Magicians, I, 298, 319
Mahal (Málé), II, 438, 447
Mahomet, visitation of sepulchre of, I, 143, 165, 336; miracle of, 145
Mahomet, Maldive King, I, 251
Mahommedanism, date of conversion of Maldives to, I, 266
Mahommedans, difficulty of converting, II, 252; *see also* **Maldives** and other titles
Maize, II, 316
Makian, island, I, 166
Makunudu, island, I, 76
Malabar, extent and kingdoms of, I, 369; distinctions of the people, 371
Malabars, assist the Maldivians, I, 247, 248; II, 476; no nobility among, 337; *i.e.*, Mahommedans, as distinguished from Nairs, I, 340, 341, 385, 444; relations with the Nairs, 340, 341; piratical traffic, 342; war with Portuguese, 444-450; II, 204; attacks upon the Cambay fleet, II, 246, 255
Malacca, description of, II, 150, 155, 156; besieged by Dutch, 151, 152; sea-fight off, 152-155; besieged by king of Achin, 160
Malacca, bishop of, II, 27
Malacca cane, I, 330
Malailli, island, I, xxiii; arrival and adventures at, 42-48
Málam (a vestibule), II, 441
Malay language, II, 156, 405
Malays, wrecked at Maldives, quarrel described, I, 294-296; their disregard of life, 295; race and language, II, 156, 405
Maldiva (Málé), II, 481
Maldives (i) THE NAME, I, 95; II, 480
—— (ii) THE ISLANDS, description of, I, 93 *et seq.*; distance from Spain and India, *ib.*; number of, 95; increase and decrease of, 96; number of, inhabited, 97; trading between, 115; external trade, 241, 242; II, 468; no walled towns, I, 118; buildings, 118, 124, 125; populations over forty governed by a Catibe, 198; invasion of, I, 310-320; civil war at, 320; Batuta's names of, II, 437; vegetables, fruits, and trees, I, 111-114; II, 365, 367-385. *See also* **Atolls**, and names of islands.
—— (iii) GOVERNMENT of the realm, I, 197; never goes to females, *sed qu.*, I, 320; II, 451, 528; of the atolls, I, 198; revenue officers, 200; the high officers of state, I, 210-215; II, 450, 451; offices of Sinhalese origin, I, 211, 212; departmental government, I, 212, 213; militia, I, 215-217; revenues and taxation, I, 227-232; mode of trading with strangers, I, 300; list of kings, II, 528 *et seq.*
—— (iv) PEOPLE, dislike of melan-

choly, I, 74; expert navigators and swimmers, 100, 101; appearance and character, 105, 106, 169, 195; compared with Sinhalese, 105, 169 *n.*; dress, 105, 109, 161-169; difference between north and south, 105, 122, 123; hair-dressing, 106-111, 164, 167; craftsmen collected in different islands, 114; freedom of women, 168; indolence of, 117, 305; lewdness, 151, 195, 304, 305-307; education, 184-186; skill in manufactures, 188, 195; ranks and dignities, 208-218; women keep their own rank on marriage, 209; children take status of mother, 209, *sed quære*, 208 *n.*; princes of the blood royal, 209; personal names, 217; dress and habits of king's wives, 226, 227; hatred of the Portuguese, 251; Ceylon origin of, 266; II, 423-425; first contact with Portuguese, II, 472-476

Maldives (v) RELIGION, I, 123 *et seq.*; mosques, 124-128; indications of preceding Buddhism, 123; belief in a flat world, 127; ablutions, *ib.*; Friday observances, 130-134; new moon, 134; Ramadhan, 134-140; the minor festival, 140; sacrifice, 140-141; the greater Beiram, 143; the *Poycacan*, 143, 144; festival in June, 144; the *Candis cacan*, 145; Moolids, 146-150; devil worship, 180; legend as to conversion, II, 446-448

—— (vi) LAW, of wreck (*see* **Wreck**); boat-stealing, I, 79, 87; legal procedure, 198-207; jurisdiction of Naibs, 198, 199; of the Pandiar, 199; of the Moucouris, *ib.*; writs used, 201; appeal to the king, 199, 201, 202; mode of pleading causes, 201, 202; debt-slavery, 202-204; crimes, 204-207; king heir to dead captain, 267-8, 281, 299; and to foreigners, 286; and to his own officers, 289; confession exacted, 295, 296; punishment of women for intercourse with unbeliever, 303; for abominable crime, 306; punishment of theft, 307

Maldives (vii) FISHERY, abundance of, I, 117, 240; popularity of sport, 188; modes of fishing, 189-194; mode of cooking fish, 188; distribution of catch, 191

—— (viii) NAVIGATION, charts, 65, 99; sails of coco-fibre, 64; skill of the natives, 100, 101; they never navigate by night, 100; use the compass only for long voyages, 100, 104; launching ships, 178; boats kept scrupulously clean, *ib.*; superstitions, 178; burial at sea, 161

—— (ix) MANNERS AND CUSTOMS, reception of persons of distinction, I, 70-72; mode of saluting the king, 77; necessity of attending court, 89; importance of receiving the king's bounty, 89, 215; love-making, 138; colouring the feet and hands, 169; at meals and entertainments, 170-173; killing animals, 173; bathing, 174, 196; exchanging betel, 174; passing in front of a person, 175; swinging the legs, 175; meeting or touching another when on a journey, 175; or going fishing, *ib.*: nursing of babes, 183, 184; modesty among kindred, 196; mode of paying visits, 196, 197; respect paid to birth, 209; customs at Durbar, 220, 221; how the king walks abroad, 225; honorifics, use of, 226; visits to ladies, 227; gallantries, 305; number of wives, 305; II, 432; fondness for flowers, I, 108, 147; II, 371; laxity of divorce, I, 153-155; II, 459

——(x) LANGUAGE, I, 122; alphabets, I, 184, 185; different forms of writing, *ib.*; numerals, I, 95; II,

417, 421; systems of notation, II, 419-422; honorifics, I, 219, 223, 226; dictionary of, II, 405-418

Mâlé, atoll, I, 97, 99

Mâlé, capital island of the Maldives, I, 57, 117; water bad, 118; harbour, 121; exempt from taxation, 169; streets not paved, 225; Portuguese fort at, 246; Ibn Batuta at, II, 449 *et seq.*; Portuguese attacks on, II, 476, 506, 507

Malé-divar (Maldivians), I, 83

Mâlé ons (Mâlé fever), I, 83

Mâlé-ragué (Maldive kingdom), I, 83

Mâli, a place in the Soudan, II, 444

Malicut. *See* **Minicoy.**

Mâlik, the Imâm, II, 448

Malik of Chaul, II, 258

Mâlosmadulu (*Malos madou*) atoll, I, 97, 99, 103

Mamale, of Cannanor, II, 474, 475, 481; islands named after, I, 323; II, 481

Mamelucos, of Brazil, II, 39

Manacuma, II, 496

Manatee, I, 47

Manâyak (admiral), I, 210, 212; II, 451

Manaye Quilague (a queen), conspiracy of, I, 255

Manchoue (*manchua*), a kind of barge, I, 342; II, 42, 90, 110, 118, 276, 283, 518

Mandioc, I, 379; II, 218, 315, 316, 322

Mandovi, river of Goa, II, 24, 28

Manet, quoted, I, 3

Mangalore, king of, sends ship to the Maldives, I, 277; fort at, II, 259

Mangas (mangos), II, 126

Mangas de veludo (velvet sleeves), birds, so-called, I, 21; II, 294

Mango, II, 126, 367

Mangue la botte, name given to a Portuguese governor, II, 323

Maniassa, name of a Banyan, I, 365, 421, 423

Maniguette (long pepper), II, 221

Manila, II, 171, 172

Manile (bracelet), I, 377

Manji. *See Manchoue.*

Manoel, Dom, ex-king of the Maldives, his letters patent, I, 90, 296; notice of his life in India, II, 493-498

Manpas (chancellor), I, 210, 211, 214

Mansaus (cloaks), II, 240

Mantes (mantles), II, 103

Manuel de Christ, Fr., a Dominican, I, 451; II, 2

Márakkár. *See Marcaire.*

Maravedis, II, 119

Marcaire (Márakkár), I, 350, 357, 365

Marcaire Costé (Márakkár Kótta), the fort of Kunháli, I, 347, 348; *and see* **Kunhâli.**

Marchpanes (*massepain*), II, 98, 101

Margon (Margão), II, 270

Marie de Medici, dedication to, I, xxix, xxx

Marie Mena, a Portuguese lady, II, 325

Marignolli, John of, quoted, I, 11

Mariners, distinguished from soldiers, II, 184, 185; status of, 190, 191

Marmelades, II, 240, 261

Marriage, at the Maldives, I, 150 *et seq.*; three wives allowed, 151; impediments to, 152; divorce, 153; re-marriage, 153-155; among the Nairs, 392-394; at Goa, II, 100, 101; Ibn Batuta on, II, 439, 441, 445; Sinhalese kinds of, II, 182

Martaban, jars of, I, 259; timber of, II, 182

Martin, François, chronicler of the voyage of the *Croissant*, I, xiv; his book, 2; quoted, 7, 52, 80, 290, 291

Mas Bandery (finance minister), I, 210, 214

Mas Ydu (Greater Beiram), I, 143

Mascarenha, the brothers, II, 155

Maspillaspoury (island), I, 275
Mass, custom at elevation of host, II, 99 ; celebration of, on carracks, 187
Masson, Jean, II, 487
Mas'udi, quoted, II, 427
Masulipatam, I, 294 ; ship of, I, 301
Matalief, Cornelis, I, xiii; his siege of Malacca and sea-fight, II, 151-155
Mata vaca, slaughtering-place, II, 56
"*Matar, Matar,*" I, 422
Mate, duties of, II, 189, 394
Mate, of the *Corbin,* taken to Málé, I, 57 ; escape of, 66, 67 ; effect thereof, 78, 81 ; subsequent fortunes of, 80, 87; death at Quilon, II, 107
Matelot, II, 396
Matelotagem (provisions), II, 181, 274, 396
Mathematics, study of, I, 186
Mats (rush) of the Maldives, I, 241, 283 ; II, 377; of Mozambique, II, 232; of Socotora, II, 237; of Cael, II, 377
Maulude (festival), I, 146-150
Maurice, Count, referred to, I, 363, 364
Mayo, island, I, 7
Mayor (*Mór*), used of a mere superintendent, II, 41
Meal-Khan, story of, II, 135
Meau, island, II, 166
Mecca, pilgrimage to, I, 110, 143
Medina, pilgrimage to, I, 110
Medu piry, a sham husband, I, 154
Melinde, I, 23 ; II, 106, 230
Mello, Garcia da, II, 21
Menates (washermen), II, 71, 72
Menezes, Fr. Aleixo, archbishop, II, xix ; governor, 2, 266; visits Cabo as a health resort, 31, 90 ; almsgiving and emoluments, 89, 90 ; his part in death of prince of Ormuz, 91 ; dignity and state, 90 ; returns to Portugal, 91 ; conflict with the Jesuits, 92 ; assists in siege of Kunháli, 514
Menezes, Dom Francisco de, captain of Cochin, I, 428 ; name given, 440
Menezes, Dom Francisco de, governor of Brazil, II, 308, 309, 324-326
Menezes, Dom Francisco de, general of fleet, II, 2
Menezes, Dom Manoel, II, 272, 277
Mercœur, Duc de, II, 229, 321
Merigne (Port. *meirinho*), a sergeant or gaoler, I, 427; II, 16, 19, 20, 42, 69
Mesquite. *See* **Mosques.**
Messmates, system of, on French ships, I, 25, 75 ; II, 396
Mestar Cogni-aly, a Malabar of *Moutingué,* I, 339, 355
Mestiço. *See Mestifs.*
Mestifs (Portuguese half-castes), I, 78, 240, 373, 374; story of the young mestif, I, 253-255; his son, 314; at Goa, II, 38 ; woman on carrack, 291
Metempsychosis, I, 379
Metifs and *Metiz.* *See Mestifs.*
Meuuare (prepared ambergris), I, 229
Michel, Julian, II, 321, 322
Middleton, Sir H., voyage, I, xiii ; II, xvii
Miladummadulu (*Milla douc madouc*) atoll, I, 97, 99
Militia of the Maldives. *See* **Soldiers.**
Millet, I, 111
Mina (Elmina), fort, II, 221, 222
Minambar (black ambergris), II, 479
Minicoy, island, I, xxvi, 322, 323 ; Buddhist remains at, I, 124
Mirabolans, I, 399 ; II, 361
Miru Baharu. *See Mirvaires.*
Mirvaires (Emir-el Bahr), I, 90, 210, 211, 213
Misdoue Quilague, revolt at, I, 252
Misericordia, fraternity of, at Goa, II, 10, 20, 46; church and house of, 51, 64; at Bahia, II, 311

Mocquet, Jean, II, xx, 274, 275
Model boats, sacrifice of, I, 177
Moet ol (*i.e.*, *Datura*), II, 114
Mogor, *i.e.*, the Great Mogul, I, 327; war with King of Bengal, *ib.*; suzerainty over Cambay, II, 246, 249; and over Chaul, 258; account of, II, 250-253
Mogor, meaning territories of the Mogul, I, 258, 278; II, 250
Mogos, the Arakanese, I, 326
Moluccas, II, xv, xvi, 166, 167
Mombasa, II, 236
Moncadon (Port. *mocadão*), II, 117
Mondou (mundu), a turban, I, 449
Money, practice of clipping, I, 61; of the Maldives, 232-240; of Goa, II, 67-69
Monfart, Count de (H. de Feynes), II, xx, 279, 280
Mongoose, I, 116
Monkeys of Madagascar, I, 35, 37; of Malabar, 401
Monomotapa, II, 219, 233
Monroys, Dom Fernando de, II, 475
Monsoons, written *monsons*, I, 257; *monssons*, *moesons*, and *muessons*, 280; II, 175, 235
Montaire, a kind of bonnet, II, 112
Montecorvino, John of, II, 433
Montesquieu, quotes Pyrard, I, 89
Moon, feast at new, I, 134
Moranque gasts (muraga tree), II, 368
Mordesin (cholera), II, 13
Moreau, Christofle, chief merchant, I, 4; quarrel with captain, I, 17; II, 398-400
Morfie (Port. *marfim*, ivory), II, 221
Morigoran, island, II, 166
Moses Chorenensis, II, 426
Mosques, at the Maldives, I, 124-128; sittings in, 125, 126; in Malabar, 396, 397
Mosquitos, I, 36, 116
Mosso da Camera and *M. do Servicio*, II, 120
Mosso Fidalguo, II, 120
Moucheron, voyage, I, 30; II, 158
Moucois, I, 385-388, 397; religion of, 389; separate temples of, 397
Moucouris (doctors), I, 199
Moudins (incumbents of mosques), I, 125, 127, 131, 212
Mouhamede Caca, a Bengal merchant, I, 259; his wife's intrigue, 260, 261; his subsequent marriage, 262, 265
Moul (a measure), I, 86
Mountebanks, I, 343
Mourning, no special garments for, I, 160
Mouscoulits (elders), I, 70, 79, 199, 200, 213, 214, 215, 254
Mouscouly auare (headman of parish), I, 200; *and see preceding*.
Mousseliman (Mussulman), I, 261
Moussey Caca, a Malabar of *Moutingué*, I, 339
Moutingué (Muṭṭungal), Malabar port, arrival of P. at, I, 336; king of, a Nair, 337; description of residence of, 337-343; mentioned, 369
Moxama (dried fish), II, 473, 478, 485
Mozambique, not touched except of necessity, II, 197; description of, 223-235; sieges of, xxi, 225-228; trade with Goa, 224, 231, 235
Mugg, the (king of Arakan), I, 326
Muhammad Takurū-fánu, rebellion of, I, 247-250
Mukkavar. *See Moucois*.
Mulaku (*Molucque*) atoll, I, 97, 99
Mulaku (island), II, 465
Mulaku, Fua (island). *See* **Fua Mulaku.**
Mulastre (Mulatto), I, 307; II, 222
Mulatto, a thief, story of, I, 307, 308
Mulattos at Goa, II, 38
Murder, at the Maldives, I, 206
Musk (deer), II, 359
Muṭṭungal, i, xxvi; *and see Moutingué*.

Naibs, I, 110; may be also Catibes, 186; chiefs and judges of atolls,

198 ; residence in their atolls not obligatory, 212
Naicles (*Naiks*), II, 42
Nairs, act as guides, I, 339 ; character of, I, 340 ; drunkenness, 358 ; reserve towards strangers, 359 ; distinguished from Malabar Mahommedans, 371 ; description of, 380-386 ; pride towards lower castes, 382 ; polyandry, 384 ; customs, 390-394 ; act as judicial referees, 407
Najib, mosque and shrine of, II, 453
Namandé (ceremonies), I, 127, 133
Names given haphazard, I, 303
Nantes, natives of, II. 324
Náos de carreira (carracks), II, 180
Narquilly (coco-tree), II, 372, 483
Natal, storm off, I, 26-28 ; passed homeward bound, II, 291
Nature worship, I, 175-178
Navie (a galiot), II, 117
Navires (Portuguese galiots), I, 345 ; II, 118
Navis d'armade (navios de armada), men-of-war, I, 438 ; II, 118
Navis de Chetie (navios de Chatins), merchantmen, I, 438 ; II, 118
Náyar, the, or governor of Calicut, I, 367
Náyars. *See* **Nairs.**
Nazareth, carrack, II, 280
Needles, Cape. *See* **Agulhas.**
Negra da Guinea, II, 66
Negro, Rio (the Zambesi), II, 233
Negroes, as slaves, II, 66; smell, *ib.*; *see also* **Slaves** and **Slave Trade.**
Nek, Van, at Amboyna in 1599, II, xv
Netherlanders. *See* **Dutch.**
Netherlands, independence of, I, xi
New Christians, name applied to Jews, II, 93, 311; applied to native converts, I, 406 ; II, 99
Nicote, a Portuguese renegade, I, 334
Nightmare, Pyrard's, I, 396
Nilandu, atoll, I, 97, 99, 252
Niort, town, II, 339
Noort, Oliver van, the circumnavigator, I, xiii; II, xiii
Noronha, Dom Henrique de, II, 154
North-west Passage, I, x, xiii
Nossa Señora da Graça, Augustinian church at Goa, II, 57
Nossa Señora da Penha de França, carrack, II, 276
Nossa Señora da Piedade, carrack, II, 277
Nossa Señora da Serra, church at Goa, II, 51
Nossa Señora da Guadaloupe, fort, II, 32, 33
Nossa Señora de Jesus, carrack, P. embarks in, II, 281 ; condition on departure, 283 ; number of crew and passengers, 284; roll-call, 287; lashed with cables, 291; rounding the Cape, 291-294; great yard breaks, 292 ; councils held, 293, 296; condition at St. Helena, 297; grounding at, 303-306 ; arrival at Bahia, 307 ; reduced number of crew, 307 ; discharged and abandoned, 308
Nossa Señora do Cabo, chapel, II, 31
Nossa Señora do Monte, church at Goa, II, 72
Nossa Señora do Monte do Carme, carrack, II, 277
Nossa Señora do Rosario, church at Goa, II, 58
Nova, João de, discoverer of St. Helena, I, 18
Nutmegs, II, 167, 169, 357

Oath, taken on biscuit, I, 279
Ocean routes, exclusive rights in, I, ix ; II, 202, 206
Odican anpou (boat-stealing), I, 79
Ody (barque), I, 70
Ogate yourabe (royal galley), I, 312
Ola (strip of palm-leaf), II, 473, 522
Oleron, island, II, 339
Onnimaus, a flower, II, 371
Onny (lime), II, 362

Onor (Hunáwar), II, 259
Ons (fever), I, 83
Ont cory or *oncory* (spleen-disease), I, 84, 182
Ophir, site of, II, 233
Ophthalmia, I, 181
Opium, I, 195, 405; great traffic in India, II, 247
Ormuz, English assist at capture of, II, xxxvi; description of, II, 238-324; trade of, 239, 240; proverb as to, 240; profits of captains of, 241; Maldivians at, 468
Ormuz, prince of (Turun Shah), II, 91, 92, 243-245
Orphan girls, retreat for, II, 52
Orta (garden), II, 28, 110
Ou du ad (white umbrella), I, 256
Ouadou. *See* **Suadiva.**
Oucourou (Friday), I, 130, 131
Oucourou misquitte (Friday, or chief mosque), I, 72
Oura (millet), I, 111
Oussaint Ranamandy Cologue (a lord), I, 69
Outisme, island. *See Utimu.*
Ouvidor (magistrate), I, 428; II, 19, 326
Oxen, at the Maldives, I, 116
Oydor da cidade (Span. = Port. *ouvidor*), I, 428; II, 19, 326
Oyster-shells, used for window-panes, II, 15, 163
Oyuarou. *See* **Currents.**

Padoes (Malabar boats), I, 325, 342, 345, 346, 347, 356, 357
Padroado, of the see of Goa, II, 26
Padua, shoals of, II, 477, 481
Padypolo atoll. *See* **Fádiffolu.**
Padzér (Bezoar), II, 484
Pae dos Christãos, priest overseer of converts, II, xi, 20, 22
Pages, on board P. ships, II, 127, 191
Pagoda (= temple), I, 414, 419
Pagoda (= idol), I, 333, 414

Paimones (sharks), I, 96; II, 350
Pain de mil (a Frenchman), II, 326
Paindouë (island). *See* **Fehendu.**
Pairaus, Malabar galiots, so called by Portuguese, I, 345; II, 117
Palandura or *Palandiva* (?), II, 479, 480
Palanquins, II, 3, 45, 75
Palladius, quoted, II, 428
Palmero, II, 28, 372
Palmito, II, 484
Pammedery, I, 210, 211, 212, 255
Pan de Mozambic (ebony), II, 224
Panan (fanam), a gold coin, I, 350, 365, 412
Panana (fruit), I, 16
Panany, town, I, 398, 409, 413
Pandanus tree, I, 369
Pandiare, chief priest of the Maldives, I, 110, 125; and chief justice, 199; preaches, 133, 137; religious ecstasy, 148; one who had a hundred wives, 155; as one of the ministers, 210, 211; mentioned by Ibn Batuta, II, 450 *et seq.*; one who was a sherif, 272, 304, 308; another married to a sister of chief queen, 276; goes to Arabia and dies there, 277, 308; name applied to a Calicut noble, I, 365
Pandoro (Port. *pão de oro*), gold ingots, II, 176
Pangim, now Nova Goa, II, 25, 31; incoming viceroy tarries at, 32, 76, 81
Panguaye (*pangaie*), I, 53
Paṇikan (fencing-master in Malabar), I, 269
Papaya tree, II, 368
Paper imported from China, II, 177
Papos. *See* **Papaya.**
Parable, of the flies, II, 87
Pardo (*paru*), a galiot, I, 345
Parasoles, II, 45
Parcintes (*precintos*), II, 248
Pardáo (Port. coin), I, 446; II, 6, 11 17, 20, 66, 83, 235

Parenae tacourou, revolt of, I, 256, 257
Parenas (an officer of state), I, 210, 213
Parmentier, Jean and Raoul, I, x, xi, 2; their visit to the Maldives, II, 486-492
Parrots, at Madagascar, I, 35, 37; generally, II, 352, 353
Partisans, II, 68
Pasme. *See* **Pepper.**
Passages (Port. *passos*), at Goa, II, 25; permits at, 33; difficulty of evading, 132
Passes (raisins), II, 73, 261, 383
Passports, system of Portuguese, II, 206, 207
Paste, a dress of, I, 165
Pastèques (water-melons), I, 33, 399, 417
Pastia (prayer = Ar. fátihah), I, 130
Pata-marakkár, a corsair, II, 476
Patána, name for atoll, I, 94; II, 481, 496
Pattimár (a boat), I, 342
Paulo, Dom, mistake for Pedro, I, 294
Pavois (screens), I, 6
Pazon, II, 484
Pearl fishery, of Ceylon, II, 143; of Persian Gulf, II, 239
Peas, from China, II, 247
Pedro, Dom, exiled Maldive prince, I, 294; II, 139, 497, 501
Pedroso. *See* **Poderoso.**
Pegu, timber of, II, 182
Peiresc, collector of notes for Le Blanc's voyages, I, xxxix
Pelican, a, visits the Maldives, II, 353, 354; used for fishing, *ib.*
Pelourinho velho (old pillory), II, 55
Pemousseré (debt-slaves), I, 203, 204
Penguins, I, 16, 97
Pensée, ship of Parmentier, I, x; II, 486
Peon. *See Pion.*
Pepin, lieutenant of *Corbin*, I, xix, xxi; death, 19
Pepper, drink seasoned with, I, 172; black and white, I, 328 *n.*; of Malabar, 400; of Cochin, 433, 437, 438; II, 213, 273; of Achin, II, 157; generally, II, 355, 356
Pepper, long, I, 328; II, 221, 356
Pérau, Abbé, his *Life of Bignon*, I, xxxvi
Periplus, quoted, II, 426
Pernambuco, II, 197, 331
Perou (turkeys), II, 316
Perrier (small cannon), I, 23; II, 183
Persia, relations with Maldives, II, 468
Persia, king of, relations with Mogul, II, 253
Persian ambassador to Spain, II, 277
Persian carpets, II, 128
Petun (tobacco), II, 313
Pezo (*peso*), II, 48
Phanans. *See Panan.*
Phare masse (reef fish), I, 194
Philip II, policy as king of Portugal, I, xi, xii
Philippe, Dom. *See* **Filippe.**
Philippine Islands, II, 171, 172
Philippus a Sanctâ Trinitate, quoted, II, 507, 508
Pig's bristles, I, 244
Pillory, II, 55, 69
Pilory viejo (old pillory), II, 69
Pilot, of the *Corbin*, I, xv, xxiii, 13; plot and death, 78, 79; status of Portuguese, II, 189; of French, II, 394, 395
Pineapples, I, 328; II, 365
Pinguy (penguins), I, 16, 97
Pinnace, timber brought for building, I, 49; uses of, *ib.*
Pion (or *peon*), I, 428, 440; II, 16
Pirates, Malabar, their ports, I, 337-344; acknowledge the Samorin, 338, 348; distribution of their prizes, 342; system of watch-towers, 344; take great booty, 345; conduct of expeditions, 346, 347; hatred of the Portuguese, 347, 349; have their own kings besides be-

vernor from Calicut, 350 ; revenge for death of Kunháli, 356
Pitourou, I, 139
Place Royale, of Paris, referred to, I, 361
Plantain (*i.e.*, ribwort), II, 362
Plantenes (plantains), II, 345 ; *see also* **Bananas.**
Plata, Rio de la, II, 219, 220; beef and hide trade of, 322, 323
Po! Po!! cry of, I, 383
Poderoso, Pedro de, I, 441; II, 2
Poecaca, a rich merchant, I, 285
Poison, slow-timed, II, 129, 275
Pollouoys, fabulous island, I, 296-299
Polo, Marco, quoted, II, 433
Polyandry, among the Nairs, I, 384
Pomegranates, I, 328
Ponambar, II, 479
Ponicmbous Thory (cinnamon), I, 301
Pontador. See Apontador.
Pontevedra, II, 336
Porcelain, vessels of, I, 170, 224 ; II, 79; imported from China, II, 176
Pork, of Brazil and Mozambique, II, 231, 316
Porpoises, I, 9
Porto Grande (Chittagong), I, 326
Porto pequeno (Sátgáuw), I, 326
Portugal, India governed from, II, 3; lack of timber, II, 181; times for setting out from, 197 ; period of subjection to Spain, II, xxvi
Portuguese, policy of, I, ix, 375 ; conduct at Annobom, 14-17; treachery towards other Europeans, 44; expeditions to the Maldives, I, 160, 245-247, 250 ; prosperity of Maldives under, 247 ; terms of treaty, 251; passports of, referred to, I, 250; in Bengal, 334; hatred of Malabars towards, 347, 349 ; expeditions to Badara, 349 ; first expedition against Kunháli, 352-354 ; second, and capture of fort, 354-356 ; plot against Pyrard at Calicut, I, 365 ; encroachments at Cochin, 375; driven out of Calicut, 405 ; relations thereafter, *ib.*; fatal policy in Ceylon, II, xiii, xiv ; *résumé* of first hundred years in India, xxiv-xxix ; only married P. allowed from Goa to mainland, 34; engage but little in trade, 74; marriage ceremonies, 100, 101; church-going, 101-104 ; pastimes, 115 ; levies of, for service in India, 118-120 ; their wars in Ceylon, 147; assumption of names and titles, 120, 121, 193 ; losses at hands of Dutch and English, 201, 203; have ceased to fight, 207, 208; hatred of Spain, 212; in Brazil, characterised, 313 ; their irruption into India, 470-472 ; first contact with Maldives, 472-477 ; garrison exterminated, 476; expedition in 1632, 506, 507
Portuguese factor, at Calicut, issues passports, I, 405
Portuguese fortresses in Ceylon, II, 143; in Western India, II, 254, 256-259
Portuguese ladies, relations with female slaves, II, 67; how they go to church, 102-104; painted, 103, 113 ; dress of, 112, 113
Portuguese lords at Goa, keep open house, II, 23, 130
Portuguese ships, one at Málé, I, 78, 239; one wrecked at the Maldives, I, 253; one captured by the Dutch, I, 292; II, 262 ; afterwards wrecked at the Maldives, *ib.*; pictures of, II, 50 ; description of, 180-184; lack of timber in Portugal, 181 ; sheathing of, 180, 305 ; loss of ships and lives on Indian voyage, II, 184, 208, 209; no private ship goes to India, 208 ; mode of lashing ship in storm, 291. *See also* **Carracks, Galions, Caravels.**
Portuguese soldiers, II xxviii, xxix ; how enrolled, II, 118; titles and dignities, 119, 121 ; highest allowance for voyage, 120 ; status

and duties on carracks, *ib.*, 184, 185 ; assumption of titles by low-born, 120, 121, 193, 200 ; unrestrained in India, 121, 122 ; pay for service on armadas, 122 ; numbers never published, *ib.*; large proportion are exiles, 124 ; boys shipped at Lisbon, *ib.*; distinction of married and unmarried, 125 ; number in Goa, *ib.*; how enlisted for service, 126 ; equipment of, 127; life at Goa, 128-131; of the unmarried, 129, 130 ; vainglory of, 130; night marauding, 131; few return, *ib.*; in Ceylon, 143

Portuguese treaties with Indian princes, II, 204-206

Potatos (*batatas*), II, 315

Potosi, mountain, II, 220

Pottery of the Maldives, I, 170 ; of Bengal, 329

Poua (areca), I, 301

Poua Molucque, atoll. *See* **Fua Mulaku**

Pouladou (island). *See* **Fuladu.**

Poulia, caste, I, 386

Poulisdous atoll. *See* **Felidu.**

Poultry at the Maldives, I, 115 ; black, at Mozambique, II, 230

Pouraddé (stranger), I, 83

Pouy tallan, a crime, I, 304

Poycacan (festival), I, 143, 144

Práhú, native vessel, I, 345

Pregoeiro (written *Pregonneur*), a crier, II, 65

Prester John, II, 236

Priests, want of, on voyage, I, xv ; natives can become, II, 61, 96; how paid in India, 96

Principe, Ilha do, II, 221

Printing in India, II, 211

Proverbs, as to Goa, II, 26 *n.*; as to India, II, 196 ; as to Ormuz, II, 240

Psalms of David, I, 148

Ptolemy, quoted, II, 426

Pulayar. *See Poulia.*

Pullobay (islands), I, 296 ; II, 496

Puntador (=apontador), II, 42

Pursers, on French ships, II, 395

Pyjamas, II, 112

Pyrard, François (the author), birth and youth, I, xvii ; office in *Corbin*, xix, xx ; summary of vol. i, xx-xxviii ; chronology of voyage (vol. i), I, xlix ; motive in embarking, 4; opinion of his fellows, 5 ; health and sickness during the voyage, I, 35, 64 ; II, 389 ; takes order from captain, I, 51; taken to Fehendu, 59; treatment there, 62-69; learns the Maldive language, 64, 73, 81; visits his companions at Fuladu, 65; sickness from eating turtle, 66 ; his special friend, 75, 87; arrives at Málé, 76; his fever, 82-85; taken to Bandos, 85 ; a second attack, 89 ; summoned before council, *ib.* ; favour with the king, 91; engages in traffic, 92, 93; suffers from night-blindness, 181 ; discourses about France, 243, 244 ; visits Guráddú, 257, 258 ; meets a Dutchman, 282 ; acts as factor for merchants, 286; friendship with Assant-Caounes, 287-8 ; meets Domburgh at Málé and Cochin, 292-3 ; his dream, 310 ; dangers during the invasion, 311-314; addressed by the king, 312; bequeaths his property, 313; consoles the queen, 316, 317; well treated by the invaders, 317; embarks in invaders' fleet, 320; arrival at Minicoy, 322; and at the Laccadives, 324; arrival at Chittagong, 326 ; reception by raja, *ib.* ; departure from Bengal, 326, 336 ; arrival at Moutingué, 336 ; leaves for Calicut, 339, 343 ; visits Badara, 344-348; also Koṭṭakkal, 349, 356 ; Coluotte (Kollam), 360 ; arrives at Calicut, 360 ; visits the Samorin, 362-365; lodged in the alfandega, *ib.*; resides eight months at Calicut, 366; his nightmare, 396 ; his favour at the Calicut court, 420 ; departure from

Calicut, 421 ; kidnapped by the Portuguese, 422 ; lands in the Châliyam territory, 425; arrives at Tanur, *ib.* ; brought to Cochin, 427; interview with captain of Cochin, 428; lodged in the Tronco, 429 ; released, 433 ; delivered to Portuguese fleet, 440; miseries of voyage to Goa, 441-443, 451; arrival at Cannanor, 443 ; at Goa, 451; in the Goa hospital, II, x-xii, 2, 5, 15-17 ; in prison, 17-23 ; visits Ceylon, II, xiii, 140; Malacca, 150 ; Bantam, 160; Tuban, 164; Madura, 164 ; Báli, 165 ; Ternaté, 167; Banda, *ib.* ; visits Diu and Cambay, II, xii, 249 ; returns to Goa, xvii, 179, 261; pressed to go to Africa, 235, 272 ; and to the North, 269 ; and to China, 272 ; again imprisoned, 269 ; released, 271 ; gets license to depart, 272, 273 ; taken before viceroy, 273 ; takes ship, 281 ; robbed, 282 ; treatment on board, 283-287; sufferings near the Cape, 291 ; taken before governor at Bahia, 309; adventures at Bahia, 324-326 ; gets passage in Flemish hulk, 330; lands at Bayona islands, 335 ; pilgrimage to Compostella, 336 ; visits Corunna, 337; arrival at La Rochelle, 339 ; and returns to Laval, *ib.*; his latter days and death, I, xxviii-xlii

Pyrard (his book), four editions, I, xxviii-xxxi ; abridgements, xxxii ; question as to authorship, xxxiii-xli ; title-page of 2nd edition, li ; scheme of division, II, ix

Pyrard (Pierre), brother of above, I, xvii, xviii

Pyrau, Abbé Duval, I, xviii

Pyraux, Claude, confused with Pyrard, I, xix

Queen, of Minicoy, I, 323

Queens of the Maldives (wives of (Sultan), inquisitiveness of, I, 77 ; dress and habits of, I, 226 ; a foreign queen, I, 258 ; the pilot's wife, 262, 264 ; the chief queen, I, 58, 263, 264 ; the Bengal merchant's wife, I, 265 ; her conspiracies, I, 274-277; the queens during the invasion, 312, 315, 316

Queens of the Maldives in their own right, errors of author, I, 320, 321; *see also* **Khadija.**

Queimadas, Islas, II, 214, 284

Quella or *quela* (bananas), I, 113, 188, 304

Quenuery (sorcery), I, 274

Quérard, M., I, xxxiii, xxxvii

Queualo, fish, II, 299 ; *and see* **Cavallo.**

Quiauany (readers), I, 158

Quicksilver, II, 177

Quilague, I, 56, 210, 250

Quilla panis (parasitical worms), I, 182

Quilon, written *Coilan*, I, 80; II, 107; *Couelan*, II, 198 ; *Coulan*, II, 259 ; *Kaulam*, II, 458; intended siege of, II, 524

Quinces, preserved, II, 261

Rachil, II, 143

Raignolles. See Reinol.

Rain, contrivances for catching, I, 98

Raisin wine, II, 73, 286

Raiso (*reis*), II, 119

Raja Sinha, of Ceylon, II, 143

Ram, ship, I, xxi, xxii, 30

Ramadhan, celebration of, I, 134-143 ; close of, 140

Rambutan fruit, II, 366

Ramos, Cabo de, II, 214 ; is the northern boundary of Malabar, *ib.*

Ramusio, I, xi

Ranabandery Tacourou, brother of chief queen, I, 58 ; incurs king's anger, 69 ; jealousy of king's nephew, 273 ; figure and accomplishments, 274; escapes to Arabia, 277; afterwards becomes king, *ib.*,

321 ; taken prisoner by invaders, 320 ; not entered in list of kings, II, 533
Rans (jointure), I, 151, 152
Rans bandery (treasurer), I, 210, 214
Ransom, of Portuguese not allowed on part of state, II, 46
Rape, punishment of, I, 205
Rasquan (king), I, 208
Rats, at the Maldives, I, 116; II, 373
Rattans, I, 207, 331
Ravery (toddy drawers), II, 376
Ray, fish, II, 351
Reals, Spanish, I, 235
Red Dragon, ship, I, xiii
Red dye, I, 169
Red wood. *See* **Brazil-wood.**
Reinol, a newcomer from Europe, II, 123
Religion, practice as to exercise of, at Goa and in Deccan, II, 133, 134
Renches (bunks), II, 283
Renderes (Port. *rendeiros*), II, 174, 178
Renequillague (queen), I, 208
Resende, Pedro B. de, his *Livro do Estado*, etc., II, xxxix
Revenge, ship, II, xx
Rhinoceros, I, 331
Ribeira das galés, II, 45
Ribeira Grande, II, 40-44
Ricci, Father, II, 37
Rice, not grown at the Maldives, I, 112; mode of cooking, *ib.*; abundance in Bengal, 327; imports of, to Goa, II, 8
Riens, Maldive measure, I, 86
Ring, silver, as badge, I, 189
Ringworm, I, 181
Rivara, J. H. da Cunha (of Goa), his Portuguese edition of Pyrard, I, xxxii ; his *Archivo Portuguez*, II, xxiii ; both works cited, *passim*
Rochelle, La, II, 339
Roda, coin, I, 439 *n.*
Rodet. *See* **Ramadhán.**
Rodet pillauay, feast at close of Ramadhán, I, 137
Rodrigues, Belchior, II, 521
Rodrigues Palhota, A., II, 521
Rodrigue, Simon, his intrigue and death, I, 260, 261
Rodriguez, island, II, 290
Rodriguez, Dom Pedro (a Spaniard), II, 22
Roll of Portuguese, sent out annually to India, II, 120
Ropemakers, II, 187; *and see Trinqueres*
Rosary, Church of the, II, 58
Rosnans (eye-ailment), I, 181
Rosquilhos (sweetmeats), II, 98, 101
Rotan (rattan), I, 207, 331
Rouen, a Jesuit of, II, 22
Roul (coco-tree), II, 113; II, 372
Round ships, II, 118
Roys, Diego de, supposed islands. *See* **Diego de Roys.**
Rua direita, street at Goa, II, 51, 52, 64
Rua dos Chapelleiros, street at Goa, II, 55
Rua Grande, street at Goa, II, 55
Rudders, removal of, to prevent escape, I, 286

Sabatz, I, 312
Sacouest (law), I, 201
Sacre, ship of Parmentier, I, x ; II, 486 *et seq.*
Sacrifice Rock, II, 527
Saffron, I, 411
Sagou (sago), II, 166
Sailor's breeches, II, 127
St. Anthony (of Padua), church at Goa, II, 58 ; image of, 304 ; church at Bahia, 307
St. Augustine, convent of, II, 57, 58
St. Augustine's Bay, arrival and adventures at, I, xxi, xxii, 30 *et seq.*; sickness at, 34 ; description of animals and people, 35-39 ; escape of sailors at, 39 ; plot to kidnap natives at, 41; departure from, *ib.*
St. Braz, fort, II, 32, 33

St. Catherine, quay of, II, 44; bust of, on arch, 47; cathedral of, 53; chapel of, 54; patroness of Goa, 56
St. Dominic. *See* **Dominicans.**
St. Francis of Assisi, church at Goa, II, xxxvii, 53
St. Francis Xavier, reference to his letters, II, xxvii, xxviii; shrine at Goa, xxxviii, 62, 63; baptised the Maldive king, 494, 495
St. Genois, Baron de, mistake as to Pyrard, I, xviii
St. George, island at Mozambique, II, 230
St. Helena, I, xxi; arrival and sojourn at, 17, 18; on homeward voyage, II, 296-304; chapel used as post-office, I, 18; II, 296, 297; description of, 298-302
St. James, feast of, II, 56; *see also* **Santiago.**
St. Jean de Luz, town, II, 336
St. John, a square at Cochin, I, 427
St. John Baptist, fort, II, 32, 33; church and street, 505; festival at Goa, *ib.*; feast of, I, 144; II, 56, 505
St. Joseph, church, II, 33
St. Lawrence. *See* **Madagascar.**
St. Lazarus, leper hospital, II, 55; campo, 55, 95
St. Louis of France, chapel at Goa, II, 56
St. Malo, expedition leaves, I, xiii, xiv, 2, 5
St. Martin, church of, in Goa hospital, II, 12
St. Monica, convent at Goa, II, 58
St. Paul, Jesuit church and college at Goa, II, 22, 55, 59, 62, 96, 505; feast of conversion of, 60, 61
St. Roch, church at Goa, II, 58, 61
St. Salvador, II, 309; *and see* **Bahia.**
St. Thomas (the Apostle), church of, at Goa, II, 55
St. Thomas, island, II, 221, 312
St. Thomas Aquinas, convent, 58
St. Vincent, river, II, 223
Sala das bragas, prison at Goa, II, xi, xii, 18-23
Salan à lescon, I, 133
Saldanha Bay, I, 22
Sallam Alecon, I, 70
Salle (*Sala das bragas*), II, 18-23
Salsette, II, 135; college, 269
Salt-fish, diseases attributed to, I, 181
Saluat, I, 130
Samorin of Calicut (written *Samory*), supremacy over pirate ports, I, 338, 348; joins Portuguese in attack upon Kunháli, 353; refuses to restrain the pirates, 356; receives Pyrard, 362-365; hasty temper of, 366, 367; his nephew creates an affray, 368; expels the Portuguese, 374, 375; greatness of, 408; description of him and his palace, 409-411, 413-418; his queen, 418, 419; warns P. as to the Portuguese, 421; anger towards Jesuits and Portuguese on capture of P., 424; II, 108; claims prisoners from Goa, II, 107
San Lazaro, Campo de, II, 95
San Thome, a gold coin, II, 69
Sandal-wood, red and white, II, 360
Sandals, only worn by the king, I, 223
Sangradores (bleeders), II, 70
Santiago, city and shrine. *See* **Compostella.**
Santiago, fort at Goa, II, 32, 33, 55
Santiago (called *S. Jacques*), island at Mozambique, II, 230
Santo Alberto, carrack, II, 280
Sarbatane, II, 165
Sardare (captain), I, 254
Sargasso weed, II, 331
Sátgánw port, I, 326
Scarlet (cloth), I, 57; red, 244; violet, II, 263
Schefer, Ch., I, xi, 2
Scurvy in the ships at Madagascar,

I, 31, 34 ; on Portuguese carracks, II, 199; generally, 389, 390-392
Sé (cathedral), at Goa, II, 53, 95 ; at Bahia, 311
Sea, king of the, worshipped, I, 176; a fish so called, 191, 192
Sea-slugs. *See* **Bêche de mer.**
Sea-urchins (sea chestnuts), I, 343
Seal (or sea-wolf), I, 244
Sebastian, king, II, xix, 267, 278
Seine, Jean de, Father, II, 36, 270, 281, 282
Selden, John, I, x
Serra, church of the, II, 51; retreat for orphan girls, 52
Seunat. *See* **Circumcision.**
Shábásh. *See Sabatz.*
Shah of Persia, II, 253
Shahíd. *See Chaydes.*
Shanuráza, Maldive king, II, 447
Sharks, I, 96 ; II, 349, 350
Sharpeigh, voyage of, I, xiii
Sheathing of ships, II, 183, 305, 388
Sheep, difference between those of Comorro and Madagascar, I, 46 ; rare at the Maldives, I, 116; II, 454, 485
Sherif. *See* **Cherife.**
Shiháb uddín, a sultan, II, 449, 453, 461-463
Ships, Indian built, I, 258 ; round and long, II, 118 ; contrast of ships of Latin and Teutonic races as to cleanliness, 196; equipment of, for Indian voyage, 387-393. *See also* **English, French, Dutch,** and **Portuguese ships.**
Shroffs (money-changers), II, 67
Siam, timber of, II, 182
Siare, I, 176
Sidi. *See Cisdy.*
Sierra Leone, I, 10
Silent bargaining, II, 178, 179
Silk, bought raw and worked up by Maldivians, I, 241; of Bengal, 328; grass silk, *ib.*
Silveira d'Aranjo, Manoel, grant to, 495, 496
Silver, valued at Madagascar, I, 33; secreted from the *Corbin*, 60 *et seq.* 72, 81 ; of E. and W. Indies, II, 174; high value in India, 193; exported to India by King of Spain, 211; mines of Monomotopa, 219
Sinhalese, described, II, 142-148
Síya (100), as a measure of Cowries, I, 237
Slaves at Maldives, condition of, I, 202 ; in Bengal, 332 ; in Brazil, II, 319; at Goa, exported to Portugal, II, 39 ; market for, 65 ; condition of, 65-67, 115; an orchestra of, 323
Slave trade, use of cowries in, I, 238; of Bengal, 332; between Africa and Brazil, II, 218-223 ; between Mozambique and Goa, 224
Small-pox, I, 181
Snake-charmers, I, 378
Snakes not killed in Malabar, I, 400; water-snakes at the Maldives, I, 116 ; II, 352
Socotora, island, II, 236, 237
Sodré, Vicente, II, 472
Sofala, endeavour to join dominion with Angola, II, 219, 235; description of, 232, 233
Soldado, II, 128. *See* **Portuguese soldier.**
Soldiers at the Maldives, I, 215-217; receive cotton cloths, I, 228 ; in Portuguese India. *See* **Portuguese soldiers.**
Solomon, king, II, 233
Solteras, II, 128
Sombreros, II, 45, 64, 75, 92
Sompas, I, 316
Sophy (Shah of Persia), II, 253
Sorberiana, quoted, I, xix, xxxiii
Sorcerers at the Maldives I, 274; in Malabar, 395
Sorcery, I, 181, 187, 274
Souadou (atoll). *See Suadiva*, I, 90, 97, 103, 122, 247
Sousa, Francisco de, II, 516, 521
Sousa, Jeronymo de, II, 475

Sousa, Dom Luis de, Maldive prince, II, 508
Soutes (bunkers), I, 60
Southern Cross, I, 9
Spain, not mentioned in India, I, 438, 439; II, 205; period of Portuguese subjection to, II, xxvi
Spaniards, not well received in India, II, 22; few or none there, 36, 212; at Manila, etc., 171-173; prohibited from trading with India, 202; hated by the Portuguese, 212
Spicy breezes, II, 170
Spleen, disease of, I, 84, 182
Spilbergen, Joris van, I, xiii, xx; his ships sighted off Guinea, 10; met at the Cape, 22-23; his account of the French ships, 23-24; one of his ships at Madagascar, 30; lands at Batticoloa, II, xiii; his ships referred to, 397, 398
Spoons, not used in India, I, 171, 378; II, 121
Sports, athletic, I, 141-143
Starfish, II, 351
Stevens, Father Thomas, II, xix, 269, 270
Stewards, on carracks, II, 192
Strappado, II, 188, 189, 287
Suadiva (*Suadou*), atoll, I, 97, 271, 312; exiles to, 90, 255; inhabited islands, 97; channel, 103; difference of speech, 122, 123; rebellion centres at, 247; fort at, 250; weavers at, I, 241; II, 485
Sugar, of China, II, 177; Bengal, Cambaye, etc., I, 328; of Brazil, II, 216, 217, 312-315; mills in Brazil, 221; adulteration of, 312. *See also* **Jaggery.**
Suleiman, traveller, quoted, II, 428
Sultan, title used by king of the Maldives, I, 95; sovereigns entitled to be called, 245
Sumatra, reached by Parmentier in 1526, I, xi; by Houtman in 1596, xiii; description of, II, 157-160

Sunda, referred to, I, 327, 328; use of the name, II, 157, 166, 168
Suppara (copra), II, 384
Sura (toddy), II, 35
Surat, river of, I, 336; II, 106
Susan, ship, I, xiii; referred to, II, 107
Suttee, practice of, I, 378, 394
Swiss, deserter, II, xxi, 229
Swords, struck to avert storm, I, 11
Sylva, Luiz da, killed at Kunhâli's fort, I, 353; II, 514-516
Sylva de Menezes, Dom Fernando da, referred to, II, 264; kindness to the author, 327, 328; captured by Barbary pirates, 329
Syphilis, I, 182-183; II, 13

Tabaquo, II, 313
Tabiran (Tambarán), I, 415
Tabriz, Persians from, I, 160
Tabu, at the Maldives, I, 57
Tacourou. *See* **Takuru.**
Tagals of the Philippines, their writing, I, 185
Takuru, I, 58, 217
Talachchenôr, or Náyar of Calicut, I, 367
Tallemant des Réaux, his *Historiettes*, I, xxxv-xl
Tamarinds, II, 361
Tanga (coin), II, 21, 68, 69
Tanur (spelt *Tananor*), a ship of, I, 266-268; II, 252; kingdom of, 369; arrival of P. at, 425
Tapestry, silk and cotton, I, 221, 232
Tarapilly (trumpets), I, 131
Tarent or *Tarens* (táran, tara), silver coin, I, 344, 387, 412
Tárikho (national record), I, 309; II, 528
Tartar, the Great, II, 251
Tartars, I, 266
Tauarcarré (coco-de-mer), I, 230-232
Tauide (charms), I, 178

Tavora, Ruy Lorenço de, viceroy, II, xviii, 77, 78, 242, 271
Taxes, exemption from, I, 169
Te Deum, sung at Goa, I, 356 ; on doubling Cape, II, 295
Teixeira de Macedo, Antonio, II, 499, 500
Tenasserim, misapplied to Ceylon, II, 140
Tengua (Tam., *tengha*), coconut, II, 372, 483
Tennis, not played at Goa, II, 112
Terceira, island, II, 332
Ternaté, island, II, xv, xvi, 166, 167, 173
Terre sigillée, I, 329, 376 ; II, 27
Terreiro dos gallos, II, 54
Terreiro grande, II, 48
Testoon, II, 174
Thaury (large boats), I, 389
Theft, punishment at the Maldives, I, 205, 307
Tibao, Sebastian, I, 334
Ticou, in Sumatra, I, x
Tidoré, island, II, xv, xvi, 166, 167
Tigers, in Malabar, I, 382, 400 ; in the Deccan, II, 136 ; described, 346, 347
Tilladummati, atoll, I, 98, 99
Tissuary, the name of Goa island, II, 25
Tithes, in India taken by the king, II, 96
Tiua (Tivar), I, 386, 387
Tobacco, of Brazil, II, 313
Tóni. See Tonny.
Tonny (boat), i, 389
Toothache, unknown at the Maldives, I, 183
Tortoiseshell, I, 240, 241, 285; II, 172, 348; cruel method of obtaining, II, 349 ; Cambay trade in, II, 478
Touladou (island), I, 73
Trade routes, Portugal and India, I, 197-201 ; India, Malacca, and China, etc., 170, 173-177 ; Spanish America and Philippines, 170-175 ; Portugal and Brazil, 215-218 ; Brazil and Angola, 218 ; East Africa and Goa, 223-225, 231, 235-237 ; Ormuz and Goa, 238-241 ; Cambay and Goa, 245; at end of 15th century, 470-472
Travados (squalls), I, 12, 48
Treasure trove, I, 229
Trigaut, Father, II, xix, 36-38, 270, 281
Trinqueres (ropemakers), II, 187, 191
Trombas (reeds), I, 20 ; II, 294
Tronco, of Cochin, I, 429-432 ; of Goa, II, 18, 24, 49
Trumpets, for use at sea, II, 398
Tuban, II, 164
Tuberons (Port., *tuberão*), a kind of shark, II, 350
Turacun, island, I, 322
Turbans, I, 165
Turk, the Grand, II, 253
Turk captain, I, 278
Turkey carpets, II, 239
Turkeys, II, 316
Turtle, sickness from eating, I, 65-66; II, 348; different kinds of, II, 347
Turun Shah, II, xxii, 91, 92, 243-245
Twelfth Night, I, 24; II, 98

Ulcers, mode of curing, I, 182
Umbrella, mark of royalty, I, 223 ; (white), I, 256
Unicorns, in Bengal, I, 331
Union (ship), I, xiii ; at the Comorros, 45 ; referred to, II, 106, 264
Utimu (island), I, 322; II, 437, 438, 452

Vadakkara. *See Badara.*
Vara de Justicia, I, 428
Varicor, I, 153 ; *and see* **Divorce.**
Varuery (revenue collector), I, 200, 213
Varugé (storehouse), I, 213
Vasconellos, Dona Francisca de, II, 500
Vater, II, 291

Vaypin. *See* **Vypeen.**
Vedon à Rouespou, I, 71
Vedor da fazenda (spelt *viador de fasienda*, etc.), II, 19, 21 ; his precinct and duties, 40, 41; frauds, 43; pays the soldiers, 126; at Cochin, 241
Velannas (admiral), I, 90, 210, 211, 213, 214, 254
Venetian glass, I, 43
Venetians, formerly many at Goa, II, 36 ; sequins, 69
Ventanes (windows), II, 115
Verd, Cape, islands, I, xx, 7; II, 222
Verhoeven, P. W., I, xiv, 364; II, xxi, 226
Vias de successao, II, 77
Viceroy, term used indiscriminately, II, 23; palace of, II, 47, 49-51; prison of, 49; the portraits of the viceroys, *ib.* ; succession and assumption of office, 76, 81 ; power and dignity of, 77, 78, 211, 212 ; reserve of, 78, 82 ; pay and emoluments, 83 ; almsgiving, 84 ; his three years of office, 85-88; parable of the flies, 87
Victualler, want of, I, xv ; II, 388
Vigia, vigia ! II, 19
Vinho de passas (raisin wine), II, 73, 383
Vintem, coin, I, 439 *n.*
Vitré, share in expedition, I, xiv, 2 ; ship's clerk from, 87
Voulos (ablutions), I, 174
Vows made at sea, II, 334
Voyages, grant of, II, 173
Vypeen, island, at Cochin, I, 435

Wadá (cowries), I, 237 ; II, 443, 444
Walendj, II, 442
War, king of, worshipped, I, 178
Water, mode of keeping on board ship, I, 258
Wax-cloth, for covering ships, I, 12
Weert, Sibalt de, I, xiii ; II, xiii, 146, 147
Wells, at the Maldives, I, 98
Whales, fishery at Brazil, II, 317, 321, 322
Wheat, not grown at the Maldives, I, 112
Whip, carried before the Pandiare, I, 199 ; used for scourging, 205 306
Whirlpool, I, 104
Whistles, silver, I, 33; II, 192
Wickham, Richard, I, 45 ; II, xviii, xix, 264, 265, 269
Wiliyán, II, 440, 443
Willekens, a Flemish pilot, I, 24, 25
Wimala Dharma, king of Ceylon, II, 144
Windowpanes, of oyster-shells, II, 15, 63
Winds, king of the, I, 175-178
Wine, used in India, II, 73 ; of the Azores, 216; of the Canaries, 316, 390; how far a necessary provision, 388-391
Winter (*i.e.*, the rainy season in India), I, 64, 104; II, 34
Woman with one breast, II, 464
Worms (parasitical), I, 181
Wreck, law of, at the Maldives, I, xxiv, 54, 62, 267-268, 294; at Calicut, 404
Wrecks at the Maldives, a Portuguese ship, I, 252; a ship of Sunda, I, 258
Writs, legal, used at the Maldives, I, 201, 207

Xavier. *See* **St. Francis Xavier.**
Xerafim, gold coin, II, 69

Yams, I, 112 ; II, 367, 368
Ybrahim. *See* **Ibrahim.**
Ydu, festival, I, 140, 157
Young, Lieut., residence at the Maldives, I, xliv, xlv

The Hakluyt Society.

REPORT FOR 1889.

SINCE the publication of our last Report we have had to deplore the loss of Sir Henry Yule, for many years President of the Society. Besides the works he edited for our series, (MARVELS DESCRIBED BY FRIAR JORDANUS; CATHAY AND THE WAY THITHER, 2 vols.; and the DIARY OF WILLIAM HEDGES, 3 vols.), he revised and assisted in several of our recent volumes. His learning in all that concerned the geography of the East and his remarkable memory made his work very valuable.

Shortly before his death he sent for Mr. Clements Markham, and expressed the wish that he should succeed him in the office of President. Mr. Markham kindly consented to undertake these duties, and was duly elected at a meeting of Council on November 27th, 1889. A graceful compliment was thus paid to one who has worked more for the Society than anybody else during the many years he held the post of Honorary Secretary.

We have also to mention with sincere regret the death of Mr. P. A. Tiele, of Utrecht, who, upon the decease of the late Dr. Coke Burnell, completed the editing of LINSCHOTEN'S VOYAGE.

The Congress of Orientalists, held at Stockholm and Christiania in 1889, afforded an opportunity to our Council of presenting a set of the Society's works to King Oscar II, Honorary President of that Congress. His Majesty was graciously pleased to accept this gift, and to express his satisfaction in adding these books to his Royal Library.

The destruction by fire of the Toronto University, when the whole of its valuable collection of books was entirely destroyed, led to an appeal being made to the learned Societies in this and other countries to come forward with gifts of their publications. The Council of the Hakluyt Society, recognising the claims so worthy an object had upon its generosity, and taking into consideration that this University was among the oldest of its subscribers, authorised the presentation of a set of its works to the Restoration Committee. This was accordingly done, and a grateful acknowledgment has been received by the Hon. Secretary.

The Council is glad to be able to announce that the following works have been undertaken: A new edition (the first being out of print) of Sir R. Schomburghk's RALEIGH'S EMPIRE OF GUIANA, edited by Mr. Everard Im Thurn, of British Guiana; THE LETTERS OF PIETRO DELLA VALLE, transcribed from the early English version by G. Havers (1665), and edited by Mr. Edward Grey, late of the Indian Civil Service; THE TRUE HISTÓRY OF THE CONQUEST OF NEW SPAIN, by Bernal Diaz, translated from the Spanish and edited by Rear-Admiral Lindesay Brine; THE VOYAGE OF ULRICH SCHMIDT TO LA PLATA, translated from the original German edition (1567); and the COMMENTARIES OF CABEZA DE VACA, GOVERNOR OF THE PROVINCE OF LA PLATA, translated from the original Spanish edition (Valladolid 1555)—the two last edited by Don Luis L. Dominguez, Argentine Minister to the Court of St. James's, are in progress—

and the VOYAGE OF FRANÇOIS LEGUAT TO THE ISLAND OF RODRIGUEZ, edited by Captain S. P. Oliver (nearly ready).

The following Members retire from Council:

Mr. CECIL S. FOLJAMBE, M.P.,
Mr. E. BURNE JONES, A.R.A., and
Mr. TYSSEN AMHERST, M.P.

The following are elected in their place:

Professor E. B. TYLER, D.C.L.,
Dr. ROBERT BROWN, M.A., Ph.D., and
Mr. E. A. PETHERICK.

The Statement of Accounts shows a balance of £235 16*s.* 11*d.* The number of Subscribers is 278.

N.B.—The election of Mr. Markham to the Presidency leaves another vacancy on the Council not yet filled.

BALANCE SHEET, 1889.

Dr.

	£	s.	d.
Brought forward from last year's Report	301	19	3
Subscriptions	224	14	0
Arrears	7	7	0
Sales of back volumes, including five sets	143	2	3
	£677	2	6

Cr.

	£	s.	d.
Banker's charge	0	0	6
Agent's account, including rent of store	42	14	8
Advertising	1	16	6
Illustrations for Hedges' Diary, vols. ii and iii ...	18	11	11
Prætorius, for portrait of Mrs. Pitt	3	10	0
Autotype Co., for portrait of Elihu Yale	5	13	9
Transcriptions for Mr. Sparling's work	8	0	0
Prætorius, engraving Molyneux Celestial Globe ...	5	5	0
Captain Oliver, for transcriptions	10	0	0
Petty Cash	10	0	0
Messrs. Whiting & Co., for printing, etc.	311	3	3
Mr. Weller, for lithographing map of Western Europe	6	10	0
Mr. Griggs, for 20 plates of Leguat's Voyage ...	18	0	0
Balance	235	16	11
	£677	2	6

PETTY CASH.

Date		£	s.	d.
1888.				
Jan. 1.	To Balance	0	9	0
Apr. 16.	Cash of R. B. Hawkins for copy of the Hawkins Voyage	0	15	0
1889.				
June 7.	Cheque	10	0	0
		£11	4	0

Date		£	s.	d.
1888.				
Apr. 2.	By an imperfect copy of North-west Fox, for Mr. M. Christy	1	10	0
Dec. 9.	„ Stamps	0	5	0
1889.				
Mar. 9.	„ paid Mr. Reeves for drawing Chart ...	6	0	0
Apr. 15.	„ paid Mr. Wilkinson, photographer ...	1	0	0
„ 20.	„ Stationery...	0	12	6
June 7.	„ an imperfect copy of Captain James' Voyage, for Mr. M. Christy	0	4	0
Aug. 27.	„ paid Mr. Prætorius, preparing specimen gore of Molyneux Terrestrial Globe ...	1	0	0
Sept. 1.	„ Stamps	0	5	0
Nov. 27.	„ Balance	0	7	6
		£11	4	0

Examined and approved,

CLEMENTS R. MARKHAM.
ALBERT GRAY.